Direct Effect in EU Law

OXFORD EU LAW LIBRARY

The aim of the series is to publish important and original studies of the various branches of EU law. Each work provides a clear, concise, and critical exposition of the law in its social, economic, and political context, at a level which will interest the advanced student, the practitioner, the academic, and government officials.

OTHER TITLES IN THE LIBRARY

EU Citizenship Law
Niamh Nic Shuibhne

EU Justice and Home Affairs Law
Fifth Edition
Steve Peers

EU Procedural Law
Second Edition
Koen Lenaerts, Ignace Maselis, Kathleen Gutman, Janek Tomasz Nowak

European Migration Law
Daniel Thym

EU Securities and Financial Markets Regulation
Fourth Edition
Niamh Moloney

EU Diplomatic Law
Sanderijn Duquet

EU Constitutional Law
Koen Lenaerts, Piet Van Nuffel, Tim Corthaut

EU Customs Law
Third Edition
Timothy Lyons

Principles and Practice in EU Sports Law
Stephen Weatherill

EU Anti-Discrimination Law
Second Edition
Evelyn Ellis, Philippa Watson

Direct Effect in EU Law

DANIELE GALLO, PHD
Full Professor of EU Law, Luiss University, Italy

OXFORD
UNIVERSITY PRESS

OXFORD
UNIVERSITY PRESS

Great Clarendon Street, Oxford, OX2 6DP,
United Kingdom

Oxford University Press is a department of the University of Oxford.
It furthers the University's objective of excellence in research, scholarship,
and education by publishing worldwide. Oxford is a registered trade mark of
Oxford University Press in the UK and in certain other countries

Published in the United States of America by Oxford University Press
198 Madison Avenue, New York, NY 10016, United States of America

British Library Cataloguing in Publication Data

Data available

Library of Congress Control Number: 2024946923

ISBN 9780192898708

DOI: 10.1093/9780191925221.001.0001

Printed and bound by
CPI Group (UK) Ltd, Croydon, CR0 4YY

MIX
Paper | Supporting
responsible forestry
FSC® C013604
FSC
www.fsc.org

The manufacturer's authorised representative in the EU for product safety is
Oxford University Press España S.A. of El Parque Empresarial San Fernando de Henares, Avenida
de Castilla, 2 – 28830 Madrid (www.oup.es/en or
product.safety@oup.com). OUP España S.A. also acts as importer into Spain
of products made by the manufacturer.

To Francesca, Ester, Matilde,
Thanking you for welcoming 'Book' with subdued happiness in the last years,
making him feel at home in the family ménage,
greeting her in the morning
and wishing him a good night before going to bed.
Thank you also for making me realize every day that taking oneself too seriously is evil and
that 'Book', despite all the love we have for her and his overflowing personality,
is just a book.

Foreword

The issue of 'direct effect' is a fundamental and enduring one in the study of European Union Law. From some of the earliest and most famous case law of the European Court of Justice in the 1960s to cases of ongoing importance about the relationship between direct effect and primacy in recent years, the doctrine of direct effect of EU law has featured prominently in the imaginary of the EU legal order. Perhaps even more than its 'twin' doctrine of supremacy or primacy, the direct effect of EU law has helped to mark out the European Union project of legal and political integration as a distinctive if not unique one, whose laws may enjoy this robust characteristic. At the same time that it has developed as a core characteristic of EU law, however, direct effect has remained a largely judge-made and court-led doctrine which political actors have mostly sidestepped and have chosen to leave to the court. Apart from an EEC Treaty reference to the 'direct applicability' of regulations, the development of direct effect as a doctrine has taken essentially place through the interaction of the case law of the Court of Justice and the responses of national courts who apply, interpret, implement or resist EU law.

Much scholarly ink has been spilt on the subject of direct effect, on its meaning, its implications, its complexity and its reception. One might imagine that there is little left to say on the topic, six decades after its introduction into EU law. But Daniele Gallo's book, building on earlier work which was published in Italian, and in a number of articles on the subject, is a fresh and welcome contribution to the canon. Revisiting the classic cases and the extensive scholarship on the subject, Gallo argues that some of the original conditions articulated for the direct effect of EU law are no longer valid, and that a simpler test can be identified. In a thorough analysis of the many twists and turns in the case law and the doctrine, including horizontal effect, exclusionary effect, 'external' direct effect (of international agreements etc) as well as internal direct effect, the obligation to disapply national law, indirect effect and more, the book seeks to clarify, explain and articulate the contours of this elusive and dynamic concept, while engaging with the wealth of existing scholarship on the topic.

Following seven comprehensive and confidently written chapters on the gradual development and expansion of direct effect through the case law of the Court of Justice, the author brings the book to a close with a brisk Conclusion recapping his main arguments and proposing some clarity and change, including by calling on the Court of Justice to resist judicial minimalism and to return to a bolder constitutional role in properly defining the contours of the doctrine. I predict that this book will be widely read, and will become a key reference point for all those interested in the nature and character of EU law, and particularly in the fundamental doctrine of direct effect.

Gráinne de Búrca
Professor of Law, European University Institute (EUI)
Florence Ellinwood Allen Professor of Law, New York University (NYU) (on leave)

Acknowledgements

I had the privilege to receive comments on an earlier draft from several colleagues, to whom I would like to express my upmost gratitude: Chiara Amalfitano, Brunessen Bertrand, Giacomo Biagioni, Andrea Biondi, Federico Casolari, Lorenzo Cecchetti, Edoardo Chiti, Andrea Circolo, Francesco Costamagna, Giacomo Di Federico, Cristina Fasone, Filippo Fontanelli, Eleni Frantziou, Stéphanie Hennette-Vauchez, Sara Iglesias Sánchez, Clara H. L. Labus, Giuseppe Martinico, François-Xavier Millet, Alessandro Nato, Fernanda Nicola, Sara Poli, and Daniel Sarmiento.

I am indebted to Justices Roberto Mastroianni (EU General Court) and Francesco Viganò (Italian Constitutional Court) for their insightful reflections on direct effect, including its practicability in proceedings before domestic courts.

I am grateful to Robert Schütze, as editor of the Series, for his constructive criticisms expressed throughout the writing period, as well as for emphasizing the need to broaden the scope of the research so as to include Chapter VII on the direct effect of international law (or lack thereof) in the EU legal order.

Additionally, thank you to Oriana Balsamo and Viola Lo Schiavo for their editing assistance, as well as to Gabrielle Saltzberg for her linguistic revision.

The usual disclaimers apply.

This study, which is inspired by and partially builds on the theoretical background set out in *L'efficacia diretta del diritto dell'Unione europea negli ordinamenti nazionali.* Una dottrina ancora controversa (Milan, Giuffrè, Jean Monnet Centre for Excellence's Series, 2018), is the result of my research and teaching on the internal effect of EU law conducted first and foremost at Luiss University (Rome), further refined at *Université Capitole I de Toulouse*, American University College of Law (Washington DC), and *Université Panthéon-Assas* (Paris). Before then, I investigated, as Jean Monnet Fellow, DAAD Fellow and R. Schuman EU Fulbright Scholar, respectively, key matters of EU law—which I later studied in depth for this volume—at the following institutions: European University Institute (Florence), *Max-Planck-Institut für ausländisches öffentliches Rech* (Heidelberg), and Fordham Law School (New York).

The publication is one of the main deliverables of my Jean Monnet Chair (Erasmus+ Programme/2020–2023) on *Understanding EU Law in Practice: EU Rights in Action before Courts* (Project Number 620360-EPP-1-2020-1-IT-EPPJMO-CHAIR). Therefore, my acknowledgements go to the European Commission (Education, Audiovisual and Culture Executive Agency) for its support and co-funding.

PRACT
EU Rights before Courts

With the support of the
Erasmus+ Programme
of the European Union

The European Commission's support for the production of this publication does not constitute an endorsement of the contents, which reflect the views only of the authors, and the Commission cannot be held responsible for any use which may be made of the information contained therein.

Brief Contents

Detailed Contents

Table of Cases

1. COURT OF FIRST INSTANCE/GENERAL COURT

2. ADVOCATES GENERAL

3. COURT OF JUSTICE

INTRODUCTION

1. Background, aims, and scope of the research

The tireless critics of the European Union (EU) have a natural inclination towards underlining the fragilities and incongruencies of both the EU legal system and the process of European integration.[1] In doing so, either knowingly or unknowingly, they tend to overlook the peculiarities and points of strength of the European legal order, as well as the extraordinary legal innovations—amongst international organizations—that were brought forth by the founding of the European (Economic) Communities. In this respect, criticism is usually grounded in an outdated (and predictable) vision of the EU. The narrative, which is often strictly ideological and dear to sovereigntists at all levels and of various kinds, describes the EU as an organization acting, more or less systematically, *ultra vires*, that is, to the detriment of Member States' sovereignty.[2]

This stance is puzzling because the above-mentioned peculiarities, points of strength, and innovations constitute the axis around which the whole integration process was formed and continues to evolve. Indeed, they represent both its original core and the principal factors of its development. The reference goes first and foremost to the judiciary-based constitutional principles governing the relationship between EU law and domestic legal orders and, more specifically, the impact of the former on the latter: direct effect, effectiveness, primacy, effective judicial protection, State liability, and consistent interpretation. These principles express their strength and *effet utile* thanks to a distinctive tool of judicial cooperation between Member States and the EU, that is, the preliminary ruling procedure laid down in Article 267 of the Treaty on the Functioning of the European Union (TFEU).

Against this backdrop, the book reflects on the content, *ratio*, scope, and extent of direct effect. In doing so, it revisits the past, present, and future of a principle that has, over the years, to an extent far greater than any other, transformed the law of the EU in synergy with other principles, theories, and doctrines. Indeed, direct effect, while placing natural and legal persons at the centre of the Treaties, giving them a substantive and procedural avenue to safeguard their interests and ensure the proper enforcement of EU rules, determines the autonomy and originality of the EU legal system. It is its driving force and *raison d'être*. Thus, writing about direct effect means delving into the essence of EU law. As a matter of fact, due to direct effect, the international law axiom, according to which individuals lack

[1] This § of the Introduction builds extensively on, or reproduces extracts from, the introductory remarks contained in D. Gallo, *Rethinking direct effect and its evolution: a proposal* (2022) 1 *European Law Open* 576, 576–580. All URLs for the Introduction were last accessed on 30 April 2024.

[2] *See*, recently, *inter alia*, the critical account by P. Anderson, *The European Coup* 42 *London Review of Books*, 17 December 2020, available at https://www.lrb.co.uk/the-paper/v42/n24/perry-anderson/the-european-coup. On the competence problem within the EU legal order *see*, *ex multis*, S. Weatherill, *Competence Creep and Competence Control* (2004) 23 *Yearbook of European Law* 1–55; P. Craig, *The ECJ and Ultra Vires Action: A Conceptual Analysis* (2011) 48 *Common Market Law Review* 395; L. Azoulai, *Introduction*, in L. Azoulai (ed.), *The question of competence in the European Union*, Oxford, Oxford University Press, 2014, 1–16.

Direct Effect in EU Law. Daniele Gallo, Oxford University Press. © Daniele Gallo 2025. DOI: 10.1093/9780191925221.003.0001

full legal personality and are generally relegated to the periphery with respect to the exercise of rights in view of seeking the setting aside of domestic laws, in fact, is overturned and radically questioned. In *Van Gend & Loos*,[3] the reasoning of the Court of Justice (CJ)[4] was inspired by '*une certaine idée d'Europe*' rather than by strictly technical arguments on points of law.[5] The Court's decision to interpret EU law in the sense of conferring rights on individuals was ultimately a political choice, since it expressed the purposes and values that, in the opinion of the Court, were to direct the process of European integration. At the same time, thanks to *Van Gend & Loos* and part of the subsequent case law, the EU judges managed to keep 'Community law out of the hands of politicians and bureaucrats and give it to the people'.[6] Direct effect, therefore, has always been and continues to be the most powerful tool to advance the European 'integration through law'[7] and through *rights*. The establishment and completion of a 'Community based on the rule of law', therefore, as it is described in the *Les Verts* case[8] and in Opinion 1/91,[9] implies the existence of a 'Community of rights'.

On the other hand, the fact that direct effect is the backbone of EU (institutional, constitutional, procedural, and substantive) law, alongside the principles of autonomy and primacy,[10] does not mean that such doctrine, nowadays, is clearly legally framed by both the CJ and the General Court (GC) in their case law. It is not, in fact, despite its pivotal status within the EU legal framework. It should be, however, since grasping if, when, and how direct effect arises affects the individuals' entitlement to invoke EU law and put it into action. In this connection, the aim of this book is to reconstruct and revisit direct effect, also beyond the *Van Gend & Loos* judgment and the doctrine originating from it, and ultimately submit solutions for its appropriate understanding and enforcement.

A further clarification on the title of the volume: 'Direct Effect *in* EU Law'. The 'in', rather than 'of', is explained by the fact that the direct effect of international law within the EU legal order is systematically evoked throughout the six chapters and the whole seven chapter is devoted to this matter.

2. Structure and outline of the chapters

The volume is divided into four main thematic sections. The first, consisting of Chapters I and II, focuses on the origins of direct effect and the relationship that links this principle to the primacy and autonomy of EU law, as well as to the preliminary ruling procedure

[3] CJ, *NV Algemene Transport-en Expeditie Onderneming van Gend & Loos*, 26/62, EU:C:1963:1.

[4] Throughout the volume the term 'CJEU' stands for both the CJ and the General Court (GC). If the allusion is made specifically to the CJ or GC, it refers to the jurisdiction and case law only of the Court that is explicitly mentioned in the text.

[5] P. Pescatore, *The Doctrine of 'Direct Effect': An Infant Disease of Community Law* (1983) 8 *European Law Review* 155, 157.

[6] F. Mancini, D. Keeling, *Democracy and the European Court of Justice* (1994) 57 *Modern Law Review* 175.

[7] M. Cappelletti, M. Seccombe, J. H. H. Weiler (eds.), *Integration through Law: Europe and the American Federal Experience*, Berlin-New York, Walter de Gruyter and Co., 1986, I.

[8] CJ, *Parti écologiste 'Les Verts'*, 294/83, EU:C:1986:166, para. 23.

[9] CJ, *Opinion delivered pursuant to the second subparagraph of Article 228 (1) of the Treaty—Draft agreement between the Community, on the one hand, and the countries of the European Free Trade Association, on the other, relating to the creation of the European Economic Area*, 1/91, EU:C:1991:490, para. 21.

[10] The CJ frequently refers to the 'essential characteristics' of EU law, as held in CJ, *Accession of the European Union to the European Convention for the Protection of Human Rights and Fundamental Freedoms*, 2/13, EU:C:2014:2454, para. 166 and CJ, *Andy Wightman*, C-621/18, EU:C:2018:999, para. 45.

governed by Article 267 TFEU. The second, consisting of Chapters III–V, strives to investigate, first, the *Van Gend & Loos* doctrine, as it has evolved over the decades, secondly, the nature of direct effect, intended in objective and exclusionary terms, that is, regardless of the conferral of rights and substitution effects, and, thirdly, the *true* core elements of direct effect, be it narrow or broad, as well as the extent of the duty to disapply. The third, consisting of Chapter VI, deals with the rationale, potential, and limits of the horizontal direct effect of EU law, with particular, but not exclusive, reference to both directives and fundamental rights. The fourth thematic section, consisting of Chapter VII, relates to the doctrine of direct effect when it comes to the penetration of international law into EU law and its invocability before both national and EU courts.

Chapter I provides a contextualized examination of the *Van Gend & Loos* case, including from a historical perspective. This chapter explains why *Van Gend & Loos* is the result of a development in the case law which began even before the establishment of the European Economic Community (EEC), that is, at the time of the European Coal and Steel Community (ECSC), thanks first and foremost to the stimulus from the Legal Service of the ECSC High Authority and from Advocate General Lagrange. On the other hand, however, it is argued that the ruling is also revolutionary because here the CJ identified for the first time the defining characteristic of the European system and of its autonomy, which it later explicitly reaffirmed in *Costa*:[11] the centrality of the individual as a subject of law, that is, as a holder of individual rights conferred by EU provisions. The chapter also clarifies that this attitude allowed the CJ to emancipate EU law, albeit not in its entirety, from international law. Furthermore, the relevance and impact of the *Van Gend & Loos* decision are captured by putting it into the political context of the Community at the time. Lastly, the chapter expounds that the *Van Gend & Loos* doctrine placed the Court, in its role as the judge of rights and duties, at the centre of the transformation of EU law, laying the foundation for the creation of two other fundamental doctrines: fundamental rights and the EU citizenship.

Chapter II dwells on the complementarity between direct effect and the preliminary ruling procedure. Indeed, the chapter explicates that through the interpretative preliminary reference mechanism and by virtue of the *erga omnes* effect of preliminary rulings, the CJ does not only exercise a monopoly over the interpretation of EU law, but has also come to perform, *de facto*, a centralized judicial review of national legislation. Using the preliminary reference procedure, the Court has given substance to the doctrine of direct effect, broadening it and reinforcing its legal significance. While not in itself new in the context of international law, this doctrine has entered the EU legal order to such an extent that, today, there is a presumption of direct effect of EU law. A direct effect theorized, defined, and ascertained by the Luxembourg Court rather than by national courts. And therein lies the monistic facet of the EU legal order.

Chapter III, first, defines subjective substitutive direct effect as it takes shape in *Van Gend & Loos* and the doctrine stemming from it. In doing so, special attention is devoted to the conferral of rights as the key element of such manifestation of direct effect, in the light of the two principles of effectiveness and effective judicial protection. It then identifies the jurisprudential milestones related to a notion as chameleon-like and iridescent as direct effect. Amongst these lies the test on direct effect, whose uncertain functioning is explored, as well as its dubious relevance, today. In particular, the ambit and potential of unconditionality are examined, and so is the merging of direct effect with direct applicability, *in concreto*.

[11] CJ, *Flaminio Costa v E.N.E.L.*, 6/64, EU:C:1964:66.

The focus is also on the implications deriving from a selective disapplication of national law conflicting with EU primary and/or secondary law.

Chapter IV illustrates why direct effect is an evolving, many-sided, and polysemic notion that cannot be traced back solely to the *Van Gend & Loos* doctrine. Indeed, it is demonstrated that direct effect does not always come along either with the immediate conferral of a right by an EU norm or with the capacity of the latter to govern the case through the replacement of a conflicting national provision. The chapter revolves around the so-called *invocabilité d'exclusion*, whereby the key feature of direct effect is not the capacity of a provision of EU law to directly confer rights on individuals and to replace a provision of national legislation as the law governing a given case. The analysis shows that objective exclusionary direct effect is the capacity of a provision of EU law to serve as a parameter of legality for national law, with exclusionary rather than substitution effects. In this sense, if the reflections on the differences between subjective substitutive direct effect and objective exclusionary direct effect seem to be only academic, advocating for a broad, rather than narrow, notion of direct effect is very important in practice since it affects whether and how individuals are entitled to invoke (and rely on) EU law, and thus to request disapplication.

Chapter V investigates the interplay between direct effect, primacy, and disapplication, and shows that justifying disapplication on the basis of primacy alone, not of primacy *and* direct effect, entails a blank proxy for EU institutions and is, ultimately, apt to undermine the logic governing the relationship between EU law and domestic legal systems. Connecting disapplication only to primacy, fortunately, is a position that has been openly rejected, in recent times, by the CJEU. The chapter also argues that a paramount quality of direct effect, along with unconditionality, is the creation of an advantage resulting from the application of EU law and the subsequent disapplication of national law. In this respect, a detailed analysis is carried out so as to explain when inverse vertical direct effect and intra-State direct effect are allowed, whereby if and when public authorities can rely on EU directly effective provisions in disputes against private parties, or different State agencies, respectively, to seek the disapplication of national law. As for regulations and those decisions that are not only addressed to States, it is explained that the enforcement of unconditional provisions enshrined therein should not be subject to the same limitations on inverse vertical direct effect which are valid for the other EU provisions, as they are directly applicable acts of general application published in the Official Journal of the EU. Furthermore, it is clarified why, notwithstanding the ambiguous EU case law, *in malam partem* disapplication of national law should occur only on condition that the principles of legal certainty and legitimate expectations are not unduly and irreparably infringed. An infringement that always occurs when directives are at stake. As far as EU primary law is concerned, it is assessed how its *pro futuro* interpretation and application by the CJEU under Article 267 TFEU could be the right avenue to safeguard the legitimate prerogatives of both natural and legal persons in inverse vertical situations. Against this backdrop, a tentative list of admissible derogations from the duty to disapply is drawn up, considering the EU case law and in contrast with the pathological derogations wrongfully invoked by Member States' authorities, including supreme and constitutional courts.

Chapter VI frames the contentious matter of horizontal direct effect of EU law, beginning with the EU Treaties and with particular regard to the freedoms of movement. It then analyses the unsatisfactory techniques designed by the CJEU to get around the no horizontal direct effect rule for directives. In this connection, the chapter dives into the inconsistencies underpinning the Court's approach towards the joint application of the EU Charter and directives. It finally argues that the CJEU, in over-extending the notion of public measure and systematically relying on a multiplicity of techniques and alternative remedies, has complicated and continues to further complicate matters in relation to such a peculiar source as the directive. Moreover, it is noted that the denial of horizontal direct effect, by depriving individuals of the possibility of invoking EU law against other individuals, ultimately jeopardizes the effectiveness of EU law, and should induce the Court to finally change its approach.

Chapter VII relates to the direct effect of international law within the EU legal order. It covers both vertical and horizontal direct effect, and both conventional and customary law. In doing so, it examines the unclear trajectories of 'external' direct effect in the EU case law and reflects upon the blurred boundaries between (broad) direct effect, legality review, and the so-called *Fediol-Nakajima* doctrine(s). It also compares the 'internal' direct effect doctrine, that is, the direct effect of EU law within domestic legal orders, and 'external' direct effect. To this end, it demonstrates to what extent the recognition of direct effect of international agreements, or lack thereof, is imbued with heavy political connotations. Finally, the chapter explores the consequences of the diminishing role of the CJEU as a 'gatekeeper' in the conceptualization and practice of 'external' direct effect resulting from the current phenomenon of precluding such effect through the insertion of clauses in EU international agreements.

The volume is updated up to 30 April 2024.

I

THE ORIGINS OF DIRECT EFFECT

VAN GEND & LOOS IN CONTEXT

1. Direct effect before *Van Gend & Loos*

The conceptual cornerstones of direct effect were identified by the Court of Justice (CJ) for the first time in *Van Gend & Loos*.[1] In the ruling, the Court acted with courage[2] through an innovative interpretation of the European Economic Communities (EEC) Treaty as a unique type of international agreement. Indeed, the revolutionary value of the judgment lies in the recognition of such uniqueness.[3] A judgment that, since the *Da Costa* ruling, rendered one month later,[4] has been confirmed and reiterated in the jurisprudence of European judges.

Whilst the analysis of the *Van Gend & Loos* decision is addressed in the following sections, in this section a connected, but distinct, set of problems will be discussed. They relate to the origins of *Van Gend & Loos*. In this respect, attention is devoted to the historical and legal context[5] in which the ruling was handed down,[6] account being made for the practice of the

[1] CJ, *NV Algemene Transport-en Expeditie Onderneming van Gend & Loos*, 26/62, EU:C:1963:1. On the relevance of the judgment for the conceptualization of direct effect by the CJ, *see*, amongst recent works, M. Rasmussen, *Revolutionizing European Law: A History of the* Van Gend en Loos *Judgment* (2014) 12 *International Journal of Constitutional Law* 136 and M. Rasmussen, *Law Meets History*, in F. Nicola, B. Davies (eds.), *EU Law Stories. Contextual and Critical Histories of European Jurisprudence*, Cambridge, Cambridge University Press, 2017, 103–120. All URLs for this chapter were last accessed on 30 April 2024.

[2] In these terms, with regard to both *Van Gend & Loos* and *Costa*, *see* R. Kovar, *La contribution de la Cour de justice à l'édification de l'ordre juridique communautaire. Cours général de droit communautaire*, in *Recueil des cours de l'Académie de droit européen*, The Hague, Martinus Nijhoff, 1995, 15–122, 21.

[3] *See* D. Sarmiento, *El Derecho de la Unión europea: medio siglo de historia. Comentario a la celebración del 50 aniversario de la sentencia* Van Gend en Loos, in *Unión Europea Aranzadi*, 2013, 37, 38.

[4] CJ, *Da Costa*, joined cases C-28–30/62, EU:C:1963:6, whereby the CJ concluded in the operative part of the judgment that there was 'no ground for giving a new interpretation' of the EEC Treaty since the answer on the same points of law had already been offered in *Van Gend & Loos*.

[5] The archive of the CJEU, on the basis of which numerous studies have been made over the last few years on the jurisprudence of the Court, includes the dossiers of case law, amongst which, of course, is the *Van Gend & Loos* ruling. It has been placed in the historical archive of the EU located at the European University Institute, in Florence. For a socio-legal-historical perspective underpinning research on the CJEU, *see* F. Bignami, *Rethinking the Legal Foundation of the European Constitutional Order: The Lessons of the New Historical Research* (2013) 28 *American University International Law Review* 1311; M. Rask Madsen, F. Nicola, A. Vauchez, *Researching the European Court of Justice. Methodological Shifts and Law's Embeddedness*, Cambridge, Cambridge University Press, 2022. On such research, from the perspective of the possible challenges it raises to the secrecy of deliberations, *see* M. Pollak, *Learning from EU Law Stories*, in F. Nicola, B. Davies (eds.), *EU Law Stories*, 577–602, 598-602; F. Nicola, *Waiting for the Barbarians: Inside the Archive of the European Court of Justice*, in C. Kilpatrick, J. Scott (eds.), *New Legal Approaches to Studying the Court of Justice*, Oxford, Oxford University Press, 2020, 62–91, 72–3, and 86; L. Clément-Wilz, *An Institutional View on the Influence of Italians Judges and Advocates General*, in D. Gallo, R. Mastroianni, F. Nicola, L. Cecchetti (eds.), *The Italian Influence on European Law: Judges and Advocates General* (1952-2000), Oxford, Hart, 2024, forthcoming.

[6] On this matter, *see* A. Vauchez, *The Transnational Politics of Judicialization.* Van Gend en Loos *and the Making of EU Polity* (2010) 16 *European Law Journal* 1; P. Grossi, *A History of European Law*, New York, John Wiley & Sons, 2010; M. Rasmussen, *Revolutionizing*; A. Vauchez, *Brokering Europe. Euro-Lawyers and the Making of a Transnational Polity*, Cambridge, Cambridge University Press, 2015, 116–146; M. Rasmussen, *Law*; W. Phelan, *Great Judgments of the European Court of Justice. Rethinking the Landmark Decisions of the Foundational Period*,

Direct Effect in EU Law. Daniele Gallo, Oxford University Press. © Daniele Gallo 2025. DOI: 10.1093/9780191925221.003.0002

ECSC's High Authority and the European Commission, as well as of the CJ and some of its Advocates General. In this regard, scholars have observed that, even before *Van Gend & Loos*, the CJ had laid the foundations for what would then become the direct effect doctrine.[7] As a matter of fact, the CJ, while employing the interpretive canons known to international law at the time,[8] was without a doubt influenced by some rulings issued prior to *Van Gend & Loos*, by a number of Advocates General's opinions, as well as by the position taken by the Legal Service of both the High Authority and the European Commission in previous cases.[9]

Along these lines, some authors have emphasized that in *Van Gend & Loos* the CJ offered the only possible logical interpretation[10] of the European Treaties in underscoring what the peculiar juridical nature of the EEC Treaty was. In short, according to them, the pioneering character of *Van Gend & Loos* should be considerably tempered. On one hand, such conclusion seems to go way too far, as will be further clarified;[11] on the other, it has the virtue of making it evident that the revolution initiated by *Van Gend & Loos* was based on several previous intuitions and ideas, which circulated between Brussels and Luxembourg, as well as on the practice that existed before the judgment. In this connection, as is apparent from historiographical research,[12] already by the mid-1950s, members of the Legal Service of the High Authority, beginning with M. Gaudet and N. Catalano,[13] in their pleadings lodged with the Registrar of the CJ,[14] had asked the latter to adopt a teleological interpretation of the EEC

Cambridge, Cambridge University Press, 2020, 31–57; T. Pavone, *The Ghostwriters: Lawyers and the Politics Behind the Judicial Construction of Europe*, Cambridge, Cambridge University Press, 2022, 129–196. More in general, amongst studies on the Community/EU case law in context *see* R. Zimmermann, *Roman Law, Contemporary Law, European Law: The Civilian Tradition Today*, Oxford, Oxford University Press, 2001; A. Cohen, *Constitutionalism without Constitution: Transnational Elites Between Political Mobilization and Legal Expertise in the Making of a Constitution for Europe (1940s–1960s)* (2007) 32 *Law and Society Inquiry* 109; B. Davies, M. Rasmussen, *Towards a New History of European Law* (2012) 21 *Contemporary European History* 305; M. Egan, *Towards a New History of European Law: New Wine in Old Bottles* (2013) 28 *American University International Law Review* 1223; A. Vauchez, B. de Witte (eds.), *Lawyering Europe: European Law as a Transnational Social Field*, Oxford, Oxford University Press, 2013; T. Herzog, *A Short History of European Law: The Last Two and a Half Millennia*, Cambridge (Mass.), Harvard University Press, 2018.

[7] *See* D. Edward, *Judicial Activism—Myth or Reality?* Van Gend en Loos, Costa v ENEL *and the* Van Duyn *Family Revisited*, in A. I. K. Campbell, M. Voyatzi (eds.), *Essays in the Honour of Lord Mackenzie-Stuart*, Trenton, New Jersey, 1996, 29–67, 36–49 and A. Cohen, *Constitutionalism*, 125–128.

[8] On this point, *see* J. H. H. Weiler, *Revisiting* Van Gend en Loos: *Subjectifying and Objectifying the Individual*, in A. Tizzano, J. Kokott, S. Prechal (Organizing Committee), *50ème anniversaire de l'arrêt Van Gend en Loos: 1963-2013: actes du colloque*, Luxembourg, 13 mai 2013, 11–22, 12.

[9] *See* the contributions in A. Vauchez, B. de Witte (eds.), *Lawyering Europe*, most notably A. Cohen, *'Ten Majestic Figures in Long Amaranth Robes': The Formation of the Court of Justice of the European Communities*, 21–42 and J. P. Jacqué, *The Role of Legal Services in the Elaboration of European Legislation*, 43–54.

[10] *See* P. Pescatore, *Rôle et chance du droit et des juges dans la construction de l'Europe* (1974) 26 *Revue internationale de droit comparé* 5.

[11] In the same vein, *see* E. Perillo, *Alberto Trabucchi: The Defender of the European Citizens' Rights and the Van Gend & Loos Ruling of the Court of Justice*, in D. Gallo, R. Mastroianni, F. Nicola, L. Cecchetti (eds.), *The Italian Influence.*

[12] *See, inter alia*, E. Stein, *Lawyers, Judges, and the Making of a Transnational Constitution* (1981) 75 *American Journal of International Law* 1 and M. Rasmussen, *Revolutionizing.*

[13] On the role performed by Gaudet and Catalano, as well as by the *Groupe de redaction* in charge of drafting the EEC Treaty, composed also by Gaudet and Catalano, as agents of the High Authority, along with Pescatore, as representative of Luxembourg, *see* M. Rasmussen, *Establishing a Constitutional Practice of European Law: The. History of the Legal Service of the European Executive (1952–65)* (2012) 21 *Contemporary European History* 375; J. Bailleux, *Michel Gaudet a Law Entrepreneur: The Role of the Legal Service of the European Executives in the Invention of EC Law (2013) 50 Common Market Law Review* 359; A. Boerger, M. Rasmussen, *The Making of European Law: Exploring the Life and Work of Michel Gaudet* (2017) 57 *American Journal of Legal History*, 51; T. Pavone, *The Ghostwriters*, 137, 145–146; T. Pavone, *Making the European Court Work: Nicola Catalano and the Origins of European Legal Integration*, in D. Gallo, R. Mastroianni, F. Nicola, L. Cecchetti (eds.), *The Italian Influence.*

[14] *See* M. Rasmussen, *Revolutionizing*, 140.

Treaty aimed at enhancing its integrationist spirit. Indeed, although the Court, in its first judgments, had adopted an approach that was almost impermeable to the considerations brought by the agents of the High Authority,[15] the rulings in *Groupement des Industries Sidérurgiques Luxembourgeoises*[16] and, to a lesser extent, *Fédération Charbonnière de Belgique*,[17] dedicated special attention to the object and scope of the ECSC Treaty beyond its letter.

Groupement des Industries Sidérurgiques Luxembourgeoises concerns an action for annulment submitted by a Luxembourg-based company against the High Authority's 'implied decision of refusal'[18] to adopt a recommendation regarding the activities of the *Office Commercial du Ravitaillement* of the Grand Duchy of Luxembourg, as well as of the *Caisse de Compensation*, aimed at requesting the cessation of the functions performed by the *Office Commercial* 'as the sole importer of coal into the Grand Duchy of Luxembourg' and the abolition of the *Caisse de Compensation.*[19]

Two aspects must be highlighted. In the first place, the CJ hinged its decision on a systematic reading of the objectives of the ECSC Treaty. In so doing, it did not see in the activities of the two Luxembourg entities, in particular in the equalization levy introduced by them, a violation of the common market's core principles, since they did not show any 'intention to distort competition'.[20] In the second place, the Court emphasized that certain provisions set forth in Article 4 of the ECSC Treaty, when not restated in any other part of the Treaty, are 'sufficient of themselves and are directly applicable', and that for those other provisions in the same article 'referred to, restated or elaborated on' in other parts of the Treaty, 'the texts relating to one and the same provision must be considered as a whole and applied simultaneously'.[21] Hence, an interpretation which was designed to consider the overall structure and final aims of the Treaty and at the same time identify the legal grounds for its immediate penetration into national legal systems.

In *Fédération Charbonnière de Belgique*, the CJ had to assess the extent of the powers attributed to, and the obligations imposed on, the High Authority for the reduction of Belgian carbon prices within the limits established by the ECSC Treaty. In this framework, the Court held that it was admissible to interpret the Treaty given that some of its provisions implicitly include 'the rules without which that treaty or law would have no meaning or could not be reasonably and usefully applied'.[22] On the basis of this consideration, the Court first made clear that, pursuant to Article 8 of the ECSC Treaty, the High Authority was responsible for achieving the objectives set forth in the Treaty and, then, that it enjoys a certain degree of autonomy in determining which implementing measures shall be enacted to that end. As a result, the decision of the High Authority considering that the ultimate purpose 'of fully and finally integrating Belgian coal into the common market' falls undoubtedly 'within the general ambit of the Treaty' was deemed legitimate by the CJ.[23]

The two rulings examined above reveal that, in the period preceding the establishment of the EEC, the CJ, being aware of the ECSC's potential and peculiarities, contributed to strengthen the powers and competences conferred by the ECSC Treaty to itself as well as to the High Authority for the purpose of ensuring the effectiveness and uniformity

15 Generally, but not always, as pointed out by D. Edward, *Judicial Activism*, 37.
16 CJ, *Groupement des Industries Sidérurgiques Luxembourgeoises*, joined cases 7/54 and 9/54, EU:C:1956:2.
17 CJ, *Fédération Charbonnière de Belgique*, 8/55, EU:C:1956:11.
18 *Groupement des Industries Sidérurgiques Luxembourgeoises* (n 16), 178.
19 *Groupement des Industries Sidérurgiques Luxembourgeoises* (n 16), 178.
20 *Groupement des Industries Sidérurgiques Luxembourgeoises* (n 16), 201.
21 *Groupement des Industries Sidérurgiques Luxembourgeoises* (n 16), 195.
22 *Fédération Charbonnière de Belgique* (n 17), 299.
23 *Fédération Charbonnière de Belgique* (n 17), 302.

of Community law. However, this case law is devoid of that constitutional ethos and advanced understanding of Community law which instead lie at the heart of the *Van Gend & Loos* judgment, as will be observed in the next sections. A spirit and understanding that, instead, define the core of AG Lagrange's opinions in the pre-*Van Gend & Loos* era.[24] Indeed, Lagrange, in his opinion in *Fédération Charbonnière de Belgique* regarding the 'individual' character of a decision pursuant to Article 33(2) of the ECSC Treaty, preferred 'a material and not merely a procedural criterion',[25] according to which interpretation should be neither narrow nor rigid, but rather driven towards clarifying the concept of 'legal interest',[26] in so far as 'any measure of uncertainty remains'.[27]

At the centre of the AG's reasoning was the consideration that strict interpretive methods, which must 'always prevail in the case of international treaties according to the practice followed before international courts such as the Court at The Hague',[28] and are based on the 'common intention of the parties',[29] cannot be naturally implemented in the ECSC context, to the extent that the CJ 'is not an international court but the court of a Community created by six States on a model which is more closely related to a federal than to an international organization'.[30] The AG thereby concluded that the Treaty represents the 'Charter of the Community'[31] and thus its rules constitute 'the internal law of that Community' and must be interpreted in broad and evolutive terms.[32]

These are suggestive and *ante litteram* observations, which are grounded in positions previously taken by Lagrange, all aimed at underlining the differences between the ECSC Treaty and 'classic' international treaties. For example, in the opinion rendered in the *France v High Authority* case,[33] Lagrange specified that the ECSC Treaty has the features of 'a public law legislation' whose main characteristic is that of having established 'a common market based on a system of free competition', having defined 'the rules for it', and having made 'institutions responsible for seeing that those rules are complied with'.[34] A similar approach can be seen in the opinion set forth in *Associazione Industrie Siderurgiche Italiane v High Authority*,[35] where AG Lagrange affirmed that ECSC Treaty rules must not 'be made to say less than' they do.[36] Even more clearly, in an essay published in 1954 in the *Revue du droit public et de la science politique en France et à l'étranger*, Lagrange observed that the Court is '*l'arbitre entre les droits des Etats membres et ceux de la Communauté*'[37] and that, on the

[24] For a recent study, *see*, *inter alia*, L. Clément-Wilz, *La Cour de justice de M. Lagrange*, in M. Mangenot (ed.), *Un légiste de Vichy à la Communauté européenne. Maurice Lagrange: une biographie professionnelle*, dossier, Civitas Europa n. 50, 2023, 101–120.

[25] Opinion of AG Lagrange of 12 June 1956, *Fédération Charbonnière de Belgique*, EU:C:1956:6, 267.

[26] Opinion of AG Lagrange, *Fédération Charbonnière de Belgique* (n 25), 268.

[27] Opinion of AG Lagrange, *Fédération Charbonnière de Belgique* (n 25), 269.

[28] Opinion of AG Lagrange, *Fédération Charbonnière de Belgique* (n 25), 277.

[29] Opinion of AG Lagrange, *Fédération Charbonnière de Belgique* (n 25), 277.

[30] Opinion of AG Lagrange, *Fédération Charbonnière de Belgique* (n 25), 277.

[31] Opinion of AG Lagrange, *Fédération Charbonnière de Belgique* (n 25), 277.

[32] Opinion of AG Lagrange, *Fédération Charbonnière de Belgique* (n 25), 277 (italics added).

[33] Opinion of AG Lagrange of 10 November 1954, *French Republic v High Authority of the European Coal and Steel Community*, 1/54, EU:C:1954:4. At the core of the case lies the interpretation of Article 60(2) of the ECSC Treaty, where it was foreseen that 'the price-lists and conditions of sale applied by undertakings within the Common Market must be made public to the extent and in the manner prescribed by the High Authority'.

[34] Opinion of AG Lagrange, *French Republic v High Authority of the European Coal and Steel Community* (n 33) 30.

[35] Opinion of AG Lagrange of 11 November 1954, *Associazione Industrie Siderurgiche Italiane (ASSIDER) v High Authority of the European Coal and Steel Community*, 3/54, EU:C:1954:6.

[36] Opinion of AG Lagrange, *ASSIDER* (n 35), 87.

[37] M. Lagrange, *La Cour de justice de la Commanauté éuropéenne du carbon et de l'acier* (1954) 70 *Revue du droit public et de la science politique en France et à l'étranger* 417, 434.

one side, the ECSC is '*un embryon d'organisation fédérale*' while, on the other, the Treaty by which it was established has a '*véritable caractère constitutionnel*'.[38]

The reasoning put forward by the members of the CJ who were contemporaries of Lagrange, even if not falling into a purely literal interpretation of the ECSC Treaty, is a long way from the concept of the ECSC system expressed by the AG and the High Authority. A change of perspective occurs, in the case law of the CJ, following the establishment of the EEC,[39] with the 1960 *Humblet v Belgium* ruling,[40] where a clear reference to the prevalence of ECSC law over national laws was made, the Court having written that the Treaty has 'the force of law in the Member States' and 'take[s] precedence over national law'.[41] Moreover, a first trace of the notion of autonomy of Community law from national legal systems arose in *Humblet* to the extent that the Court affirmed that 'the Treaties sought to reinforce the independence of the administrative departments of the Community vis-à-vis the national powers'.[42] This stance is ingrained in the judges' belief, constantly reflected in *Humblet*, that 'it is not sufficient for the Court to adopt the literal interpretation' of the text of the treaties.[43] Moreover, as far as the transfer of powers and competences from the States to the Community institutions is concerned, in the *De Gezamenlijke Steenkolenmijnen in Limburg v High Authority* ruling,[44] the CJ stated that 'the institutions of the Community have been endowed with exclusive authority',[45] a phrase which would be reiterated by European judges in their jurisprudence.

The autonomy of Community law became more visible in the *De Geus v Bosch*[46] judgment. In that case, the Court, while rejecting the idea that that Community rules were in principle self-executing, affirmed that national law and Community law are two 'separate and distinct legal orders'[47] and, consequently, independent from one another.

That said, a significant evolution took place thanks to the appointment as judge, in May 1962, of Robert Lecourt,[48] who would share Antonio Trabucchi's understanding of Community law,[49] as far as the relationship between the latter and domestic legal systems is concerned. Indeed, as remarked in the literature,[50] Lecourt and Trabucchi were very close to each other, albeit coming from different professional and legal backgrounds: Lecourt was a former politician and public law jurist, Trabucchi an academic and a private law scholar. They had in common a clear attachment to European ideals and were both strongly

[38] M. Lagrange, *La Cour de justice*, 434.

[39] An impressive survey on the biographies of the then-judges and advocates general at the CJ has been undertaken by V. Fritz, *Juges et avocats généraux de la Cour de Justice de l'Union européenne (1952-1972): une approche biographique de l'histoire d'une révolution juridique*, Frankfurt, Klostermann, 2018.

[40] CJ, *Jean-E. Humblet*, 6/60, EU:C:1960:48. On the case, *see* A. Arena, *How European Law Became Supreme: The Making of Costa v ENEL*, Jean Monnet Working Paper Series, 2018, 1, 19, available at https://jeanmonnetprogram.org/wp-content/uploads/JMWP-05-Amedeo-Arena.pdf; A. Arena, *The Twin Doctrines of Primacy and Pre-emption*, in R. Schütze, T. Tridimas (eds.), *Oxford Principles of European Union Law: The European Union Legal Order: Volume I*, Oxford, Oxford University Press, 2018, 300–349, 302, 309, and 310.

[41] *Humblet* (n 40), 569.

[42] *Humblet* (n 40), 577.

[43] *Humblet* (n 40), 575.

[44] CJ, *De Gezamenlijke Steenkolenmijnen in Limburg*, 30/59, EU:C:1961:2.

[45] *De Gezamenlijke Steenkolenmijnen* (n 44), 22.

[46] CJ, *Kledingverkoopbedrijf de Geus en Uitdenbogerd*, 13/61, EU:C:1962:11.

[47] *De Geus v Bosch* (n 46), 50.

[48] On the legal philosophy of Lecourt, as well as on its major influence, first as judge and then as President, on the work by the Court, *see* W. Phelan, *Supremacy, Direct Effect, and Dairy Products in the Early History of European law* (2016) 14 *International Journal of Constitutional Law* 6; W. Phelan, *The Revolutionary Doctrines of European Law and the Legal Philosophy of Robert Lecourt* (2017) 28 *European Journal of International Law* 935. *See* also P. Pescatore, *Robert Lecourt (1908-2004)* (2005) 3 *Revue trimestrielle de droit européen* 589.

[49] Trabucchi was appointed in March 1962.

[50] *See* V. Fritz, *Juges*, 325–329.

devoted to the development of the process of European integration.[51] As a matter of fact, in *Commission v Luxembourg and Belgium*,[52] with Judge-Rapporteur Lecourt, the Court embraced a teleological interpretation of the EEC Treaty, notably of its Articles 9 and 12, in relation to customs duties and charges having an equivalent effect. In fact, it was observed that to understand the meaning of 'equivalent' 'it is important to consider . . . the objectives of the Treaty',[53] including Article 3, where it prescribes that competition should not be distorted. As such, this is an interpretation which anticipates *Van Gend & Loos* and the subsequent case law. The Court notes, for that matter, 'the essential nature' and 'the clarity, certainty and unrestricted scope'[54] of those two articles.

Considering the above, there can be no doubt that the *Van Gend & Loos* decision was the product of an evolution of case law,[55] rooted in the cutting-edge viewpoint of AG Lagrange, as well as in the approach embraced by the High Authority and, later, by the European Commission. However, the fact that there has been a conceptual ripening cannot lead to an underestimation of the importance of *Van Gend & Loos*. In the first place, where the Court places at the heart of *Van Gend & Loos* the idea that Community law penetrates immediately into the national legal systems, a turning point has been traversed, despite the existence of a 'softer' alternative, that is, relying on the monistic view which existed and still exists today in the Dutch legal system.[56] In the second place, the systematic and teleological interpretation of primary law, that is, of both the ECSC Treaty and the EEC Treaty, as well as the identification of direct effect's premises, are placed in the context of a broad reflection on the effectiveness of Community law, for the first time, only with *Van Gend & Loos*. Thirdly, it is only in this judgment that the internal effect of Community law is associated for the first time with the need to ensure its uniform application amongst Member States. Lastly, *Van Gend & Loos* is the first occasion in which the CJ dwelled on the central relevance that the preliminary rulings procedure plays in the European legal order, above all from the standpoint of its impact on the enhancement of the judicial protection of individual rights.[57]

2. Direct effect in *Van Gend & Loos*

2.1 The actors at play

The facts which gave rise to the *Van Gend & Loos* decision, the most historic among the historic rulings of the CJ,[58] are well-known. Here is a summary: the company N.V. Algemene

[51] For an overview on the protagonists of the *Van Gend & Loos* ruling, *see* the next §.

[52] CJ, *Commission v Luxembourg and Belgium*, joined cases 2–3/62, EU:C:1962:45. On such judgment, read along with *Van Gend en Loos* and *Costa*, see W. Phelan, *The Troika: The Interlocking Roles of Commission v Luxembourg and Belgium, Van Gend en Loos and Costa v ENEL in the Creation of the European Legal Order* (2015) 21 *European Law Journal* 116.

[53] *Commission v Luxembourg and Belgium* (n 52), 432.

[54] *Commission v Luxembourg and Belgium* (n 52), 431–432.

[55] *Contra, see* P. Neill QC, *The European Court of Justice: A Case Study in Judicial Activism, European Policy Forum/Frankfurter Institut - Stiftung Marktwirtschaft und Politik*, London, European Policy Forum, 1995, 1.

[56] *See* Article 66, at the time, of the Dutch Constitution, amended and then transposed into Article 93 due to the constitutional reform of 1981, as clarified by B. de Witte, *Relire* van Gend en Loos (2012) 3 *Il Diritto dell'Unione europea* 513.

[57] On this matter *see* §§ 1 and 4 of Chapter II.

[58] *See*, *ex multis*, F. Mancini, D. Keeling, *Democracy and the European Court of Justice* (1994) 57 *Modern Law Review* 175, 183, who underlined that 'if the European Community still exists 50 or 100 years from now, historians will look back on *Van Gend en Loos* as the unique judicial contribution to the making of Europe'; A. Tizzano, *I 'grands arrêts' della giurisprudenza dell'Unione europea*, Turin, Giappichelli, 2012, 16. According to D. Chalmers,

Transport-en Expeditie Onderneming Van Gend & Loos imported into the Netherlands, in September 1960, a shipment of urea formaldehyde (urea resin) from the Federal Republic of Germany. The goods were immediately subject to an *ad valorem* import duty of 8 per cent. The company lodged an objection against the application of the duty with the Inspector of Customs and Excise of Zaandam. The objection was dismissed after several months. In April 1961, Van Gend & Loos appealed this decision before an administrative court, that is the *Tariefcommissie* of Amsterdam. In the applicant's view, the Dutch authorities had violated Article 12 of the EEC Treaty,[59] currently Article 30 TFEU, since—it was claimed—they had unlawfully imposed an import duty on those foreign products. The *Tariefcommissie*, in the hearing of 21 May 1962, chose not to resolve the matter on its own and, by order of August 1962, referred the question to the CJ for a preliminary ruling, pursuant to Article 177 of the EEC Treaty, currently Article 267 TFEU, formulating the following (interpretive) question: 'whether Article 12 of the EEC Treaty has direct application within the territory of a Member State, in other words, whether nationals of such a State can, on the basis of the Article in question, lay claim to individual rights which the courts must protect'.[60]

The crux of the matter lies in finding out if and when Community rules, of primary law, attribute rights to individuals in such a way that they may invoke them before the national authorities, especially courts.

Reasoning about direct effect implies reflecting on the deep legal nature of the European legal order, including on its rules from the point of view of their ability to create subjective legal positions.[61] Such an investigation necessarily intersects with the issue of direct applicability of Community law since verifying if a certain provision attributes rights cannot be kept separate from a reflection on its suitability to enter, without mediation, the domestic legal orders and be immediately applied by the national authorities.[62] Furthermore, in addition to direct applicability, in *Van Gend & Loos* the stone guest was the principle of primacy, most notably the role it plays within the EEC and in conjunction with direct effect.

Verifying if and to what extent Article 12 of the EEC Treaty was equipped with 'direct internal effect'[63] required the CJ to evaluate if Community law belonged to international law and, therefore, whether the EEC Treaty was a 'standard international treaty'.[64] In other words, the Court had to choose between two opposing hermeneutical approaches: a literal interpretation of Article 12 of the EEC Treaty that would have led to denying its direct effect,

G. Davies, G. Monti, *European Union Law. Text and Materials*, 4th ed., Cambridge, Cambridge University Press, 2019, 15, the judgment is 'arguably the most important decision ever given' by the CJ. *See* also S. Weatherill, *Cases and Materials on EU Law*, Oxford, Oxford University Press, 2014, 81; J. H. H. Weiler, Van Gend en Loos: *The Individual as Subject and Object and the Dilemma of European Legitimacy* (2014) 12 *International Journal of Constitutional Law* 94; W. Phelan, *Great Judgments*, 40.

[59] On the legal and academic background of the appellant's attorneys—Hans Stibbe, an international law lawyer, and Ter Kuile, a member of the *Fédération Internationale pour le Droit Européen* (FIDE) entrusted by the latter with the task of identifying the EEC Treaty's directly effective provisions—*see* A. Vauchez, *Judge-Made Law: aux origines du modèle politique communautaire (retour sur* Van Gend en Loos *et* Costa c. ENEL), in O. Costa, P. Magnette (eds.), *Une Europe des élites? Réflexions sur la fracture démocratique de l'Union européenne*, Brussels, Bruylant, 2007, 139–166, 14.

[60] *Van Gend & Loos* (n 1), 3.

[61] Conferral of a right implies, normally but not always, that an EU provision is endowed with direct effect; *see* extensively Chapter IV.

[62] On the interplay, in *Van Gend & Loos*, between direct effect and direct applicability *see* F. C. Mayer, Van Gend en Loos: *The Foundation of a Community of Law*, in M. Poiares Maduro, L. Azoulai (eds.), *The Past and Future of EU Law: The Classics of EU Law Revisited on the 50th Anniversary of the Rome Treaty*, Oxford, Hart, 2010, 16–25, 17–18. On the *de facto* coincidence between these two concepts in part of EU case law, *see* § 7 of Chapter III.

[63] *Van Gend & Loos* (n 1), 8.

[64] *Van Gend & Loos* (n 1), 8.

lacking the express conferral of subjective rights, or its systematic and teleological interpretation that would have led to admitting that individual rights, and not only obligations on States, derive from that provision.

Written observations were presented, in addition to those of Van Gend & Loos and of the government of the Netherlands, also by the Commission and the governments of Belgium and the Federal Republic of Germany. Moreover, at the hearing of November 1962 before the Court, only the appellant company and the Commission made oral interventions. With respect to the Netherlands, its arguments were embedded in the conceptual and practical dissociation between the concept of internal effect and that of direct effect. At the core of the Dutch government's reasoning was the conviction that the EEC Treaty 'does not differ from a standard international treaty'.[65] In its view, a provision of primary law could be granted internal effect only when it would be possible to infer this characteristic from the intent of the Contracting Parties and the actual contents of the provision. In this respect, the government simply pointed out that the wording of Article 12 of the EEC Treaty, especially when compared with that of other rules, 'only places an obligation on Member States', who would remain, in this way, free to decide how they intend to fulfil their obligations.[66] Not having internal effect, Article 12 of the EEC Treaty would not, '*a fortiori*, have direct effect'[67] and, even if it were to consider the imposition of an obligation on the Member States as an internal effect, the provision—as clarified by the Dutch government—would not have direct effect in the sense of 'permit[ing] nationals of Member States to assert subjective rights'.[68] And in any case—the Dutch government stressed in its submission to the Court—the issue of the direct effect of Article 12 of the EEC Treaty would require an interpretation of Dutch constitutional law and, therefore, should be kept outside the scope of the CJ's jurisdiction. The *originalist* conclusion[69] presented by the Dutch government was that the attribution of internal immediate effects, that is direct effect, to Article 12 of the EEC Treaty 'would upset the system which the authors of the Treaty intended to establish',[70] also because it would subject States to a system of control different from the infringement procedures set forth in Articles 169 and 170 of the EEC Treaty, currently Articles 258 and 259 TFEU.

As to Belgium, the observations revolved around the assumption that the matter brought before the CJ was one of national constitutional law and thus should be resolved by virtue of monism,[71] which was in force at the time in the Dutch legal system. More specifically, the Belgian government first noted that the directly effective provisions of the EEC Treaty were an exception, then, that Article 12 was not among those provisions and, last, that such norm, far from determining the invalidity of all the newly introduced customs duties, would prompt the national authorities 'only' to refrain from taking such measures. Nationals, therefore, could not invoke, demand, or enforce compliance since, as is the case with the majority of rules of primary law, Article 12 of the EEC Treaty 'requires action at a later date'[72] by the Dutch government to attain the objectives laid down in the Treaty in order to ensure the fulfilment of the obligations deriving from it. Therefore, it would be inadmissible to request the

[65] *Van Gend & Loos* (n 1), 8.
[66] *Van Gend & Loos* (n 1), 8.
[67] *Van Gend & Loos* (n 1), 8.
[68] *Van Gend & Loos* (n 1), 8.
[69] On the meaning of 'originalist' interpretation of the law, *see*, *inter alia*, J. Rubenfeld, *Freedom and Time—A Theory of Constitutional Self-Government*, New Heaven, Yale University Press, 2001, 61–67.
[70] *Van Gend & Loos* (n 1), 8.
[71] On the contested terms 'monism' and 'dualism', *see* the considerations in § 3 of Chapter II and § 1 of Chapter VII.
[72] *Van Gend & Loos* (n 1), 8.

intervention of national courts, who, instead, must decide, solely in terms of national law, if and how an international rule can be incorporated in the domestic legal order.

The German government's position emphasized that Article 12 of the EEC Treaty imposed on the States an international obligation which had to be executed by national authorities endowed with legislative powers in the field of customs policy. The doubt raised by the *Tariefcommissie*, according to Germany, consisted in the evaluation of whether certain internal provisions, adopted to fulfil Community obligations, corresponded to their intended purpose. In this vein, as the interpretation of national law was the true, sole object of the reference, Germany argued that the Court could not render a preliminary ruling since the question referred by the Dutch court was not about interpretation of the Treaty.

At the other extreme, the appellant company considered that Article 12 of the EEC Treaty had internal—and, according to the company, direct—effect, and was thus suitable for immediate application by the national courts for two principal reasons. Firstly, the prohibition enshrined in the law, although addressed to States rather than individuals, requires the latter to be safeguarded against the illegitimate behaviour of domestic authorities. If this were not the case, they would not be guaranteed the right to invoke key economic rights arising from Community law. In the second place, Article 12 of the EEC Treaty, to be implemented, did not need to be transposed into national law because it dictated a *non facere* on the national authorities.

The Commission's position also stood in stark contrast with the claims made by the intervening governments: the central idea is that the internal effect of the Community rules within the national systems cannot be determined by virtue of what is foreseen in the law of each State. This would, consequently, be a problem for interpretation of the Treaty, as the Member States not only intended to assume 'mutual commitments' but also wanted to establish 'a system of Community law'.[73] The need for Community law to be applied 'effectively and uniformly'[74] throughout all the Member States lies at the heart of the Commission's reasoning.[75] For this to happen, two conditions shall be fulfilled: *(i)* the internal effect of the EEC provisions in the domestic legal orders must be specified by Community—not national—law; and *(ii)* the Member States are required, where possible, to apply the Community law directly even if it conflicts with internal rules that were 'passed later'.[76] The point of departure of the Commission's reasoning is that the possible reliance upon an EEC rule by an individual cannot be denied simply because, 'as regards its form',[77] it is directed at the Member States. In its pleadings presented at the hearing, the Commission wrote that, '[*É*]*tant par la volonté des Etats membres une norme de la Communauté en fonction de laquelle chacun est tenu de régler son comportement, la règle de droit communautaire crée pour chacun le droit à obtenir son application*'.[78] More specifically, with regard to Article 12 of the EEC Treaty, the Commission pointed out that the rule was capable of being applied in practice by the national courts as it is a 'perfectly clear'[79] and 'complete and self-sufficient provision',[80] in the sense that it imposes upon national authorities 'a specific and unambiguous obligation',[81]

[73] *Van Gend & Loos* (n 1), 7.
[74] *Van Gend & Loos* (n 1), 7.
[75] A survey on the Commission's arguments is carried out by A. Vauchez, *Judge-Made Law*, 144 and M. Rasmussen, *Revolutionizing*, 152–155.
[76] *Van Gend & Loos* (n 1), 7.
Van Gend & Loos (n 1), 7.
[77] *Van Gend & Loos* (n 1), 7.
[78] As reported by A. Vauchez, *Judge-Made Law*, 145.
[79] *Van Gend & Loos* (n 1), 7.
[80] *Van Gend & Loos* (n 1), 7.
[81] *Van Gend & Loos* (n 1), 7.

since 'it does not require on a Community level any new measure to give concrete form to the obligation which it defines'.[82]

The position set forth by AG Roemer differed considerably from that of the Commission. Roemer, who was influenced by the jurisprudence of German courts according to which rights enshrined in international treaties could be invoked on the sole condition that they be embedded in express provisions,[83] proposed to the CJ to declare that 'Article 12 only contains an obligation on the part of the Member States'.[84] The AG's stance, while consistent with the core of the arguments advanced by the governments of the Netherlands, Belgium, and the Federal Republic of Germany, only partially coincides with their reasoning. In fact, Roemer contested that the question, in his opinion incorrectly formulated by the *Tariefcommissie*,[85] could be resolved solely on the basis of Dutch constitutional law. According to him, the problem was rooted also, *but not only*, in constitutional law. As the AG saw it, it was a constitutional law issue since Article 66 of the Dutch Constitution in force at the time, as interpreted by the judiciary, including the Constitutional Court, established that international treaties prevail over internal rules provided that their provisions were intended to be made directly applicable.[86] The essential point was whether Article 12 of the EEC Treaty had this feature and thus directly conferred a justiciable right to individuals, or whether it contained an obligation only for the States, the violation of which would not, however, entail the setting aside of conflicting national laws. Therefore, the question would not simply be a constitutional law one because the effects of an international treaty, in accord with Roemer, would depend above all on the juridical character which its authors intended to grant to its provisions. The main concern for the AG, thus, was to prevent the CJ from acting *ultra vires* and misinterpreting the EEC Treaty.

Having put forward this premise, Roemer, deviating from the more clear-cut arguments of the three national governments, even though opposed to recognizing the direct effect of Article 12 of the EEC Treaty, in essence considered valid the Commission's claim that the Treaty could not be interpreted only in the light of general principles of international law. More specifically, in the opinion of the AG, from one side, Community law 'does not just consist of contractual relations between a number of States considered as subjects of the laws of nations',[87] while from the other, it consists of a series of binding acts and measures which apply also to individuals. In this framework, Roemer observed that the EEC Treaty encompasses provisions which are clearly directly effective, such as those regarding competition law, or provisions 'designed to produce direct effects at a later stage', such as the provisions regarding the free movement of persons, services, and capital.[88] On the other hand, continued the AG, in addition to Article 12 of the EEC Treaty, there were many other primary law provisions that merely referred to the obligations imposed on the national authorities, including those regulating customs matters, tax duties, and State monopolies: their wording would demonstrate that direct effect cannot be asserted. Even where the EEC Treaty laid down a prohibition addressed at domestic authorities or provided that a given attitude of the States was 'incompatible with the Common Market',[89] the concerned rules could not be

[82] *Van Gend & Loos* (n 1), 7.
[83] As observed by F. C. Mayer, Van Gend en Loos, 17–18.
[84] Opinion of AG Roemer of 12 December 1962, *Van Gend & Loos*, EU:C:1962:42, 30.
[85] Opinion of AG Roemer, *Van Gend & Loos* (n 84), 18–19.
[86] Opinion of AG Roemer, *Van Gend & Loos* (n 84), 26.
[87] Opinion of AG Roemer, *Van Gend & Loos* (n 84), 20.
[88] Opinion of AG Roemer, *Van Gend & Loos* (n 84), 20.
[89] Opinion of AG Roemer, *Van Gend & Loos* (n 84), 21.

considered directly applicable because they were subject to a subsequent 'clarifying' intervention by the Commission.

The AG then focused on the organization of the administration of justice in the Community legal order, noting that at its core laid not the principle of internal direct effect/applicability but rather the public enforcement through the Commission's action. This being said, Roemer emphasized that, albeit Article 12 of the EEC Treaty having 'in a certain sense'[90] direct legal effect, such effect was not able to 'penetrate into the national legal field and lead to its direct application by the administrative authorities and courts of Member States'.[91] In fact, according to the AG, Article 12 of the EEC Treaty would deploy its effects only vis-à-vis the governments of the Member States, who were the addressees of the rule and, at least at the time, enjoyed significant discretional regulatory power in the customs sector. In support of his argument, Roemer observed that Article 12 of the EEC Treaty was 'very complex'[92] and that, where it contemplated a fluid concept such as the charge having equivalent effect, it lacked clarity because it could not be applied 'in every case without creating problems'.[93] Roemer explained, moreover, that if the direct effect of Article 12 of the EEC Treaty were to be permitted, given the diversity of the national regimes regarding the relationships between supranational rules and internal rules, its violation would determine, only in domestic monistic legal orders, such as the Netherlands, the questioning of their customs rules, while in others, of a dualistic nature, such precedence could not be guaranteed. The AG then concluded his reasoning by relying on a 'subjectivist' interpretive method, seeking to find the parties' actual intentions through a review of the preparatory work, clarifying that 'the authors of the Treaty' were aware[94] of the risks of disparity arising from the idea, argued by Van Gend & Loos and the Commission, pursuant to which Community rules should be directly applied in the national legal systems and held inapplicable because in conflict with Community law.

2.2 The key role of teleological interpretation

The CJ, composed of the then-President A. M. Donner and Justices L. Delvaux, R. Rossi, O. Riese, C. L. Hammes, A. Trabucchi, and R. Lecourt, rejected the AG's approach. As written in the literature, 'the driving force behind the judgment' was Trabucchi,[95] who had recently arrived at the Court and, in opposition[96] to the minimalism of Judge Rapporteur Hammes,[97]

[90] Opinion of AG Roemer, *Van Gend & Loos* (n 84), 22.
[91] Opinion of AG Roemer, *Van Gend & Loos* (n 84), 22.
[92] Opinion of AG Roemer, *Van Gend & Loos* (n 84), 22.
[93] Opinion of AG Roemer, *Van Gend & Loos* (n 84), 22.
[94] Opinion of AG Roemer, *Van Gend & Loos* (n 84), 24.
[95] R. van Leuken, *Private Law and the Internal Market*, Cambridge, Intersentia, 2017, footnote 10, 15. On the role performed by Trabucchi in the Court's drafting of *Van Gend & Loos*, *see* M. Cartabia, *Fundamental Rights and the Relationship among the Court of Justice, the National Supreme Courts and the Strasbourg Court*, in A. Tizzano, J. Kokott, S. Prechal (Organizing Committee), *50ème anniversaire*, 155–169, 155–156 and R. Barents, *Van Gend &. Loos en Costa/Enel*, in T. W. B. Beukers, H. J. van Harten, S. Prechal (eds.), *Het recht van de Europese Unie in 50 klassieke arresten*, The Hague, Boom Juridische Uitgevers, 2010, 22–28, 26–27. For a recent survey on Trabucchi and his role at the CJ, from the perspective of one of his *référendaires*, *see* E. Perillo, *Alberto Trabucchi.*
[96] *See* P. Gori, *Quindici anni insieme ad Alberto Trabucchi alla Corte di giustizia CE*, in *La formazione del diritto europeo – Quaderni della Rivista di diritto civile*, Padua, Cedam, 2008, 71–83, 76.
[97] Supported by Justices Riese and Donner. In this respect, it shall be recalled the internal conflict that existed at the time at the Court, as demonstrated by the resignation of President Donner immediately after the *Costa* ruling, who observed that he had lost the support of the other judges; *see* V. Fritz, *Juges*, 116–117.

together with Lecourt,[98] pleaded in favour of direct effect. Indeed, in a *note en délibéré*,[99] he asserted the idea that the EEC was a new legal construct that 'placed individuals centre stage'.[100] Both Trabucchi and Lecourt managed to convince Delvaux and Rossi[101] to support that position and in this way reached a majority within the Court.[102]

In the original text (Dutch),[103] like in the French,[104] German,[105] and English,[106] translations of the *Van Gend & Loos* ruling, it was stressed that Article 12 of the EEC Treaty produces direct effect (Dutch) or direct effects (French, German, and English).[107] In the French text there is a reference also to '*effets immédiats*', while in the Italian translation the term 'direct effect(s)' is absent, but a reference is made rather to the preceptive force ('*valore precettivo*') of the rule, intended to confer on 'nationals of Member States [the possibility to] lay claim to rights which the national court must protect'.[108]

With respect to the nature of the analysis conducted by the Court, it is teleological and systematic, freed from a mere examination of the Contracting Parties' intent.[109] A look at the 'spirit' and 'general scheme'—not only at the 'wording'—of the Treaty,[110] allowed European judges to affirm that rights are conferred by the EEC Treaty also when they impose obligations only on States, with the result that, in essence, the granting of individual rights—that is, of rights arising from Community law '[i]ndependently from the legislation of Member

[98] For a different reconstruction, tailored on highlighting the crucial role of R. Lecourt as well as the private enforcement element implied in direct effect, *see* W. Phelan, *The Revolutionary Doctrines of European Law*.

[99] On the contents of the *délibéré* and on the impact it had on the Court at the time, *see* E. Perillo, *Alberto Trabucchi*, who also recalled that such document was disclosed, many years later, 'by his *référendaire*, Professor Paolo Gori, who officially announced this discovery at the 50th VGL anniversary Conference organized by the Court of Justice'.

[100] In these terms, *see* K. Lenaerts, J. A. Gutiérrez-Fons, '*Van Gend en Loos*: A Star is Born', in P. Craig, R. Schütze (eds.), *Landmark Cases in EU Law*, Oxford, Hart, 2025, forthcoming.

[101] Notwithstanding their differing political origins and attitudes towards the project of European integration, Trabucchi and Rossi got along very well; on this point, *see* A. Arena, '*Notre Nestor, Monsieur le Juge Rossi' (1889-1974): An Internationalist's Contribution to the Making of a Supranational Legal Order*, in D. Gallo, R. Mastroianni, F. Nicola, L. Cecchetti (eds.), *The Italian Influence*.

[102] M. Rasmussen, *The Origins of a Legal Revolution—The Early History of the European Court of Justice* (2008) 14 *Journal of European Integration History* 77, 94. In this regard, *see* P. Gori, *Souvenirs d'un survivant*, in A. Tizzano, J. Kokott, and S. Prechal (Organizing Committee), *50ème anniversaire*, 29–35, 30, who was, along with E. Perillo, mentioned above, the legal secretary of Judge Trabucchi, and observed that the judgment was the result of a four-judge majority. For further insights on the debate, and contrasts, which arose at the Court at the time, *see* also A. Vauchez, *The Transnational Politics*.

[103] '*Artikel 12 van het Verdrag tot oprichting van de Europese Economische Gemeenschap heeft directe werking en schept rechten ten bate der justitiabelen, welker handhaving aan de nationale rechters kan worden gevraagd*'.

[104] '*L'article 12 du traité instituant la Communauté économique européenne produit des effets immédiats et engendre dans le chef des justiciables des droits individuels que les juridictions internes doivent sauvegarder*'.

[105] '*Artikel 12 des Vertrages zur Gründung der Europäischen Wirtschaftsgemeinschaft erzeugt unmittelbare Wirkungen und begründet individuelle Rechte der Einzelnen, welche die staatlichen Gerichte zu beachten haben*'.

[106] 'Article 12 of the Treaty establishing the European Economic Community produces direct effects and creates individual rights which national courts must protect'. As is known, the English translation dates back to several years after the publication of the ruling, inasmuch as neither the UK nor Ireland were members of the EEC at the time; on this aspect, *see* B. de Witte, *The Continuous Significance of* Van Gend en Loos, in M. Poiares Maduro, L. Azoulai (eds.), *The Past*, 9–15, footnote 14, 11.

[107] English text, 11. As recalled by P. Gori, *Souvenirs d'un survivant*, 34, '*la version française qui [. . .] tout en n'étant pas la version faisant foi, est celle qui en fait a été délibérée par la Cour*'.

[108] French text, 25 and 28; Italian text, 27 and 22, whereby there is also a reference to '*diritti soggettivi*'.

[109] Conversely, *see* PCIJ, *Jurisdiction of the Courts of Danzig (Pecuniary Claims of Danzig Railway Officials who have passed into the Polish Service, Against the Polish Railways Administration)*, Reports, Series B, No. 15, 3 March 1928, 3. On this matter, *see* C. Blumann, L. Dubouis, *Droit institutionnel de l'Union européenne*, 6th ed., Paris, Lexis Nexis, 2016, footnote 61, 558. On the *travaux préparatoires* as a basis for investigating the intent of the Contracting Parties that drafted the European Treaties, *see* S. Lattanzi, *I 'travaux préparatoires' del diritto dell'Unione Europea: tassonomia, ruolo e funzioni*, Padua, Cedam, 2022.

[110] *Van Gend & Loos* (n 1), 12

States'[111]—need not be made explicit in the text of the law.[112] What emerges from the reconstruction carried out by the CJ is that the recognition of direct effect (of certain provisions) of the EEC Treaty, confirmed by the reference to the peoples, in addition to the governments, in the Treaty's Preamble, appears functional to the pursuit of its final goal, namely the establishment of a common market. A common market which, as emphasized by the Court, 'is of direct concern to interested parties in the Community'[113] and does not merely create 'mutual obligations between the contracting states'.[114] In this connection, the CJ departed from the standard rule of interpretation that both international and national courts normally had recourse to at that time, and still do today.[115]

As a matter of fact, the Court chose an objective, rather than a subjective[116] and literal, interpretation of the European Treaties.[117] 'Objective' means that the intent of the Contracting Parties disappears as such[118] from the written norm, which shall be interpreted first and foremost by the CJ in the light of the structure and objectives of the European Treaties. As held by J. A. Winter, 'it seems that the spirit of the Treaty amounts to the imputed objective will of the Contracting Parties: *i.e.*, not what the drafters of the Treaty had in mind but what they ought to have had in mind'.[119] This way, not only has the Court taken away from domestic authorities the power to determine the extent of their obligations pursuant to EU law, but it has also 'seized complete control over the question of interpretation of the direct applicability of Treaty law'.[120]

That direct effect is a founding, constitutional principle of European law can be derived also from the institutional structure of the Community, in particular by the transfer

[111] *Van Gend & Loos* (n 1), 12.

[112] On teleological interpretation, seen also in the light of the other methods of interpretation employed by the CJ, *see* G. D'Agnone, *L'interpretazione soggettiva nella giurisprudenza della Corte di giustizia dell'Unione europea*, Turin, Giappichelli, 2020, 12–21; K. Lenaerts, J. A. Gutiérrez-Fons, *Les méthodes d'interprétation de la Cour de justice de l'Union européenne*, Brussels, Bruylant, 2020, 54–61; R. Schütze, *European Union Law*, Oxford, 3rd ed., Oxford University Press, 2021, 135–136.

[113] *Van Gend & Loos* (n 1), 12.

[114] *Van Gend & Loos* (n 1), 12.

[115] In the literature, amongst the first authors to examine the nexus between rules of interpretation and the doctrine of direct effect, *see* V. D. Degan, *L'interprétation des accords en droit international*, The Hague, Martinus Nijhoff, 1963. For a more recent study, *see* M. Forteau, *The Role of the International Rules of Interpretation for the Determination of Direct Effect of International Agreements*, in H. P. Aust, G. Nolte (eds.), *The Interpretation of International Law by Domestic Courts*, 2016, 96–112. Doubts about the existence of manifest divergences between principles of interpretation belonging to the realm of international law and those known to EU law were expressed by A. Peters, *The Position of International Law within the European Community Legal Order* (1997) 40 *German Yearbook of International Law* 9–77, 24–25.

[116] Generally, on the subjective interpretation of the CJ, *see* the in-depth volume by G. D'Agnone, *L'interpretazione*.

[117] For an account, *see* P. Pescatore, *L'ordre juridique des Communautés européennes*, Liège, Presses universitaires de Liège, 1975, 133–135 and W. Ganhof van der Meersch, *L'ordre juridique des Communautés européennes et le droit international*, Alphen aan den Rijn, Sijthoff & Noordhoff, 1979, 273–294. *See* also J. H. H. Weiler, *Revisiting* Van Gend en Loos, 12; P. Mengozzi, *Rapporto tra Stato e individui nella giurisprudenza comunitaria*, in *La formazione del diritto europeo* (n 96) 111–115, 111; P. Mengozzi, *Quelques réflexions sur les origines de l'arrêt* Van Gend en Loos (2013) 4 *Il Diritto dell'Unione Europea* 679, 687. In this framework, J. H. H. Weiler, *Rewriting* Van Gend en Loos: *Towards a Normative Theory of ECJ Hermeneutics*, in O. Wiklund (ed.), *Judicial Discretion in European Perspective*, Stockholm, Kluwer Law International, 2003, 150–164, argued that the Court could have reached the same conclusion as in *Van Gend & Loos* on the basis of the ordinary interpretive principles of international law.

[118] *See* above in this § about the opposition to the recognition of direct effect expressed by the intervening governments (Belgium, Germany, and the Netherlands).

[119] J. A. Winter, *Direct Applicability and Direct Effect. Two Distinct and Different Concepts in Community Law* (1972) 9 *Common Market Law Review* 425, 433.

[120] J. A. Winter, *Direct Applicability*, 431. *See* also A. Bleckmann, *L'applicabilité directe du droit communautaire*, in Waelbroeck M., Velu J. (eds.), *Les recours des individus devant les instances nationales en cas de violation du droit européen*, Brussels, Larcier, 1978, 85–130, 108 and J. H. H. Weiler, *The Community System: The Dual Character of Supra-Nationalism* (1981) 1 *Yearbook of European Law* 267–306, 270.

of sovereign powers, 'the exercise of which affects Member States and also their citizens',[121] from the States to the Community bodies. The role granted to the CJ by Article 177 of the EEC Treaty confirms the States' willingness to acknowledge Community law's 'authority'[122] such as to allow it to be invoked by individuals before the national authorities, *in primis* before the courts. The Community thereby constitutes 'a new legal order of international law'[123] which recognizes as legal subjects not only the States but also their citizens, to the benefit of which the domestic authorities have self-imposed limits in their transfer of a part of their sovereignty. The originality of European law consists in its ability to affect individuals, intended as holders of legal positions stemming from Community law, rather than as third parties and beneficiaries of legal relationships existing between the Parties who have signed and ratified the treaties.

In short, the Court showed that it had a conception of Europe inspired by the need to pursue a greater integration among the legal orders, and it is this idea, rather than simply a technical and strictly legal answer to the issues brought in the case,[124] which induced it to take a first, major step towards the creation 'of an ever-closer union among the peoples of Europe'.[125] This is the reason why the *Van Gend & Loos* decision constitutes the cornerstone of Community law, as written by Trabucchi,[126] the importance of which had been anticipated, prior to its publication, by R. M. Chevalier, legal secretary[127] of Lecourt.[128] This is also the reason why the key role of *Van Gend & Loos* in the whole legal architecture of European law has been asserted in a series of writings, on the basis of an informal coordination, by judges, former judges (even those who had originally taken a different view), and Advocates General of the Court, by the most senior officials of the High Authority, the Commission, and the European Parliament, that is, by all the major players of the time,[129] including A. M. Donner,[130] M. Gaudet,[131] the then-President of the Commission W. Hallstein,[132] M. Lagrange,[133] R. Lecourt,[134] N. Catalano,[135] and

[121] *Van Gend & Loos* (n 1), 12.
[122] *Van Gend & Loos* (n 1), 12.
[123] *Van Gend & Loos* (n 1), 12. *See* recently, amongst others, CJ, *Euro Box Promotion*, joined cases C-357/19, C-379/19, C-547/19, C-811/19, and C-840/19, EU:C:2021:1034, para. 245.
[124] As also recalled in the Introduction, P. Pescatore, *The Doctrine of 'Direct Effect': An Infant Disease of Community Law* (1983) 8 *European Law Review* 155, 157, observed that the CJ built its reasoning on '*une certaine idée d'Europe*' rather than on 'legal technicalities of the matter'. For a critical appraisal of the legal arguments used by the CJ in *Van Gend & Loos*, *see* A. Arnull, *The European Union and Its Court of Justice*, Oxford, Oxford University Press, 1999, 168–170 and R. Schütze, *European Constitutional Law*, Cambridge, Cambridge University Press, 2016, 80.
[125] *See* Preamble and Article 1(1) TEU.
[126] A. Trabucchi, *Incidenza del diritto comunitario sul diritto interno in Italia*, in V. Rizzo (ed.), *Diritto privato comunitario*, Naples, Editoriale Scientifica, 1997, 77–87, on which, *see* the observations by P. Mengozzi, *Quelques réflexions*, 681.
[127] *See* the account by A. Cohen, '*Ten Majestic Figures in Long Amaranth Robes*'.
[128] M. Chevalier, *Commentaire d'arrêt* (1963) 1 *Gazette du Palais* 1.
[129] *See* J. Ziller, *Les réactions des milieux institutionnels*, 39–40 and 42, who speaks of '*dédoublement fonctionnel*' (42). *See* also E. Stein, *Lawyers*, footnote 4, 2.
[130] A. M. Donner, *National Law and the Case Law of the Court of Justice of the European Community* (1963) 1 *Common Market Law Review* 8.
[131] M. Gaudet, *Incidences des Communautés européennes sur le droit interne des Etats membres*, in *Annales de la Faculté de droit de Liège*, 1963, 5, 24.
[132] W. Hallstein, *Communautés Européennes*, Luxembourg, 1964.
[133] M. Lagrange, *L'organisation, le fonctionnement et le rôle de la Cour de justice des Communautés européennes* (1963) 13–14 *Bulletin de l'Association des juristes européens*, 10; M. Lagrange, *The Court of Justice as a factor in European Integration* (1966-1967) 15 *American Journal of Comparative Law* 709.
[134] R. Lecourt, *L'Europe dans le prétoire*, *Le Monde*, 23 February 1963, 1.
[135] N. Catalano, *L'inserimento diretto delle disposizioni contenute nel Trattato istitutivo della Comunità economica europea negli ordinamenti giuridici degli Stati membri* (1963) 5 *Il Foro padano* 33. *See* also Catalano's

A. Trabucchi.[136] More in general, 1as regards the reception of *Van Gend & Loos* in the literature,[137] there is no doubt that the judgment, together with the *Costa* case, lies at the origins of the dissemination of studies on European law in various Member States and of the creation of important European law institutes and research centres,[138] as well as of some of the most authoritative law journals in the field.[139]

2.3 The rights-driven hard core

In the *Van Gend & Loos* decision, the CJ, acknowledging the points raised by the referring court—which in turn was influenced by the arguments submitted by the applicant—and by the Commission, singled out the crucial features of the Community legal order. In doing so, the Court laid the foundations of the doctrine of direct effect, which not only contributed to defining the European legal order and shaping 'the history of European Integration'.[140] To the contrary, the principle of direct effect has generated and moulded Community law in its current state and not vice versa.[141] In this respect, it defines and constitutes the 'European transnational constitution'.[142] As is also remarked by the Court, in fact, *Van Gend & Loos* shall be intended as a 'source of and a framework for the principles which have shaped the constitutional structure of the European Union'.[143] In the judgment, the Court touched upon

textbook published in 1965, whose reprinted version has been published in 2024: N. Catalano, *Manuel de droit des Communautés européennes*, Brussels, Bruylant, 2024.

[136] A. Trabucchi, *Un nuovo diritto* (1963) 1 *Rivista di diritto civile* 259. *See* also the work by one of his legal secretaries: P. Gori, *Una pietra miliare nell'affermazione del diritto europeo* (1963) 4 *Giurisprudenza italiana* 49.

[137] Amongst contributions published in the days, weeks, and months after the release of the ruling, *see*, in addition to those cited in the footnotes above, *inter alia*, F. Durante, *Giudizio pregiudiziale, rapporti tra ordinamenti e principio di effettività nella recente giurisprudenza della Corte di giustizia delle Comunità europee* (1963) 46 *Rivista di diritto internazionale* 415; D. Ehle, *Van Gend & Loos* (1963) 16 *Neue Juristische Wochenschrift* 974; P. Hay, *Van Gend & Loos* (1963) 12 *American Journal of Comparative Law* 404; F.-C. Jeantet, *Droit communautaire et juridictions internes* (1963) 147–148 *Le Barreau de France* 25; N. S. Marsh, *Some Reflections on Legal Integration in Europe, Europe* (1963) 12 *International and Comparative Law Quarterly* 1411; A. Migliazza, *Ordinamento comunitario e ordinamenti nazionali* (1963) 4 *Rivista di diritto processuale* 651; F. Rigaux, *Van Gend & Loos* (1963) 12 *Journal des tribunaux* 190; J. Robert, *Sur une égalité des droits devant la Communauté économique européenne des ressortissants des Etats membres avec ces Etats eux-mêmes*, in *Recueil Sirey*, 1963, 29; N. Ronzitti, *L'art. 12 del Trattato istitutivo della CEE ed i rapporti tra ordinamento comunitario ed ordinamento degli Stati membri* (1964) 4 *Il Foro italiano* 98; W. Wengler, *Van Gend & Loos* (1963) 16 *Neue Juristische Wochenschrift* 1751. For a comprehensive analysis of these pieces, *see* M. Rasmussen, *Law*, 107–111.

[138] A. Vauchez, *Judge-Made Law*, 155, mentions Cologne, Leiden, and Liège.

[139] A. Vauchez, *Judge-Made Law*, 155, whereby a reference is made to the *colloques* of FIDE and, as for law journals, to the following ones: *Common Market Law Review, Europarecht, Il Foro Italiano, Cahiers de droit européen,* and *Revue trimestrielle de droit européen. See* also J.-V. Louis, *Conclusions générales*, in A. Tizzano, J. Kokott, S. Prechal (Organizing Committee), *50ème anniversaire*, 205–228, 207.

[140] As noted by I. Pernice, *The Autonomy of the EU Legal Order—Fifty Years after* Van Gend, in A. Tizzano, J. Kokott, S. Prechal (Organizing Committee), *50ème anniversaire*, 55–81, 55, *Van Gend & Loos* 'in some way, shaped the history of European integration more than any other policy, leader or judgment'.

[141] *See* J. H. H. Weiler, *Revisiting* Van Gend en Loos, 11 and J. H. H. Weiler, Van Gend en Loos*: The Individual*, 103, whereby it is affirmed that '*Van Gend* is Europe'. *See* also D. Gallo, *L'effetto diretto quale dottrina fondante dell'ordinamento dell'Unione Europea* (2020) 3 *Rivista internazionale di filosofia del diritto* 537, 537–561.

[142] Accordingly, E. Stein, *Lawyers. See* J. H. H. Weiler, *The Transformation of Europe* (1990-1991) 100 *Yale Law Journal* 2403. For an historical analysis, *see* M. Rasmussen, *Constructing and Deconstructing European 'Constitutional' European Law. Some Reflections on How to Study the History of European Law*, in K. Hagel-Sørensen, H. Koch, U. Haltern, J.H.H. Weiler (eds.), *Europe. The New Legal Realism*, Copenhagen, Djøf Forlag, 2010, 639–660 and the special issues of the following three journals: *Journal of European Integration History*, 14(2), 2008; *Contemporary European History*, 21(3), 2012; and *American University International Law Review*, 28(5), 2013.

[143] *See* http://curia.europa.eu/jcms/jcms/P_95693/en/.

the main points which the CJ and the GC would face in the years ahead. Indeed, the subsequent case law sought to clarify, whether explicitly or implicitly, the contents of the *Van Gend & Loos* rule of reason, to extend its scope and, more generally, attempted to define the relationship between European law and national law as systematically as possible.

A quick reading of the above-mentioned observations submitted by the interested parties, the governments, the AG, and the Commission, as well as of the arguments of the CJ, makes it clear that all these actors were aware of the potential impact of the issues at hand on the future of the Community. Indeed, the Commission highlighted the 'importance'[144] of the matter, whose resolution would likely have an impact on the interpretation of other EEC Treaty provisions that were 'as clear and complete'[145] as Article 12.

'Direct effect(s)', as already mentioned, appears in the original Dutch version of the judgment, in the French and German (but not Italian) translations, in Roemer's opinion, as well as in the later English version. Moreover, the Court used various other expressions, amongst which most notably: internal effect; immediate effects; direct application; direct applicability. All these terms are not explicitly considered equivalent to the notion of direct effect, yet they revolve around the ability for individuals, as noted by the Court, to directly draw on rights stemming from Community law. The creation/attribution of rights, therefore, lies at the heart of the CJ's reasoning. In this regard, it was asserted by authoritative (though isolated) doctrine[146] that the Court's use in *Van Gend & Loos* of the conjunction '*en*', '*et*', '*und*', 'and', and '*e*' in the texts of the decision with regard to the production of direct effects (or, in the Italian version, of the preceptive nature of Article 12 of the EEC Treaty) *and* the granting of rights, would refute the existence of an inseparable link between direct effect and creation of rights. The latter would not be an 'essential component' of direct effect at the time.[147] Thus, according to these scholars, the conferral of a right, in *Van Gend & Loos*, would be a variable and not a constant of direct effect.

The argument that there is no structural connection between the doctrine of direct effect and the granting of rights, in itself, is correct: there is an objective aspect of direct effect, as will be comprehensively set forth in Chapter IV of this book, in addition to a subjective one, that justifies a *broad* notion of such doctrine. That, however, this dissociation between direct effect and rights was already set forth in *Van Gend & Loos* and, thus, that, according to the Court, at the time, the two elements had to be considered separate from one another, seems to prove too much.[148] As Hilson and Downes put it, the obligation imposed by Article 12 of

[144] *Van Gend & Loos* (n 1), 7.

[145] *Van Gend & Loos* (n 1), 7.

[146] *See* P. Craig, G. de Búrca, *EU Law. Text, Cases, and Materials*, Oxford, Oxford University Press, 2020, 218, according to whom '[t]he ECJ's case law supports both a broad or a narrow definition of direct effect. The broader definition, which can arguably be derived from *Van Gend en Loos*, can be expressed as the capacity of a provision of EU law to be invoked before a national court. This is sometimes referred to as "objective" direct effect. The normal consequence of a legal provision being invoked, as in Van Gend en Loos, is that it confers a legal right on the individual who invokes it, but this is not, on the broader definition, an essential component of direct effect.' *See* also R. Kovar, *L'intégrité de l'effet direct du droit communautaire selon la jurisprudence de la Cour de Justice de la Communauté*, in R. Bieber, D. Nickel (eds.), *Das Europa der Zweiten Generation: Gedächtnisschrift für Christoph Sasse*, Baden-Baden, Nomos, 1981, I, 151–163, 161, who affirmed, with regard to *Van Gend & Loos*, that '*la creation de droits individuels s'étant [...] qu'une des manifestations de l'effet immediat*', and R. Kovar, *La contribution*, 70, whereby it is clarified that '*la formule* Van Gend *autorise à penser que la création de droits ou d'obligations n'est qu'une des manifestations possibles de l'effet direct du droit communautaire*'.

[147] P. Craig, G. de Búrca, *EU Law*, 219.

[148] In this vein, *see* I. Sebba, *The Doctrine of Direct Effect: A Malignant Disease of Community Law* (1995) 22 *Legal Issues of Economic Integration* 35, 40; D. Edward, *Direct Effect, the Separation of Powers and the Judicial Enforcement of Obligations*, in *Scritti in onore di Giuseppe Federico Mancini*, Milan, Giuffrè, 1998, 423–445, 426; C. Hilson, T. Downes, *Making Sense of Rights: Community Rights in EC Law* (1999) 24 *European Law Review* 121, 124; S. Prechal, *Does Direct Effect Still Matter?* (2000) 37 *Common Market Law Review* 1047, 1050, according to whom 'initially, in the slipstream of the *Van Gend en Loos* judgment, direct effect was often defined

the EEC Treaty, in *Van Gend & Loos*, from the perspective of the CJ, entails the conferral of rights—which the national courts must protect— 'and this was synonymous with Article 12 being directly effective'.[149] It can be seen in all the versions of the judgment[150] that the notion of direct/immediate effect implies the granting of rights to individuals and, consequently, the creation of a subjective legal position. The conjunction 'and' simply aims to strengthen and clarify what the 'core' of direct effect is. Nowhere is direct effect interpreted as meaning that a Community rule can be invoked before a national court regardless of the existence of a right. The existence of a right as a precondition of direct effect is clear where the Court affirmed that '[i]ndependently of the legislation of Member States, Community law therefore not only imposes obligations on individuals but is also intended to confer upon them rights which become part of their legal heritage'.[151]

A further argument shall be laid out in this connection. In the sixties, under international law, the concept of direct effect was regarded as being naturally tied with the granting of an enforceable right to the individual. It suffices to recall, in this regard, the opinion of the Permanent Court of International Justice (PCIJ) in the *Jurisdiction of the Courts of Danzig* case,[152] where it was stated that 'it cannot be disputed that the very object of an international agreement, according to the intention of the contracting Parties, may be the adoption by the Parties of some definite rules creating individual rights and obligations and enforceable by the national courts'.[153] In short, if the Court had wished to introduce, with *Van Gend & Loos*, a different, innovative concept of direct effect, it should have said so explicitly, not indirectly, incidentally, and, ultimately, implicitly, with a 'mere' conjunction.[154]

In addition to the points described above, in *Van Gend & Loos* the CJ crystalized a number of further considerations which recur in subsequent case law. There are three aspects in particular: while two are discussed in this section, the third, on the relationship between primacy and direct effect, is examined in the next section of this chapter. The first aspect foreshadowing what the Court would later affirm in future judgments within and

as the creation of rights'; B. de Witte, *Direct Effect, Primacy and the Nature of the Legal Order*, in P. Craig, G. de Búrca (eds.), *The Evolution of EU Law*, 3rd ed., Oxford, Oxford University Press, 2021, 187–227, 191 (but B. de Witte in *The Continuous Significance*, 12, wrote that *Van Gend & Loos* may be read 'as not excluding the possibility that other provisions than Article 12 EEC Treaty could have *effet immédiat* without necessarily creating individual rights'); M. Blanquet, G. Isaac, *Droit général de l'Union européenne*, Paris, Dalloz, 2012, 375; S. Robin-Olivier, *The Evolution of Direct Effect in the EU: Stocktaking, Problems, Projections* (2014) 12 *International Journal of Constitutional Law* 165, 176; J. H. Jans, M. J. M. Verhoeven, *Europeanisation via Consistent Interpretation and Direct Effect*, in J. H. Jans, S. Prechal, R. J. G. M. Widdershoven (eds.), *Europeanisation of Public Law*, 2nd ed., Groningen, Europa Law Publishing, 2015, 71–132, 94. J. A. Winter, *Direct Applicability*, 438, observed that 'the use of two elements in this formula (direct effects and the creation of individual rights) is explained by the fact that at its inception the formula was a reply adjusted to the manner in which the Dutch Tariefcommissie had phrased its request for interpretation of Article 12 of the Treaty in the *Van Gend en Loos* case'.

[149] C. Hilson, T. Downes, *Making Sense*, 124.

[150] *See* D. Edward, *Direct Effect, the Separation*, 425–426.

[151] *Van Gend & Loos* (n 1), 12.

[152] For a joint analysis of the opinion and the *Van Gend & Loos* judgment, *see* S. Prechal, *Does Direct*, 1050. *See* also M. Forteau, *The Role.*

[153] *Jurisdiction of the Courts of Danzig* (n 109), 17.

[154] An example of an early international tribunal that admitted, in its case law, the direct enforcement of international law rules by private parties is the 1923 Treaty establishing the Tangier International Zone, as observed by M. Erpelding, *International Law and the European Court of Justice: The Politics of Avoiding History* (2020) 22 *Journal of the History of International Law* 446, 460–465, and T. Pavone, *Making*, who focuses on the role of Catalano, as former chief legal adviser to the Zone. More recently, for a rare example of a recognition of direct effect by an international court with regard to a treaty, *see* International Court of Justice, *Germany v United States (LaGrande)*, Reports, Series B, No. 4, 27 June 2001, 77 and 89–90, about Article 36 of the Convention on Consular Relations.

beyond free movement of goods is as follows: the prohibition set out in Article 12 of the EEC Treaty is 'clear and unconditional',[155] due to its very nature which 'makes it ideally adapted to produce direct effects in the legal relationship between Member States and their subjects'.[156] Explicit reference is thus made to the conditions of direct effect, namely clarity and unconditionality.[157] The prohibition set forth in Article 12 is defined as clear and unconditional, according to the CJ, in particular because the obligation arising therefrom is negative.[158] One cannot infer from the Court's reasoning, however, the intent to preclude the extension of such prohibition also to the (positive) obligations to act. As a matter of fact, this extension was made in the decisions following *Van Gend & Loos*.[159]

With regard to the second aspect, it is revealing that the CJ focused on the prerequisite of unconditionality and, in doing so, placed it in close correlation with direct applicability of Article 12 of the EEC Treaty.[160] Indeed, the Court observed that the prohibition/unconditioned obligation contained therein, which is a necessary element of direct effect, 'is not qualified by any reservation on the part of states which would make its implementation conditional upon a positive legislative measure enacted under national law'[161] and, therefore, that, for its implementation, no State legislative intervention was required. Hence, between the two concepts of direct applicability and direct effect exists a connection so close that the first seems to represent the prerequisite of the second, that is, the precondition for the granting of a right. Indeed, in several passages of the judgment, as well as in the AG's opinion,[162] the two concepts overlap, merging into one.[163]

2.4 The complementarity with the principles of primacy and autonomy, in the light of *Costa*

As briefly observed in the previous section, the third significant innovation introduced in *Van Gend & Loos*, which is at the heart of the judgments that will follow, concerns the relevance attributed to the principle of primacy and its ties with direct effect. A reading of *Van Gend & Loos* indicates that the Court's reasoning was based on the principle of primacy in the way it was later explained in *Costa*.[164] Direct effect presupposes, for its '*matérialisation*',[165] the respect of primacy, although this term was missing in the text of the judgment. The '*principe de la priorité*'[166] was recalled as a hidden pivotal principle implied in the *Van Gend & Loos* ruling by P. Gori, legal secretary to Justice Trabucchi at the time. *Van Gend & Loos*, therefore,

[155] *Van Gend & Loos* (n 1), 13.
[156] *Van Gend & Loos* (n 1), 13.
[157] *Van Gend & Loos* (n 1), 13.
[158] *Van Gend & Loos* (n 1), 13.
[159] For a reconstruction of the case law on direct effect's core elements after *Van Gend & Loos*, *see* extensively Chapter III.
[160] *Van Gend & Loos* (n 1), 13.
[161] *Van Gend & Loos* (n 1), 13.
[162] Opinion of AG Roemer, *Van Gend & Loos* (n 84), 18–19.
[163] On such merger, *see* § 7 of Chapter III.
[164] On the origins of the *Costa* decision, *see*, recently, A. Arena, *From an Unpaid Electricity Bill to the Primacy of EU Law: Gian Galeazzo Stendardi and the Making of Costa v. ENEL* (2019) 30 *European Journal of International Law* 1017; W. Phelan, *Great Judgments*, 58–83.
[165] P. Pescatore, *Monisme, dualisme et 'effet utile' dans la jurisprudence de la Cour de Justice de la Communauté Européenne*, in N. Colneric N., D. Edward, J-P. Puissochet, D. R.-J. Colomer (eds.), *Une communauté de droit—Festschriftfür G.C. Rodríguez Iglesias*, Berlin, Berliner Wissenschafts-Verlag, 2003, 329–359, 331.
[166] P. Gori, *Souvenirs d'un survivant*, 30.

presupposes[167] the '*Costa* rule' even if, at the time, the Court did not make explicit what was clearly later affirmed, for the first time, only in *Costa*.[168] Of course, an individual is entitled to directly invoke a European provision not only in the presence of a conflict with domestic law and not only when they intend to challenge an earlier provision of national law.[169] However, in practice, the useful effect of direct effect[170] would disappear if one were to make direct effect depend only on the principle *lex posterior derogat legi priori*.[171] Indeed, the primacy principle exerts its force beyond the temporal criterion governing the relationship between sources of law and, in that sense, constitutes, together with direct effect, the core of the originality and autonomy of European law. It is a '*condition existentielle*'[172] of the European legal order: its denial 'would be tantamount to reducing the Community to a cipher'.[173] Without primacy the treaties would be 'deprived of [their] character as Community law'[174] and 'the very foundations of the Community' would be irreparably called into question. In fact, 'recourse to provisions of the domestic legal systems to restrict the scope of the provisions of Community law would have the effect of impairing the unity and efficacy of that law'.[175]

That being said, if the principle of direct effect presupposes, for it to be effective, the primacy of Community law, the reverse is not true.[176] In fact, the CJ never said that the EEC Treaty rules, since they prevail over national provisions, are *per se* directly effective. Only some are directly effective. Hence, the *summa divisio*, in doctrine, between rules that are directly effective and those which are not.[177]

The nexus between direct effect and primacy of Community law was captured by AG Roemer where he wrote, in his opinion in *Van Gend & Loos*, that the direct application of Article 12 of the EEC Treaty would imply 'a review of legislative acts by the administrative authorities and the courts of Member States'.[178] On the other hand, Roemer acknowledged that the negative obligation set forth in Article 12 of the EEC Treaty 'would not result in the national laws being ineffective'.[179] While the AG excluded that the domestic legal order may yield to Community law, at least in matters, such as customs, largely governed by national

[167] As stressed by R. Joliet, *La protection juridictionnelle des particuliers contre les manquements étatiques* (1994) 10 *Revue Française de Droit Administratif* 647, 653, '*la doctrine de l'effet direct contenait déjà en germe celle de la primauté*'. In similar terms, *see* also J.-V. Louis, *Le droit de la CEE*, vol. 10 (*La Cour de Justice, Les actes des institutions*), 2nd ed., Brussels, Bruylant, 1993, 522; *contra* B. Cortese, *A la recherche d'un parcours d'autoconstitution de l'ordre juridique interindividuel européen: essai d'une lecture pluraliste 50 ans après* Van Gend en Loos *et* Costa contre ENEL (2015) 2 *Il Diritto dell'Unione europea* 271.

[168] In the opinion of G. Bebr, *Les dispositions de droit communautaire directement applicables: développement d'une notion communautaire* (1970) 1 *Cahiers de droit européen* 3, 8–9, '*la notion de disposition directement applicable a toujours été etroitement, fonctionnellement liée à la notion de primauté du droit communautaire*'.

[169] It is possible that EU directly effective provisions are invoked although they are not in conflict with domestic law, as explained by B. de Witte, *Retour à* Costa. *La primauté du droit communautaire à la lumiere du droit international* (1984) 20 *Revue trimestrielle de droit européen* 425, 440. *See* also B. de Witte, *Retour à* Costa, 427, who refers to '*primauté interne*'.

[170] On the importance of *Van Gend & Loos*, seen in the light of EU law's *effet utile*, *see* U. Villani, *Una rilettura della sentenza* Van Gend en Loos *dopo cinquant'anni* (2013) 2 *Studi sull'integrazione europea* 225, 235.

[171] *Contra* B. Cortese, *A la recherche*, 277.

[172] P. Pescatore, *L'ordre*, 227.

[173] CJ, *Acciaierie San Michele S.p.A.*, 9/65, EU:C:1965:63, 36.

[174] CJ, *Flaminio Costa v E.N.E.L.*, 6/64, EU:C:1964:66, 594.

[175] CJ, *Commission v Belgium*, 149/79, EU:C:1980:297, para. 19.

[176] *See* the account by L.-J. Constantinesco, *L'applicabilité directe dans le droit de la CEE*, Brussels, Bruylant, 2006, 14–18 and B. de Witte, *The Impact of* Van Gend en Loos *on Judicial Protection at European and National Level: Three Types of Preliminary Questions*, in A. Tizzano, J. Kokott, S. Prechal (Organizing Committee), *50ème anniversaire*, 93–101, 94–95; L. Daniele, *Diritto dell'Unione europea*, 8th ed., Milan, Giuffrè, 2022, 279.

[177] *See* L.-J. Constantinesco, *L'applicabilité directe*, 5–50. On the existence of such dichotomy in the ECSC Treaty, *see* G. Morelli, *Appunti sulla CECA* (1954) 1 *Rivista di diritto internazionale* 3 and G. Sperduti, *La CECA, ente sopranazionale*, Padua, Cedam, 1960, 20-22.

[178] Opinion of AG Roemer, *Van Gend & Loos* (n 84), 20.

[179] Opinion of AG Roemer, *Van Gend & Loos* (n 84), 20.

laws,[180] the Commission, very clearly understanding what was at stake, on the basis of a thorough analysis of the 'legal structure of the Treaty',[181] concluded that the national court 'is bound to ensure that the rules of Community law prevail over conflicting national laws even if they are passed later'.[182] Consequently, the Commission linked direct effect and primacy with two other fundamental principles of Community law,[183] whose relevance would be repeatedly highlighted by the CJ in subsequent case law: effectiveness and uniformity. In *Simmenthal*,[184] for example, the Court wrote that direct applicability, which was equated to direct effect, had to be understood as meaning that the provisions of Community law must fully produce their effects 'uniformly . . . in all the Member States'.[185] As a matter of fact, the synergy between primacy and direct effect prevents the then Community law, now EU law, from being properly enforced only in some countries and not in others, with serious consequences in terms of consistency[186] in the compliance of domestic legal orders with the European Treaties, and, as noted in the doctrine, with possible infringement of the principle of equality.[187] Moreover, if direct effect presupposes primacy, primacy implies that EU law shall be effectively, as well as uniformly, enforced. In this sense, primacy and direct effect are two ramifications of the principle of effectiveness of EU law.[188]

The fact that direct effect necessarily rests on primacy emerges also from the tone of the criticisms levelled in the literature in the period immediately following the issuance of the *Costa* judgment. They are, in fact, reactions which indirectly respond to the *Van Gend & Loos*[189] logic rather than 'simply' to that set out in *Costa*.

Concerning the *Costa* decision, the link between direct effect and primacy is made clear where the CJ, in interpreting Articles 37 and 53 of the EEC Treaty, currently Articles 37 and 60 TFEU, on government monopolies and freedom of establishment, respectively, affirmed that the obligations imposed therein on the States are legally complete, thereby capable of entailing direct effects, and that for this reason they are 'part of the law'[190] of the national legal orders. It is the combination of direct effect and primacy, explained in *Costa*, which makes Community law unique.[191] The Court stated that, '[b]y contrast with ordinary international treaties, the EEC Treaty has created its own legal system which, upon the entry into force of the Treaty, became an integral part of the legal systems of the Member States'.[192] This is an assertion which detaches Community law from international law even more so than occurred in *Van Gend & Loos*, where it was placed in the realm of 'international law'.[193] As affirmed in

[180] Opinion of AG Roemer, *Van Gend & Loos* (n 84), 22.
[181] Opinion of AG Roemer, *Van Gend & Loos* (n 84), 7.
[182] Opinion of AG Roemer, *Van Gend & Loos* (n 84), 7.
[183] In this vein, *see* V. Colcelli, *Individual Rights as Construction of the EU Legal System*, in R. Arnold, V. Colcelli (eds.), *Europeanization through Private Law Instruments*, Regensburg, Schnell & Steiner, 2015, 35–38, 35.
[184] CJ, *Amministrazione delle Finanze dello Stato v Simmenthal SpA*, 106/77, EU:C:1978:49.
[185] *Simmenthal* (n 184), 14.
[186] *See* C. Blumann, L. Dubouis, *Droit institutionnel*, 531–532 and F. Capotorti, *Il diritto comunitario dal punto di vista del giudice nazionale* (1977) 13 *Rivista di diritto internazionale privato e processuale* 497, 500.
[187] This point is raised by J. Robert, *Sur une égalité* and, more recently, by I. Pernice, *The Autonomy*, 58.
[188] *See* N. Póltorak, *European Union Rights in National Courts*, Alphen aan den Rijn, Kluwer Law International, 2015, 7.
[189] A. Vauchez, *The Transnational Politics*, 19–21 and J. Ziller, *Les réactions des milieux institutionnels, nationaux et scientifiques de l'époque*, in A. Tizzano, J. Kokott, S. Prechal (Organizing Committee), *50ème anniversaire*, 37–48, 48, assuming that direct effect lies at the roots of primacy, demonstrate that the reactions vis-à-vis *Costa* were also an indirect response to *Van Gend & Loos*.
[190] *Costa* (n 174), 596.
[191] A combination that is '*essentielle à toute notion de communauté*': R. Lecourt, *Quel eut été le droit des Communautés sans les arrêts de 1963 et 1964?*, in *Mélanges Jean Boulouis: l'Europe et le droit*, Paris, Dalloz, 1991, 349–350. *See* also G. Contaldi, *Effetto diretto e primato*, in S. Cassese (ed.), *Dizionario di diritto pubblico*, vol. III, Milan, Giuffrè, 2006, 2124.
[192] *Costa* (n 174), 593.
[193] *Van Gend & Loos* (n 1), 12.

the literature,[194] the EU is indeed 'based on a conception of divided sovereignty' and is, 'in strictness, neither an international nor a national Constitution, but a composition of both', representing 'an (inter) national phenomenon that stands on - federal - middle ground'.[195]

The unique character of Community/EU law was confirmed in the subsequent case law. It was stated, in opinion 1/91 on the Draft Agreement between the European Community and the countries of the European Free Trade Association regarding the creation of the European Economic Area,[196] that the EEC Treaty, albeit concluded in the form of an international agreement, constitutes 'the constitutional charter of a Community based on the rule of law', and that its fundamental, morphological characteristics[197] are, in particular, 'its primacy over the law of the Member States' and 'the direct effect of a whole series of provisions which are applicable to their nationals and to the Member States themselves'.[198] In opinion 2/13 on the Accession of the EU to the European Convention on Human Rights it was emphasized that 'these essential characteristics of EU law have given rise to a structured network of principles, rules and mutually interdependent legal relations linking the EU and its Member States, and its Member States with each other'.[199]

Community/EU law, as was perceived by several scholars even before *Van Gend & Loos* and *Costa*,[200] is independent from international law[201] as well as from national legal orders,

[194] On the different theses (the so-called '*sui generis* theory' and the so-called 'international law theory') about the origins and nature of the then Community, now European Union, *see* the critical account by R. Schütze, *European Union Law*, 41–71. *See* also R. Schütze, *On 'Federal' Ground: The European Union as an (Inter)national Phenomenon* (2009) 46 *Common Market Law Review* 1069; R. Schütze, *Constitutionalism and the European Union*, in C. Barnard, S. Peers (eds.), *European Union Law*, Oxford, Oxford University Press, 2020, 71–96, 75. In the literature, amongst those who focus on the *sui generis* idea implied in the Community legal order, *see* H. L. Mason, *The European Coal and Steel Community: Experiment in Supranationalism*, The Hague, Martinus Nijhoff, 1955, 121–145 and J. H. H. Weiler, *Federalism without Constitutionalism: Europe's Sonderweg*, in K. Nikoilaidis, R. Howse (eds.), *The Federal Vision: Legitimacy and Levels of Governance in the United States and the European Union*, Oxford, Oxford University Press, 2002, 54–72, 54; L. F. Pace, *La natura giuridica dell'Unione europea*, Bari, Cacucci, 2021, 36–70. Amongst those who stress the limits of the characterization of the Community as a supranational institution, *see* P. Hay, *Federalism and Supranational Organizations*, Urbana, University of Illinois Press, 1966, 37–44. Amongst the first to point out the differences between the Community and other international organizations, *see* G. Morelli, *Stati ed individui nelle organizzazioni internazionali* (1957) 1 *Rivista di diritto internazionale* 3, 22 and R. Kovar, *La contribution*, 21. On the content and limits of European supranationalism, *see*, *ex multis*, P. Pescatore, *The Law of Integration: Emergence of a New Phenomenon in International Relations*, The Hague, Martinus Nijhoff, 1974, 58 and J. H. H. Weiler, *The Community System*, 267.

[195] R. Schütze, *Constitutionalism*, 73, quoting A. Hamilton, J. Madison, and J. Jay, *The Federalist*, 1787-1788, 187. *See* also R. Schütze, *From Dual to Cooperative Federalism: The Changing Structure of European Law*, Oxford, Oxford University Press, 2009, 70. On the definition of European law as a *quasi* federal system, *see* J. L. Kunz, *Supra-national Organs* (1952) 46 *American Journal of International Law* 697; G. Héraud, *Nature juridique de la Communauté Européenne d'après le projet de Statut du 10 mars 1953* (1953) 69 *Revue du Droit Public et de la Science Politique en France et à l'Etranger* 581; N. Catalano, *La Comunità economica europea e l'EURATOM*, Milan, Giuffrè, 1959, 12. For an early analysis, *see* G. Jaenicke, *Die Europäische Gemeinschaft für Kohle und Stahl—Struktur und Funktionen ihrer Organe* (1952) 13 *Zeitschrift für ausländisches öffentliches Recht und Völkerrecht* 727. E. H. Mosler, *Der Vertrag über die Europäische Gemeinschaft für Kohle und Stahl* (1951–1952) 14 *Zeitschrift für ausländisches öffentliches Recht und Völkerrecht* 8; P. Hay, *Federalism*.

[196] CJ, *Opinion delivered pursuant to the second subparagraph of Article 228 (1) of the Treaty—Draft agreement between the Community, on the one hand, and the countries of the European Free Trade Association, on the other, relating to the creation of the European Economic Area*, 2/13, EU:C:1991:490.

[197] In these terms, *see* L.-J. Constantinesco, *Traité de droit comparé*, I, Paris, Librarie générale de droit et de jurisprudence, 1972, 213. On the matter, *see* also K. Lenaerts, *Federalism: Essential Concepts in Evolution—The Case of the European Union* (1998) 21 *Fordham International Law Journal* 746 and M. Bobek, *The Effects of EU Law in the National Legal Systems*, in C. Barnard, S. Peers (eds.), *European Union*, 154–189, 155–156.

[198] CJ, *Opinion delivered pursuant to the second subparagraph of Article 228 (1) of the Treaty—Draft agreement between the Community, on the one hand, and the countries of the European Free Trade Association, on the other, relating to the creation of the European Economic Area*, 1/91, EU:C:1991:490, para. 21.

[199] CJ, *Accession of the European Union to the European Convention for the Protection of Human Rights and Fundamental Freedoms*, EU:C:2014:2454, para. 167.

[200] *See*, for instance, P. A. Sereni, *Diritto internazionale*, II, Milan, Giuffrè, 1960, 1177; R. Monaco, *Primi lineamenti di diritto pubblico europeo*, Milan, Giuffrè, 1962, 61; G. Morelli, *Stati*, 22.

[201] On direct effect, autonomy, and originality of EU law, *see*, *ex multis*, D. Simon, *Les fondements*; K. Lenaerts, J.-A. Gutiérrez-Fons, S. Adam, *Exploring the Autonomy of the European Union Legal Order* (2021) 1 *Zeitschrift für ausländisches öffentliches Recht und Völkerrecht* 47.

precisely because of the specific features[202] underpinning the European 'legal system' as a whole, not only the European Treaties.[203] The peculiarity and originality of the European legal order, at the heart of the *Costa* judgment and subsequent case law,[204] revolves around the strengthening of individual rights enshrined in *Van Gend & Loos*, particularly where it was observed, as has been already recalled in sections 2 and 3, that Community law, independently from national legal systems, creates individual rights.[205] Independence means autonomy,[206] observance of which is ensured by the CJ 'by virtue of the exclusive jurisdiction'[207] conferred on it by the Treaties. An autonomy which implies a separation among legal systems.[208] A separation which implies the existence of an inherently pluralistic[209] relationship between sources, to the extent that the independence of one from the other does not preclude that there is interaction,[210] interdependence, and fertilization between the two.

[202] R. Kovar, *La contribution*, 25, noted that '*l'acte fondateur de l'ordre juridique de la Communauté a été l'affirmation de sa spécificité et de son autonomie*'. On the autonomy of European law, *see*, *ex multis*, P. Pescatore, *L'ordre*, 122–135; R. Kovar, *L'application directe du droit Communautaire* (1973) 100 *Journal du droit international* 279; J. H. H. Weiler, U. Haltern, *The Autonomy of the Community Legal Order: through the Looking Glass* (1996) 37 *Harvard International Law Journal* 411; R. Barents, *The Autonomy of Community Law*, Alphen aan den Rijn, Kluwer Law International, 2004; B. de Witte, *European Union Law: How Autonomous is its Legal Order?* (2010) 65 *Zeitschrift fur öffentliches Recht* 141; J. W. Van Rossem, *The Autonomy of EU Law: More is less?*, in R.A. Wessel, S. Blockmans (eds.), *Between Autonomy and Dependence: The EU Legal Order Under the Influence of International Organizations*, The Hague, Martinus Nijhoff, 2013, 13–46; G. Martinico, *The Autonomy of EU Law: A Joint* Kadi II—Van Gend en Loos *Celebration*, in M. Avbelj, F. Fontanelli, G. Martinico (eds.), Kadi *on Trial: A Multifaceted Analysis of the* Kadi *Judgment*, Abindgon, Routledge, 2014, 157–171; A. Rosas, *International Law—Union Law—National Law: Autonomy or Common Legal System?*, in D. Petrlik, M. Bobek, J. M. Passer, A. Masson (eds.), *Évolution des rapports entre les orders juridiques de l'Union européenne, international et nationaux: Liber amicorum Jiří Malenovský*, Brussels, Bruylant, 2020, 261–282; A. Adinolfi, *Trattati dell'Unione e 'comuni trattati internazionali': il carattere atipico dei Trattati istitutivi nella giurisprudenza della Corte di giustizia*, in A. Annoni, S. Forlati, P. Franzina (eds.), *Il diritto internazionale come sistema di valori*, Naples, Jovene, 2021, 213–234; J. Lindeboom, *The Autonomy of EU Law: A Hartian View* (2021) 13 *European Journal of Legal Studies* 37; J. Lindeboom, R. A. Wessel (eds.), *The Autonomy of EU Law, Legal Theory and European Integration*, Special Issue (2023) 8 *European Papers* 1247; L. Lionello, *L'autonomia dell'ordinamento giuridico dell'Unione europea*, Turin, Giappichelli, 2024.

[203] On the necessity to consider the European system in its entirety, not 'simply' the European Treaties, *see* F. G. Jacobs, Speech for the Walther Schücking Institute/Institute for International Law, University of Kiel, April 1983, available at https://www.uni-kiel.de/en/law/research/wsi; R. Schütze, *On 'Middle Ground'. The European Union and Public International Law*, in R. Schütze, *Foreign Affairs and the EU Constitution*. Selected essays, Cambridge, Cambridge University Press, 2014, 47–90, 48.

[204] *See*, e.g., *Acciaierie San Michele S.p.A.* (n 173); CJ, *Firma Molkerei-Zentrale Westfalen/Lippe GmbH*, 28/67, EU:C:1968:17; CJ, *F.lli Variola SpA*, 34/73, EU:C:1973:101.

[205] *Contra* G. Balladore Pallieri, *Le Comunità europee e gli ordinamenti interni degli Stati membri* (1961) 1 *Diritto internazionale* 3.

[206] On this point, *see* I. Pernice, *The Autonomy*, 56 and P. Pescatore, *Van Gend en Loos, 3 February 1963—A View from Within*, in M. Poiares Maduro, L. Azoulai (eds.), *The Past*, 3–8, 5.

[207] CJ, *Yassin Abdullah Kadi and Al Barakaat International Foundation*, joined cases C-402/05 P and C-415/05 P, EU:C:2008:461, para. 282.

[208] *See* R. Barents, *The Autonomy*, 169; *contra* M. Blanquet, G. Isaac, *Droit*, 368.

[209] *See* Pernice, *The Autonomy*, 60–61. On constitutional pluralism, *see*, *inter alia*, N. MacCormick, *Beyond the Sovereign State* (1993) 56 *Modern Law Review* 1; N. Walker, *The Idea of Constitutional Pluralism* (2002) 65 *Modern Law Review* 317; M. Barber, *Legal Pluralism in the European Union* (2006) 12 *European Law Journal* 306; N. Krisch, *Beyond Constitutionalism: The Pluralist Structure of Postnational Law*, Oxford, Oxford University Press, 2013; K. Tuori, *European Constitutionalism*, Cambridge, Cambridge University Press, 2015, 78-107; N. Walker, *Constitutional Pluralism Revisited* (2016) 22 *European Law Journal* 333. With a focus on EU law, *see* M. Poiares Maduro, *Contrapunctual Law: Europe's Constitutional Pluralism in Action*, in N. Walker (ed.), *Sovereignty in Transition*, Oxford, Hart, 2003, 501–537; M. Avbelj, J. Komárek, *Introduction*, in M. Avbelj, J. Komárek (eds.), *Constitutional Pluralism in the European Union and Beyond*, Oxford, Hart, 2012, 1–17; A. Bobić, *The Jurisprudence of Constitutional Conflict in the European Union*, Oxford, Oxford University Press, 2022, 25–72.

[210] They are independent '*par leur naissance, mais concurrents pour ce qui est de leur application, car ils s'addressent aux memes sujets de droit*' : L.-J. Constantinesco, *La spécificité*, 11.

Pluralism, however, does not mean, as noted in the literature,[211] that one could not speak of a hierarchical relationship between EU and the national legal systems when disputes fall under the scope of application of European Treaties.[212] Indeed, such reconstruction clashes with the very extent of the primacy principle.[213] It is, in this regard, sufficient to recall a passage in *Costa*, where the CJ clarified that the national courts are bound to observe the rules which make up the Community legal order. A legal order that forms a 'body of law which binds'[214] both the Member States and their citizens and which cannot be overridden by 'domestic legal provisions, however framed, without being deprived of [their] character as Community law' and without 'the legal basis of the Community itself being called into question'.[215]

To conclude, before moving on, in the next section, to a political contextualization of *Van Gend & Loos*, any investigation on direct effect shall consider that Community law originated as an interstate phenomenon, grounded in international law,[216] and then, because of primacy and direct effect,[217] freed itself,[218] although not *in toto*,[219] from international legal categories,[220] being 'an independent source of law'.[221]

[211] *See* J.-V. Louis, *La primauté du droit de l'Union, un concept dépassé*, in G. Cohen Jonathan, V. Constantinesco, V. Michel (eds.), *Mélanges en l'honneur de Jean Paul Jacqué*, Paris, Dalloz, 2010, 443–461; B. Cortese, *A la recherche*, 274; A. von Bogdandy, *I principi fondamentali dell'Unione europea*, Naples, Editoriale Scientifica, 2011, 77.

[212] L.-J. Constantinesco, *La spécificité*, 3, wrote that the '*collision*' is inescapable. On the scope of application of EU law and the possible conflicts between the EU legal system and national laws, see M. E. Bartoloni, *Ambito d'applicazione del diritto dell'Unione europea e ordinamenti nazionali*, Naples, Editoriale Scientifica, 2018.

[213] In the frame of a comparative study on the US and European legal orders, see M. Cappelletti, D. Golay, *Judicial Branch in the Federal and Transnational Union*, in M. Cappelletti, M. Seccombe, J. H. H. Weiler (eds.), *Integration through Law: Europe and the American Federal Experience*, Berlin-New York, Walter de Gruyter and Co., 1986, II, 261–351, 263, argued that, in transnational and federal systems, there must be an 'acceptance of legal hierarchy' because, lacking primacy, 'the federal or transnational can have no direct integrative force'.

[214] *Costa* (n 174), 593.

[215] *Costa* (n 174), 594.

[216] Moreover, as will be further explained in § 3 of Chapter II, direct effect was a doctrine not unknown to international law at the time.

[217] *See* S. M. Carbone, *Organi comunitari, controllo di legittimità e soggetti privati*, Padua, Cedam, 1973, 1–12. D. Simon, *Les fondements de l'autonomie du droit communautaire. Rapport général*, in *Droit international et Droit communautaire. Perspectives actuelles Actes du colloque de la SFDI 1999*, Paris, Pedone, 2000, 207–249, 220–221, emphasized the degree of emancipation of EU law from international law and the risks of trivialization associated with a different conceptualization of the relationship between the two legal systems.

[218] F. G. Jacobs, K. Karst, *The 'Federal' Legal Order: The USA and Europe Compared—A Juridical Perspective*, in M. Cappelletti, M. Seccombe, J. H. H. Weiler (eds.), *Integration*, 169–243, 171, considered that direct effect is the clearest sign of the federal nature of the EEC. On this matter, for a quite different perspective, *see* § 1 of Chapter V and the Conclusion.

[219] Even the 'integrationist' scholar *par excellence* affirmed that EU law presents 'features of an inter-state nature'; in these terms, *see* P. Pescatore, *International Law and Community Law—A Comparative Analysis* (1970) 7 *Common Market Law Review* 167, 178. D. Wyatt, *New Legal Order, or Old?* (1982) 7 *European Law Review* 147, 150, recalled that several principles of international law, of both substantive and interpretive nature, apply to EU law. In the same vein, *see* also B. de Witte, *EU law: Is It International Law?*, in C. Barnard, S. Peers (eds.), *European Union*, 177–197. On the relative originality of EU law compared to international law, *see*, in the vast literature, W. Ganhof van der Meersch, *L'ordre juridique*, 248–252; S. Amadeo, *Norme comunitarie, posizioni giuridiche soggettive e giudizi interni*, Milan, Giuffrè, 2002, 3–14; J. H. H. Weiler, *Revisiting* Van Gend en Loos, 11; M. Blanquet, G. Isaac, *Droit*, 377. On the international law foundations of European law and its conceptualization as both international and supranational law, *see* D. Wyatt, *New Legal Order*; A. Pellet, *Les fondements juridiques internationaux du droit communautaire*, in *Recueil des cours de l'Académie de droit européen*, The Hague, Martinus Nijhoff, 1997, V, 2, 193–271; E. Triggiani, *Sopranazionalità ed internazionalità nell'evoluzione dell'Unione*, in M. L. Tufano (ed.), *Cantiere Europa—Le riforme istituzionali dell'Europa*, Naples, Editoriale Scientifica, 2004, 37–54; U. Villani, *Il diritto dell'Unione Europea è ancora materia per internazionalisti?* (2011) 66 *La Comunità Internazionale* 533; F. Martucci, *Droit de l'Union européenne*, 3rd ed., Paris, Dalloz, 2021, 39–73, who writes that '*si l'Union présente indéniablement une nature internationale originelle, elle connaît néanmois une mutation constitutionnelle*' (50).

[220] On the reluctancy of Member States to yield to the integrationist breakthrough represented by *Van Gend & Loos* and *Costa*, *see* A. B. Capik, *Five Decades Since* Van Gend *and* Costa *Came to Town: Primacy and Indirect Effect Revisited*, in A. Lazowski, S. Blockmans (eds.), *Research Handbook in EU Institutional Law*, Cheltenham, Edward Elgar, 2016, 379–420, footnote 7, 381.

[221] *Costa* (n 174), 594.

2.5 Politics and the constitutionalization of the CJ

Van Gend & Loos marks a key moment for having transformed European law and its relationship with both national law and international law, as has been explained so far. However, the relevance and impact of the decision can be fully captured only by putting it into the political context of the Community at the time. As a matter of fact, *Van Gend & Loos*, on the one hand, was also the result of a 'political' move taken by the CJ,[222] while on the other, it had an impact even on the political relationships between the Community institutions and Member States.[223] Indeed, the CJ, while rejecting the path suggested by AG Roemer,[224] indirectly responded, although only with a bare majority,[225] to the strong intergovernmental petitions made by several countries, *in primis* France, which, at the time, had brought about the first true crisis of the fledgling process of European integration. A crisis that would lead in 1965–1966 to the so-called empty chair policy and the Luxembourg compromise,[226] and that was the product of two opposing conceptions of the European Communities.[227] On one side, there was the state-centred and 'sovereigntist' vision of the Community project, which was the expression of the Gaullist revival on the French political scene and of the so-called 'Fouchet Plan',[228] to a large extent inspired by ideals far away from the traditions of Jean Monnet and Robert Schumann. On the other side, there was a more ambitious and 'Communitarian' vision of Europe and European policy. Therefore, a conflict emerged between the France of Charles de Gaulle, the greatest proponent of the idea of a '*Europe des patries*',[229] and the other five founding States, including the Germany of Konrad Adenauer,[230] who had rejected that Plan.

Against this background, in *Van Gend & Loos* the CJ emphasized the originality of the Community legal order, placed the individual's rights at the heart of it, and put in writing

[222] On this matter, *see* P. Piva, *Giudice nazionale e diritto dell'Unione europea. L'efficacia diretta e il primato*, Naples, Editoriale Scientifica, 2008, 96–99.

[223] On this issue, *see* the critical studies released in the same period of *Van Gend & Loos* by P. Hay, *Federal Jurisdiction of the Common Market* (1963) 12 *American Journal of Comparative Law* 21 and R. M. Buxbaum, S. A. Riesenfeld, *N. V. Algemene Transport—En Expeditie Onderneming van Gend & Loos v. Administration Fiscale Néerlandaise: A Pioneering Decision of the Court of Justice of the European Communities* (1964) 12 *American Journal of Comparative Law* 152.

[224] *See* §§ 1–2 of this chapter.

[225] *See* § 1 of this chapter, for a brief reference to the contrasts between Justices Delvaux, Lecourt, Rossi, and Trabucchi, on the one hand, and, on the other, Donner, Hammes, and Riese.

[226] *See* P. Pescatore, *Van Gend en Loos*, 5, footnote 2. On the crisis of the 1960s, *see* J. Newhouse, *30 juin 1965: crise à Bruxelles*, Paris, Dalloz, 1969 and, more recently, N. P. Ludlow, *The European Community and the Crises of the 1960s: Negotiating the Gaullist Challenge*, London, Routledge, 2006. On this point, *see* also K. Lenaerts, J. A. Gutiérrez-Fons, *Van Gend.*

[227] *See* P. Gori, *Retrospettiva sulla genesi dei principi dell'applicabilità diretta e della preminenza del diritto comunitario: le sentenze* Costa c. Enel e Van Gend & Loos (2014) 4 *Diritto comunitario e degli scambi internazionali* 653, 653–655. For a different position, which shows that at stake were more than the two conceptions outlined above, *see* N. P. Ludlow, *Making the New Europe: European Integration Since 1950*, in M. Gordon, (ed.), *A Companion to International History 1900 - 2001. Blackwell Companions to History*, Oxford, Blackwell, 2007, 327–339 and L. Warlouzet, *Competitivenss and Solidarity in the History of the EU* (1957–2017), in P. Chiocchetti, F. Allemand (eds.), *Competitiveness and Solidarity in the European Union. Interdisciplinary Perspectives*, Abingdon, Routledge, 2019, 54–72, 56.

[228] Christian Fouchet was a French diplomat and a Minister between 1962 and 1967. The Fouchet Plan was an unsuccessful plan drafted by Mr. Fouchet, then endorsed and proposed by French President Charles de Gaulle in 1961. The plan included a three-power directorate, consisting of France, the United Kingdom, and the United States, aiming at forming a new Union of States, that is, an intergovernmental alternative to the European Communities.

[229] *See* the statement pronounced by De Gaulle on 15 May 1962, available at http://www.ina.fr/video/I00012372.

[230] J. Ziller, *Les réactions des milieux institutionnels*, 38. *See* also M. Wathelet, *Arrêt* Van Gend en Loos*: 50 ans déjà* (2013) 200 *Journal de droit européen* 213.

its distancing from the objectives of intergovernmental cooperation which were the basis of French politics at the time.[231] The *Van Gend & Loos* doctrine, as judge-made law, like the other constitutional core pillars of EU law, including primacy, thus places the CJ as the true actor of change and '*giudice dei doveri e diritti dei singoli*' ('arbiter of individual duties and rights').[232]

With *Van Gend & Loos*, the European judges gave extraordinary impetus to the Community integration process, identifying in the doctrine of direct effect the supranational basis of the European Communities and the engine of European integration.[233] The very same purpose of integration '*postule l'applicabilité*'[234] of direct effect, which is the 'essence of EU law'[235] and the principle best suited to 'impinge directly on the lives of individuals'.[236] Hence, the CJ, beginning with *Van Gend & Loos*, albeit not in explicit terms and by one step at the time,[237] initiated the process of its own constitutionalization in the Community legal order[238] and, in so doing, constitutionalized the treaties.[239] This had been highlighted by AG Lagrange in his above-cited doctrinal piece, where reference was made to the '*rôle constitutionnel*'[240] of the Court, made explicit in his opinion in the *Da Costa*[241] case where he stressed that the treaties 'can be considered as true constitutions for each of the Communities which they institute',[242] and later confirmed outright by the CJ in several other rulings, starting with *Les Verts*.[243] Indeed, in such case, the Court, anticipating what would be made clear in the above-mentioned 1/91 opinion, underscored that 'the European Economic Community is a Community based on the rules of law, inasmuch as neither its

[231] More generally, *see* J. H. H. Weiler, *Journey to an Unknown Destination: A Retrospective and Prospective of the European Court of Justice in the Arena of Political Integration* (1993) 31 *Journal of Common Market Studies* 417; W. Mattli, A.-M. Slaughter, *Revisiting the European Court of Justice*, (1998) 52 *International Organization* 177. With particular regard to *Van Gend & Loos*, *see* M. Rasmussen, *Law*, 108.

[232] G. Tesauro, *Alcune riflessioni sul ruolo della Corte di giustizia nell'evoluzione dell'Unione europea*, in *Il Diritto dell'Unione europea*, 2013, 483, 492.

[233] *See* F. Mancini, D. Keeling, *Democracy*, 183 and R. Adam, A. Tizzano, *Lineamenti di diritto dell'Unione europea*, Turin, Giappichelli, 2022, 257.

[234] G. Isaac, *Droit communautaire général*, 3rd ed., Paris, Dalloz, 1990, 157.

[235] K. Lenaerts, *Some Thoughts on the State of the European Union as a Rights-Based Legal Order* (2015) 1 *Il Diritto dell'Unione europea* 5, 7: 'by heralding the doctrine of direct effect, Van Gend demonstrated that the EU is a rights-based legal order . . . [T]he very essence of EU law is the principle that the individual rights it creates are directly enforceable before national courts and prevail over conflicting national norms.'

[236] *See* F. Mancini, D. Keeling, *Democracy*, 183.

[237] As noted by B. Davies, F. Nicola, *Introduction to EU Law Stories. Contextual and Critical Histories in European Jurisprudence*, in F. Nicola, B. Davies (eds.), *EU Law Stories*, 1–18, 3–4.

[238] On the constitutional role of the CJ in the light of *Van Gend & Loos* and *Costa*, *see*, *inter alia*, A. Vauchez, *The Transnational Politics*, 1–2. *See* also D. Simon, *Retour au mythe du gouvernement des juges?* (2006) *JurisClasseurEurope*, February, 1 and L. Azoulai, *Le rôle constitutionnel de la Cour de justice des Communautés européennes tel qu'il se dégage de sa jurisprudence* (2008) 1 *Revue trimestrielle de droit européen* 29, 30.

[239] In the extensive literature, *see*, amongst many others, J. H. H. Weiler, *The Constitution of Europe: 'Do the New Clothes Have an Emperor?' and Other Essays on European Integration*, Oxford, Oxford University Press, 1999; K. J. Alter, *Establishing the Supremacy of European Law. The Making of an International Rule of Law in Europe*, Oxford, Oxford University Press, 2001; A. Stone Sweet, *The Judicial Construction of Europe*, Oxford, Oxford University Press, 2004; F. Amtenbrink, P. van den Berg (eds.), *The Constitutional Integrity of the European Union*, The Hague, TMC Asser Press, 2010; T. Isiksel, *Europe's Functional Constitution: A Theory of Constitutionalism Beyond the State*, Oxford, Oxford University Press, 2016. Amongst textbooks, *see* E. Dubout, *Droit constitutionnel de l'Union européenne*, Brussels, Bruylant, 2021, 7, 33, 219. For a recent critique, 'emphasising . . . the inherent tensions' in the process of constitutionalization, 'which continue to complicate the efficiency of European law', *see* M. Rasmussen, D. S. Martinsen, *EU Constitutionalisation Revisited: Redressing a Central Assumption in European Studies* (2019) 25 *European Law Journal* 1,1.

[240] M. Lagrange, *La Cour*, 435.

[241] Opinion of AG Lagrange of 13 March 1963, *Da Costa en Schaake NV, Jacob Meijer NV, Hoechst-Holland NV v Netherlands Inland Revenue Administration*, joined cases 28–30/62, EU:C:1963:2.

[242] Opinion of AG Lagrange, *Da Costa* (n 241), 43.

[243] CJ, *Parti écologiste 'Les Verts' v European Parliament*, 294/83, EU:C:1986:166.

States nor its institutions can avoid a review of the question whether the measures adopted by them are in conformity with the basic constitutional charter, the Treaty'.[244] *Van Gend & Loos* is, to the Community legal order, what *Marbury v Madison*[245] is to the US legal system. Just as the Supreme Court gave life and substance to the system of judicial review with a view to the progressive strengthening of judicial protection for individuals, the CJ laid the foundations for an integrated system of protection of rights, between Luxembourg and the national courts, placing itself in the middle of this system through the advocation of an interpretative monopoly.

The words of Trabucchi, in his 1963 article, perfectly illustrate the function carried out by the Court in those years. Trabucchi wrote that Community law represented '*una nuova realtà giuridica che va sempre più affermandosi nel senso di una unità irreversibile*' ('a new legal reality which was increasingly establishing itself as an irreversible unity'), whose importance became clear at the time when '*l'ideale, o almeno il problema dell'unificazione europeo [...] è dominato da preoccupazioni nazionalistiche o da convenienze di difesa*' ('the ideal, or at least the problem of European unification [...] is dominated by nationalist concerns or by strategic conveniences of defence'). Trabucchi continued, concluding that '*la solidarietà di fatto tra i popoli europei, di cui parlava Schumann, è felicemente diventata un'unità di diritto sotto un controllo che ha la Corte di giustizia su tutti gli atti*' ('the *de facto* solidarity among the European populations, which Schumann referred to, has successfully become a unity of laws under one control that the Court of Justice has over all the legal acts'), a '*controllo*' which also constitutes '*una professione di fede nel diritto*' ('a declaration of faith in the law').[246]

In conclusion, the making of a legal principle by the CJ is something different from dangerous judicial activism.[247] Far from being the result of a creative action of the CJ, the *Van Gend & Loos* doctrine was the result of a gradual assumption of responsibility and jurisprudential awareness.[248] It is such awareness that pushed the Court to interpret Community law beyond a textual reading of the norm, in order to advance, reinforce, and complete the process of communitarization underpinning the European Treaties and secondary legislation.

[244] *Les Verts* (n 243), para. 23. *See* also, *inter alia*, CJ, *Beate Weber*, C-314/91, EU:C:1993:109, para. 8.

[245] US Supreme Court, 5 U.S. 1 Cranch 137, 1803. *See* D. Halberstam, *Pluralism in* Marbury *and* Van Gend, in M. Poiares Maduro, L. Azoulai (eds.), *The Past*, 26–36 and K. Lenaerts, J. A. Gutiérrez-Fons, *Van Gend*; F. Nicola, C. Fasone, D. Gallo, *Comparing the Effects of US Unconstitutionality and EU's Preliminary Interpretative Rulings: Disapplication, Resistance and Coordination Procedures*, in D. Gallo, L. Cecchetti (eds.), *The Preliminary Ruling Procedure, Today: Revisiting Article 267 TFEU's Constitutional Backbone* Special Issue (2023) 15 *European Journal of Legal Studies* 147, 151–152.

[246] A. Trabucchi, *Un nuovo diritto*, 272.

[247] On the risks of judicial activism within the EU, *see* H. Rasmussen, *On Law and Policy in the European Court of Justice: a Comparative Study in Judicial Policymaking*, The Hague, Martinus Nijhoff, 1986; D. Sarmiento, *Poder judicial e integración europea*, Madrid, Civitas, 2004, 284–338; K. J. Alter, *The European Court's Political Power*, Oxford, Oxford University Press, 2009; M. Dawson, B. de Witte, E. Muir (eds.), *Judicial Activism at the European Court of Justice*, Cheltenham, Edward Elgar, 2015; S. Sauregger, F. Terpan, *The Court of Justice of the European Union and the Politics of Law*, London, Palgrave, 2016; L. Clément-Wilz (ed.), *Le rôle politique de la Cour de justice de l'Union européenne*, Brussels, Bruylant, 2018; K. Lenaerts, J. A. Gutiérrez-Fons, *Les méthodes*, 61–75.

[248] *See* H. Rasmussen, *On Law and Policy*; J. H. H. Weiler, *The Court of Justice on Trial* (1987) 24 *Common Market Law Review* 555; D. Edward, *Judicial Activism*; T. Tridimas, *The Court of Justice and Judicial Activism* (1996) 21 *European Law Review* 21; W. van Gerven, *The Role and Structure of the European Judiciary Now and in the Future* (1996) 21 *European Law Review* 211; E. Benvenisti, G. W. Downs, *The Premises, Assumptions, and Implications of* Van Gend en Loos: *Viewed from the Perspectives of Democracy and Legitimacy of International Institutions* (2014) 25 *European Journal of International Law* 85; C. Fasone, D. Gallo, J. Wouters, *Re-connecting Authority and Democratic Legitimacy in the EU: Introductory Remarks* (2020) 5 *European Papers* 175, 176–177. *Contra*, criticizing the creativity of the CJ, *see* the reflections by P. Neill, *The European Court of Justice—A Case Study in Judicial Activism, European Policy Forum*, London, European Policy Forum, 1995 and T. Hartley, *The European Court, Judicial Objectivity and the Constitution of the EU* (1996) 112 *Law Quarterly Review* 95.

Moreover, as suggested in the literature, 'it is not simply the *telos* of the rules to be interpreted that matters but also the *telos* of the legal context in which those rules exist'.[249] As a matter of fact, the ability of the European legal system to create rights (and obligations) directly for the individuals, rather than 'only' for the Contracting Parties, as occurs in all other regional integration projects,[250] is structurally plugged into the existential role played by the CJ in the EEC/European Community (EC)/EU legal order.[251]

3. The subjectification of the European Treaties and the twin doctrines of fundamental rights and EU citizenship

The *Van Gend & Loos* doctrine is at the origin of a legal order aimed at safeguarding, initially, the socio-economic prerogatives of the individual-*homo oeconomicus*, subsequently and progressively up to the present, the prerogatives of individuals as holders of rights derived not only from norms inspired by 'market integration' purposes but also from 'policy integration norms'.[252] Norms that natural and legal persons can immediately invoke before national courts against the State or other private parties. The CJ, through a subjectification of the European Treaties and while placing the individual, as a subject of law, at the centre of the Community order,[253] despite there being no express reference in the EEC Treaty to the terms 'rights' or 'individuals', has greatly strengthened the democratic dimension of the European integration project. As a matter of fact, the transformation of the Community legal order brought forward by the CJ led to the formulation of two other doctrines that lie at the heart of the evolution of Community/EU law: the protection of fundamental rights,[254] and the general principles linked to them,[255] and the principle of effective judicial protection, of which direct effect is a necessary complement.[256] Indeed, rulings such as *Internationale Handelsgesellschaft*,[257] on the one hand, and *Johnston* on the other, rest on *Van Gend & Loos*, that is, on the ability of natural and legal persons to directly invoke European law through

[249] M. Poiares Maduro, *Interpreting European Law: Judicial Adjudication in a Context of Constitutional Pluralism* (2007) 1 *European Journal of Legal Studies* 137, 140. *See* also M. Lasser, *Judicial Deliberations: A Comparative Analysis of Judicial Transparency and Legitimacy*, Oxford, Oxford University Press, 2009, 227–236.

[250] Including in an advanced integrated legal order such as the European Free Trade Association (EFTA).

[251] A. Nollkaemper, *The Duality of Direct Effect of International Law* (2014) 25 *European Journal of International Law* 105, 106–107, wrote that regional integration projects like the Association of Southeast Asian Nations (ASEAN), the Economic Community of West African States (ECOWAS), the Caribbean Community (CARICOM), and MERCOSUR, 'are unlikely to embrace a top-down principle of direct effect any time soon'.

[252] In these terms, *see* B. de Witte, *Direct Effect*, 225. On direct effect and the invocability of European norms imbued with facets of both economic and non-economic character, *see* R. Lecourt, *Quel eut été*, 360–361 and N. Reich, *A European Constitution for Citizens: Reflections on the Rethinking of Union and Community Law* (1997) 3 *European Law Journal* 131, 131–133.

[253] On this matter, *see* recently, amongst monographs, J. Rondu, *L'individu, sujet du droit de l'Union européenne*, Brussels, Bruylant, 2020.

[254] According to T. Cottier, *A Theory of Direct Effect in Global Law*, in A. von Bogdandy, P. C. Mavroidis, Y. Mény (eds.), *European Integration and International Co-ordination*, Alphen aan den Rijn, Kluwer Law International, 2002, 99–124, 99, direct effect is the 'most significant step', together with fundamental rights, 'in fostering the post World War II legal order'. In the same vein, *see* also F. C. Mayer, Van Gend en Loos, 20 and J. H. H. Weiler, *The Transformation*, 1213–1219.

[255] For a parallelism between direct effect and general principles, as two core non-written EU law doctrines, *see* G. Gaja, P. Hay, D. Rotunda, *Instruments for Legal Integration in the European Community—A Review*, in M. Cappelletti, M. Seccombe, J. H. H. Weiler (eds.), *Integration*, 113–160, 141–142.

[256] On the interplay between direct effect, effectiveness, and effective judicial protection, *see* § 3 of Chapter II.

[257] CJ, *Internationale Handelsgesellschaft mbH v Einfuhr- und Vorratsstelle für Getreide und Futtermittel*, 11/70, EU:C:1970:114, para. 3.

direct effect as the core of Community autonomy. The same is true for European citizenship,[258] insofar as direct effect allows the individual to enforce their right of residence flowing from Article 20 TFEU which 'precludes national measures which have the effect of depriving citizens of the Union of the genuine enjoyment of the substance of the rights conferred by virtue of their status as citizens of the Union'.[259] This is what the CJ itself observed in its May 1995 Report on certain aspects of the application of the TEU, whereby, in section 4, it is written that, 'even before there was the idea of citizenship of the Union',[260] the Court had identified direct effect as the backbone of the new European legal order. By recognizing natural and legal persons, if not the Treaty masters, as its natural and immediate recipients, the CJ found in the principle of direct effect the most powerful avenue to adapt, shape and transform EU law, enabling it to depart from 'so many other international organisations whose existence passes unnoticed by ordinary citizens'[261] and evolve over the decades, despite moments of political stagnation and crisis.

[258] On the importance of *Van Gend & Loos* and direct effect for the construction of the European citizenship, *see* A. Epiney, *L'arrêt* Van Gend en Loos *et la citoyenneté de l'Union*, in A. Tizzano, J. Kokott, S. Prechal (Organizing Committee), *50ème anniversaire*, 135–153, 136 and J. H. H. Weiler, *Revisiting* Van Gend en Loos, 14. For a recent account on EU citizenship, *see* N. N. Shuibhne, *EU Citizenship Law*, Oxford, Oxford University Press, 2023.

[259] CJ, *Gerardo Ruiz Zambrano*, C-34/09, EU:C:2011:124, para. 42.

[260] *See* the Report available at https://www.cvce.eu/content/publication/2003/4/2/3644862f-2e8f-4170-9616-e573a41b61c5/publishable_en.pdf.

[261] F. Mancini, D. Keeling, *Democracy*, 183.

II
EVOLUTIVE DIRECT EFFECT AND THE PRELIMINARY REFERENCE PROCEDURE

1. Private enforcement through multi-faceted direct effect and Article 267 TFEU

In *Van Gend & Loos*, the Court of Justice (CJ) forged the doctrine of direct effect in relation to the rules of the European Economic Community (EEC) Treaty, as observed in Chapter I. In the jurisprudence which followed, the EU judges further developed what had been established in *Van Gend & Loos* and, in that manner, extended their reasoning, to differing degrees, to secondary legislation, international agreements, general principles of EU law, and the Charter of Fundamental Rights.[1] The absolute majority of these decisions have one thing in common: they were brought in the context of preliminary ruling proceedings under Article 267 of the Treaty on the Functioning of the EU (TFEU), most notably within the framework of interpretative judgments.[2] As a matter of fact, without the '*genius*'[3] of Article 267 TFEU, as the 'keystone' of the EU judicial system[4] and the 'jewel in the Crown' of the Court's jurisdiction,[5] direct effect would lose most of its usefulness, as was affirmed by AG Lagrange, even before *Van Gend & Loos*, in his opinion in *De Geus v Bosch*, with respect to the EEC Treaty and regulations.[6]

The same can be affirmed for the principle of primacy, the doctrine of consistent interpretation, the principles of effectiveness and effective judicial protection, and the State

[1] *See* Chapter III, § 3. All URLs for this chapter were last accessed on 30 April 2024.

[2] On the origins of the preliminary rulings procedure, the role of Catalano within the *Groupe de redaction* in charge of drafting the EEC Treaty, and the interplay between the then Article 177 of the EEC Treaty and direct effect, *see* T. Pavone, *Making the European Court Work: Nicola Catalano and the Origins of European Legal Integration*, in D. Gallo, R. Mastroianni, F. Nicola, L. Cecchetti (eds.), *The Italian Influence on European Law: Judges and Advocates General (1952-2000)*, Oxford, Hart, 2024, forthcoming, and, for further reflections on the debate underpinning the insertion of that article in the EEC Treaty, A. Arena, A. Rosanò, *Nicola Catalano (1910-1984): padre del rinvio pregiudiziale d'interpretazione e apostolo del primato del diritto comunitario* (2024) 1 *Eurojus* 89.

[3] J. H. H. Weiler, *Revisiting* Van Gend en Loos: *Subjectifying and Objectifying the Individual*, in A. Tizzano, J. Kokott, S. Prechal (Organizing Committee), *50ème anniversaire de l'arrêt Van Gend en Loos: 1963-2013: actes du colloque*, Luxembourg, 13 mai 2013, 11-22, 12.

[4] CJ, *Opinion 2/13, Accession of the European Union to the European Convention for the Protection of Human Rights and Fundamental Freedoms*, EU:C:2014:2454, para. 176. As highlighted by R. Schütze, *European Union Law*, 3rd ed., Oxford, Oxford University Press, 2021, 359, this procedure must be regarded as 'the central pillar of the Union's cooperative federalism for it combines the central interpretation of Union law by the Court of Justice with the decentralized application of European law by the national courts'; *see* also R. Schütze, *Conclusion: Article 267 TFEU and EU Federalism*, in D. Gallo, L. Cecchetti, *The Preliminary Ruling Procedure, Today: Revisiting Article 267 TFEU's Constitutional Backbone*, Special Issue (2023) 15 *European Journal of Legal Studies* 221.

[5] P. Craig, G. de Búrca, *EU Law. Text, Cases, and Materials*, 7th ed., Oxford, Oxford University Press, 2020, 496; J. Langer, *Article 267 TFEU: Celebrating the Jewel in the Crown of the Community Legal Architecture and Some Hot Potatoes*, in F. Ambtenbrink, G. Davies, D. Kochenov, J. Lindeboom (eds.), *The Internal Market and the Future of European Integration. Essays in Honour of Laurence W. Gormley*, Cambridge, Cambridge University Press, 2019, 455–469.

[6] Opinion of AG Lagrange of 27 February 1962, *De Geus v Bosch*, EU:C:1962:3, 114.

Direct Effect in EU Law. Daniele Gallo, Oxford University Press. © Daniele Gallo 2025. DOI: 10.1093/9780191925221.003.0003

liability remedy, amongst others.[7] Indeed, *Van Gend & Loos* and direct effect, seen also in the light of such principles and doctrines, cannot be detached from one of the inherent features of the European legal order, that is, from the need to guarantee the uniform and effective enforcement of primary and secondary law.[8] A need that lies at the heart of the preliminary rulings procedure,[9] the importance of which was repeatedly emphasized by the CJ in its case law,[10] since its foundations. A procedure, moreover, that has been the landscape where the Court reinforced the protection of individual rights and, in so doing, clarified the content and scope of European law.[11]

The biggest novelty of *Van Gend & Loos* regards direct effect as a tool of rights' protection and as an effective, efficient, and operational alternative to public enforcement of EU law assured by the European Commission pursuant to Article 258 TFEU.[12] By placing individuals at the centre of the EU legal order, as explained in Chapter I, direct effect renders them the true enforcers of EU law. Through litigation, natural and legal persons can complain that States have failed to fulfil their obligations under the European Treaties. As R. Lecourt remarked in his *L'Europe des juges*, 'when the individual applies to a judge to ensure that their treaty rights are recognised, they are not acting in their own interest alone, but by this behaviour the individual becomes a type of auxiliary agent of the Community'.[13] Moreover, the individuals are not the only trigger for the development and fair enforcement of EU law. Almost all landmark decisions of the CJ shall be considered, at least partially, also the fruit of national courts' intuitions diluted in their preliminary references, as well as of individuals aiming to vindicate their interests before domestic judges. Indeed, normally, national courts turn to the CJ on the basis of Article 267 TFEU in the context of disputes initiated by natural and legal persons asking a judge to safeguard rights—first and foremost through direct effect

[7] The preliminary ruling procedure has been defined as the 'most important aspect of the work of the Court' by L. Neville Brown, F. G. Jacobs, *The Court of Justice of the European Communities*, London, Sweet & Maxwell, 1977, 131. *See* also the account in D. Gallo, L. Cecchetti, *Introduction: Article 267 TFEU, today*, in D. Gallo, L. Cecchetti, *The Preliminary Ruling*, 1 and R. Schütze, *Conclusion*.

[8] On this aspect *see* A. Arnull, *The European Union and Its Court of Justice*, Oxford, Oxford University Press, 1999, 159–161.

[9] On Article 267 TFEU (past and present) *see*, in the copious literature, A. Barav, *Études sur le renvoi préjudiciel dans le droit de l'Union européenne*, Brussels, Bruylant, 2010; R. Mastroianni, *Pregiudiziale comunitaria*, in *Digesto delle discipline pubblicistiche*, vol. IV, Turin, UTET, 2010, 399; C. Naomé, *Le renvoi préjudiciel en droit de l'Union*, 2nd ed., Brussels, Bruylant, 2010; E. D'Alessandro, *Il procedimento pregiudiziale interpretativo dinanzi alla Corte di giustizia: oggetto ed efficacia della pronuncia*, Turin, Giappichelli, 2012; J. Pertek, *Coopération entre juges nationaux et Cour de justice de l'UE. Le renvoi préjudiciel*, Brussels, Bruylant, 2013; G. Vandersanden, *Renvoi préjudiciel en droit européen*, Brussels, Bruylant, 2013; E. Neframi (ed.), *Renvoi préjudiciel et marge d'appréciation du juge national*, Brussels, Bruylant, 2015; C. Kovács, *Die temporale Wirkung von Urteilen des EuGH im Vorabentscheidungsverfahren*, Baden-Baden, Nomos, 2015; X. Arzoz Santisteban, *La garantía constitucional del deber de reenvío prejudicial*, Madrid, Centro de Estudios Políticos y Constitucionales, 2020; C. Iannone, F. Ferraro (eds.), *Il rinvio pregiudiziale*, Turin, Giappichelli, 2020; C. Lacchi, *Preliminary References to the Court of Justice of the European Union and Effective Judicial Protection*, Brussels, Larcier, 2020; M. Broberg, N. Fenger, *Preliminary References to the European Court of Justice*, 3rd ed., Oxford, Oxford University Press, 2021; J. Krommendijk, *National Courts and Preliminary References to the Court of Justice*, Elgar, Cheltenham, 2021; J. Pertek, *Le renvoi préjudiciel. Droit, liberté ou obligation de coopération des juridictions nationales avec la CJUE*, 2nd ed., Brussels, Bruylant, 2021; S. Barbieri, *Il rinvio pregiudiziale tra giudici ordinari e Corte costituzionale*, Naples, Jovene, 2023.

[10] *See*, amongst others, CJ, *Melki*, joined cases C-188-189/10, EU:C:2010:363; *Accession of the European Union to the European Convention for the Protection of Human Rights and Fundamental Freedoms*, para. 176.

[11] *See* the observations by P. Pescatore, *International Law and Community Law—A Comparative Analysis* (1970) 7 *Common Market Law Review* 167, 175–177 and B. de Witte, *Retour à* Costa. *La primauté du droit communautaire à la lumiere du droit international* (1984) 20 *Revue trimestrielle de droit européen* 425, 448–450.

[12] Recently, on Article 267 TFEU, recognition of individual rights and private enforcement, *see* R. Adam, *Il rinvio pregiudiziale tra tutela dei diritti soggettivi e controllo delle inadempienze statali*, in J. Alberti, G. De Cristofaro (eds.), *Il rinvio pregiudiziale come strumento di sviluppo degli ordinamenti*, Pisa, Pacini, 2023, 3–26.

[13] R. Lecourt, *L'Europe des juges*, Brussels, Bruylant, 1976, 260.

and disapplication—which they feel they deserve protection under EU law.[14] Furthermore, in addition to the two interrelated facets of *Van Gend & Loos*, that is, the direct justiciability of EU rights and the role of individuals as enforcers, another central contribution of the judgment is that it allowed Member States 'to give up the use of interstate retaliation and reciprocity mechanisms to enforce European treaty obligations'.[15] As a matter of fact, the then Article 177 of the EEC Treaty, currently Article 267 TFEU, was the trigger to achieve this result.

Against this background, the CJ, as it did several years later with regard to fundamental rights, conceived a doctrine that was not expressly acknowledged in the Treaties.[16] And unlike what happened, thanks to the Treaty of Maastricht, with the inclusion of Article 6 of the EU Treaty, the principle of direct effect never became black letter law. Besides, the Declaration No. 17, annexed, together with the opinion of the Council's Legal Service of 22 June 2007, to the Treaty of Lisbon,[17] is devoted to primacy, while no reference is made to direct effect either in the European Treaties or in secondary law, or even in the acts, political in nature, adopted by the EU and/or the Member States at the Treaties revision intergovernmental conferences which took place beginning in the eighties.

Now, the absence of an express provision in the Treaties providing for the doctrine of direct effect, is not in itself a limit. To the contrary, this absence enables said doctrine to mature and evolve,[18] so that the European institutions, in particular the CJ and GC, can intercept and frame situations and transformations that would otherwise be excluded *ab origine* from EU law. Indeed, the EU legal system is inherently in progress and direct effect acts as a motor for its evolution.[19] The circumstance that this evolution is above all the result of the action carried out by the CJ is not surprising. In fact, it is the position that Article 267 TFEU, read together with Article 19 TEU, grants to the CJ to justify its role as protagonist and *primus inter pares* actor in the establishment and shaping of EU law. The procedure set forth in Article 267 TFEU reassures national courts that they are not necessarily left on their own to interpret a law external to 'their' legal order.[20] From this point of view, it is a 'centralized' system to the extent that the EU courts are endowed with a monopoly for the interpretation of primary and secondary EU law. In this context, the judicial origins of constitutional

[14] On the essential role performed by parties' attorneys within domestic proceedings *see*, besides authors cited in § 1 of Chapter I, footnote 59, A. Vauchez, *Introduction. Euro-lawyering, Transnational Social Fields and European Polity-Building*, in A. Vauchez, B. de Witte (eds.), *Lawyering Europe: European Law as a Transnational Social Field*, Oxford, Oxford University Press, 2013, 1–20, 1, footnote 4, and, in the same volume, K. D. Kelemen, *Eurolegalism and the European Legal Field*, 221–242. *See* the recent inspiring research by T. Pavone, *The Ghostwriters: Lawyers and the Politics Behind the Judicial Construction of Europe*, Cambridge, Cambridge University Press, 2022, 129–240.

[15] W. Phelan, *Great Judgments of the European Court of Justice. Rethinking the Landmark Decisions of the Foundational Period*, Cambridge, Cambridge University Press, 2020, 52–53. In this respect, Phelan stressed the importance of CJ, *Commission v Luxembourg and Belgium*, joined cases 2-3/62, EU:C:1962:45, 224–240, arguing that in this judgment the CJ 'had rejected self-help retaliation and safeguard mechanisms thirty years before the Court was first granted or first employed its power to fine the member states, and it is instead the pervasive granting of direct effect to European law within the national legal systems that has primarily acted as a substitute for self-help and unilateral safeguards within the European legal order' (225).

[16] *See* Chapter I, § 3.

[17] *See*, respectively, Declaration concerning primacy in OJEU, C 202/01 of 7 June 2016, 343–344, and Council, Opinion of the Legal Service on the Primacy of EC law, 11197/07 JUR 260, Brussels, 22 June 2007, 1.

[18] On this aspect *see* M. Bobek, *The Effects of EU Law in the National Legal Systems*, in C. Barnard, S. Peers (eds.), *European Union Law*, Oxford, Oxford University Press, 2020, 154–189, 155.

[19] L.-J. Constantinesco, *Actes officiels du Congrès international d'études sur la Communauté européenne du charbon et de l'acier*, II, Milan, Giuffrè, 1958, 236, refers to a process '*en marche*', not being rooted in a '*structure définitivement cristallisée*'.

[20] In these terms J. H. H. Weiler, *Revisiting* Van Gend en Loos, 14.

principles and their refinement over the years enables direct effect not to remain static as it would if it were based on written sources of law.

From the time when in *Van Gend & Loos* and the subsequent case law it was affirmed that it is not European law in its entirety but only those of its provisions apt to entail direct effects, the relationship between the national courts and the EU courts has been one of clear dependency of the former upon the latter.[21] It is the CJ's task to assess, in the frame of Article 267 TFEU, whether and according to what terms an EU rule produces direct effect.[22] This has allowed the Court to impose[23] a certain vision of European law regardless of the constitutional law's constraints on the individual Member States.[24] Already in *Van Gend & Loos*, the CJ was bold in stating that the question regarding the direct or indirect effect of an EU provision is not a purely internal matter.[25] After all, from a reading of the subsequent case law it may be concluded that what shall be considered 'purely internal', that is, falling within the exclusive jurisdiction of the national courts, is very little.[26]

The key innovative aspect of *Van Gend & Loos* and the doctrine originating from it is not only the recognition, as directly effective, of the EEC rules but rather the fact that such recognition was removed from the courts of Member States.[27] *Van Gend & Loos* clearly shows that domestic courts have no margin of appreciation in the qualification of an EU provision as non-directly effective.[28]

The ties between direct effect and preliminary ruling proceedings are so close that the two are practically ingrained in one another since they both ensure that EU law is correctly applied across all Member States[29] and that this application shall cause, if needed, the

[21] According to G. Bebr, *Court of Justice: Judicial Protection and the Rule of Law*, in D. Curtin, T. Heukels (eds.), *Institutional Dynamics of European Integration—Essays in Honour of Henry G. Schermers*, Dordrecht-Boston, Martinus Nijhoff, II, 1994, 303–333, 307, the CJ has transformed the preliminary reference procedure 'into an indirect means of protecting individual Community rights based on directly effective provisions which had been infringed by the member States'.

[22] As observed by J. H. Jans., J. M. Prinssen, *Direct Effect: Convergence or Divergence?*, in J. M. Prinssen, A. Schrauwen (eds.), *Direct Effect: Rethinking a Classic of EC Legal Doctrine*, Groningen, European Law Publishing, 2002, 106–126, 119, 'the ECJ should have the monopoly in terms of shaping the contours of the doctrine as such; it is the ECJ that rules exclusively on the question whether and, if so, under what circumstances, a Community law provision does or does not have direct effect'.

[23] For an insightful account, *see* M. Claes, *The Impact of* Van Gend en Loos *beyond the Scope of EU law*, in A. Tizzano, J. Kokott, S. Prechal (Organizing Committee), *50ème anniversaire*, 103-110, 104.

[24] For an interesting parallelism between the US Supreme Court and the CJ in 'filling the gap' when domestic constitutional law is not conclusive, *see* M. Claes, *The Impact. See* also D. Halberstam, *Internal Legitimacy and Europe's Piecemeal Constitution: Reflections on* Van Gend *at 50*, in A. Tizzano, J. Kokott, S. Prechal (Organizing Committee), *50ème anniversaire*, 111–117, 114.

[25] This implies that the Court can autonomously endow an EU provision with direct effect by giving substance to it in spite of how it is formualted, while it cannot refrain from considering an EU provision directly effective, should direct effect's premises be fulfilled.

[26] *See* L. Potvin-Solis, *Qualification des situations purement internes*, in E. Neframi (ed.), *Renvoi*, 39–100, 62.

[27] *See* A. Trabucchi, *Un nuovo diritto* (1963) 1 *Rivista di diritto civile* 259, 268–269 and B. de Witte, *The Impact of* Van Gend en Loos *on Judicial Protection at European and National Level: Three Types of Preliminary Questions*, in A. Tizzano, J. Kokott, S. Prechal (Organizing Committee), *50ème anniversaire*, 93–101, 93. On the importance of the preliminary reference procedure for the evolution of direct effect, beginning with *Van Gend & Loos*, *see* M. Cremona, *The Judgment—Framing the Argument*, in A. Tizzano, J. Kokott, S. Prechal (Organizing Committee), *50ème anniversaire*, 23–27, 26. On this topic, *see* also § 4 of this chapter.

[28] On Article 267 TFEU and the margin of discretion, *see* E. Neframi, *Le rôle du juge national dans le cadre du renvoi préjudiciel: une marge d'appréciation?*, in E. Neframi (ed.), *Renvoi*, 21–38.

[29] For further reflections, *see* F. C. Mayer, Van Gend en Loos: *The Foundation of a Community of Law*, in M. Poiares Maduro, L. Azoulai (eds.), *The Past and Future of EU Law: The Classics of EU Law Revisited on the 50th Anniversary of the Rome Treaty*, Oxford, Hart, 2010, 16–25, 23 and M. de Visser, M. Claes, *Courts United? On European Judicial Networks*, in A. Vauchez, B. de Witte (eds.), *Lawyering Europe*, 75–100. On the need for a close relationship between national courts and the CJ in the frame of Article 267 TFEU *see*, amongst early judgments, CJ, *Firma G. Schwarze*, 16/65, EU:C:1965:117, para. 922. More recently, *see* CJ, *SMW Winzersekt GmbH*, C-306/93, EU:C:1994:407, para. 15; CJ, *Criminal proceedings against Claude Laguillaumie*, C-116/00, EU:C:2000:350, para. 21; CJ, *J. Slob*, C-496/04, EU:C:2006:570, para. 34; CJ, *Creation of a unified patent litigation system*, 1/09,

disapplication of national law.[30] There is profound complementarity between Article 267 TFEU and direct effect[31] because the trigger of the preliminary ruling procedure is generally the individual,[32] who acts as 'legal vigilante',[33] 'agent',[34] and '*sentinelle*',[35] 'on behalf' of the EU institutions,[36] in ensuring compliance with EU law and consistency in its enforcement.[37] Direct effect, therefore, is not only instrumental for the safeguarding of rights, at a judicial level, but is also a key tool through which the application of EU law is secured in domestic legal orders. In that regard, a clear difference exists between Article 267 TFEU, as far as interpretative preliminary ruling proceedings are concerned, and the judicial review mechanisms governed by Articles 263 and Article 267 TFEU on the validity of EU acts, as well as the infringement actions pursuant to Articles 258–260 TFEU. In all these proceedings, national measures (Articles 258–260 TFEU) and EU legislation (Articles 263 and 267 TFEU on validity) can be challenged 'without questions of direct effect arising'.[38]

In this context, it is important to note that the doctrine of direct effect, while normally availed by a natural/legal person, does not always presuppose that the latter is the one invoking EU law. As a matter of fact, the enforcer of EU law could ultimately be one of the State agencies, who relies on an EU provision against a private party, while seeking disapplication of a conflicting national law. This is a problematic doctrine of EU law generally known as 'inverse vertical direct effect'. Precedents in which the CJ has recognized such effect are quite rare, though. Some are convincing, as in the case of generally applicable measures such as regulations, while others raise several concerns, first and foremost due to the possible infringement of the principles of legal certainty and legitimate expectations.[39]

In other situations a public authority invokes an EU norm to challenge the behaviour of other public bodies who are deemed responsible for the violation of EU provisions. In fact, this kind of situation has arisen in very few cases, including one, recently, about seaside concessions in Italy. Indeed, in the *Autorità Garante della Concorrenza e del Mercato* preliminary ruling of April 2023,[40] the CJ recognized the direct effect of Article 12 of Directive 123/2006/CE and deemed it could apply also in a domestic dispute involving the Italian Competition Authority against a local municipality, that is, a public authority against another public authority. Hence, by this judgment, direct effect was affirmed, although the

EU:C:2011:123, para. 84; CJ, *Consorzio Italian Management*, C-561/19, EU:C:2021:799, para. 29. As a matter of fact, *Van Gend & Loos* and all other preliminary rulings concerning the protection of individual rights, as well as the scope of direct and indirect effect, reveal that there isn't only one 'hero' or 'protagonist' in the cases at hand, since national courts, in submitting the references to the CJ, 'w[ere] already opening the conceptual (and political) door to the Court' (J. H. H. Weiler, *Revisiting* Van Gend en Loos, 12).

[30] On the extent of disapplication within the EU legal order, *see* extensively Chapter V.

[31] In these terms V. Skouris, *Allocution*, in A. Tizzano, J. Kokott, S. Prechal (Organizing Committee), *50ème anniversaire*, 7–9, 9.

[32] As noted by P. Pescatore, *Van Gend en Loos, 3 February 1963—A View from Within*, in M. Poiares Maduro, L. Azoulai (eds.), *The Past*, 3–8, 7 and B. de Witte, *The Impact*, 94–95.

[33] J. H. H. Weiler, *Revisiting* Van Gend en Loos, 13. *See* also M. Cremona, *The Judgment*, 27.

[34] F. C. Mayer, Van Gend en Loos, 24.

[35] J. Roux, *Droit général de l'Union européenne*, 10th ed., Paris, LexisNexis, 2016, 333.

[36] M. Poiares Maduro, *We the Court. The European Court of Justice and the European Economic Constitution*, Oxford, Oxford University Press, 1998, 9.

[37] On the deterrent effect of the preliminary reference procedure, *see* G. Tesauro, *Art. 19 TUE*, in A. Tizzano (ed.), *Trattati dell'Unione europea. Commentario*, 2nd ed., Milan, Giuffrè, 2014, 195–215, 208–210.

[38] R. Dunbar, *The Application of International Law in the Court of Justice of the European Union: Proportionality Rising* (2021) 22 *German Law Journal* 557, 566.

[39] On direct effect, disapplication, and inverse vertical effect, *see* § 3.2 of Chapter III and §§ 2 and 5–10 of Chapter V.

[40] CJ, *Autorità Garante della Concorrenza e del Mercato*, C-348/22, EU:C:2023:301. On this and other rulings, *see* §§ 3 and 7 of Chapter III, § 4 of Chapter V, and § 5.1 of Chapter VI.

plaintiff in the internal dispute was a branch of the State and notwithstanding the risks for legal certainty resulting from a situation in which the former relies on an EU directive, in a dispute against another public authority, with the aim of setting aside a conflicting national law and, simultaneously, applying the EU directive *in malam partem*.[41]

Lastly, as remarked by Joseph H. H. Weiler,[42] direct effect and preliminary ruling procedures should also be seen in the light of the principle of subsidiarity, as the latter makes sure that EU law is applied in a manner which meets, as close as possible, the needs not only of the States but also of the citizens, that is, those who are most directly and immediately involved in its enforcement. In the words of Weiler, subsidiarity 'is built into the system given the fundamental role which individuals come to play as a result of Direct Effect combined with the Preliminary Reference'.[43] A principle of subsidiarity, in this sense, *ante litteram* since it appears, ultimately, as a manifestation of both direct effect and the preliminary ruling procedure.

2. The *de jure erga omnes* effect of preliminary rulings

Article 267 TFEU, which is 'activated' by domestic courts in the frame of individuals' actions frequently involving EU directly effective provisions, performs a crucial function within the EU legal order first and foremost because preliminary rulings are not merely declaratory[44] and their effect is *erga omnes.*[45] *Erga omnes* means that the ruling binds not only the referring court[46] but all the authorities of all the Member States, including domestic judges.[47] However, considering the lack of clear and explicit stances taken by the CJ on the personal scope of preliminary rulings beyond the referring court[48] among scholars[49] there are

[41] On this problem, *see* extensively Chapter V.

[42] J. H. H. Weiler, *Revisiting* Van Gend en Loos, 13: 'the demand for legal rights and their enforcement is a bottom up phenomenon, emanating from and close to, the most immediate stake holders'.

[43] H. H. Weiler, *Revisiting* Van Gend en Loos, 13.

[44] As remarked by W. Phelan, *Great Judgments*, 50.

[45] *See*, amongst early commentators, A. M. Donner, *National Law and the Case Law of the Court of Justice of the European Community* (1963) 1 *Common Market Law Review* 8, 15. Most recently, *see* the account by A. Correra, *Natura ed effetti delle sentenze pregiudiziali della Corte di giustizia*, Naples, Editoriale Scientifica, 2023; G. Martinico, *Retracing Old (Scholarly) Path. The* Erga Omnes *Effects of the Interpretative Preliminary Rulings*, in D. Gallo, L. Cecchetti, *The Preliminary Ruling*, 37. For a different critical perspective, *see* E. Cimiotta, *L'ambito soggettivo di efficacia delle sentenze pregiudiziali della Corte di giustizia dell'Unione europea. L'efficacia nei confronti dei giudici diversi dal giudice del rinvio*, Turin, Giappichelli, 2023, 283–326.

[46] For judgments explicitly affirming that preliminary rulings are binding for the referring courts, *see*, *ex multis*, CJ, *Luigi Benedetti*, 52/76, EU:C:1977:16, para. 26; CJ, *Fazenda Pública v Câmara Municipal do Porto*, C-446/98, EU:C:2000:691, para. 49; CJ, *Georgi Ivanov Elchinov*, C-173/09, EU:C:2010:581, para. 29.

[47] In this regard, it is interesting what the CJ writes in the disclaimers of the press releases regarding its preliminary rulings. *See*, e.g., press release No. 208/23, CJ, *G. K.*, C-281/22, EU:C:2023:1018, available at https://curia.europa.eu/jcms/upload/docs/application/pdf/2023-12/cp230208en.pdf: 'A reference for a preliminary ruling allows the courts and tribunals of the Member States, in disputes which have been brought before them, to refer questions to the Court of Justice about the interpretation of EU law or the validity of an EU act. The Court of Justice does not decide the dispute itself. It is for the national court or tribunal to dispose of the case in accordance with the Court's decision, which is similarly binding on other national courts or tribunals before which a similar issue is raised.'

[48] On such uncertainty, *see* the opinion of AG Darmon of 18 November 1987, *Fratelli Pardini SpA*, 338/85, EU:C:1987:495, para. 4; the opinion of AG Lenz of 29 April 1989, *Fratelli Costanzo*, 103/88, EU:C:1989:166, para. 35; the opinion of AG Lenz of 29 June 1989, *Torfaen Borough Council*, C-145/88, EU:C:1989:279, para. 8. In the literature, for a detailed analysis illustrating the CJ's tendency to grant *erga omnes* binding effects to its preliminary rulings, *see* D. Anderson, M. Demetriou, *References to the European Court*, London, Sweet & Maxwell, 2002, 331–332; K. Lenaerts, K. Gutman, J. T. Nowak, *EU Procedural Law*, 2nd ed., Oxford, Oxford University Press, 2023, 264–267.

[49] For an overview of the divergent doctrinal positions on the internal effects of preliminary rulings, *see* A. Barav, G. Vandersanden, *Contentieux Communautaire*, Paris, Pedone, 1977, 312–315; G. Martinico, *Le sentenze*

opposing views to the recognition of such effect. The assumption some authors generally move from is that the interpretive preliminary rulings, differently from those on validity, have binding force *ultra partes* exclusively *de facto* 'simply' because of—it would appear they infer—the authority vested in the CJ by the European Treaties,[50] above all through the medium of the reference preliminary ruling procedure. Following this approach to the letter, therefore, only the referring judge shall abide by the preliminary ruling. Notably, some scholars,[51] while denying the *de jure* character of the rulings' *erga omnes* effects, underscore that a new reference would be *de facto* unnecessary given the existence of a previous preliminary ruling on the same matter of EU law.[52]

On the opposite side, according to a different doctrinal trend, inspired by the Anglo-Saxon tradition, interpretive rulings entail *erga omnes* effects[53] in accordance with the principle of *stare decisis*, thus they serve ('formally') as a precedent.[54]

In this book the stance that preliminary rulings produce *de jure erga omnes* effects is upheld. However, a few clarifications are needed. First of all, they do not constitute precedent in the strict sense for the overall structure of the European judicial order is different from the Anglo-Saxon system.[55] As a matter of fact, two components of a precedent-like system are missing: the hierarchical relationship between the CJ and domestic courts,[56] and the duty

interpretative della Corte di giustizia come fonte di produzione normativa (2004) 9 *Rivista di diritto costituzionale* 249, 250–256; E. D'Alessandro, *Il procedimento pregiudiziale*, 211–311; M. Broberg, N. Fenger, *Preliminary References*, 399–409; E. Cimiotta, *L'ambito soggettivo*, 57–102; G. Martinico, *Retracing*, 41–53.

50 *See, inter alia*, L. Ferrari Bravo, *Art. 177*, in R. Quadri, R. Monaco, A. Trabucchi (eds.), *Trattato istitutivo della Comunità economica europea. Commentario*, Milan, Giuffrè, 1965, 1310–1335, 1332; A. G. Toth, *The Authority of Judgments of the European Court of Justice: Binding Force and Legal Effects* (1984) 4 *Yearbook of European Law* 1–77; M. Waelbroeck, D. Waelbroeck, *Article 177*, in J. Mégret, J. V. Louis, D. Vignes, W. Waelbroeck (eds.), *Commentaire Mégret. Le droit de la Communauté économique européenne*, 2nd ed., vol. X, Brussels, Bruylant, 1993, 197–210; C. Baudenbacher, *The Implementation of Decisions of the ECJ and of the EFTA Court in Member States' Domestic Legal Orders* (2005) 40 *Texas International Law Journal* 383, 397, who refers to 'factual *erga omnes*', i.e. to a 'factual precedent for all national courts'.

51 *See* M. Dauser, *Das Vorabentscheidungsverfahren nach Artikel 177 EG-Vertrag*, Munich, C. H. Beck, 1995, 156.

52 E. D'Alessandro, *Il procedimento pregiudiziale*, 292.

53 A. Arnull, *The Use and Abuse of Article 177 ECC* (1989) 52 *Modern Law Review* 622, 624; F. G. Jacobs, *The Effect of Preliminary Rulings in the National Legal Order*, in M. Andenas (ed.), *Article 177 References to the European Court—Policy and Practice*, London, Butterworths, 1994, 29–45, 30; J. Combrexelle, *L'impact de l'arrêt de la Cour: étendue et limites des pouvoirs du juge national*, in V. Christianos (ed.), *Evolution récente du droit judiciaire communautaire*, Maastricht, European Institute of Public Administration, vol. I, 1994, 113–115; F. Ghera, *Pregiudiziale comunitaria, pregiudiziale costituzionale e valore di precedente delle sentenze interpretative della Corte di giustizia* (2000) 4 *Giurisprudenza costituzionale* 1193; K. Lenaerts, K. Gutman, J. T. Nowak, *EU Procedural Law*, 265–266; M. Broberg, N. Fenger, *Preliminary References*, 406–406.

54 *See*, amongst others, A. Arnull, *The European Union*, 625; P. Craig, G. de Búrca, *EU Law*, 530. On CJ precedents, *see* also T. Koopman, Stare decisis *in European Law*, in D. O'Keeffe, H. G. Schermers (eds.), *Essays in European Law and Integration*, Leiden, Kluwer, 1982, 11; G. Slynn, *The Court of Justice of the European Communities* (1984) 33 *International and Comparative Law Quarterly* 409, 423; J. Barceló, *Precedent in European Community Law*, in N. MacCormick, R. S. Summers (eds.), *Interpreting Precedents—A Comparative Study*, London, Routledge, 1997, 407–436; J. Komárek, *Precedent and Judicial Lawmaking in Supreme Courts: The Court of Justice Compared to the US Supreme Court and the French Cour de Cassation* (2009) 11 *The Cambridge Yearbook of European Legal Studies* 399–433; T. Tridimas, *Precedent and the Court of Justice: A Jurisprudence of Doubt?*, in J. Dickson, P. Eleftheriadis (eds.), *Philosophical Foundations of European Union Law*, Oxford, Oxford University Press, 2012, 307–330; U. Šadl, S. Hink, *Precedent in the* Sui Generis *Legal Order: A Mine Run Approach*' (2014) 20 *European Law Journal* 544; D. Simon, A. Rigaux, *Le 'précédent' dans la jurisprudence du juge de l'Union*, in C. Mestre (ed.), *Europe(s), droit(s) européen(s), Une passion d'universitaire*, Brussels, Bruylant, 2015, 547–578; R. Mańko, *Preliminary reference procedure, Briefing of the European Parliamentary Research Service*, EPRS, European Parliament, 608.628, July 2017; S. Rodin, *La valeur des précédents dans la jurisprudence de la Cour* (2017) 4 *Il Diritto dell'Unione Europea* 661.

55 As explained by G. Bebr, *Development of Judicial Control of the European Communities*, The Hague, Martinus Nijhoff, 1981, 9, and A. G. Toth, *The Authority*, 2–3. *See* also J. Barceló, *Precedent*, 416 and G. Martinico, *Retracing*, 42–43.

56 On this matter, *see* P. Biavati, *Diritto processuale dell'Unione europea*, Milan, Giuffrè, 2015, 433–434.

to openly justify the reasons in case a *revirement* is made.[57] Secondly, there is no provision in either primary or secondary law which provides that preliminary rulings are an autonomous source of law, separate from the provisions that they interpret, as would instead be the case if it were a formal system of precedents. Thirdly, the United Kingdom, as is well known, acceded to the EU in 1973: prior to that, only States following a civil law system were represented.[58] The idea that preliminary rulings, as per their effects, were originally designed based on common law jurisdictions and traditions, of consequence, cannot be shared. Lastly, rulings under Article 267 TFEU lack the force of *res judicata* in the strict sense because, unlike preliminary rulings on validity (and judgments on annulment *ex* Article 263 TFEU),[59] subsequent interpretative preliminary rulings could be delivered on a new interpretation of the EU rule that was at stake in the previous judgment(s).[60]

What, then, would be the *erga omnes de jure* effect of interpretive preliminary rulings? In line with a part of the francophone doctrine,[61] it could be argued that they produce *erga omnes* effects as '*autorité de la chose interprétée*',[62] *par incorporation*,[63] that is, by virtue of the binding nature of the provisions interpreted by the CJ in its judgments.[64] This means that the exact contents and contours of a rule are not static and can change over time. Moreover, a given provision, consisting of several parts, could be subject to a new interpretation about different profiles and other parts than the one(s) which had already been deciphered by the Court. As noted by some scholars, authority is one thing, while immutability is another.[65] Preliminary rulings thus become one with the EU rule they interpret.[66]

Additionally, it shall be highlighted that the *effet utile* of EU law, the effectiveness of judicial protection, and uniformity in the enforcement of EU law, as well as the respect of direct effect, would be jeopardized if the preliminary rulings were devoid of *erga omnes* effects. Furthermore, such effects are not limited to the operative part of the judgment but are extended to the whole reasoning developed therein.[67] As a matter of fact, limiting the effect to the decision only, that is, to the specific point(s) of law raised before the CJ with respect to specific provisions,

[57] On the need to openly perform overrulings, in the presence of conflicts, *see* opinion of AG Bobek of 23 September 2021, *NE*, C-205/20, EU:C:2021:759, paras 133–139. An explicit overruling has been recently undertaken by the CJ, regarding the direct effect of the principle of proportionality of penalties (which was explicitly neglected in CJ, *Link Logistic*, C-384/17, EU:C:2018:810) in CJ, *NE*, C-205/20, EU:C:2022:168, para. 29. For a recent, innovative, and in-depth classification of overruling techniques, *see* D. Sarmiento, *The 'Overruling Technique' at the Court of Justice of the European Union*, in D. Gallo, L. Cecchetti (eds.), *The Preliminary Ruling*, 107.

[58] On this matter, *see* F. Nicola, *Luxemburg judicial style with or without the UK* (2017) 41 *Fordham International Law* 1506.

[59] *Contra* G. Martinico, *Le sentenze interpretative*, 265.

[60] E. D'Alessandro, *Il procedimento pregiudiziale*, 249–250.

[61] In the same vein, in Italy, *see* M. Condinanzi, R. Mastroianni, *Il contenzioso dell'Unione europea*, Turin, Giappichelli, 2009, 231–237.

[62] J. Boulouis, *A propos de la fonction normative de la jurisprudence. Remarques sur l'oeuvre jurisprudentielle de la Cour de justice des Communautés européennes* (1999) 1 *Recueil d'Etudes, Droit communautaire et droit français* 99–111, 107.

[63] *See* F.-C. Jeantet, *Originalité d'interprétation du traité de Rome* (1966) 1 *La Semaine juridique* I-1987; A. Pepy, *Le rôle de la Cour de justice des Communautés européennes dans l'application de l'article 177 du Traité de Rome* (1966) 2 *Cahiers de droit européen* 459, 484–487; G. Vandersanden, *De l'autorité de chose jugeé des arrêts préjudiciels d'interprétation rendus par la Cour de Justice des Communautés européennes* (1972) 25 *Revue critique de jurisprudence belge* 508; K. Lenaerts, K. Gutman, J. T. Nowak, *EU Procedural Law*, 266. *See* extensively A. Turmo, *L'autorité de la chose jugée en droit de l'Union européenne*, Brussels, Bruylant, 2017.

[64] M. Condinanzi, R. Mastroianni, *Il contenzioso*, 232.

[65] *See* A. Trabucchi, *L'effet* erga omnes *des décision préjudicielles rendues par la Cour de justice des Communautés européennes* (1974) 10 *Revue trimestrielle de droit européen* 56.

[66] D. Simon, *Le système juridique communautaire*, Paris, Puf, 1997, 234, considered such rulings an autonomous source of law.

[67] *Contra* L. Plouvier, *Le dècisions de la Cour de Justice des Communautés Européennes et leur effects Juridiques*, Brussels, Bruylant, 1975, 240.

would make little sense[68] since the CJ, in interpreting EU law, often develops doctrines and principles which are at the core of (and enhance) the EU legal order beyond the judgment. Amongst many others, an example is the recognition by the Court of directives' direct effect in its jurisprudence—from *van Duyn*[69] onwards—rendered pursuant to Article 267 TFEU.

The attribution of *erga omnes de jure* effects is also essential because it prevents the occurrence of discrimination among individuals that may result from the divergences in the compliance (or lack thereof) by the courts of the Member States with the preliminary rulings rendered by the CJ. Were the effects not *erga omnes*, the principle of sincere cooperation, as set forth in Article 4(3) TEU, requiring national courts to abstain from infringements of EU law, would be called into question. Lastly, from a joint reading of Article 267 TFEU together with Article 19 TEU one can see that the CJ's role as the final arbiter of EU law would risk being plunged into crisis if the decisions it renders were not binding *de jure ultra partes*.[70] Arguing otherwise would jeopardize the 'jurisdictional autonomy' enjoyed by the CJ within the composite judicial structure of the Union enshrined in Article 19 TEU, whereby, by that expression, reference is made to the Court's 'exclusive jurisdiction over the definitive interpretation of EU law'.[71] Should the ruling be binding *de jure* for the referring court only, the very sense of '*definitive* interpretation', to which the Court attached significant consequences in its opinion 2/13,[72] would be questionable, and the Court's function in the preliminary ruling mechanism would amount, in practice, to acting as a sort of legal advisor with the task of assisting national jurisdictions for settling the dispute in the main proceedings.

3. The CJ's *de facto* legality review of national laws

The discussion outlined in the previous section regards the nature and effects of preliminary rulings. Another closely connected issue concerns the scope of control over domestic internal legal orders exercised by the CJ through Article 267 TFEU. In this regard, it should be recalled that the EU judges adopt general interpretations of EU law.[73] As a matter of fact, private enforcement of EU law does not mean that the Court, on the basis of Article 267 TFEU, formally holds the power to assess whether a specific *national* law is valid or not in the light of EU law. Quite to the contrary, its jurisdiction is limited to the interpretation, at least formally, of EU primary and (also the validity of) secondary law. In the context of preliminary ruling procedures, the CJ cannot declare the annulment of any domestic provision. Under EU law, the only exception is foreseen for the governance of the European System of Central Banks, a rather specific area regulated by the Statute of the European System of Central Banks under its Article 14(2), whereunder the CJ once annulled the decision of the Central Bank of Latvia to temporarily suspend its Governor, Mr. Rimšēvičs.[74] Aside from this, the invalidation of

[68] In the same vein M. Broberg, N. Fenger, *Preliminary References*, 408–409.

[69] CJ, *Yvonne van Duyn*, 41/74, EU:C:1974:133.

[70] M. Broberg, N. Fenger, *Preliminary References*, 408, explicitly affirmed that the individual is entitled to bring an action before a domestic judge and seek compensation for the damages suffered from the decision taken by a national court not to comply with the legal principle and the interpretation of EU law rendered by the CJ pursuant to Article 267 TFEU; accordingly, *see* F. G. Jacobs, *The role of the ECJ in the Development of Uniform Law*, in N. Jareborg (ed.), *Towards Universal Law—Trends in National, European and International Lawmaking*, Iustus Forlag, 1995, 193–210, 207.

[71] C. Vajda, *Achmea and the Autonomy of the EU Legal Order*, in *LAwTTIP Working Papers No 1/2019*, 2019, 10.

[72] *Opinion 2/13* (n 4), paras 236–248.

[73] *See* also G. Vandersanden, *De l'autorité*, 519.

[74] CJ, *Rimšēvičs*, joined cases C-202 and 238/18, EU:C:2019:139; *see* §§ 3.3 of Chapter III and 3 of Chapter V.

internal legislation is a task for domestic courts only. Typically, preliminary rulings should not address the merits of the case, from the standpoint of national law, nor should they set the application of EU law to specific facts. In addition, from the *Cilfit* decision onwards, it has been clearly stated that the preliminary ruling procedure 'does not constitute a means of redress available to the parties to a case pending before a national court'.[75] This implies that direct effect of EU law cannot lead the CJ, in principle, through the national court and thus Article 267 TFEU, to interpret the legal order of a Member State, verify its lawfulness under EU law, and decide whether the EU provision 'is applicable in the case brought before it'.[76]

A different conception of Article 267 TFEU from the one described above was submitted by a committee of experts—all jurists, inspired by an unequivocal 'integrationist' vision of the preliminary ruling procedure, including Catalano, Gaudet, and Pescatore—appointed in the early 1950s by the (then) Member States in order to draft the text of relevant articles to be included in the EEC Treaty.[77] Such solution, however, was never upheld by the national governments. Consequently, the Court has made it clear, on a number of occasions, that:

> It is not for the Court . . . to determine whether national provisions are compatible with Community law. However, the Court may provide the national court with all the criteria for the interpretation of Community law which may enable it to assess whether those provisions are so compatible in order to give judgment in the proceedings before it.[78]

In fact, the CJ avoids making direct reference to the compatibility of the national law with EU law in both the substantive and operative parts of the ruling.[79] By way of example, among the many, in the *Argenta Spaarbank NV v Belgium* judgment the Court held that Article 49 TFEU 'must be interpreted as precluding national legislation in force of which, for purposes of the calculation of a deduction granted to a company subject to full tax liability in a Member State, the net value of the assets of a permanent establishment situated in another Member State which is not taken into account'.[80] On the other hand, in several decisions[81] the Court affirmed that a certain EU provision must be interpreted as precluding (or not precluding) a Member State's legislation, 'such as that in the main proceedings',[82] or that a given national behaviour/provision 'is incompatible'[83] with EU law. These are cases where the Court seems to decide, not so implicitly, on the compatibility of the specific national law

[75] CJ, *CILFIT*, 283/81, EU:C:1982:335, para. 9; *see* also CJ, *International Air Transport Association and European Low Fares Airline Association*, C-344/04, EU:C:2006:10, para. 28.

[76] As recalled in CJ, *Procureur de la Republique v Gérard Tissier*, 35/85, EU:C:1986:143, para. 9; CJ, *Angelo Bagli Pennacchiotti*, C-315/88, EU:C:1990:139, para. 10; CJ, *Società cooperativa Madonna dei miracoli*, C-81/13, EU:C:2013:655, para. 15; CJ, *'CHEZ Elektro Bulgaria' AD v Yordan Kotsev and 'FrontEx International' EAD*, joined cases C-427-428/16, EU:C:2017:890, para. 30.

[77] On this Committee, *see* M. Rasmussen, *Revolutionizing European law: A History of the* Van Gend en Loos *Judgment* (2014) 12 *International Journal of Constitutional Law* 136, 144.

[78] *See*, amongst others, CJ, *Fendt Italiana*, joined cases C-145-146/06, EU:C:2007:411, para. 30.

[79] On the limit of the CJ's jurisdiction to rule on such compatibility *see* K. Lenaerts, K. Gutman, J. T. Nowak, *EU Procedural Law*, 253–254.

[80] CJ, *Argenta Spaarbank NV*, C-350/11, EU:C:2013:447, para. 59.

[81] On this aspect *see* F. Nicola, C. Fasone, D. Gallo, *Comparing the Effects of US Unconstitutionality and EU's Preliminary Interpretative Rulings: Disapplication, Resistance and Coordination Procedures*, in D. Gallo, L. Cecchetti (eds.), *The Preliminary Ruling*, 147, 154 and 166. In truth, the approach recalled in the text above does not seem as 'exceptional' as it is affirmed in K. Lenaerts, K. Gutman, J. T. Nowak, *EU Procedural Law*, footnote 116, 254.

[82] *See*, *inter alia*, CJ, *OTO*, C-130/92, EU:C:1994:288, para. 21; CJ, *Anton Las*, C-202/11, EU:C:2013:239, para. 34.

[83] *See*, for instance, CJ, *Allianz*, C-185/07, EU:C:2009:69, para. 34.

at stake with EU law,[84] ruling *de facto* on its validity. Therefore, even when the EU judges expressly recall, with a 'modest' amount of self-restraint, what the limits to their jurisdiction are or demand the task of verifying the proportionality of a measure with EU law to the national courts, the focus is always (or almost always) on, essentially, the compliance of a national provision with EU law.[85]

The fact that the CJ takes account, in depth, of the national law when giving a preliminary ruling does not come as a surprise. Indeed, pursuant to Article 94 of the Court's Rules of Procedure, the preliminary reference must contain a detailed and self-standing description of the national rules at stake.[86] As a matter of fact, there are cases, rare but striking, where, as rightly pointed out by Broberg and Fenger, the Court has '*de facto* set aside the interpretation that a national court has given of rules from its own legal system'[87] on the basis, in essence, of the observations submitted by the Commission, the Member States' governments, and the parties in the main proceedings, like in *Roquette Frères*[88] and *Lenz*.[89] Additionally, as has been very clearly argued, 'although the ECJ does not have the power to rule on the validity of national measures or apply the law on particular facts, preliminary references serve in fact as the principal way of constitutional review of State action ... ECJ rulings on interpretation thus become a proxy for constitutional review'.[90] Hence, a *sui generis* European centralized review of national law, a detour of the role conferred by the European treaties to the CJ,[91] and the blurring of the distinction between 'interpretation' and 'application' of EU law.[92] This is true to the extent that AG Warner, in his opinion in the *Foglia I* case, surprisingly and openly affirmed that the Court can be entrusted with 'the question of the compatibility with Community law' of a rule or administrative practice by means of two types of proceedings: the first set forth in then Article 169 of the EEC Treaty, currently Article 258 TFEU, to be initiated by the Commission, and the second brought 'by a reference under Article 177 [currently Article 267 TFEU] made by a court or tribunal of that State in proceedings in which the appropriate authority of that State is a party'.[93]

[84] On this issue, *see* the reflections by F. C. Mayer, Van Gend en Loos, 23. *See* also M. Broberg, *Preliminary References as a Means for Enforcing EU Law*, in A. Jakab, D. Kochenov (eds.), *The Enforcement of EU Law and Values: Ensuring Member States' Compliance*, Oxford, Oxford University Press, 2017, 99–111, where he highlighted that in some judgments the CJ rephrases the question so that it reads whether EU law 'precludes' a national law such as that of the Member State. Should the rephrased question be answered in the affirmative, 'the Member State is obliged to amend its national law so [that] in practice there is no real difference between the original question and the rephrased one' (99). *See*, amongst others, CJ, *Wienand Meilicke, Heidi Christa Weyde and Marina Stöffler*, C-292/04, EU:C:2007:132.

[85] *See* the account by B. de Witte, *The Impact*, 97–101.

[86] M. Broberg, N. Fenger, *Preliminary References*, 283–290.

[87] M. Broberg, N. Fenger, *Preliminary References*, 334–338.

[88] CJ, *Roquette Frères SA*, C-88/99, EU:C:2000:652, paras 16–19, where the Court held that the question raised must be rephrased since, although 'the national court based itself on the premiss that the national provision at issue in the main proceedings draws a distinction between actions arising from a finding by a national court that a provision of domestic law is unlawful in the light of a superior rule of national law and those arising from a finding by the Community judicature that a provision of domestic law is unlawful in the light of Community law', 'the wording of the second and third paragraphs of Article L190 of the Livre des Procédures Fiscales draws no such distinction' (paras 16–17).

[89] CJ, *Anneliese Lenz*, C-315/02, EU:C:2004:446, paras 51–55, where the Court concluded that there was no need to reply to the preliminary question since 'the tax legislation in force at the date of the facts in the main proceedings did not allow the identification of a deduction such as that indicated by the referring court, even on a broad interpretation of the law' (para. 53).

[90] T. Tridimas, *Constitutional Review of Member State Action: The Virtues and Vices of an Incomplete Jurisdiction* (2011) 9 *International Journal of Constitutional Law* 737, 738.

[91] L.-J. Constantinesco, *L'applicabilité directe dans le droit de la CEE*, Brussels, Bruylant, 2006, 41, speaks of '*déviation fonctionnelle*'.

[92] M. Broberg, N. Fenger, *Preliminary References*, 138–139.

[93] Opinion of AG Warner of 23 January 1980, *Foglia I*, 104/79, EU:C:1980:22, para. 766.

In this context, as stressed by AG Jacobs, the 'detailed answers to very specific [fact and national law-oriented] questions will not always promote [the] uniform application [but] may merely provoke further questions'.[94] In his opinion delivered in *Consorzio Italian Management*, AG Bobek advocated in favour of a paradigm shift with regard to the duty to refer under Article 267(3) TFEU. The duty, therefore, should be restricted to situations where there is an 'objective divergence detected in the case law at the national level thereby threating the uniform interpretation of EU law within the European Union'.[95] For the purpose of this analysis, it is worth mentioning that the first condition to be met (that is, to be under a duty to refer) has been identified by the AG in the fact, for last instance national courts, of being confronted with a 'general or generalizable issue of interpretation of EU law', thereby bringing back this cooperation mechanism to what it 'has always been about' in sharp contrast with the above-mentioned common practice.[96] Such a proposal has not been endorsed by the CJ.

Overall, what seems to define the role of the CJ, as illustrated by its case law, is a recurrent ambivalence, inherent not 'simply' in the atypical design set forth in Article 267 TFEU, but also and above all in the very nature of the European legal order. On the one hand, the order of reference must always bear relation to the 'actual nature of the case or to the subject-matter of the main action'[97] and contain elements demonstrating a connection between the dispute and EU law.[98] Moreover, it cannot rest on general or hypothetical questions[99] or aim at seeking a ruling on the interpretation of points of law related to the domestic legal system.[100] The judgment of the CJ must thus be connected to an existing concrete dispute at the national level. On the other hand, the CJ does not, formally and institutionally, have the power to verify the lawfulness of national law in the light of EU law. An assessment, however, that is carried out, in practice, by the Court in many of its rulings.

In the light of the above, the *erga omnes* effects of preliminary rulings, associated with the *nomophiliac* role performed by the CJ, as the body responsible for conducting *de facto*, together with domestic courts, a centralized syndicate of legality of national law, strengthens the *effet utile* of direct effect. Indeed, the recognition of direct effect by the CJ through its preliminary rulings endowed with *erga omnes* effect, *in primis Van Gend & Loos*, enormously increased the enforceability of EU directly effective provisions and their uniform application across domestic legal orders. Direct effect, therefore, by its nature, is intertwined with preliminary rulings inasmuch as one reinforces the value of the other within the European legal system.

In this context, it is undeniable that the 'expansionism' of the preliminary ruling procedure has, over time, resulted in a gradual process of constitutionalization of the CJ.[101]

[94] Opinion of AG Jacobs of 10 July 1997, *Wiener S.I. GmbH v Hauptzollamt Emmerich*, C-338/95, EU:C:1997:352, para. 50.

[95] Opinion of AG Bobek of 15 April 2021, *Consorzio Italian Management*, C-561/19, EU:C:2021:291, paras 131 and 133. On such opinion, as well as on the Court's ruling, *see* M. Broberg, N. Fenger, *If You Love Somebody Set Them Free: On the Court Of Justice's Revision of The Acte Clair Doctrine* (2022) 59 *Common Market Law Review* 711; L. Cecchetti, D. Gallo, *The Unwritten Exceptions to the Duty to Refer after Consorzio Italian Management II: 'CILFIT Strategy' 2.0 and its Loopholes* (2022) 15 *Review of European Administrative Law* 29; F.-X. Millet, Cilfit *Still Fits* (2022) 18 *European Constitutional Law Review* 533; F.-X. Millet, *How to Enforce 'Mild' Obligations under EU law? Proceduralising the Weak Duty to Refer as a Strong Duty to State Reasons*, in D. Gallo, L. Cecchetti (eds.), *The Preliminary Ruling*, 7.

[96] Opinion of AG Bobek, *Consorzio Italian Management* (n 95), para. 139.

[97] CJ, *Salonia*, 126/80, EU:C:1981:136, para. 6.

[98] CJ, *Ullens de Schooten*, C-268/15, EU:C:2016:874, paras 55–56.

[99] CJ, *Kamberaj*, C-571/10, EU:C:2012:233, paras 44–46.

[100] CJ, *NI*, C-799/19, EU:C:2020:960, para. 45.

[101] On such process, from the standpoint of direct effect, *see* Chapter I, §§ 2.5 and 3.

However, the Court could have acquired even greater centrality, not only with respect to its role within EU law but also in its relationships with European citizens, in the case where the preliminary ruling procedure had been conceived in more federalist terms,[102] that is to say, had the CJ been institutionally, explicitly, and formally granted the power to lawfully decide upon the validity of a national law, as had been suggested by top European officials and authoritative scholars.[103] In this respect, there is no doubt that the EU legal framework governing the CJ features several characteristics which differ very much from the way the Supreme Court of the United States operates, with its powers of constitutional review and its competence to disregard federal law conflicting with the Constitution since the *Marbury v Madison* judgment.[104] Indeed, the US Constitution, in the Supremacy Clause, established the power of federal law over conflicting State laws, and this power translates judicially to the Supreme Court's ability to invalidate State laws in conflict with the Constitution, as well as with international treaties and federal laws.[105] Generally speaking, the US Supreme Court rules on the constitutionality of the provision(s) at hand as a matter of law and then remands the law back to a State court to determine the correct rewrite or excision of unconstitutional sections. This competence has allowed the citizens of the US to understand the constitutional importance of the Supreme Court and the magnitude of the impact of its jurisprudence on the protection of individual rights.[106] In that regard, notwithstanding what has been said in section 2.5 of Chapter I on the revolutionary twist represented by *Van Gend & Loos*, this awareness does not have the same breadth in Europe with respect to the CJ,[107] in some cases not even among judges and legal practitioners.

[102] On this point, *see* extensively P. Allott, *Preliminary Rulings—Another Infant Disease* (2000) 5 *European Law Review* 538, 542; J. Komárek, *In the Courts We Trust? On the Need for Hierarchy and Differentiation in the Preliminary Ruling Procedure* (2007) 32 *European Law Review* 467, 471; T. de la Mare, C. Donnelly, *Preliminary Rulings and EU Legal Integration: Evolution and Stasis*, in P. Craig, G. de Búrca (eds.), *The Evolution of EU Law*, 3rd ed., Oxford, Oxford University Press, 2021, 228–274 and 255–256.

[103] On this matter, *see* § 2 of this chapter. In the literature, *see* A. Bleckmann, *L'applicabilité directe du droit communautaire*, in Waelbroeck M., Velu J. (eds.), *Les recours des individus devant les instances nationales en cas de violation du droit européen*, Brussels, Larcier, 1978, 85–130, 141.

[104] As already mentioned in Chapter I, § 2.5. For comparative studies on the EU and the US from a juridical perspective, *see* J. C. Cohen, *The European Preliminary Reference and U.S. Supreme Court Review of State Court Judgments: A Study in Comparative Judicial Federalism* (1996) 44 *American Journal of Comparative Law* 421; L. F. Goldstein, *Constituting Federal Sovereignty: The European Union in Comparative Context*, Baltimore, The Johns Hopkins University Press, 2001, 16; M. Rosenfeld, *Comparing Constitutional Review by the European Court of Justice and the U.S. Supreme Court* (2006) 4 *International Journal of Constitutional Law* 618; K. Lenaerts, *Interpretation and the Court of Justice: A Basis for Comparative Reflection* (2007) 41 *International Lawyer* 1011; M. L. Wells, *European Union Law in the Member State Courts: A Comparative View*, University of Georgia School of Law Research Paper Series, Paper No. 2021-11, 2021, available at https://papers.ssrn.com/sol3/papers.cfm?abstract_id=3911155. On divergences but also assonances between the CJ's power to issue preliminary rulings and the Supreme Court's power, *see* F. Nicola, C. Fasone, D. Gallo, *Comparing*.

[105] Article VI, clause 2: 'This Constitution, and the Laws of the United States which shall be made in Pursuance thereof; and all Treaties made, or which shall be made, under the Authority of the United States, shall be the supreme Law of the Land; and the Judges in every State shall be bound thereby, any Thing in the Constitution or Laws of any State to the Contrary notwithstanding.' On the importance of *Fletcher v Peck*, 10 U.S. 87, 3 L. Ed. 162 (1810) and *Martin v Hunter's Lessee*, 14 U.S. 304 (1816) for the achievement of the judicial power described above, *see* F. Nicola, C. Fasone, D. Gallo, *Comparing*, 153–154 and 173–174.

[106] *See* the analysis by C. Barnard, Van Gend en Loos *to(t) the Future*, in A. Tizzano, J. Kokott, S. Prechal (Organizing Committee), *50ème anniversaire*, 117–122, 118.

[107] This lack of awareness exacerbates the problems connected to the so-called democratic deficit and the broadening of the CJEU's competences in areas which for decades have been excluded from the scope of EU law. On this issue, *see* F. Mancini, *Democracy and Constitutionalism in the EU*, Oxford, Oxford University Press, 2000, 31–51 and C. Tomuschat, *Introduction*, in A. Tizzano, J. Kokott, S. Prechal (Organizing Committee), *50ème anniversaire*, 49–54, 54.

4. The direct effect/preliminary reference procedure duo as a motor of integration and the presumption of direct effect

AG Roemer, in his opinion in the *Van Gend & Loos* case, remarked that the question before the Dutch court, regarding the direct effect of Article 12 of the EEC Treaty, was an issue of constitutional law and, consequently, could not be tackled by the CJ. In fact, he first recalled that the relationships between international law and national legislation are shaped differently from one Member State to another and then emphasized that the recognition of internal effect of Article 12 would result in 'breaches [that] would render the national customs laws ineffective and inapplicable in only a certain number of Member States'. This would be the case in the Netherlands, Luxembourg, and—the AG noted—'it may be, in France'.[108] The AG's reasoning focused on the fact that only in monistic systems could European rules penetrate and prevail over national legislation or, as affirmed in his opinion, enjoy 'a superior status to that of national law'.[109] This conclusion depends on two factors: (*i*) the Court would not have jurisdiction to make decisions regarding the nature, more or less directly effective, of Community law; (*ii*) direct effect, if asserted by the CJ regardless of the type of national constitutional legal system, would necessarily presuppose the primacy of the Treaty over the national legal orders.

As highlighted in Chapter I,[110] the CJ, in *Van Gend & Loos*, affirmed that it was within its competence, and not the competence of the national courts, to verify the internal effect of the EEC provisions. This held true despite the Dutch legal order[111] recognizing the superiority of self-executing provisions contained in international treaties over national law, including successive norms,[112] as demonstrated by Article 66, currently Article 94, of the Constitution, which lies at the heart of the referral made by the *Tariefcommissie* of Amsterdam. In short, *Van Gend & Loos* is revolutionary because it is one thing to recognize that international norms are apt to produce direct effects, as was already the case in some legal orders at the time (notwithstanding the reluctance of national authorities to 'exploit' this avenue, particularly in judicial proceedings).[113] It is another to admit, as the CJ did, *(i)* that it is the supranational/international norm which directly confers rights to individuals, *(ii)* that an authority other than the national judge is the only one entrusted with making such recognition, and *(iii)* that the external rule should take precedence over the internal legal system. To this end, the CJ, on the one hand, imposed a European monistic view of the relations between external (European) sources and domestic law,[114] while on the other, asserted the immediate application of Community law in the Member States' legal orders regardless of whether they are monistic or dualistic.

After all, if the question concerning the internal effect of Article 12 TEEC had come from a judge of a dualistic State, like Italy or Germany or Belgium and not from a 'monistic'

[108] CJ, *NV Algemene Transport-en Expeditie Onderneming van Gend & Loos*, 26/62, EU:C:1963:1, 23.
[109] *Van Gend & Loos* (n 108), 23.
[110] *See* Chapter I, § 2.5.
[111] On the active role exercised by Dutch lawyers and judges, also through preliminary references aimed at obtaining clarification from the Court on the question of direct effect, *see* A. Vauchez, *The Transnational Politics of Judicialization.* Van Gend en Loos *and the Making of EU Polity* (2010) 16 *European Law Journal* 1, 10; M. Rasmussen, *Revolutionizing*, 147.
[112] On the impact of *Van Gend & Loos* on the Dutch legal system as well as on the techniques of 'denial of direct effect' employed by Dutch courts, *see* M. Claes, *The impact*, 105.
[113] On such reluctance, *see* M. Claes, *The Impact*, 105 and 107–108 and J. H. H. Weiler, *Revisiting* Van Gend en Loos, 13–15.
[114] On international law's direct effect within the EU legal system, from the perspective of monism, *see* § 1 of Chapter VII.

country like the Netherlands, the CJ would have been obliged to reflect, explicitly and from the outset, on primacy.[115] In this sense, one can only share Pescatore's opinion, according to which *Van Gend & Loos* represents the founding act of Community monism.[116] In this sense, his words are enlightening insofar as he affirmed that the European legal order and national legal systems are the two pillars of a '*système juridique global*', to the extent that primacy and direct effect draw their strength from the '*droit tout court*'.[117] A monism-based system of integration, moreover, whose core lies in direct effect, primacy, and the qualification of national courts as '*juge de droit commun de l'ordre communautaire*'.[118]

In the aftermath of *Van Gend & Loos*, the Court made more explicit the need to consider direct effect and primacy in complementary terms, for example where it observed in *Simmenthal*[119] that Community law, unlike classic international law, 'is not just foreign law',[120] as it is an 'integral part of, and take[s] precedence in, the legal order applicable in the territory of each of the Member States'.[121] *Simmenthal*, which represents the peak of the early jurisprudence on the joined application of the principles of direct effect and primacy,[122] implies an '*intégration immédiate*',[123] to the extent that the Community rules penetrate the internal legal orders, without any domestic act of transposition. F. Dumon spoke distinctly of the integration of Community law into national legal systems, where, as President of the FIDE (*Fédération Internationale pour le Droit Européen*) Congress tasked with providing

[115] As happened in *Costa* in respect to Italy. On such matter, *see* J. Ziller, *Les réactions des milieux institutionnels, nationaux et scientifiques de l'époque*, in A. Tizzano, J. Kokott, S. Prechal (Organizing Committee), *50ème anniversaire*, 37–48, 48.

[116] P. Pescatore, *Monisme, dualisme et 'effet utile' dans la jurisprudence de la Cour de Justice de la Communauté Européenne*, in N. Colneric N., D. Edward, J-P. Puissochet, D. R. Colomer (eds.), *Une communauté de droit—Festschriftfür G.C. Rodríguez Iglesias*, Berlin, Berliner Wissenschafts-Verlag, 2003, 329–359, 331, wrote that *Van Gend & Loos* is the '*acte judiciaire fondateur du monisme communautaire*'; *contra* A. Arnull, *The European Union*, 168.

[117] P. Pescatore, *Discussion*, in M. Waelbroeck, J. Velu (eds.), *Les recours*, 185.

[118] CJ, *Pigs Marketing Board*, 83/78, EU:C:1978:214, para. 25. The expression 'national courts as "ordinary" courts within the European Union legal order' has been used for the first time by the CJ in CJ, *Opinion on the creation of a unified patent litigation system*, 1/09, EU:C:2011:123, para. 80, on which, *see* R. Baratta, *National Courts as 'Guardians' and 'Ordinary Courts' of EU Law: Opinion 1/09 of the ECJ* (2011) 38 *Legal Issues of Economic Integration* 297. Before this opinion, on the constitutional implications of the role exercised by domestic courts as European courts, *see* I. Maher, *National Courts as European Community Courts* (1994) 14 *Legal Studies* 226; M. Bobek, *The Impact of the European Mandate of Ordinary Courts on the Position of Constitutional Courts*, in M. Claes, M. de Visser, P. Popelier, C. Van de Heyning (eds.), *Constitutional Conversations in Europe: Actors, Topics and Procedures*, Cambridge-Oxford, Interesentia-Hart, 2012, 287–308. In the recent case law, *see Consorzio Italian Management* (n 29), para. 29. In the literature, *see*, amongst monographs/edited volumes, A. Barav, *La fonction communautaire du juge national*, Strasbourg, Université R. Schuman, 1983; M. Claes, *The National Courts' Mandate in the European Constitution*, Oxford, Hart, 2006; J. Temple Lang, *The Development by the Court of Justice of the Duties of Cooperation of National Authorities and Community Institutions Under Article 10 EC* (2007) 31 *Fordham International Law Journal* 1483; A. Rosas, *The National Judge as EU Judge*, in P. Cardonnel, A. Rosas, N. Wahl (eds.), *Constitutionalising the EU Judicial System-Essays in Honour of Pernilla Lindh*, Oxford, Oxford University Press, 2012, 105–121; N. Fennelly, *The National Judge as Judge of the European Union*, in A. Rosas, E. Levits, Y. Bot (eds.), *The Court of Justice and the Construction of Europe: Analyses and Perspectives on Sixty Years of Case-law*, Berlin, Springer, 2013, 61–80; G. Di Federico, *Il giudice italiano come giudice europeo*, in G. Di Federico (ed.), *Ordinamento giudiziario. Uffici giudiziari, CSM e governo della magistratura*, Bologna, Bononia University Press, 2019, 237–265. Conversely, on the relevance of national law for the construction and formation of EU law, *see* M. Prek, S. Lefèvre, *The EU Courts as 'National Courts': National Law in the EU Judicial Process* (2017) 54 *Common Market Law Review* 369; A. Rosas, *International Law*, 261–282; A. Rosas, *EU Law and National Law: A Common Legal System*, AEL working paper, 2024, available at https://cadmus.eui.eu/handle/1814/76744.

[119] *See* also Chapter I, § 2.4.

[120] M. Claes, *The National Courts' Mandate*, 60.

[121] CJ, *Amministrazione delle Finanze dello Stato v Simmenthal SpA*, 106/77, EU:C:1978:49, 17.

[122] On the conceptual ties between *Simmenthal* and the subsequent recent case law on disapplication as a result of primacy and direct effect, *see* § 1 of Chapter V.

[123] M. Blanquet, G. Isaac, *Droit général de l'Union européenne*, Paris, Dalloz, 2012, 371.

a definition of '*norme directement applicable*',[124] placed emphasis, in the Congress' final report, on the ability of directly effective rules to generate effects '*dans les relations juridiques*' between States and individuals.[125] In other words, the *raison d'être* of Community law[126] lies in the integration, or rather, in the creation of effects in the internal legal orders, of an '*ordre juridique commun*'.[127] The departure from international law lies in the overturning[128] of traditional dualism,[129] which has guided and still steers the jurisprudence of international courts. This is true first of all for the Permanent Court of International Justice (PCIJ), which, in its (already mentioned) opinion in the *Jurisdiction of the Courts of Danzig* case, while acknowledging that rules contained in international treaties can confer individual rights and obligations 'according to the intention of the contracting Parties',[130] ruled out that such conferral derives directly from the former—as occurs in Community law in relation to the European Treaties—arising instead from the internal rules adopted by the Parties to the Treaty.[131] This is the first crucial difference between direct effect of EU law and the

[124] F. Dumon, *La notion de 'disposition directement applicable' en droit européen* (1968) 4 *Cahiers de droit européen* 369, 381.

[125] F. Dumon, *La notion*, 381.

[126] On this point, *see* P. Pescatore, *Le droit de l'intégration*, Brussels, Bruylant, 2005. For further insights, *see* A. Tizzano, *Dall'unità nazionale all'integrazione sopranazionale* (2012) 3 *Il Diritto dell'Unione europea* 621.

[127] F. Dumon, *La notion*, 393. E. Stein, *Lawyers*, 1, observed that the CJ 'has fashioned a constitutional framework for a federal-type structure in Europe', has framed the Community 'in a constitutional mode rather than employing the traditional international methodology', and, of consequence, has entailed the 'direct integration of Community law' in the Member States' legal orders.

[128] U. Villani, *Una rilettura della sentenza* Van Gend en Loos *dopo cinquant'anni* (2013) 2 *Studi sull'integrazione europea* 225, 230.

[129] In the words of G. de Búrca, *The European Court of Justice and the International Legal Order after* Kadi (2009) 51 *Harvard International Law Journal* 1, 1, footnote 2: 'in more technical legal parlance, however, the term dualist is generally used to refer to a legal system in which international law requires transposition before it becomes part of that domestic legal order.' Amongst early seminal writings on dualism in international law, *see*, *ex multis*, H. Triepel, *Völkerrecht und Landesrecht*, Leipzig, C. L. Hirschfeld, 1899; D. Anzilotti, *Il diritto internazionale nei diritti interni*, Naples, ESI, 1905. On monism, *see* H. Kelsen, *Les rapports de système entre le droit interne et le droit international public*, in *Recueil des Cours*, vol. 14, 1926, 226–331; A. Verdross, *Die Verfassung der Völkerrechtsgemeinschaft*, Berlin, Springer, 1926. For more recent contributions, *see* G. Arangio-Ruiz, *Dualism Revisited: International Law and Interindividual Law* (2003) 86 *Rivista di Diritto Internazionale* 909; C. Amrhein Hofmann, *Monismus und Dualismus in den Volkerrechtslehren*, Berlin, Duncker & Humblot Gmbh, 2003; H. Keller, *Rezeption des Völkerrechts*, Berlin, Springer, 2003; J. Nijman, A. Nollkaemper (eds.), *New Perspectives on the Divide between International and National Law*, Oxford, Oxford University Press, 2007; M. Mendez, *The Legal Effects of EU Agreements*, Oxford, Oxford University Press, 2013, 37–47; P. Gragl, *Legal Monism: Law, Philosophy, and Politics*, Oxford, Oxford University Press, 2018. For a critique on monism, as a 'moribund notion' that 'should be put to rest', and dualism, 'that should be overcome and developed into a theory of legal pluralism', *see* A. von Bogdandy, *Pluralism, Direct Effect, and the Ultimate Say: On the Relationship between International and Domestic Constitutional Law* (2008) 6 *International Journal of Constitutional Law* 397, 398. In the same vein, *see* C. Tomuschat, *International Law Ensuring the Survival of Mankind on the Eve of a New Century: General Course on Public International Law*, in *Recueil des Cours*, vol. 281, 1999, 9–438, 363–364; B. Conforti, *International Law and the Role of Domestic Legal Systems*, The Hague, Martinus Nijhoff, 1993, 26–28; *contra*, *see* R. Higgins, *Problems & Process: International Law and How We Use It*, Oxford, Clarendon Press, 1995, 206–217; P. Koutrakos, *EU International Relations Law*, 2nd ed., Oxford, Hart, 2015, 257. For an historical contextualization of the two theories, *see* C. Focarelli, *Introduzione storica al diritto internazionale*, Milan, Giuffrè, 2021. On monism and dualism, from the perspective of the effects of international law in the EU legal order, including for further references, *see* § 1 of Chapter VII.

[130] PCIJ, *Jurisdiction of the Courts of Danzig (Pecuniary Claims of Danzig Railway Officials who have passed into the Polish Service, Against the Polish Railways Administration)*, Reports, Series B, No. 15, 3 March 1928, 3, 18. On the twist entailed by such recognition, *see* H. Lauterpacht, *The Development of International Law by the International Court*, London, Stevens, 1958, 173–175; *contra*, *see*, amongst others, D. Anzilotti, *Cours de droit international*, Paris, Sirey, 1929, 333–534, 407.

[131] On this point, *see* T. Buergenthal, *Self-Executing and Non-Self-Executing Treaties in National and International Law*, in *Recueil des Cours*, vol. 235, 1992, 303–400, 327 and, recently, M. Mendez, *The Legal Effects*, 11. In this regard, A. Nollkaemper, *The Direct Effect of Public International Law*, in J. M. Prinssen, A. Schrauwen (eds.), *Direct Effect*, 156–180, 168–169, noted that 'rule[s] of international law that are accepted as part of the national legal order remain fully subject to the secondary rules of international law, including interpretation, modification and termination'.

possible, yet rare, direct effect of international law in the frame of other international organizations: while within the EU, direct effect is a matter of EU law, direct effect of (public) international law in national legal orders is a matter of each Member State's constitutional law. As Trabucchi wrote in his 1963 article (published the same year as the release of *Van Gend & Loos*), it goes without saying that rights conferred by Community law 'have an autonomous source, outside the national legal systems' and that such source shall continue to be autonomous thanks to the removal of the interpretation of Community law from the national judicial authorities.[132] Moreover, it has been brilliantly held in the literature that 'what fundamentally changed the discourse was that a sizeable group of States accepted that the direct effect of future rules of unknown content and scope was no longer under their exclusive control, but was determined by EU law'.[133] Likewise, the acknowledgement of the peculiarity of Community law and of its autonomy from purely international legal constructs carried out by the CJ in *Van Gend & Loos*, *Costa*, and subsequent judgments, enables the Court to reassure the dualistic Member States that monism is innate to Community law and not to international law as a whole.

There is a second fundamental divergence[134] between European law and classic international law:[135] in the former direct effect[136] is the rule, while in the latter it is the exception.[137] In fact, one can infer from a reading of the advisory opinion of the PCIJ in the *Jurisdiction of the Courts of Danzig* case that under international law there is a presumption of a lack of direct effect. In that case, the PCIJ, while admitting *ab abstracto* that the Danzig-Polish Agreement of October 1921 could entail direct effects,[138] as has been already recalled, held that 'according to a well-established principle of international law, ... an international agreement, cannot, as such, create direct rights and obligations for private individuals'.[139] Conversely, as far as European law is concerned, 'because of the particular character of the Community Treaty, any presumption must be held to work in favour of,

[132] In Italian: '*trovano una fonte autonoma, al di fuori degli ordinamenti giuridici statali*'; *see* A. Trabucchi, *Un nuovo diritto*, 268.

[133] A. Nollkaemper, *The Duality of Direct Effect of International Law* (2014) 25 *European Journal of International Law* 105, 106.

[134] An additional divergence consists, as recalled in § 2.2 of Chapter I, in the objectivist interpretive method applied by the CJ, as opposed to the subjectivist approach taken by international courts, such as the PCIJ and the International Court of Justice (ICJ).

[135] *See* H. P. Ipsen, *Über Supranationalität*, in H. Ehmke, J. H. Kaiser, W. A. Kewenig, K. M. Meessen, W. Rüfner (eds.), *Festschrift für Ulrich Scheuner zum 70. Geburtstag*, Berlin, Duncker & Humblot, 1973, 211–225, 220.

[136] On the originality of European law compared to international law, from the perspective of their internal effect, *see* also § 1 of this chapter.

[137] For case reports and surveys drafted by a worldwide network of academics and practitioners who demonstrate that domestic courts, in some countries more than others, frequently rely on direct effect to enforce international law, *see* A. Nollkaemper, A. Reinisch, *Oxford Reports on International Law in Domestic Courts*, available at https://opil.ouplaw.com/page/212. For a (relatively recent) casebook, *see* A. Nollkaemper, A. Reinisch, R. Janik, F. Simlinger, *International Law in Domestic Courts. A Casebook*, Oxford, Oxford University Press, 2018. For a website collecting relevant case law, *see* the *American Journal of International Law* (*AJIL*)'s interest group called *International Law in Domestic Courts*, available at https://opil.ouplaw.com/display/10.1093/law/9780198739746.001.0001/law-9780198739746.

[138] Here is the apparent paradox: it is international law that, as admitted *ab abstracto* by the PCIJ, has generated a doctrine which, incorporated at the Community level by the CJ with the *Van Gend & Loos* decision, enabled the Court to distinguish European law from international law, making direct effect the key rule governing the relationship between EEC/EC/EU law and Member States' legal orders.

[139] *Jurisdiction of the Courts of Danzig* (n 130), 17. For a comparison between the opinion and *Van Gend & Loos*, *see* S. Prechal, *Does Direct Effect Still Matter?* (2000) 37 *Common Market Law Review* 1047, 1050; M. Mendez, *The Legal Effects*, 4–5 and 10–11. More in general, about the opinion, in the light of the peculiarities of European law, *see* M. Waelbroeck, *Traités internationaux et juridictions internes dans les pays du Marché commun*, Brussels, Bruylant, 1969, 165 and 185–186; A. Bleckmann, *Self-Executing Treaty Provisions*, in *Encyclopedia of Public International Law*, IV, 2000, 374.

rather than against, direct effect'.[140] A presumption, thus, inverted if compared with international law,[141] in respect to bilateral and multilateral treaties.[142] This means that '[i]n view of the maxim *in dubio, pro* direct effect national courts should be very cautious about denying the direct effect of a given provision of Community law and, in cases of real doubt, should refer the case to the ECJ'.[143] There are also those who write that EU provisions, unless proved otherwise, are to be considered directly effective, that is, invocable in judicial proceedings and able to entail disapplication, since otherwise natural and legal persons could not effectively safeguard their prerogatives. As noted by Pescatore, the operative nature of EU justiciable provisions could be assured only by considering direct effect as 'nothing but the ordinary state of the law'.[144] Just like States, and international organizations, as the only *full* subjects of law according to international law, are (their creators and for this reason) *normally* the only recipients of justiciable and enforceable treaty provisions,[145] European treaties can be invoked directly by individuals, the latter being subjects of law within the EU legal order, that is, recipients of (most of) its primary and secondary law provisions.

5. Iridescent chameleon-like direct effect

The judge-made origin of direct effect by virtue of the CJ's rulings delivered pursuant to Article 267 TFEU, while ensuring that such doctrine can evolve and equip individuals with the substantive and judicial means to adequately safeguard their prerogatives, means also that the CJ shall be as clear as possible in its conceptualization and characterization. Unfortunately, as will be demonstrated in the following chapters, the case law is not at all clear-cut.[146] There is uncertainty about the understanding, scope, and consequences of direct effect, and this is also the result of massive argumentative minimalism, contradictions, and more or less implicit *revirements* in the EU case law.[147]

[140] E. Stein, *Lawyers*, 9–10.

[141] On this matter, *see* also § 2.2 of Chapter I.

[142] In this vein, *see* B. de Witte, *The Continuous Significance*, 10 and, for a detailed analysis, F. Martines, *Direct Effect of International Agreements of the European Union* (2014) 25 *European Journal of International Law* 12. From this angle, on the differences between international law and EU law, *see* R. Luzzatto, *La diretta applicabilità del diritto comunitario*, Milan, Giuffrè, 1983, 23; P. Pescatore, *International Law*, 174–175; M. Wathelet, *Du concept de l'effet direct à celui de l'invocabilité au regard de la jurisprudence récente de la Cour de justice*, in M. Hoskins, W. Robinson (eds.), *A True European. Essays for Judge David Edward*, Oxford, Oxford University Press, 2004, 367–390, 368–369; J. Roux, *Droit*, 330. On such topic, *see* also § 4 of Chapter I.

[143] J. H. Jans., J. M. Prinssen, *Direct Effect*, 119.

[144] P. Pescatore, *The Doctrine of 'Direct Effect': An Infant Disease of Community Law* (1983) 8 *European Law Review* 155, 177.

[145] 'Full' and 'normally' are in italics since the matter of the international legal personality of individuals within international law is highly contentious; *see*, amongst recent studies, A. Kjeldgaard-Pedersen, *The International Legal Personality of the Individual*, Oxford, Oxford University Press, 2018; A. Peters, T. Sparks, *The Individual in International Law. History and Theory*, Oxford, Oxford University Press, 2024.

[146] M. Bobek, *The Effects*, 155, observed that direct effect is 'a purely judicial world of remedies that may suffer from lack of clarity, internal contradictions, and hidden reversals, which result in a perceived or real lack of predictability and foreseeability of the law'. J. Bengoetxea, *Is Direct Effect a General Principle of European Law?*, in U. Bernitz, J. Nergelius, C. Cardner (eds.), *General Principles of EC Law in a Process of Development*, The Hague, Wolters Kluwer, 2008, 3–24, 8, mentions the 'twists and turns taken by the theory or doctrine of direct effect'.

[147] On such uncertainties, as well as on the consequence of direct effect and the unclear scope of the remedy of disapplication, *see* Chapter III, §§ 3.3–5 and Chapters IV–V. For a brilliant analysis on judicial minimalism and the CJEU, *see* D. Sarmiento, *Half a Case at a Time: Dealing with Judicial Minimalism at the European Court of Justice*, in M. Claes, M. De Visser, P. Popelier, C. van de Heyning (eds.), *Constitutional Conversations*, 13–40.

In the literature, most of the authors who, directly or indirectly, have specifically dealt with the doctrine of direct effect tend to focus only on the positive implications of the relevant case law. However, there is a significant group of scholars[148] who ponder the different facets of direct effect and its most controversial features.[149] These authors, nonetheless, are divided on the scope of direct effect, its premises, and its consequences.[150] Thus, on one hand, what largely brings together academics is the description of direct effect as an indispensable tool of integration with a knock-on effect for completing and refining the process of European integration. A further common thread is the awareness about the twofold nature of direct effect, that is, ensuring the effective enforcement of EU law and safeguarding individuals'

[148] M. Bobek, *Van Gend en Loos +50: The Changing Social Context of Direct Effect*, in A. Tizzano, J. Kokott, S. Prechal (Organizing Committee), *50ème anniversaire*, 181–187, 182, pointed out that 'the principle of direct effect remains astonishingly unexplored, even today'.

[149] *See* F. Dumon, *La notion*; A. Bleckmann, *L'applicabilité directe*; G. Bebr, *Les dispositions de droit communautaire directement applicables: développement d'une notion communautaire* (1970) 1 *Cahiers de droit européen* 3; M. Waelbroeck, *L'immédiateté communautaire, caractéristique de la supranationalité: quelques consequences pour la pratique*, in C. Rousseau (ed.), *Le droit international demain*, Neuchâtel, Edition Ides et Calendes, 1974, 81–89; C. W. A. Timmermans, *Directives: their Effect within the National Legal Systems* (1979) 16 *Common Market Law Review* 533; R. Kovar, *L'intégrité de l'effet direct du droit communautaire selon la jurisprudence de la Cour de Justice de la Communauté*, in R. Bieber, D. Nickel (eds.), *Das Europa der Zweiten Generation: Gedächtnisschrift für Christoph Sasse*, Baden-Baden, Nomos, 1981, I, 151–163; R. Luzzatto, *La diretta applicabilità*; P. Pescatore, *The Doctrine*; G. Isaac, *L'effet direct du droit Communautaire, Répertoire européen Dalloz*, 1997, 1, 4; Y. Galmot, J.-C. Bonichot, *La Cour de Justice des Communautés européennes et la transposition des directives en droit national*, (1988) 1 *Revue française de droit administratif* 1; P. Eleftheriadis, *The Direct Effect of Community Law: Conceptual Issues* (1996) 16 *Yearbook of European Law* 205–221; *see* I. Sebba, *The Doctrine of Direct Effect: A Malignant Disease of Community Law* (1995) 22 *Legal Issues of Economic Integration* 35; M. Ruffert, *Rights and Remedies in European Community Law: A Comparative view* (1997) 34 *Common Market Law Review* 307; S. Prechal, *Does Direct*; D. Edward, *Direct Effect, the Separation of Powers and the Judicial Enforcement of Obligations*, in *Scritti in onore di Giuseppe Federico Mancini*, Milan, Giuffrè, 1998, 423–445; S. Amadeo, *Norme comunitarie, posizioni giuridiche soggettive e giudizi interni*, Milan, Giuffrè, 2002; D. Edward, *Judicial Activism—Myth or Reality?* Van Gend en Loos, Costa v ENEL *and the* Van Duyn *Family Revisited*, in A. I. K. Campbell, M. Voyatzi (eds.), *Essays in the Honour of Lord Mackenzie-Stuart*, Trenton, New Jersey, 1996, 29–67; D. Edward, *Direct Effect: Myth, Mess or Mystery?*, in J. M. Prinssen, A. Schrauwen (eds.), *Direct Effect*, 1–13; T. Eijsbouts, *Direct Effect, the Test and the Terms*, in J. M. Prinssen, A. Schrauwen (eds.), *Direct Effect*, 237–249; S. Prechal, *Direct Effect Reconsidered, Redefined and Rejected*, in J. M. Prinssen, A. Schrauwen (eds.), *Direct Effect*, 15–41; J. Bengoetxea, *Direct Applicability or Effect*, in M. Hoskins, W. Robinson (eds.), *A True European*, 353–366; T. Eilmansberger, *The Relationship between Rights and Remedies in EC Law: In Search of the Missing Link* (2004) 41 *Common Market Law Review* 1199; M. Wathelet, *Du concept de l'effet direct*; S. Prechal, *Directives in EC Law*, 2nd ed., Oxford, Oxford University Press, 2005, 97–106; M. Dougan, *When Worlds Collide! Competing Visions of the Relationship between Direct Effect and Supremacy* (2007) 44 *Common Market Law Review* 931; S. Prechal, *Direct Effect, Indirect Effect, Supremacy and the Evolving Constitution of the European Union*, in C. Barnard (ed.), *The Fundamentals of EU Law Revisited. Assessing the Impact of the Constitutional Debate*, Oxford, Oxford University Press, 2007, 35–69; J. Bengoetxea, *Is Direct Effect*; S. Prechal, *Protection of Rights: How Far?*, in S. Prechal, B. Van Roermund (eds.), *The Coherence of EU Law. The Search for Unity in Divergent Concepts*, Oxford, Oxford University Press, 2008, 155–182; C. W. A. Timmermans, *Un nouveau chapitre sur l'invocabilité des directives*, in *Mélanges en l'honneur de Jean-Pierre Puissochet—L'Etat souverain dans le monde d'aujourd'hui*, Paris, Pedone, 2008, 291–302; B. de Witte, *Direct Effect, Primacy and the Nature of the Legal Order*, in P. Craig, G. de Búrca (eds.), *The Evolution*, 187–227; J. Ziller, *Relire* van Gend en Loos (Reading Van Gend en Loos *Once Again)* (2012) 3 *Il Diritto dell'Unione europea* 513; M. Bobek, *Van Gend en Loos*; D. Chalmers, L. Barroso, *What* Van Gend en Loos *Stands for* (2014) 12 *International Journal of Constitutional Law* 105; S. Robin-Olivier, *The Evolution of Direct Effect in the EU: Stocktaking, Problems, Projections* (2014) 12 *International Journal of Constitutional Law* 165; J. H. Jans, M. J. M. Verhoeven, *Europeanisation via Consistent Interpretation and Direct Effect*, in J. H. Jans, S. Prechal, R. J. G. M. Widdershoven (eds.), *Europeanisation of Public Law*, 2nd ed., Groningen, Europa Law Publishing, 2015, 71–132; C. Wohlfahrt, *Die Vermutung unmittelbarer Wirkung des Unionsrechts. Ein Plädoyer für die Aufgabe der Kriterien hinreichender Genauigkeit und Unbedingtheit*, Heidelberg, Springer, 2016; R. Schütze, *Direct Effects and Indirect Effects of Union Law*, in R. Schütze, T. Tridimas (eds.), *Oxford Principles of European Union Law: The European Union Legal Order: Volume I*, Oxford, Oxford University Press, 2018, 265–299; L. Squintani, J. Lindeboom, *The Normative Impact of Invoking Directives: Casting Light on Direct Effect and the Elusive Distinction between Obligations and Mere Adverse Repercussions* (2019) 38 *Yearbook of European Law* 18–72.

[150] As remarked by Edward D., *Direct Effect: Myth*, 3 and K. Lenaerts, T. Corthaut, *Of Birds and Hedges: The Role of Primacy in Invoking Norms of EU Law* (2006) 31 *European Law Review* 287, 297.

rights against public bodies and/or other natural and legal persons. As a matter of fact, there is agreement on the past of direct effect. On the other hand, regarding the present and the future, however, there is no consensus, as will be clarified in the following chapters of this book. As to the present, there are divergences regarding how the doctrine of direct effect is interpreted and applied by the CJEU. As to the future, there is no consensus on the role that the doctrine should play in the relationships between EU and domestic law: several scholars keep underlining its potential, while others, in a more or less provocative way, stress its limits or even its outdatedness.

Several authors hold that the notion of direct effect is always intertwined with the conferral of a right upon the individual and, as such, should be limited to the *Van Gend & Loos* model. Others, instead, favour a wider comprehension of direct effect, irrespective of a nexus with the creation of a right, arguing that such doctrine rests on the concepts of invocability and justiciability and thus comprises the so-called objective exclusionary (or oppositive) effect.[151] Moreover, while some authors point out the incongruences implied in the direct effect test,[152] others wonder what would be the *effet utile* of direct effect in itself.[153] Furthermore, there are those who always connect disapplication, especially by virtue of the *Simmenthal* case[154] and, today, *Popławski II*,[155] to both primacy and direct effect, and those who, to the contrary, have been arguing—much less so, due to recent case law—that primacy on its own should be able to trigger the duty to disapply. The latter academics are, furthermore, generally the same ones who, while finding an inseparable bond between direct effect and the attribution of an individual right, do not connect the objective-exclusionary effect to direct effect, considering, instead, that disapplication could be treated as a consequence of primacy alone.[156] Lastly, some authors advocate in favour of directives' horizontal direct effect, while others, in line with the EU case law, challenge such possibility. Also, concerns do arise in respect to horizontality of fundamental rights, as well as to the recognition of inverse vertical direct effect of EU law to EU primary law sources.[157]

The existence of a variety of scholarly approaches reveals that the concept of direct effect is ever-changing[158] and 'diluted'.[159] Direct effect is a 'chameleon concept',[160] multi-faceted and constantly evolving.[161] It is not 'carved in stone'[162] and, as a matter of fact, has been subject, in the EU case law, to a progressive '*diversification et gradation*'[163] of its effects. Hence, direct effect is a very imprecise notion, difficult to frame in a legal sense, particularly

[151] *See* extensively Chapter IV.
[152] *See* extensively Chapter III, § 4.
[153] *See* Conclusion.
[154] *Simmenthal* (n 121).
[155] CJ, *Criminal proceedings against Popławski*, C-573/17, EU:C:2019:530.
[156] *See* extensively Chapter V, § 1.
[157] *See* extensively Chapter III, § 3.2 and Chapter V, §§ 2 and 5–10, for what concerns inverse vertical direct effect; Chapter VI, §§ 2–6, as regards horizontal direct effect.
[158] According to T. Eijsbouts, *Direct Effect*, 240, direct effect, firstly, 'is ever unfinished', secondly, is not a doctrine 'seeking perfection but one seeking to inspire and channel evolution'. *See* also, in the same vein, J. Bengoetxea, *Is Direct Effect*, 3 and D. Chalmers, L. Barroso, *What* Van Gend en Loos, 106.
[159] S. Prechal, *Direct Effect Reconsidered*, 23.
[160] Expression borrowed from J. Steiner, *Direct Applicability in EEC Law—A Chameleon Concept* (1982) 98 *Law Quarterly Review* 229; *see* also J. Steiner, *From Direct Effects to Francovich: Shifting Means of Enforcement of Community Law* (1993) 18 *European Law Review* 2.
[161] W. N. Hohfeld, *Some Fundamental Legal Conceptions as Applied in Judicial Reasoning* (1913) 23 *Yale Law Journal* 16, defined rights as 'chameleon-hued words'.
[162] M. Bobek, *Van Gend en Loos*, 181.
[163] R. Kovar, *La contribution de la Cour de justice à l'édification de l'ordre juridique communautaire. Cours général de droit Communautaire*, in *Recueil des cours de l'Académie de droit européen*, Alphen aan den Rijn, Kluwer Law International, 1995, 15, 68.

in its ambit of application and objectives. In some cases, a risk arises of 'charging' with a certain meaning the CJEU's choice to employ one word rather than another in defining a directly effective EU provision and, therefore, a risk of falling into what has been defined a 'nominalist fallacy'.[164] It has been underlined that this uncertainty would transform direct effect from a legal cornerstone of EU law into a 'virus',[165] capable of potentially infecting any theoretical elaboration regarding the interplay between EU law and the legal systems of the Member States. Furthermore, the doctrinal disagreements also originate from the asymmetries existing between national legal traditions: the variety of interpretations given to the concept of 'individual right' is proof of this phenomenon.[166] In short, direct effect, albeit 'a Community concept *par excellence*',[167] reveals different facets depending on the relevant national legal tradition (be it doctrinal or jurisprudential), which, inevitably, represent a starting point for the legal interpreter. The same, obviously, holds true not only for the scholarship and the national courts but also for the CJEU and the members of the Commission as well as of other EU institutions, who are certainly influenced by the nature of the legal order of their Member State of origin.

[164] D. Edward, *Direct Effect: Myth*, 3.
[165] D. Edward, *Direct Effect: Myth*, 3.
[166] In this regard, *see* S. Prechal, *Does Direct Effect*, 1057; S. Prechal, *Directives*, 97. Extensively, on the concept of individual rights in EU law, *see* B. Thorson, *Individual Rights in EU Law*, Berlin, Springer, 2016; H. K. Ellingsen, *Standing to Enforce European Union Law before National Courts*, Oxford, Hart, 2021, 105–122, who, while explaining the meaning of 'Union Rights', identified the differences between direct effect, invocability, standing, and effective judicial protection.
[167] S. Prechal, *Direct Effect Reconsidered*, 20.

III
TRANSFORMATIVE DIRECT EFFECT
THE *VAN GEND & LOOS* DOCTRINE, *TODAY*

1. Conferral of rights as the backbone of subjective substitutive direct effect

As clarified in Chapter I, section 2.3, the conferral of a right is a constitutive element of direct effect expounded by the CJ in *Van Gend & Loos* and in the doctrine which, over the years, has developed based on the judgment. The conferral may be explicitly asserted in the EU provision or recognized by the CJEU in its jurisprudence. In this sense, direct effect is *subjective* since it results from the attribution of a subjective legal position stemming directly from EU law,[1] as the counterpart of the obligation enshrined therein.

The nexus between the creation of a right and direct effect is apparent in most judgments. In *Salgoil* it was affirmed that the prohibition set forth in Article 31 of the EEC Treaty, currently Article 34 TFEU, by its very nature, 'lends itself perfectly to producing direct effects on the legal relationships between Member States and those subject to their jurisdiction' and, 'thus', attributes rights which the national courts are bound to protect.[2] In *Ferwerda* it was observed that individuals' rights are protected 'through the direct effect of the Community law'.[3] In the *Comitato per la difesa della cava* case, the CJ excluded the direct effect of Article 4 of Council Directive 75/442,[4] concerning waste management, precisely because it 'is not capable of conferring rights on which individuals may rely as against the State'.[5] Moreover, as far as the Charter's provisions are concerned, their direct effect has always been recognized in the EU case law on the condition that the EU rule was 'sufficient in itself to confer a right',[6] such conferral being a structural premise of direct effect.[7]

As a corollary, the individual invoking the right safeguarded by the EU directly effective provision seeks the application of EU law and the resulting replacement of domestic law governing the case before the national court. Subjective direct effect, therefore, in creating an actionable right, produces *substitutive* effects.

In this context, the preliminary question to be asked is what the meaning of 'right' is from the perspective of EU law. In truth, a definition does not exist in either the case law or in

[1] As mentioned already in §§ 4 and 5 of Chapter II, and will be carefully demonstrated in Chapter IV, direct effect has a different, objective dimension. In this sense, direct effect shall be intended broadly inasmuch as it has both a subjective and objective character. This applies to direct effect of EU law in domestic legal systems and, arguably, also to direct effect of international law in EU law, as will be claimed in §§ 3 and 5 of Chapter VII. All URLs for this chapter were last accessed on 30 April 2024.

[2] CJ, *Salgoil*, 13/68, EU:C:1968:54, 612.

[3] CJ, *H. Ferwerda BV*, 265/78, EU:C:1980:66, para. 10.

[4] Council Directive 75/442/EEC of 15 July 1975 on waste (L 194, 25/07/1975, 39).

[5] CJ, *Comitato di coordinamento per la difesa della Cava*, C-236/92, EU:C:1994:60, para. 14.

[6] CJ, *Association de médiation sociale*, C-176/12, EU:C:2014:2, para. 47; for further judgments, *see* §§ 5.3–5.5 of Chapter VI.

[7] In these terms, *see* S. Prechal, *Horizontal Direct Effect of the Charter of Fundamental Rights of the EU* (2020) 66 *Revista de Derecho Comunitario Europeo* 407, 410, and 415.

Direct Effect in EU Law. Daniele Gallo, Oxford University Press. © Daniele Gallo 2025. DOI: 10.1093/9780191925221.003.0004

primary and secondary law.[8] This is fully understandable[9] given the necessity, for the EU institutions, including the CJEU, to not favour one or another domestic legal reconstruction.[10] In *Cilfit*, in fact, it was noted that Community law uses unique terminology and that European concepts do not necessarily have 'the same meaning in Community law and in the law of the various Member States'.[11]

The EU judges employ a variety of terms.[12] In this respect, both the CJ and the GC rely on the word 'right'[13] essentially as a synonym for 'legal position/situation'[14] and generally prefer to refrain from a further characterization.[15] Moreover, the preference for one word over another does not impact the content and extent of direct effect, that is, the conditions that an EU provision must fulfil to be invoked by natural and legal persons. The CJEU, thus, does not make use of one concept rather than another in order to inflect the effects of direct effect. Indeed, much depends on how the referrals for preliminary rulings are framed by the courts of the Member States[16] and the level of completeness of the EU norm. Subjective substitutive direct effect, therefore, can assume different gradations. That is not to say, however, that where the CJ interpreted an EU rule to grant a right, this is automatically endowed with direct effect.[17] As a matter of fact, the CJ regards the suitability of an EU provision to attribute rights as one of the prerequisites for bringing a State liability action, even when not directly effective EU provisions are at stake.[18]

Furthermore, on the one hand, there is no doubt that the various expressions employed by the EU judges must be contextualized and read in the light of the case brought to their attention and of the national legal framework. What is 'inside' the right should be identified and filled in by the domestic authorities, particularly by the courts. The CJ, beginning with the *Salgoil* case, where it was asked by the referring judge to take a position on the qualification of certain legal concepts, made it clear that it is for the legal order of each Member State 'to classify rights with reference to the criteria of national law'.[19] In this respect, EU law has a

[8] *See* S. Prechal, *Does Direct Effect Still Matter?* (2000) 37 *Common Market Law Review* 1047, 1057 and S. Prechal, *Directives in EC Law*, 2nd ed., Oxford, Oxford University Press, 2005, 97. On the matter, *see amplius* B. Thorson, *Individual Rights in EU Law*, Berlin, Springer, 2016, 191–346.

[9] According to W. van Gerven, *Of Rights, Remedies and Procedures* (2000) 37 *Common Market Law Review* 501, 502, defining concepts such as 'rights', 'remedies', and 'procedures' is a 'mission impossible.' The need to rely on a European notion of 'right' is highlighted by S. Beljin, *Rights in European Union Law*, in S. Prechal, B. van Roermund (eds.), *The Coherence of EU Law. The Search for Unity in Divergent Concepts*, Oxford, Oxford University Press, 2008, 91–121, 91, and 93.

[10] For a historical account, *see*, from a European perspective, M. Graziadei, *Rights in the European Landscape. A Historical and Comparative Profile*, in S. Prechal, B. van Roermund (eds.), *The Coherence*, 63–91.

[11] *Srl CILFIT and Others and Lanificio di Gavardo SpA v Ministero della sanità*, 283/81, EU:C:1982:335, para. 19.

[12] For instance, with respect to environmental law, S. Prechal, L. Hancher, *Individual Environmental Rights: Conceptual Pollution in EU Environmental Law?* (2002) 2 *Yearbook of European Environmental Law* 89–115, 91, referred to 'conceptual ambiguity.'

[13] *See* W. van Gerven, *Bridging the Gap between Community and National Laws: Towards a Principle of Homogeneity in the Field of Legal Remedies?* (1995) 32 *Common Market Law Review* 679, 679–680.

[14] As was remarked already by A. Trabucchi, *Un nuovo diritto* (1963) 1 *Rivista di diritto civile* 259, 266, according to whom the notion of 'right' ('*diritto*') was to be intended broadly as a 'subjective legally safeguarded situation' ('*situazione giuridicamente protetta*').

[15] *See*, amongst others, CJ, *Hansen GmbH & Co.*, 91/78, EU:C:1979:65, paras 15–17.

[16] *See*, amongst others, *Comitato per la difesa della cava* (n 5), para. 5, whereby the referring judge referred to 'subjective right' ('*diritto soggettivo*').

[17] On the similarities and divergences between direct effect and State liability, from the standpoint of the notion of 'rights', *see* S. Prechal, *Member State Liability and Direct Effect: What's the Difference after All?* (2006) 17 *European Business Law Review* 299, 303–306.

[18] *See, inter alia*, CJ, *Andrea Francovich and Danila Bonifaci and Others v Italian Republic*, joined cases C-6/90 and C-9/90, EU:C:1991:428, para. 40. The CJ associated for the first time the State liability remedy with EU directly effective provisions in CJ, *Brasserie du Pêcheur*, joined cases C-46–48/93, EU:C:1996:79, para. 51.

[19] *Salgoil* (n 2), 615.

different role: guaranteeing the effectiveness of a European norm and, at the same time, the full judicial protection of individuals. To this end, the recognition of direct effect is essential for the exercise of a remedy that an individual can bring before the courts.[20] As emphasized by AG Mengozzi in his opinion in the *Gestoras* case, the rule of law is 'based not so much on rules and the proclamation of rights as on mechanisms that make it possible to ensure respect for rules and rights'.[21]

On the other hand, the concept of 'right' cannot be construed purely by virtue of national law. The CJEU's reasoning is independent of whether the legal position stemming from EU law is a subjective right *stricto iure*. A 'right' arising under the EU legal order, that is, with *causa petendi* in one or more of its rules, thus, cannot be categorized[22] as that which the civil law tradition defines as a subjective right, *droit subjectif, Individualrechtsschutz/subjektive Rechte, diritto soggettivo*.[23]

2. Direct effect as a complement to the principles of effectiveness and effective judicial protection

As is well-known, there is no EU comprehensive legal framework providing remedies which individuals can use to wield their rights recognized under EU law provisions, whether they are directly effective or not.[24] This implies that, in large part, procedural law is not harmonized, falling as it does under the competence of Member States. There exists, therefore, a wide

[20] As noted by B. Hofstötter, *Non-Compliance of National Courts: Remedies in European Community Law and Beyond*, The Hague, TMC Asser Press, 2005, 20, who observed that 'the maximum of *ubi ius, ibi remedium* holds true for the Community order as well, even if combined with an element of rigorous decentralisation'.

[21] Opinion of AG Mengozzi of 26 October 2006, *Gestoras Pro Amnistía*, C-354/04 P, EU:C:2006:667, para. 101.

[22] For some reflections grounded in a comparative legal discourse, *see* S. Prechal, *Direct Effect Reconsidered, Redefined and Rejected*, in J. M. Prinssen, A. Schrauwen (eds.), *Direct Effect: Rethinking a Classic of EC Legal Doctrine*, Groningen, European Law Publishing, 2002, 15–41, 20, and A. Ward, *More than an 'Infant Disease': Individual Rights, EC Directives, and the Case for Uniform Remedies*, in J. M. Prinssen, A. Schrauwen (eds.), *Direct Effect*, 43–75, 49–50.

[23] *See* M. Ruffert, *Subjektive Rechte im Umweltrecht der Europäischen Gemeinschaft. Unter besonderer Berücksichtigung ihrer prozessualen Durchsetzung*, Heidelberg, University of Heidelberg (dissertation), 1996 and M. Ruffert, *Rights and Remedies in European Community Law: A Comparative View* (1997) 34 *Common Market Law Review* 307. *See* also the analyses by J. A. Winter, *Direct Applicability and Direct Effect. Two Distinct and Different Concepts in Community Law* (1972) 9 *Common Market Law Review* 425; J. Coppel, *Rights, Duties and the End of* Marshall (1994) 57 *Modern Law Review* 859; C. Hilson, T. Downes, *Making Sense of Rights: Community Rights in EC Law* (1999) 24 *European Law Review* 121; S. Prechal, *Directives*, 97–105. Amongst early authors, *see* W. N. Hohfeld, *Some Fundamental Legal Conceptions as Applied in Judicial Reasoning* (1913) 23 *Yale Law Journal* 16. With particular reference to the German doctrine, S. Prechal, *Protection of Rights: How Far?*, in S. Prechal, B. Van Roermund (ed.), *The Coherence*, 155–182, 158, wrote that if the very restrictive conception of this doctrine were valid, the CJ, in its jurisprudence on the protection of the environment, would not have been able to infer from any directives rights exercisable by individuals. In the same direction, *see* T. Lock, *Is Private Enforcement of EU Law through State Liability a Myth? An assessment 20 years after* Francovich (2012) 49 *Common Market Law Review* 1675, 1689. As per the Anglo-Saxon tradition, the essential idea is that there cannot be a right without a legal remedy so that the aphorism *ubi ius ibi remedium*, dear to the traditions of civil law countries, shall be reversed. On the relationship and overlaps between the two concepts of 'remedy' and 'right', *see* C. Harlow, *A Common European Law of Remedies?*, in C. Kilpatrick, T. Novitz, P. Skidmore (eds.), *The Future of Remedies in Europe*, Oxford, Oxford University Press, 2000, 69–86, 72–75. *See* also T. Heukels, J. Tib, *Towards Homogeneity in the Field of Legal Remedies: Convergence and Divergence*, in P. Beaumont, C. Lyons, N. Walker (eds.), *Convergence and Divergence in European Public Law*, Oxford, Hart, 1997, 111–129, 113; F. Ferraro, *La responsabilità risarcitoria degli Stati per violazione del diritto dell'Unione*, Milan, Giuffrè, 2008, 33–34.

[24] K. Lenaerts, *The Decentralised Enforcement of EU Law: The Principles of Equivalence and Effectiveness*, in U. Leanza, A. Tizzano, T. Vassalli di Dachenhausen, R. Mastroianni, P. De Pasquale, R. Ciccone (Organizing Committee), *Scritti in onore di Giuseppe Tesauro*, Naples, Editoriale Scientifica, vol. II, 2014, 1057–1085, 1057, acknowledged the existence of a 'division of functions between the EU and national legal systems, with the former providing the rights, and the latter the remedies'.

margin of procedural autonomy[25] for national authorities in establishing remedies which enable substantive rights deriving from EU law to find judicial redress through indirect/decentralized domestic avenues.[26] As a matter of fact, the CJ observed that, 'in the absence of Community rules on this subject', it is for the legal system of each Member State 'to designate the courts having jurisdiction and to determine the procedural conditions' governing the actions intended to ensure the protection of the rights 'which citizens have from the direct effect of Community law'.[27] After all, the Treaty was not designed 'to create new remedies in the national courts to ensure the observance of Community law other than those already laid down by national law'.[28]

The procedural autonomy of Member States is justified because a thorough EU framework of remedies and procedural rules would presuppose the establishment of fully harmonized mechanisms for the administration of justice which, at present, do not exist. Such integration, if realized, should lead the EU institutions to disregard the different procedural traditions of the States, which are imbued with countervailing redistributive choices, for example regarding the determination of the damages caused by, and suffered from, the infringement of EU law.[29] In short, national procedural autonomy originates, upstream, from the principle of conferral set forth in Article 5(1) TEU, read together with Article 4(1) TFEU. The point of departure for any analysis on the relationship between the EU legal order and the procedural law of the States is accordingly the awareness about the absence of a legal basis, at the EU level, for ensuring full uniformity amongst Member States' procedural laws.[30]

Nonetheless, it would be wrong to neglect the progressive relativization of such procedural autonomy that the GC and the CJ have performed over the years[31] through a

[25] On such notion, *see*, amongst early studies, *ex multis*, T. Hartley, *The Effects in National Law of Judgments of the European Court* (1980) 5 *European Law Review* 366; J. Bridge, *Procedural Aspects of the Enforcement of European Community Law through the Legal Systems of the Member States* (1984) 9 *European Law Review* 28; D. Curtin, *Directives: The Effectiveness of Judicial Protection of Individual Rights* (1990) 27 *Common Market Law Review* 709; S Weatherill, *Beyond EC Law Rights, National Remedies*, in A. Caiger, D. A. Floudas (eds.), *Onwards: Lowering the Barriers Further*, Chichester, Chancery Law, 1996, 233–254; C. N. Kakouris, *Do the Member States Possess Judicial Procedural 'Autonomy'?* (1997) 34 *Common Market Law Review* 1389; J. Lonbay, A. Biondi (eds.), *Remedies for Breach of EC Law*, London, Wiley, 1997; M. Brealey, M. Hoskins, *Remedies in EC Law*, London, Sweet & Maxwell, 1998; J. M. Kendrick, *Modifying Procedural Autonomy: Better Protection for Community Rights* (2000) 8 *European Review of Private Law* 565; R. Rodriguez Iglesias, *Sui limiti dell'autonomia procedimentale e processuale degli Stati membri nell'applicazione del diritto comunitario* (2001) 1 *Rivista italiana di diritto pubblico comunitario* 5; M. Dougan, *National Remedies before the Court of Justice: Issues of Harmonisation and Differentiation*, Oxford, Oxford University Press, 2004.

[26] In these terms, *see* J. Schwarze, *European Administrative Law*, London, Sweet & Maxwell, 2006, clxxii; R. Crauford Smith, *Remedies for Breaches of EU Law in National Courts: Legal Variation and Selection*, in P. Craig, G. de Búrca (eds.), *The Evolution of EU Law*, 3rd ed., Oxford, Oxford University Press, 2021, 287–320, 287; M. Dougan, *National Remedies*, 1.

[27] *See*, amongst others, CJ, *Rewe-Zentralfinanz eG and Rewe-Zentral AG*, 33/76, EU:C:1976:188, para. 5; CJ, *Comet BV*, 45-76, EU:C:1976:191, para. 13; CJ, *Peterbroeck, Van Campenhout & Cie SCS*, C-312/93, EU:C:1995:437, para. 12; CJ, *Courage*, C-453/99, EU:C:2001:465, para. 29; CJ, *Safalero*, C-13/01, EU:C:2003:447, para. 49.

[28] *See*, amongst others, *Rewe* (n 27), para. 44; CJ, *Unibet (London) Ltd and Unibet (International) Ltd*, C-432/05, EU:C:2007:163, para. 40.

[29] D. Chalmers, G. Davies, G. Monti, *European Union Law. Text and Materials*, 4th ed., Cambridge, Cambridge University Press, 2019, 315. *See* also D. Caruso, *The Missing View of the Cathedral: The Private Law Paradigm of European Legal Integration* (2002) 8 *European Law Journal* 3.

[30] In the opinion of K. Lenaerts, K. Gutman, J. T. Nowak, *EU Procedural Law*, 2nd ed., Oxford, Oxford University Press, 2023, 119, EU law 'piggybacks on the national judicial system'.

[31] On such relativization, *see*, for early analyses, A. P. Tash, *Remedies for European Community Law Claims in Member State Courts: Toward a European Standard* (1993) 31 *Columbia Journal of Transnational Law* 377; E Szyszczak, *Making Europe More Relevant to Its Citizens: Effective Judicial Process* (1996) 21 *European Law Review* 351. *See* also, more recently, A. Perrin, *Droit européen et droit communautaire: Que reste-t-il de l'autonomie procédurale des états membres?* (2008) 124 *Revue de droit public* 1661; G. Vitale, *Diritto processuale nazionale e diritto dell'Unione europea, L'autonomia procedurale degli Stati membri in settori a diverso livello di 'europeizzazione'*,

case-by-case approach[32] in order to achieve a minimum level of harmonization, a set of procedural common standards,[33] and ultimately, consistency across domestic legal systems.[34] Such an attitude on the part of the EU judges has even led a part of the scholarship to question the existence *per se* of said autonomy.[35] Actually, there can be little doubt that this process of relativization is gradual and unavoidable, to the extent that the very idea that a genuine presumption of said autonomy[36] still exists clashes with the EU jurisprudence.[37] The process is unavoidable because it constitutes, ultimately, a consequence of the primacy principle.[38] Furthermore, we have witnessed the adoption of EU secondary law instruments, in particular in the areas of public procurement, environmental law, intellectual property, competition law, and anti-discrimination law,[39] designed to harmonize domestic remedies and procedures. In this respect, the narrowing of national procedural autonomy results

Catania, Ed.It, 2010; A. M. Romito, *La tutela giurisdizionale nell'Unione europea tra effettività del sistema e garanzie individuali*, Bari, Cacucci, 2015, 62–75. With a focus on EU secondary law, rather than on the case law, *see* especially F. G. Wilman, *The end of the absence? The Growing Body of EU legislation on Private Enforcement and the Main Remedies it Provides for* (2016) 53 *Common Market Law Review* 887.

[32] The State liability remedy is the clearest example. In this regard, *see, inter alia*, R. Caranta, *Judicial Protection against Member States: A New* Jus Commune *Takes Shape* (1995) 32 *Common Market Law Review* 703; P. Craig, Francovich, *Remedies and the Scope of Damages Liability* (1993) 109 *Law Quarterly Review* 595; C. Harlow, Francovich *and the Problem of the Disobedient State* (1996) 2 *European Law Journal* 199; M. Dougan, *The* Francovich *Right to Reparation: Reshaping the Contours of Community Remedial Competence* (2006) 12 *European Public Law* 103; J. Talberg, *Supranational Influence in EU Enforcement: The ECJ and the Principle of State Liability* (2000) 7 *Journal of European Public Policy* 104; N. Reich, *Horizontal Liability in EC Law: Hybridization of Remedies for Compensation in case of Breaches of EC Rights* (2007) 44 *Common Market Law Review* 705, 708–709, who highlighted the existence of a hybridization of remedies which on the one hand are based on national law as basis for a claim on compensation ('*Anspruchsgrundlage*'), but this national law is reshaped under the influence of EC law. *See* also T. Tridimas, *The General Principles of EU Law*, Oxford, Oxford University Press, 2006, 456–461; M.-P. Granger, *National Applications of* Francovich *and the Construction of a European Administrative* Ius Commune (2007) 32 *European Law Review* 157; A. Biondi, M. Farley, *The Right to Damages in European Law*, Austin (Texas), Wolters Kluwer, 2009; T. Lock, *Is Private Enforcement*; F. Ferraro, *La responsabilità*, 125–184.

[33] On the interplay between effectiveness and uniform application of EU law, *see* C. Plaza Martin, *Furthering the Effectiveness of EC Directives and the Judicial Protection of Individual Rights Thereunder* (1994) 43 *International and Comparative Law Quarterly* 26; M. Hoskins, *Tilting the Balance: Supremacy and National Procedural Rules* (1996) 21 *European Law Review* 365; C. M. G. Himsworth, *Things Fall Apart: The Harmonisation of Community Judicial Procedural Protection Revisited* (1997) 22 *European Law Review* 291; A. Biondi, *The European Court of Justice and Certain National Procedural Limitations: Not Such a Tough Relationship* (1999) 36 *Common Market Law Review* 1271; A. Ward, *Judicial Review and the Rights of Private Parties in EU Law*, Oxford, Oxford University Press, 2007, 86–92; D. Leczykiewicz, *Compensatory Remedies in EU Law: The Relationship between EU Law and National Law*, in P. Giliker (ed.), *Research Handbook on EU Tort Law*, Cheltenham, Edward Elgar, 2017, 63–92, 71.

[34] K. Lenaerts, *The Decentralised Enforcement*, 1065, claimed that a 'basic threshold of judicial protection' is achieved thanks to the case law of the CJEU.

[35] In this vein, *see* extensively C. N. Kakouris, *Do the Member States*; W. van Gerven, *Of Rights*, 502, who wrote of 'procedural competence of the Member States' rather than of procedural autonomy; D. U. Galetta, *Procedural Autonomy of EU Member States: Paradise Lost? A Study on the 'Functionalized Procedural Competence' of EU Member States*, Heidelberg, Springer, 2009; M. Bobek, *Why There is No Principle of 'Procedural Autonomy' of the Member States*, in H.-W. Micklitz, B. de Witte (eds.), *The European Court of Justice and the Autonomy of the Member States*, Oxford, Intersentia, 2012, 305–322; B. Bertrand, J. Sirinelli, *Droit du contentieux de l'Union européenne*, Paris, LGDJ, 2022, 598–607.

[36] M. Dougan, *The Vicissitudes of Life at the Coalface: Remedies and Procedures for Enforcing Union Law before the National Courts*, in P. Craig, G. de Búrca (eds.), *The Evolution*, 407–438, 412, noted that there exists a tension between such presumption and the principle of effectiveness. *See* also the further reflections by P. Wattel, *National Procedural Autonomy and Effectiveness of EC Law* (2008) 35 *Legal Issues of Economic Integration* 109 and F. Episcopo, *The Vicissitudes of Life at the Coalface: Remedies and Procedures for Enforcing Union Law before the National Courts*, in P. Craig, G. de Búrca (eds.), *The Evolution*, 275–305.

[37] *See* also D. U. Galetta, *Procedural Autonomy*, 2, who emphasized the existence of a 'pre-supposed procedural autonomy'.

[38] On this point, *see* J. S. Delicostopoulos, *Towards European Procedural Primacy in National Legal Systems* (2003) 9 *European Law Journal* 599, 599, who referred to 'European procedural primacy'.

[39] As observed by P. Craig, G. de Búrca, *EU Law: Text, Cases, and Materials*, 7th ed., 2020, footnote 1, 262; R. Adam, A. Tizzano, *Manuale di diritto dell'Unione europea*, 2nd ed., Turin, Giappichelli, 2017, 358.

also from the pre-emption principle[40] since the CJ, in several judgments, beginning with *Roquette*,[41] has clarified that Member States lose their freedom to legislate in the areas not falling under the exclusive competence of the EU that turn out to be governed by EU law.[42]

In light of the above, reflecting upon direct effect means also looking at the interplay between this doctrine and the principles of effectiveness[43] and effective judicial protection,[44] as means to enforce EU law and safeguard individuals[45] from the standpoint of procedural rather than substantive law.[46] The conformity of national law with EU law, therefore, implies the respect of these two interconnected principles, so that effective judicial protection represents a development of the principle of effectiveness, as it emerges from the EU case law,[47] starting with the *Johnston*[48] ruling.[49] Effective judicial protection,[50] indeed, became

[40] *See*, recently, A. Arena, *Exercise of EU Competences and Pre-emption of Member States' Powers in the Internal and the External Sphere: Towards 'Grand Unification'?* (2016) 35 *Yearbook of European Law* 28–105.

[41] CJ, *Roquette Frères SA*, C-94/00, EU:C:2002:603. *See* also CJ, *Hans Just I/S*, 68/79, EU:C:1980:57.

[42] On pre-emption and procedural law, *see* J. Mertens de Wilmars, *L'efficacité des différentes techniques nationales de protection juridique contre les violations du droit communautaire par les autorités nationales et les particuliers* (1982) 18 *Cahiers de Droit Européen* 379, 400–401.

[43] For an analysis devoted to the interplay between the principle of effectiveness and national procedural autonomy, *see* M. Accetto, S. Zleptnig, *The Principle of Effectiveness: Rethinking its Role in Community Law* (2005) 11 *European Public Law* 375.

[44] In these terms, *see* R. Schütze, *European Union Law*, 3rd ed., Oxford, Oxford University Press, 2021, 409–414. G. Tesauro, *The Effectiveness of Judicial Protection and Cooperation between the Court of Justice and National Courts* (1993) 13 *Yearbook of European Union Law* 1–17, 5, wrote that 'the right to effective protection, in so far as it may be relied on by any person who considers that, under Community law, he enjoys a legal position which constitutes a right, is closely linked with the principle of direct effect'. *See* also D. Leczykiewicz, *Effectiveness of EU Law before National Courts*, in *Oxford Handbook of European Union Law*, Oxford, Oxford University Press, 2015, 212–248, 224.

[45] On the importance of Tesauro's opinions for the design of the principle of effective judicial protection, and on its close relationship with direct effect, *see* R. Mastroianni, M. Condinanzi, *Giuseppe Tesauro—Advocate General at the ECJ—1988-1998. A Paladin of Effective Judicial Protection*, in D. Gallo, R. Mastroianni, F. Nicola, L. Cecchetti (eds.), *The Italian Influence on European Law: Judges and Advocates General* (1952–2000), Oxford, Hart, 2024, forthcoming. For an overview on the key role performed by Italian judges and AGs in conceiving the two principles as a duo, *see* F. Nicola, R. Mastroianni, D. Gallo, L. Cecchetti, *Conclusions*, in D. Gallo, R. Mastroianni, F. Nicola, L. Cecchetti (eds.), *The Italian Influence on European Law: Judges and Advocates General* (1952–2000), Oxford, Hart, 2024, forthcoming.

[46] For what concerns direct effect as a means of private enforcement, *see* Chapter II, § 1.

[47] *See* M. Bobek, *The Effects of EU Law in the National Legal Systems*, in C. Barnard, S. Peers (eds.), *European Union Law*, Oxford, Oxford University Press, 2020, 154–189, 182–183.

[48] CJ, *Marguerite Johnston*, 222/84, EU:C:1986:206, paras 18–19. On the importance of the ruling, from the viewpoint of the principle of effective judicial protection, *see*, *ex multis*, E. Szyszczak, *Making Europe*, 353, and I. Pernice, *The Right to Effective Judicial Protection and Remedies in the EU*, in A. Rosas, E. Levits, Y. Bot (eds.), *The Court of Justice and the Construction of Europe: Analyses and Perspectives on Sixty Years of Case-law*, Berlin, Springer, 2013, 381–396, 382. *See* also CJ, *Union nationale des entraîneurs et cadres techniques professionnels du football (Unectef) v Georges Heylens*, 222/86, EU:C:1987:442, para. 14; CJ, *Commission v Austria*, C-424/99, EU:C:2001:642, para. 45; CJ, *Unión de Pequeños Agricultores*, C-50/00 P, EU:C:2002:462, para. 39; CJ, *Eribrand*, C-467/01, EU:C:2003:364, para. 61; CJ, *Lesoochranárske zoskupenie VLK*, C-243/15, EU:C:2016:838, para. 50.

[49] A. Barav, *Applicabilité directe*, in A. Barav, C. Philip, C. Boutayeb (eds.), in *Dictionnaire juridique des Communautés européennes*, Paris, Pedone, 1993,179, noted that the CJEU considers '*l'effectivité de la protection des droits tirés par les particuliers des règles communautaires comme le pendant barométrique de l'effectivité du droit communautaire lui-même*'. On the close relationship between effectiveness and effective judicial protection, *see* G. Tesauro, *The Effectiveness*, 6, and S. M. Carbone, *Principio di effettività e diritto comunitario*, Naples, Editoriale Scientifica, 2010, 25–62; A. Tizzano, *La tutela dei privati nei confronti degli Stati membri dell'Unione europea* (1995) 4 *Il Foro italiano* 14; S. Prechal, *EC Requirements for an Effective Remedy*, in J. Lonbay, A. Biondi (eds.), *Remedies for Breach of EC Law*, London, Wiley, 1997, 3–13; A. Arnull, *The Principle of Effective Judicial Protection in EU Law: An Unruly Horse?* (2011) 36 *European Law Review* 51.

[50] For a description of the principle, and the related case law, *see*, e.g., T. Tridimas, *The General Principles*, 443–456; M. Safjan, D. Dusterhaus, *A Union of Effective Judicial Protection: Addressing a Multi-Level Challenge through the Lens of Article 47 CFREU* (2014) 33 *Yearbook of European Law* 3–40; K. Gutman, *Article 47: The Right to an Effective Remedy and to a Fair Trial*, in M. Bobek, J. Adams-Prassl (eds.), *The EU Charter of Fundamental Rights in the Member States*, Oxford, Hart, 2020, 371–384; T. Lock, D. Martin, *Article 47 CFEU*, in M. Kellerbauer, M. Klamert, J. Tomkin (eds.), *The EU Treaties and the Charter of Fundamental Rights. A Commentary*, Oxford,

the main tool to guarantee the effectiveness of EU law by safeguarding subjective legal positions stemming from the EU legal order thanks to the judicial recognition of an ever-wider core of procedural rights. Such rights comprise both the right/power of access to the courts (*jus standi*) and the right to an effective remedy (*jus locus standi in judicio*),[51] which lie at the heart of Article 19 TEU and Article 47 of the Charter.[52]

As to the legal status of effectiveness, at times the CJ has classified it as a general principle of EU law,[53] while in the great majority of cases[54] it has not identified a specific legal framing.[55] Irrespective of its definition in the jurisprudence, what can be easily affirmed is that the principle of effectiveness, also due to its inherent flexibility,[56] lies at the foundation of the EU legal system.[57] After all, it has been correctly observed that '[E]verything in the treaty is about effectiveness'.[58] Moreover, as affirmed by the CJ in *Factortame*, it is for the national courts, in application of the principle of cooperation, 'to ensure the legal protection which persons derive from the direct effect of provisions of Community law'.[59] In this regard, M. Ross remarked that direct effect requires that internal legal orders, especially the rules governing the judiciary, 'must ensure that a remedy is available for infringement of directly effective rights' and that such remedy is designed in compliance with the twin principles of equivalence and effectiveness[60] inasmuch as it shall not be 'less favourable or more difficult to achieve that than provided by domestic law'.[61]

Against this backdrop, a tension between direct effect and national procedural autonomy may arise because certain domestic procedural rules, as well as the lack of a specific remedy in the legal order of a Member State, can impair the exercise of a right arising from directly effective EU norms. The diminishing of autonomy, consequently, serves to ensure the *effet utile* of direct effect implied in those norms, that is, their effectiveness.[62] For that matter,

Oxford University Press, 2019, 2214–2225; D. Domenicucci, F. Filpo, *Diritto a un ricorso effettivo e a un giudice imparziale*, in R. Mastroianni, O. Pollicino, S. Allegrezza, F. Pappalardo, O. Razzolini (eds.), *Carta dei diritti fondamentali dell'Unione europea*, Milan, Giuffrè, 2017, 864–883; A. Ward, *Article 47—Right to an Effective Remedy*, in S. Peers, T. Hervey, J. Kenner, A. Ward (eds.), *The EU Charter of Fundamental Rights: A Commentary*, 2nd ed., Oxford, Hart, 2021, 1285–1344.

[51] On such two core elements, *see* T. Tridimas, *The General Principles*, 443–455, and N. Póltorak, *European Union Rights in National Courts*, Alphen aan den Rijn, Kluwer Law International, 2015, 101–144 and 239–262.

[52] These rights shall be reconstrued in the light of the constitutional traditions common to the Member States as well as of the ECHR, most notably of its Articles 6 and 13. *See*, amongst others, *Johnston* (n 48), para. 18. On effective judicial protection in light of the ECHR and the Charter, *see*, *inter alia*, S. Prechal, *The Court of Justice and Effective Judicial Protection: What Has the Charter Changed?*, in C. Paulussen, T. Takacs, V. Lazic, B. van Rompuy, (eds.), *Fundamental Rights in International and European Law*, The Hague, TMC Asser Press, 2015, 143–157.

[53] *Brasserie* (n 18), para. 95.

[54] On this matter, *see* T. Tridimas, *The General Principles*, 418–422.

[55] For instance, *see* CJ, *Gerhard Köbler*, C-224/01, EU:C:2003:513, para. 33.

[56] The interdisciplinary character is remarked by F. Snyder, *The Effectiveness of European Community Law. Institutions, Processes, Tools and Techniques* (1993) 56 *Modern Law Review* 19, 19, and 24–27. *See* also M. Ross, *Effectiveness in the European Legal Order(s):Beyond Supremacy to Constitutional Proportionality?* (2006) 31 *European Law Review* 476, 479.

[57] In the same vein *see* M. Ross, *Effectiveness*, 476.

[58] J. Bengoetxea, *Is Direct Effect a General Principle of European Law?*, in U. Bernitz, J. Nergelius, C. Cardner (eds.), *General Principles of EC Law in a Process of Development*, Alphen aan de Rijn, Kluwer Law International, 2008, 3–24, 22.

[59] CJ, *The Queen v Secretary of State for Transport, ex parte: Factortame Ltd and Others*, C-213/89, EU:C:1990:257, para. 19.

[60] *See Rewe* (n 27), para. 5.

[61] M. Ross, *Beyond Francovich* (1993) 56 *Modern Law Review* 55, 56.

[62] The ties between effectiveness and direct effect are illustrated by P. Pescatore, *The Doctrine of 'Direct Effect': An Infant Disease of Community Law* (1983) 8 *European Law Review* 155, 177; R. Kovar, *La contribution de la Cour de justice à l'édification de l'ordre juridique communautaire. Cours général de droit Communautaire*, in *Recueil des cours de l'Académie de droit européen*, Alphen aan den Rijn, Kluwer Law International, 1995, 15, 67;

direct effect and effectiveness are two naturally interconnected legal categories, so much so that some scholars,[63] where they refer to direct effect, mean 'immediate effectiveness'[64] of EU law. There are also those who note that the general principle of direct effect is rooted in the general principle of effectiveness.[65]

As already observed with regard to the *Van Gend & Loos* judgment, the CJ was clear, starting from its earliest case law, in asserting that the duty of national courts is to shield the rights that EU law grants to individuals in order to give full effect to the rules of primary and secondary law.[66] Notably, in the *Commission v Luxembourg*[67] and *Lück*[68] judgments, the CJ transferred the core of the reasoning developed in *Van Gend & Loos* to procedural law. In *Commission v Luxembourg* it wrote that the Treaty 'expressly provides means and special procedures'[69] permitting Community rules to generate their effects. Therefore, Community law attributes rights, like those stemming from Article 12 of the EEC Treaty, which lie at the core of *Van Gend & Loos*, but it also requires the establishment of procedures enabling those subjective legal situations to be effectively invoked and enforced.[70] In *Lück* the CJ highlighted that domestic courts must apply those remedies, enshrined in national law, that are 'appropriate for the purpose of protecting the individual rights'[71] bestowed by Community law.[72] The same approach was taken and further refined in the *Lorenz* case, where it was stated that the direct effect of the prohibition set forth in a Community rule, in that case Article 93(3) of the EEC Treaty, currently Article 108(3) TFEU, could not be 'excluded' by rules of national law of any kind whatsoever, including domestic procedural provisions.[73]

E. Szyszczak, *Making Europe*, 357; C. Kilpatrick, *The Future of Remedies in Europe*, in C. Kilpatrick, T. Novitz, P. Skidmore (eds.), *The Future*, 1–31; M. Dougan, *The Vicissitudes of Life*, 409–410; S. M. Carbone, *Principio di effettività*, 14–19; P. Piva, *Il principio di effettività della tutela giurisprudenziale del diritto dell'Unione europea*, Naples, Editoriale Scientifica, 2012, 3 and 6–7; D. Chalmers, G. Davies, G. Monti, *European Union*, 296. There is equivalence between effectiveness and *effet utile*, as underlined by the great majority of authors, amongst whom: D. Curtin, K. J. M. Mortelmans, *Application and Enforcement of Community Law by the Member States*, in D. Curtin, T. Heukels (eds.), *Institutional Dynamics of European Integration—Essays in Honour of Henry G. Schermers*, Dordrecht-Boston, Martinus Nijhoff, II, 1994, 423–466, 453; M. Claes, *The National Courts' Mandate in the European Constitution*, Oxford, Hart, 2006, 66–67; X. Groussot, *General Principles of Community Law*, Groningen, Europa Law Publishing, 2006, 240; C. Pesce, *Il principio dell'effetto utile e la tutela dei diritti nella giurisprudenza dell'Unione* (2014) 2 *Studi sull'integrazione europea* 359; U. Šadl, *National courts and the effectiveness of EU law*, in B. de Witte, J. A. Mayoral, U. Jaremba, M. Wind, K. Podstawa (eds.), *National Courts and EU Law: New Issues, Theories and Methods*, Cheltenham, Edward Elgar, 2016, 68–103, 68. *Contra* M. Ross, *Effectiveness*, 481; O. Dubos, *Que reste-t-il de l'autonomie procédurale du juge national? Histoire de l'attribution d'une compétence au nom de l'effectivité et de l'efficacité du droit de l'Union*, in E. Neframi (ed.), *Renvoi préjudiciel et marge d'appréciation du juge national*, Brussels, Bruylant, 2015, 159–182, 171–172; D. U. Galetta, *Procedural Autonomy*, 17.

[63] D. Curtin, *Directives: The Effectiveness*, 728, observed that the duty of national judges in ensuring the effectiveness of EU law 'entails the faithful application hand in glove of the paramount doctrines of direct effect and supremacy of Community law'.

[64] P. Pescatore, *International Law and Community Law—A Comparative Analysis* (1970) 7 *Common Market Law Review* 167, 174–175.

[65] J. Bengoetxea, *Is Direct Effect*, 20–21 and N. Póltorak, *European Union Rights*, 7.

[66] On early judgments, *see* S. Prechal, *National Courts in EU Judicial Structures* (2006) 25 *Yearbook of European Law* 429–450.

[67] CJ, 13 November 1964, *Commission v Luxembourg and Belgium*, joined cases 90–91/63, EU:C:1964:80.

[68] CJ, *Firma Gebrüder Lück*, 34/67, EU:C:1968:24.

[69] *Commission v Luxembourg* (n 67), 634.

[70] On the relevance of such ruling, *see* R. Kovar, *La contribution*, 25.

[71] *Lück* (n 68), 251.

[72] On this aspect, *see* W. Ganhof van der Meersch, *L'ordre juridique des Communautés européennes et le droit international*, Alphen aan den Rijn, Sijthoff & Noordhoff, 1979, 260.

[73] CJ, *Gebr. Lorenz GmbH*, 120/73, EU:C:1973:152, para. 9.

Thus, Member States must put in place remedies giving substance to EU rights.[74] If this is not the case and EU rights remain deprived of corresponding remedies, a violation of EU law occurs.[75] In fact, if an EU right exists but there is not a national remedy which would permit its exercise, the right remains unheeded and the effective judicial protection is undermined.[76] In this sense, it is necessary that the EU legal order establish limits to the States' procedural autonomy, which, otherwise, if understood in broad terms, would entail a discrepancy between the legal situations stemming from EU law and their projection at the level of national procedural remedies.[77] Indeed, a procedural issue was also the focus of the *Simmenthal* case,[78] whereby a national constitutional practice granting the Constitutional Court sole jurisdiction to declare unconstitutional Italian provisions conflicting with Community law, rather than allowing domestic judges to set aside such provisions, was deemed incompatible with EU law.[79] Furthermore, in the *post-Simmenthal* case law, the CJ expanded that approach beyond the realm of disapplication by paying increasing attention to the effectiveness of EU law, above all of EU provisions endowed with direct effect, in particular regarding the remedies that Member States should establish to ensure the enforcement of EU law.[80]

In conclusion, the attainment of effectiveness necessarily requires direct effect and the latter, in turn, cannot be realized without the principle of effective judicial protection, and vice versa. The positive obligation on the Member States to provide effective remedies, as enshrined in Article 19(2) TEU—which has been granted direct effect by the CJ—[81] can be fully enforced only through direct effect that renders rights enforceable before national authorities, including, first and foremost, the courts. Therefore, effectiveness, direct effect, and effective judicial protection are mutually instrumental and interrelated principles: they all serve to safeguard rights and secure the uniform and fair enforcement of EU law.

3. The milestones of a concept in flux

The *Van Gend & Loos* doctrine, in its evolution over time, has taken on, sometimes in unexpected ways,[82] new contours compared to the letter of the *Van Gend & Loos* decision. Today it presents features which mark a clear dilation of its scope.[83] One need only think, by way of example, of the gradual attribution of direct effect, including in horizontal relationships, carried out by the CJ from the seventies onwards, to the rules on freedoms of movement.

[74] *See* also J. Mertens de Wilmars, *L'efficacité*, 398–401. *See*, amongst early judgments, CJ, *Norddeutsches Vieh- und Fleischkontor GmbH*, 39/70, EU:C:1971:16, para. 4; CJ, *Markmann KG*, 121/73, EU:C:1973:153, para. 7 of the maxim.

[75] As noted by T. Eilmansberger, *The Relationship between Rights and Remedies in EC Law: In Search of the Missing Link* (2004) 41 *Common Market Law Review* 1199, 1206.

[76] As affirmed by R. Schütze, *European Union Law*, 412, rights without remedies are like 'pie in the sky'.

[77] *See* the observations by R. Caranta, *Judicial Protection*.

[78] CJ, *Amministrazione delle Finanze dello Stato v Simmenthal SpA*, 106/77, EU:C:1978:49, para. 23. Recently, *see*, in similar terms, amongst others, CJ, *YP*, joined cases C-615/20 and C-671/20, EU:C:2023:562, para. 62, whereby an express reference is made to Article 4(3) TEU.

[79] As explained by R. Schütze, *European Union Law*, 410–411.

[80] *See*, *inter alia*, *Factortame* (n 59), paras 18–22; CJ, *Gervais Larsy*, C-118/00, EU:C:2001:368, para. 65.

[81] CJ, *A.B.*, C-824/18, EU:C:2021:153, para. 146.

[82] In such terms, *see* the thoughts by P. Craig, *Once upon a Time in the West: Direct Effect and the Federalization of EEC Law* (1992) 12 *Oxford Journal of Legal Studies* 453, 461–463.

[83] On this matter, *see* the observations by D. Simon, *L'interprétation judiciaire des traités d'organisations internationales (Morphologie des conventions et fonction juridictionnelle)*, Paris, Pedone, 1981, 509.

Even where, for how they are drafted, they do not seem to be fully clear, precise, and unconditional[84] and thus require the enactment of further measures, the CJ held otherwise.

Direct effect is a dynamic concept, as are the legal constructs of jurisprudential origin, through which ever-developing social phenomena are intercepted and legally framed. Indeed, the fact that such legal constructs are connected to the exercise of individual, including fundamental, rights cannot lead to them being considered immutable in their nature and extent. From this perspective, there is no reason why direct effect should necessarily be limited to that which resulted from the *Van Gend & Loos* judgment. Indeed, the enforcement of EU law through the protection of rights could not be dissociated from the constant development and refinement of direct effect by the CJ. To the contrary, on the one hand, direct effect has evolved into a broader legal category than it was at the outset of the process of European legal integration. On the other, several elements have consolidated over the decades so that a constant fulfilment of direct effect's content has been carried out by the EU courts. In this framework, there are some milestones arising from the EU case law, considering its evolution up to the present day, and at the heart of an almost boundless literature, regarding the content and boundaries of direct effect. They are milestones but are not carved in stone since, although the jurisprudence is abundant, doubts persist in several respects.

3.1 EU sources of law and direct effect

The first milestone has already been examined in section 1 of this chapter: the conferral of rights is an essential element of direct effect in its subjective-substitutive dimension. This does not mean, however, that other dimensions of direct effect do not exist. In this connection, the process of objectification of direct effect deserves separate consideration, where both the direct granting of a right by the EU rule and the application of the latter in place of the national law are missing, giving rise to so-called objective-exclusionary direct effect. These two taxonomies, that is, subjective-substitutive direct effect and objective-exclusionary direct effect, have theoretical relevance to grasp the essence of broad, rather than narrow, direct effect, yet they are less decisive in terms of direct effect's practicability. The topic is addressed in Chapter IV.

The second milestone has already been explored in section 1 of this chapter and incidentally in section 5 of Chapter II, whereby it was observed that the doctrine of direct effect has two rationales: firstly, safeguarding the rights of individuals who invoke EU law before domestic authorities and, secondly, ensuring the fair enforcement of EU provisions, principles, and judgments in national legal orders. As for the nexus between these two dimensions, the doctrine of direct effect, while normally tied to the invocability of EU law by natural/legal persons, can rarely be relied on by a branch of the State against other public bodies[85] and less rarely by the State against private parties when at stake there are regulations. Such invocability by public authorities can occur also, under strict conditions, when at issue are other EU law sources which are addressed (also or exclusively) to natural/legal persons, that is, different than directives and those decisions that are addressed only at Member States.

[84] On the premises of clarity, precision, and unconditionality, *see* §§ 3.2 and 4 of this chapter.

[85] For three examples, *see* CJ, *Ufficio distrettuale delle imposte dirette di Fiorenzuola d'Arda ed altri v Comune di Carpaneto Piacentino*, joined cases 231/87 and 129/88, EU:C:1989:381; CJ, *Salzburger Flughafen GmbH v Umweltsenat*, C-244/12, EU:C:2013:203; CJ, *Autorità Garante della Concorrenza e del Mercato*, C-348/22, EU:C:2023:301.

The reference goes to primary law, written and unwritten, as well as to decisions addressed to natural/legal persons.[86] In other words, the matter of invocability of an EU right by a natural/legal person does not fully merge with that of direct effect. Especially when EU directly effective provisions are invoked by subjects other than private parties, the 'enforcing element' takes on decisive importance, while the 'rights component' remains in the background.

The third milestone: the EU rule need not be formally construed to apply to individuals for it to be considered directly effective. In *Van Gend & Loos* it was observed that rights arise not only where 'they are expressly granted by the Treaty, but also by reason of obligations which the Treaty imposes . . . upon the Member States'.[87] It is sufficient that the rule be addressed to the States and thereby impose upon them, either directly or indirectly, not necessarily in an express manner, one or more obligations to act[88] or to refrain from a certain action:[89] each obligation has, in fact, a counterpart[90] in the allocation of a right to natural persons and legal entities. Consequently, individuals can enforce this subjective legal position, arising directly from EU law,[91] in internal proceedings against public authorities (vertical direct effect). And, as will be mentioned later in this section and carefully illustrated in Chapter VI, (some) EU rules could be invoked and enforced possibly also against private parties (horizontal direct effect).[92]

This means that most of the precepts set out in the European Treaties,[93] today, can entail direct effects, provided they are clear, precise, and unconditional.[94] Exceptions, nevertheless, do exist, as in the case of provisions on common foreign and security policy (CFSP).[95] Direct effect is also excluded when EU rules are addressed at the EU institutions and bodies (rather than at the Member States),[96] or because they are inherently too vague in their content and scope, and their direct effect thus cannot be granted by the EU judges. In this regard, the EU case law is not at all clear about when an EU rule is to be considered devoid of direct effect due to its programmatic character. For instance, in *Zaera*, the CJ affirmed, with respect to Article 2 of the EEC Treaty, that the provision, due to its 'general terms', cannot 'impose legal obligations on Member States or confer rights on individuals'.[97] On the other hand, upon reading the *Savas* judgment,[98] one can infer that Article 12 of the Agreement between Turkey, on the one side, and the Community and Member States, on the other, to the extent to that it provides that the Contracting Parties 'agree to be guided by Articles 48, 49 and 50 of the Treaty establishing the Community for the purpose of progressively securing freedom of movement for workers between them', contains provisions which are not directly

[86] On this such issue, *see* § 5 of Chapter V, whereby a reference is also made to the recent ruling CJ, *Infraestruturas de Portugal SA*, C-66/22, EU:C:2023:1016, in which it seems that directives' inverse vertical direct effect has been surprisingly (and incomprehensibly) admitted for the first time by the CJ, in contrast with its previous consolidated case law.

[87] CJ, *NV Algemene Transport-en Expeditie Onderneming van Gend & Loos*, 26/62, EU:C:1963:1, 23.

[88] *See*, by way of example, on Article 101 TFEU, CJ, *Firma Alfons Lütticke GmbH*, 57/65, EU:C:1966:34.

[89] *See*, by way of example, on Article 34 TFEU, CJ, *Iannelli & Volpi SpA*, 74/76, EU:C:1977:51.

[90] The term '*parallélisme*' is employed by L. Azoulai, *Le rôle constitutionnel de la Cour de justice des Communautés européennes tel qu'il se dégage de sa jurisprudence* (2008) 1 *Revue trimestrielle de droit européen* 29, 34.

[91] *See*, amongst others, CJ, *IN.CO.GE.*, joined cases C-10–22/97, EU:C:1998:498, para. 21.

[92] *See*, amongst others, CJ, *Walrave*, 36/74, EU:C:1974:140.

[93] P. Craig, G. de Búrca, *EU Law*, 219.

[94] *See* further in this § and in § 3.3 of this chapter.

[95] On this matter, *see* later, in this §.

[96] *See*, amongst others, CJ, *Maurits Casteels*, C-379/09, EU:C:2011:131.

[97] CJ, *Fernando Roberto Giménez Zaera v Instituto nacional de la seguridad social y Tesorería General de la Seguridad Social*, 126/86, EU:C:1987:395, para. 11.

[98] CJ, *The Queen v Secretary of State for the Home Department, ex parte Abdulnasir Savas*, C-37/98, EU:C:2000:224.

effective since Article 12 identifies, in exhortatory and not peremptory terms, abstract purposes and 'essentially serves to set out a programme'.[99] Moreover, in respect to Article 71(1) of the EEC Treaty, now repealed, according to which 'Member States shall endeavour to avoid introducing within the Community any new exchange restrictions which affect the movement of capital and current payments connected with such movement, and making existing rules more restrictive', in fact, the CJ, in *Guerrino Casati*,[100] noted that, '[B]y using the term "shall endeavour", the wording of the provision departs noticeably from the more imperative forms of wording employed in other similar provisions concerning' free movement of goods, persons, and services.[101]

The case of Article 4(3) TEU is representative: the obligation of cooperation provided therein is operative *in concreto* only to the extent to which it is enforced in conjunction with other rules of EU law. On the other hand, direct effect was expressly denied in *Raffinerie Mediterranee* in relation to Article 174 of the EC Treaty, currently Article 191 TFEU, where it states that 'Community policy on the environment is to aim at a high level of protection and is based, *inter alia*, on the principle that "the polluter should pay" ', because this rule 'is confined to defining the general environmental objectives of the Community' and thus 'cannot be relied [upon] as such by individuals in order to exclude the application of national legislation'.[102] Although the EU judges do not explicitly say so, the lack of direct effect depends precisely on the programmatic nature of Article 174 of the EC Treaty.

Now, without entering into terminological and doctrinal disputes on the meaning of 'programmatic rules' and their debated justiciability,[103] as well as on their peculiarities compared to other non-directly effective provisions, it should be noted that, when an EU rule contains no obligation of result for the Member States or individuals, the function it performs is purely interpretive.[104] If, however, the rule contains an obligation of result, then the recognition of its direct effect by the CJ is possible; in this case, the result will be mediated by the joined application of the rule with another provision of EU law. Proof of this is the EU case law on the combined application of the Charter with the directives, which relates to some 'rights' contained in the Charter and possibly also for the 'principles' enshrined therein.[105]

With respect to provisions of secondary law, the CJ has acknowledged that they can produce direct effect so long as they are binding.[106] For what concerns regulations—whose

[99] *Savas* (n 98), para. 41.

[100] CJ, *Casati*, 203/80, EU:C:1981:261.

[101] *Casati* (n 100), para. 19.

[102] CJ, *Raffinerie Mediterranee (ERG) SpA, Polimeri Europa SpA e Syndial SpA*, C-378/08, EU:C:2010:126, paras 45–46.

[103] *See, inter alia*, in Italian constitutional law, V. Crisafulli, *La Costituzione e le sue disposizioni di principio*, Milan, Giuffrè, 1952; R. Bin, *Atti normativi e norme programmatiche*, Milan, Giuffrè, 1988. Under EU law, *see* S. Amadeo, *Norme comunitarie, posizioni giuridiche soggettive e giudizi interni*, Milan, Giuffrè, 2002, 142–148; C. F. von Gerber, *Grundzüge eines Systems des deutschen Staatsrechts*, Leipzig, Nabu Press, 1865, 44–46; P. L. Verdú, *Curso de Derecho Político*, Vol. II, Madrid, Tecnos, 1977, 431–432; P. L. Murillo de la Cueva, *Normas programáticas, estatutos y autonomía comunitaria* (1984) 1 *Revista de Derecho Político* 7; P. Montalivet, *Les objectifs de valeur constitutionnelle*, in *Cahiers du Conseil Constitutionnel*, 20 June 2006, available at https://www.conseil-constitutionnel.fr/nouveaux-cahiers-du-conseil-constitutionnel/les-objectifs-de-valeur-constitutionnelle; L. Goldsmith, *A Charter of Rights, Freedoms and Principles* (2001) 38 *Common Market Law Review* 1201.

[104] An example is the application of Article 151 TFEU in CJ, *Sloman Neptun Schiffahrts AG*, joined cases C-72–73/91, EU:C:1993:97, paras 25–26.

[105] The reference goes to the distinction foreseen in Articles 51(1) and 52(5) of the Charter. On the potential implied in the Charter's principles, *see* § 5.5 of Chapter VI.

[106] On soft law instruments in judicial review and their effects, *see* R. Gordon, R. Moffatt, *EU Law in Judicial Review*, 2nd ed., Oxford, Oxford University Press, 2014, 21.

use by the EU institutions is by far the most frequent among acts of secondary law—,[107] these are generally directly effective because they can be immediately enforced within domestic legal orders.[108] Such recognition occurred, subject to a number of conditions, in the *Grad* case, for decisions,[109] and, on the basis of similar considerations, in the *Van Duyn* case, for directives.[110]

As to directives, a specific requirement must be fulfilled for them to be invoked by individuals and applied by the national authorities: the directive must have been implemented in a manner contrary to EU law and/or after the deadline for its incorporation in domestic legal systems, or not transposed *tout court*. Therefore, unlike regulations and decisions, directives generate direct effect only if and from the moment in which a breach has occurred, in their execution, on the part of the State, that is, if and only from the time in which the term for transposition has expired or if and only from the time in which they are implemented late or inconsistently within the internal legal order.[111] Prior to that time the obligation imposed by the directive on the States is that of standstill, whereby national authorities cannot adopt measures that would contrast with the directive's objectives.[112] After expiration of the time limit, instead, if the transposition has been correctly made, the internal legal provision(s) will apply.

Upstream, there lie the two main and peculiar[113] characteristics of directives, as acknowledged in Article 288(3) TFEU: *(i)* the act is not directly applicable and *(ii)* the act is addressed only at the States, which is why direct effect is precluded in horizontal relationships.[114] In other words, directives are 'indirect' sources[115] since they require the adoption of implementing measures by Member States, that are free to choose the most appropriate 'form and methods'.[116] Directives, thus, are both a sign of the dualist character of EU law and a symptom of their origins rooted in international law.[117] On the other hand, the distinction between regulations

[107] For a comparative quantitative account on regulations and directives, *see* R. Schütze, *European Union Law*, 81 and M. Ovádek, *Legislative Output of the European Union. An Automatically Updated Overview of the EU's Legislative Activity*, available at https://michalovadek.github.io/eulaw/.

[108] *See*, amongst early judgments, CJ, *Politi*, 43/71, EU:C:1971:122.

[109] CJ, *Franz Grad*, 9/70, EU:C:1970:78, para. 1 of the operative part.

[110] CJ, *Yvonne van Duyn*, 41/74, EU:C:1974:133, paras 2 of the operative part and 12. For an historical account, *see* M. Rasmussen, *How to Enforce European Law? A New History of the Battle over the Direct Effect of Directives 1958-1987* (2017) 23 *European Law Journal* 290 and, more recently, *see* W. Phelan, *Great Judgments of the European Court of Justice. Rethinking the Landmark Decisions of the Foundational Period*, Cambridge, Cambridge University Press, 2020, 152–170. *See* also S. Prechal, *Van Duyn and the Nature of Directives*, in P. Craig, R. Schütze (eds.), *Landmark Cases in EU Law*, Oxford, Hart, 2025, forthcoming.

[111] CJ, *El Dridi*, 28 April 2011, C-61/11 PPU, EU:C:2011:268, para. 46.

[112] *See*, amongst others, CJ, *Inter-Environnement Wallonie ASBL (Inter-Environnement Wallonie I)*, 129/96, EU:C:1997:628, paras 45–50.

[113] On the peculiar character of directives, *see*, *ex multis*, J. Boulouis, *Sur une catégorie nouvelle d'actes juridiques: 'les directives'*, in *Mélanges Eisenmann*, Paris, Pedone, 1975, 191–203, 192; R. Kovar, *Observations sur l'intensité normative des directives*, in R. Kovar, *Itinéraire d'un juriste européen*, Brussels, Bruylant, 2010, 141–154, 141–143; F. Capotorti, *Legal Problems of Directives, Regulations and their Implementation*, in S. Heinrich, Z. Jacques (eds.), *Making European Policies Work: The Implementation of Community Legislation in the Member States*, London, Sage, 1988, I, 151–168; D. Simon, *La directive européenne*, Paris, Pedone, 1997; S. Prechal, *Directives*, 13–40.

[114] *See* further this § and §§ 4 and 7 of this chapter, on direct applicability, and extensively Chapter VI, §§ 3–6, on directives' lack of horizontal direct effect.

[115] *See*, amongst others, CJ, *Commission v Belgium*, 102/79, EU:C:1980:120, paras 3–16 and CJ, *Government of Gibraltar v Council*, C-298/89, EU:C:1993:267, para. 16.

[116] Article 288(3) TFEU.

[117] As observed by R. Schütze, *European Union Law*, 58 and 169. On the 'indirect nature' of directives, *see* also N. Catalano, *La Comunità*, 59; D. Simon, *La directive*, 58, and D. Gallo, *La* vexata *quaestio dell'efficacia interna delle direttive: l'insostenibile leggerezza del divieto di effetti diretti orizzontali*, in E. Moavero Milanesi, G. Piccirilli (eds.), *Attuare il diritto dell'Unione europea in Italia. Un bilancio a 5 anni dall'entrata in vigore della legge n. 234 del 2012*, Bari, Cacucci, 2018, 17–36, 17. For an early historical contextualization of directives, *see* H. P. Ipsen, *Richtlinien-Ergebnisse*, in W. Hallstein, H. J. Schlochauer (eds.), *Zur Integration Europas. Festschrift für Carl*

and directives is ever more blurred due to the increasing use of self-executing directives, that is, acts which are more precise and detailed than 'standard' directives.[118] Indeed, such trend renders directives different from how they were originally designed pursuant to Article 288 TFEU, according to which the choice of form and methods belongs to national authorities and thus effects on individuals could only arise from the implementing measures.

Against this background, from *Van Duyn* onwards,[119] the CJ has clarified that the lack of direct applicability of a directive[120] does not preclude its direct effect.[121] As a matter of fact, direct effect shall be attributed to directives due to their binding legal force and their inclusion in the scope of the preliminary reference procedure.[122] If rights enshrined therein were never enforceable via their invocability by private parties, national authorities could simply ignore the directives.[123] Indeed, where an unimplemented directive could not be relied on by individuals, the States would have the power to impair its effectiveness by preventing natural and legal persons from exercising the rights protected under EU law. Furthermore, in *Ratti* the CJ built its reasoning on an additional argument, which can be traced back to the so-called estoppel doctrine: without directives' direct effect, national authorities would be induced to not implement the directives, or to implement them incorrectly, and could paradoxically benefit from their nonfulfillment.[124] As explained by AG Slynn in *Marshall I*, a directive 'comes into play *only* to enable rights to be claimed by individuals against the State in default' which 'cannot rely on its own failure to confer those rights', with the result that citizens 'can assert them against the State either as a sword or as a shield'.[125]

One could criticize the soundness of the estoppel argument observing that it presupposes that the States must have failed in their duty to comply with EU law before the deadline for the implementation of the directive, even though a distinctive feature of directives is precisely that there is no failure before such date. There exists, however, a counterargument: directives have legal effects as soon as they enter into force, that is, even during the transition period. Actually, as has already been recalled in this section, during that period domestic authorities, pursuant to Article 4(3) TEU, 'must refrain from taking any measures liable seriously to compromise the result prescribed by the directive'.[126] Another objection against the estoppel principle is that only the legislator, and less frequently the executive, has the primary responsibility to transpose the directive, which means that, in practice, other bodies, including decentralized municipalities, end up being responsible for something that cannot be ascribed to them. The CJ has repeatedly, and in an agreeable way, responded to this argument, however, by observing that the obligations arising under the provisions contained in

Friedrich Ophüls aus Anlass seines siebzigsten Geburtstages, Karlsruhe, Verlag CF Müller, 1965, 67–84, and S. Prechal, *Directives*, 1–5.

[118] For a detailed discussion, *see* S. Prechal, *Directives*, 73–91.

[119] *van Duyn* (n 110), para. 12.

[120] CJ, *Criminal proceedings against Tullio Ratti*, 148/78, EU:C:1979:110. On the coincidence, *de facto*, between direct effect and direct applicability *see* § 7 of this chapter.

[121] *See* the observations by P. Pescatore, *L'effet des directives communautaires—une tentative de démythification*, in *Recueil Dalloz-Sirey*, XXV, 1980, 171–176, and H. G. Schermers, *No Direct Effect for Directives* (1997) 3 *European Public Law* 527.

[122] *van Duyn* (n 110), para. 12.

[123] *van Duyn* (n 110) para. 12.

[124] See *Ratti* (120), para. 22. *See*, amongst others, CJ, *Ursula Becker*, 8/81, EU:C:1982:7.

[125] Opinion of AG Slynn of 18 September 1985, *M. H. Marshall*, 152/84, EU:C:1985:345, 734 (italics added). On pros and cons of directives' direct effect, *see* S. Prechal, *Directives*, 216–226 and 253–270.

[126] *Commission v Belgium* (n 115), para. 62 and *Inter-Environnement Wallonie I* (n 112), para. 45 and CJ, *Stichting Zuid-HollandseMilieufederatie*, C-138/05, EU:2006:577, para. 42.

the directives 'are binding upon all the authorities of the Member States'.[127] The recognition of direct effect to directives, therefore, does not lead *per se* to legal uncertainty[128] and does not upset the system of EU acts as established in Article 288 TFEU.[129]

A last observation relates to directives when they are harmonization acts within the meaning of Articles 114 or 115 TFEU. In the fields covered by these acts, it is only the rules contained therein that shall apply rather than the internal market/competition/sectorial rules contained in the Treaties, with the consequence that, where they have direct effect, the individual will have to invoke the directive, rather than the Treaties, as the CJ explained in *Promoimpresa*, whereby Directive 2006/123/EC was applied rather than Article 49 TFEU.[130]

Apropos of decisions, it shall be recalled that EU institutions, over the decades, have regularly adopted *sui generis* non-binding decisions not corresponding to the type indicated by Article 288(4) TFEU, such as organizational and operational decisions. As they are not binding legal acts, they are never directly effective.[131] Secondly, as is the case for all secondary legislation, decisions are legislative acts when EU law associates them with a legislative procedure, as set forth in Article 289(3) TFEU and affirmed in the *Slovakia and Hungary v Council* judgment.[132] As a matter of fact, such association is explicitly made only in Article 311 TFEU, which entrusts the Council, acting 'in accordance with a special legislative procedure . . . unanimously and after consulting the European Parliament', with the power to enact a 'decision laying down the provisions relating to the system of own resources of the Union'.[133] Of course, not all legislative decisions are directly effective. In fact, whether they are or not depends on the features of their provisions.

It is well-known that there are two different categories of binding decisions, as can be easily inferred from Article 288(4) TFEU,[134] whereby they are defined in these terms: 'A decision shall be binding in its entirety. A decision which specifies those to whom it is addressed shall be binding only on them.' The first group is represented by specifically addressed decisions, which are binding only on their addressees, be they natural/legal entities and/or Member States.[135] As for decisions addressed to private parties, they are normally adopted, outside a legislative procedure, by the Commission, especially (but not only, of course) under competition rules[136] and can be regarded as individual administrative acts aimed at executing 'a

[127] CJ, *Fratelli Costanzo*, 103/88, EU:C:1989:256, paras 30–31.

[128] Amongst those who highlight the weak legal discourse put forward by the CJ to admit directives' direct effect, *see* S. Weatherill, *Cases and Materials on EU Law*, Oxford, Oxford University Press, 2014, 112; R. Schütze, *European Constitutional Law*, Cambridge, Cambridge University Press, 2016, 97; D. Chalmers, G. Davies, G. Monti, *European Union*, 307–310. On the political rationale implied in *van Duyn*'s reasoning, *see* W. Phelan, *Great Judgments*, 158.

[129] Yet, the direct effect of directives has been opposed by several governments, such as the UK in its observations rendered in the *van Duyn* case, as well as by several jurisdictions in the seventies, as remarked by M. Rasmussen, *How to Enforce*, 295. Amongst national documents, *see Report Select Committee on the European Communities, House of Lords*, February 1975; amongst national judgments, *see Conseil d'Etat, Assemblée du 22 décembre 1978*, 11604, *Cohn Bendit*. For an historical account, from the viewpoint of Member States, *see* F. Costamagna, *Diritti fondamentali e rapporti tra privati nell'ordinamento dell'Unione europea*, Turin, Giappichelli, 2022, 22–27.

[130] CJ, *Promoimpresa*, joined cases C-458/14 and C-67/15, EU:C:2016:558. On the saga of Italian seaside concessions, *see* especially § 11 of Chapter V.

[131] F. Cherubini, *Decisions under the Law of European Union: 'You May Be Six People, but I Love You'* (2022) 41 *Yearbook of European Law* 117–161, 119.

[132] CJ, *Slovak Republic and Hungary v Council of the European Union*, joined cases C-643/15 and C-647/15, EU:C:2017:631, paras 57–61 and 146.

[133] F. Cherubini, *Decisions*, 125.

[134] For an account, *see* R. Schütze, *European Union Law*, 167–169 and extensively F. Cherubini, *Decisions*, 139–159.

[135] *See*, amongst others, CJ, *Mensch und Natur AG v Freistaat Bayern*, C-327/09, EU:C:2011:249.

[136] As written by F. Cherubini, *Decisions*, 142.

Union norm by applying it to an individual situation'.[137] In the case of decisions addressed at Member States, which are generally adopted by the Council or the Commission, while they seem to overlap, in their content, with directives, a distinction can be made since the latter are not, unlike the former, entirely binding. Furthermore, while they can be legislative or non-legislative—such as delegated decisions—when they are addressed at all Member States, they are always non-legislative when addressed at individual Member States.

The second group of decisions encompasses those not addressed at specific subjects.[138] They normally do not follow a legislative procedure,[139] yet they are often substantially legislative in their content and similar to regulations,[140] so that the CJ has defined them as 'regulatory act[s]' within the meaning of Article 263(4) TFEU.[141] This is highlighted by several scholars, who hold that they should be treated as legislative acts.[142]

As to the matter of direct effect, there are no express indications in EU primary law. With regard to decisions addressed at States, as acknowledged in the previously mentioned *Grad* case regarding a Council Decision on the harmonization of certain provisions affecting competition in the transport sector[143] and confirmed in the subsequent case law concerning decisions addressed at all Member States[144] or at (only) some of them,[145] they can create direct effect, but only in vertical relationships.[146] In fact, in *Grad* it has been stated that the decision 'to exclude in principle the possibility that persons affected may invoke the obligation imposed by a decision' would conflict with the binding effect conferred by Article 288 TFEU.[147] Indeed, if an act is binding in its entirety, it is likely that it may be directly enforced in national legal orders, that is, directly applicable. This is often, but not always, the case: an act, while binding in its entirety, could be deprived of direct applicability due to the inability of its own norms to autonomously govern the case. Evidence that the two concepts of direct applicability and 'binding in entirety' are different can be found in Article 288(2) TFEU, whereby it is foreseen that a regulation shall be 'binding in its entirety *and* directly applicable in all Member States'. Therefore, decisions, when they are acts falling under the scope of Article 288(4) TFEU, that is, binding in their entirety, are normally directly applicable, and thus, as explained later in this section and in section 8, directly effective, provided that their norms have a number of characteristics enabling them to be self-executing and produce direct effects.

137 R. Schütze, *Direct Effects and Indirect Effects of Union Law*, in R. Schütze, T. Tridimas (eds.), *Oxford Principles of European Union Law: The European Union Legal Order: Volume I*, Oxford, Oxford University Press, 2018, 265–299, 276.

138 *See* extensively J. Bast, *Grundbegriffe der Handlungsformen der EU: entwickelt am Beschluss als praxisgenerierter Handlungsform des Unions- und Gemeinschaftsrechts*, Heidelberg, Springer, 2006.

139 With few exceptions, as demonstrated by F. Cherubini, *Decisions*, 148, with regard to the association of overseas countries.

140 *See*, amongst others, CJ, 6 October 2015, *Maximillian Schrems*, C-362/14, EU:C:2015:650. R. Schütze, *European Union Law*, 156, wrote that those decisions have been increasingly employed over the decades in lieu of regulations.

141 *See*, amongst others, GC, 25 October 2011, *Microban International Ltd and Microban (Europe) Ltd*, T-262/10, EU:T:2011:623, para. 25.

142 According to M. Bobek, *The Effects*, 164, the decisions indicated in the text 'amount to a legislative act in all but name.'

143 *Grad* (n 109), para. 9.

144 *See* CJ, *Transports Lesage & Cie SA v Hauptzollamt Freiburg*, 20/70, EU:C:1970:84 and CJ, *Erich Haselhorst v Finanzamt Düsseldorf-Altstadt*, 23/70, EU:C:1970:85, both regarding the very same decision scrutinized in *Grad*. *See* also CJ, 10 November 1992, *Hansa Fleisch Ernst Mundt GmbH & Co. KG*. C-156/91, EU:C:1992:423.

145 *See*, amongst others, CJ, *Foselev Sud-Ouest SARL*, C-18/08, EU:C:2008:647, paras 11-19, whereby the CJ, albeit not asserting the direct effect of a decision addressed at France, made an assessment on clarity, precision, and above all unconditionality.

146 On this aspect, *see* § 7 of Chapter VI.

147 *Grad* (n 109), para. 5.

With respect to decisions addressed at natural and legal persons, there seems to be no doubt regarding their possible direct effect due to their binding effect and the self-sufficiency of their norms. In this case, thus, such decisions are *naturally* directly effective in horizontal relationships, unless they are too vague to be directly enforced in domestic legal orders. Moreover, while a decision that is addressed to a private party will only be binding on its addressee, it could entail (horizontal) direct effect also vis-à-vis other private parties subject to a number of conditions.[148]

As regards non-addressed decisions, the matter of direct effect is controversial since there is no case law on this issue and most of the scholarship has not directly examined it. In this respect, it could be asserted that, the act being binding in its entirety and legislative in substantive terms, the provisions contained therein can have direct effect, as occurs in relation to regulations, that is, acts binding in their entirety and of general application.[149]

Regarding the secondary legal acts enacted under the former third pillar (police and judicial cooperation in criminal matters) and the CFSP,[150] direct effect is precluded. This was expressly provided for, prior to the entry into force of the Treaty of Lisbon, in the former Article 34(2) TEU, on the decisions and the framework decisions. To date, the exclusion of direct effect with regard to the decisions and framework decisions continues to be the rule since Article 9 of Protocol No. 36 on transitional provisions requires that '[t]he legal effects of the acts of the institutions, bodies, offices and agencies of the Union adopted on the basis of the Treaty on European Union prior to the entry into force of the Treaty of Lisbon shall be preserved until those acts are repealed, annulled or amended in implementation of the Treaties'. This formula certainly 'covers' also the lack of direct effect.

As for general principles of EU law,[151] it seems that the express recognition of direct effect, or the reliance on the test for its assessment,[152] has been undertaken by the CJ always in conjunction with written EU law sources, be they primary or secondary law. The reason lies in the very fact that principles are unwritten sources of law, that is, sources not easily detectable and identifiable in their contents[153] and that, in the early case law, disapplication was not always deemed as an immediate outcome stemming from direct effect.[154] The EU judges have recognized direct effect to some general principles of EU law that relate to the protection of fundamental rights,[155] to some general principles of EU law not related to fundamental

[148] *See* § 7 of Chapter VI.

[149] *See* § 7 of Chapter VI.

[150] On CFSP's acts, *see* extensively R. Schütze, *European Union Law*, 87 and R. Schütze, *Direct Effects*, 265–299.

[151] For a ground-breaking categorization of general principles of EU law, *see* T. Tridimas, *The General Principles*, 1–58. For a different classification, with a focus on fundamental rights, *see* C. Amalfitano, *General Principles of EU Law and the Protection of Fundamental Rights*, Cheltenham, Edward Elgar, 2018, 110–146.

[152] For a specific account on the test, *see* § 4 of this chapter.

[153] There is no reference to direct effect, e.g. in neither CJ, *Internationale Handelsgesellschaft mbH*, 11/70, EU:C:1970:114, nor in CJ, *J. Nold, Kohlen- und Baustoffgroßhandlung*, 4/73, EU:C:1974:51.

[154] This issue is examined in § 3.3 of this chapter and especially in § 1 of Chapter V.

[155] Such recognition was rarely asserted explicitly in respect to vertical relationships and outside the realm of the Charter. An example is *Johnston* (n 48), paras 18–19 and 58–59, where the requirement of judicial control was deemed the source for disapplying a national law not providing an effective remedy to persons wronged by sex discrimination since, according to the Court, such requirement, stipulated by Article 2(1) of Council Directive No. 76/207/EEC of 9 February 1976 on the implementation of the principle of equal treatment for men and women (OJ L 39, 14.2.1976, 40), 'reflects a general principle of law' (para. 18). In the same vein, *see* also CJ, *Heylens*, 222/86, EU:C:1987:442, para. 14. Direct effect was attributed to the general principle of non-discrimination on the basis of age, in combination with EU secondary law, in a horizontal relationship, for instance, in CJ, *Werner Mangold*, C-144/04, EU:C:2005:709, para. 77, where at stake were also Council Directive 1999/70/EC of 28 June 1999 concerning the framework agreement on fixed-term work concluded by ETUC, UNICE and CEEP (OJ L 175, 10.7.1999, 43), and Council Directive 2000/78/EC of 27 November 2000 establishing a general framework for equal treatment in employment and occupation (OJ L 303, 2.12.2000, 16). *See* extensively §§ 5.3–5.5 of Chapter VI for the case law relating to (general) principles of EU law—most notably, the principle of non-discrimination (on

rights,[156] and to some provisions of the Charter,[157] most notably to Articles 21, 31(2), 47, and 50.[158,159]

As interestingly observed by AG Trstenjak in her opinion in *Dominguez*, direct effect can be granted also to provisions on fundamental rights which are worded 'in a legally abstract fashion in order to take account of political and social changes', as is particularly clear in the case of social rights since the level of their protection is contingent 'upon *de facto* economic possibilities of the State'.[160] For example, in *Association de médiation sociale* it was observed that the principle of non-discrimination based on age, enshrined in Article 21(1) of the Charter, at the heart (not of the *Association de médiation sociale* ruling, which mainly concerned Article 27 of the Charter, but rather) of *Kücükdeveci*,[161] 'is sufficient in itself to confer on individuals an individual right which they may invoke as such'.[162] This means that such provision, like others in the Charter, including Article 50, in *Åkerberg Fransson*,[163] and Article 47, in *État luxembourgeois*[164] or *K.L.*,[165] amongst recent judgments, is directly effective, even if lacking, in the reasoning of the CJ, a specific assessment on the premises of direct effect and even if it is explicitly affirmed that directives 'give concrete expression' to the Charter, for instance in respect to Article 21.[166] In any case, on more than one occasion the CJ has decided to not choose, abstaining from clarifying whether the provisions of the Charter can create, by themselves or in conjunction with other EU legal sources, direct effect. In some other cases, the CJ only implicitly granted direct effect, as occurred in *NE*, whereby Article 20 of Directive 2014/67 concerning posted workers was deemed to be directly effective immediately after having observed that such provision 'merely reiterates'

grounds of sex, age, and religion), the right to an effective remedy and to a fair trial, and the right to paid annual leave—, the Charter, and horizontal relationships.

[156] *See*, e.g. CJ, *NE*, C-205/20, EU:C:2022:168, para. 57, where the principle of proportionality of penalties has been applied in combination with Article 20 of Directive 2014/67/EU of the European Parliament and of the Council of 15 May 2014 on the enforcement of Directive 96/71/EC concerning the posting of workers in the framework of the provision of services and amending Regulation (EU) No. 1024/2012 on administrative cooperation through the Internal Market Information System ('the IMI Regulation') (OJ L 159, 28.5.2014, 11).

[157] On the relationship between general principles of EU law and the Charter, *see* extensively C. Amalfitano, *Il diritto non scritto nell'accertamento dei diritti fondamentali dopo la riforma di Lisbona* (2016) 1 *Il diritto dell'Unione europea* 21, 22–23; C. Amalfitano, *General Principles*, 96–110. *See* also T. Tridimas, *The General Principles*, 298–369; D. Sarmiento, *Who's Afraid of the Charter? The Court of Justice, National Courts and the New Framework of Fundamental Rights Protection in Europe* (2013) 50 *Common Market Law Review* 1267, 1269–1277; T. Tridimas, *Fundamental Rights, General Principles of EU Law, and the Charter* (2014) 16 *Cambridge Yearbook of European Legal Studies* 361–392; E. Hancox, *The Relationship between the Charter and General Principles: Looking Back and Looking Forward* (2022) 24 *Cambridge Yearbook of European Legal Studies* 233–257. According to M. Dougan, *In Defence of* Mangold?, in A. Arnull, C. Barnard, M. Dougan, E. Spaventa (eds.), *A Constitutional Order of States—Essays in Honour of Alan Dashwood*, Oxford, Oxford University Press, 2010, 219–244, 223, not every Charter's provision codifies a general principle of EU law; *contra*, *see* E. Spaventa, *The Horizontal Application of Fundamental Rights as General Principles of Union Law*, in A. Arnull, C. Barnard, M. Dougan, E. Spaventa (eds.), *A Constitutional Order*, 199–218, 218.

[158] On the direct effect of these provisions, *see* further in this § and in §§ 5.3–5.5 of Chapter VI.

[159] On the increased importance of the Charter in the EU case law, *see* G. de Búrca, *After the EU Charter of Fundamental Rights: The Court of Justice as a Human Rights Adjudicator?* (2013) 20 *Maastricht Journal of European and Comparative Law* 168 and, from the perspective of the national judiciaries, *see* the contributions in L. Bougorgue-Larsen (ed.), *La Charte des droits fondamentaux saisie par les juges en Europe*, Paris, Pedone, 2017, and A. Adinolfi, *La rilevanza della Carta dei diritti fondamentali nella giurisprudenza interna: qualche riflessione per un tentativo di ricostruzione sistematica* (2018) 1 *Studi sull'integrazione europea* 29.

[160] *See* the opinion of AG Trstenjak of 8 September 2011, *Dominguez*, EU:C:2011:559, para. 78.

[161] CJ, *Seda Kücükdeveci*, C-555/07, EU:C:2010:21.

[162] *Association de médiation sociale* (n 6), para. 47.

[163] CJ, *Åklagaren v Hans Åkerberg Fransson*, C-617/10, EU:C:2013:105.

[164] CJ, *État luxembourgeois v B and État luxembourgeois v B and A.*, joined cases C-245–246/19, EU:C:2020:795.

[165] CJ, *État luxembourgeois v B and État luxembourgeois* (n 164).

[166] CJ, *K.L.*, C-715/20, EU:C:2024:139, para. 80.

Article 49(3) of the Charter, according to which the severity of penalties must not be disproportionate to the offence and, thus, is 'mandatory in nature'.[167] Finally, in other cases the CJ has expressly rejected direct effect.[168]

In this framework, a problem (still) on the table is that of the internal effect of the norms of the Charter containing 'principles', which, on the basis of its Article 51(1), must be 'observed' and 'promoted', rather than 'respected' as it envisaged for 'rights'. Moreover, Article 52(5) states that the provisions of the Charter which contain 'principles' 'may be implemented . . . by acts of Member States when they are implementing Union law' and 'shall be judicially cognisable only in the interpretation of such acts and in the ruling on their legality'.[169,170] As affirmed by AG Cruz Villalón in *Association de médiation sociale*,[171] the reference to 'principles', as opposed to rights, served 'not only to facilitate a broad consensus amongst States', but it also ensures 'the practical implementation of the provisions of the Charter',[172] considering the experience of some Member States, where a similar distinction to the one foreseen in the Charter 'had allowed full justiciability of "rights" and a reduced, or in some cases no, justiciability of "principles"'.[173] Most notably, at the origins of Article 52(5) of the Charter[174] is the fear on the part of some States that the 'recognition of particular economic and social

[167] *NE* (n 156), para. 31.

[168] *See*, e.g., *Association de médiation sociale* (n 6), para. 47, and some of the rulings on horizontal disputes examined in §§ 5.4–5.5 of Chapter VI. On the Charter and its internal effect, *see* the interesting reflections by L. S. Rossi, *'Same Legal Value as the Treaties'? Rank, Primacy, and Direct Effects of the EU Charter of Fundamental Rights* (2017) 18 *German Law Journal* 771.

[169] On Article 51, *see* M. Borowsky, *Artikel 51—Anwendungsbereich*, in J. Meyer (ed.), *Charta der Grundrechte der Europäischen Union*, Baden-Baden, Nomos, 2014, 743–760; F. Fontanelli, *National Measures and the Application of the EU Charter of Fundamental Rights—Does curia.eu Know iura.eu?* (2014) 14 *Human Rights Law Review* 231; C. Schubert, *Art 51 GRC*, in M. Franzen, I. Gallner, H Oetker (eds.), *Kommentar zum europäischen Arbeitsrecht*, 4th ed., Munich, Beck, 2024; N. Lazzerini, *La Carta dei diritti fondamentali dell'Unione europea. I limiti di applicazione*, Milan, Franco Angeli, 2018; T. Lock, *Article 51 CFR*, in M. Kellerbauer, M. Klamert, J. Tomkin (eds.), *The EU Treaties*, 2241–2246; S. Iglesias Sanchez, *Article 51: The Scope of Application of the Charter*, in M. Bobek, J. Adams-Prassl (eds.), *The EU Charter*, 401–420; G. Biagioni, *The EU Charter of Fundamental Rights: in bad need of instructions for use?*, in A. M. Mancaleoni, E. Poillot (eds.), *National Judges and the Case Law of the Court of Justice of the European Union*, Rome, Roma Tre Press, 2021, 165–182.

[170] In the Explanations relating to the Charter (OJ 2007 C 303/17, 32), it is written that 'principles may be implemented through legislative or executive acts (adopted by the Union in accordance with its powers, and by the Member States only when they implement Union law); accordingly, they become significant for the Courts only when such acts are interpreted or reviewed'. On the scope and limits of the Explanations, *see* J. Ziller, *Le fabuleux destin des* Explications *relative à la Charte des droits fondamentaux*, in G. Cohen Jonathan, V. Constantinesco, V. Michel (eds.), *Chemins d'Europe—Mélanges en l'honneur de Jean Paul Jacqué*, Paris, Pedone, 2010, 765–781

[171] Opinion of AG Cruz Villalón of 18 July 2013, *Association de médiation sociale*, EU:C:2013:491.

[172] Opinion of AG Cruz Villalón (n 171), para. 47.

[173] Opinion of AG Cruz Villalón (n 171), para. 49.

[174] On the rationale of the distinction implied in Article 52(5), *see* R. Schütze, *Three 'Bills of Rights' for the European Union* (2011) 30 *Yearbook of European Law* 131–158, 146–147; E. Dubout, *Principes, droits et devoirs dans la Charte des droits fondamentaux de l'Union européenne* (2014) 50 *Revue trimestrielle de droit européen* 409; D. Guðmundsdóttir, *A Renewed Emphasis on the Charter's Distinction between Rights and Principles: Is a Doctrine of Judicial Restraint More Appropriate?* (2015) 52 *Common Market Law Review* 685; J. Krommendijk, *Principled Silence or Mere Silence on Principles? The Role of the EU Charter's Principles in the Case Law of the Court of Justice* (2015) 11 *European Constitutional Law Review* 321; M. Condinanzi, *Diritti, principi e principi generali nell'ordinamento giuridico dell'Unione europea*, in L. D'Andrea, G. Moschella, A. Ruggeri, A. Saitta (eds.), *La Carta dei diritti dell'Unione europea e le altre Carte (ascendenze culturali e mutue implicazioni)*, Turin, Giappichelli, 2016, 71–85; T. Lock, *Article 52*, in M. Kellerbauer, M. Klamert, J. Tomkin (eds.), *The EU Treaties*, 2248–2260; S. Peers, S. Prechal, *Article 52—Scope of Guaranteed Rights*, in S. Peers, T. Hervey, J. Kenner, A. Ward (eds.), *The EU Charter*, 1611–1674; S. Douglas-Scott, *Fundamental Rights and the Union*, in R. Schütze, T. Tridimas (eds.), *Oxford Principles*, 383–422, 396–397; F. Ferraro, N. Lazzerini, *Art. 52. Portata e interpretazione dei diritti e dei principi*, in R. Mastroianni, O. Pollicino, S. Allegrezza, F. Pappalardo, O. Razzolini (eds.), *Carta*, 1062–1083; T. Lock, *Rights and Principles in the EU Charter of Fundamental Rights* (2019) 56 *Common Market Law Review* 1201; R. Palladino, *Diritti, principi ed effetto diretto orizzontale delle disposizioni (in materia sociale) della Carta dei diritti fondamentali dell'Unione europea* (2019) 1 *Il Diritto dell'Unione europea* 175; M. Brkan, S. Imamovic, *Article 52: Twenty-Eight Shades of Interpretation?*, in M. Bobek, J. Adams-Prassl (eds.), *The EU Charter*, 401–420.

rights would result in the judicialization of public policy, particularly in areas of significant budgetary importance'.[175] For sure,[176] creating justiciable standards[177] related to the enforcement of social rights[178] was a cause of concern for several Member States[179] since such rights were and still are deemed different in nature from civil and political rights due to a number of characteristics. First, they are *normally*[180] attached to positive, rather than negative, obligations imposed upon public authorities and attached to decisions on the allocation of State resources. Secondly, their indeterminate nature and complex regulation presupposes the take-up of political choices and shall not be left to judicial review and democratically unaccountable judges.

Against this background, it is well understood by EU law scholars that at the core of the matter of justiciability lies the controversial issue of (lack of) direct effect of 'principles'. The pivotal question is whether the Charter's 'principles' governing social rights are sufficiently

[175] Opinion of AG Cruz Villalón, *Association de médiation sociale* (n 171), para. 49.

[176] As known, there are many general legal theory and political science studies on the justiciability of social rights and on the need to include the issue of social rights' legal force in the broader discourse on the availability of State resources, the exercise of legislative power, and the limits underpinning the democratic legitimacy of constitutional judicial review. *See*, *inter alia*, the pivotal works by M. S. Giannini, *Stato Sociale: una nozione inutile* (1977) 42 *Il Politico* 205; R. Plant, *Modern Political Thought*, Oxford, Basil Blackwell, 1991, 268–270; J. Rawls, *Political Liberalism*, New York, Columbia University Press, 1993, 229–230 and 267; L. Ferrajoli, *Diritti fondamentali. Un dibattito teorico*, Rome-Bari, Laterza, 2001, 5–33; R. Alexy, *A Theory of Constitutional Rights* (translated by Julian Rivers), Oxford, Oxford University Press, 2002, 334–348; J. Waldron, *The Core Case against Judicial Review* (2006) 115 *Yale Law Journal* 1346, 1352–1353; S. Fredman, *Human Rights Transformed. Positive Rights and Positive Duties*, Oxford, Oxford University Press, 2008; D. M. Davis, *Socio-Economic Rights*, in M. Rosenfeld, A. Sajó (eds.), *The Oxford Handbook of Comparative Constitutional Law*, Oxford, Oxford University Press, 2012, 1020–1035. For an EU law perspective, *see* O. Gerstenberg, *The Justiciability of Socio-economic Rights, European Solidarity, and the Role of the Court of Justice of the EU* (2014) 33 *Yearbook of European Law* 245–276. Among the works on political economy, *see* A. Sen, *Resources, Values and Development*, Cambridge (Mass.), Harvard University Press, 1984, 307–325, and A. Sen, *Development as Freedom*, New York, Oxford University Press, 1999, 111–146 and 282–299.

[177] On the limited degree of justiciability relating to principles and social rights, *see* the opinion of AG Cruz Villalón, *Association de médiation sociale* (n 171), paras 50–55 and, in the literature, C. Hilson, *Rights and Principles in EU Law: A Distinction without Foundation?* (2008) 15 *Maastricht Journal of European and Comparative Law* 193, 194–199; T. Lock, *Rights*, 1214–1218; F. Ferraro, N. Lazzerini. S. Peers, S. Prechal, *Article 52*, 1611–1674, 1662, regard 'principles' as justiciable, although their justiciability is not as full as that of 'rights'; similarly, *see* S. Prechal, *Rights v. Principles, or How to Remove Fundamental Rights from the Jurisdiction of the Courts*, in J. De Zwaan, F. A. Nelissen, J. H. Jans, S. Blockmans (eds.), *The European Union: An Ongoing Process of Integration*, The Hague, TMC Asser Press, 2004, 177–184. Arguing that 'principles' containing social rights should not be treated differently than 'rights', *see* N. Jääskinen, *Fundamental Social Rights in the Charter—Are They Rights? Are They Fundamental?*, in S. Peers, T. Hervey, J. Kenner, A. Ward (eds.), *The EU Charter*, 1885–1870.

[178] Generally, on social rights and the Charter, *see*, in addition to the references in footnotes 176–177 above, Editorial comments, *The EU Charter of Fundamental Rights still under discussion* (2001) 1 *Common Market Law Review* 1, 3; L. Goldsmith, *A Charter*; J. C. Hunt, *Fair and Just Working Conditions*, in T. Hervey, J. Kenner (eds.), *Economic and Social Rights under the EU Charter of Fundamental Rights. A Legal Perspective*, Oxford, Hart, 2003, 45–65; E. Paciotti, *Libertà—Solidarietà*, in L. S. Rossi (eds.), *Carta dei diritti fondamentali e Costituzione dell'Unione europea*, Milan, Giuffrè, 2002, 95–108,; S. O'Leary, *Solidarity and Citizenship Rights in the Charter of Fundamental Rights of the European Union*, in G. de Búrca (ed.), *EU Law and the Welfare State: In Search of Solidarity*, Oxford, Oxford University Press, 2005, 39–88, 50–54; S. Robin-Olivier, *La contribution de la Charte des droits fondamentaux à la protection des droits sociaux dans l'Union européenne: un premier bilan après Lisbonne* (2013) 1 *Journal européen des droits de l'homme* 109; A.-O. Cozzi, *Diritti e principi sociali nella Carta dei diritti fondamentali dell'Unione Europea—Profili costituzionali*, Naples, Jovene, 2017; G. Pino, *Il costituzionalismo dei diritti*, Bologna, Il Mulino, 2017, 165–196; C. Barnard, *Are Social 'Rights' Rights?* (2020) 11 *European Labour Law Journal* 351; M. Manfredi, *Enhancing Economic and Social Rights within the Internal Market through Recognition of the Horizontal Effects of the European Charter of Fundamental Rights* (2021) 6 *European Papers* 293.

[179] As observed by E. Frantziou, *The Horizontal Effect of Fundamental Rights in the European Union*, Oxford, Oxford University Press, 2019, 89.

[180] On this point, *see*, amongst others, G. Braibant, *La Charte des droits fondamentaux de l'Union européenne*, Paris, Éditions du Seuil, 2001, 44–46. 'Normally', as written in the text, not *always* since, while there are some social rights which entail only negative obligations, like the right to strike, some civil and political rights, such as the right to vote, presuppose the fulfillment of a number of positive obligations by the State, as remarked by T. Lock, *Rights*, 1210.

'accomplished', in legal terms, to entail direct effects. The easiest answer is that they are devoid of such effect since they would appear to be non-self-sufficient provisions, thus incapable of autonomously governing the case before the court: as written in the Explanations to the Charter, 'principles' do not 'give rise to direct claims for positive action'. However, if, on the one hand, they cannot be 'directly relied on before the courts', on the other, they are 'endowed with normative force at the constitutional level allowing the review of acts, primarily those of a legislative nature'.[181] Hence, 'principles' create 'one-sided non-relational'[182] general duties on public authorities, which are compelled to make them enforceable 'in the cases and under the conditions provided for by Union law and national laws and practices', that is, through additional implementing acts aimed at determining 'the objective content' and 'certain outcomes' stemming from the 'principles'.[183] The issue of direct effect, in this sense, necessarily passes through the joint application of the 'principles', as non-autonomous legal sources,[184] with other rules of EU law, primarily directives. And such an application tends to intervene, as demonstrated by the CJ in its jurisprudence, when disputes are between private parties, which is why the question related to the operability and justiciability of the 'principles' is explored in sections 5.3–5.5 of Chapter VI. Moreover, the joint application of the Charter with directives also frequently occurs in the case law on 'rights' enshrined in the Charter. At this stage, what shall be noted is that the recognition of justiciability, thus of direct effect, to some social rights enshrined in the Charter, such as Article 31(2), shows, from one side, the inexistence of structural divergences between those rights and other types of rights, and from the other, the thinness of the boundaries between 'rights' and 'principles' and consequently the need to relativize such a divide.[185] In fact, *in concreto*, is there really a big difference between recognizing direct effect to EU rules and admitting their autonomous enforceability on paper while enforcing them most of the times jointly with directives ('rights'), on one hand, and, on the other, asserting the invocability of EU rules via their joint application with directives ('principles')?[186] The answer seems to be negative as the 'principles' do stipulate both a duty and a correlating claim-right. A right that stems from the joint application of the Charter's provision with the implementing measure that makes it enforceable and directly effective.

More generally, irrespective of the rights–principles dichotomy, there are doubts as to whether the provisions of the Charter, whose scope of application is activated by pre-existent EU law under Article 51, in particular but not only by secondary law, are capable of autonomously generating direct effects. Looking at the practice, the impression, in fact, is that, in terms of the intensity of their precepts, the Charter adds little to primary and secondary EU law. Despite the CJ's reiterated narrative, also examined in sections 5.3–5.5 of Chapter VI, on the direct effect of the Charter and its self-sufficient character, it is not the provisions of the Charter that are directly effective in and of themselves; instead, *in concreto*, it is the rules

[181] Opinion of AG Cruz Villalón, *Association de médiation sociale* (n 171), para. 49.
[182] T. Lock, *Rights*, 1216.
[183] Opinion of AG Cruz Villalón, *Association de médiation sociale* (n 171), para. 54.
[184] In these terms, *see* C. Hilson, *Rights*, 204–206. *See* also T. Lock, *Rights*, 1217, who writes that, 'in contrast to rights', principles 'are not automatically justiciable'.
[185] *Contra*, T. Lock, *Rights*, 1225.
[186] In this vein, *see* the reflections in D. Gallo, *L'efficacia diretta del diritto dell'Unione europea negli ordinamenti nazionali. Una dottrina ancora controversa*, Milan, Giuffrè, 2018, 343–347, in which it was argued, already in the *pre-Bauer/Max Planck* case law, that Article 31(2) of the Charter had all the characteristics to be granted (horizontal) direct effect. *See* also the observations by E. Triggiani, *La complessa vicenda dei diritti sociali fondamentali nell'Unione europea*, in U. Leanza, A. Tizzano, T. Vassalli di Dachenhausen, R. Mastroianni, P. De Pasquale, R. Ciccone (Organizing Committee), *Scritti*, 693–725, 716. On such matter, *see* also the outstanding in-depth examination by AG Cruz Villalón, *Association de médiation sociale* (n 171), paras 57–78.

of EU law that enable the Charter to apply. One only has to think of the indifference shown by the Court over the past year to Article 34 on social security. In both the *UB* ruling on the Slovak legislation restricting the grant of an additional benefit for sportspersons who have represented the State to the citizens of that State and the *INPS* ruling on the Italian maternity and birth allowances, once it has been ascertained that EU secondary legislation was directly effective and liable to lead to disapplication,[187] Article 34 was only briefly mentioned. Certainly, there are (rare) situations in which the Charter applies autonomously in the context of vertical relationships, as shown by a number of judgments, firstly *Åkerberg Fransson* and, more recently, *Menci*, both in relation to Article 50, and *Luxembourg v B*, concerning the right to an effective remedy under Article 47. These are, however, cases concerning rights corresponding to fundamental rights long recognized by the ECHR and detailed in the case law of the Strasbourg Court.

Lastly, while Chapter VII will explore in detail the complexities and incongruencies underpinning the EU case law on the direct effect of international law, at this stage, it shall be pointed out that, since the *Bresciani* ruling,[188] international agreements, and the decisions of the bodies established by such agreements since *Sevince*,[189] as well as customary law, can be recognized as directly effective by the CJ, provided that several (quite strict) conditions are fulfilled.[190]

3.2 Content of direct effect

While the above analysis related to the position of direct effect in the variety of EU sources of law, this section dwells more in detail on the very content and scope of the *Van Gend & Loos* doctrine of direct effect.[191]

The first milestone of the *Van Gend & Loos* doctrine as it emerges in the EU case law is that not only both directly effective and non-directly effective provisions can be envisaged in EU primary and secondary law. It may also be the case that the same provision, due to the heterogeneity of the obligations it imposes, is comprised of both types of norms.[192] For instance, under EU internal market law, there are several provisions, such as Article 56 TFEU, that include elements 'which are directly applicable and others which could not have such effect',[193] whereby, on the one hand, they lay out a prohibition and, on the other, they empower EU institutions to enact legislation.

[187] *See*, respectively, CJ, *UB v Generálny riaditel' Sociálnej poisťovne Bratislava*, C-447/18, EU:C:2019:1098, and CJ, *O.D., R.I.H.V., B.O., F.G., M.K.F.B., E.S., N.P, S.E.A. v Istituto nazionale della previdenza sociale* (*INPS*), C-350/20, EU:C:2021:659, on which *see* D. Gallo, *Assegni di natalità e maternità nella recente sentenza della Corte di giustizia: riflessioni 'a caldo'* (2023) 1 *Eurojus* 9 September 2023, 1; D. Gallo, *Migrants' Social Rights in the Dialogue between the CJEU and the Italian Constitutional Court: Long Live Article 267 TFEU!*, EU Law Live, 8 September 2021, available at https://eulawlive.com/op-ed-migrants-social-rights-in-the-dialogue-between-the-cjeu-and-the-italian-constitutional-court-long-live-article-267-tfeu-by-daniele-gallo/.

[188] CJ, *Bresciani*, 87/75, EU:C:1976:18.

[189] CJ, *Sevince*, C-192/89, EU:C:1990:322.

[190] It seems that a clear recognition of direct effect of customary law can be traced, for the first and apparently only time, in CJ, *Air Transport Association of America*, C-366/10, EU:C:2011:864.

[191] On the direct effect of international law within the EU legal order, *see* extensively Chapter VII.

[192] *See*, e.g., Article 31(2) of the Charter, as stated by the CJ in CJ, *Pensions-Sicherungs-Verein VVaG v Günther Bauer*, C-168/18, EU:C:2019:1128, para. 85 and CJ, *Max-Planck-Gesellschaft zur Förderung der Wissenschaften*, C-684/16, EU:C:2018:874, para. 74. With regard to directives, S. Prechal, *Directives*, 250, even affirmed that 'a provision has direct effect in some cases, but not in others'.

[193] *See, inter alia*, P. Pescatore, *The Doctrine*, 162.

The second milestone: when the obligation deriving from EU law is addressed to the State—and this is frequently the case—, the latter shall be intended at any level,[194] also in consideration of the principle of loyal cooperation set forth in Article 4(3) TEU.[195] As a matter of fact, legal entities are to be deemed 'public' for the purposes of EU law also when they are governed by private law, provided that they are under public control and perform essential services of general interest.[196]

Exceptionally, measures of secondary law, most notably directives, can explicitly and specifically identify in detail the public bodies which are their addressees and/or which must ensure their implementation. The case of directives related to public procurement is illustrative insofar as the characteristics that a body governed by public law must possess to fall within the scope of application of the directive are clearly listed therein.[197] Nonetheless, the general identification of the recipients is normally the rule. It is therefore up to the EU institutions, beginning with the CJEU, to verify, case by case, in the last resort, whether the subject falls within, or outside, the ambit of EU law, regardless of its formal legal status. It should also be noted that, in the case of a rule having direct effect in horizontal relationships, where the respondent to the claim is a private party, the public authorities of the State in which the (mainly, but not only, judicial) proceedings were initiated are in any case required to verify and ensure that the private party complies with the requirements prescribed by EU law.[198]

The third milestone: the CJ did not 'only' grant direct effect in vertical relationships. To the contrary, horizontal direct effect has been affirmed by the CJ with respect to EU binding primary law, as well as to secondary law, with the exception of directives and some decisions. The topic, which has been briefly mentioned at the beginning of the previous section, is examined in Chapter VI in detail and with regard to the different EU legal sources.[199] At this stage, several preliminary considerations can be made on horizontality and inverse vertical (direct) effect.

Generally, individuals are not expressly bound by the obligations set forth in the European Treaties. *Generally*, but not always, given that, in matters of antitrust law, for example, the undertakings, rather than the States, are subject to a set of substantive and procedural obligations, as provided in Articles 101 and 102 TFEU. Conversely, the rules on freedoms of movement, which were designed to challenge the protectionist policies of the States, have been originally interpreted as being directed at the public authorities. This fact has not, however, prevented the EU judges from recognizing their horizontal direct effect, yet explicitly 'only' with respect to persons, workers, establishment, and services, as will be observed in section 2 of Chapter VI.

The CJ has also asserted the horizontal direct effect of the general principles of EU law, as well as of some of the Charter's provisions. In truth, the issue of their horizontality has not been resolved systematically by the Court, but on a case-by-case basis, given that, to date, in addition to the principles of non-discrimination on grounds of nationality under

[194] *See*, amongst others, CJ, *Günter Fuß*, C-243/09, EU:C:2010:609.

[195] As remarked by J. Temple Lang, *Article 10 EC—The Most Important 'General Principle' of Community Law*, in U. Bernitz, J. Nergelius, C. Cardner (eds.), *General Principles*, 75–113, 77.

[196] *See*, amongst others, CJ, *Foster*, C-188/89, EU:C:1990:313.

[197] *See*, amongst others, Article 2 of Directive 2014/24/EU of the European Parliament and of the Council of 26 February 2014 on public procurement and repealing Directive 2004/18/EC (OJ L 94, 28.3.2014, 65).

[198] S. Rodin, *Les effets horizontaux du droit de l'Union européenne*, in A. Tizzano, A. Rosas, R. S. de Lapuerta, K. Lenaerts, J. Kokott (eds.), *La Cour de justice de L'Union européenne sous la présidence de Vassilios Skouris (2003-2015)*. Liber amicorum *Vassilios Skouris*, Brussels, Bruylant, 2015, 491–508, 504–506.

[199] On international law's direct effect within the EU legal order and horizontality, *see* § 4 of Chapter VII.

EU internal market freedoms of movement, 'only' the principles of non-discrimination on grounds of sex, age, and religion, enshrined in Article 21 of the Charter, as well as the right to paid annual leave (Article 31(2) of the Charter) and the rights to an effective remedy and to a fair trial (Article 47 of the Charter), have been explicitly granted horizontal direct effect.[200] As for regulations, there is no doubt that the provisions they contain are both vertically and horizontally directly effective, being acts of general application. As for directives, the CJ, notwithstanding several unclear and problematic judgments, has repeatedly formally ruled out that these acts could produce horizontal direct effect, being acts addressed only at the States, who abide by a duty of transposition.[201] Lastly, a further problem is whether decisions addressed at States and non-addressed decisions can generate horizontal, in addition to vertical, direct effect. The CJ's answer is negative for the former, while it is still unclear for the latter.[202] Overall, it shall be recalled that horizontal direct effect implies that not only EU law can indirectly impose obligations on individuals[203] but also that prohibitions can directly stem from EU primary and secondary law and apply to them. The question of the effect, therefore, merges with that of the personal scope of the EU provisions.[204]

A similar, yet not identical, matter is that of inverse vertical direct effect, that is, a situation in which direct effect is affirmed in the frame of disputes where a State invokes an EU provision against an individual, imposing obligations on the latter, and aims at obtaining the disapplication of domestic laws. In this regard, for the same reasons sketched out above, and more in general in conformity with the principles of legal certainty and legitimate expectations, according to the CJ, directives and decisions addressed only at States[205] cannot apply in inverse vertical situations and cannot trigger the disapplication of inconsistent domestic law, also but not exclusively when criminal law is at issue and may affect the individuals.[206]

[200] On the horizontality of directly effective EU law norms, including the general principles of EU law and the Charter, *see* the detailed analysis in Chapter VI, also for case law and bibliography.

[201] *See* extensively Chapter VI, especially § 3–4 and 6.

[202] *See* extensively § 6 of Chapter VI.

[203] As noted by R. Schütze, *European Union Law*, 162, 'indirectly' since individuals 'lose their right to rely on a national law that violates European Law'.

[204] R. Schütze, *European Union Law*, 162, instead, distinguishes these two dimensions in so far as he writes that the 'question whether a Treaty provision has horizontal direct effect must, however, be distinguished from the question of whether it also outlaws private party actions'.

[205] 'Allegedly' since it seems that there is no case law in this regard; yet, there is no reason why the reasoning regarding directives shall not apply also to decisions.

[206] Quite surprisingly, the GC applied this reasoning to a very different situation in GC, *Francesca Corneli*, T-502/19, EU:T:2022:627 (appeal pending before the CJ in case C-777/22 P), whereby it was ruled that the European Central Bank (ECB) infringed EU law when it imposed, as prudential supervisor, a measure of temporary administration on *Banca Carige* through which three administrators were appointed and then renewed until the situation of the bank was stabilized. The GC imposed on the ECB 'a strict adherence to national law, even in cases in which national law may be in breach of the Directive it is bound to transpose' (D. Sarmiento, *Setting the limits of implementation of national law by EU Institutions: the Corneli v ECB case (T-502/19)*, 24 October 2022, available at https://eulawlive.com/op-ed-setting-the-limits-of-implementation-of-national-law-by-eu-institutions-the-corneli-v-ecb-case-t-502-19-by-daniel-sarmiento/) and annulled the ECB's contested decision. The GC transferred the CJ's approach towards the prohibition of (horizontal direct effect and) inverse vertical direct effect of directives into a situation where an EU institution—rather than a State—relied on an unimplemented directive, with negative side-effects for natural and legal persons. Indeed, as observed by D. Sarmiento, *Setting*, 'an EU Institution is not in the same position as a Member State that refuses to transpose a Directive and immediately after tries to rely on that Directive in a claim against a private party. Quite the contrary: an EU Institution is under a specific duty to, above all, uphold Union law, and although it is not the addressee of a Directive, it is not a private individual either, but an EU Institution with duties of enforcement that introduce significant variants that do not exist for a Member State or an individual.' On the matter of legal standing and effective judicial protection within the Banking Union, *see* M. Simoncini, *Different Shades of Legal Standing and the Right to Judicial Protection of Private Parties in the Banking Union:* Trasta Komercbanka (2020) 57 *Common Market Law Review* 1867.

At least, this was the rule until few weeks ago, when the CJ seems to have, albeit implicitly and hypothetically, admitted the possible inverse vertical direct effect of directives.[207]

As for inverse vertical situations and regulations, while a clear stance on this by the CJ is still lacking and in spite of the concerns attached to the above-mentioned 'estoppel argument',[208] due to their general application, their direct applicability and their ability to set aside conflicting domestic provisions once entered into force, inverse vertical direct effect could be asserted. Indeed, those acts are published, immediately enforceable, and, thus, do not raise issues of legal certainty and legitimate expectations: individuals must know the existence of regulations and be aware that they are direct sources of EU law *and* national law. The same applies *mutatis mutandis* to decisions that are not only addressed at States.

As for the application of Treaty provisions and general principles of EU law/Charter provisions in inverse vertical disputes, the matter is controversial since at stake are problems of legal certainty and legitimate expectations, the levying of disadvantages for the parties to the dispute stemming from inverse vertical direct effect, and the estoppel argument.[209] Indeed, the crux of the question is that the CJ has never directly dealt with the contours and limits of inverse vertical direct effect when EU primary law is in hand.

In any event, the situation outlined above is different than the one involving the strand of rulings on tax law of a few years ago.[210] Most notably, the CJ, in the *N Luxembourg, X Denmark, C Danmark, Z Denmark* case,[211] pointed out that 'there is, in EU law, a general legal principle that EU law cannot be relied on for abusive or fraudulent ends'[212] and that such principle applies 'irrespective of whether the rights and advantages that are abused have their basis in the Treaties, in a regulation or in a directive'.[213] It follows that the State can rely on such principle against a person who invokes certain rules of EU law providing for an advantage in a manner which is not consistent with the objectives underpinning those rules.[214] The principle cannot be excluded also when the State refuses the taxable person the right to a number of exemptions listed in EU law, such as Directive 2003/49 on a common system of taxation applicable to interest and royalty payments made between associated companies of different Member States, even in the absence of provisions of specific and distinct national law providing for such refusal, that is, domestic or agreement-based anti-abuse provisions. Indeed, the application of the principle of EU law that abusive practices are prohibited 'is not—as the provisions of the directive are—subject to a requirement of transposition'.[215] In such a case, then, the directives do not create by themselves obligations for individuals. The refusal of an advantage foreseen in a directive, in fact, is 'merely the consequence of the finding that the objective conditions required for obtaining the advantage

[207] *See*, recently, *Infraestruturas de Portugal SA* (n 86). On inverse vertical direct effect and directives, including on that case, *see* extensively § 5 of Chapter V.

[208] As a matter of fact, the State invokes an EU provision to disapply its own laws that are inconsistent with EU law and aims at obtaining a benefit resulting from such disapplication.

[209] According to the estoppel doctrine, already mentioned in the previous section of this chapter and as remarked in the previous footnote 208 with regard to regulations, the State could not rely on an EU primary rule to take advantage of its infringement of EU law and, simultaneously, pursue the disapplication of domestic law. *See* generally §§ 4-10 of Chapter V.

[210] CJ, *Schoenimport 'Italmoda' Mariano Previti*, joined cases C-131/13 and C-163-164/13, EU:C:2014:2455, para. 62; CJ, *Cussens*, C 251/16, EU:C:2017:881, para. 33.

[211] CJ, *N Luxembourg, X Denmark, C Danmark, Z Denmark*, joined cases C-115/16, C-118–119/16, C-299/16, EU:C:2019:134.

[212] *N Luxembourg* (n 211) para. 96.

[213] *N Luxembourg* (n 211), para. 101.

[214] *N Luxembourg* (n 211), para. 102.

[215] *N Luxembourg* (n 211), para. 105.

sought, prescribed by the directive as regards that right, are met only formally'.[216] That is to say, the denial of a benefit is the result of the violation of a general principle of EU law. The *N Luxembourg, X Denmark, C Danmark, Z Denmark* ruling, therefore, is not about either inverse vertical *direct* effect of a directive or, *stricto senso*, inverse vertical *direct* effect of a general principle. If it is true that the State relies on a general principle, rather than on a directive, it does so not in order to disapply a domestic law and, by that means, affect pre-existing individuals' rights attached to the directive itself. Instead, it is the State that refuses to grant an exemption enshrined in a directive by virtue of a general principle of EU law—a principle that has been infringed by the private party willing to invoke a directive. There isn't, therefore, an issue of legitimate expectations for the companies as the latter have engaged in fraudulent and abusive conduct.

Finally, on the fourth milestone: as will be anticipated in section 3 of Chapter V and further explored in sections 4 and 6–10 of the same chapter, in this book it is argued that, as a rule, for EU law other than regulations and those decisions that are not only addressed to States, inverse vertical direct effect, and the related *in malam partem* disapplication, should not be admissible. However, inverse vertical direct effect can be asserted if the CJ, through a *pro futuro* interpretation of its rulings, ensures the respect of the principle of legitimate expectations. This depicts a form of prospective inverse vertical direct effect.

The fifth milestone: the obligation to apply the EU directly effective provision, as well as the justiciability by an individual of the right recognized therein, do not depend on the request made by said individual to the national judge (and the administration) to proceed with the enforcement of EU law and the disapplication of the conflicting domestic rule. To the contrary, domestic courts (and administrations) must *ex officio* apply the EU rule, regardless of whether it has been expressly invoked by the party to the internal proceeding.[217]

The sixth milestone: the need to ensure the effective judicial protection of individuals and consistency in the enforcement of EU law across Member States' jurisdictions implies the power of the national courts to issue interim and/or provisional measures aimed at suspending the application of an internal provision, pending the preliminary ruling of the CJ pursuant to Article 267 TFEU.[218]

The seventh milestone on the content and scope of direct effect: the CJ, in its case law,[219] as incidentally recalled in Chapter I and above in this section, generally identifies the following conditions for direct effect: clarity, precision, and unconditionality. This means that the obligation enshrined in the EU provision must be sufficiently determined and complete, that is, 'legally perfect',[220] so that the individuals may piece together its content and invoke the EU norm before the national authorities. Regarding clarity and precision, the CJ believes them to be integrated once the provision 'sets out an obligation in unequivocal terms'.[221] To this end, the EU judges have left aside a purely formalistic approach, choosing instead a

[216] *N Luxembourg* (n 211), para. 119.

[217] *See*, amongst others, CJ, *Van Schijndel v Stichting Pensioenfonds voor Fysiotherapeuten*, joined cases C-430–431/93, EU:C:1995:441; *Peterbroeck, Van Campenhout & Cie SCS* (n 27); CJ, *Aannemersbedrijf P.K. Kraaijeveld BV*, C-72/95, EU:C:1996:404. On such issue, *see* S. Prechal, *Community Law in National Courts: The Lessons from Van Schijndel* (1992) 5 *Leiden Journal of International Law* 681.

[218] *See*, amongst others, *Factortame* (n 59), paras 21–22; CJ, *RH*, C-8/19 PPU, EU:C:2019:110, para. 43. *See* E. Sharpston, *Interim Relief in the National Courts*, in J. Lonbay, A. Biondi (eds.), *Remedies for Breach of EC Law*, London, Wiley, 1997, 47–54; K. Lenaerts, K. Gutman, J. T. Nowak, *EU Procedural Law*, 166–168.

[219] *See, ex multis, Ratti* (n 120), para. 23.

[220] *See, inter alia*, CJ, *Heinz Kühne v Finanzamt München III*, 50/88, EU:C:1989:262, para. 26.

[221] *See, ex multis*, CJ, *Cooperativa Agricola Zootecnica S. Antonio and Others v Amministrazione delle finanze dello Stato*, joined cases C-246/94, C-247/94, C-248/94, and C-249/94, EU:C:1996:329, para. 19; CJ, *RTS*, C-387/19, EU:C:2021:13, para. 46.

flexible interpretation, knowing that it is much easier to apply a rule of law where 'there is no doubt regarding its content' and it is thus able to 'create legal effects by itself'.[222] In *Defrenne II*, in fact, the contents of the obligation set forth in Article 141 of the EC Treaty, currently Article 157 TFEU, were considered sufficiently clear, to the extent that the Member States must ensure 'the application of the *principle* that men and women should receive equal pay for equal work',[223] despite the use of the term 'principle' and that there was, at the time, relative uncertainty about the concept of 'equal work' as well as that of 'work of equal value'. To date, what was noted in the *Francovich* judgment (where, as known, direct effect was not recognized in the case at hand) still holds true. In *Francovich* it was stated that an EU provision is clear and precise if there exist, cumulatively, three elements: *(i)* the determination of the person(s) entitled to benefit from the provision; *(ii)* the determination of the person(s) obliged to grant the right/advantage implied therein; and *(iii)* the content of such right/advantage-obligation duo.[224] Said in other words, individuals must be able to ascertain what their rights and/or obligations are,[225] and national authorities must be able to apply the provision(s) to the case at hand.

With respect to the prerequisite of unconditionality,[226] according to the CJ, whether the application of the EU provision is subject 'in its implementation or effects'[227] to additional integrative and/or implementing measures by the Member States' authorities or the EU institutions must be assessed.[228] If it is, the EU rule would not be deemed (sufficiently) unconditional.

3.3 Consequences of direct effect

Three milestones can be identified on the consequences of direct effect in the light of the EU case law.

First, direct effect implies that the national authorities, if consistent interpretation cannot be performed,[229] must set aside any conflicting internal rules,[230] including those provisions with constitutional status.[231] A consequence of disapplication is that EU law normally replaces national law in governing the case at hand. 'Normally', not always, as shown by the consequences stemming from objective-exclusionary direct effect investigated in detail in Chapter IV. Furthermore, the remedy of disapplication does not necessarily affect the

[222] *See* the opinion of AG Léger of 11 January 2000, *Grand Duchy of Luxemburg v Berthe Linster, Aloyse Linster and Yvonne Linster*, C-287/98, EU:C:2000:3, para. 38.

[223] CJ, *Gabrielle Defrenne v Société anonyme belge de navigation aérienne Sabena, 43/75*, EU:C:1976:56, para. 16 (italics added); more recently, *see* CJ, *Tesco Stores*, C-624/19, EU:C:2021:429.

[224] *Francovich* (n 18), para. 26.

[225] On the concept of 'ascertainability' in the context of direct effect, *see* S. Prechal, *Directives*, 283. *See* also the opinion of AG Tesauro of 28 November 1995, *Erich Dillenkofer*, joined cases C-178-179/94, and C-188-190/94, EU:C:1995:410, para. 18.

[226] *See* extensively §§ 4–7 of this chapter.

[227] *G. Pohl-Boskamp GmbH & Co. KG v Gemeinsamer Bundesausschuss*, C-317/05, EU:C:2006:684, para. 41.

[228] *See*, *inter alia*, CJ, *Commissioners for Her Majesty's Revenue & Customs against GMAC UK plc*, C-589/12, EU:C:2014:2131, para. 30; CJ, *Gassmayr*, C-194/08, EU:C:2010:386, para. 45; CJ, *Spetsializirana prokuratura*, C-569/20, EU:C:2022:401, para. 28; CJ, *Towercast SASU*, C-449/21, EU:C:2023:207, paras 43–53.

[229] *See*, e.g., CJ, *XR*, C-107/19, EU:C:2021:722, para. 45. On the interplay between consistent interpretation and direct effect, *see* § 3 of Chapter IV.

[230] *See*, amongst others, CJ, *Solred SA*, C-347/96, EU:C:1998:87, paras 30–31 and para. 2 of the operative part. Recently, *see* CJ, *A*, C-716/17, EU:C:2019:598, paras 38–40; CJ, *UY*, C-615/18, EU:C:2020:376, paras 69 and 75; CJ, *Braathens Regional Aviation*, C-30/19, EU:C:2021:269, paras 58–59; CJ, *ZX*, C-282/20, EU:C:2021:874, paras 39–41. On disapplication, primacy, and direct effect, *see* extensively Chapter V.

[231] Recently, *see* CJ, *Pelham and Others*, C-476/17, EU:C:2019:624, para. 78.

concerned domestic legislation in its entirety. Disapplication, thus, can be 'only' selective. Indeed, in *NE*, regarding the internal effect of the proportionality principle of penalties laid down in Article 20 of Directive 2014/67, it was stated that the principles of primacy and direct effect impose on national authorities the obligation to disapply national legislation contrary to the requirement of proportionality of penalties 'only to the extent necessary to enable the imposition of proportionate penalties'.[232] Therefore, they cannot go further than that: 'when an effective and dissuasive penalty may still be applied, [domestic] courts should do so'.[233] As a result, judges should adjust the sanctioning regime in question, by virtue of partial disapplication. Upstream, the decentralized operability of the duty to disapply rests on the identification of the national rules that are in contrast with EU law. The implication is obvious: national authorities are not compelled to disapply the entire legislation in so far as disapplication is required exclusively for internal provisions that are precluded by EU law.[234]

Disapplication does not trigger the invalidity of the national law, as might be wrongfully construed from a superficial reading of the *Simmenthal* case, where it was held that, in accordance with the primacy principle, directly effective provisions have the effect 'not only by their entry into force [of] render[ing] automatically inapplicable' the internal law, but also of 'preclud[ing] the valid adoption of new national legislative measures' which would be incompatible with Community provisions.[235] Although consequences stemming from a conflict between EU law and national law shall be determined autonomously by each Member State,[236] disapplication can never bring about the annulment or repeal of the internal provision(s).[237] In *IN.CO.GE.*, for example, the CJ, in rejecting the approach proposed by the Commission, stated that it cannot be inferred from the '*Simmenthal* rule' that the incompatibility with Community law of a subsequent provision of national law has the effect of 'rendering that rule ... non-existent'.[238] EU law does not have the capacity to render domestic laws void within their own legal system and the CJ does not have the power to rectify that which, instead, shall be done by Member States through legislative interventions. This is the rule. However, in the literature, Dougan suggested reading some recent cases as proof that there are 'exceptional circumstances when the unity and effectiveness of EU law might propel the Court to insist that primacy entails legal consequences going beyond mere disapplication'. Such consequences would be, in the eyes of Dougan, that certain incompatible domestic acts become 'null and void' as a result of the CJ's judgment.[239] He refers, most notably, to the *Rimšēvičs*[240] and *W.Ż.*[241] rulings, which concern two peculiar situations

[232] *NE* (n 156), para. 34. On selective disapplication, exemplified by the application of the proportionality principle of penalties at the core of the *NE* judgment, as a manifestation of exclusionary direct effect, *see* also §§ 1.1 and 1.2 of Chapter IV.

[233] *See* the opinion of AG Emiliou of 10 November 2022, *T.A.C.*, C-40/21, EU:C:2022:873, para. 71.

[234] *See* the comments by S. Montaldo, *Handle with Care! The Direct Effect of the Requirement of Proportionality of Sanctions and the Remedy of Disapplication:* NE v. Bezirkshauptmannschaft Hartberg-Fürstenfeld (2023) 60 *Common Market Law Review* 863 and M. Lanotte, *La proporzionalità della sanzione: un principio ritrovato? Note a margine della sentenza* NE, Serie Speciale (2023) 17 *Quaderni AISDUE* 367.

[235] *Simmenthal* (n 78), para. 3 of the operative part.

[236] *Firma Gebrüder Lück* (n 68), 333–335.

[237] *See* CJ, *Krzysztof Filipiak*, C-314/08, EU:C:2009:719, para. 82, where the Court held that 'pursuant to the principle of the primacy of Community law, a conflict between a provision of national law and a directly applicable provision of the Treaty is to be resolved by a national court applying Community law, if necessary by refusing to apply the conflicting national provision, and not by a declaration that the national provision is invalid, the powers of authorities, courts and tribunals in that regard being a matter to be determined by each Member State'.

[238] *IN.CO.GE.* (n 91), para. 21. *See* also *Filipiak* (n 237), para. 82.

[239] *See* M. Dougan, *The Primacy of Union Law over Incompatible National Measures: Beyond Disapplication and Towards a Remedy of Nullity?* (2022) 59 *Common Market Law Review* 1301, 1321.

[240] CJ, *Rimšēvičs*, joined cases C-202 and 238/18, EU:C:2019:139. *See* also Chapter II, § 3.

[241] CJ, *W.Ż.*, C-487/19, EU:C:2021:798.

and are very different from each other.[242] They are special and different since with the first the CJ annulled the decision suspending the Governor of the Central Bank of Latvia from office (on account of the serious misconduct that was imputed to him in the context of a preliminary criminal investigation concerning acts of bribery and corruption). Most notably, the actions brought by Mr. Rimšēvičs and the European Central Bank against that decision represent the first and only case which the CJ has heard on the basis of the jurisdiction conferred to it by the second subparagraph of Article 14(2) of the Statute of the European System of Central Banks (ESCB) and of the European Central Bank to review decisions relieving the governors of the national central banks from office.

The *W.Ż.* judgment was delivered in the frame of a preliminary ruling procedure triggered by the reference stemming from the Polish Supreme Court (Civil Chamber) concerning a resolution by which the National Council of the Judiciary declared that there was no need to adjudicate on the challenge brought by a judge, W.Ż., against a decision adopted by the President of the Regional Court of K. Such decision ordered W.Ż. to be transferred from one division of that court to another. More specifically, the question raised before the CJ was whether Articles 2, 6(1) and (3), and the second subparagraph of Article 19(1) TEU, in conjunction with Article 47 of the Charter and Article 267 TFEU, were to be interpreted as meaning that 'a court composed of a single person who has been appointed to the position of judge in flagrant breach of the laws of a Member State applicable to judicial appointments . . . is not an independent and impartial tribunal previously established by law within the meaning of EU law'.[243]

Now, it is precisely due to the special character of the two rulings that their findings cannot be generalized. In fact, in *Rimšēvičs* the domestic measure was annulled by the CJ pursuant to a Treaty provision that explicitly confers upon it the power to review its lawfulness. This is a derogation rooted not in a judicial decision taken by the CJ, but in primary law, outside the realm and logic of direct effect. As clarified by the Court, Article 14(2) 'derogates from the general distribution of powers between the national courts and the courts of the European Union as provided for by the Treaties and in particular by Article 263 TFEU'. However, that derogation 'can be explained by the particular institutional context of the ESCB within which it operates', the ESCB being 'a novel legal construct in EU law which brings together national institutions, namely the national central banks, and an EU institution, namely the ECB'.[244] Nothing extraordinary, then, occurs in *Rimšēvičs*, from the standpoint of the role and competence of the CJ, but just the application of a *sui generis* EU law provision.

As for *W.Ż.*, whereby the nullity was required by the CJ and had to be declared by a national court, as explained by Dougan himself, the case remains 'just as unusual, in terms of its factual and legal anchoring to the specific procedural features of Polish law'.[245] This is so

[242] Dougan, *The Primacy*, 1309–1313, while reflecting upon the *Berlusconi* ruling (CJ, *Berlusconi*, C-219/17, EU:C:2018:1023) and noting that 'it adds something to the established case law' (1310), excluded that such ruling has the same potential as the two other judgments mentioned above. In this respect, he writes that, in *Berlusconi*, 'the preparatory national act is part of a procedure that leads to the adoption of a definitive Union act, and the competent Union institution ultimately retains full decision-making power—so that the prior national act is not binding as such on the Union institution (i.e. the latter could nevertheless decide to disclose the relevant documents)—it falls to the ECJ to exercise exclusive jurisdiction over the legality of the final Union act and to ensure the effective judicial protection of affected individuals. In that context, the Court itself will examine any defects vitiating the national preparatory act that could affect the validity of the definitive Union measure' (1310). On the *Berlusconi* ruling, *see* also F. B. Bastos, *Derivative illegality in European composite administrative procedures* (2018) 55 *Common Market Law Review* 101.

[243] *W.Ż.* (n 241), para. 51.

[244] *W.Ż.* (n 241), para. 69.

[245] M. Dougan, *The Primacy*, 1331.

because the Court concluded that Article 19(1) TEU and the principle of primacy must be interpreted as meaning that a national court seized of an application for recusal shall 'declare to be null and void an order by which a court, ruling at last instance and comprising a single judge, has dismissed' the action by a judge holding office in a court aimed at challenging a decision to transfer them without their consent. In this respect, that appointment must have taken place 'in clear breach of fundamental rules which form an integral part of the establishment and functioning of the judicial system concerned', and the integrity of the outcome of that procedure must have been 'undermined, giving rise to reasonable doubt in the minds of individuals as to the independence and impartiality of the judge concerned, with the result that that order may not be regarded as being made by an independent and impartial tribunal previously established by law, within the meaning of the second subparagraph of Article 19(1) TEU'.[246] As has been observed with regard to *Rimšēvičs*, *W.Ż.* cannot be seen as a revolutionary twist with respect to the previous case law of the CJ on the nature of the remedy of disapplication. Indeed, by that ruling the CJ did not mandate the annulment of a national law, but rather of an order issued by a domestic court that was manifestly in breach of the domestic legal system.

In continuing the analysis on the extent of disapplication, it shall be highlighted that disapplying national law implies *a fortiori*, from *Factortame*[247] onwards, that the jurisprudence, including that generated by constitutional and higher national courts which interpret and apply the domestic rule, so far as it contrasts with the EU legal order, shall also be set aside. Furthermore, the duty to disapply does not apply only to the judiciary. In fact, beginning with the *Fratelli Costanzo* judgment,[248] the EU judges extended it to State administration (central or local), which is thus treated in the same way, from this point of view, *mutatis mutandis*, as the domestic courts. Moreover, regardless of the existence of an obligation placed on them by national legislation which conflicts with EU law, the administrative authorities of that country must act on their own initiative to observe the EU rules and, therefore, abstain from implementing the relevant internal law. In short, they cannot 'hide' behind the non-compliance of the legislature.[249] Obviously, in order to avoid that a variable-geometry application of EU law (i.e. one that is too decentralized and, consequently, apt to undermine consistency and coherence) creates untenable legal uncertainty, those same national administrations shall '*as far as possible*'[250] use the national procedures and the tool of consistent interpretation in order to resolve the possible conflict. As a matter of fact, at closer look, if at stake are judicial or administrative practices, even originating from higher/constitutional courts and key State agencies, consistent interpretation is the proper means best able apt to recompose the conflict with EU law, disapplication being not indispensable.

Lastly, by combining what was written on the role of disapplication with the reflections made in the previous section on horizontality (and on inverse vertical direct effect), direct effect does not always trigger the disapplication of a public law measure, be it a parliamentary bill or another type of legislation. In fact, direct effect can cause the disapplication of

[246] *W.Ż.* (n 241), para. 161.
[247] *Simmenthal* (n 78), paras 22–23; CJ, *Factortame* (n 59), paras 19–21.
[248] *Fratelli Costanzo* (n 127); CJ, C-378/17, *The Minister for Justice and Equality, The Commissioner of the Garda Síochána v Workplace Relations Commission*, EU:C:2018:979.
[249] In these terms, *see* J. H. Jans, M. J. M. Verhoeven, *Europeanisation via Consistent Interpretation and Direct Effect*, in J. H. Jans, S. Prechal, R. J. G. M. Widdershoven (eds.), *Europeanisation of Public Law*, 2nd ed., Groningen, Europa Law Publishing, 2015, 71–132, 126–127.
[250] J. H. Jans, M. J. M. Verhoeven, *Europeanization*, 126.

private law measures,[251] which often, but not always,[252] are adopted following laws/measures enacted by public bodies admitting[253] or imposing[254] inconsistent private actions. Should those private law measures be adopted in compliance with State measures, the latter shall be seen at the origins of the former and, of course, shall be set aside, too.

Regarding the second milestone, the setting aside does not exempt the legislator from amending or repealing the incompatible national law.[255] In fact, should national authorities fail to proceed with such removal—whose practical functioning varies in each Member State[256]—infringement proceedings could be initiated by the European Commission pursuant to Article 258 TFEU.[257] The rationale of this possible action, of course, is to counter the uncertainty, to the detriment of individuals, judges, and the administration, which would otherwise occur without a reparatory *erga omnes* legislative intervention.[258]

In respect of the last milestone, the violation of a directly effective rule implies the conferral, to individuals, (also) of the right to seek compensation for the damages suffered from the violation of EU law by a Member State. This is a right which, as is known, the CJ initially developed in relation to EU provisions devoid of direct effect[259] and which, from the *Brasserie*[260] judgment onwards, was extended to EU directly effective provisions, qualifying it as its 'necessary corollary',[261] 'complementing' or 'supplementing' direct effect,[262] and to the remedy of disapplication attached to it. This holds true although, as observed by Prechal, direct effect operates 'at the level of primary norms and, in terms of rights, primary rights', while State liability is a 'second level sanctioning norm or, again when put in terms of rights, a sanctioning right', being the result of a breach of an EU law obligation rather than originating from the EU law provision 'itself'.[263]

4. The direct effect test's outdatedness

The questions one should ask when confronting the contents of the test on direct effect briefly outlined in section 2.3 of Chapter I and section 3.2 of this chapter[264] are as follows:[265] what do precision, clarity, and unconditionality actually mean? Are such conditions genuinely

[251] On this matter, from the viewpoint of standing in proceedings against private parties, *see* H. K. Ellingsen, *Standing to Enforce European Union Law before National Courts*, Oxford, Hart, 2021, 181–197, 183.

[252] e.g. *Defrenne II* (n 223) and CJ, *International Transport Workers' Federation and Finnish Seamen's Union v Viking Line ABP and OÜ Viking Line Eesti*, C-438/05, EU:C:2007:772.

[253] e.g. CJ, *IR*, C-68/17, EU:C:2018:696.

[254] e.g. *Mangold* (n 155) and CJ, *Cresco Investigation*, C-193/17, EU:C:2019:43.

[255] L. Daniele, *Diritto dell'Unione europea*, 8th ed., Milan, Giuffrè, 2022, 302–303. *See*, recently, CJ, *Grossmania*, C-177/20, EU:C:2022:175, para. 36.

[256] By way of example *see*, as for the Italian legal system, Law 234/2012.

[257] CJ, *Commission v France*, 167/73, EU:C:1974:35, para. 41; CJ, *Commission v Italy*, 104/86, EU:C:1988:171, para. 13; CJ, *Commission v Germany*, 74/86, EU:C:1988:198, paras 280–286. *See* also T. Hartley, *Direct Applicability and the Failure to Repeal Incompatible National Legislation* (1975) 1 *European Law Review* 53.

[258] As noted by M. Dougan, *The Primacy*, 1306.

[259] CJ, *Francovich* (n 18).

[260] *Brasserie* (n 18).

[261] *Brasserie* (n 18), para. 22.

[262] In these terms, *see* S. Prechal, *Member State Liability*, 301–302.

[263] S. Prechal, *Member State Liability*, 301. On the interplay between direct effect and State liability, from the standpoint of EU rights, *see* also L. Boch, *European Community Law in National Courts: A Continuing Contradiction* (1992) 5 *Leiden Journal of International Law* 171. *See* also § 1 of this chapter.

[264] *See* also the reasoning developed in D. Gallo, *L'efficacia*, 177-211; D. Gallo, *Effetto diretto del diritto dell'Unione europea e disapplicazione*, oggi (2019) 1 *Osservatorio sulle Fonti* 1, 6–11.

[265] On the peculiarities underpinning the test, from the angle of international law's direct effect in EU law, *see* § 5 of Chapter VII.

used by the CJEU to verify the direct effect of EU law? Do they have the same relevance in the case law? Does their assessment vary due to the characteristics of the EU provision(s) at stake? Are they still, in practice, useful for an appropriate understanding of direct effect and, if not, is the test ultimately unclear, outdated, and ineffective?[266]

In the first place, nowadays, in many rulings, the concept of clarity, which was normally referred to in past case law,[267] is not even recalled.[268] Indeed, clarity and precision seem to have the same meaning: using both terms as core elements of direct effect, as if they were two distinct premises, is a sophisticated intellectual exercise, yet redundant and misleading.[269]

In the second place, the interpretation of the conditions of direct effect made by the CJEU is usually very extensive.[270] Provisions which, upon an initial reading, are not clear, precise, or unconditional, have been considered as such by the EU judges through a flexible and teleological interpretation. As a matter of fact, in the case law reference is often made to norms which are 'sufficiently' ('*suffisamment*' in French) precise,[271] that is, norms that are precise *in substance* rather than simply formally for how they are worded, and/or unconditional also when they leave a certain discretion to the national authorities who are called upon to apply them.[272] Such an approach is evident in the *Van Gend & Loos* judgment, as has been extensively explored in Chapter I, and is even more so in the subsequent case law, starting with the *Reyners*[273] and *Defrenne II*[274] cases, where the test was further 'relaxed',[275] 'loosened',[276] and 'broadened'[277] by the CJ so as to avoid that even less accomplished provisions than Article 12 of the EC Treaty could not satisfy it. AG Bobek was right in observing that the clear and precise character of a provision is a 'rather elastic concept' and that those requirements can actually be met also in presence of 'undefined or even vague concepts or indeterminate legal notions'.[278]

In the third place, the fact that the CJEU, in its case law, often verifies the presence of precision, clarity, and unconditionality does not mean that it always employs the test nor that it employs it with reference to all sources of EU law. As to negative obligations, at times the test has been blandly applied or not even mentioned. The *Costa* ruling is paradigmatic: the Court, after noting that Article 37(2) of the EEC Treaty, currently Article 37(2) TFEU, on re-organization of state monopolies of a commercial nature, established an 'absolute obligation', concluded, quite sharply, that the prohibition contained therein is 'capable of producing direct effects on the legal relations between the Member States and their nationals'.[279]

[266] *See* also D. Gallo, *Rethinking Direct Effect and its Evolution: a Proposal* (2022) 1 *European Law Open* 576, 596–599.

[267] *See*, for instance, CJ, *Carmine Capolongo v Azienda Agricole Maya*,77/72, EU:C:1973:65, para. 11.

[268] *See*, for instance, *NE* (n 156), para. 18, and *Autorità Garante della Concorrenza e del Mercato* (n 85), para. 63.

[269] A. Bleckmann, *L'applicabilité directe du droit communautaire*, in Waelbroeck M., Velu J. (eds.), *Les recours des individus devant les instances nationales en cas de violation du droit européen*, Brussels, Larcier, 1978, 85–130, 98, points out that '*bien quel les arrêts emploient parfois ces notions concurrement, elles se réfèrenet à un meme contenu*'.

[270] *See*, explicitly, P. Craig, G. de Búrca, *EU Law*, 223–224; R. Schütze, *European Union Law*, 159–161; A. B. Capik, *Five Decades Since Van Gend and Costa Came to Town: Primacy and Indirect Effect Revisited*, in A. Lazowski, S. Blockmans (eds.), *Research Handbook in EU Institutional Law*, Cheltenham, Edward Elgar, 2016, 379–420, 387; M. Bobek, *The Effects*, 158–159.

[271] e.g. CJ, *M.D.*, C-528/21, EU:C:2023:341, para. 94.

[272] On this point, *see* further, in this §.

[273] CJ, *Jean Reyners v Belgian State*, 2/74, EU:C:1974:68.

[274] CJ, *Defrenne II* (n 223).

[275] D. Chalmers, G. Davies, G. Monti, *European Union*, 293.

[276] R. Schütze, *European Union Law*, 158.

[277] D. Chalmers, G. Davies, G. Monti, *European Union*, 293; R. Schütze, *European Union Law*, 161.

[278] Opinion of AG Bobek of 23 September 2021, *NE v Bezirkshauptmannschaft Hartberg-Fürstenfeld*, C-205/20, EU:C:2021:759, para. 36.

[279] CJ, *Flaminio Costa v E.N.E.L.*, 6/64, EU:C:1964:66, 597.

The CJ's simplistic affirmation in the *Molkerei-Zentrale Westfalen/Lippe GmbH* case that EU provisions which contain a prohibition are 'by their nature'[280] sufficiently precise, unconditional, and, therefore, directly effective, still stands today in most of the EU case law.

In respect of positive obligations, the assessment on the conditions of direct effect generally tends to play a more decisive role since these are provisions which confer a subjective legal position enabling the individual to obtain a benefit vis-à-vis the State (or private subjects). In this framework, without anticipating too much the reasoning developed in Chapter IV, it is worth mentioning the different attitude shown by the EU judges vis-à-vis the assessment on conditions of direct effect, depending on whether it is of the substitutive or exclusionary type, that is, whether the EU norm replaces the national provision or 'only' generates the disapplication of the latter, respectively. Indeed, it seems that, where the EU norm penetrates the national legal order, substituting itself for the pre-existing domestic provision, the test is generally carried out, while the same cannot be said in relation to those EU provisions which do not directly confer subjective legal positions and which aim at 'simply' avoiding, in exclusionary terms, the application of conflicting internal norms.[281] By way of example, in the *Verbond*,[282] *ENKA*,[283] *Delkvist*,[284] *Cowan*,[285] *Kraaiejveld*,[286] *WWF*,[287] *Linster*,[288] *Unilever*,[289] *Landelijke*[290], *FNV*,[291] *Moormann*,[292] *Tögel*,[293] *Großkrotzenburg*,[294] *Pafitis*,[295] *Bernáldez*,[296] *Melki*, *Schwibbert*,[297] *Ivansson*,[298] and *Ince*[299] cases, the test is not even mentioned. The reason seems to be the necessity for the CJEU, the legal interpreter, and the national operators (companies, individuals etc.), to have better 'guidance' in the cases in which the external EU provision takes the place of the internal one, as happens with substitutive direct effect, rather than what generally happens where an EU provision is invoked by the individual 'only' as a parameter of legality of national law, as occurs in exclusionary direct effect.[300] As observed by AG Léger in *Linster*, the limits regarding the role of the legislator when the effect is exclusionary 'are not the same when it is called upon to assess the validity of a rule of domestic law in the light of the relevant Community rule'.[301] This does not always occur, however. In the *CIA Security International* case regarding the exclusionary

[280] CJ, *Firma Molkerei-Zentrale Westfalen/Lippe GmbH v Hauptzollamt Paderborn*, 28/67, EU:C:1968:17, para. 207.

[281] *See* Opinion of AG Léger, *Linster* (n 222) paras 41 and 50.

[282] CJ, *Verbond van Nederlandse Ondernemingen v Inspecteur der Invoerrechten en Accijnzen*, 51/76, EU:C:1977:12.

[283] CJ, *Enka BV v Inspecteur der Invoerrechten en Accijnzen Arnhem*, 38/77, EU:C:1977:190.

[284] CJ, *Knud Oluf Delkvist v Anklagemyndigheden*, 21/78, EU:C:1978:213.

[285] CJ, *Ian William Cowan v Trésor public*, 186/87, EU:C:1989:47.

[286] *Kraaijeveld* (n 217).

[287] CJ, *World Wildlife Fund (WWF)*, C-435/97, EU:C:1999:418.

[288] CJ, *Grand Duchy of Luxemburg v Berthe Linster and Others*, C-287/98, EU:C:2000:468.

[289] *Österreichische Unilever GmbH v Smithkline Beecham Markenartikel GmbH*, C-77/97, EU:C:1999:30.

[290] CJ, *Landelijke Vereniging tot Behoud van de Waddenzee and Nederlandse Vereniging tot Bescherming van Vogels v Staatssecretaris van Landbouw, Natuurbeheer en Visserij*, C-127/02, EU:C:2004:482.

[291] CJ, *Netherlands v Federatie Nederlandse Vakbeweging*, C-71/85, EU:C:1986:465.

[292] CJ, *Oberkreisdirektor des Kreises Borken und Vertreter des öffentlichen Interesses beim Oberverwaltungsgericht für das Land Nordrhein-Westfalen v Handelsonderneming Moormann BV*, 190/87, EU:C:1988:424.

[293] CJ, *Walter Tögel*, C-76/97, EU:C:1998:432.

[294] CJ, *Commission v Germany*, C-431/92, EU:C:1995:260.

[295] CJ, *Panagis Pafitis*, C-441/93, EU:C:1996:92.

[296] CJ, *Bernáldez*, C-129/94, EU:C:1996:143.

[297] CJ, *Karl Josef Wilhelm Schwibbert*, C-20/05, EU:C:2007:652.

[298] CJ, *Lars Ivansson*, C-307/13, EU:C:2014:2058.

[299] CJ, *Sebat Ince*, C-336/14, EU:C:2016:72.

[300] On this point, *see* also S. Prechal, *Direct Effect Reconsidered*, 21.

[301] *Linster*, Opinion of AG Léger (n 222), para. 73.

effect, *par excellence*, of an EU provision,[302] for example, it was explicitly observed that the provisions of Directive 83/189/EEC are unconditional and sufficiently precise.[303]

In the fourth place, the impression is that the Court, when it has applied the three criteria (i.e. clarity, precision, unconditionality), did so often vaguely and in a shifting and evanescent manner, without steady guiding principles.

In the light of the four arguments above, the GC and the CJ, in their more recent case law, seem to scrutinize, if at all, the presence of precision and unconditionality especially in relation to the provisions of directives, when applied alone or with other EU primary law sources.[304] At times, the CJ has applied these criteria without making any mention of direct effect.[305] At others, it has explicitly affirmed direct effect without making reference to the criteria.[306] In a large number of cases, the Court has made no mention of either direct effect or the criteria.[307] This absence leads to a reassessment/relativization of the three premises at the core of the test on direct effect, as confirmed by the case law on fundamental rights, which have penetrated EU law as general principles since the seventies and were then codified in the Charter. In fact, as anticipated in section 3.1 of this chapter, unless when applied in conjunction with written sources of EU law, the CJ does not refer explicitly to direct effect or use the test with regard to general principles of EU law, due to their inherently indefinite character. As for the Charter, in several rulings[308] a reference to the conditions of direct effect and/or the test itself is lacking, although direct effect is indeed implied in the reasoning of the Court, as is the duty to disapply. In this connection, the EU legal order would risk appearing schizophrenic if, on the one hand, it were affirmed that the Charter, as provided for in Article 6 TEU, has binding legal force equal to the Treaties, and, on the other hand, that its normative intensity would be inferior due to a *a priori* lack of direct effect.[309] To deny *sic et simpliciter* the direct effect of the Charter's rules would mortify the role that EU law attributes to the Charter as the main instrument for protecting fundamental rights.

In the fifth place, and as a specification of the argument above, the Court, in allowing individuals to rely directly on the Charter against national rules, does not seem to make any distinction between directly effective rules of the Charter and other types of rules with direct effect.[310] In this view, disapplication is a characteristic of the (direct) effect of certain provisions of the Charter, as well as of all other directly effective sources of EU law. In *Åkerberg Fransson*, to give an example, it is specified that the national court, within the scope of its jurisdiction, in the event of a conflict between national law and rights recognized by the Charter, 'is obliged to ensure the full effectiveness of [the Charter's] rules, by disapplying where necessary, on its own initiative, any conflicting provisions of national law'.[311] This obligation shall apply provided that that conflict clearly results 'from its wording or from the

[302] *See* §§ 1–2 of Chapter IV.

[303] CJ, *CIA Security International SA v Signalson SA and Securitel SPRL*, C-194/94, EU:C:1996:172, para. 44.

[304] On this aspect, as well as on the peculiar facets of directives in relation to the premises of direct effect, *see* L. Coutron, *Retour fataliste aux fondements de l'invocabilité des directives* (2015) 51 *Revue trimestrielle de droit européen* 39. *Contra see*, among others, F. Picod, *Le statut des particuliers, désormais titulaires de droits individuels*, in A. Tizzano, J. Kokott, S. Prechal (eds.), *50ème anniversaire de l'arrêt Van Gend en Loos: 1963-2013: actes du colloque*, Luxembourg, 13 mai 2013, 81–92, 82.

[305] e.g. *WWF* (n 287); *El Dridi* (n 111).

[306] e.g. *Verbond* (n 282).

[307] e.g. *Aziz Melki and Sélim Abdeli*, C-188/10 and C-189/10, EU:C:2010:363; *Åkerberg Fransson* (n 163); *Bernáldez* (n 296); *Unilever* (n 289).

[308] But not in all of them; *see*, e.g., CJ, *Pensions-Sicherungs-Verein VVaG v Günther Bauer*, C-168/18, EU:C:2019:1128, paras 70–72, 77, and 85; *Max-Planck* (n 192), paras 63–68.

[309] In the same vein, *see* P. Craig, G. de Búrca, *EU Law*, 196.

[310] See, *ex multis*, CJ, *Digital Rights Ireland Ltd*, joined cases C-293/12 and C-594/12, EU:C:2014:238.

[311] *Åkerberg Fransson* (n 163), para. 45.

relevant case law, since it deprives the national court of the power to fully assess, where appropriate with the cooperation of the Court of Justice of the European Union, the compatibility of that provision with the Charter'.[312]

In the sixth place, regarding the usefulness of the test on direct effect, in the literature, two authors in particular challenge the very need to keep it as it is designed by the CJ. Most notably, Prechal highlights the need to rely on a '*contextual approach*' in testing the conditions '*in concreto*' and for the specific purposes of the case, while Pescatore rejects the idea that direct effect depends on the 'intrinsic quality of the rules concerned'.[313]

In the seventh place, not only is the interpretation of the three criteria for direct effect generally very flexible, but the lines between them have become thinner. As AG van Gerven observed in his opinion in the *Banks* case, 'on closer scrutiny, the case law of the Court exhibits several minor differences as regards the wording of those conditions'.[314] *In concreto*, the 'precision' does not seem to be a stand-alone requirement, as unintentionally demonstrated in the *NE* ruling regarding the enforcement of Article 20 of Directive 2014/67 on the proportionality of penalties, whereby the reasoning on the degree of discretion is even used by the CJ to define what a precise obligation is, rather than to fill with content the notion of 'unconditionality'.[315] As a matter of fact, the Court held that the assessment on the proportionality of penalties had to be carried out in the light of the discretion left to public authorities in defining the rules on those penalties applicable in the event of infringements of the national provisions adopted pursuant to Directive 2014/67. In this connection, direct effect was asserted since that discretion was limited by the prohibition, laid down by Article 20 of the Directive in a general manner and in unequivocal terms, on imposing disproportionate penalties.[316] The concept of discretion, thus, lies also at the core of precision, and not only of unconditionality. It could not be otherwise: the criterion of unconditionality, in fact, absorbs clarity/precision. In other words, if a norm is clear/precise, it is not necessarily unconditional, while if a norm is unconditional, it is inevitably clear/precise. If there is no need for the adoption of a further internal legal act to make the EU provision applicable, then the obligation contained therein, due to its unconditional character, is also *in re ipsa* clear/precise. Proof of this lies in the case law of the CJ on the horizontal direct effect of the Charter,[317] most notably in those judgments in which a reference to direct effect was made, whereby the only requirement whose presence has been assessed was the unconditionality of the EU rule at hand, that is, whether or not the latter makes a *renvoi* to 'the cases and under the conditions provided for by European Union law and national laws and practices'.[318]

[312] *Åkerberg Fransson* (n 163), paras 48–49.

[313] *See*, respectively, S. Prechal, *Does Direct Effect*, 1063–1064; S. Prechal, *Directives*, 252–253; P. Pescatore, *The Doctrine*, 177. On the contextualization of direct effect, from the twofold perspective of its core constitutive elements and the duty of disapplication, *see* Chapter V, § 3.

[314] Opinion of AG van Gerven of 27 October 1993, *Banks*, C-128/92, EU:C:1993:860, para. 27.

[315] *NE* (n 156), para. 27: 'as regards, in the second place, whether Article 20 of Directive 2014/67 is sufficiently precise, in that it lays down the requirement that penalties must be proportionate, it must be held that, although that provision leaves the Member States a certain discretion in defining the rules on penalties applicable in the event of infringements of the national provisions adopted pursuant to that directive, that discretion is limited by the prohibition, laid down by that provision in a general manner and in unequivocal terms, on imposing disproportionate penalties.' On this aspect, see L. Cecchetti, *L'efficacia diretta delle direttive negli ordinamenti nazionali, oggi: questioni ancora aperte alla vigilia del 50° anniversario della sentenza* van Duyn (2023) 3 *Eurojus* 151, 159.

[316] *NE* (n 156), para. 27.

[317] For a similar approach, *see* E. Frantziou, *The Horizontal Effect of the Charter: Towards an Understanding of Horizontality as a Structural Constitutional Principle?* (2020) 22 *Cambridge Yearbook of European Legal Studies* 208–232, 218. *See* also *Association de médiation sociale* (n 6), para. 45; CJ, *Egenberger*, C-414/16, EU:C:2018:257, para. 76; *IR* (n 253), para. 77; *Cresco Investigation* (n 254), para. 76; *Bauer* (n 308), para. 85; *Max Planck* (n 192), para. 74.

[318] *Association de médiation sociale* (n 6), para. 44.

5. Unconditionality as the *sine qua non* premise of direct effect

What is the meaning of unconditionality as the key and only premise of the test on direct effect?[319] First of all, it is clear that the distinction, made above all in the earliest literature,[320] between unconditionality, seen as the requirement that the obligation be '*dégagé de toute condition particulière*',[321] and the necessity for further implementing measures, cannot be upheld: an obligation is unconditional if it can produce its effects irrespective of the adoption of subsequent measures for its enforcement.[322] In the *Commissioners for Her Majesty's Revenue and Customs* judgment, in fact, the CJ wrote that a provision of EU law is unconditional if it lays down an obligation 'not qualified by any condition, or subject, in its implementation or effects, to the taking of any measure either by the institutions of the European Union or by the Member States'.[323] As pointed out by AG Bobek in his opinion in the *NE* case, unconditionality 'implies that the EU provision does not require the adoption of any further measure to be applied'.[324] A provision is unconditional if 'no further elaboration is necessary for its application'.[325]

In this context, what is the essential parameter to affirm or deny the unconditionality of a provision? The answer lies in the degree of discretion[326] left to the States[327] in the application of EU law.[328] As AG Léger remarked in *Linster*, 'review of the way in which the Member State has exercised its discretion remains alone at the heart' of the analysis of the case carried out by the CJ.[329] After all, the inquiry on the discretionary power can be summed up, in essence, as an inquiry on the unconditionality of an EU provision, which means that the review of a State's discretion merges into that on unconditionality.

The matter at this point is how the CJEU defines the concept of discretion. In this regard, three observations can be made. The first is that 'an unconditional provision is one which leaves no discretion to the Member States'.[330] There is no discretion when an EU provision is construed so as to limit the freedom of the Member States in its application.[331] This is the

[319] On this matter, *see* D. Gallo, *L'efficacia*, 202–211.
[320] G. Bebr, *Les dispositions*, 19.
[321] G. Bebr, *Les dispositions*, 19.
[322] For such definition, *see* D. Edward, R. Lane, *Edward and Lane on European Union Law*, Cheltenham, Edward Elgar, 2014, 295; R. Schütze, *European Union Law*, 158.
[323] *Commissioners for Her Majesty's Revenue & Customs v GMAC UK plc* (n 228), para. 30.
[324] Opinion of AG Bobek, *NE* (n 278), para. 41.
[325] S. Prechal, *Horizontal Direct Effect*, 420, 424.
[326] On the importance of such parameter, *see* M. Brand, *Discretion, Divergence, and Unity*, in S. Prechal, B. van Roermund (eds.), *The Coherence*, 217–232. On unconditionality, discretion, and direct effect, *see* G. Isaac, *L'effet direct du droit Communautaire, Répertoire européen Dalloz*, 1997, 1, 3; M. Blanquet, G. Isaac, *Droit général de l'Union européenne*, Paris, Dalloz, 2012, 379. With respect to directives, *see* W. Ganhof van der Meersch, *L'ordre juridique*, 258; P. Pescatore, *L'ordre juridique des Communautés européennes*, Liège, Presses universitaires de Liège, 1975, 161; P. Manin, *De l'utilisation des directives communautaires par les personnes physiques ou morales* (1994) 4 *Actualité juridique. Droit admnistratif* 259, 262; S. Amadeo, *Norme comunitarie*, 127–131.
[327] *See*, amongst others, CJ, *M. H. Marshall v Southampton and South-West Hampshire Area Health Authority (Teaching)*, 152/84, EU:C:1985:345, para. 55.
[328] T. Vandamme, *Democracy and Direct Effect: EU and National Perceptions*, in S. Prechal, B. van Roermund (eds.), *The Coherence*, 271–290, wrote: 'MS discretion, or rather its absence, is after all the core element of the clarity and unconditionality test that the ECJ and national courts use to argue direct effect' (273); 'EC law requirements of sufficient clarity and unconditionality both seem derivatives of the basic requirement of absence of discretion, the "true" ground for direct effect' (284).
[329] Opinion of AG Léger, *Linster* (n 222), para. 50.
[330] *See*, amongst others, CJ, *Peter Kaefer and Andrea Procacci*, joined cases C-100–101/89, EU:C:1990:456, para. 26.
[331] *See*, amongst others, *Comitato per la difesa della cava* (n 5), para. 13.

case regardless of the type of EU source of law at stake, including regulations, as exemplified in the *Abdullahi* case.[332]

The second is that it is possible that an EU norm could be considered directly effective albeit in the presence of a certain margin of discretion. As noted by the EU judges, the existence of such a margin does not necessarily imply that the provision is *per se* deprived of direct effect.[333] Indeed, unconditionality is not an absolute concept and this means that an EU provision is directly effective also when Member States enjoy a degree of latitude in enforcing EU rules.[334] Hence, if there is no discretion, there is direct effect; if, on the other hand, there is discretion, direct effect may eventually arise all the same.[335] More specifically, the CJ has held that direct effect is compatible with the freedom left to States to select[336] and specify the obligations that are provided for under EU law.[337] Accordingly, if a provision grants Member States a certain degree of discretion, it 'does not alter the precise and unconditional nature of the obligation' set forth therein.[338] As shown in the *Van Binsbergen* case, where it was affirmed, as proof of their directly effective nature, that Articles 59 and 60 of the EEC Treaty, currently Articles 56 and 57 TFEU, 'impose a well-defined obligation, the fulfilment of which by the member States cannot be delayed or jeopardized',[339] the fact that certain notions referred to in an EU provision should be specified in more detail by the domestic authority applying them does not preclude *per se* the recognition of their direct effect. After all, there is no doubt that Article 34 TFEU, for example, has direct effect, even though it contains two concepts, that of a quantitative restriction and that of a measure having equivalent effect, which were not clear at all when the CJ had to interpret them for the first time.[340]

With respect to directives, the Court has held that, even though a directive leaves the Member States a certain degree of latitude when they adopt rules in order to implement it,[341] a provision of that act may be regarded as directly effective[342] when, as affirmed in *NE*, it can be considered 'unconditional and precise' in so far as 'it imposes on Member States in unequivocal terms a precise obligation as to the result to be achieved, which is not coupled with any condition regarding application of the rule laid down by it'.[343] Moreover, direct effect shall be asserted provided that it is possible to determine the 'minimum rights' and the minimum protection' stemming from the EU provision.[344] This holds true also when

[332] CJ, *Shamso Abdullahi*, C-394/12, EU:C:2013:813.

[333] In the opinion of P. Craig, G. de Búrca, *EU Law*, 223, the fact that direct effect 'could apply even where the Member States possessed discretion ... represented a significant juridical shift in thinking about direct effect'.

[334] *See*, for instance, *RTS infra BVBA and Aannemingsbedrijf Norré-Behaegel v Vlaams Gewest*, C-387/19, EU:C:2021:13, para. 47.

[335] *See*, for instance, CJ, *M. Helen Marshall v Southampton and South-West Hampshire Area Health Authority (Marshall II)*, C-271/91, EU:C:1993:335, para. 36. *See* also CJ, *Sindicato de Médicos de Asistencia Pública (Simap) v Conselleria de Sanidad y Consumo de la Generalidad Valenciana*, C-303/98, EU:C:2000:528, para. 68; CJ, *Firma Fink-Frucht GmbH*, 27/67, EU:C:1968:22, 309.

[336] In these terms, *see* G. Di Federico, *Il recepimento delle direttive nella giurisprudenza della Corte di Giustizia*, in G. Di Federico, C. Odone (ed.), *Il recepimento delle direttive dell'Unione europea nella prospettiva delle regioni italiane. Modelli e soluzioni*, Naples, Editoriale Scientifica, 2010, 1–68, 49.

[337] Accordingly, J. H. Jans, M. J. M. Verhoeven, *Europeanization*, 91–92.

[338] CJ, *Almos Agrárkülkereskedelmi Kft v Nemzeti Adó- és Vámhivatal Közép-magyarországi Regionális Adó Főigazgatósága*, C-337/13, EU:C:2014:328 , para. 34.

[339] CJ, *van Binsbergen*, 33/74, EU:C:1974:131, para. 26.

[340] *See Iannelli* (n 89), para. 2 of the operative part.

[341] As recalled in CJ, *Impact v Minister for Agriculture and Food*, C-268/06, EU:C:2008:223, para. 62: 'such latitude is not apt to question the direct effect of a directive in so far as EU law does not in any way confer on Member States the right, when transposing it into domestic law, to limit the scope of the prohibition laid down therein.'

[342] *Autorità Garante della Concorrenza e del Mercato* (n 85), para. 64

[343] *Autorità Garante della Concorrenza e del Mercato* (n 85), para. 29.

[344] *See*, to that effect, CJ, *Paola Faccini Dori v Recreb Srl*, C-91/92, EU:C:1994:292, para. 17; *Simap* (n 335), para. 68; *RTS* (n 334), para. 49; *Autorità Garante della Concorrenza e del Mercato* (n 85), para. 64.

domestic authorities must adopt the 'material and procedural conditions' aimed at applying the EU rules at stake, as recently stated in *RTS*[345] with regard to the so-called 'self-cleaning principle' enshrined in Article 57(6) of Directive 2014/24 of 26 February 2014 on public procurement and repealing Directive 2004/18/EC. Actually, in that case, it was stated that any economic operator that is in one of the situations listed in paragraphs 1–4 of Article 57(6) 'may provide evidence to the effect that measures taken by him are sufficient to demonstrate its reliability' to avoid being excluded from a tender they had participated in.[346] Such provision, according to the CJ, 'is not dependent on transposition into national law in order to be invoked by the economic operator concerned and applied to its benefit' and 'provides, for the benefit of that economic operator, a minimum level of protection irrespective of the margin of discretion left to Member States in determining the procedural conditions of that provision'.[347]

In the same vein, in *Autorità Garante della Concorrenza e del Mercato*, about the compatibility of Italian law on seaside concessions with Article 12 of Directive 2006/123,[348] the CJ, first, clarified that, 'where the number of authorisations available for a given activity is limited because of the scarcity of natural resources', the domestic authorities 'must apply a selection procedure to potential candidates which provides full guarantees of impartiality and transparency'.[349] Secondly, the CJ affirmed, on the one hand, that the Member States retain a degree of latitude if they decide to adopt provisions intended specifically to ensure the impartiality and transparency of a selection procedure, while on the other hand, that, by requiring the organization of an impartial and transparent selection procedure, Article 12(1) of Directive 2006/123 shall be interpreted as a norm prescribing, 'unconditionally and sufficiently precisely, content comprising minimum protection in favour of potential candidates'.[350] As for Article 12(2) of Directive 2006/123, the CJ observed that, while providing that an authorization, such as a concession for the occupation of State-owned maritime property, 'is to be granted for an appropriate limited period and may not be open to automatic renewal',[351] that provision has direct effect in so far as it prohibits, in unequivocal terms, the Member States from providing for automatic and general extensions of such concessions. Moreover, as noted by the CJ, the fact that the obligation to apply an impartial and transparent selection procedure to potential candidates and the prohibition of the automatic renewal of the authorization apply only in cases where the number of authorizations available for a given activity is limited because of the scarcity of available natural resources cannot question the direct effect of Article 12 even though such scarcity must be determined by reference to a factual situation assessed by the competent authority and subject to review by a national court.[352] To this effect, the analysis on the unconditionality of a norm shall not be confused with that on the necessity of its transposition into the domestic legal order through a further national implementing measure. Furthermore, as can be inferred from the *NE* ruling, direct effect

[345] *RTS* (n 334), paras 43–50, on which, *see* D. Gallo, L. Cecchetti, *La prassi regolatoria e giurisprudenziale italiana in materia di self-cleaning è compatibile con il diritto dell'Unione Europea?* (2021) 2 *Rivista della Regolazione dei Mercati* 244.
[346] *RTS* (n 334), para. 48.
[347] *RTS* (n 334), paras 48 and 49.
[348] *See* § 4 of Chapter V.
[349] *Autorità Garante della Concorrenza e del Mercato* (n 85), para. 66.
[350] *Autorità Garante della Concorrenza e del Mercato* (n 85), para. 67.
[351] *Autorità Garante della Concorrenza e del Mercato* (n 85), para. 68.
[352] *Autorità Garante della Concorrenza e del Mercato* (n 85), paras 69–71.

shall be recognized only if the question of whether the national authorities exceeded their discretion can be judicially reviewed.[353]

The above reflections hold true also when the assessment of complex economic circumstances is brought to the CJ's attention: as acknowledged in the *Comune di Carpaneto* judgment, unlike what was done in previous decisions,[354] such an assessment 'is not exempt from judicial review'[355] and, therefore, the EU provision shall not be considered deprived of direct effect. Also, in *Van Duyn* it was confirmed that the existence of doubts regarding the EU provisions under examination by the CJ, and their resolution through the procedure under Article 267 TFEU,[356] do not preclude their recognition as directly effective. As emphasized by AG Jacobs in *Lindopark*, even though a provision can be regarded as directly effective, its meaning need not be 'beyond dispute'; the very fact that the court is called upon to interpret a provision before applying it grants it a certain discretionary power.[357] The ambiguity of a provision, as stated by AG Warner in *Regina v Secretary of State for Home Affairs*, does not prevent the attribution of direct effect.[358] As pointed out by Szyszczak, direct effect is about how EU rules 'interact with national laws in order to provide effective enforcement of substantive Community measures', as long as EU law and national law 'in tandem' can create 'justiciable solutions'.[359] In fact, EU provisions, much more often than it is normally assumed, are not fully self-executing, that is, they need additional specifications, at the domestic level, to be directly invoked by natural and legal persons and enforced by State authorities.[360]

The third observation: the assessment on the margin of discretion, that is, on the scope of direct effect, on the one hand, may encroach upon the principle of equality in so far as it is applied differently by the various national courts[361] while, on the other, it may breach the separation of powers, notably (but not only) between the legislator and the judiciary. In fact, where the EU provision is directly effective, the domestic court is required to disapply the national provision and replace it in order to comply with EU law. Direct effect grants to courts the power to directly apply EU provisions without the intermediation of the legislator.[362] The application of EU disrectly effective provisions may also affect the separation between legislative and executive powers, besides the judiciary, given that direct effect can require the court to review the legality of administrative practice rather than of national legislation.[363]

[353] *NE* (n 156), para. 23; *van Duyn* (n 110), paras 7 and 13. *See* also *Kraaijeveld* (n 217), para. 59; *Impact* (341), para. 64; CJ, *Salzburger Flughafen*, C-244/12, EU:C:2013:203, paras 29 and 31. *See*, more recently, CJ, *Secretary of State for the Home Department v Muhammad Sazzadur Rahman and Others*, C-83/11, EU:C:2012:519, para. 25; *NE*, opinion of AG Bobek (n 278), para. 36. *See*, in that regard, *Linster* (n 222), para. 37.

[354] *See*, amongst others, CJ, *Madeleine Muller*, 10/71, EU:C:1971:85. But exceptions do exist also in the early case law, as demonstrated by *Firma Molkerei* (n 280), 207.

[355] *Comune di Carpaneto* (n 85), para. 32.

[356] *van Duyn* (n 110), para. 14.

[357] Opinion AG Jacobs of 26 September 2000, *Lindöpark*, C-150/99, EU:C:2000:504, para. 44.

[358] Opinion AG Warner of 27 February 1980, *Regina v Secretary of State for Home Affairs, ex parte Mario Santillo*. 131/79, EU:C:1980:58, 1611.

[359] *See* E. Szyszczak, *Making Europe*, 358.

[360] As per EU primary law, it has been observed by G. Beck, *The Legal Reasoning of the Court of Justice of the EU*, Oxford, Hart, 2012, 438, that 'EU primary law [itself] is characterized by a high degree of vagueness and pervasive norm collision across most of its substantive areas'.

[361] *See* the opinion by AG Emiliou, *T.A.C.* (n 233), para. 64.

[362] The EU provision enters, therefore, in the 'judicial province of judges', as highlighted by D. Edward, *Direct Effect: Myth, Mess or Mystery?*, in J. M. Prinssen, A. Schrauwen (eds.), *Direct Effect*, 1–13, 3–4. *See* also the reflections in D. Edward, *Direct Effect, the Separation of Powers and the Judicial Enforcement of Obligations*, in *Scritti in onore di Giuseppe Federico Mancini*, Milan, Giuffrè, 1998, 423-445, 424-425.

[363] C. W. A. Timmermans, *Directives: their Effect within the National Legal Systems* (1979) 16 *Common Market Law Review* 533, 541, affirmed that the judge 'would usurp governmental or administrative powers' in the application of an EU provision which leaves too great a margin of discretion to Member States for its enforcement.

In this context, the principle of separation of powers is potentially challenged by an incorrect and too narrow interpretation of 'discretionary margin'.[364] The application of EU law should not subvert this principle.[365] Such subversion would materialize where the vagueness of the EU norm compels the judge to fill the gap through interpretation to the extent of eroding the legislator's competence. The principle of separation of powers, moreover, is connected with that of legal certainty and predictability: individuals must be able to determine the effects that EU provisions can entail in their subjective legal spheres. Beneficiaries of legal positions arising from EU laws must thus be able 'to ascertain the full extent of their rights and, where appropriate, rely on them before the national courts'[366] and the application of said norms 'must be foreseeable by those subject to them'.[367] Ultimately, what emerges from an analysis of the EU case law is that unconditionality, as the only true condition for which a provision is considered to be directly effective, is realized when natural and legal persons can understand and invoke it and the national authorities can enforce it. As AG van Gerven observed in his opinion in *Banks*, the completeness of the EU rule and its independence from discretionary implementing measures are 'merely aspects of one and the same characteristic feature which that rule must exhibit, namely it must be capable of being applied by a court to a specific case'.[368] It is this enquiry on the degree of discretion inherent in the EU rule, that is, on its unconditionality and possible application to the specific case, which must steer both national courts and the CJEU.

6. Proportionality of penalties as a privileged *sedes materiae* for assessing the selective disapplication of national law

A thorny and topical issue emerges from a reading of recent EU jurisprudence: whether and to what extent is the general principle of proportionality[369] of penalties[370] sufficiently unconditional to be considered directly effective and generate the disapplication of conflicting national law? Such a principle, in fact, is the privileged *sedes materiae* to understand the complexities underpinning the definition of unconditionality and the scope of the duty to disapply resulting from direct effect. Indeed, when the field is criminal law, the risks associated with the immediate application of an ill-defined EU rule or principle, as well as the consequent disapplication of the national rule that follows, are not negligible. They are not from

[364] On this topic, *see* A. Bleckmann, *L'applicabilité directe*, 99–100; P. Pescatore, *L'ordre juridique*, 161; P. J. Kuijper, *Epilogue; Symbiosis?*, in J. M. Prinssen, A. Schrauwen (eds.), *Direct Effect*, 252–267, 254; J. H. Jans, M. J. M. Verhoeven, *Europeanization*, 91; S. Amadeo, *Norme comunitarie*, 20–21 and 152–157.

[365] S. Amadeo, *Norme comunitarie*, footnote 41, 20.

[366] *Almos* (n 338), para. 21.

[367] CJ, *Traum EOOD*, C-492/13, EU:C:2014:2267, para. 28.

[368] Opinion of AG van Gerven, *Banks* (n 314), para. 27.

[369] On the principle of proportionality as a general principle of EU law, *see Internationale Handelsgesellschaft* (n 153), paras 6–13, and more recently CJ, *The Queen v Ministry of Agriculture, Fisheries and Food, ex parte FEDESA and Others*, C-331/88, EU:C:1990:391, para. 13. In the literature, *see* N. Emiliou, *The Principle of Proportionality in European Law: A Comparative Study*, Alphen aan de Rijn, Kluwer Law International, 1996; X. Groussot, *General Principles*, 20–23; T.-I. Harbo, *The function of the Proportionality Principle in EU Law* (2010) 16 *European Law Journal* 159; W. Sauter, *Proportionality in EU Law: A Balancing Act?* (2013) 15 *Cambridge Yearbook of European Legal Studies* 439–466; P. De Pasquale, *Art. 5 TUE*, in A. Tizzano (ed.), *Trattati dell'Unione europea. Commentario*, 2nd ed., Milan, Giuffrè, 2014, 50–54; T. Tridimas, *The Principle of Proportionality*, in R. Schütze, T. Tridimas (eds.), *Oxford Principles*, 243–264.

[370] *See*, amongst judgments on this principle, CJ, *Farkas*, C-564/15, EU:C:2017:302, para. 59; CJ, *Commission v Spain*, C-788/19, EU:C:2022:55, para. 48. On its qualification as general principle of EU law, *see* CJ, *Repsol Butano*, joined cases C-473/17 and C-546/17, EU:C:2019:308, para. 39 and *NE* (n 156), para. 31.

three points of view: the discretion left to the judge-enforcer of EU law; the implications for the respect of the principle of separation of powers; and the rights of individuals subject to the application of the penalty regime provided for in national law.

Since the *Greek Maize* case,[371] the CJ has affirmed that domestic authorities have a duty to adopt 'effective, proportionate and dissuasive' sanctions with regard to infringements of EU law or national laws implementing it.[372] After thirty-three years, such formula was granted direct effect in the (above-mentioned) *NE* case, whereby Austrian provisions imposing excessively harsh sanctions were deemed inconsistent with EU law, notably with Article 20 of Directive 2014/67 concerning the posting of workers, and thus subject to disapplication. More specifically, the Austrian regime envisaged several predetermined minimum and maximum fines which were applied in relation to each posted worker and possibly subject to accumulation (with no maximum amount to cap the accumulation of individual pecuniary sanctions) and, in respect to such legal framework, the Austrian Constitutional Court and the Supreme Administrative Court took divergent stances as to which national rules were to be set aside. The former had opted to disapply *in toto* the relevant internal provisions, while the latter had selectively set aside only the words 'in relation to each worker concerned', which had allowed for the unlimited accumulation of individual fines.[373] Against this background, the Regional Administrative Court of Styria asked the CJ if the requirement of proportionality laid down in Article 20 of Directive 2014/67 was endowed with direct effect and, if so, what the consequences would be for the national courts. On this second matter, the problem, in practice, was whether the domestic legislation as a whole had to be disapplied or only some of its provisions so that the remaining rule would be aligned with the principle of proportionality. While the principle of proportionality of penalties, as well as the *NE* judgment, will be analyzed in section 1.1 of Chapter IV from the standpoint of the objective exclusionary form of direct effect, in this section the focus is on the characteristics of direct effect and on the role of the judiciary in disapplying, *selectively*, domestic norms which are in conflict with EU law endowed with direct effect.

As for the characteristics of direct effect, the CJ openly departed from its previous *Link Logistik* ruling[374] and the paradox which arose in that case: the imposition of a duty to disapply outside the realm of direct effect, that is, by virtue of EU provisions deprived of precision, clarity, and/or unconditionality.[375] According to the CJ, although the content of the principle of proportionality is *per se* more indeterminate than other principles/rules and is necessarily connected to a certain degree of discretion, the obligation imposed upon Member States to avoid disproportionate penalties was to be deemed sufficiently clear, precise, and unconditional first and foremost because it is not subject to any terms.[376] Proof of this is that such principle has been codified in the very short, yet determined, Article 49(3) of the Charter, which states that 'the severity of penalties must not be disproportionate to the criminal offence', and merely 'reiterated'[377] by Article 20 of Directive 2014/67. In the words of AG Bobek, Article 49(3) is 'a far more qualified candidate for direct effect' than were other

[371] CJ, *Commission v Greece* (Greek Maize), 68/88, EU:C:1989:339, para. 24.

[372] For a reconstruction of the principle of proportionality of penalties in the light of the *NE* ruling, as well as of the EU case law, *see* S. Montaldo, *Handle with Care!*, 863–864 and M. Lanotte, *La proporzionalità*, 367–374.

[373] In these terms, *see* S. Montaldo, *Handle with Care!*, 865.

[374] CJ, *Link Logistic*, C-384/17, EU:C:2018:810, para. 56.

[375] On the overruling technique, *see* § 2 of Chapter II.

[376] *NE v Bezirkshauptmannschaft Hartberg-Fürstenfeld II*, para. 29. This ruling brings a novelty since for decades direct effect has not been affirmed, as occurred in CJ, *Amsterdam Bulb*, 50/76, EU:C:1977:13, para. 32; *Casati* (n 100), para. 27.

[377] *NE* (n 156), para. 31.

less intelligible and clear/precise/unconditional Charter provisions. In this vein, the denial of direct effect of Article 49(3) 'would be a rather surprising outcome'.[378] Moreover, as stressed again by Bobek, there aren't sound grounds for possibly distinguishing between the way the proportionality requirement, as a directly effective principle, functions under the EU internal market and the way such requirement acts under EU criminal law in respect to more specific rules on posted workers.[379]

As for the object and extent of the duty to disapply, the CJ affirmed that the cumulation of the various characteristics of the Austrian legislation, in particular the accumulation without an upper limit of fines which may not be lower than a predefined minimum amount, breached the requirement of proportionality of penalties.[380] As not every single characteristic had been considered able to question the effectiveness of that requirement, the CJ observed that national courts had 'to disregard that part of the national legislation from which the disproportionate nature of the penalties stems in such a way as to result in the imposition of proportionate penalties, which are at the same time effective and dissuasive'.[381] Disapplication, therefore, shall concern only those national provisions[382] which prevent the imposition of proportionate penalties,[383] as was argued also by the European Commission in its observations and by AG Bobek.[384] Moreover, the same approach had been taken by the Austrian Supreme Administrative Court, as recalled by the referring court.[385] A partial disapplication, therefore, is justified in so far as a selection of inconsistent domestic rules can be performed.[386]

Against this backdrop, a connected problem is whether national judges, by partially setting aside national laws, could do something that they would not be allowed to do, that is, integrate the internal legislation and, in this way, unduly replace the legislator. At stake is the compliance with the principles of legality, legal certainty, and equality. In this respect, the CJ dismissed the concerns raised, not only by the referring court, but also by the Czech and Polish governments, according to which a partial disapplication of national law would have caused an infringement of such principles.[387] To this end, the Court, first, clarified that the principle of legal certainty requires that individuals may 'ascertain unequivocally what their rights and obligations are'.[388] Then, it recalled that the principle of legality and proportionality of criminal offences and penalties implies 'that legislation must clearly define offences and the penalties which they attract'.[389] Afterwards, and more importantly, the CJ focused on the principle of non-retroactivity of criminal law in order to highlight that this principle, on the one hand, means 'that a court cannot, in the course of criminal proceedings, aggravate the rules on criminal liability of those against whom such proceedings are brought', and, on the other, does not preclude 'the imposition of lighter penalties on them'.[390]

[378] Opinion of AG Bobek, *NE* (n 278), para. 48.
[379] Opinion of AG Bobek, *NE* (n 156), paras 49–52.
[380] For a critique, *see* F. Viganò, *La proporzionalità della pena tra diritto costituzionale italiano e diritto dell'Unione europea: sull'effetto diretto dell'art. 49, par. 3, della Carta alla luce di una recentissima sentenza della Corte di giustizia* (2022) *Sistema Penale.it* 1. By the same author, *see* extensively F. Viganò, *La proporzionalità della pena. Principi di diritto penale e costituzionale*, Turin, Giappichelli, 2021.
[381] *NE* (n 156), para. 42.
[382] For the identification of these provisions, *see* opinion of AG Bobek, *NE* (n 278), paras 77–79.
[383] *NE* (n 156), para. 44
[384] Opinion of AG Bobek, *NE* (n 278), paras 75–85 and 112–117.
[385] As remarked above, this court adopted a different approach than the one taken by the Constitutional Court; on this matter, *see* the opinion of AG Bobek, *NE* (n 278), paras 77–85.
[386] A case not related to criminal law, whereby selective disapplication has been imposed by the CJ, is *K.L.* (n 166).
[387] *NE* (n 156), paras 45–57.
[388] *NE* (n 156), para. 46.
[389] *NE* (n 156), para. 47.
[390] *NE* (n 156), para. 48.

Where the perspective is the principle of legal certainty, a problem, however, must be addressed to the extent that the individual would see penalties applied (by the judge) which are unknown to them insofar as they are not provided for by law. A closely related critical issue relates to the scope of the principle of separation of (judicial, administrative, legislative) powers, in particular, of its corollary, in the field of criminal law, represented by the principle '*nulla poena sine lege*', the strict application of which should not allow either the courts or the administrative bodies to determine *ex post* the amount of the penalty, in place of the legislature. More specifically, on the predictability of the penalties, a consequence of *NE* is that both the judiciary and administrative bodies would be endowed with the power to modulate, by means of interpretation, the national rules regarding the amount of sanctions. This would happen since, once acknowledged that EU law can penetrate domestic criminal legal systems, it would be unavoidable that judges would take advantage with a certain degree of discretion to correctly draw the line between applicable and non-applicable domestic rules. The establishment of the criteria determining the amount of the penalty by the judge (or the administrative bodies), on the basis of a partial disapplication of domestic law, could give the latter too much leeway, as observed by the Czech and Polish governments,[391] lacking a proper legal basis. However, if disapplication does not affect the prerogatives that the individual has already acquired, such *in bonam partem* judicial intervention should not be *a priori* stigmatized. As a matter of fact, when the disapplication of domestic laws is *in bonam partem*, as happens when EU law imposes a reduction of the severity of penalties compared to those provided for by national criminal law, the situations at hand must be treated differently than when the disapplication is *in malam partem*.[392] In any event, the CJ seems to have acted correctly also because, even if a national authority disregards certain parts of the national legislation relating to some penalties, 'the fact remains that the penalty thus adopted will remain so under that legislation'.[393] Additionally, as observed by Bobek, the recognition of direct effect to a given norm 'does not imply that every aspect is expressly set out in advance therein', as such a scenario is 'simply not realistic'.[394]

As to the principle of equality, it seems that its possible violation is unlikely to concretize, in practice, since national authorities, including courts, shall always apply the requirement of proportionality. Differences in the amount of penalties would naturally occur as they are the result of the varying levels of seriousness of the offences committed and of the need for the determination of the sanctions, accordingly.[395] Moreover, as remarked by Bobek, a problem of equality could arise 'only if the two offenders were in an identical situation. Yet, as stressed in his *NE* opinion, 'life tends to be infinitely variable' and this is the reason 'why both administrative and criminal law, when setting out penalties or sanctions in general, at least in modern law, normally do not proceed by a "one size fits all" approach, but by setting a permissible range, within which administrative or judicial discretion is exercised'.[396]

In conclusion, the CJ made the right choice in making the principle of proportionality operational through direct effect and the surgical *in bonam partem* disapplication of national law. However, it may happen that, in some legal orders, due to a stricter conception of

[391] *NE* (n 156), para. 45.
[392] On this issue, *see* the analysis in § 3 of Chapter V.
[393] *NE* (n 156), para. 52.
[394] Opinion of AG Bobek, *NE* (n 278), para. 108.
[395] S. Montaldo, *Handle with Care!*, 870.
[396] Opinion of AG Bobek, *NE* (n 278) para. 107.

the principle of legality and to a wide perimeter of the principle of separation of powers, the disapplication could be triggered only after an *erga omnes* clarification by the apex court of that State. In this vein, a derogation from the immediate enforcement of the duty to disapply is conceivable: a suspension of such disapplication, possibly grounded in the respect of the national identity pursuant to Article 4(2) TEU,[397] would then be performed.

Having highlighted the crucial role performed by the premise of unconditionality and taken the principle of proportionality of penalties as a privileged tool of analysis, the next question to be addressed, at the core of the following section, is the interplay between direct effect, whose test ultimately revolves around unconditionality, and direct applicability.

7. Merging direct effect with direct applicability, in practice

As to the relationship between direct effect and direct applicability,[398] scholars often tend to exclude the possibility that these two concepts coincide.[399] The assumption is that, while direct applicability refers to an objective quality of an EU provision not requiring a further implementing act, direct effect, instead, is about the justiciability of EU law by the individual. As noted in the literature, there is a need to distinguish between direct applicability and direct effect because the former indicates the way EU law is implemented in the legal order of the Member States as the 'law of the land', while the latter is concerned with how said 'law of the land' can be invoked by private subjects before national courts.[400]

Such reconstruction is theoretically correct. The fact that there is a close connection implies, indeed, upstream, that, at least in theoretical terms, these are two different categories. The existence of a correlation, and thus a non-coincidence between direct effect and direct applicability, can be inferred by reading some of the most important and oldest decisions of the CJ. From an analysis of *Van Gend & Loos*, it can be seen, in fact, that direct effect and direct applicability have different meanings. In particular, the Court, right after it observed that Article 12 of the EEC Treaty is aimed at producing 'direct effects in the legal relationship between Member States and their subjects', noted that the provision 'does not require any legislative intervention on the part of the states', and then concluded that it produces 'direct effects' and creates 'individual rights which national courts must protect'.[401] Direct applicability and direct effect of Article 12, thus, are inextricably interconnected. This logically entails that, in theoretical terms, one does not identify itself in the other. From the analysis of *Van Gend & Loos* it flows that the recognition of direct applicability seems to act as a precondition for the production of direct effect, as happens in other decisions, both recent and past.[402] In *van Duyn*, in particular, the CJ stated that, as regulations are directly applicable

[397] *See* also §§ 7 and 11 of Chapter V.

[398] On such matter in respect to the legal effects of international law within the EU legal system, *see* §§ 1–2 and 5 of Chapter VII.

[399] However, amongst international law scholars, many, consciously or unconsciously, superimpose the concept of direct effect with that of direct applicability. For instance, M. J. M. Verhoeven, *La notion d'applicabilité directe' du droit international* (1980) 13 *Revue belge de droit international* 243, 243, wrote that: '*l'applicabilité directe peut être entendue de l'aptitude d'une règle de droit international à conférer par elle-même aux particuliers, sans requérir aucune mesure interne d'exécution, des droits dont ils puissent se prévaloir devant les autorités (juridictionnelles) de l'Etat où cette règle est en vigueur*.'

[400] J. A. Winter, *Direct Applicability*, 425. *See* also A. Rosas, L. Armati, *EU Constitutional Law: An Introduction*, 3rd ed., Oxford, Hart, 2018, 72–73.

[401] *Van Gend & Loos* (n 87), paras 3 and 13.

[402] According to R. Schütze, *European Union Law*, 154–155, 'direct applicability' is 'broader' than direct effect and the latter is not the precondition for the former.

pursuant to (then) Article 189 of the EC Treaty, currently Article 288 TFEU, they 'may by their very nature have direct effects'.[403] In other words, direct applicability means that a provision directly infiltrates into the national legal order, but is only potentially and in principle capable of producing practical effects, that is, be relied upon by individuals before the national authorities and, in this regard, applied in the specific case.[404] From *van Duyn* we may conclude that, if a norm is also enforceable, then, in addition to being directly applicable, it will also have direct effect. Thus, we may affirm that not all directly applicable acts produce direct effects. According to such line of reasoning, direct applicability would be one thing, linked to the nature of the legal source of the legislative instrument, while direct effect, as it pertains to the nature of the provision included within that source of law, would be a different thing.[405] In this regard, if the perspective is that of theoretical reconstruction, an objection must be raised: following the reasoning above, directives, being (considered) always deprived of direct applicability, should not be able to entail direct effects, which is just not true, as observed in section 3.1 of this chapter.

The perspective we shall choose must not be only theoretical/reconstructive. In fact, the problem regarding the relationship between direct effect and direct applicability must be examined first and foremost from a practical point of view. And by using this approach, the evidence demonstrates that direct effect and direct applicability cannot be deemed as distinct legal categories for two reasons.[406] The first crucial reason why direct effect and direct applicability merge is the result of what has been explained in the previous section: the presence or lack of unconditionality of an EU provision depends on the nature and extent of discretion left to national authorities in its enforcement. Unconditionality means that an EU provision does not require further acts of implementation and is thus directly applicable by national authorities for the governing of the case, that is, unconditionality means direct applicability. If unconditionality means direct applicability and if direct applicability/unconditionality, by 'absorbing' the conditions of clarity and precision, is the only core element of the test on direct effect,[407] direct effect and direct applicability end up being, in practice, the same thing rather than 'simply' inter-connected.[408]

The second reason is that from an analysis of EU and national case law it appears that direct effect and direct applicability merge: what really matters[409] is whether an EU provision is justiciable, that is, applicable to the dispute at issue. For instance, in the *Reyners* case, regarding the (then) Article 52 of the EEC Treaty, currently Article 49 TFEU, concerning freedom of establishment, the norm was defined as 'directly applicable'/'*directement applicable*',[410] even though at stake was the justiciability of that provision.[411]

In light of the above, aside from issues of terminology, direct applicability is a feature of regulations, but it can also be part of the other EU legal sources, under the guise of their

[403] *van Duyn* (n 110), para. 12.
[404] In these terms, *see* S. Prechal, *Directives*, 227–229.
[405] This argument is submitted by J. Bengoetxea, *Direct Applicability or Effect*, in M. Hoskins, W. Robinson (eds.), *A True European. Essays for Judge David Edward*, Oxford, Oxford University Press, 2004, 353–366, 354–355, and 363.
[406] *See* also D. Gallo, *Rethinking*, 599.
[407] On the attribution of an advantage as the other core element of (and precondition for) direct effect, *see* § 3 of Chapter V.
[408] *Contra see*, amongst others, R. Schütze, *Direct Effects*, 266–268.
[409] *See* G. Tesauro, *Diritto dell'Unione europea*^{7}, Padua, Cedam 2012, 165; R. Kovar, *L'intégrité*, 161–162.
[410] *Reyners* (n 273), para. 32.
[411] As to the concepts of direct applicability and direct effect in respect to the incorporation and legal effects of international law within the EU legal order, *see* §§ 1–2 and 5 of Chapter VII.

unconditional character, including directives. There are no significant differences between the effects of regulations and unimplemented directives when national acts are not needed for their enforcement.[412] Just as direct effect/applicability of regulations does not *a priori* exclude that provisions contained therein should be implemented, through further acts, at the domestic level,[413] other EU legal sources, both primary and secondary, including directives, albeit not defined as directly applicable by the Treaties or the CJEU, may contain obligations which, to be unconditional, do not require the adoption of additional measures.[414] In such situations direct effect arises and, as a consequence, so does direct applicability. In short, there is no reason why AG Reischl's thesis in *Ratti*, according to which only regulations could be reputed directly applicable,[415] should be upheld.

In conclusion, an EU norm is directly effective if it is unconditional and thus immediately/directly applicable. In line with Pescatore, direct effect shall be identified with the concept of justiciability of a provision[416] and with its ability to be directly applied. In the words of Edward, the doctrine of direct effect, 'using that expression in a broad way', provides the criteria 'for selecting or rejecting the norms to be applied and for clarifying the scope of judicial competence'.[417] Hence, at the heart of direct effect lies the concept of *immédiateté*,[418] that is, the capacity of an EU provision to govern the case at hand. As proof of the practical nature of direct effect,[419] AG Van Gerven correctly affirmed that, 'provided and in so far as a provision of [Union] law is sufficiently operational in itself to be applied by a court, it has direct effect',[420] and, in the same vein, more recently, AG Bobek observed that 'direct effect is the ability of an EU law rule to be justiciable at national level, directly before the national judge, without the need for any further "intermediary" of national law'.[421]

[412] *Contra see* G. Bebr, *Directly Applicable Provisions of Community Law: The Development of a Community Concept* (1970) 19 *International and Comparative Law Quarterly* 257, 283–298, and J. A. Winter, *Direct Applicability*, 437. For a criticism of Bebr's and Winter's stances, *see* J. Steiner, *Direct Applicability in EEC Law—A Chameleon Concept* (1982) 98 *Law Quarterly Review* 229, 231–232.

[413] *See* Opinion of AG Warner of 19 November 1974, *Filippo Galli*, 31/74, EU:C:1974:126, para. 70.

[414] *See* K. Lenaerts, *Le juge et la Constitution aux États-Unis d'Amérique et dans l'ordre juridique européen*, Brussels, Bruylant, 1988, 560.

[415] Opinion of AG Reischl of 5 April 1979, *Ratti*, EU:C:1979:44, 1650.

[416] According to P. Pescatore, *International Law*, 174 and 177, direct effect is always a 'matter of justiciability', which is crucial to verifying whether an EU provision is 'capable of judicial application'.

[417] D. Edward, *Direct Effect, the Separation*, 13.

[418] As pointed out by M. Waelbroeck, *L'immédiateté communautaire, caractéristique de la supranationalité: quelques consequences pour la pratique*, in C. Rousseau (ed.), *Le droit international demain*, Neuchâtel, Edition Ides et Calendes, 1974, 81–89, 85–89.

[419] X. Groussot, A. Loxa, *Of The Practicability of Direct Effect and the 'Doctrine of Change'*, in *EU Law Live*, 29 March 2022, available at https://eulawlive.com/op-ed-of-the-practicability-of-direct-effect-and-the-doctrine-of-change-by-xavier-groussot-and-alezini-loxa/.

[420] Opinion of AG van Gerven, *Banks* (n 314), para. 27.

[421] Opinion of AG Bobek, *NE* (n 278), para. 32.

IV
BROAD DIRECT EFFECT

1. Decoupling direct effect and rights

1.1 The EU case law

In the *Van Gend & Loos* ruling, the conferral of a right is the core element of the doctrine of direct effect. As a corollary to this conferral, in *Van Gend & Loos* and the related doctrine, directly effective provisions, which are invoked by natural and legal persons,[1] replace domestic norms when it comes to governing a case under the scrutiny of a national court. Disapplication, in the light of the *Van Gend & Loos* judgment and the subjective substitutive direct effect originating from it, therefore, presupposes the existence of a right created by EU law, while triggering the application of an EU norm in place of a domestic provision.

As has been anticipated[2] and will be extensively demonstrated in this section, the abovementioned conventional narrow understanding of direct effect, while valid for the *Van Gend & Loos* ruling and doctrine, cannot be generalized. After all, direct effect does not necessarily mean that individuals exercise rights conferred by EU law on them, nor does it always entail substitutive effects, whereby a norm of EU law replaces a provision of domestic law. Direct effect has a different, objective, facet, in so far as it also reveals the capacity of EU law to serve as a parameter (or standard) of legality of national law,[3] with exclusionary effect, regardless of the creation of a right stemming directly from the EU legal order. Direct effect is thus broader than the *Van Gend & Loos* doctrine. In those situations, EU law generally[4] does not serve to replace the void left by the national provisions that were rendered inapplicable. In fact, the cases often end up being regulated (only) by those internal rules which have not been set aside and, for this reason, continue to apply to the extent that they do not conflict with the EU legal order. In other words, under objective exclusionary direct effect the key matter is that of justiciability and invocability, regardless of the creation of a right.[5]

[1] But *see* § 3.1 of Chapter III and §§ 4–6 of Chapter V on public bodies invoking EU directly effective provisions against other public bodies or private parties. All URLs for this chapter were last accessed on 30 April 2024.

[2] *See* also Chapter III, §§ 1 and 3.1.

[3] On the two visions of narrow and broad direct effect of international law within the EU legal order, *see* § 3 and 5 of Chapter VII.

[4] *See* L. Squintani, J. Lindeboom, *The Normative Impact of Invoking Directives: Casting Light on Direct Effect and the Elusive Distinction between Obligations and Mere Adverse Repercussions* (2019) 38 *Yearbook of European Law* 18–72, footnote 100, 34, according to whom, 'the emphasis on the obligation of national institutions to exclude, i.e. disapply, any national provision conflicting with an EU provision that is invoked by an individual, seems to suggest that the substitution–exclusion distinction is broadly similar to the distinction between subjective and objective direct effect'. They point out, however, that this equation would be mistaken 'since some instances of "objective direct effect" require substitution of the directive provision'. In fact, the only exception, as recalled by the two authors themselves, seems to be the following case: CJ, *Salzburger Flughafen GmbH v Umweltsenat*, C-244/12, EU:C:2013:203.

[5] On direct applicability, invocability, and justiciability as the distinctive feature(s) of direct effect, *see* § 7 of Chapter III.

Direct Effect in EU Law. Daniele Gallo, Oxford University Press. © Daniele Gallo 2025. DOI: 10.1093/9780191925221.003.0005

From this angle, direct effect shall be deemed as the capacity of a provision to be invoked before a national authority, that is, justiciable and enforceable. What the individuals claim, in practice, is the obligation enshrined in EU law and imposed on the States and/or other individuals. Thus, they invoke an EU norm not to exercise a right attached to it, but rather to obtain a review of legality of national law. In doing this, individuals seek to vindicate an advantage/interest through disapplication. As will be further discussed, the advantage entailed by disapplication shall be intended as an interest or a 'privilege', borrowing from Hohfeld's re-conceptualization of 'subjective legal situations'.[6]

The complexity of the matter is increased due to the EU case law on direct effect, which is far from straightforward, as mentioned several times in this book. Moreover, the boundaries between the different forms of direct effect (subjective, objective, substitutive, exclusionary), which have been discussed by a few Advocates General,[7] have not been explicitly dealt with by either the CJ or the GC to this day. There is, therefore, great uncertainty on the matter.

Against this backdrop, the CJEU's case law, particularly the rulings on directives, will be interpreted, in this section, in the sense of favouring a broad interpretation of direct effect that is inclusive of objective exclusionary direct effect.[8] On the other hand, the collateral implications from this understanding of direct effect for the relativization of the prohibition of horizontal direct effect of directives will be discussed in sections 3–6 of Chapter VI. In this framework, the starting point in the process of objectification of direct effect is the *Becker* judgment,[9] regarding Article 13(B)(d)(1) of the Sixth Directive 77/388/EEC on the harmonization of Member States' law in relation to the turnover tax.[10] In paragraph 25, the existence of two manifestations of direct effect (subjective and objective)[11] is clear where it is stated that, wherever the provisions of a directive appear to be unconditional and sufficiently precise, those provisions may 'be relied upon as against any national provision which is incompatible with the directive *or* in so far as the provisions define rights which individuals

[6] *See*, *amplius*, W. N. Hohfeld, *Fundamental Legal Conceptions as Applied in Judicial Reasoning* (1917) 26 *Yale Law Journal* 710, and, on this point, *see* S. Prechal, *Does Direct Effect Still Matter?* (2000) 37 *Common Market Law Review* 1047, 1058–1059. *See* also § 3 of this chapter.

[7] Amongst Advocates General, on the subjective substitutive/objective exclusionary dichotomy, *see* Opinion of AG van Gerven of 26 January 1993, *Marshall II*, C-271/91, EU:C:1993:30; opinion of AG Jacobs of 27 January 1994, *Vaneetveld v Le Foyer SA*, C-316/93, EU:C:1994:32; opinion of AG Lenz of 9 February 1994, *Faccini Dori v Recreb Srl*, C-91/92, EU:C:1994:45; opinion of AG Léger of 11 January 2000, *Grand Duchy of Luxemburg v Berthe Linster, Aloyse Linster and Yvonne Linster*, C-287/98, EU:C:2000:3; opinion of AG Saggio of 16 December 1999, *Océano Grupo Editorial*, joined cases C-240–244/98, EU:C:1999:620; opinion of AG Alber of 18 January 2000, *Renato Collino and Luisella Chiappero v Telecom Italia SpA*, C-343/98, EU:C:2000:23; opinion of AG Colomer of 5 October 2004, *Pfeiffer*, joined cases C-397–403/01, EU:C:2003:245; opinion of AG Bot of 7 July 2009, *Seda Kücükdeveci v Swedex GmbH & Co. KG*, C-555/07, EU:C:2009:429; opinion of AG Bobek 26 June 2018, *Dooel Uvoz-Izvoz Skopje Link Logistic N&N v Budapest Rendőrfőkapitánya*, C-384/17, EU:C:2018:494; opinion of AG Sánchez-Bordona of 27 November 2018, *Openbaar Ministerie v Daniel Adam Popławski*, C-573/17, EU:C:2018:957; opinion of AG Bobek of 23 September 2021, *NE v Bezirkshauptmannschaft Hartberg-Fürstenfeld*, C-205/20, EU:C:2021:759.

[8] *See* also, extensively, D. Gallo, *L'efficacia diretta del diritto dell'Unione europea negli ordinamenti nazionali.* Una dottrina ancora controversa, Milan, Giuffrè, 2018, 213–255 and D. Gallo, *Rethinking Direct Effect and its Evolution: A Proposal* (2022) 1 *European Law Open* 576, 581–588.

[9] *See* S. Prechal, *Directives in EC Law*, 2nd ed., Oxford, Oxford University Press, 2005, 231–237. *See* CJ, *Ursula Becker v Finanzamt Münster-Innenstadt*, 8/81, EU:C:1982:7, on which, *see* J. Usher, *Direct Effect of Directives: The European Court Holds Firm* (1982) 7 *European Law Review* 193, and, recently, L. Squintani, J. Lindeboom, *The Normative Impact*, 22–24.

[10] Sixth Council Directive (ECC) 77/388 on the harmonization of the laws of the Member States relating to turnover taxes—Common system of value added tax: uniform basis of assessment [1977] (OJ L 145, 13.6.1977, 1).

[11] As noted in Editorial, *Horizontal direct effect—A law of diminishing coherence?* (2006) 1 *Common Market Law Review* 1, 4, it is not a 'false dichotomy.' *See* also L. Squintani, J. Lindeboom, *The Normative Impact*, 23.

are able to assert against the State'.[12] This formula has been reiterated multiple times in the case law of the CJEU, although it is rarely used in the most recent judgments.[13]

In any event, the emergence of a direct effect different from subjective substitutive direct effect is not traceable only in those decisions where the '*Becker* formula' was expressly applied. A good example is *Direktsia 'Obzhalvane i upravlenie na izpalnenieto'* on the interpretation of Articles 314 and 320(1), first paragraph, and (2) of Directive 2006/112 on the common system of value-added tax. The Court noted that, owing to the precision and unconditionality of these provisions, the direct effect resulting therefrom consists in authorizing individuals to invoke them before domestic courts in the context of a dispute against the Member State's national tax authorities, such as that in the main proceedings, 'for the purposes of having national legislation which is incompatible with those provisions disapplied'.[14] It has also occurred that a provision, considered deprived of subjective substitutive direct effect, was regarded by the CJ as having direct effect in the objective exclusionary sense. The *Rahman* case,[15] with respect to the interpretation of Article 3(2) of Directive 2004/38 on the right of citizens of the Union and their family members to move and reside freely within the territory of the Member States,[16] seems illustrative. Here the EU judges, from the one side, noted that the wording used in this provision 'is not sufficiently precise to enable an applicant for entry or residence to rely directly on that provision in order to invoke criteria which should in his view be applied when assessing his application', while from the other, stated that such an applicant has the right nonetheless to a 'judicial review of whether the national legislation and its application have remained within the limits of the discretion set by that directive'.[17] The consequence is that, if these limits have been exceeded and the prescribed conditions have not been satisfied, the national legislation must be disapplied.[18]

[12] For a thorough analysis of the case law, *see* S. Prechal, *Does Direct Effect*, 1049–1058. In similar terms, *see* R. Schütze, *Direct Effects and Indirect Effects of Union Law*, in R. Schütze, T. Tridimas (eds.), *Oxford Principles of European Union Law: The European Union Legal Order: Volume I*, Oxford, Oxford University Press, 2018, 265–299, 270.

[13] *Becker* (n 9), para. 25 (italics added); *see* also CJ, *Fratelli Costanzo SpA v Comune di Milano*, 103/88, EU:C:1989:256, para. 13; CJ, *Acciaierie and Ferriere Busseni SpA*, C-221/88, EU:C:1990:84, para. 22; CJ, *Ufficio distrettuale delle imposte dirette di Fiorenzuola d'Arda and Others v Comune di Carpaneto Piacentino and Others*, 231/87 and 129/88, EU:C:1989:381, para. 30; CJ, *A. Foster and Others v British Gas plc*, C-188/89, EU:C:1990:313, para. 16; CJ, *Andrea Francovich and Danila Bonifaci and Others v Italian Republic*, joined cases C-6/90 and C-9/90, EU:C:1991:428, para. 11; CJ, *Braathens Sverige AB v Riksskatteverket*, C-346/97, EU:C:1999:291, para. 29; CJ, *Connect Austria*, C-462/99, EU:C:2003:297, para. 114; CJ, *Ambulanter Pflegedienst Kügler GmbH*, C-141/00, EU:C:2002:473, para. 51; CJ, *Radiosistemi Srl v Prefetto di Genova*, joined cases C-388/00 and C-429/00, EU:C:2002:390, para. 49; CJ, *Christoph-Dornier-Stiftung für Klinische Psychologie*, C-45/01, EU:C:2003:595, para. 78; JC, *Finanzamt Eisleben v Feuerbestattungsverein Halle eV*, C-430/04, EU:C:2006:374, para. 28; CJ, *Rieser Internationale Transporte GmbH*, C-157/02, EU:C:2004:76, para. 22; CJ, *Meiland Azewijn BV*, C-292/02, EU:C:2004:499, para. 57. Amongst Advocates General, *see* opinion of AG Kokott of 1 March 2007, *JP Morgan Fleming Claverhouse Investment Trust plc and The Association of Investment Trust Companies v The Commissioners of HM Revenue and Customs*, C-363/05, EU:C:2007:125, para. 52, and, more recently, opinion of AG Saugmandsgaard Øe delivered on 18 June 2020, *BY and CZ*, C-321/19, EU:C:2020:480, para. 75.

[14] CJ, *Direktsia 'Obzhalvane i upravlenie na izpalnenieto'—Varna v Auto Nikolovi OOD*, C-203/10, EU:C:2011:118, para. 64.

[15] CJ, *Secretary of State for the Home Department v Muhammad Sazzadur Rahman and Others*, C-83/11, EU:C:2012:519.

[16] Directive 2004/38/EC of the European Parliament and of the Council of 29 April 2004 on the right of citizens of the Union and their family members to move and reside freely within the territory of the Member States amending Regulation (EEC) No. 1612/68 and repealing Directives 64/221/EEC, 68/360/EEC, 72/194/EEC, 73/148/EEC, 75/34/EEC, 75/35/EEC, 90/364/EEC, 90/365/EEC, and 93/96/EEC (Text with EEA relevance) (OJ L 158, 30.4.2004, 77).

[17] *Rahman* (n 15), para. 25.

[18] *Rahman* (n 15), para. 26.

As brilliantly observed in the literature, two types of situations make it clear why the existence of a dichotomy between subjective substitutive direct effect and objective exclusionary direct effect can be useful, in reconstructive terms, to explore the contents of direct effect:[19] *(i)* the national legal order comprises a derogation, that is, a provision that deviates from a rule enshrined in the domestic legal order and, for that reason, causing a breach of EU law; *(ii)* the national legal order comprises trade-related technical rules amending the domestic technical rules already in force, which were not notified by the Member State to the Commission, in contrast with EU obligations, and are thus unenforceable in judicial proceedings. In both situations, the individual relies on EU law and seeks the disapplication of (some) national provisions. There is neither the direct conferral of a right stemming from an EU provision nor the replacement of national law by EU law. Indeed, the dispute is governed by domestic provisions which remain applicable since they have not been affected by the remedy of disapplication. In this vein, as pointed out in by some authors, EU law 'immunizes' the individual from a provision or an action of the State[20] and, in doing so, serves as a 'shield' rather than a 'sword'.[21] Hence, the defendant(s) would be blocked from relying on domestic rules which are inconsistent with EU law.[22] In addition to these two situations there seems to be a third one, which materializes where the disapplication entailed by direct effect is selective. There is neither a conferral of rights nor the creation of substitutive effects since it is national law that finds room for application. This occurs in the *NE* ruling, with respect to the recognition of the principle of proportionality of direct effect penalties, whose analysis will be carried out (on different profiles) in section 6 of Chapter III, to which reference is made.

As examples of the first strand of rulings, two are worth mentioning.[23] The first is *Johnston*,[24] which regards the interpretation of Directive 76/207/EEC on equal treatment of men and women.[25] In the judgment, the CJ first discussed the interpretation of national law in conformity with EU law.[26] Subsequently, 'in the event that the question should still arise whether an individual may rely on the directive as against a derogation laid down by national legislation',[27] in recalling the *Becker* judgment, the Court affirmed that the individuals may demand, vis-à-vis the State authority, the application of the principle of equal treatment between men and women as enshrined in Article 2, paragraph 1 of Directive 76/207, to the conditions of access to work and access to professional and further training, 'in order to have a derogation from that principle under national legislation set aside'.[28] The effect, in the case, is direct because the application of EU law entails the disapplication of national law. Direct effect is objective in nature since the EU provision does not explicitly confer a right upon the

[19] *See* extensively S. Prechal, *Does Direct Effect.*

[20] In these terms, *see* C. Hilson, T. Downes, *Making Sense of Rights: Community Rights in EC Law* (1999) 24 *European Law Review* 121, 132.

[21] In these terms, *see* B. de Witte, *The Continuous Significance of* Van Gend en Loos, in M. Poiares Maduro, L. Azoulai (eds.), *The Past and Future of EU Law: The Classics of EU Law Revisited on the 50th Anniversary of the Rome Treaty*, Oxford, Hart, 2010, 9–15, 12. *See* also S. Prechal, *Does Direct Effect*, 1059–1064.

[22] *See* L. Squintani, J. Lindeboom, *The Normative Impact*, 29 and C. Hilson, T. Downes, *Making Sense*, 137–138.

[23] On the case law, *see* extensively L. Squintani, J. Lindeboom, *The Normative Impact*, 33–35 and S. Prechal, *Directives*, 234–241.

[24] CJ, *Marguerite Johnston v Chief Constable of the Royal Ulster Constabulary*, 222/84, EU:C:1986:206.

[25] Council Directive (EEC) 76/207 on the implementation of the principle of equal treatment for men and women as regards access to employment, vocational training and promotion, and working conditions [1976] L 39/76, 40.

[26] *Johnston* (n 24), paras 51–53.

[27] *Johnston* (n 24), para. 54.

[28] *Johnston* (n 24), para. 57.

individual and is 'simply' exclusionary (rather than substitutive) since it is national law that finally applies, in conformity with EU law, provided that the derogation enshrined therein is removed.

The second ruling is *Bernàldez*[29] on Directive 72/166/EEC concerning the approximation of the laws of the Member States relating to insurance against civil liability regarding the use of motor vehicles and enforcement of the obligation to insure against such liability.[30] In the case at hand, the CJ urged the referring judge to interpret the Directive as disapplying a Spanish provision, *rectius*, a derogation, according to which the insurer could not be deemed liable for damage to property and for personal injuries caused to third parties if the driver of the insured vehicle was intoxicated.

Two examples of the second strand of rulings are well-known in the literature and, like many others, will also be discussed in another part of this book, notably in section 5.1 of Chapter VI on the lack of horizontal direct effect of directives. The first is *CIA Security International*,[31] concerning Directive 83/189/EEC on the provision of information in the field of technical standards and regulations. In the ruling, the CJ observed that Articles 8 and 9 of the Directive—according to which Member States are required to notify to the Commission any draft of technical regulations falling under the sphere of application of the Directive—were sufficiently precise and unconditional to be invoked by the individuals before a national judge 'which must decline to apply a national technical regulation which has not been notified in accordance with the directive'.[32] As a matter of fact, the Directive contains provisions of a procedural character that can be relied on by individuals to obtain the freezing of domestic technical rules—that should have been notified but were not—and do not directly confer any individual right because they 'simply' entail exclusionary effects. In other words, there is no substitutive effect since EU law does not replace domestic legislation.

The second example, with regard to Article 9 of Directive 83/189/EEC, is the *Unilever* judgment, in which neither direct effect nor its conditions were mentioned. In this regard, the Court's assertion that Directive 83/189 'creates neither rights nor obligations for individuals'[33] has been interpreted in the sense of denying the direct effect of the provisions contained in the Directive.[34] This denial holds true only if one considers direct effect as always linked to the creation of a right. However, this is a preconceived assumption, not an argument. Instead, if one supports, as this book does, the idea of a possible dissociation between direct effect and the creation of a right, building upon the arguments set forth above and further developed in the following sections, the reasoning in the *Unilever* case—which is based on that elaborated in the *CIA Security International* ruling—cannot be of any surprise. The invocation of Directive 83/189/EEC by Unilever SpA and its subsequent enforcement

[29] CJ, *Criminal proceedings against Rafael Ruiz Bernáldez*, C-129/94, EU:C:1996:143, paras 23–25.

[30] Council Directive (EEC) 72/166 on the approximation of the laws of Member States relating to insurance against civil liability in respect of the use of motor vehicles, and to the enforcement of the obligation to insure against such liability [1972] L 103/72, 1.

[31] CJ, *CIA Security International SA v Signalson SA and Securitel SPRL*, C-194/94, EU:C:1996:172. *See* also CJ, *A. Verholen and Others v Sociale Verzekeringsbank Amsterdam*, joined cases C-87–89/90, EU:C:1991:314; CJ, *World Wildlife Fund (WWF) and Others v Autonome Provinz Bozen and Others*, C-435/97, EU:C:1999:418; CJ, *Aannemersbedrijf P.K. Kraaijeveld BV e.a. v Gedeputeerde Staten van Zuid-Holland*, C-72/95, EU:C:1996:404.

[32] *CIA Security International* (n 31), para. 32.

[33] CJ, *Österreichische Unilever GmbH v Smithkline Beecham Markenartikel GmbH*, C-77/97, EU:C:1999:30, paras 51–52.

[34] *See* M. Dougan, *When Worlds Collide! Competing Visions of the Relationship between Direct Effect and Supremacy* (2007) 44 *Common Market Law Review* 931, 960–963. In M. Dougan, *Case C-443/98, Unilever Italia v. Central Food* (2001) 38 *Common Market Law Review* 1503, 1507, however, the author affirmed that disapplication is the result of primacy 'triggered' by direct effect.

by the Italian courts ultimately triggered the disapplication of domestic technical regulations in relation to the labelling of foodstuffs, thereby causing a disadvantage for Central Food and, simultaneously, an advantage for Unilever. Of consequence, the effect arising from the application of unconditional EU provisions is direct in so far as it imposed upon national authorities the duty to apply old domestic technical standards rather than new technical rules in force at the time in Italy, which had not been notified to the European Commission, as they should have been, by domestic authorities. It is direct effect, yet it neither generated substitutive effects nor conferred immediate individual rights.[35]

1.2 The academic literature

Having discussed the case law, at this point the literature shall be examined, noting that some authors have changed their approach over time in view of the evolution of the case law: Timmermans[36] and de Búrca,[37] for example, have abandoned the strict view of direct effect which inspired their early writings, refraining, in more recent works, from any reference to the existence of a structural link between direct effect and attribution of rights.

At the roots of the objective form of direct effect lies the reasoning developed in the seventies by Waelbroeck, who identified two distinct categories of direct effect: the '*effet direct positif ou immédiateté*' and the '*effet direct simple ou négatif*'.[38] Still in the seventies, Bleckmann, even more boldly than Waelbroeck, anticipating what the CJ would have argued in *Becker* and its subsequent case law, speculated about the existence of a broader type of direct effect not necessarily linked to the conferral of an individual right. While underlining that the various formulas employed by the CJ revolved around '*effets directs*' and '*effets immédiats*', Bleckmann acknowledged that '*la Cour de justice emploie le terme d'effet direct dans le sens plus large d'applicabilité par le juge*'. In this vein, he pointed out that '*la création de droits est un simple cas d'application de cette notion plus large*'.[39]

Building upon Bleckmann's studies and the German scholarship of that time,[40] Prechal was the first, in the nineties, to undertake an in-depth analysis of direct effect and its perimeter. In her 1995 masterpiece monograph on directives—which has been frequently mentioned in this work—reviewed and updated in 2005, she observed that the definition

[35] In Editorial, *Horizontal direct effect*, 1, it is observed that 'the disapplication of the Italian legislation created a "disability" for the purchaser and a correlative "immunity" for the seller'.

[36] *See* C. W. A. Timmermans, *Directives: their Effect within the National Legal Systems* (1979) 16 *Common Market Law Review* 533, 544–551, and, subsequently, C. W. A. Timmermans, *Un nouveau chapitre sur l'invocabilité des directives*, in *Mélanges en l'honneur de Jean-Pierre Puissochet—L'Etat souverain dans le monde d'aujourd'hui*, Paris, Pedone, 2008, 291–302, 295.

[37] *See* G. de Búrca, *Giving Effect to European Community Directives* (1992) 55 *Modern Law Review* 215 and, subsequently, as co-author, P. Craig, G. de Búrca, *EU Law*, 222–225.

[38] M. Waelbroeck, *L'immédiateté communautaire, caractéristique de la supranationalité: quelques consequences pour la pratique*, in C. Rousseau (ed.), *Le droit international demain*, Neuchâtel, Edition Ides et Calendes, 1974, 81–89, 85–90.

[39] A. Bleckmann, *L'applicabilité directe du droit communautaire*, in Waelbroeck M., Velu J. (eds.), *Les recours des individus devant les instances nationales en cas de violation du droit européen*, Brussels, Larcier, 1978, 85–130, 89–90.

[40] *See* A. Scherzberg, *Die Innerstaatlichen Wirkungen von EG-Richtlinien* (1993) 15 *Juristische Ausbildung* 225, 229; A. Epiney, *Unmittelbare Anwendbarkeit und Objektive Wirkung von Richtlinien* (1996) 111 *Deutsches Verwaltungsblatt* 409, 412; M. Pechstein, *Die Anerkennung der Rein Objektiven Unmittelbaren Richtlinienwirkung* (1996) 7 *Europäisches Wirtschafts- und Steuerrecht* 261; C. Calliess, *Zur unmittelbaren Wirkung der EG-Richtlinie über die Umweltverträglichkeitsprüfung und iherer Umsetzung im deutschen Immissionsschutzrecht* (1996) 9 *Neue Zeitschrift für Verwaltungsrecht* 339; N. Reich, '*System der subjektiven öffentlichen Rechte*' *in the Union: A European Constitution for Citizens of Bits and Pieces*, in *Recueil des cours de l'Académie de droit européen*, 1998, 157–236.

of direct effect 'in terms of the creation of individual or subjective rights as understood in national law will often be, if not impossible, then rather artificial and, moreover, unnecessary'.[41] In 1997, Ruffert, in an article based on his 1996 monograph (in German), noticed that it could be possible to infer from the EU case law that the CJ built the 'objective direct effect as a new form of direct effect ... whereas the ordinary "subjective" direct effect should remain conditional upon the existence of an individual right'.[42] Edward reflected upon the existence of an objective direct effect and, in the light of this, deemed it useful 'to adopt the German distinction between objective and subjective direct effect'.[43] A few years later, van Gerven, recalling the German literature, referred to the trend of objectification characterizing the EU case law and observed that a provision of a directive could be invoked to seek the disapplication of national provisions which are incompatible with the said directive 'in themselves, meaning, objectively without reference to any specific right granted to the claimant under the directive'.[44] In similar terms, more recently, Bobek[45] has explicitly argued in favour of 'objective justiciability'.

2. Broadening direct effect through invocability and justiciability

At the heart of the literature theorizing a narrow concept of direct effect—limited to its subjective substitutive dimension—,[46] we find the works by Winter, who, in the early seventies, affirmed that 'the direct effects and the creation of individual rights ... seem to be inseparable and to stand to each other in a Yin-Yang relationship'.[47] Generally, in the literature, with the few exceptions mentioned in the previous section and later in this section, such connection is taken for granted or strongly emphasized.[48] According to Dumon, direct effect consists

[41] S. Prechal, *Directives*, 99.

[42] M. Ruffert, *Rights and Remedies in European Community Law: A Comparative View* (1997) 34 *Common Market Law Review* 307, 320.

[43] D. Edward, *Direct Effect, the Separation of Powers and the Judicial Enforcement of Obligations*, in *Scritti in onore di Giuseppe Federico Mancini*, Milan, Giuffrè, 1998, 423–445, 442.

[44] W. van Gerven, *Of Rights, Remedies and Procedures* (2000) 37 *Common Market Law Review* 501, 506.

[45] M. Bobek, *The Effects of EU Law in the National Legal Systems*, in C. Barnard, S. Peers (eds.), *European Union Law*, Oxford, Oxford University Press, 2020, 154–189, 161. *See* also F. Becker, A. I. L. Campbell, *The Direct Effect of European Directives: Towards the Final Act?* (2007) 13 *Columbia Journal of European Law* 401, 405.

[46] Among those who explicitly argue in favour of a narrow conception of direct effect, *see* T. Dal Farra, *L'invocabilité des directives communautaires devant le juge national de la légalité* (1992) 28 *Revue trimestrielle de droit européen* 631; D. Simon, *La directive européenne*, Paris, Pedone, 1997, 95–96; D. Alland, *L'applicabilité directe du droit international considerée du point de vue de l'office du juge: des habits neufs pour une nouvelle dame?* (1998) 2 *Revue générale de droit international public* 203, 235–237; S. Amadeo, *L'efficacia 'obiettiva' delle direttive comunitarie ed i suoi riflessi nei confronti dei privati. Riflessioni a margine delle sentenze sui casi* Linster *e* Unilever (2001) 1 *Il Diritto dell'Unione europea* 95; S. Amadeo, *Norme comunitarie, posizioni giuridiche soggettive e giudizi interni*, Milan, Giuffrè, 2002, 168–169; A. La Pergola, *Il giudice costituzionale italiano di fronte al primato e all'effetto diretto del diritto comunitario: note su un incontro di studio* (2003) 4 *Giurisprudenza costituzionale* 2419; M. Wathelet, *Du concept de l'effet direct à celui de l'invocabilité au regard de la jurisprudence récente de la Cour de justice*, in M. Hoskins, W. Robinson (eds.), *A True European. Essays for Judge David Edward*, Oxford, Oxford University Press, 2004, 367–390; K. Lenaerts, T. Corthaut, *Of Birds and Hedges: The Role of Primacy in Invoking Norms of EU Law* (2006) 31 *European Law Review* 287, 310; J. Dickson, *Directives in EU Legal Systems: Whose Norms are They Anyway?* (2011) 17 *European Law Journal* 190, 199–206; U. Villani, *Istituzioni di diritto dell'Unione europea*, 6th ed., Bari, Cacucci, 2020, 273–277, 275; E. Cannizzaro, *Il diritto dell'integrazione europea*, 4th ed., Turin, Giappichelli, 2022, 119–121. Even Y. Galmot, J.-C. Bonichot, *La Cour de Justice des Communautés européennes et la transposition des directives en droit national* (1988) 1 *Revue française de droit administratif* 1, 2–7, who are the first to openly speak of an objective exclusionary character implied in the internal effect of EU directives, do not refer to direct effect.

[47] J. A. Winter, *Direct Applicability and Direct Effect. Two Distinct and Different Concepts in Community Law*, in *Common Market Law Review*, 1972, 425, 438.

[48] *See* C. Hilson, T. Downes, *Making Sense*, 130.

in the determination of subjective legal positions deriving directly from an EU norm. The author wrote that '*sont des dispositions directement applicables celles qui, dans l'ordre interne, déterminent la position juridique des sujets de droit*'.[49] In the words of Lenaerts and Corthaut, direct effect must be considered as 'the technique which allows individuals to enforce a subjective right'.[50] Von Danwitz claimed that the '*conséquence juridique réelle de l'effet direct*' is the creation '*d'un droit dans la personne du citoyen de l'Union*' invoking EU law.

The narrative on direct effect as a doctrine inherently linked to the conferral of a right interweaves with the theorization, conducted particularly in the French public law literature,[51] about the distinction between the so-called *invocabilité de substitution* and *invocabilité d'exclusion*. Such *invocabilité d'exclusion* amounts to the invocability by a natural and legal person of an EU provision, which, rather than creating a right and governing the dispute through the replacement of a domestic provision, 'only' obliges the national authority to exclude/set aside the conflicting internal law.[52] In this vein, it was observed that the exclusion, *rectius* disapplication, stemming from this form of invocability, should not be seen as the result of direct effect, but *only* of the principle of primacy.[53] It was also noted that this dissociation becomes possible since direct effect is regarded as a sufficient condition '*pour entraîner le double effet d'exclusion et de substitution, mais que rien ne permet d'affirmer qu'il s'agit d'une condition necessaire*'.[54] Moreover, it was affirmed that '*pour écarter une norme nationale contraire, point n'est besoin, pour le juge national, de lui reconnaitre un effet direct*'.[55]

There are some recurring arguments put forward by the scholars challenging a broad definition of direct effect. First, they affirm that only when EU law confers a right to the individual which the latter may then exercise before the national authorities, the provision can fill the gap left by the (inapplicable) national law, and thus be considered directly effective. According to Wathelet, the *invocabilité de substitution* would consist in the true and only form of direct effect since '*c'est la règle communautaire et uniquement elle que le juge national est invité à appliquer pour garantir le droit conféré par l'ordre juridique communautaire au justiciable*'.[56] Second, scholars hold that, in the case of exclusionary effect, the EU provision

[49] F. Dumon, *La notion de 'disposition directement applicable' en droit européen* (1968) 4 *Cahiers de droit européen* 369, 376.

[50] *See* K. Lenaerts, T. Corthaut, *Of Birds*, 310, who are less explicit in K. Lenaerts, T. Corthaut, *Towards an Internally Consistent Doctrine on Invoking Norms of EU Law*, in S. Prechal, B. van Roermund (eds.), *The Coherence of EU Law. The Search for Unity in Divergent Concepts*, Oxford, Oxford University Press, 2008, 495–515, 509, whereby the reference is to direct effect '*sensu stricto*'.

[51] *See*, amongst others, Y. Galmot, J.-C. Bonichot, *La Cour de justice*, and D. Simon, *La directive*.

[52] Opinion of AG Léger, *Linster* (n 7); opinion of AG Ruiz-Jarabo Colomer, *Pfeiffer* (n 7); opinion of AG Kokott of 14 October 2004, *Berlusconi*, joined cases C-387/02, C-391/02, and C-403/02, EU:C:2004:624.

[53] On the matter, from the standpoint of horizontal direct effect, *see* Chapter VI, § 5.1. In the literature, *see* the following authors: C. W. A. Timmermans, *Directives*, P. Manin, *L'invocabilité des directives: quelques interrogations* (1990) 26 *Revue trimestrielle de droit européen* 669; K. Lenaerts, *L'égalité de traitement en droit Communautaire* (1991) 1–2 *Cahiers de droit européen* 3; P. J. Slot, *Annotation of CIA Security International SA* (1996) 33 *Common Market Law Review* 1035; C. W. A. Timmermans, *Community Directives Revisited* (1997) 17 *Yearbook of European Law* 1–28; A. Barav, *Rapport Général*, in XVIII Congrès FIDE, Stockholm, 3–6 June 1998, *Les directives communautaires: effets, efficacité, justiciabilité*, 418; M. Dougan, *When Worlds Collide!*, 933; G. Di Federico, *Il recepimento delle direttive nella giurisprudenza della Corte di Giustizia*, in G. Di Federico, C. Odone (ed.), *Il recepimento delle direttive dell'Unione europea nella prospettiva delle regioni italiane. Modelli e soluzioni*, Naples, Editoriale Scientifica, 2010, 1–68, 55; R. Mastroianni, G. Strozzi, *Diritto dell'Unione europea: Parte istituzionale*, 8th ed., Turin, Giappichelli, 2019, 314–315. *See* also, amongst French scholars, M. Blanquet, G. Isaac, *Droit général de l'Union européenne*, Paris, Dalloz, 2012, 375. In the case law, *see* Opinion of AG Léger, *Linster* (n 7), para 73; opinion of AG Saggio, *Océano* (n 7), paras 37–39; opinion of AG Bot, *Kücükdeveci* (n 7), para. 63; opinion of AG Sánchez-Bordona, *Popławski II* (n 7), para. 117; opinion of AG Bobek, *Link Logistic* (n 7), para. 93.

[54] D. Simon, *La directive*, 95–96.

[55] M. Wathelet, *Du concept de l'effet direct*, 372.

[56] M. Wathelet, *Du concept de l'effet direct*, 370. In similar terms, *see* E. Cannizzaro, *Il diritto*, 119–120.

would create 'limited effects' which are dissociated from the 'claimable rights'[57] and, for this reason, it could not have true subjective repercussions (*'ricadute soggettive'*)[58] on the individual. In short, the EU rule would not be suitable *'à completer directement le patrimoine juridique des particuliers de droits subjectifs et/ou d'obligations'.*[59] Third, few commentators believe that an EU provision generating exclusionary effects could not be applied directly by the national authorities, particularly by the national courts. For this reason, the exclusionary effect should fall within the concept of indirect effect. In this vein, such form of invocability would be similar to the State liability remedy and to the duty of consistent interpretation.[60] Fourth, some authors note that the disapplication, as a result of exclusionary direct effect, is limited to cases involving directives concerned with duties of a technical or procedural nature.[61]

The above arguments are not conclusive. Indeed, there are four reasons why direct effect should be intended in a broad sense as comprising an objective exclusionary dimension and why this form of direct effect could not be rejected *per se*. The first is that invocability-justiciability, in its exclusionary facet, is not something new. It is not unusual in domestic legal systems. Indeed, the so-called *invocabilité d'exclusion* is an essential element, for instance, in the French, Belgian, and Dutch traditions.[62]

The second reason is that relevant legal effects for individuals can also be entailed in EU provisions that do not directly confer rights upon natural and legal persons.[63] As a matter of fact, the effects stemming from an EU provision are not only the result of a right created by EU law; a directly effective norm does not necessarily generate one type of effect. As observed by Hohfeld, alongside the concept of 'right in the proper sense' there lie other concepts, such as 'privilege', 'power', and 'immunity',[64] which are part of the broader notion of *interest*. Two situations are worth mentioning, as pointed out by Prechal:[65] *(i)* any right is directly and immediately attributed whereby the individual invokes an EU provision to 'defend' themselves from a criminal proceeding that started against them at the national level; and *(ii)* any right is directly and immediately attributed whereby the individual relies on EU law as a parameter of legality for challenging a State's action in the context of administrative proceedings.

Prechal managed to frame the problem correctly. First, she observed that 'direct effect is a broader concept, in the sense that a directly effective provision of Community law may be relied upon for several purposes'. Second, she noted that 'to equate the concept of direct effect with the creation of rights does not do justice to the diversity of the effects which directly effective provisions may produce'.[66] As maintained by Bleckmann,[67] the remedy of legality review is a form of direct effect. Moreover, Isaac wrote that direct effect is *'la capacité à être une source de la légalité en vigueur dans l'ordre juridique national'.*[68] Ruffert proved a point,

[57] J. A. Winter, *Direct Applicability*, 437.
[58] S. Amadeo, *Norme comunitarie*, 174.
[59] M. Blanquet, *Droit général de l'Union européenne*, 11th ed., Paris, Sirey, 2018, 552.
[60] *See* M. Wathelet, *Du concept de l'effet direct*, 370–371.
[61] E. Cannizzaro, *Il diritto*, 120–121. *See* also Opinion of AG Mazák of 15 February 2007, *Félix Palacios de la Villa*, C-411/05, EU:C:2007:106, paras 127–128.
[62] On this point, *see* S. Prechal, *Does Direct Effect*, 1052.
[63] *See* the reflections made by P. Eleftheriadis, *The Direct Effect of Community Law: Conceptual Issues* (1996) 16 *Yearbook of European Law*, 205–221, 207–210.
[64] W. N. Hohfeld, *Fundamental Legal Conceptions*, 710.
[65] S. Prechal, *Directives*, 98–100.
[66] S. Prechal, *Directives*, 99.
[67] A. Bleckmann, *L'applicabilité directe*, 89–90.
[68] G. Isaac, *L'effet direct du droit Communautaire, Répertoire européen Dalloz*, 1997, 1, 4.

too, when he remarked that 'the direct effect of a directive provision is not dependent on the existence of an individual right that should be enshrined in the protective content or intent of the provision'.[69] Bobek's understanding of direct effect can be shared in so far as the 'granting of individual rights' is not seen as being 'in itself' 'one of the general conditions for direct effect'.[70] In the same vein, Schütze rightly affirmed that 'direct effect does not depend on a European norm granting a subjective right, but to the contrary, the subjective right is a result of a directly effective norm'.[71]

As a matter of fact, the conferral of a right is a possible consequence caused by a directly effective EU provision, not its precondition. When the effect is objective, the justiciability of the EU provision serves the purpose of protecting the interest of an individual that can take shape only through its application and, therefore, the neutralization of the conflicting domestic provisions. Thus, there exists an interest, which is decoupled with the 'attribution of a benefit to individuals'[72] and is incapable of representing a direct source for the creation of a right. Along these lines, the EU provision acts as a 'standard for reviewing the legality of Member State action'.[73] What the individual invokes before national courts is the EU provision which, although not directly creating individual rights, imposes obligations—generally towards the States. The EU provision is invoked as a means of safeguarding the individual interest deriving from its fair application, even if not linked to the existence of a right recognized therein. The reliance on EU law, therefore, aims at enforcing the obligation(s) laid down in the EU norm.[74] This means that the conferral of a right is not an indispensable element *per se*; at the heart of a directly effective EU provision always lies an obligation and likely, but not necessarily, also a right. In this respect, AG Tesauro, in the *Brasserie* case, noted that 'the obligations of the Member States and Community institutions are directed *above all*, in the system which the Community system has sought and sets out to be, to the creation of rights of individuals'.[75] 'Above all', not always. Direct effect implies that the EU provision creates an obligation upon the State and/or an individual, and a corresponding advantage for a non-State party, which is not necessarily an individual right in the strict sense. As clarified by Bengoetxea, 'the analysis of the legal relation involved in direct effect should always start with the obligation, i.e., an obligation on someone, to do or secure something to somebody in some given circumstances and by some time'.[76]

The third reason is as follows: holding that the immediate application of EU law occurs *only* when the effect is substitutive because the EU provision would be fully self-sufficient *only* in this case, assumes, tautologically, that the exclusionary effect is a *minor* manifestation of internal effect which lacks one of direct effect's alleged constitutive elements, that is, the replacement of national law with EU law. This is incorrect for, through exclusionary effect, domestic provisions can be applied and govern the case at hand autonomously, as has been

[69] M. Ruffert, *Rights*, 321.

[70] M. Bobek, *The Effects*, 161.

[71] R. Schütze, *European Union Law*, 3rd ed., Oxford, Oxford University Press, 2021, 161.

[72] B. de Witte, *Direct Effect, Primacy and the Nature of the Legal Order*, in P. Craig, G. de Búrca (eds.), *The Evolution of EU Law*, 3rd ed., Oxford, Oxford University Press, 2021, 187–227, 193.

[73] B. de Witte, *Direct Effect*, 193.

[74] On the relevance of the concept of 'obligation' within the doctrine of direct effect, *see* D. Edward, *Direct Effect, the Separation of Powers*, 442–443 and W. van Gerven, *Of Rights*, 506–507.

[75] Opinion of AG Tesauro of 28 October 1995, *Brasserie*, joined cases C-46/93 and C-48/93, EU:C:1995:407, para. 39.

[76] J. Bengoetxea, *Is Direct Effect a General Principle of European Law?*, in U. Bernitz, J. Nergelius, C. Cardner (eds.), *General Principles of EC Law in a Process of Development*, Alphen aan de Rijn, Kluwer Law International, 2008, 3–24, 7.

shown with respect to, among others, the *Bernàldez* and *Johnston* cases. Moreover, it shall be recalled that even a directly effective norm conferring a right upon the individual and apt to replace a domestic provision rarely fully takes the place of the national law that is at odds with the EU legal order. In other words, as already highlighted in Chapter III, section 3.3, an EU provision is rarely perfectly autonomous. Additional clarifications, at the level of national (or EU) law, are normally necessary.[77] Furthermore, an EU law provision does not generally produce identical effects throughout the legal orders of the Member States.[78] Hence, it is impossible to mark a clear and preconceived boundary between subjective and objective direct effect.

The fourth reason challenges the argument according to which an exclusionary effect, combined with the disapplication of national law, would come into play only regarding directives containing provisions of a technical nature. In fact, as clarified above in this section and will be demonstrated in section 5.1 of Chapter V, from the *Becker* judgment onwards the CJ recognized the existence of exclusionary effects also in relation to EU legal acts deprived of such technical character.

In short, considering the twofold form of direct effect, both objective and subjective, Prechal's stance shall be embraced insofar as she defines direct effect as 'the obligation of a court or another authority to apply the relevant provision of Community law, either as a norm which governs the case at hand or as a standard for legal review'.[79] Direct effect, thus, means invocability and justiciability. Invocability and justiciability, in turn, mean that EU provisions can be relied upon to review national legislation. They often, not always, create enforceable rights: this creation, therefore, is not a precondition for the recognition of direct effect.[80]

In conclusion, the common element between substitutive subjective direct effect and objective exclusionary direct effect is the occurrence of the exclusion, that is, the disapplication of national law. When engaging with a directly effective EU provision, national authorities, being bound by the obligation of disapplication, always settle the case by virtue of a different provision than the one that would have applied if, *ab astracto*, EU law had not been applicable: *(i)* in the case of subjective substitutive direct effect, the EU provision instead of the national one; *(ii)* in the case of objective exclusionary direct effect, a national norm different from the one originally envisaged to govern that specific case, that had to be set aside by the judge (or the administration).[81] The fundamental divergence between substitutive subjective direct effect and objective exclusionary direct effect, instead, is that the exclusion is always present within subjective direct effect *together* with a substitutive effect because the EU provision directly creates a legal position governing the case at stake in place of the internal law provision. Conversely, within objective exclusionary direct effect the effect is 'only' exclusionary since the dispute is governed by the internal law which outlives (and was not affected by) the disapplication, not by EU law.

[77] *See*, in this respect, on Article 31(2) of the Charter, with similar implications for other sources of law, CJ, *Max-Planck-Gesellschaft zur Förderung der Wissenschaften*, C-684/16, EU:C:2018:874, paras 73–75.

[78] In this regard, *see* the observations made by M. Dougan, *When Worlds Collide!*, 937–942.

[79] S. Prechal, *Direct Effect, Indirect Effect, Supremacy and the Evolving Constitution of the European Union*, in C. Barnard (ed.), *The Fundamentals of EU Law Revisited. Assessing the Impact of the Constitutional Debate*, Oxford, Oxford University Press, 2007, 35–69, 37–38.

[80] S. Prechal, *Does Direct Effect*, 1050.

[81] *See* Editorial, *Horizontal direct effect*, 4 and A. Dashwood, *From Van Duyn to Mangold via Marshall: Reducing Direct Effect to Absurdity?* (2007) 9 *The Cambridge Yearbook of European Legal Studies* 81–109.

3. Filling *lacunae* stemming from objective exclusionary direct effect

In the doctrine contrary to the recognition of the *invocabilité d'exclusion* as a form of direct effect there are those who maintain that such invocability is apt to cause '*vides juridiques*'.[82] These *lacunae* would be an inevitable outcome of the inapplicability of the national law incompatible with EU law and would necessarily require, for their resolution, the enactment of further implementing measures at the internal level. In addition, this same doctrine highlights that the problem exists in particular with respect to the directives, to the extent that they contain provisions which often tend to be insufficiently precise and not unconditional.[83]

With regard to the unavoidability of legal vacuums deriving from disapplication as a result of exclusionary direct effect and thus necessitating a further and subsequent intervention of national and/or EU law, it could be reaffirmed what has been observed in the previous sections: it is certainly possible for an EU provision to be invoked for opposing a national rule whose removal would entail that the situation shall be governed by the domestic legal order which outlived the disapplication.[84] The *Pfeiffer* case, in which the CJ affirmed that EU law, in the case of vertical relationships, precludes legislations such as that in force in Germany at that time, is worth mentioning. In that case, it was stated that, while provisions of German law allowing for the forty-eight-hour maximum period of weekly working time to be exceeded had to be set aside, the remaining domestic provisions could remain in force and were applicable insofar as they did not establish this excess. Disapplication, thus, can be partial and this also applies to subjective and substitutive direct effect.[85]

The above reflections do not suggest, however, that the unsuitability of domestic law regulating the individual case under the scrutiny of the national court, in the context of exclusionary effect, is itself a negligible matter. The problem exists. The question to ask is what happens when the legal order of a Member State, deprived of those norms incompatible with directly effective EU provisions, fails to effectively regulate a given case.[86] In short, the issue is that of understanding what the options available to the national courts are should the vacuum effect resulting from disapplication of national provisions arise. In the case in which EU law acts as a parameter of legitimacy of the administrative or judicial action, the question, understandably, does not exist. In fact, in the case where administrative measures and/or judgments have been removed, the national law, which did 'not suffer' from any removal, continues to apply.[87] Conversely, in the case where EU law, while not replacing the conflicting national law, operates 'only' as a parameter of legitimacy of the latter, the problem does exist. In this respect, there are four different scenarios. In the first the domestic judge could use the tool of consistent interpretation, grasping all its underlying potential. A tool which would allow them to consider the national legal order as a whole and leverage a systematic interpretation of the law: the conflicting domestic law is removed from the internal legal order, because of exclusionary direct effect, and no issue of interpretation

[82] T. von Danwitz, *Effets juridiques des directives selon la jurisprudence récente de la Cour de justice—Effet anticipé, antérieur à l'expiration du délai de transposition, interprétation conforme aux directives, primauté et application 'combinée' avec les principes généraux du droit* (2007) 4 *Revue trimestrielle de droit européen* 575, 578.

[83] C. W. A. Timmermans, *Directives*, 550.

[84] On this point, *see* G. Di Federico, *Il recepimento*, 50.

[85] On the extent of partial disapplication, *see* also Chapter III, §§ 3.2–3.3 and 6, as well as § 2 of Chapter V.

[86] The problem is explicitly acknowledged by S. Prechal, *Direct Effect, Indirect Effect*, 42–43.

[87] *See, inter alia, Kraaijeveld* (n 31).

contra legem[88] would arise in practice. In this vein, the outlived domestic law would apply thanks to interpretation, with the result that the court would use different pieces of legislation than those it would have relied on where disapplication did not occur.

In the second scenario, which arises if the first does not occur, the court would apply, by analogy, EU directly effective provisions additional to the rule triggering the setting aside of national law and tasked with governing the case: the substitutive direct effect, therefore, would come to the rescue of an exclusionary direct effect unable to provide the necessary legal framework.[89] This means that the national court must 'go hunting' for EU provisions other than those which are at the heart of the dispute before it and which are suitable to confer rights upon individuals. Consequently, the interpretation of EU law must be carried out systematically, taking into account the European legal order in its entirety.

In the third scenario, the national court would consult with the CJ in the context of Article 267 TFEU for the purpose of obtaining clarifications regarding the internal legal effect of the EU rule seeking clearer guidance on its structure, object, and scope.

In the fourth and final scenario, the national court, rather than referring the case to the CJ in accordance with Article 267 TFEU, in those countries equipped with a centralized system of constitutional review,[90] could turn to the Constitutional Court, which would then render an *erga omnes* judgment striking down the conflicting domestic provision(s) to the extent that neither the EU nor the internal legal orders are self-sufficient to govern the case. Instead, in those countries lacking a centralized system of constitutional review,[91] the antinomy would be resolved through the involvement of their ordinary courts and possibly up to their supreme courts.[92]

4. Objective exclusionary direct effect and subjective substitutive direct effect as valuable theoretical taxonomies with limited practicability

What can we infer from the previous sections? Theoretically, the existence of two different boxes, that is, objective exclusionary direct effect and subjective substitutive direct effect, is comprehensible, just as it is useful to reason about both of these manifestations of direct effect. It is so since it makes it possible to explain why a narrow reconstruction of direct effect, as proposed by several scholars and some Advocates General, should be rejected. Moreover, such boxes are valuable in so far as they allow us to grasp the complexities of direct effect and its multiple forms, as further proof and confirmation of what has already been said on the evolving and multifaceted nature of such doctrine.

On the other hand, in practice, the boundaries between the two above categories are much more blurred than one might think, and their practicability could be legitimately

[88] *See* CJ, *Sumal*, C-882/19, EU:C:2021:800, para. 72 and the case law cited therein. On the notion of consistent interpretation, in the light of direct effect, *see* § 5.2 of Chapter VI. On the *contra legem* limitation, *see*, recently, A. Arnull, *European Union Law and the* Contra Legem *Principle* (2022) 47 *European Law Review* 291.

[89] In these terms, *see* P. Craig, *The Legal Effect of Directives: Policy, Rules and Exceptions* (2009) 34 *European Law Review* 349, 368.

[90] This is the case of countries such as France, Germany, Italy, Belgium, and Spain.

[91] This is the case of countries such as Finland, Ireland, and Sweden. On the identification of, and differences amongst, systems of constitutional review in Europe, *see* A. Bobić, *The Jurisprudence of Constitutional Conflict in the European Union*, Oxford, Oxford University Press, 2022, 15–21.

[92] For a comparative study on constitutional review in Europe, *see* M. De Visser, *Constitutional Review in Europe. A Comparative Analysis*, Oxford, Hart, 2014.

questioned. In many situations, whether direct effect generates substitutive effects and is grounded in the conferral of rights stemming from an EU provision is not easily understandable. In fact, rights are only rarely explicitly and directly created by EU law, the conferral often being the result of the CJ's case law. Overall, the dividing frontier between the two concepts is dependent on the factual and legal background of each specific case.[93] Disapplication could be a sufficient tool in some national legal orders, but not in others, depending on the existence, internally, of normative elements able to govern disputes and fill the void entailed by the application of EU law, and the related disapplication of national law. Therefore, on the one hand, a reflection on the objective exclusionary/subjective substitutive dichotomy should not lead us to make such taxonomies the key drivers towards the recognition or denial of the direct effect since their practicability is doubtful. On the other hand, a study on the theoretical taxonomies of direct effect is justified to challenge the idea that direct effect should always be intended in narrow terms, leaving aside situations which, albeit not belonging to the classic *Van Gend & Loos* scheme, in fact, do fall under the realm of direct effect, as explicitly clarified in *Poplawski II*. This applies to three situations above all, as previously remarked: (*i*) when to be disapplied is a derogation enshrined in a domestic provision, which sets forth an exception to a rule that is consistent with EU law; (*ii*) when to be disapplied are new technical rules introduced in national legal orders that have not been notified to the European Commission as requested by EU law; (*iii*) when the disapplication resulting from disapplication is selective, as held by the CJ with regard to the principle of proportionality of penalties.

In conclusion, advocating for a broad understanding of direct effect, as done in the volume, has evident practical implications since it expands the scope of intervention of a doctrine of EU law as key as it is direct effect. Indeed, choosing between broad or narrow direct effect is very important *in concreto* since it affects whether and how individuals are entitled to invoke (and rely on) EU law, and thus to request disapplication.This is a more useful perspective than merely reflecting on the assonances and dissonances between subjective substitutive direct effect and objective exclusionary direct effect, which are likely to act as taxonomies with limited practicability.

[93] *See* opinion of AG Bobek, *NE* (n 7), paras 118–124.

V
DIRECT EFFECT'S CORE CONDITIONS AND THE EXTENT OF DISAPPLICATION

1. Primacy *and* direct effect as the (only) legitimate source of the *duty* to disapply

This chapter, while partially building upon Chapter IV's findings on the objective exclusionary dimension of direct effect, aims to investigate the relationship between primacy, direct effect, and disapplication. Most notably, the reflection on a narrow or broad conception of direct effect already made in the previous chapter is a good starting point for venturing into the role and scope of the remedy of disapplication. This remedy[1] comes into play in the case of incompatibility between the internal legal order of Member States and EU law and stipulates that every national court must, in a case within its jurisdiction, 'apply Community law in its entirety and protect rights which the latter confers on individuals and must accordingly set aside any provision of national law which may conflict with it, whether prior or subsequent to the Community rule'.[2] Moreover, national laws cannot impair the effectiveness of EU law by withholding from ordinary judges 'the power to do everything necessary at the moment of its application to disregard a national provision or practice which might prevent directly effective EU rules from having full force and effect'.[3] Such domestic rules and practices would be incompatible with the principle of loyal cooperation stated in Article 4(3) TEU, as well as with 'the requirements which are the very essence of EU law'.[4] This would be the case in the event of a conflict between a provision of EU law and a national law 'if the solution of the conflict were to be reserved for an authority with a discretion of its own, other than the court called upon to apply EU law'.[5] Moreover, as already clarified in section 3.3 of Chapter III, disapplication does not always relate to a public law measures, including legislation enacted by national parliaments. To the contrary, direct effect can also trigger the setting aside of measures issued by private actors adopted on the basis of domestic laws/administrative/judicial practice, or independently from a public law measure.

In such framework, this section aims at understanding whether disapplication, given the evolution of EU case law, is always the result of the joint application of primacy and direct effect, or whether disapplication can also occur regardless of the latter.[6] To this

[1] On the principal characteristics of such remedy, in the light of the EU case law, *see* Chapter III, § 3.3 and § 2 of this chapter. All URLs for this chapter were last accessed on 30 April 2024.

[2] *See*, amongst many others, CJ, *Amministrazione delle Finanze dello Stato v Simmenthal SpA*, 106/77, EU:C:1978:49, para. 22 and CJ, *NE*, C-205/20, EU:C:2022:168, para. 37.

[3] *See Simmenthal* (n 2), para. 23; CJ, *Criminal proceedings against PM and Others* (*Euro Box Promotion and Others*), joined cases C-357/19, C-379/19, C-547/19, C-811/19 and C-840/19, EU:C:2021:1034, para. 258; CJ, *RS*, C-430/21, EU:C:2022:99, para. 63.

[4] *See Simmenthal* (n 2), para. 22.

[5] *See Simmenthal* (n 2), para. 23. See also CJ, *Aziz Melki and Sélim Abdeli*, C-188/10 and C-189/10, EU:C:2010:363, para. 44; *RS* (n 3), para. 63.

[6] On the derogations from the duty to disapply, *see* §§ 6–9 of this chapter.

Direct Effect in EU Law. Daniele Gallo, Oxford University Press. © Daniele Gallo 2025. DOI: 10.1093/9780191925221.003.0006

end,[7] neither primary law, including Declaration No. 17, annexed to the Lisbon Treaty, nor secondary law, provides a clear answer. We should thus delve into the literature and the EU case law.

With regard to the literature, we need not recall the abundant scholarship, including textbooks, which assumes that the duty to disapply is a product of primacy and direct effect together.[8] As affirmed by Bleckmann, '*d'après la Cour de justice, seul le droit européen directement applicable a la force de repousser une loi national contraire*'.[9] More recently, amongst others, Curtin has underlined that EU law 'entails the disapplication by a national judge of a rule or judicial mechanism of national law which would prevent the directly effective right from being fully applied'.[10] On the other hand, it has been observed in sections 1–2 of Chapter IV that several Advocates General and authors have argued that disapplication cannot be regarded as always being the product of both primacy and direct effect. They claim that in the EU case law on objective exclusionary effect only the principle of primacy would apply and cause the disapplication of domestic provisions. The exclusionary effect would simply act as a 'corollary' of primacy. As noted by AG Léger in the *Linster* case, where one of the parties does not aim to obtain recognition of an individual right, the matter of direct effect 'tends to be eclipsed by that of primacy' because the problem of integration of the EU provision in the national legal order would remain 'a confrontation between the different rules' while ignoring the rule regarding the application of the said norms to the subjects of rights.[11] The result is a real disconnection between direct effect and primacy as far as disapplication is concerned. This dissociation becomes possible since direct effect is deemed to be a sufficient condition '*pour entraîner le double effet d'exclusion et de substitution, mais que rien ne permet d'affirmer qu'il s'agit d'une condition necessaire*'.[12] Moreover, it has been affirmed that '*pour écarter une norme nationale contraire, point n'est besoin, pour le juge national, de lui reconnaitre un effet direct*'.[13] One could also argue that the recognition of direct effect as a precondition for disapplication could dangerously restrict the *effet utile* of EU law, with the additional risk of improperly expanding the scope of the remedies of consistent interpretation and State liability to compensate for situations where disapplication cannot be performed due to a lack of direct effect.

Furthermore, several scholars[14] and Advocates General[15] have claimed that embedding exclusionary effect within direct effect would call into question the well-known (yet,

[7] *See* also, extensively, D. Gallo, *Rethinking direct effect and its evolution: a proposal* (2022) 1 *European Law Open* 576, 589–593.

[8] *See*, by way of example, amongst textbooks, D. Sarmiento, *El Derecho de la Unión europea*, 4th ed., Madrid, Marcial Pons, 2022, 357–408, 362. As pointed out by R. Kovar, *La contribution de la Cour de justice à l'édification de l'ordre juridique communautaire. Cours général de droit Communautaire*, in *Recueil des cours de l'Académie de droit européen*, Alphen aan den Rijn, Kluwer Law International, 1995, 15, 64: '*lorsqu'est en cause une règle de droit communautaire d'effet direct, le principe de la primauté lui permet de l'emporter sur toute norme de droit interne qui lui est contraire*.'

[9] A. Bleckmann, *L'applicabilité directe du droit communautaire*, in Waelbroeck M., Velu J. (eds.), *Les recours des individus devant les instances nationales en cas de violation du droit européen*, Brussels, Larcier, 1978, 85–130, 124.

[10] D. Curtin, *Directives: The Effectiveness of Judicial Protection of Individual Rights* (1990) 27 *Common Market Law Review* 709, 728; L. Daniele, *Diritto dell'Unione europea*, 8th ed., Milan, Giuffrè, 2022, 279.

[11] Opinion of AG Léger of 11 January 2000, *Grand Duchy of Luxemburg v Berthe Linster, Aloyse Linster and Yvonne Linster*, C-287/98, EU:C:2000:3, para. 73.

[12] D. Simon, *La directive européenne*, Paris, Pedone, 1997, 95–96.

[13] M. Wathelet, *Du concept de l'effet direct à celui de l'invocabilité au regard de la jurisprudence récente de la Cour de justice*, in M. Hoskins, W. Robinson (eds.), *A True European. Essays for Judge David Edward*, Oxford, Oxford University Press, 2004, 367–390, 372.

[14] *See*, amongst others, M. Dougan, *When Worlds Collide! Competing Visions of the Relationship between Direct Effect and Supremacy* (2007) 44 *Common Market Law Review* 931, 936 and 957–963.

[15] *See, inter alia*, opinion of AG Bot of 7 July 2009, *Seda Kücükdeveci v Swedex GmbH & Co. KG*, C-555/07, EU:C:2009:429, paras 63–64.

problematic) axiom of EU law recognized from the *Faccini Dori* ruling[16] onwards, that is, the prohibition of horizontal direct effect.[17] In other words, they highlight that tracing back the objective exclusionary effect, and disapplication, to primacy alone, rather than to direct effect and primacy, would solve the problems arising from cases such as *CIA Security International* and *Unilever*.[18] Indeed, in this case law the disapplication entailed by EU directives affects *de facto*, although in incidental terms, the private individuals who had benefited from the Member State's 'guilty' omission in the notification of new domestic technical standards. The principle on the prohibition of directives' horizontal direct effect would then be infringed because of exclusionary *direct* effect. Conversely, scholars have affirmed that leaving out exclusionary effect from direct effect would make such infringement *a priori* impossible. According to AG Bot in his opinion in the *Kücükdeveci* case, 'disconnecting the horizontal direct effect of directives from the right to plead them to exclude contrary national law' may constitute a 'palliative' for the lack of direct effect, whereby the application of an EU directive would cause adverse effects for individuals in horizontal relationships.[19]

The above reasoning cannot be accepted: the primacy principle would be the only trigger of disapplication if one were to embrace a strict interpretation of direct effect, which has been challenged and rejected already in Chapter IV.

As to the nexus between direct effect, primacy, and disapplication from the standpoint of the EU case law, the matter has never been openly and precisely unveiled in most of the CJEU's rulings for decades. However, in spite of such uncertainties, two landmark judgments explain once and for all that direct effect is always the precondition for the duty to disapply: *Popławski II*[20] and *NE*,[21] which are both discussed in several parts of this book.[22] These decisions have clarified the meaning of the famous *Simmenthal* ruling, whereby it was, first, affirmed that 'the relationship between provisions of the Treaty and directly applicable measures of the institutions on the one hand and the national law of the Member States on the other is such that those provisions and measures . . . by their entry into force render automatically inapplicable any conflicting provision of current national law'.[23] Secondly, it was held that 'every national court must, in a case within its jurisdiction, apply Community law in its entirety and protect rights which the latter confers on individuals and must accordingly set aside any provision of national law which the latter confers on individuals'.[24] Regardless of the confusion that may arise due to the reference to the concept of direct applicability, rather than direct effect, and the lack of an explicit link between direct effect and the remedy of disapplication, *Simmenthal* seems to reveal that disapplication, while being a manifestation of primacy, is triggered by the application of EU directly applicable/effective provisions. On the other hand, it can be inferred from the judgment that there is a situation where direct

[16] CJ, *Faccini Dori v Recreb Srl*, C-91/92, EU:C:1994:292.

[17] On this matter, *see* Chapter III, § 3.1 for some preliminary remarks and, for an in-depth analysis, *see* §§ 3–6 of Chapter VI.

[18] *See* Chapter IV, § 1.1 and § 5.1 of Chapter VI.

[19] Opinion of AG Bot, *Kücükdeveci* (n 15), paras 63–64.

[20] CJ, *Criminal proceedings against Daniel Adam Popławski* (*Popławski II*), C-573/17, EU:C:2019:530.

[21] *NE* (n 2). For a detailed analysis of the relationship between primacy, direct effect, and disapplication in the light of the CJ's case law, *see* D. Gallo, *Rethinking*, 590–593, and F. Nicola, C. Fasone, D. Gallo, *Comparing the Effects of US Unconstitutionality and EU's Preliminary Interpretative Rulings: Disapplication, Resistance and Coordination Procedures*, in D. Gallo, L. Cecchetti (eds.), *The Preliminary Ruling Procedure, Today: Revisiting Article 267 TFEU's Constitutional Backbone*, Special Issue (2023) 15 *European Journal of Legal Studies* 147, 154–165.

[22] *See* also § 3.3 of Chapter III.

[23] *Simmenthal* (n 2), para. 17.

[24] *Simmenthal* (n 2), para. 21.

effect does not operate as a *condicio sine qua non* of disapplication. This occurs when EU provisions 'preclude the valid adoption of new national legislative measures to the extent to which they would be incompatible with Community provisions'.[25]

In *Popławski II* it was stated that the principle of primacy cannot 'have the effect of undermining the essential distinction between provisions of EU law which have direct effect and those which do not and, consequently, of creating a single set of rules for the application of all the provisions of EU law by the national courts'.[26] Furthermore, the CJ, in harsh contrast with the position adopted by AG Sánchez-Bordona in his opinion in the case,[27] affirmed that 'a provision of EU law which does not have direct effect may not be relied on, as such, in a dispute coming under EU law in order to disapply a provision of national law that conflicts with it'.[28] Finally, EU judges observed that 'a national court is not required, solely on the basis of EU law, to disapply a provision of its national law which is contrary to a provision of EU law if the latter provision does not have direct effect'.[29] Consequently, the *Popławski II* ruling interprets the *Simmenthal* judgment in the sense that, just as domestic authorities have a *duty* of disapplication only when the EU provision is directly effective and can for this reason replace the conflicting national law, in the same way, a domestic judge has the *discretion* to disapply when direct effect is lacking. In this latter case, however, the legal subjective positions of those affected by disapplication shall be sufficiently safeguarded through the internal legal order, given the fact that EU law alone, lacking direct effect, cannot govern the case.

The judgment delivered by the CJ in the *Thelen Technopark* case upholds this reasoning, clarifying that national authorities can (*not must*) 'disapply, on the basis of domestic law, any provision of national law which is contrary to a provision of EU law that does not have such effect'.[30] This approach was followed by the CJ in the *Commission v Spain* ruling:[31] while affirming that national courts were *not required*, solely on the basis of *EU* law, to disapply a provision of national law contrary to a non-directly effective provision of EU law, the Court admitted such possibility and connected this to the discretionary power of domestic judges, to be exercised by virtue of national, rather than EU, law. Moreover, very recently, the CJ made it clear that such disapplication rooted in national law is above all a means for national authorities to apply correctly unimplemented directives, thus achieve the results laid down therein, in horizontal situations, when domestic provisions allow them to do so. In such a situation, 'the obligation thus imposed on private parties is based not on EU law, but on national law, and therefore does not constitute an obligation additional to those provided for by that law'.[32] Indeed, the Court explained that 'while, under EU law, a directive

[25] *Simmenthal* (n 2), para. 21.

[26] *Popławski II* (n 20), para. 60. On this point, *see* the reflections by I. Anrò, J. Alberti, *Riflessioni sull'effetto diretto, sul primato e sulla disapplicazione del diritto nazionale*, in M. Graziadei, C. Iannone, B. Nascimbene, L. Salvato, E. Vincenti (eds.), *Il diritto europeo e il giudice nazionale*, Rome, SSM, 2023, 51–85, 80.

[27] Opinion of AG Sánchez-Bordona of 27 November 2018, *Criminal proceedings against Daniel Adam Popławski*, C-573/17, EU:C:2018:957, para. 117.

[28] *Popławski II* (n 20), para. 62.

[29] *Popławski II* (n 20), para. 68. In the same, vein *see* CJ, *David Smith v Patrick Meade and Others*, C-122/17, EU:C:2018:631, para. 49.

[30] CJ, *Thelen Technopark*, C-261/20, EU:C:2022:33, para. 33. The provision at stake was Article 15 of Directive 2006/123/EC of the European Parliament and of the Council of 12 December 2006 on services in the internal market. *See* also D. Gallo, *Rethinking*, 593.

[31] CJ, *Commission v Spain*, C-278/20, EU:C:2022:503, para. 141. *See* also CJ, *K.L. v X sp. z o.o.*, C-715/20, EU:C:2024:139, para. 74.

[32] CJ, *Gabel Industria Tessile*, C-316/22, EU:C:2024:301, para. 23. *See* also the interesting reflections by AG Emiliou, in his opinion of 16 November 2023, *Gabel Industria Tessile*, EU:C:2023:885, paras 23–32. For a first comment, see J. Lindeboom, *Another Episode on Horizontal Direct Effect of Directives, Or: Who Should Clean Up the Mess? Case C-316/22 Gabel Industria Tessile*, EU Law Live, 30 April 2024, available at https://eulawlive.com/

cannot, of itself, impose obligations on a private party . . . a Member State may, on the other hand, confer on the national courts the power to disapply, on the basis of its domestic law, any provision of national law which is contrary to a provision of EU law that does not have direct effect'.[33] This means, for example, as stated in *Gabel Industria Tessile*, that a national court may allow a private party to seek the neutralization of the additional economic burden stemming from the payment of a tax which is unlawful pursuant to a directive and which had been 'wrongly passed on to it by a supplier' if 'such a possibility is provided for by national legislation, which, in the case at issue in the main proceedings, it is for the referring court to determine'.[34]

In this regard, besides the specifics of that case, it is not fully clear when and how, in practice, a national authority could disapply an internal provision only on the basis of national law only when such provision conflicts with non-directly effective EU provisions. Such situations can surely occur if there is an antinomy within the domestic legal order and either the judge, or the administration, confronted with conflicting national provisions, decides to set aside a national law not in compliance with EU law and consequently applies another domestic rule which is compatible with EU norms. This might be the case if there are different types of legal sources essentially regulating the same issue.

If the antinomy arises between an EU-friendly superior domestic norm, such as a statute passed by the national parliament, and an inferior norm, like a national regulation passed by the executive, which stands in contrast to EU law, the problem is easily solved in terms of hierarchy of norms. This is even more clear when a declaration of unconstitutionality is made, in respect to those legal orders which foresee such remedy. If such declaration ensures, ultimately, compliance with EU law, it is irrelevant whether this has been made on the basis of national law rather than EU law. Effectiveness of EU law is at the core of the CJ's role, regardless of the legal source generating the removal of inconsistent domestic law. Additionally, the *Popławski II-Thelen Technopark* formula could apply also in situations where the antinomy arises between sources of equal standing. In this case, every Member State's legal order would provide the courts with adequate substantive and procedural mechanisms to resolve the conflict. A harmony that would be achieved, through the recognition of the precedence of one law over another, by ensuring the fair enforcement of (non-directly effective) EU norms.

In *NE* the CJ confirmed boldly, and further elaborated on, what was already incidentally observed in *Bank BGZ BNP Paribas, E.sp.zo.o.sp.k.*,[35] *Asociația 'Forumul Judecătorilor din România' and Others*,[36] *IS*,[37] and *Euro Box Promotion*:[38] the national court shall 'give full effect to the requirements of that law in the dispute before it, if necessary disapplying of its own motion any national legislation or practice, even if adopted subsequently, which is contrary to a provision of EU law with direct effect'.[39] It did so through an open overruling

op-ed-another-episode-on-horizontal-direct-effect-of-directives-or-who-should-clean-up-the-mess-case-c-316-22-gabel-industria-tessile-by-justin-lindeboom/.

[33] *Gabel Industria Tessile* (n 32), para. 24.
[34] *Gabel Industria Tessile* (n 32), para. 25.
[35] *See*, respectively, CJ, *Bank BG BNP Paribas*, C-183/18, EU:C:2020:153, para. 62, and CJ, *E. Sp. z o.o. Sp. k.*, C-335/19, EU:C:2020:829, para. 51.
[36] CJ, *Asociația 'Forumul Judecătorilor din România' and Others v Inspecția Judiciară and Others*, joined cases C-83/19, C-127/19, C-195/19, C-291/19, C-355/19 and C-397/19, EU:C:2021:393, para. 247.
[37] CJ, *IS*, C-564/19, EU:C:2021:949, para. 80.
[38] *Euro Box Promotion* (n 3), para. 252.
[39] *NE* (n 2), para. 37.

of the *Link Logistic* case, whereby the qualification of direct effect as a source for imposing disapplication had been challenged in explicit terms, following, in this respect, the opinion by AG Bobek.[40] More specifically, in *Link Logistic* the EU judges, while excluding direct effect with regard to the principle of proportionality of penalties in Article 9a of Directive 1999/62,[41] affirmed that domestic authorities shall 'disapply any national provision in so far as its application would, in the circumstances of the case, lead to a result contrary to EU law'.[42] Such statement is stunning and unprecedented because it stands in contrast with the *Simmenthal* ruling, as also demonstrated by the misleading references to the EU case law made by the CJ in support of its vision of direct effect. For instance, the *Pöpperl* judgment that the EU judges mentioned twice in their ruling, in which an obligation was imposed upon domestic courts to disapply national law if consistent interpretation was not feasible, concerns directly effective provisions, unlike the EU rules and principles at the core of the *Link Logistic* ruling that the Court deemed to be non-directly effective.[43]

From the above analysis we can deduce that both *Popławski II* and *NE* mark a firm and definitive point in the interplay between direct effect, primacy, and disapplication, making explicit the stance underpinning *Simmenthal*. More specifically, as clarified by AG Bobek in the *NE* case,[44] the *Popławski II* ruling has 'authoritatively settled the issue of whether the setting aside of national law may be only the consequence of primacy, or of primacy of EU law in conjunction with the direct effect of the EU law provision that is to be applied'.[45] A further consequence is that the EU judges, albeit implicitly, cut to the chase with regard to the characterization of objective exclusionary effect: it is direct effect, and there is no doubt about it, since it triggers the disapplication of conflicting domestic law.[46]

In this connection, we shall conclude that if the principle of direct effect presupposes, to be effective, the primacy of EU law, the reverse is not true.[47] The argument according to

[40] Opinion of AG Bobek of 26 June 2018, *Dooel Uvoz-Izvoz Skopje Link Logistic N&N v Budapest Rendőrfőkapitánya*, C-384/17, EU:C:2018:494, paras 55–56.

[41] Directive 1999/62/EC of the European Parliament and of the Council of 17 June 1999 on the charging of heavy goods vehicles for the use of certain infrastructures (OJ L 187, 20.7.1999, 42).

[42] CJ, *Dooel Uvoz-Izvoz Skopje Link Logistic N&N v Budapest Rendőrfőkapitánya*, C-384/17, EU:C:2018:810, para. 62.

[43] CJ, *Joachim Pöpperl*, C-187/15, EU:C:2016:550.

[44] Opinion of AG Bobek of 23 September 2021, *NE v Bezirkshauptmannschaft Hartberg-Fürstenfeld*, C-205/20, EU:C:2021:759, para. 73. For a comment on the opinion, *see* D. Gallo, L. Cecchetti, *The principle of proportionality of penalties and the inextricable knot between primacy, direct effect and disapplication*, EU Law Live, 30 September 2021, available at https://eulawlive.com/op-ed-the-principle-of-proportionality-of-penalties-and-the-inextricable-knot-between-primacy-direct-effect-and-disapplication-by-daniele-gallo-and-lorenzo-cecchetti/.

[45] In the opinion of M. Dougan, *The Primacy of Union Law over Incompatible National Measures: Beyond Disapplication and Towards a Remedy of Nullity?* (2022) 59 *Common Market Law Review* 1301, 1308: 'it was only in the *Popławski* judgment of 2019 that the Court finally settled a decades-old dispute about the underlying relationship between the fundamental principles of direct effect and primacy, by clarifying that the latter's capacity to procure the disapplication of incompatible national rules ultimately depends on the former attribute first attaching to the relevant provision of Union law, a proposition that had been consistently rejected by a significant proportion of the scholarship, and indeed challenged by several of the Court's own advocates general.' *See* also D. Gallo, *La disapplicazione è sempre figlia dell'effetto diretto, non del (solo) primato: Poplawski*, in F. Caruso, F. Medico, A. Morrone (eds.), *Granital* revisited?, Bologna, Bologna University Press, 2020, 81–89, and D. Miasik, M. Szwarc, *Primacy and Direct effect—Still Together*: Popławski II (2021) 58 *Common Market Law Review* 571.

[46] Opinion of AG Bobek, *NE* (n 44), paras 118 and 119. *Contra, see* L. S. Rossi, *Effetti diretti delle norme dell'Unione europea ed invocabilità di esclusione: i problemi aperti dalla seconda sentenza Popławski*, in *Giustizia Insieme*, 3 February 2021, available at https://www.giustiziainsieme.it/it/diritto-ue/1517-effetti-diretti-delle-norme-dell-unione-europea-ed-invocabilita-di-esclusione-i-problemi-aperti-dalla-seconda-sentenza-poplawski.

[47] As clarified by B. de Witte, *The Impact of* Van Gend en Loos *on Judicial Protection at European and National Level: Three Types of Preliminary Questions*, in A. Tizzano, J. Kokott, S. Prechal (Organizing Committee), *50ème anniversaire de l'arrêt Van Gend en Loos: 1963-2013: actes du colloque, Luxembourg*, 13 mai 2013, 93–101, 94–95.

which the obligation to disapply could be a result of primacy alone forgets that the primacy principle has a larger sphere, when compared to direct effect, insofar as also non-directly effective provisions impose duties towards national authorities. As is known, while all EU provisions prevail over the internal legislation of the Member States, only some of them are directly effective. This is the *summa divisio* that was conceptualized in the literature decades ago and still stands today.[48]

Against this background, why should direct effect be considered the precondition for disapplication and, for this reason, the most effective tool to 'bite' at the national level, notwithstanding the risk that the courts, including the CJ, could declare indiscernibly 'any and every provision of EU law directly effective'?[49] The answer is that direct effect ensures that the EU principle of conferral and the related principle of subsidiarity are not called into question by a generalized, unrestrained use of the principle of primacy. Justifying disapplication based on primacy alone would be dangerous and potentially fatal for the whole dialogue between EU institutions and Member States. It would entail a blank proxy to the EU capable of undermining the fertile relationship between EU law and domestic legal systems for good, as well as the mutual cooperation between the EU and national authorities.[50] Moreover, direct effect continues to be an essential doctrine capable of shaping, in its interaction with primacy, in proto-federalist terms, a legal order that, albeit juridically mature and unique in its kind, is not a federal union. Should the EU ever become a federal union, direct effect, as a filter[51] and *sine qua non* condition for ensuring the enforcement of EU law through the remedy of disapplication, would no longer be necessary in its current form. Only then would the national courts have to handle EU law in the same way they handle domestic law and, therefore, apply EU provisions, regardless of their nature, as directly effective norms. As a matter of fact, the EU and domestic legal systems, although closely interconnected, are separate.[52] This is also the reason why disapplication is the most complete form of effective judicial protection and a distinctive characteristic of EU law: direct effect enables EU provisions to apply in domestic legal systems and serve as cognizable norms to be enforced by national authorities, including judges. Disapplication is the true and only means for challenging inconsistent domestic provisions. Lastly, arguing that the duty to disapply cannot arise outside the realm of direct effect, whether it be substitutive or exclusionary, does not mean, of course, that consequences stemming from the application of the primacy principle shall not occur where the EU law at stake is deprived of direct effect. To the contrary, aside from the avenue provided by Article 267 TFEU, individuals and national authorities—including courts—have at their disposal the remedies offered by the combination of the EU and national legal orders: consistent interpretation, if the interpretative tool can be effectively pursued; State liability; the referral to domestic constitutional courts for

[48] *See* L.-J. Constantinesco, *L'applicabilité directe dans le droit de la CEE*, Brussels, Bruylant, 2006, 5–50.

[49] M. Bobek, *Why Is It Better to Treat Every Provision of EU Directives as Having Horizontal Direct Effect?* (2023) 39 *International Journal of Comparative Labour Law and Industrial Relations* 211, 216.

[50] By focusing on the interplay between direct effect and the principle of subsidiarity, J. H. H. Weiler, *Revisiting* Van Gend en Loos: *Subjectifying and Objectifying the Individual*, in A. Tizzano, J. Kokott, S. Prechal (Organizing Committee), *50ème anniversaire*, 11–22, 13, remarked that subsidiarity 'is built into the system given the fundamental role which individuals come to play as a result of Direct Effect combined with the Preliminary Reference' and that 'the demand for legal rights and their enforcement is a bottom up phenomenon, emanating from and close to, the most immediate stake holders'. More generally, on the relationships between direct effect, primacy, and general principles of EU law, *see* K. Lenaerts, José A. Gutiérrez-Fons, *The constitutional allocation of powers and general principles of EU law* (2010) 47 *Common Market Law Review* 1629.

[51] Dougan, *The Primacy*, 1323, referred to direct effect as an 'essential passerelle'.

[52] Dougan, *The Primacy*, 1323–1324.

an *erga omnes* decision on the incompatibility of national law with the EU legal system, in case of domestic centralized mechanisms of constitutional review; and the involvement of ordinary courts up to supreme courts, should the constitutional review foreseen in those Member States be decentralized, as it has been recalled in section 3 of Chapter IV.

2. Stocktaking on the scope of disapplication and the problems of inverse vertical direct effect in a nutshell

Before delving into the core elements of the doctrine of direct effect and the complexities relating to the remedy of disapplication, it is worth recalling the main points arising from the analysis conducted in section 1 of this chapter, as well as in other chapters, also with respect to the scope of the duty to disapply.

First, direct effect is necessarily intertwined with neither the conferral of a right by an EU provision nor the replacement of a domestic norm by the latter. More particularly, the reflection on the distinction between objective exclusionary direct effect and subjective substitutive direct effect, albeit with limited practical effect, serves to challenge the idea that direct effect is a narrow notion. A broad definition of direct effect, thus, shall be endorsed.[53] Second, unconditionality, which means direct applicability, is the core element of, stands for, and merges with direct effect.[54] Third, direct effect and direct applicability, albeit theoretically distinct, coincide in practice.[55] Fourth, the decentralized remedy of disapplication entails the duty for ordinary/common domestic judicial and administrative authorities to set aside national laws conflicting with EU law. When at stake is the (inconsistent) practice of domestic administrative bodies and/or courts, rather than disapplication one should speak of consistent interpretation if this new EU-friendly interpretation is not *contra legem*.[56] Fifth, disapplication, in horizontal relationships, causes the setting aside of private behaviours/regulations, which often comes along with the setting aside of public measures when the latter induce private actors to infringe EU law.[57] Sixth, disapplication may affect the entire legislation, or only some of its parts. Thus, it could be selective, leaving to the national judge and administration the task of possibly integrating the void resulting from the setting aside of domestic normative elements inconsistent with EU law.[58] Seventh, only if an EU provision is directly effective, can disapplication occur. Primacy, alone, cannot trigger such consequence.[59] Eighth, if an EU provision is not directly effective, national judges/administrations can—not must—still set aside domestic provisions if the internal legal order so allows.[60]

In addition to these points, three further key arguments will be made in the following sections. First, direct effect, and the related duty to disapply, as a rule, can be asserted only if the application of EU law entails advantages for *at least* one private party to the dispute, that is, it is *in bonam partem*, or, lacking the attribution of an advantage, if it does not have the effect of worsening the condition all private parties involved in the dispute were in before the enforcement of EU law. In short, disapplication, if it is *in malam partem* for all private parties

[53] *See* Chapter IV.
[54] *See* § 5 of Chapter III.
[55] *See* § 7 of Chapter III.
[56] *See* § 3.3 of Chapter III.
[57] *See* § 3.3 of Chapter III.
[58] *See* §§ 3.3 and 6 of Chapter III, as well as § 3 of Chapter IV.
[59] *See* § 1 of this chapter.
[60] *See* § 1 of this chapter.

involved in the dispute, is inadmissible because, upstream, direct effect does not come into play. Second inverse vertical direct effect can be affirmed and *in malam partem* disapplication of national law can be asserted only if the principle of legitimate expectations is respected.[61] Third, there are situations in which the knot between direct effect and disapplication can come undone. This is the case when national authorities, especially courts, invoke physiological derogations from the duty to disapply, that is, derogations deemed legitimate by the CJ.[62] Conversely, there are other situations where this knot has been autonomously undone by Member States, but this should not have happened given that no justification had been provided by the CJ. A justification that is necessary, however, since the Court is the last guardian of the respect of the principles of primacy and direct effect, as well as of the duty to disapply.[63]

3. Contextualizing direct effect in vertical and horizontal relationships: the advantage for the individual as the second cumulative premise in addition to unconditionality

When is an EU provision directly effective? It seems that the presence of two cumulative requirements must be verified by the national judge (or the administrative authority). The first, as already discussed in detail, is that the EU norm is unconditional and thus immediately/directly applicable, that is, justiciable and, for this reason, internally enforceable to govern the dispute.[64]

What is claimed in this book is that a second condition, in both vertical and horizontal relationships, exists.[65] As a rule, the application of the EU provision in *lieu* of the national norm (subjective substitutive direct effect), or as its parameter of legality (objective exclusionary direct effect), must not be purely/exclusively detrimental for the private parties to the dispute, including for the plaintiff invoking EU law before the national authorities.[66] This means that the doctrine of direct effect, being conceived *mainly*[67] as a means at the disposal of natural and legal persons to actively safeguard their own prerogatives and, at the same time, assure the fair enforcement of EU law, cannot entail *only* a disadvantage for the individuals involved in the dispute. The minimum requirement (and *condicio sine qua non*) for the emergence of direct effect is the existence of an advantage/interest,[68] which occurs

[61] *See* §§ 3, 5, and 8-10 of this chapter.
[62] *See* §§ 6-7 of Chapter V.
[63] *See* § 11 of Chapter V.
[64] *See* Chapter III, § 5.
[65] *See* also, extensively, D. Gallo, *Rethinking*, 600–603.
[66] On such aspect of direct effect, from the viewpoint of international law, *see* § 5 of Chapter VII.
[67] On direct effect and the 'private enforcement element', *see* Chapter II, § 1. On the origins of direct effect, from the standpoint of the private enforcement of EU law, *see* P. Craig, G. de Búrca, *EU Law: Text, Cases, and Materials*, 7th ed., 2020, 223–224, and P. Craig, *Once upon a Time in the West: Direct Effect and the Federalization of EEC Law* (1992) 12 *Oxford Journal of Legal Studies* 453.
[68] P. Pescatore, *L'ordre juridique des Communautés européennes*, Liège, Presses universitaires de Liège, 1975, 163, affirmed that direct effect arises '*chaque fois que des justiciables ont intérêt à invoquer les règles du droit communautaire devant une juridiction nationale*'. The concept of interest shall be preferred over the concept of right in the opinion of C. Hilson, T. Downes, *Making Sense of Rights: Community Rights in EC Law* (1999) 24 *European Law Review* 121, 132–133; S. Prechal, *Directives in EC Law*, 2nd ed., Oxford, Oxford University Press, 2005, 97–110; J. Bengoetxea, *Is Direct Effect a General Principle of European Law?*, in U. Bernitz, J. Nergelius, C. Cardner (eds.), *General Principles of EC Law in a Process of Development*, Alphen aan de Rijn, Kluwer Law International, 2008, 3–24, 8. On the similarities and divergences between these two notions, *see* R. von Jhering, *Der Zweck im Recht*, Leipzig, Druck und Verlag Von Breitkopf & Härtel, 1877.

as a result of the application of EU law and the subsequent disapplication of domestic law. Or, alternatively, lacking such an advantage/interest, in order for direct effect to be asserted, the application of EU law should, at least, not worsen for all private parties the condition they were in before EU law was enforced. This is so regardless of whether said advantage/interest is (subjective substitutive direct effect) or is not (objective exclusionary direct effect) conferred directly by the same EU norm and regardless of whether—in addition to the benefit for the individual—there simultaneously lies a constraint of personal prerogatives for someone else, as happens in horizontal disputes. In short, if the enforcement of an EU provision, in vertical or horizontal relationships, is entirely *in malam partem*, lacking the creation of an advantage for any of the parties to the dispute or anyway affecting all private parties' prerogatives, direct effect does not arise and, therefore, disapplication shall not play any role. Indeed, the content of the doctrine of direct effect cannot be reconstructed without putting it in context in the light of the consequences stemming from disapplication. If it is true that the doctrine of direct effect was also created to guarantee that, through the individual, EU law is implemented in the national legal orders and, thus, uniformly and consistently applied, there can be no doubt that direct effect, placing the individual at the core of the EU legal system, cannot prescind from the strengthening of subjective prerogatives as a result of the enforcement of EU law.[69]

These reflections imply that in (vertical and horizontal) situations where the application of EU law is exclusively detrimental for the individual, direct effect does not come into play. In this vein, direct effect is not *ex se* a quality of the provision. Such attention to the outcomes of the application of the EU rule in each individual case has been recently acknowledged by AG Bobek in *NE* with respect to the principle of proportionality of penalties. And this is clear to the extent that Bobek observed that it would be not only incoherent, but also 'morally questionable', to deny direct effect to the proportionality principle, while asserting the direct effect of Article 325 TFEU, as done by the CJ in the *Taricco* case, where a duty to disapply had been affirmed, on the basis of that provision, in respect to national rules that were more favourable to the individuals than the interpretation of EU law offered in the judgment.[70] Should direct effect not been recognized in *NE*, the consequence would have been a denial of the disapplication of domestic laws breaching the principle of proportionality and making the sanctions less effective, while admitting, as occurred in *Taricco*, the disapplication of internal provisions which were instead more favourable to the sanctioned individuals.[71] In this sense, recognizing the direct effect of the obligation to protect the EU's financial interests (also) by means of effective sanctions incumbent on the Member States pursuant to Article 325 TFEU, while excluding disapplication of disproportionate penalties, would be unjustifiable. A similar position was taken by AG Emiliou commenting upon the *NE* ruling in so far as the latter observed that, in that case, direct effect had to be affirmed because otherwise 'individuals may continue to be subject to disproportionate penalties' and 'may be unable to challenge, before domestic courts, the incompatibility of [national] legislation with the EU provision in question'.[72] This focus on the consequences for the individuals resulting from a disapplication (*in bonam partem*) of national law can be

[69] But *see*, in this chapter, § 4 on intra-State direct effect and §§ 8 and 9 on admissible inverse vertical direct effect.

[70] Opinion of AG Bobek, *NE* (n 44), paras 53–54.

[71] On the *Taricco* saga, *see* § 9 of this Chapter. '*Taricco*' stands for two famous rulings by the CJ: CJ, *Ivo Taricco and Others*, C-105/14, EU:C:2015:555; CJ, *M.A.S. and M.B*, C-42/17, EU:C:2017:936.

[72] Opinion of AG Emiliou of 10 November 2022, *T.A.C. v Agenția Națională de Integritate (ANI)*, C-40/21, EU:C:2022:873, paras 60–61.

transferred into other realms of the EU legal system and lies beyond the specific matter of the proportionality of penalties.[73] Indeed, such reasoning on the *in bonam partem/malam partem* divide implied in the duty to disapply shall hold true for all areas of law, not only the criminal sector.

Contextualizing direct effect means taking into consideration the implications deriving from the enforcement of EU law in the domestic legal system, with reference to the case at hand, from the standpoint of the effects produced by the disapplication of the conflicting domestic norm. Already Pescatore and Prechal had pleaded for 'a contextual approach' (Prechal) and for the qualification of direct effect as a doctrine which shall not depend on the 'intrinsic quality of the rules concerned' (Pescatore).[74] However, they did so by reflecting, most notably, upon the partial usefulness of the test of direct effect, whereby, in practice and *in concreto*, the conditions of clarity, precision, and unconditionality were found 'of a relatively limited value only'.[75] The perspective chosen in this book develops and extends their reasoning: while only unconditionality, as observed several times,[76] remains a valuable tool for testing direct effect (the classical test being outdated and ineffective), focusing on the context of the case is crucial first and foremost with regard to the effects on the individuals resulting from disapplication. As a matter of fact, the attention paid to the practical *ex post* consequences for individuals stemming from the recognition of direct effect, and the resulting duty to disapply, are at the heart of the whole CJ (problematic and unsteady) narrative on the lack of horizontality of directives: very similar, if not identical, EU rules, that are directly effective in vertical relationships, are not so when they must be enforced in horizontal disputes amongst private parties. This is a confirmation that direct effect is not a fixed and predetermined qualitative feature of EU law.

Objecting to the above reconstruction that direct effect could come into play regardless of the creation of an advantage for the individual since such doctrine originated also to ensure the enforcement of EU law, in addition to the (public) enforcement by the European Commission pursuant to Article 258 TFEU, is misleading. Indeed, it is one thing to acknowledge that direct effect is a tool used by the individual to both safeguard their rights (and seek redress) through disapplication of inconsistent internal provisions and enforce EU law, while it is quite another to claim that direct effect may serve, in practice, also as a means, only for the State, to apply EU law and disapply its own rules while diminishing the rights for all private parties to the dispute who legitimately relied on those rules. As a matter of fact, should a clear conflict between EU and domestic law arise which is unsolvable by virtue of (consistent) interpretation, the State, lacking a ruling by the CJ, has other means (than disapplication) for complying with EU law and enforcing the principle of primacy, while respecting the principles of legality and legitimate expectations. As explained in section 3 of Chapter IV, most notably, while in those countries equipped with a centralized system of constitutional review the remedy is represented by a referral to the Constitutional Court, in the other countries lacking such a review mechanism, ordinary courts, as well as supreme courts, would be involved.

[73] Opinion of AG Bobek, *NE* (n 44), para. 38.

[74] On the need to use a 'contextual approach', yet with regard to the premises of direct effect, *see* S. Prechal, *Directives*, 252; S. Prechal, *Does Direct Effect Still Matter?* (2000) 37 *Common Market Law Review* 1047, 1064; P. Pescatore, *The Doctrine of 'Direct Effect': An Infant Disease of Community Law* (1983) 8 *European Law Review* 155, 177. For an insight on this issue, *see* § 4 of Chapter III.

[75] S. Prechal, *Directives*, 252. S. Prechal, *Does Direct Effect*, 1064, write that she 'would like . . . to propose to drop the examination of the conditions together'.

[76] *See* § 2 of this chapter and more extensively Chapter III, § 5.

4. Recognizing intra-State direct effect

The creation of advantages for the individual resulting from the application of EU directly effective provisions shall not be confused with the matter of their invocability. This means that even if the subject relying on those provisions against a branch of the State, whether central, regional, or local, is public, then, the doctrine of direct effect may come into play all the same, provided, of course, that the requirement of unconditionality is fulfilled. The invoked EU provisions would create 'only' indirectly adverse repercussions, rather than directly imposing obligations on individuals/companies who are not parties to the dispute. Albeit in very few cases, this possibility, which seems inspired by a logic similar to the one underpinning the CJ's approach toward the so-called triangular/incidental effects of directives, as will be observed in section 5.1 of Chapter VI, was affirmed by the CJ in its jurisprudence. In *Comune di Carpaneto*, the Court, in a dispute between a local district office for direct taxes and a municipality, for the first time in such an explicit way, affirmed that 'bodies governed by public law, which ... [are] assimilated to individuals' are 'entitled to rely on' EU law to seek disapplication of domestic laws.[77] In fact, the reference to the assimilation of public bodies to individuals as a precondition for the invocability of an EU provision (and for triggering direct effect), which was not replicated in the subsequent case law, arguably can be interpreted as allowing the State to invoke/rely on EU law when it acts in the performance of activities normally carried out by individuals, that is, governed by private law. The problem, in *Comune di Carpaneto*, was the status of the legal entity involved, in the light of Article 4(5) of Council Directive 77/388 of 17 May 1977 on the harmonization of the laws of the Member States relating to turnover taxes.[78] Most notably, in the case at hand, the issue was whether the municipalities that were parties to the dispute could be considered taxable persons 'in respect of the activities or transactions in which they engage as public authorities, even where they collect dues, fees, contributions or payments in connection with [them]', unless 'treatment as non-taxable persons would lead to significant distortions of competition'.[79] This meant that the only way for municipalities not to be subject to taxation was to be treated as public authorities, not private entities. The well-known '*acta jure gestionis/jure authoritate*' divide, thus, was not the theory the CJ could use to make the Directive applicable since the reasoning developed in *Comune di Carpaneto* was built on completely different rationales. What remains from the *Comune di Carpaneto* ruling, therefore, is the obscurity of a quite incomprehensible passage that has never been clarified nor upheld in any of the CJ's subsequent rulings.

Recently,[80] as confirmation of the possibility of using direct effect and imposing disapplication, the CJ, in the *Autorità Garante della Concorrenza e del Mercato* preliminary ruling

[77] CJ, *Ufficio distrettuale delle imposte dirette di Fiorenzuola d'Arda ed altri v Comune di Carpaneto Piacentino*, joined cases 231/87 and 129/88, EU:C:1989:381, paras 29–33.

[78] Sixth Council Directive 77/388/EEC of 17 May 1977 on the harmonization of the laws of the Member States relating to turnover taxes—Common system of value added tax: uniform basis of assessment (OJ L 145, 13.6.1977, 1).

[79] Article 4.5.

[80] For another case involving, as plaintiff and defendant, two State agencies, *see* CJ, *Salzburger Flughafen GmbH v Umweltsenat*, C-244/12, EU:C:2013:203, concerning a dispute between Salzburger Flughafen GmbH, a German publicly owned company, and the Administrative Chamber for Environmental Matters with regard to the obligation to subject certain projects which expand the infrastructure of the airport of Salzburg to an environmental impact assessment. In the more very recent *Infraestruturas de Portugal SA* case, which has been already cited several times in the book, the CJ, *ab abstracto* and theoretically, admitted the possibility that Article 57(4) of Directive 2014/24/EU of the European Parliament and of the Council of 26 February 2014 on public procurement and repealing Directive 2004/18/EC (OJ 2014 L 94, 28.3.2014, 65), can be invoked by a public body against another, with

about an Italian dispute involving two public bodies,[81] granted direct effect to Article 12 of Directive 2006/123/EC. By that means, the Court, siding with the Italian Competition Authority, obliged Italy, including the resistant local municipality in the internal dispute that gave impulse to the preliminary reference, to apply an impartial and transparent selection procedure to potential candidates. Thus, it prohibited the automatic renewal of concessions for the occupation of State-owned maritime property which was decided by that municipality.[82]

In conclusion, in disputes involving different public bodies, whereby, upstream, there is no EU norm invoked by a private party to obtain an individual advantage, direct effect can play a role since *in malam partem* disapplication, from the standpoint of individuals, is excluded, as the parties to the dispute include only State agencies. This holds true for all kinds of disputes involving such bodies. On the other hand, of course, in practice, negative repercussions for individuals, albeit not stemming directly from the disapplication of national law, may arise. In this connection, the reference goes, as previously noted, to the EU case law on directives and triangular/incidental effects, whose analysis will be carried out in section 5.1 of Chapter VI.

5. Questionable inverse vertical direct effect: the case of directives

A more complicated issue than intra-State disputes, examined in the previous section, arises when the realm is that of inverse vertical relationships.[83] In such situations,[84] should we strictly follow the reconstruction made in section 3 of this chapter, direct effect could not come into play since all private parties involved in the dispute are affected by the application of EU law, and the related disapplication of national law, at the benefit of the State. Moreover, it is quite rare, *in concreto*, for the State to rely on an EU provision against an individual and seek its enforcement through the disapplication of its *own* national law, which had been

negative repercussions for the individual. In truth, the main issue is that of (in)admissible inverse vertical direct effect and this is why it will be examined in the next § of this chapter.

[81] The request has been made in proceedings between the *Autorità Garante della Concorrenza e del Mercato* (Competition and Markets Authority, Italy) (AGCM) and the *Comune di Ginosa* (Municipality of Ginosa, Italy) concerning the latter's decision to extend, in its territory, concessions for the occupation of State-owned maritime property until 31 December 2033. For some remarks on the case, *see* also § 1 of Chapter II and § 5 of Chapter III. In the literature, on the 'purely' public law dimension of the dispute giving rise to the preliminary ruling and then to the CJ's judgment, *see* A. Nato, *Le concessioni balneari, tra mercato interno, armonizzazione e tutela della proprietà: primato, effetto diretto e disapplicazione nella causa Autorità garante della Concorrenza e del Mercato c. Comune di Ginosa* (2023) 2 *Eurojus* 22. *See* also C. Curti Gialdino, *La sentenza della Corte di giustizia europea del 20 aprile 2023 in tema di concessioni balneari: spunti critici e proposte per chiudere una storia infinita*, in *Ordine internazionale e diritti umani*, 2023, 455; D. Diverio, *Nulla di nuovo . . . sotto il sole? Qualche considerazione a prima lettura sulla sentenza della Corte di giustizia nella causa* AGCM c. Comune di Ginosa, *Blog DUE*, 28 April 2023, available at https://www.aisdue.eu/davide-diverio-nulla-di-nuovo-sotto-il-sole-qualche-considerazione-a-prima-lettura-sulla-sentenza-della-corte-di-giustizia-nella-causa-agcm-c-comune-di-ginosa/ and G. Greco, *La Corte di giustizia ritorna sulle concessioni balneari precisandone le regole: problemi superatie problemi ancora aperti in sede di applicazione nazionale del diritto UE* (2023) 14 *Federalismi.it* 125.

[82] *See* CJ, *Autorità Garante della Concorrenza e del Mercato v Comune di Ginosa*, C-348/22, EU:C:2023:301, paras 60–75.

[83] On inverse vertical direct effect, *see* also Chapter II, § 1, Chapter III, § 3.2 and § 2 of this chapter.

[84] For some considerations on why the *N Luxembourg, X Denmark, C Danmark, Z Denmark* case (CJ, *N Luxembourg 1 and Others v Skatteministeriet*, C-115/16, C-118-119/16 and C-299/16, EU:C:2019:134), which relates more to general principles of EU law than to directives, should be deemed outside the scope of inverse vertical direct effect, *see* § 3.2 of Chapter III and § 8 of this chapter.

followed by that individual. On the other hand, one might challenge that reconstruction and maintain that direct effect could be asserted also when disapplication, rather than creating advantages for the plaintiff or the defendant in the dispute, entails only *in malam partem* effects for private parties to the dispute. After all, it could be alleged that there are advantages for the State and/or for the community at large resulting from the disapplication of national law. Disapplication could then be considered *in bonam partem lato sensu* as a way to pursue the general interest, rather than *in malam partem*.

The above approach raises serious concerns: as anticipated in sections 2 and 3 of this chapter, where the enforcement of EU law, through disapplication, affects the rights of all private parties to the dispute, the principle of legitimate expectations (and consequently legal certainty) turns out to be necessarily infringed.[85] The law, thus, does not operate as it should since it does not protect against illegitimate changes of policy by a public power. Hence, to be infringed, when criminal law is at stake, are also the principle of legality and the connected principle of non-retroactivity. This (not so trivial) matter has been partially tackled by the CJ. 'Partially' since an analysis of EU case law shows that the problems associated with inverse vertical direct effect have been grasped by the Court quite rarely and only with regard to directives, especially (but not only) in relation to the criminal law sphere. To this end, the CJ superimposed the plane of horizontal effect to inverse vertical effect,[86] using the prohibition of the former as the basis for pleading the prohibition of inverse vertical direct effect. Indeed, the Court, unexpectedly, relied on the case law concerning the invocation of directives in the context of disputes between private parties, not between the State and a private party.[87] In any event, when it did so, it found inverse vertical direct effect prohibited. In short, albeit in very few rulings, the CJ did affirm that inverse vertical direct effect of directives shall be prohibited in EU law.[88] The CJ addressed this issue for the first time in the field of criminal law in *Pretore di Salò*[89] and then in *Kolpinghuis*, *X*,[90] *Tombesi*,[91] *Arcaro*, *Niselli*, and *Berlusconi, Adelchi and Dell'Utri*.[92]

In these judgments, the public authority, in the course of internal judicial proceedings—leading to the use of Article 267 TFEU—, invoked provisions of directives which, if they were implemented, would cause adverse consequences for individuals who were defendants in criminal proceedings. Reiterating that, from *Becker* onwards, its own case law allows individuals to rely on the provisions of a directive against the State 'both when the latter fails to adapt national law to the directive in due time and when it fails to implement it correctly',[93]

[85] On the relevance and status of legal certainty and legitimate expectations within the EU legal order, *see* CJ, *Vereniging voor Energie, Milieu en Water*, C-17/03, EU:C:2005:362, paras 73–75; CJ, *Test Claimants*, C-362/12, EU:C:2013:834, paras 44–45; CJ, C-98/14, *Berlington Hungary Tanácsadó és Szolgáltató kft*, EU:C:2015:386, para. 77; CJ, C-342/14, *X-Steuerberatungsgesellschaft*, EU:C:2015:827, para. 59.

[86] On this matter, *see* G. Betlem, *The Doctrine of Consistent Interpretation—Managing Legal Uncertainty* (2002) 22 *Oxford Journal of Legal Studies* 397, 414 and A. Arnull, *Annotation of Kolpinghuis* (1988) 13 *European Law Review* 42, 44. On the need to distinguish horizontality from inverse vertical effect, *see* Chapter VI, §§ 1 and 6.

[87] *See*, e.g., CJ, *Riunione Adriatica di Sicurtà SpA (RAS)*, C-233/01, EU:C:2002:621, para. 19, and CJ, *Maribel Dominguez v Centre informatique du Centre Ouest Atlantique and Préfet de la région Centre*, C-282/10, EU:C:2012:33, para. 37.

[88] *See* the account by D. Gallo, *L'efficacia diretta del diritto dell'Unione europea negli ordinamenti nazionali. Una dottrina ancora controversa*, Milan, Giuffrè, 2018, 363–375.

[89] CJ, *Pretore di Salò*, 14/86, EU:C:1987:275.

[90] CJ, *X*, joined cases C-74/95 and C-129/95, EU:C:1996:491.

[91] CJ, *Tombesi (C-304/94), Roberto Santella (C-330/94), Giovanni Muzi e altri (C-342/94) e Anselmo Savini (C-224/95)*, joined cases C-304/94, C-330/94, C-342/94, and C-224/95, EU:C:1997:314.

[92] CJ, *Silvio Berlusconi (C-387/02), Sergio Adelchi (C-391/02) and Marcello Dell'Utri a. (C-403/02)*, joined cases C-387/02, C-391/02 and C-403/02, EU:C:2005:270.

[93] CJ, *Kolpinghuis*, 80/86, EU:C:1987:431, para. 7.

the Court concluded that a Member State which has not adopted the implementing measures required by the directive within the time-limit cannot benefit from its own failure, and infringement of EU law, to fulfil the obligations foreseen therein.[94] Thus, in the opinion of the Court, a national authority could not enforce against an individual 'a provision of a directive for which the necessary transposition into national law has not yet taken place'.[95] The Court pointed out, moreover, that if that was the case, it would not even be necessary to ascertain whether the directive contained unconditional and sufficiently precise provisions.[96] The conclusion, therefore, was that EU directives cannot have, 'independently of a State's domestic law, the effect of determining or aggravating the criminal liability of those who act in violation of its provisions'.[97] It was, in fact, specified in *X*, as to the possible extension of liability in criminal law arising under legislation adopted for the specific purpose of implementing a directive, that 'the principle that a provision of the criminal law may not be applied extensively to the detriment of the defendant' precluded bringing criminal proceedings in respect of 'conduct not clearly defined as culpable by law'.[98] In the same vein, in the *Berlusconi, Adelchi and Dell'Utri* case, which concerned the interpretation of First Council Directive 68/151/EEC, Fourth Council Directive 78/660/EEC, and Seventh Council Directive 83/349/EEC,[99] the CJ imposed the enforcement of EU law in place of the Italian legislation at hand that should have applied based on the principle *tempus regit actum* because the latter contained stricter sanctioning provisions in relation to the offences prosecuted in the criminal proceedings pending in Italy at the time. At the heart of the case was the compliance with the principle of the retroactive application of the more lenient penalty as 'part of the constitutional traditions common to the Member States'.[100] This is a principle which prevents the authorities of a Member State from invoking Directive 68/151—whose transposition had taken place in a timely manner and in accordance with EU law—against private individuals since that directive 'cannot, of itself and independently of national legislation adopted by a Member State for its implementation, have the effect of determining or increasing the criminal liability' of those accused persons who were also subject to the domestic criminal proceedings.[101]

The prohibition of inverse vertical direct effect in respect to directives has been examined by the CJ in areas other than criminal law in four judgments. The first is *Beuttenmüller*,[102] relating to a dispute between an Austrian national and the Land Baden-Württemberg concerning the refusal of the Stuttgart Secondary Education Office to recognize the equivalence

[94] CJ, *Arcaro*, C-168/95, EU:C:1996:363, para. 36.
[95] *Kolpinghuis* (n 93), para. 10.
[96] *Arcaro* (n 94), para. 36.
[97] *Pretore di Salò* (n 89), para. 18.
[98] *X* (n 90), para. 25.
[99] First Council Directive 68/151/EEC of 9 March 1968 on coordination of safeguards which, for the protection of the interests of members and others, are required by Member States of companies within the meaning of the second paragraph of Article 58 of the Treaty, with a view to making such safeguards equivalent throughout the Community (OJ L 65, 14.3.1968, 8) ('the First Companies Directive'), in particular Article 6 thereof; Fourth Council Directive 78/660/EEC of 25 July 1978 based on Article 54(3)(g) of the Treaty on the annual accounts of certain types of companies (OJ L 222, 14.8.1978, 11) ('the Fourth Companies Directive'), in particular Article 2 thereof; Seventh Council Directive 83/349/EEC of 13 June 1983 based on Article 54(3)(g) of the Treaty on consolidated accounts (OJ L 193, 18.7.1983, 1) ('the Seventh Companies Directive'), in particular Article 16 thereof.
[100] *Berlusconi, Adelchi and Dell'Utri* (n 92), para. 68. *See* also CJ, *Michel Mulliez and Giuseppe Momblano (C-23/03 e C-52/03), Alessandro Nizza and Giacomo Pizzi (C-133/03), Fabrizio Barra (C-337/03) and Adelio Aggio. (C-473/03)*, joined cases C-23/03, C-52/03, C-133/03, C-337/03, and C-473/03, EU:C:2006:285. On this matter, *see* A. Biondi, R. Mastroianni, *Annotation of Berlusconi* (2006) 43 *Common Market Law Review* 553; C. Amalfitano, M. Condinanzi, *Unione europea: fonti, adattamento e rapporti tra ordinamenti*, Turin, Giappichelli, 2015, 62.
[101] *See*, amongst others, *Berlusconi, Adelchi and Dell'Utri* (n 92), para. 74.
[102] CJ, *Ingeborg Beuttenmüller*, C-102/02, EU:C:2004:264.

between her primary school teaching diploma, obtained in Austria, and the qualification required for a teaching career in primary and secondary schools in that Land. The questions referred by the Stuttgart Administrative Court concerned the interpretation of Council Directive 89/48/EEC on a general system for the recognition of higher-education diplomas awarded on completion of professional education and training of at least three years' duration and Council Directive 92/51/EEC on a second general system for the recognition of professional education and training to supplement Directive 89/48.[103] With regard to the derogation provided for in the last paragraph of Article 3 of Directive 92/51, which at the time was not timely transposed into German law, according to which the host Member State would not always be obliged to admit, within its territory, access to or the pursuit of a regulated profession, the Court stated that public authorities which have failed to fulfil their obligation to transpose the provisions of a directive could not rely upon the limitations laid down therein against EU citizens.[104]

The second judgment, *Kofoed*,[105] concerns the interpretation of Articles 2(d), 8, and 11 of Council Directive 90/434/EEC on the common system of taxation applicable to mergers, divisions, transfers of assets, and exchanges of shares concerning companies of different Member States.[106] The reference was made by the Danish *Østre Landsret* (Eastern Regional Court) in the context of proceedings between Mr. Kofoed and the Danish Ministry of Fiscal Affairs about the charging of income tax on an exchange of shares. The question was whether, in the absence of a specific national provision transposing Article 11(1)(a) of Directive 90/434 into Danish law, the latter provision, according to which a Member State may refuse to apply certain rules of that directive or withdraw the benefit of those rules where it appears that the exchange of shares has tax evasion or tax avoidance as its principal objective or as one of its principal objectives, could nevertheless be applied in the main proceedings. The CJ answered by reaffirming the '*Berlusconi* rule' and recalling first that 'Member States may choose the form and methods for implementing directives' and secondly that 'the transposition of a directive into national law does not necessarily require legislative action in each Member State',[107] provided that 'the legal situation arising from the national transposition measures is sufficiently precise and clear' to enable the persons concerned 'to know the full extent of their rights and obligations'.[108]

The third case is the *Accardo* ruling[109] about the interpretation of Articles 5, 17, and 18 of Council Directive 93/104/EC on certain aspects of the organization of working time.[110] The reference was made in proceedings between Mr. Accardo and others and the Turin Municipal Council regarding a claim for compensation for harm allegedly suffered for almost twenty years as a result of a failure to comply with requirements pertaining to weekly rest periods which—it was alleged—should have been granted to officers of the municipal

[103] Council Directive 89/48/EEC of 21 December 1988 on a general system for the recognition of higher-education diplomas awarded on completion of professional education and training of at least three years' duration (OJ L 019, 24/01/1989, 16) and Council Directive 92/51/EEC of 18 June 1992 on a second general system for the recognition of professional education and training to supplement Directive 89/48/EEC (OJ L 209, 24.7.1992, 25).

[104] *Beuttenmüller* (n 102), para. 63.

[105] CJ, *Kofoed*, C-321/05, EU:C:2007:408.

[106] Council Directive 90/434/EEC of 23 July 1990 on the common system of taxation applicable to mergers, divisions, transfers of assets and exchanges of shares concerning companies of different Member States (OJ L 225, 20.8.1990, 1).

[107] *Kofoed* (n 105), para. 43.

[108] *Kofoed* (n 105), para. 44.

[109] CJ, *Accardo*, C-227/09, EU:C:2010:624.

[110] Council Directive 93/104/EC of 23 November 1993 concerning certain aspects of the organization of working time (OJ L 307, 13.12.1993, 18).

police employed by the *Comune di Torino*. In particular, the referring court sought to establish whether the municipality of Turin, and thus the Italian State, may rely on the derogating provisions at issue directly against the applicants in the main proceedings. In that regard, it was stated that, in so far as those derogations may not have been validly transposed, 'the authorities of a Member State which has not exercised that option cannot rely on that State's own failure to do so in order to refuse individuals . . . entitlement to a weekly rest period'.[111]

The fourth ruling is *OSA* concerning the interpretation of Articles 3 and 5 of Directive 2001/29/EC on the harmonization of certain aspects of copyright and related rights in the information society, of Article 16 of Directive 2006/123/EC on services in the internal market, and of Articles 56 TFEU and 102 TFEU.[112] The request was made in proceedings between a musical works copyright collecting society and a company managing a non-State health establishment providing spa treatment services. The main question was whether Directive 2001/29 could be interpreted as not permitting an exception prohibiting authors from being remunerated for the communication of their work, by means of television or radio broadcasts, to patients in the rooms of a spa establishment. The additional question was whether provisions of the directive could be relied on before the national courts, in a dispute between private individuals, by the management bodies, where a State has not correctly transposed Directive 2001/29 into its national law. In that regard, the Court observed that Directive 2001/29 must be interpreted as meaning that 'it cannot be relied on by a collecting society in a dispute between individuals for the purpose of setting aside national legislation contrary to that provision'.[113]

Against this background, until very recently, there was no doubt that the prohibition of inverse vertical direct effect applied to directives since the latter, as recalled in section 3.1 of Chapter III and carefully examined in Chapter VI, are addressed only to States. Additionally, individuals' legitimate expectations would be irremediably challenged, should directives' inverse vertical direct effect be admitted. Moreover, the rationale of this prohibition seems much more comprehensible than the one relating to the possible application of directives in horizontal situations. As a matter of fact, inverse vertical situations are different from horizontal situations, whereby two parties are involved and a balance of individual advantages/interests shall be necessarily performed, with the ultimate unavoidable consequence that one of the two will have to be 'sacrificed' in favour of the other.[114] Stated otherwise, in inverse vertical situations it is not a matter of choosing whose individual rights to protect. A further conclusive argument confirming the prohibition—with no exception—of inverse vertical direct effect in relation to directives relates to the estoppel doctrine: how could the State, by invoking a directive, legitimately benefit from its lack of transposition and, while doing this, simultaneously affect the individual, who is not responsible for such noncompliance?[115] It could not, it should not: inverse vertical direct effect must always be rejected when unimplemented directives are at stake.

[111] *Kofoed* (n 105), para. 46.

[112] Directive 2001/29/EC of the European Parliament and of the Council of 22 May 2001 on the harmonisation of certain aspects of copyright and related rights in the information society (OJ L 167, 22/06/2001,10) and Directive 2006/126/EC of the European Parliament and of the Council of 20 December 2006 on driving licences (Recast) (OJ L 403, 30.12.2006, 18).

[113] CJ, *OSA—Ochranný svaz autorský pro práva k dílům hudebním o.s. v Léčebné lázně Mariánské Lázně a.s*, C-351/12, EU:C:2014:110, paras 46 and 48.

[114] *See* also § 1 of Chapter VI.

[115] In this respect, A. Arnull, *Annotation*, 44, affirmed that, only within inverse vertical effect, 'MS clearly cannot be allowed to have their cake by failing to implement directives and at the same time to eat it by enforcing them against private parties when it suits them'.

It has been written above that the prohibition of inverse vertical direct effect in relation to directives held true 'until very recently'. Has, then, anything changed, *recently*? The answer is that probably the Grand Chamber's *Infraestruturas de Portugal SA* ruling of 21 December 2023—which will also be examined with regard to directives' triangular effects in section 5.1 of Chapter VI—put the basis for a possible velvet revolution, with multiple side effects on the admissibility of horizontal direct effect and, more generally, on the acceptance of the idea that directives can indeed create direct obligations upon natural and legal persons.[116] For what concerns inverse vertical direct effect, these are obligations invoked by the State against private parties and, by that means, may entail the disapplication of domestic rules inconsistent with the invoked EU directive. The revolution will be real, in practice, however, if the CJ's reasoning is confirmed in other judgments in explicit terms, eventually in areas beyond public procurement, which is at the core of *Infraestruturas de Portugal SA*.

More in detail, in the judgment above-mentioned, the CJ, with regard to the interpretation of one of the facultative grounds for exclusion enshrined in the first subparagraph of Article 57(4) of Directive 2014/24/EU, made a clear U-turn. As a matter of fact, the Court recognized that a systematic analysis of (d) of that subparagraph[117] shows that 'contrary to what is apparent from' several of its judgments,[118] 'the Member States are under the obligation to transpose that provision into their national law'.[119] By overruling its established jurisprudence, the CJ did something unexpected and surprising by observing, first, that, as to the objective pursued by Directive 2014/24 in so far as concerns the facultative grounds for exclusion, 'the EU legislature intended to confer on the contracting authority, and on it alone, the task of assessing whether a candidate or tenderer must be excluded from a procurement procedure during the stage of selecting the tenderers'.[120] Subsequently, the CJ affirmed that it shall be ensured 'that contracting authorities have, in all Member States, the possibility of excluding economic operators who are regarded as unreliable by those authorities'.[121] The Court did not challenge the way a Member State transposes Directive 2014/24, which would have had a considerable impact 'only' on the substantive law facet implied in the ruling, from the standpoint of public procurement law. In fact, the CJ, albeit only *ab abstracto*, *pro futuro*, and in theoretical terms through a long preliminary *obiter dictum*,[122] admitted that contracting (public) authorities can use an EU directive to *directly* affect private parties' prerogatives, creating upon them obligations whose existence such parties could not possibly

[116] On the implications of the case, *see* D. Sarmiento, S. Iglesias Sanchez, *Is Direct Effect Morphing into Something Different?*, EU Law Live, 4 March 2024, available at http:/eulawlive.com/insight-is-direct-effect-morphing-into-something-different-by-daniel-sarmiento-and-sara-iglesias-sanchez/; A. Sanchez-Graells, *Transposing Directives no longer so discretionary! The Court of Justice forces transposition of discretionary exclusion grounds and hints at 'intra-State' vertical direct effect (C-66/22)*, EU Law Live, 27 February 2024, available at https://eulawlive.com/op-ed-transposing-directives-no-longer-so-discretionary-the-court-of-justice-forces-transposition-of-discretionary-exclusion-grounds-and-hints-at-intra-state-vertical-dire/.

[117] It is stated therein that contracting authorities may exclude from participation in a procurement procedure any economic operator 'where the contracting authority has sufficiently plausible indications to conclude that the economic operator has entered into agreements with other economic operators aimed at distorting competition'.

[118] *See* CJ, *Meca*, C-41/18, EU:C:2019:507, para. 33; CJ, *Tim*, C-395/18, EU:C:2020:58, paras 34 and 40; CJ, *Rad Service*, C-210/20, EU:C:2021:445, para. 28.

[119] CJ, *Infraestruturas de Portugal, SA and Futrifer Indústrias Ferroviárias, SA v Toscca—Equipamentos em Madeira Lda*, C-66/22, EU:C:2023:1016, para. 50.

[120] *Infraestruturas de Portugal SA* (n 119), para. 55.

[121] *Infraestruturas de Portugal SA* (n 119), para. 57.

[122] *Infraestruturas de Portugal SA* (n 119), paras. 41–64, where the CJ concluded that 'it is therefore appropriate to answer the questions referred for a preliminary ruling while taking the preceding preliminary observations into consideration'. Indeed, in the case at hand, a private party was invoking the directive against the State, not vice versa.

be aware of. New direct obligations are, thus, invoked by part of the State's administration to challenge national laws to the detriment of companies, which had legitimately relied on that State's legislation, that is, in full defiance, not only of the EU consolidated jurisprudence on the nature and personal scope of directives, but also of the principle of legitimate expectations. This reasoning, if confirmed and applied *in concreto* to answer the specific preliminary rulings possibly posed by national judges, seems to be a clear departure from the CJ's constitutional narrative on directives' internal effect. As will be shown in section 6 of Chapter VI, *a fortiori*, such approach, if reiterated and made more explicit, could, *rectius* should, be held also in regard to horizontal direct effect of directives.

6. Limits of direct effect and derogations from the duty to disapply

While disapplication, as an obligation stemming from EU law, should take place only in the context of directly effective EU provisions, it is not true that direct effect always implies necessarily, automatically, and/or immediately the disapplication of the conflicting domestic norm. Some derogations can be identified.[123] These are legitimate, 'physiological' derogations from the principle of primacy, *rectius*, from the duty to disapply attached to both the principles of primacy and direct effect, since the CJ itself finds them compatible with the EU legal system. Only the Court is endowed with the power to identify such situations since 'rules of national law, even of a constitutional order, cannot be allowed to undermine the unity and effectiveness of EU law'.[124] Indeed, the CJ affirmed that 'even assuming that overriding considerations of legal certainty are capable of leading, by way of exception, to a provisional suspension of the ousting effect which a directly applicable rule of EU law has on national law that is contrary thereto, the conditions of such a suspension can be determined solely by the Court'.[125]

A tentative list of derogations admitted by the CJ is drawn up in the following. By these derogations, the Court, through its preliminary rulings, enables national judges not to disapply, or to suspend/postpone such disapplication. In section 8 the focus is on inverse vertical situations in relation to sources of EU law other than directives.[126] It is there submitted that in those situations direct effect can be asserted normally for regulations and decisions not addressed only to States, and exceptionally for EU primary law sources, even if no advantages for the natural and legal persons who are parties to the dispute stem from the applicable EU law provisions. As for EU primary law, more in particular, the legal avenue to admit direct effect is the compliance with the principle of legitimate expectations so that disapplication could take place only for future cases raising the same problems of compatibility with EU law tackled by the CJ with its judgment, a judgment which gave rise to a new interpretation of the EU provision(s) at stake. Such reasoning would apply also to the *Taricco* saga, the legacy that originated from it, as well as to the recent strand of case law on the (inverse vertical) direct effect of EU criminal law, as explained in section 9. The CJ followed, in *Taricco* and other rulings, a different casuistic reasoning tailored on the specific national

[123] For a less detailed account, *see* also D. Gallo, *Rethinking*, 593.

[124] *See* CJ, *Melloni*, C-399/11, EU:C:2013:107, para. 59, and CJ, *Pelham GmbH and Others v Ralf Hütter and Florian Schneider-Esleben*, C-476/17, EU:C:2019:624, para. 78.

[125] *See*, *inter alia*, CJ, *Winner Wetten*, C-409/06, EU:C:2010:503, paras 61 and 67; CJ, *B*, C-439/19, EU:C:2021:504, para. 135.

[126] For inverse vertical effect and directives, *see* § 5 of this chapter.

legal system affected by its ruling, which does not seem to be the right track for safeguarding fundamental rights, while ensuring the enforcement of EU law. More in particular, it is argued that, while the Court's approach is commendable in so far as the EU judges detected some derogations from the duty to disapply, their framing should have been done differently. In section 10 the analysis is devoted to the study of a quite isolated strand of rulings that seem to have been traced back by the CJ to direct effect and the duty to disapply, while generating a systematic violation of the principle of legitimate expectations caused by the disapplication *in malam partem* of national law. The reference goes to the Court's case law on the relativization of the *res judicata* principle. Finally, section 11 aims to identify the clearest attempts pursued by supreme/constitutional courts of Member States to illegitimately and expressly derogate from the duty to disapply, notwithstanding the countervailing obligation imposed by EU law, as interpreted by the Court, to give precedence to, and ensure application of, EU directly effective provisions.

7. (Tentative) list of 'physiological' derogations permitted by the CJ

A first derogation from the duty to disapply is rooted in the relationship between the EU legal order and national procedural autonomy.[127] Most notably, when the application of EU law is apt to challenge *res judicata*, national courts are normally not compelled to set aside domestic rules in conflict with EU directly effective provisions. Indeed, the CJ itself considers the principle of *res judicata* one of the pillars of EU law.[128] As affirmed in the EU case law, 'in order to ensure both stability of the law and of legal relations and the sound administration of justice', judicial decisions which have become definitive after all rights of appeal have been exhausted or after the passing of the time limits provided for in that connection 'can no longer be called into question'. Consequently, 'EU law does not require a national court to disapply domestic rules of procedure conferring finality on a judgment, even if to do so would make it possible to remedy a domestic situation which is incompatible with EU law'. This also means that a judicial body cannot 'automatically reverse a judgment having the authority of *res judicata* in order to take into account the interpretation of a relevant

[127] On national procedural autonomy and its progressive relativization, *see* R. Caranta, *Judicial Protection against Member States: A New* Jus Commune *Takes Shape* (1995) 32 *Common Market Law Review* 703; C. N. Kakouris, *Do the Member States Possess Judicial Procedural 'Autonomy'?* (1997) 34 *Common Market Law Review* 1389; J. M. Kendrick, *Modifying Procedural Autonomy: Better Protection for Community Rights* (2000) 8 *European Review of Private Law* 565; M. Dougan, *National Remedies before the Court of Justice: Issues of Harmonisation and Differentiation*, Oxford, Oxford University Press, 2004; A. Perrin, *Droit européen et droit communautaire: Que reste-t-il de l'autonomie procédurale des états membres?* (2008) 124 *Revue de droit public* 1661; D. U. Galetta, *Procedural Autonomy of EU Member States: Paradise Lost? A Study on the 'Functionalized Procedural Competence' of EU Member States*, Heidelberg, Springer, 2009; G. Vitale, *Diritto processuale nazionale e diritto dell'Unione europea, L'autonomia procedurale degli Stati membri in settori a diverso livello di 'europeizzazione'*, Catania, Ed.It, 2010; M. Bobek, *Why There is No Principle of 'Procedural Autonomy' of the Member States*, in H.-W. Micklitz, B. de Witte (eds.), *The European Court of Justice and the Autonomy of the Member States*, Oxford, Intersentia, 2012, 305–322; A. M. Romito, *La tutela giurisdizionale nell'Unione europea tra effettività del sistema e garanzie individuali*, Bari, Cacucci, 2015, 62–75.

[128] On the status of the principle in EU law, *see*, *inter alia*, A. Kornezov, Res judicata *of national judgments incompatible with EU Law: Time for a major rethink?* (2014) 50 *Common Market Law Review* 809; A. Turmo, *National* res judicata *in the European Union: Revisiting the tension between the temptation of effectiveness and the acknowledgement of domestic procedural law* (2021) 58 *Common Market Law Review* 361; M. Bolognese, *Il giudicato nazionale nel diritto dell'Unione europea e della CEDU*, Naples, Editoriale Scientifica, 2023; A. Turmo, Res Judicata *in European Union Law*, Madrid, EU Law Live, 7 March 2023, available at https://eulawlive.com/book-launch-res-judicata-in-european-union-law-by-araceli-turmo/. For an account of the *Lucchini* case and the subsequent case law, see § 10 of this chapter.

provision of EU law' adopted by the CJ.[129] Moreover, in the absence of EU detailed primary and secondary laws in this field, 'the rules implementing the principle of *res judicata* are a matter for the national legal order, in accordance with the principle of the procedural autonomy of the Member States'. However, those rules 'must not be less favourable than those governing similar domestic actions (principle of equivalence), nor may they be framed in such a way as to make it in practice impossible or excessively difficult to exercise the rights conferred by EU law (principle of effectiveness)'.[130] In any event, as will be discussed and critically observed in section 10 of this chapter, the intangibility of *res judicata* is not always a common thread in the case law of the CJ in so far as the principles of primacy and effectiveness, according to the Court, in some situations, shall take precedence even on the 'finality' of the judgments rendered by domestic jurisdictions.

A second derogation arises whereby the CJ, despite the directly effective nature of one or more EU provisions, chooses to refer the matter to the national judge who is deemed to be better equipped for achieving a fair balance of interests implied in the enforcement of EU law. This means that the bond between direct effect and immediate disapplication breaks when EU judges, even though confronted with EU directly effective provisions, refrain from conducting a balancing of interests that they deem fall instead within the competence of the national court submitting the reference for a preliminary ruling and ultimately refrain from imposing a duty to disapply. An example is the *Österreichischer Rundfunk* case, whereby the CJ, while stating that the articles of Directive 95/46/EC at stake were directly effective and thus 'may be relied on by an individual before the national courts', concluded that it was 'up to the national judge' to verify, pursuant to the principle of proportionality, whether it was necessary to immediately oust the application of domestic law.[131] In this regard, when the matter is the protection of fundamental rights, should the CJ refuse to issue an *erga omnes* interpretation of EU law leading to the disapplication of national law, the national judge could seek an *erga omnes* ruling by referring the matter to the national Constitutional Court in systems that foresee such mechanism, as was done in Italy by the Constitutional Court in its judgment 20/2019.[132] In these types of proceedings, thus, the decoupling of direct effect and disapplication is viable due to a previous *non liquet* coming from the CJ.

A third derogation occurs whereby the CJ recognizes that ordinary judges can exceptionally and temporarily suspend the ousting effect which an EU directly effective provision has on national law so long as a number of conditions are fulfilled.[133] First, the measure whose disapplication is excluded must be one that correctly transposes a directive. Second, the adoption and entry into force of the new national measure would not enable the adverse effects resulting from the disapplication of the contested measure to be avoided. Third, the legal vacuum resulting from disapplication would lead to the attainment of objectives which run specifically counter to the fundamental objective of the directive. Fourth, the effects produced by the contested measure are exceptionally maintained only for the period of time which is strictly necessary to adopt the measures apt to undo the irregularity that led to the

[129] *See* CJ, *Hochtief Solutions AG Magyarországi Fióktelepe*, C-620/17, EU:C:2019:630, paras 54–56 and CJ, *Călin*, C-676/17, EU:C:2019:700, paras 26–29.

[130] *See* CJ, *Cabinet de avocat UR*, C-424/19, EU:C:2020:581, para. 25. On the principles of equivalence and effectiveness, as well as on the principle of *res judicata*, *see* CJ, *Ibercaja Banco SA*, C-600/19, EU:C:2022:394, paras 41–44.

[131] CJ, *Österreichischer Rundfunk*, joined cases C-465/00, C-138/01, and C-139/01, EU:C:2003:294, paras 88–101. *See* Directive (EC) 95/46 of the European Parliament and of the Council on the protection of individuals with regard to the processing of personal data and on the free movement of such data [1995] L 281/95, 31.

[132] Italian Constitutional Court, No. 20/2019, 23 January 2019.

[133] For recent insights on this case law, *see* M. Dougan, *Primacy and the Remedy of Disapplication* (2019) 56 *Common Market Law Review* 1459.

emergence of a contrast with the EU legal order.[134] In any event, the provisional suspension of disapplication should be confined to situations of an exceptional nature, considering the repercussions that it has on the scope of the primacy principle. Moreover, as recently observed in *G.D.*,[135] such derogation, while aimed at safeguarding principally legal certainty, could not 'seriously interfere with the fundamental rights of the persons', amongst whom, those 'whose data have been retained', as affirmed in that case.[136] In this vein, a derogation from a derogation has been asserted.

This derogatory rule of reason has been admitted, to date, only in the field of environment and energy supply, whereby the CJ relied on 'imperative reasons of overriding public interest' as the only trigger for deeming legitimate the suspension of the remedy of disapplication.[137] Most recently,[138] in *A and others*,[139] the CJ, in the first place, held that, while taking into account the existence of an overriding consideration relating to the protection of the environment, a national court

> may exceptionally be authorised to make use of a national provision empowering it to maintain certain effects of a national measure the procedure for the adoption of which did not comply with Directive 2001/42/EC [on the assessment of the effects of certain plans and programmes on the environment], where there is a risk that the annulment of that measure could create a legal vacuum that is incompatible with that Member State's obligation to adopt measures to transpose another act of EU law concerning the protection of the environment.[140]

In the second place, the CJ specified that considerations such as the security of electricity supply could justify maintaining the effects of national measures adopted in breach of the obligations under EU law 'only if, in the event that the effects of those measures were annulled or suspended, there was a genuine and serious threat of disruption to the electricity supply of the Member State concerned which could not be remedied by any other means or alternatives, particularly in the context of the internal market'.[141]

[134] *See* CJ, *Inter-Environnement Wallonie ASBL and Terre wallonne ASBL (Inter-Environnement Wallonie II)*, C-41/11, EU:C:2012:103, paras 58–62, on which, *see* T. Lock, *Are There Exceptions to a Member State's Duty to Comply with the Requirements of a Directive?: Inter-Environnement Wallonie* (2013) 50 *Common Market Law Review* 217.

[135] CJ, *G.D.*, C-140/20, EU:C:2022:258.

[136] *G.D.* (n 135), para. 122.

[137] *Inter-Environnement Wallonie II* (n 134), para. 58. *See* also CJ, *Association France Nature Environnement v Premier ministre, Ministère de l'Écologie, du développement durable et de l'Énergie*, C-379/15, EU:C:2016:603, para. 43, and CJ, *Inter-Environnement Wallonie and Bond Beter Leefmilieu Vlaanderen (Inter-Environnement Wallonie III)*, C-411/17, EU:C:2019:622, paras 146–159, on which, *see* L. Clément-Wilz, *L'office du juge interne pour moduler les effets de l'annulation d'un acte contraire au droit de l'Union. Reflexions sur l'arrêt* Association France Nature Environnement *du Conseil d'Etat français* (2017) 2 *European Papers* 259, 265–266; F. Pani, *L'obbligo (flessibile) di rinvio pregiudiziale e i possibili fattori di un suo irrigidimento. Riflessioni in margine alla sentenza* Association France Nature Environnement (2017) 2 *European Papers* 384; K. Sowery, *Reconciling primacy and environmental protection:* Association France Nature Environnement (2017) 54 *Common Market Law Review* 1, and G. Gentile, Inter-Environnement *Expanded: Another Brick Out of the Wall of EU Law Supremacy?* (2017) 2 *European Papers* 321; A. Circolo, *La disapplicazione del primato: le eccezioni della Corte di giustizia all'efficacia prevalente del diritto dell'Unione sul diritto interno. Note a margine della pronuncia* Inter Environnement Wallonie II, in *dirittounioneeuropea.eu*, 11 November 2019, available at https://www.dirittounioneeuropea.eu/Tool/Evidenza/Single/view_html?id_evidenza=900; M. Dougan, *Primacy*; F. Martucci, *Les principes de sécurité juridique et de confiance légitime dans la jurisprudence de la Cour de justice de l'Union européenne* (2020) 5 *Titre VII—Les Nouveaux Cahiers du Counseil costitutionnel* 70–78.

[138] Although only in principle, the above-mentioned derogation was admitted in CJ, *GRDF*, C-236/18, EU:C:2019:1120, paras 41–52.

[139] CJ, *A and Others*, C-24/19, EU:C:2020:503.

[140] *A and Others* (n 139), para. 90.

[141] *A and Others* (n 139), para. 92.

On the other hand, from the whole reasoning developed by the CJ in the *Winner Wetten GmbH*[142] and *Inter-Environnement Wallonie III* rulings it can be inferred that the provisional suspension of disapplication is not necessarily limited to the protection of environment and energy supply.[143] Indeed, in *Inter-Environnement Wallonie III*, the CJ explicitly observed that the derogation from disapplication comes into play 'on a case-by-case basis ... with due regard to the conditions laid down by the Court's case-law'.[144] As a matter of fact, the expansion of the scope *ratione materiae* of such a derogation from the duty to disapply is now a reality and has been performed, even if only as a principle, in several more recent judgments concerning a variety of sectors and directives, including the application of VAT to healthcare services; the protection of privacy in the electronic communications sector; the Community code relating to veterinary medicinal products; the processing of personal data, and the obligation of carriers to communicate passenger data; as well as the use of passenger name record (PNR) data for the prevention, detection, investigation, and prosecution of terrorist offences and serious crime.[145]

A fourth derogation takes place in so far as the CJ, while denying room for disapplication, even though the EU law at stake is directly effective, imposes an obligation upon ordinary judges to extend temporarily to individuals—pending an *ad hoc* domestic provision enabling the removal of the incompatibility of the national law with EU law—rights and advantages that national law already grants to specific groups of subjects. This exception occurs specifically in the field of equality and non-discrimination, as shown by the *Cresco Investigation* case,[146] in which the disapplication of a national law granting certain employees (with a particular religious affiliation) a supplementary day's holiday—that the Court found discriminatory pursuant to Article 21(1) of the Charter—would have entailed a generalized reduction of guarantees for all individuals, while not attributing any benefit to the disadvantaged group of employees who belonged to other churches and were not included in the scope *ratione personae* of the domestic provision whose disapplication had been suspended by the CJ.

A fifth derogation[147] occurs when the CJ approves the invocability of the national identity clause foreseen in Article 4(2) TEU[148] by the referring court in its reference pursuant to

[142] *Winner Wetten GmbH* (n 125), para. 67, on which, see T. Beukers, *Case C-409/06, Winner Wetten GmbH v. Bürgermeisterin der Stadt Bergheim, Judgment of the Court (Grand Chamber) of 8 September 2010*, in *Common Market Law Review*, 2011, 1985.

[143] *Winner Wetten GmbH* (n 125), para. 67.

[144] *Inter-Environnement Wallonie III* (n 137), para. 178.

[145] *See*, respectively, CJ, *Belgisch Syndicaat van Chiropraxie and Bart Vandendries*, C-597/17, EU:C:2019:544, paras 53 and 63; CJ, *La Quadrature du Net*, joined cases C-511-512/18 and 520/18, EU:C:2020:791, paras 217–220; CJ, *An tAire Talmhaíochta Bia agus Mara, Éire agus an tArd-Aighne*, C-64/20, EU:C:2021:207, paras 33–39; *G.D.* (n 135), paras 118–123; CJ, *Ligue des droits humains*, C-817/19, EU:C:2022:491, paras 294–296.

[146] CJ, *Cresco Investigation GmbH v Markus Achatzi*, C-193/17, EU:C:2019:43, para. 3, on which, *see* L. Cecchetti, *Gli strumenti del giudizio di eguaglianza della Corte di giustizia alla prova del divieto di discriminazione sulla base della religione: il caso* Cresco Investigation (2020) 2 *Il Diritto dell'Unione europea* 317 and P. Sabau, J. Ramón, *La sentencia del TJUE de 22 de enero de 2019 en el asunto* Cresco Investigation GmbH: *una nueva muestra de la irrelevancia del art. 17 del Tratado de Funcionamiento de la Unión Europea* (2020) 49 *Revista General de Derecho Europeo* 242.

[147] Amongst the first authors to reflect upon the mitigation of the principle of primacy due to the application of the identity clause, *see* A. von Bogdandy, S. Schill, *Overcoming Absolute Primacy: Respect for National Identity under the Lisbon Treaty* (2011) 48 *Common Market Law Review* 1417; B. Guastaferro, *Beyond the Exceptionalism of Constitutional Conflicts: The Ordinary Functions of the Identity Clause*, in *Yearbook of European Law*, vol. 31, 2012, 263–318; B. Guastaferro, *Legalità sovranazionale e legalità costituzionale. Tensioni costitutive e giunture ordinamentali*, Turin, Giappichelli, 2013; F.-X. Millet, *L'Union européenne et l'identité constitutionnelle des Etats membres*, Paris, LGDJ, 2013; G. Di Federico, *L'identità nazionale degli Stati membri nel diritto dell'Unione europea. Natura e portata dell'art. 4, par. 2, TUE*, Naples, Editoriale Scientifica, 2017. On such clause, from a comparative perspective, *see* P. Faraguna, *Constitutional Identity in the EU—A Shield or a Sword?* (2018) 19 *German Law Journal* 1617.

[148] In the literature, on the identity clause, including for detailed accounts on the EU case law, *see* L. D. A. Corrias, *Populism in a Constitutional Key: Constituent Power, Popular Sovereignty and Constitutional Identity* (2016) 12 *European Constitutional Law Review* 6; C. Calliess, G. Van Der Schyff (eds.), *Constitutional Identity in a Europe*

Article 267 TFEU and/or by the State involved in the proceeding before the EU judges, which often takes place in the context of Article 267 TFEU. As a matter of fact, such invocability is frequently (but not necessarily) grounded in the position that had been taken, in the course of domestic proceedings, by the constitutional/supreme Court. If the invocability is asserted by the CJ, the principle of primacy is derogated and disapplication cannot take place, regardless of the directly effective character of EU law. Of course, as affirmed mildly in *Torresi*[149] and *Coman*[150] and bluntly in the *Pancharevo*[151] and *RS*[152] rulings, such derogation can be admitted only by the CJ because the latter is the ultimate interpreter of a Treaty provision such as Article 4(2) TEU, in spite of the *renvoi* provided therein to national identities, that is, first and foremost to constitutional legal orders of Member States. This reconstruction of the national identity clause shows to what extent the process of European integration developed in *quasi* federal terms, with two major implications. First, the CJ, in attracting in its exclusive competence Article 4(2) TEU, as a parameter of legality of EU law, through Article 267 TFEU and the preliminary reference proceeding on validity, inevitably puts at the centre of its analysis the domestic legal order and its validity, thus expanding the scope of the preliminary ruling. A ruling which, being *erga omnes*, as is known, should in principle concern the interpretation and validity of EU law, not national law.[153] Second, the CJ, by virtue of a provision, such as Article 4(2) TEU, that refers to (all) the domestic legal orders of Member States, gets to be the only and ultimate interpreter, not only of EU law, but also of the twenty-seven national legal systems, insofar as their national/constitutional identities come into conflict with the principle of primacy. In this way, the Court assumes new and increased responsibilities, as the concept of national identity is naturally evolutive and changeable.

The sixth derogation arises when the CJ limits the temporal effects of its judgment ruling upon the interpretation of EU law sought by the referring domestic court pursuant to Article 267 TFEU. In such case, the disapplication of national law, as a consequence stemming from the application of EU directly effective provisions, is limited, rather than ruled out, postponed, or suspended. This scenario materializes where the Court decides, in its first very

of Multilevel Constitutionalism, Cambridge, Cambridge University Press, 2019; G. Di Federico, *The Potential of Article 4(2) TEU in the Solution of Constitutional Clashes Based on Alleged Violations of National Identity and the Quest for Adequate (Judicial) Standards* (2019) 25 *European Public Law* 347; F. Fabbrini, A. Sajó, *The Dangers of Constitutional Identity* (2019) 25 *European Law Journal* 457; L. D. Spieker, *Framing and Managing Constitutional Identity Conflicts: How to Stabilize the Modus Vivendi Between the Court of Justice and National Constitutional Courts* (2020) 57 *Common Market Law Review* 361; L. F. M. Besselink, *The Persistence of a Contested Concept: Reflections on Ten Years Constitutional Identity in EU Law* (2021) 27 *European Public Law* 597; M. Bonelli, *National Identity and European Integration Beyond 'Limited Fields'* (2021) 27 *European Public Law* 537; M. Claes, *National Identity and the Protection of Fundamental Rights* (2021) 27 *European Public Law* 517; B. de Witte, *Article 4(2) TEU as a Protection of Institutional Diversity of the Member States* (2021) 27 *European Public Law* 559; P. Faraguna, *On the Identity Clause and its Abuses: Back to the Treaty* (2021) 27 *European Public Law* 411; D. Fromage, *National Constitutional Identity and its Regional Dimension Post-Lisbon as Part of a General Trend Towards Multilevel Governance within the EU* (2021) 27 *European Public Law* 497; D. Fromage, B. de Witte, *National Constitutional Identity Ten Years on: State of Play and Future Perspectives* (2021) 27 *European Public Law* 411; G. Martinico, *Taming National Identity: A Systematic Understanding of Article 4.2 TUE* (2021) 27 *European Public Law* 447; F.-X. Millet, *Successfully Articulating National Constitutional Identity Claims: Strait Is the Gate and Narrow Is the Way* (2021) 27 *European Public Law* 571; J. Scholtes, *Abusing Constitutional Identity* (2021) 22 *German Law Journal* 534.

149 CJ, *Torresi*, C-58-59/13, EU:C:2014:2088, paras 53–55 and 58.
150 CJ, *Coman*, C-673/16, EU:C:2018:385, paras 42–43.
151 CJ, *Pancharevo*, C-490/20, EU:C:2021:1008, paras 53–54 and 69.
152 *RS* (n 3), paras 49, 69–71 and 78.
153 *See* Chapter II, §§ 2–3.

same preliminary ruling interpreting EU law,[154] to derogate from the general rule that interpretative declaratory judgments generate retroactive effects.[155] Therefore, the Court, although only occasionally, has mitigated its approach by limiting the temporal effect of a preliminary ruling to an *ex nunc* effect in order to comply with the principle of legal certainty.[156] At stake lies the quest for a fair equilibrium between two conflicting needs: effective judicial protection of the rights violated as a result of the internal misapplication of EU law, on the one side, and the protection of legitimate expectations regarding legal situations that were formed before the Court issued its ruling *ex* Article 267 TFEU, on the other. A limitation can take place only if the CJ concludes, on a case-by-case basis, that two conditions are respected, as recognized for the first time in *Defrenne II*: *(i)* the risk of serious difficulties for those concerned by the CJ's interpretation of EU law, that is, of serious negative economic repercussions owing to a large number of legal relationships; and *(ii)* the good faith expectations which arose on the basis of the national rules considered at that time to be validly in force.[157] Moreover, the CJ identified a further restrictive factor that should be taken into account for activating the *ex nunc* temporal limitation of preliminary rulings: it must have appeared that individuals and national authorities had been led to adopt practices inconsistent with EU law, to which the conduct of other Member States and/or the Commission

[154] On the need that the temporary limitation is carried out in the first judgment ruling on the interpretation sought, *see* CJ, *Bruno Barra v Belgian State and City of Liège*, C-309/85, EU:C:1988:42, para. 13; CJ, *Wienand Meilicke, Heidi Christa Weyde and Marina Stöffler v Finanzamt Bonn-Innenstadt*, C-292/04, EU:C:2007:132, paras 36–37; CJ, *Nelson and Others*, joined cases C-581/10 and C-629/10, EU:C:2012:657, para. 91; CJ, *O'Brien*, C-432/17, EU:C:2018:879, para. 34; CJ, *Proceedings brought by B*, C-439/19, EU:C:2021:504, para. 133. In the literature, *see* M. Broberg, N. Fenger, *Preliminary References to the European Court of Justice*, 3rd ed., Oxford, Oxford University Press, 2021, 412: 'the limitation can be laid down only in the first judgment ruling on the interpretation sought, but not in later rulings. Indeed, there must necessarily be one single occasion when a decision is made on the temporal effects of the requested interpretation of the EU provision in question. Otherwise, both the need for equal treatment of the Member States and of other persons subject to EU law and the requirements arising from the principle of legal certainty would be jeopardized.'

[155] On the rationale of limiting the *ex tunc* effects of preliminary rulings, see, *ex multis* and amongst early studies, G. Bebr, *Preliminary rulings of the Court of Justice: Their Authority and Temporal Effect* (1981) 18 *Common Market Law Review* 475. Amongst recent studies, *see* T. Maciejewski, J. Theilen, *Temporal Aspects of the Interaction between National Law and EU Law: Reintroducing the Protection of Legitimate Expectations* (2017) 42 *European Law Review* 707; M. Broberg, N. Fenger, *Preliminary References*, 411–422; L. Cecchetti, *The Scope* Ratione Temporis *of the Interpretive Rulings of the ECJ: Should the Temporal Limitation Still be a Strict Derogation from Retroactive Effects?*, in D. Gallo, L. Cecchetti (eds.), *The Preliminary Ruling*, 71; K. Lenaerts, K. Gutman, J. T. Nowak, *EU Procedural Law*, 2nd ed., Oxford, Oxford University Press, 2023, 267–271.

[156] CJ, *Gabrielle Defrenne v Société anonyme belge de navigation aérienne Sabena*, 43/75, EU:C:1976:56, para. 74. On the novelties regarding the temporal effects of preliminary rulings stemming from the judgment, *see* D. Wyatt, *Prospective Effect of a Holding of Direct Applicability* (1975–1976) 1 *European Law Review* 399; W. van Gerven, *Contribution de l'arret Defrenne au développement du droit Communautaire*, in *Cahiers de droit européen*, 1977, 131; M. Waelbroeck, *May the Court of Justice Limit the Retrospective Operation of Its Judgments?*, in *Yearbook of European Law*, vol. 1, 1981, 115–123.

[157] For the first condition, *see*, *inter alia*, CJ, *Vroege*, C-57/93, EU:C:1994:230, para. 21; CJ, *Legros*, C-163/90, EU:C:1992:326, para. 30; CJ, *Grzelczyk*, C-184/99, EU:C:2001:458, para. 53; CJ, *EKW and Wein*, C-437/97, EU:C:2000:110, para. 57; CJ, *Brzeziński*, C-313/05, EU:C:2007:33, para. 56; CJ, *Rēdlihs*, C-263/11, EU:C:2012:497, para. 59; CJ, *Santander*, joined cases C-338-347/11, EU:C:2012:286, para. 59; CJ, *Skanska*, C-724/17, EU:C:2019:204, para. 56; CJ, *WESTbahn Management*, C-210/18, EU:C:2019:586, para. 45; CJ, *Schuch-Ghannadan*, C-274/18, EU:C:2019:828, para. 61; *B* (n 125), para. 132. For the second condition, *see*, *inter alia*, CJ, *Blaizot*, 24/86, EU:C:1988:43, paras 31–33; CJ, *Ampafrance*, joined cases C-177/99 and C-181/99, EU:C:2000:470, para. 66; CJ, *Griesmar*, C-366/99, EU:C:2001:648, para. 76; CJ, *Bidar*, C-209/03 EU:C:2005:169, para. 69; CJ, *Paper Consult*, C-101/16, EU:C:2017:775, para. 65. For a detailed analysis, *see* D. Düsterhaus, *Eppur si muove! The Past, Present and (possible) Future of Temporal Limitations in the Preliminary Reference Procedure*, in *Yearbook of European Law*, vol. 36, 2017, 237–274, and L. Cecchetti, *The Scope* Ratione Temporis *of the Interpretive Rulings of the ECJ: Should the Temporal Limitation Still be a Strict Derogation from Retroactive Effects?*, in D. Gallo, L. Cecchetti (eds.), 'The Preliminary Ruling Procedure, Today: Revisiting Article 267 TFEU's Constitutional Backbone', Special Issue (2023) 15 *European Journal of Legal Studies* 71, 81–100.

may even have contributed.[158] In this connection, it is worth mentioning that, with regard to situations where an immediate application of EU law, as interpreted by means of a preliminary ruling, would infringe the *lex mitior* principle and the requirement of legal certainty in criminal matters, AG Bobek proposed to the CJ to rule out the remedy of disapplication. According to Bobek, this 'would just carve out a narrow exception for the individual ongoing criminal cases, while leaving the general normative consequences of the incompatibility untouched'.[159] This solution was in no way endorsed by the CJ.

A last derogation relates to inverse vertical relationships when they raise issues of criminal law in the context of EU primary law. It occurs, especially from the *Taricco* saga onwards, when *in malam partem* disapplication arises as a result of the application of EU law. While the matter will be carefully investigated in sections 8 and 9, at this stage, it shall simply be recalled that, on the one hand, according to the CJ, if the primacy of EU directly effective provisions over a national legal order entails a violation of the principle of legality and consequently of fundamental rights attached to such principle, disapplication must not be imposed upon domestic authorities. As explicitly stated in *Kolev*, 'it is for the national courts to give full effect to Article 325(1) TFEU, by disapplying that legislation, as necessary, while also ensuring respect for the fundamental rights of the persons accused'.[160] On the other hand, while the aim pursued by that derogation certainly seems agreeable, in section 9 it will be shown that the type of reasoning employed by the Court for its justification is still problematic.

8. Admissible inverse vertical direct effect beyond directives through the lens of the principle of legitimate expectations and by virtue of *pro futuro* preliminary rulings

As for EU sources of law other than directives, the CJ has never explicitly dealt with the admissibility of inverse vertical direct effect. In situations where the application of EU law replacing national law entails disadvantages for the private parties to the dispute while creating an advantage only for the State, as plaintiff invoking EU provisions and acting as their ultimate enforcer (and possibly for natural and/or legal persons who are not parties to the dispute), direct effect, and consequently disapplication, in principle, should not come into play if the reconstruction carried out in section 3 were to be followed. However, what has been observed in relation to directives and decisions addressed only to States cannot be transposed *sic et simpliciter* to EU primary law, including Treaty provisions, the Charter, general principles of EU law, as well as to regulations and to those decisions which are not addressed only to States. As a matter of fact, if an unconditional EU law provision is addressed also (or only) to individuals (like antitrust provisions such as Articles 101 and 102 TFEU), direct effect should not be excluded. Here the rule is invoked by the State against natural and/or legal persons since the latter can be subject to EU law-based obligations as occurs within horizontal direct effect. In this lies a key difference between directives (and decisions addressed

[158] *See Santander* (n 157), paras 59–60; CJ, *Maruko*, C-267/06, EU:C:2008:179, para. 77; CJ, *Bressol*, C-73/08, EU:C:2010:181, paras 91–93.

[159] Opinion of AG Bobek of 13 July 2017, *Scialdone*, C-574/15, EU:C:2017:553, para. 181.

[160] CJ, *Kolev*, C-612/15, EU:C:2018:392, para. 76; CJ, *Ministerul Lucrărilor Publice, Dezvoltării şi Administraţiei*, C-360/20, EU:C:2021:856, para. 36.

only to States) and the other sources of EU law that have a wider personal scope, that is, not limited to Member States' authorities.

Against this backdrop, it is here submitted that, as far as EU primary law is concerned, in inverse vertical situations direct effect can be asserted and the duty to disapply should occur provided that the principle of legitimate expectations, as well as the principle of legal certainty of which it is a corollary, are respected.[161] In this respect, these two general principles of EU law are often 'connected in many legal systems'[162] and frequently merge in the EU case law.[163] According to Craig, legal certainty implies that EU rules should be clear 'so that individuals may be able to ascertain unequivocally what their rights and obligations are and may take steps accordingly'.[164] In this sense, as underlined by Tridimas, legal certainty has a 'static character whereas legitimate expectations are enjoyed for the future'[165] since the latter requires 'the Community legislature and the other Community organs ... to exercise their powers over a period of time in such a way that situations and relationships lawfully created under Community law are not affected in a manner which could not have been foreseen by a diligent person'.[166] In this book, the two principles have been, and will continue to be, mentioned together. If not, the fact that the principle of legitimate expectations alone is referred to, in this chapter as well as in Chapter VI, does not mean, of course, that the principle of legal certainty is irrelevant. The opposite is true precisely because the principle of legitimate expectations, as previously observed, is its corollary.

More particularly, it is proposed here that the CJ limit *ratione temporis* the effects of its ruling in which it offered an interpretation of EU law that, until that moment, was not foreseeable. This implies that such interpretation would not apply from that very same judgment issued by the Court, unlike what occurs when preliminary rulings are granted *ex nunc* effects in compliance with *Defrenne II* and the subsequent judgments.[167] In the latter strand of cases, in fact, the CJ applies the EU provision *from that ruling onwards*, not *afterwards* as is hereby alleged with respect to the applicability of EU primary law provisions in inverse vertical situations.[168] In the latter situations, the interpretation of EU law is

[161] This is a re-elaboration, development, and refinement of what has been already argued in D. Gallo, *L'efficacia*, 351–361; D. Gallo, *Effetto diretto del diritto dell'Unione europea e disapplicazione, oggi*, (2019) 1 *Osservatorio sulle Fonti* 1, 28–30; D. Gallo, *L'effetto diretto quale dottrina fondante dell'ordinamento dell'Unione Europea* (2020) 3 *Rivista internazionale di filosofia del diritto* 537, 556–561; D. Gallo, *L'evoluzione dell'effetto diretto e dei suoi rapporti con il primato e l'immediata applicazione del diritto UE negli ordinamenti nazionali*, in G. Palmisano (ed.), *Il diritto internazionale ed europeo nei giudizi interni*, Naples, Editoriale Scientifica, 2020, 131–168, 162–166; D. Gallo, *Rethinking*, 600–603.

[162] P. Craig, *EU Administrative Law*, 3rd ed., Oxford, Oxford University Press, 2018, 600. T. Tridimas, *The General Principles of EU Law*, Oxford, Oxford University Press, 2006, 242, noted that '[A] specific expression of legal certainty is the protection of legitimate expectations.' According to X. Groussot, *General Principles of Community Law*, Groningen, Europa Law Publishing, 2006, 24, 'the clearest application of the principle of legal certainty is represented by the principle of legitimate expectations'.

[163] T. Tridimas, *The General Principles*, 242, who referred to several rulings, such as CJ, 12 November 1981, *Salumi*, joined cases 212-217/80, EU:C:1981:270, para. 10. *See* also *Test Claimants* (n 85), para. 44.

[164] P. Craig, *EU Administrative Law*, 600. *See, inter alia*, CJ, *Stichting ROM-projecten*, C-158/06, EU:C:2007:370, paras 24–26.

[165] T. Tridimas, *The General Principles*, 252.

[166] *See* the opinion of AG Cosmas of 8 June 1995, *Fintan Duff*, C-63/93, EU:C:1995:170, para. 25.

[167] *See* § 7 of this chapter, where the opinion of AG Bobek, *Scialdone* (n 159), paras 178–181, is recalled.

[168] Moreover, *ex nunc* effects ensure that the State, most often grappling with the drastic consequences associated with the retroactive effect of the Court's taxpayer-friendly rulings, is not overly affected by countless payments in favour of such taxpayers. In inverse vertical situations, instead, the *pro futuro* temporal limitation of the judgment serves to protect the individual, rather than the State.

pro futuro:[169] through the principle of primacy, domestic authorities are obliged to modify the national legal order accordingly[170] and, also through the principle of direct effect, are required to disapply, for all *new* cases, the conflicting domestic rule. In this respect, there lies an exception to what is affirmed in section 3 of this chapter about one of the two cumulative core elements of direct effect, that is, the inexistence of only disadvantages for individuals, who are parties to the dispute, stemming from the application of EU law (and the related disapplication of national law) as an additional core premise to unconditionality. Put differently, direct effect's effects, instead of immediate, are postponed. At the same time, however, such exception should be interpreted strictly and can work on the sole condition that individual legitimate expectations are safeguarded. An exception that does not come into play in cases such as *N Luxembourg, X Denmark, C Danmark, Z Denmark*, whereby, as already demonstrated in section 3.2 of Chapter III, the principle of legitimate expectations has not been infringed since at the roots of the disadvantage for the individual—stemming from the non-application of exemptions in Directive 2003/49—was their abusive and fraudulent behaviour.

As for regulations and those decisions that are not only addressed to States, the enforcement of unconditional provisions enshrined therein[171] should not be subject to the same limitations on inverse vertical direct effect which are valid for the other EU provisions, as they are directly applicable acts of general application published in the *Official Journal* of the EU. Indeed, once enacted, both regulations and decisions immediately replace the conflicting domestic provisions, and thus provide natural and legal persons with clear guidance on the rules to comply with: the principles of legal certainty and legitimate expectations, thus, are respected. A clear example is Regulation 1/2003 on the application of Articles 101 and 102 TFEU, which is legitimately enforced by public authorities, first and foremost by domestic competition authorities, against private parties.[172]

In conclusion, when EU directives are not at stake, in inverse vertical relationships, unlike what happens in vertical and horizontal relationships, direct effect can come into play also where there is no advantage for the individual deriving from disapplication of national law. However, the duty to disapply could not materialize if the principles of legal certainty and legitimate expectations are infringed. It could, instead, occur if the principle of legitimate expectations is respected through the publication of the EU act, like for regulations and decisions not addressed only at States, or by virtue of prospective/*pro futuro* interpretation of EU primary law provisions and principles by the CJ.

[169] *See* also § 7 for the strand of case law which begun with *Winner Wetten* and CJ, *Inter-Environnement Wallonie ASBL* (*Inter-Environnement Wallonie I*), 129/96, EU:C:1997:628. On the differences between *ex tunc*, *ex nunc*, and *pro futuro* effects beyond EU law, *see* S. Verstraelen, *The Temporal Limitation of Judicial Decisions: The Need for Flexibility Versus the Quest for Uniformity* (2013) 14 *German Law Journal* 1687. For a comparative study of the temporal effects of judicial decisions, *see* also E. Steiner (ed.), *Comparing the Prospective Effect of Judicial Rulings Across Jurisdictions*, Heidelberg, Springer, 2015.

[170] *Pro futuro* effects have been advocated also by AG Jacobs in his opinion of 17 March 2005, *Banca Popolare di Cremona*, C-475/03, EU:C:2005:183, paras 84–87.

[171] On decisions, *see* § 3.1 of Chapter III and § 7 of Chapter VI.

[172] Council Regulation (EC) No. 1/2003 of 16 December 2002 on the implementation of the rules on competition laid down in Articles 81 and 82 of the Treaty (OJ L 1, 4.1.2003, 1).

9. Justifying *Taricco* and prospective inverse vertical direct effect of EU criminal law

The iconic *Taricco* saga—mentioned already in sections 6 and 7 of this chapter—is mainly constituted by *Taricco I* and *Taricco II*, as well as by the response offered by the Italian Constitutional Court to the CJ in two decisions, respectively, of 2017[173] and 2018,[174] aimed at challenging the so-called '*Taricco* rule', as designed in *Taricco I* and refined in *Taricco II*. More particularly, the saga[175] began with the criminal proceedings brought before Italian courts against Mr. Taricco and six other individuals for forming and organizing a conspiracy to commit various offences in relation to VAT from 2005 to 2009. At stake was a conflict between, on the one hand, the Italian legal order and, on the other, the obligation to counter VAT fraud, foreseen in both EU primary and secondary law, VAT being the first tax which was broadly harmonized at the EU level and a key source of revenue constituting its own resource within the EU general budget.[176] The conflict arose due to the difficulties for Italian authorities to effectively prosecute tax evaders, that is, subjects who purchased goods VAT-free by virtue of shell companies and false documents. As a matter of fact, for the identification and prosecution of such crimes, long and complex cross-border investigations had to be carried out, with the result that the proceedings had already taken up a considerable amount of time at the preliminary investigation stage. Thus, it was extremely difficult,[177] in practice, to undertake and conclude such investigations within the maximum limitation period for criminal offences set forth in Articles 160 and 161 of the Italian Criminal Code, read in conjunction with Articles 157 and 158. Overall, the duration of the entire proceeding was such that in Italy *de facto* impunity was the rule, rather than the exception. Consequently, it was often impossible for the Italian tax authorities to recover the amount of the taxes evaded through the offences at hand in the *Taricco* saga. While the subsequent chapters of the saga featured different cases, in Italy and before the CJ, involving other private parties, the entire saga has been generally labelled in the literature with the name *Taricco*, to emphasize the continuity of the underlying legal issues.

As anticipated in section 7, the *Taricco* saga and the case law that followed provide the perfect occasion to reflect on the extent and limits of the duty to disapply in the context of inverse vertical direct effect. In fact, the CJ's approach taken in *Taricco I* and partially also in *Taricco II* has been generally[178] subject to tough criticism by Italian constitutional law

[173] ICC, Decision No. 24 of 26 January 2017.

[174] ICC, Decision No. 115 of 31 May 2018.

[175] *See*, in the greater literature, amongst edited volumes in Italian, A. Bernardi, C. Cupelli (eds.), *Il caso* Taricco *e il dialogo tra le corti*, Naples, Jovene, 2017; C. Amalfitano (ed.), *Primato del diritto dell'Unione europea e controlimiti alla prova della 'saga* Taricco', Milan, Giuffrè, 2018. For journal articles in English on the whole saga, *see*, *inter alia*, F. Viganò, *Supremacy of EU Law vs. (Constitutional) National Identity: A New Challenge for the Court of Justice from the Italian Constitutional Court* (2017) 7 *European Criminal Law Review* 103; M. Bonelli, *The* Taricco *saga and the Consolidation of Judicial Dialogue in the European Union* (2018) 25 *Maastricht Journal of European and Comparative Law* 357; V. Manes, *Some Lessons from the* Taricco *Saga* (2018) 9 *New Journal of European Criminal Law* 12; V. Mitsilegas, *Judicial Dialogue in Three Silences. Unpacking* Taricco (2018) 9 *New Journal of European Criminal Law* 38; G. Piccirilli, *The 'Taricco Saga': The Italian Constitutional Court Continues its European journey* (2018) 14 *European Constitutional Law Review* 814; C. Rauchegger, *National Constitutional Rights and the Primacy of EU law:* M.A.S. (2018) 55 *Common Market Law Review* 1521; G. Scaccia, *The Lesson Learned from the Taricco Saga: Judicial Nationalism and the Constitutional Review of E.U. Law* (2020) 35 *American University International Law Review* 821.

[176] *See* Article 2(1) (b) of Council Decision 2007/436/EC, Euratom of 7 June 2007 on the system of the European Communities' own resources (OJ L 163, 23.6.2007, 17).

[177] In the *Taricco* saga at stake was Law No. 251 of 5 December 2005, subsequently replaced, initially, by Law No. 148 of 14 September 2011 and subsequently by Law No. 103 of 23 June 2017.

[178] On the positive side-effects drawing from the *Taricco I* ruling, in terms of tax enforcement, *see* E. Lupo, *La* primauté *del diritto dell'UE e l'ordinamento penale nazionale. Riflessioni sulla sentenza* Taricco (2016) 2 *Diritto*

and criminal law scholars for not having considered the implications for the domestic legal order stemming from the duty to disapply asserted in *Taricco I*.[179] As for EU law scholars, the *Taricco* saga, while seen in positive terms for being the trigger towards a structural transformation of the Italian legal system on VAT-related crimes,[180] has not been generally welcomed either, having been especially criticized for the reasoning developed therein on the (alleged) direct effect of Article 325 TFEU.[181] In this framework, the saga deserves attention for three main reasons. First, the CJ, initially, in *Taricco I*, recognized the direct effect of Article 325 TFEU,[182] without caring about the *in malam partem* consequences for the individual caused by the disapplication of domestic law, which were instead highlighted by the Italian government, who participated in the proceedings before the Court, and before then by the tax administration, the public prosecutor, and the referring judge, that is, the Tribunal of Cuneo (Italy). Second, the CJ, in the later *Taricco II* judgment, made aware through Article 267 TFEU, by the Italian Constitutional Court, of the negative implications of the CJ's first judgment regarding the respect of the principle of legality in criminal matters, changed its attitude and introduced a derogation from the duty of disapplication, based on fundamental rights and, albeit only implicitly, on the national and constitutional identity of the Italian legal system. Third, the combination of *Taricco I* and *Taricco II* is at the origin of a consolidated strand of rulings giving rise to a true legacy, which raises perplexity from the point of view of respect for the principles of legal certainty and legitimate expectations. More particularly, in *Taricco II*, the CJ devised a derogation from the obligation to disapply, tailored to the peculiarities of the Italian legal system. In this respect, the Court's approach is not satisfactory. Nor is it satisfactory where the Court has ordered disapplication in *post-Taricco II* cases, as will be clarified further in this section. An alternative to the stance taken by the Court was and is possible and rests on the solution—illustrated in the previous section—centred on the temporal *pro futuro* limitation of the preliminary ruling with which the CJ had the opportunity to clarify for the first time the scope of some EU rules, innovating their meaning compared to what had been done until then.

In *Taricco I* the CJ, in imposing a duty to disapply upon domestic authorities, handed down a blunt decision, which was guided by the ultimate purpose of preserving the financial

penale contemporaneo 217; F. Viganò, *Il caso* Taricco *davanti alla Corte costituzionale: qualche riflessione sul merito delle questioni e sulla reale posta in gioco* (2016) *Diritto penale contemporaneo* 9 May 2016, 1.

[179] *See* R. Bin, Taricco, *una sentenza sbagliata: come venirne fuori?* (2016) *Diritto penale contemporaneo* 4 July 2016; M. Luciani, *Il brusco risveglio. I controlimiti e la fine mancata della storia costituzionale* (2016) 1 *Rivista AIC* 13; M. Caianiello, *Processo penale e prescrizione nel quadro della giurisprudenza europea. Dialogo tra sistemi o conflitto identitario?* (2017) *Diritto penale contemporaneo*, 24 February 2017.

[180] *See* R. Mastroianni, *Supremazia del diritto dell'Unione e 'controlimiti' costituzionali* (2016) *Diritto penale contemporaneo* 7 November 2016.

[181] *See* C. Amalfitano, *Il ruolo dell'art. 325 TFUE nella sentenza Taricco e le sue ricadute sul rispetto del principio di legalità penale*, in *forumcostituzionale.it*, 5 October 2016, 9; C. Amalfitano, *La vicenda* Taricco *e il dialogo (?) tra giudici nazionali e Corte di giustizia* (2018) 1 *Il Diritto dell'Unione europea* 153. *See* also the reflections already made in the following works: D. Gallo, *Controlimiti, identità nazionale e i rapporti di forza tra primato ed effetto diretto nella saga* Taricco (2017) 2 *Il Diritto dell'Unione europea* 249, 257–262; D. Gallo, *La Corte costituzionale chiude la 'saga Taricco': tra riserva di legge, opposizione de facto del controlimite e implicita negazione dell'effetto diretto* (2017) 2 *European Papers* 885, 892–893; D. Gallo, *Challenging EU Constitutional Law: The Italian Constitutional Court's New Stance on Direct Effect and the Preliminary Reference Procedure* (2019) 25 *European Law Journal* 434, 454–455; D. Gallo, *The* Taricco *Saga: When Direct Effect and the Duty to Disapply Meet the Principle of Legality in Criminal Matters*, in P. Craig, R. Schütze (eds.), *Landmark Cases in EU Law*, Oxford, Hart, 2025, forthcoming.

[182] Article 325 TFEU's two paragraphs state that 'The Union and the Member States shall counter fraud and any other illegal activities affecting the financial interests of the Union through measures to be taken in accordance with this Article . . .' (para. 1) and 'Member States shall take the same measures to counter fraud affecting the financial interests of the Union as they take to counter fraud affecting their own financial interests' (para. 2).

interests of the EU. Indeed, since the EU's own resources include revenue from application of a uniform rate to the harmonised VAT assessment bases determined according to EU rules,[183] the CJ observed, at the outset, in the light of *Åkerberg Fransson*,[184] that Member States are under a general obligation to both take all measures appropriate for ensuring collection of the VAT due on their territory and to fight against tax evasion,[185] including through effective and dissuasive criminal penalties involving the deprivation of liberty.[186] This holds true especially for cases of serious fraud like those in question in the *Taricco* saga.[187] The CJ, thus, noted that, since the application of the Italian Criminal Code seems to entail that, 'in a considerable number of cases, the commission of serious fraud will escape criminal punishment'—as can be inferred from the referring court's reasoning—, the measures laid down by national law should not be regarded as effective and dissuasive.[188] As a consequence, the national courts should 'ensure that EU law is given full effect, if need be by disapplying' domestic provisions, 'without having to request or await the prior repeal of those articles by way of legislation or any other constitutional procedure'.[189] Therefore, the CJ found that the provisions of Article 325(1) and (2) TFEU, as a result stemming from the principle of primacy, were apt to render 'automatically inapplicable, merely by their entering into force, any conflicting provision of national law'.[190] Consequently, the national court 'must give full effect to Article 325(1) and (2) TFEU, if need be by disapplying the provisions of national law the effect of which would be to prevent the Member State concerned from fulfilling its obligations under Article 325(1) and (2) TFEU'.[191]

If Article 325 TFEU's direct effect were not affirmed, all problems relating to the impact on national constitutional principles resulting from disapplication, which arose in Italy and triggered the response(s) by the ICC, could have been circumvented. Indeed, direct effect should not have had a role in the *Taricco* saga because Article 325 TFEU is not a clear, precise, and unconditional provision nor is the '*Taricco* rule' elaborated by the CJ sufficiently determined. The Court, in *Taricco I* and *Taricco II*, says the opposite but does so without any explanation. And this approach has been upheld in the following jurisprudence, where a legacy stemming from the *Taricco* saga emerged. In this vein, the CJ has been an activist, in substance, but minimalistic in its legal reasoning. Such argumentative minimalism is evident where the test on clarity, precision, and unconditionality is simply evoked but not, in practice, carried out. As a matter of fact, the Court, in para. 38 of *Taricco I*, merely noted that Article 325 TFEU imposes on Member States 'a precise obligation as to the result to be achieved that is not subject to any condition regarding application of the rule'. Furthermore, the '*Taricco* rule' conceived in *Taricco I* and superficially refined in *Taricco II* by the Court is too vague to successfully fill the lacunae implied in the indeterminacy of EU primary law and render Article 325 TFEU a self-standing/self-executing norm which could be directly and immediately applied by national authorities (whether the administration or the judiciary). The minimalism, therefore, lies in the lack of an assessment on the alleged direct effect of Article 325 TFEU and of any further detail regarding the content, scope, and extent of the '*Taricco* rule'. More particularly, the Court did not provide explanations as to the

183 CJ, *Criminal proceedings against Ivo Taricco and Others* (*Taricco I*), C-105/14, EU:C:2015:555, para. 38.
184 CJ, *Åklagaren v Hans Åkerberg Fransson*, C-617/10, EU:C:2013:105, para. 26.
185 *Åkerberg Fransson* (n 184), para. 36.
186 *Åkerberg Fransson* (n 184), paras 39 and 40.
187 *Åkerberg Fransson* (n 184), paras 41 and 42.
188 *Åkerberg Fransson* (n 184), para. 47.
189 *Åkerberg Fransson* (n 184), para. 49.
190 *Åkerberg Fransson* (n 184), para. 52.
191 *Åkerberg Fransson* (n 184), para. 58.

meaning of either 'a significant number of cases' or 'serious fraud', as the two core elements of such judiciary-based rule of reason.[192] The *Taricco* saga, therefore, shows the outdatedness of the test on direct effect as well as the lack of its *effet utile*. It confirms that the classic test for assessing whether an EU norm is directly effective is not a pillar in the conceptualization and practice of direct effect.[193]

From the reading of the Italian Constitutional Courts's two *Taricco* decisions it can be easily inferred that the most controversial issues concern the dangerous relations between the principle of direct effect and legal certainty. Paragraphs 10–14 of the Italian Constitutional Court's Decision No. 115/2018, rendered in the aftermath of *Taricco II*, are noteworthy whereby it was stated that 'recognizing that the crimes are time-barred on the sole basis of the *M.A.S. and M.B.* [*Taricco II*] judgment would, in any case, mean applying the "*Taricco* rule", even if only to specify its temporal limits'.[194] And that would be inadmissible because, as pointed out by the constitutional judges, 'regardless of whether the facts occurred before or after 8 September 2015, the referring ordinary courts cannot apply the "*Taricco* rule" to them' since it is contrary to the principle of legal certainty.[195] In this way, through a peculiar interpretation of the *Taricco II* judgment, the Constitutional Court was able to rely on the requirement of certainty in order to rule, once and for all and with *erga omnes* effects, that neither the '*Taricco* rule' nor Article 325 justify, under any circumstances, the disapplication of national law. Firstly, because in situations covered by such provision, criminal courts have no reliable interpretation criteria available from which to derive a clearly defined rule that, as such, may be applied to individual cases. Secondly, because Article 325 TFEU 'does not allow persons to foresee whether or not the "*Taricco* rule" will apply'.[196] According to the Constitutional Court, the *Taricco* rule is worded in terms too general to be regarded as a sufficiently defined EU provision. This will hold true even if the CJ should further specify the contents of that rule in its future case law, for instance in relation to the notion of 'a significant number of cases' or to that of 'serious fraud'.[197] The conceptual core of the Constitutional Court's approach lies in the consideration that criminal policy measures, such as the extension of limitation periods, are matters for the legislature alone, and not for the courts, whether national or European. It does not matter that the CJ is the only body that can provide, pursuant to Article 267 TFEU, an authentic, final interpretation of the EU treaties that is binding on all national authorities of the Member States. Nothing could 'make up for a potential original lack of precision in the criminal precept'.[198]

The Constitutional Court's line of reasoning evokes the 'elephant in the room'—which already surfaced in Decision No. 24/2017[199]—of the *Taricco* saga: the principle of the separation of powers, together with the related 'primary legislation requirement' (*riserva di legge*). In Decision No. 115/2018, this requirement is functionally linked with the doctrine of direct effect. According to the Constitutional Court, neither Article 325 TFEU nor the *Taricco* rule are sufficiently determined: the former because of its wording, while the latter because it originates in the case law and, for this reason, in the eyes of the Court, by filling

[192] On minimalism and activism in the *Taricco* saga, *see* D. Gallo, *Challenging* (n 181), 455–456; D. Gallo, *Efficacia diretta del diritto UE, procedimento pregiudiziale e Corte Costituzionale: una lettura congiunta delle sentenze n. 269/2017 e 115/2018* (2019) 1 *Rivista AIC* 219, 244–245; D. Gallo, *The* Taricco *Saga*.

[193] *See* § 4 of Chapter III.

[194] Italian Constitutional Court, Decision No. 115/2018, para. 10.

[195] Decision No. 115/2018 (n 194), para. 10.

[196] Decision No. 115/2018 (n 194), para. 11.

[197] *Taricco I* (n 183), para. 58.

[198] Decision No. 115/2018 (n 194), para. 11.

[199] Italian Constitutional Court, Decision No. 24/2017, para. 5.

a Treaty provision with content through interpretation, it is in itself incapable of producing direct effect.[200] No jurisprudential rule can replace 'the *praevia lex scripta*, which is intended to ensure that people have the legal certainty of free and consenting choices of action'.[201]

The connection between legal certainty, *riserva di legge*, and direct effect becomes clear when the Constitutional Court, after reiterating that 'it is the exclusive competence of the Court of Justice to provide a uniform interpretation of EU law and to specify whether or not it has direct effect', and thus formally anchoring its reasoning in EU case law, affirms, right afterwards, that 'an interpretive outcome that does not comply with the principle of legal certainty in criminal matters has no place in our legal system'.[202] Italian law is impenetrable to Article 325 TFEU and to the *Taricco* rule precisely because their application would not be apt, due to their vagueness, to confer justiciable interests or rights.

In finding that the *Taricco* rule does not comply with the principle of legal certainty, the Constitutional Court *de facto* denies that it is sufficiently clear, precise, and, most importantly, unconditional, that is, directly effective. Rather than identifying a new condition for direct effect, the Constitutional Court uses a different reasoning to reach the same conclusion. On closer inspection, the respect of the principle of certainty, which lies at the heart of the Constitutional Court's understanding of the domestic effect of Article 325 TFEU, insofar as it is associated with the principle of *riserva di legge*, seems to act as a counter-limit—implicit, general, and *pro futuro*—to the recognition of the direct effect of a provision of EU law (Article 325 TFEU) and of the jurisprudence interpreting it (the *Taricco* rule), rather than 'simply' to the penetration of an EU law provision into the Italian legal system.[203] In this connection, it is surprising that the Constitutional Court chose to place in its hands the power to define what is directly effective and to exclude the possibility that a rule of the Treaty could become sufficiently enforceable as a result of the interpretation of the CJ. In fact, as has been already observed, the idea that a provision can acquire direct effect thanks to the CJ is a fundamental characteristic of EU law.[204]

On the merits, however, the Constitutional Court's reasoning, with regard to the direct effect of Article 325 TFEU, as clarified above, is correct. Indeed, it seems to be in line with what such doctrine should require: an EU provision lacks direct effect if it is not unconditional. Furthermore, although there is no explicit reference to this issue in the ruling by the Constitutional Court, *Taricco* is very problematic since disapplication stemming from Article 325 TFEU is only *in malam partem*. In short, the obligation to disapply national law, identified by the CJ in *Taricco I*, seems to constitute a deviation from the rationale implied in direct effect. As a matter of fact, direct effect should not have had a role because unconditionality was not fulfilled *and* because a contextualization of the *Taricco* rule, from the

[200] Decision No. 115/2018 (n 194), para. 11.
[201] Decision No. 115/2018 (n 194), para. 12.
[202] Decision No. 115/2018 (n 194), para. 12.
[203] According to the counter-limits doctrine, EU law cannot prevail over conflicting national law where its application results in a violation of any of the supreme principles of the Italian constitutional order. The term '*controlimiti*' was used for the first time by the constitutional law scholar P. Barile, *Ancora su diritto comunitario e diritto interno*, in *Studi per il XX anniversario dell'Assemblea costituente*, Florence, Vallecchi, 1969, 35–54, 45. On such doctrine, *see* M. Cartabia, *Principi inviolabili e integrazione europea*, Milan, Giuffrè, 1995, and P. Faraguna, *Ai confini della Costituzione. Principi supremi e identità costituzionale*, Milan, Franco Angeli, 2015. In English, *see* D. Paris, *Limiting the 'Counter-Limit': National Constitutional Courts and the Scope of the Primacy of EU Law*, in P. Faraguna, C. Fasone, G. Piccirilli (eds.), *Constitutional Adjudication in Europe between Unity and Pluralism*, Special Issue (2018) 10 *Italian Journal of Public Law* 206; P. Faraguna, *Unamendability and Constitutional Identity in the Italian Constitutional Experience* (2019) 21 *European Journal of Law Reform* 329. In the ICC's case law, see ICC, Decision No. 183 of 18 December 1973, para. 9 (the so-called '*Frontini* case'). On the doctrine as an avenue to derogate from the duty to disapply, *see* § 11 of this chapter.
[204] *See* Chapter II, § 1 and Chapter III, § 1.

standpoint of the individuals' prerogatives, clearly illustrates that the principles of legal certainty and legitimate expectations have been fully challenged as a result of an *in malam partem* disapplication of national law. Such disapplication shall be rejected particularly when criminal law is at stake.

Taricco I was significantly tempered in *Taricco II*. The CJ did so in open contrast with AG Bot's opinion, which even expanded the material scope of *Taricco I* and was fully indifferent toward the needs underlined by the referring national court.[205] The question to be asked is thus whether such relaxation was sufficient to take due account of the effects of the *in malam partem* disapplication of national law. *Taricco II* was not an overruling, yet it is clear that the CJ, in the judgment, chose to sooth its tones and did so by endorsing the core of the Italian Constitutional Court's reasoning, whereby it was highlighted that rules on temporary limitations shall be considered, in the Italian legal order, part of the principle of legality in criminal matters, hence subject to the obligations of foreseeability and non-retroactivity. In this vein, the CJ clarified, first, that disapplication, in the case at hand and within the Italian legal order, seemed to produce a breach of such principle—and of the fundamental rights of the accused persons—, and for that reason concluded that it was up to the national judges to ultimately define its scope and boundaries.

Indeed, the Court added that the protection of the financial interests of the Union by the enactment of criminal penalties 'falls within the shared competence of the Union and the Member States within the meaning of Article 4(2) TFEU'[206] and that, at the material time for the main proceedings, 'the limitation rules applicable to criminal proceedings relating to VAT had not been harmonised by the EU legislature, and harmonisation has since taken place only to a partial extent by the adoption of Directive (EU) 2017/1371 of the European Parliament and of the Council of 5 July 2017 on the fight against fraud to the Union's financial interests by means of criminal law (OJ 2017 L 198, 29)'.[207] Then the CJ made two important observations. The first is new with respect to the *Taricco I* ruling: Italian authorities are free to provide that in their legal system the criminal rules on temporary limitations 'form part of substantive criminal law' and, thus, are 'subject to the principle that offences and penalties must be defined by law'.[208]

The second is a more clear and direct confirmation of what was incidentally stated in *Taricco I*: Italian authorities, before disapplying the provisions of the criminal code, are 'required to ensure that the fundamental rights of persons accused of committing criminal offences are observed'.[209] They might apply national standards of protection of fundamental rights, unless the level of protection provided for by the Charter is compromised.[210] This led the CJ to assert that Italian law and EU law must not necessarily be seen as conflicting since not only the former, but also the latter, give great relevance 'to the principle that offences and penalties must be defined by law, as to its requirements concerning the foreseeability, precision and non-retroactivity of the criminal law applicable',[211] as enshrined in Article 49 of the Charter.[212] Indeed, both domestic and EU law require that, where the imposition of criminal

[205] Opinion of AG Bot of 18 July 2017, *Criminal proceedings against M.A.S. and M.B.* (*Taricco II*), C-42/17, EU:C:2017:564, paras 118–187.

[206] CJ, C-42/17, *Criminal proceedings against M.A.S. and M.B.* (*Taricco II*), EU:C:2017:936, para. 43.

[207] *Taricco II* (n 206), para. 44.

[208] *Taricco II* (n 206), para. 45.

[209] *Taricco II* (n 206), para. 46.

[210] *Åkerberg Fransson* (n 184), para. 29 and *Taricco II* (n 206), para. 47.

[211] *Taricco II* (n 206), para. 51.

[212] *Taricco II* (n 206), para. 53; for references to the European Court of Human Rights' case law, *see Taricco II* (206), paras 54 and 55.

penalties is concerned, 'the rights of defendants flowing from the principle that offences and penalties must be defined by law are guaranteed'.[213] In that respect, the Court pointed out that, according to the referring court, in the case of disapplication, those rights would be infringed for two main reasons: first of all, the persons concerned 'could not reasonably foresee before the delivery of the *Taricco* judgment that that Article 325 TFEU requires the national court to disapply those provisions in the circumstances set out in that judgment'.[214] Secondly, the national court would not be able 'to define the particular circumstances in which it would have to disapply those provisions, namely where they prevent the imposition of effective and deterrent penalties in a significant number of cases of serious fraud, without exceeding the limits imposed on its discretion by the principle that offences and penalties must be defined by law'.[215] The fact that the requirements of foreseeability, precision, and non-retroactivity inherent in the principle of legality apply also, in the Italian legal system, to the limitation rules for criminal offences relating to VAT implies that it is for the national judge to ascertain whether the '*Taricco* rule' is liable to be in breach of EU law. Should this be the case, the domestic court would not be obliged to set aside the provisions of the Criminal Code at stake in the *Taricco* saga.[216] Therefore, according to the CJ, disapplication was not necessarily a duty stemming from EU law. It was then first and foremost for the Italian Constitutional Court to make the assessment on the practicability of such duty to disapply and on its possible side effects for the protection of the fundamental rights of individuals.

Against this background, it shall be noted that rulings on the very same subject at stake in the *Taricco* saga relating to the qualification of the rules on temporary limitations in domestic legal orders and the principle of legality in criminal matters, with respect to Article 325 TFEU, were not handed down by the CJ in the years between 2017 and 2024. However, from an analysis of the Court's recent case law it can be inferred that a '*Taricco* legacy' is surreptitiously gaining ground thanks to a number of judgments and Advocates General's opinions regarding EU criminal law and several facets of Article 325 TFEU.[217] Nevertheless, unlike the Advocates General's opinions, such judgments are quite cryptic, being inspired by a great argumentative self-restraint.[218] As a matter of fact, the CJ tends to abstain from directly tackling questions and doubts raised by the Advocates General, first and foremost with regard to the contours of the exact conditions triggering the '*Taricco* rule'. Overall, on the

[213] *Taricco II* (n 206), para. 48.
[214] *Taricco II* (n 206), para. 49.
[215] *Taricco II* (n 206), para. 50.
[216] *Taricco II* (n 206), para. 59.
[217] On this matter, *see* extensively D. Gallo, *The* Taricco *Saga*. The only judgment on EU criminal law not concerning Article 325 TFEU in which the *Taricco* reasoning was developed is CJ, *Consiliul Concurenţei v Whiteland Import Export SRL*, C-308/19, EU:C:2021:47, paras 37–65, on Article 101 TFEU and Council Regulation (EC) No. 1/2003 of 16 December 2002 on the implementation of the rules on competition laid down in Articles [101 and 102 TFEU] (OJ L 1, 4.1.2003, 1). For the case law on Article 325 TFEU, read jointly with Council Directive 2006/112/EC of 28 November 2006 on the common system of value added tax (OJ L 347, 11.12.2006, 1; 'the VAT Directive') and the Convention drawn up on the basis of Article K.3 of the Treaty on European Union, on the protection of the European Communities' financial interests, signed in Brussels on 26 July 1995 (OJ C 316, 27.11.1995, 49; 'the PFI Convention'), *see* opinion of AG Bobek, *Scialdone* (n 159), paras 25 and 29; *Kolev* (n 160), paras 50–72; CJ, *Dzivev*, C-310/16, EU:C:2019:30, paras 26–41; *Consiliul Concurenţei v Whiteland Import Export SRL* (n 217), paras 37–65; *Euro Box Promotion* (n 3), paras 65, 182, 203, 254; *NE* (n 2), paras 26–40; CJ, *Lin*, C-107/23 PPU, EU:C:2023:606, paras 95–137. *See* also opinion of AG Bobek of 25 July 2018, *Criminal proceedings against Petar Dzivev and Others*, C-310/16, EU:C:2018:623, paras 62–80 and 92–112; opinion of AG Bobek of 4 March 2021, *PM*, joined cases C-357/19, C-379/19, C-547/19, C-811/19, and C-840/19, EU:C:2021:170, paras 169–196; opinion of AG Pitruzzella of 3 September 2020, *Consiliul Concurenţei v Whiteland Import Export SRL*, C-308/19, EU:C:2020:639, paras 27–98; opinion of AG Campos Sánchez-Bordona of 29 June 2023, *C.I*, C-107/23 PPU, EU:C:2023:532, paras 84–160.
[218] As remarked several times in this work about the CJ's case law on direct effect.

one hand, the stance taken by the CJ in *Taricco I*, further refined and softened in *Taricco II*, still raises problems, especially with respect to the unconditionality of the '*Taricco* rule' and its prompt enforcement by national courts in the field of criminal law. On the other hand, two (relatively) firm points can be made: *(i)* the principle of legality in criminal matters may comprise (substantive, rather than merely procedural) rules on temporary limitations, if this is embraced in national legal orders, even when EU provisions other than Article 325 TFEU are at stake,[219] since Member States can foresee more advanced regimes on the protection of fundamental rights than the one implied in Article 49 of the Charter, in accordance with its Article 53;[220] *(ii)* outside the realm of prescription, the principle of primacy must be interpreted as requiring a national court to interpret domestic provisions consistently with Article 325 TFEU[221] or, in conjunction with the doctrine of direct effect, to set aside those provisions,[222] provided that such an interpretation or disapplication does not entail a breach of the principle of legality of criminal offences and penalties and an infringement of fundamental rights.

Recently, in *Lin* the CJ confirmed that in the balance between the protection of the Union's financial interests and that of fundamental rights, the latter shall be given precedence over the former. More specifically,

> while the Member States are free to choose the applicable penalties, which may take the form of administrative penalties, criminal penalties or a combination of the two, they must nonetheless ensure, pursuant to Article 325(1) TFEU, that cases of serious fraud or other serious illegal activities affecting the financial interests of the European Union are punishable by criminal penalties that are effective and that act as a deterrent,[223]

including with respect to limitation periods. However, in addressing the principle of legality, as 'an essential element of the rule of law identified in Article 2 TEU both as a founding value of the Union and as a value common to the Member States',[224] the CJ concluded that, notwithstanding the existence of a systemic risk of impunity arising from national legislation, Article 325(1) TFEU does not require the setting aside of national judgments which invalidate a national provision setting out limitation periods where said judgments protect the principle of legality in criminal matters.[225]

A connected matter, therefore, nowadays is—and will be in the future—how the fair balancing of interests between primacy/direct effect/disapplication, on the one hand, and, on the other, core domestic/EU constitutional principles shall be effectively enforced by national jurisdictions so that a derogation from the duty of consistent interpretation as well as from the duty to disapply arising from Article 325 TFEU and/or other primary/secondary law provisions could be deemed admissible in the light of EU law.[226]

As explained in section 8, rather than creating a derogation from the duty to disapply due to the peculiarities of the domestic legal systems at stake, including the Italian one on

[219] As explained in the opinion of AG Pitruzzella, *Consiliul Concurenței v Whiteland Import Export SRL* (n 217), para. 88, the line of reasoning of *Taricco I* and *II* could also be considered applicable to penalties in competition cases.

[220] *Consiliul Concurenței v Whiteland Import Export SRL* (n 217), para. 37.

[221] *Ministerul Lucrărilor Publice, Dezvoltării și Administrației* (n 160), paras 36–40.

[222] *Kolev* (n 160), para. 76.

[223] *See Lin* (n 217), para. 62.

[224] *See Lin* (n 217), para. 114.

[225] *See Lin* (n 217), para. 1 of the operative part.

[226] *See* also D. Gallo, *The* Taricco *Saga*.

temporary limitations, the CJ could have opted for a different avenue in order to recognize direct effect, while safeguarding the principle of legitimate expectations. Indeed, in *Taricco II* and in most of the following judgments on Article 325 TFEU and criminal law, the Court should have derogated from the rule on retroactive effects of its preliminary rulings since, generally speaking, the Court's interpretation of Article 325 TFEU was new and not foreseeable by individuals.[227] In practice, thus, a derogation from the duty to disapply grounded in the protection of fundamental rights and also in the principles of legal certainty and legitimate expectations serves to address the negative side effects stemming from a possible *in malam partem* application of EU law/disapplication of national law.[228] This means that the remedy described above in section 8 aimed at making new interpretations of the law applicable prospectively for future disputes—with the connected obligation imposed upon Member States to change their laws—shall apply also in the *Taricco* saga.

Lastly, in addition to the derogatory reasoning implied in the case law giving rise to the *Taricco* legacy, a brief remark can be made regarding the possible establishment of a second derogation from the duty of immediate disapplication in the field of criminal law, when at stake is an *in bonam partem*—rather than *in malam partem*, like in *Taricco*—disapplication of national law. It relates to the principle of proportionality of penalties as a general principle of EU law whose content has been already examined in section 5 of Chapter III. While such derogation has never been admitted by the CJ, it has already been recalled in this work that in the *T.A.C.* case AG Emiliou, with respect to a national law providing for disproportionate penalties for infringements of domestic norms 'that implement EU law',[229] affirmed that the approach adopted by the CJ in *Taricco II* could find room for application since national authorities and courts should in principle remain free to apply different (higher) standards for the protection of fundamental rights and this might potentially include stricter visions of the principle of legality of sanctions.[230] More specifically, in the opinion of Emiliou, 'where the national legal system offers lower courts the possibility to seek immediate guidance from higher courts, for example via specific mechanisms of referral', EU law does not preclude 'such mechanisms, if the national court considers it useful'.[231] In other words, disapplication shall not be necessarily and immediately carried out, but a referral to that Member State's Supreme/Constitutional Court could be submitted. It remains to be seen whether this stance, which was not endorsed by the CJ in *T.A.C.*, will play a role in its future case law.

10. An unjustifiable deviation from direct effect: challenging *Lucchini* and its legacy

To understand the limits of a conception of direct effect which disregards the consequences of disapplication for individuals in inverse vertical relationships, the *Lucchini* case, as well as the strand of case law that followed, are particularly useful. Indeed, *Lucchini* lies at the origins of those few judgments in which the CJ has questioned Member States' procedural

[227] *See* also § 8 of this chapter.
[228] An excellent analysis of the tense relationships between direct effect, *in malam partem disapplication*, and criminal law is performed, recently, by A. Bernardi, *Il rinvio pregiudiziale in ambito penale e i problemi posti dalle sentenze interpretative della Corte di giustizia*, in J. Alberti, G. De Cristofaro (eds.), *Il rinvio pregiudiziale come strumento di sviluppo degli ordinamenti*, Pisa, Pacini, 2023, 309–365.
[229] Opinion of AG Emiliou (n 72), para. 4.
[230] *T.A.C.* (n 229), para. 74.
[231] *T.A.C.* (n 229), para. 77.

autonomy by eroding the principle of *res judicata*.[232] In this respect, the tangibility of the so-called *exceptio rei iudicatae* has links with the matter of direct effect since the disapplication triggered by EU law challenges the national legislations on *res judicata*.[233]

Prior to the landmark *Lucchini* judgment, the CJ affirmed in several rulings the key status of the principle of *res judicata* in EU procedural law, as well as in Member States' judicial systems.[234] It did so in the light of the principles of equivalence and effectiveness, as occurred in *Köbler*[235] and *Kapferer*[236] in the field of civil law, and, albeit indirectly,[237] in *Kühne*,[238] with respect to administrative law.[239] In *Köbler*,[240] the preliminary question by the *Landesgericht für Zivilrechtssachen* of Vienna (Regional Civil Court, Vienna), concerning the potential

[232] CJ, *Ministero dell'Industria, del Commercio e dell'Artigianato v Lucchini SpA*, C-119/05, EU:C:2007:434, on which *see*, *inter alia*, J.-H. Huglo, *Primauté du droit communautaire et autorité de la chose jugée par les juridictions nationales* (2007) 53 *Gazette du Palais* 18; A. Biondi, *Ministero dell'Industria, del Commercio e dell'Artigianato v Lucchini SpA* (2008) 45 *Common Market Law Review* 1459; P. Bříza, *Lucchini SpA—Is There Anything Left of Res Judicata Principle?* (2008) 27 *Civil Justice Quarterly* 40; C. Consolo, *La sentenza Lucchini della Corte di Giustizia: quale possibile adattamento degli ordinamenti processuali interni e in specie del nostro?* (2008) 63 *Rivista di diritto processuale* 225; E. Fontana, *Qualche osservazione in margine al caso Lucchini. Un tentativo di spiegazione* (2008) 22 *Diritto del commercio internazionale* 193; P. Nebbia, *Do the Rules on State Aids Have a Life of Their Own? National Procedural Autonomy and Effectiveness in the Lucchini Case* (2008) 33 *European Law Review* 427; G. Peroni, *Il diritto comunitario prevale sul giudicato sostanziale* (2008) 22 *Diritto del commercio internazionale* 221; G. Vitale, *Il recupero degli aiuti di Stato illegittimamente erogati tra autorità del giudicato ed incompatibilità con il mercato comune in una recente sentenza della Corte di Giustizia* (2008) 3 *Il Diritto dell'Unione europea* 595; A. Tizzano, B. Gencarelli, *Union Law and Final Decisions of National Courts in the Recent Case Law of the Court of Justice*, in A. Arnull, C. Barnard, M. Dougan, E. Spaventa (eds.), *A Constitutional Order of States— Essays in Honour of Alan Dashwood*, Oxford, Oxford University Press, 2010, 267–280.

[233] R. Kovar, *L'incidence du droit communautaire sur l'intangibilité des décisions nationales définitives*, in A. De Walsche, A. Lévy (eds.), *Promenades au sein du droit européen. Mélanges en hommage à Georges Vandersanden*, Brussels, Bruylant, 2008, 203–243, 204.

[234] The first references of *res judicata* as part of EEC procedural law appear in CJ, *Raymond Elz*, joined cases 22-23/60, EU:C:1961:17, 188–189 and CJ, *Società Industriale Acciaierie San Michele*, joined cases 2-10/63, EU:C:1963:59, 330 and 339. For the first reference to the principle as a pillar of national constitutional and procedural legal orders, *see* CJ, *Eco Swiss China Time*, C-126/97, EU:C:1999:269, para. 46.

[235] CJ, *Gerhard Köbler v Republik Österreich*, C-224/01, EU:C:2003:513.

[236] CJ, *Kapferer*, C-234/04, EU:C:2006:178, on which, *see* E. Adobati, *La sentenza di un giudice nazionale passata in giudicato non può più essere rimessa in discussione anche se viola il diritto comunitario* (2006) 1 *Diritto comunitario e degli scambi internazionali* 83; M. Ludwigs, *Der Schutz der Rechtskraft im Gemeinschaftsrecht* (2006) 47 *Zeitschrift für Rechtsvergleichung, internationales Privatrecht und Europarecht* 191; S. C. Wasserer, *Rechtskraft contra Gemeinschaftstreue: Überprüfbarkeit einer rechtskräftigen, gemeinschaftsrechtswidrigen Entscheidung eines innerstaatlichen Gerichts* (2006) 6 *European Law Reporter* 198; E. Broussy, F. Donnat, C. Lambert, *Stabilité des situations juridiques et droit Communautaire* (2006) *L'actualité juridique. Droit administrative* 2275.

[237] *See* further in this §.

[238] CJ, *Kühne & Heitz NV*, C-453/00, EU:C:2004:17, on which *see* V. Atripaldi, *Leale cooperazione comunitaria ed obbligo degli Stati al riesame degli atti amministrativi definitivi contrari al diritto comunitario* (2004) 4 *Diritto pubblico comparato ed europeo* 883; R. Caranta, *Case Note on* Kühne (2005) 42 *Common Market Law Review* 179; G. Gattinara, *Il ruolo comunitario delle amministrazioni nazionali alla luce della sentenza* Kühne & Heitz (2004) 4 *Diritto comunitario e degli scambi internazionali* 489; D. De Pretis, *'Illegittimità comunitaria' dell'atto amministrativo definitivo, certezza del diritto e potere di riesame* (2004) 10 *Giornale di diritto amministrativo* 725; D. Simon, *Obligation de réexamen d'une décision administrative définitive. L'autorité d'un arrêt préjudiciel en interprétation postérieur à une décision administrative devenue définitive impose la prise en compte de la demande de retrait de celle-ci*, (2004) *Europe Mars* 14; F. Urlesberger, *Zur Rechtskraft im Gemeinschaftsrecht* (2004) 22 *Zeitschrift für Rechtsvergleichung, internationales Privatrecht und Europarech* 99; Z. Peerbux-Beaugendre, *Une administration ne peut invoquer le principe de la force de chose définitivement jugée pour refuser de réexaminer une décision dont une interprétation préjudicielle ultérieure a révélé la contrariété avec le droit communautaire. Commentaire de l'arrêt de la CJCE du 13 janvier 2004* (2004) 8 *Revue du droit de l'Union européenne* 559.

[239] On the differences between *res judicata* and finality of administrative acts, *see* the Opinion of AG Tizzano of 10 November 2005, *Kapferer*, EU:C:2005:674, paras 22 and 25. On the topic, *see* the contributions in F. Spitaleri, *L'incidenza del diritto comunitario sugli atti definitivi della Pubblica Amministrazione*, in F. Spitaleri (ed.), *L'incidenza del diritto comunitario e della CEDU sugli atti amministrativi nazionali*, Milan, Giuffrè, 2009, 7-34 notably C. Schepisi, *Atti amministrativi in contrasto con il diritto dell'Unione europea e poteri del giudice nazionale*, 17–58.

[240] *See*, *inter alia*, P. Wattel, *Köbler, CILFIT and Welthgrove: We Can't Go On Meeting Like This* (2004) 41 *Common Market Law Review* 177. *See* also CJ, *Traghetti del Mediterraneo SpA*, C-173/03, EU:C:2006:391.

and limits of the *Francovich/Brasserie* case law, came about in the context of an action for liability brought by a natural person against Austria for an infringement of a provision of EU law by the *Verwaltungsgerichtshof* (Supreme Administrative Court). The CJ stated that the full effectiveness of the EU rules would be called into question 'if individuals were precluded from being able, under certain conditions, to obtain reparation when their rights are affected by an infringement of Community law attributable to a decision of a court of a Member State adjudicating at last instance'.[241] According to the Court, since normally a violation of subjective rights resulting from a decision of a judicial body of last instance could no longer be the subject of compensation, having become final, 'individuals cannot be deprived of the possibility of rendering the State liable in order in that way to obtain legal protection of their rights'.[242]

The problem with this approach, as stressed by the governments which intervened in the proceedings before the Court,[243] is that the application of the State liability principle to infringements committed by a court of last instance, with regard to its final judgments, would infringe the principle of legal certainty, seen as a corollary to that of *res judicata*.[244] The Court, from one side, reiterated that 'the importance of the principle of *res judicata* cannot be disputed', in line with its previous case law,[245] in particular with the *Eco Swiss* case,[246] whereby it was asserted that EU law does not require 'a national court to disapply domestic rules of procedure conferring finality on a decision'.[247] On the other side, the Court held that the recognition of the principle of State liability for the decision of a judicial organ of last resort was not capable of eroding such judgment. The CJ noted that the parties in proceedings which gave rise to a decision having acquired the status of *res judicata* were not necessarily the same of those involved in an action for non-contractual liability. Further, the applicant in a State liability action, if successful, obtains an order for reparation of the damage incurred, but not 'necessarily a declaration invalidating the status of *res judicata* of the judicial decision which was responsible for the damage'.[248] And, in any case, the principle of State liability requires monetary compensation, not a revision of the judicial decision.[249] In short, the *causa petendi* is different.[250]

In *Kapferer*, the reference for a preliminary ruling concerned the interpretation of Article 10 TEC, currently Article 4(3) TEU, and Article 15 of Regulation 44/2001 on the jurisdiction and recognition and enforcement of judgments in civil and commercial matters.[251] The reference was issued in the frame of a dispute between an Austrian citizen and a German company regarding an action seeking an order requiring the latter to deliver winnings to the former since the company, with a personally addressed letter, had given the Austrian citizen the impression that she had won a prize. At issue was understanding whether, and if so, under what conditions, the principle of sincere cooperation requires national courts to review and annul a final judicial decision where it is contrary to Community law. Like in

[241] *Köbler* (n 235), para. 33.
[242] *Köbler* (n 235), para. 34.
[243] *Köbler* (n 235), paras 16–29.
[244] *Köbler* (n 235), para. 37.
[245] *Köbler* (n 235), para. 38.
[246] *Eco Swiss China Time* (n 234), para. 46.
[247] *Eco Swiss China Time* (n 234), paras 46–47.
[248] *Köbler* (n 235), para. 39.
[249] *Köbler* (n 235), paras 39–40.
[250] On this point, *see* P. Biavati, *La sentenza* Lucchini: *il giudicato nazionale cede al diritto comunitario*, in *Rassegna tributaria*, 2007, 1591.
[251] Council Regulation (EC) No. 44/2001 of 22 December 2000 on jurisdiction and the recognition and enforcement of judgments in civil and commercial matters (OJ L 012, 16.01.2001, 1).

Köbler, the EU judges underlined that the principle of *res judicata* guarantees both the stability of the law and legal relationships as well as the fair administration of justice.[252] From this the CJ inferred that Community law does not require national courts to disapply internal procedural rules attributing *res judicata* to a judicial decision, 'even if to do so would enable it to remedy an infringement of Community law by the decision at issue'.[253]

The *Kühne* case concerned administrative matters, with reference not to a final judgment but rather to the intangibility of administrative measures which—once confirmed by domestic courts—have become final.[254] Notwithstanding this peculiar feature of the case, *Kühne*, which followed *Köbler* but preceded *Kapferer*, must be given particular significance since the CJ, with respect to the interpretation of Article 10 TEC, currently Article 4(3) TEU, regarding payment of export refunds, explicitly acknowledged, even if only in principle, that national administrative bodies have an obligation to review a final administrative decision provided that four conditions are cumulatively fulfilled: *(i)* under national law, the administrative body has the power to reopen that decision; *(ii)* the administrative decision in question 'has become final as a result of a judgment of a national court ruling at final instance'; *(iii)* the judgment is, 'in the light of a decision given by the [CJ] subsequent to it, based on a misinterpretation of Community law which was adopted without a question being referred to the Court for a preliminary ruling'; and *(iv)* the person concerned 'complained to the administrative body immediately after becoming aware of that decision of the Court'.[255] While the CJ's ruling did not entail the disapplication of the internal rules governing *res judicata*, the conclusion reached by the Court caused the revocation of administrative decisions even if third party rights were adversely affected[256] and despite the formation of *res judicata* on the administrative act.

In short, there is a common thread, in practice, which guides the pre-*Lucchini* case law. Despite the (implicit) mitigations set forth in *Köbler* and especially in *Kühne*, from the reasoning on the scope of *res judicata* performed by the EU judges, inspired by the opinions of the Advocates general,[257] it clearly emerges that the need for legal certainty overrides the effectiveness of EU law. As observed in the literature, since *Kapferer*, the CJ has constantly linked EU and national rules related to *res judicata* and the intertwined principle of legal certainty[258] through a formula that highlights 'the importance, both in the legal order of the European Union and in national legal systems, of the principle of *res judicata*'.[259]

[252] *Kapferer* (n 236), para. 20.
[253] *Kapferer* (n 236), para. 21.
[254] For a confirmation of the reasoning developed in the judgment, *see* CJ, *Willy Kempter KG*, C-2/06, EU:C:2008:78, on which, *see* X. Groussot, T. Minssen, Res Judicata *in the Court of Justice Case-Law: Balancing Lgal Certainty with Legality?* (2007) 3 *European Constitutional Law Review* 385.
[255] *Kühne* (n 238), para. 26.
[256] In these terms E. Scoditti, *Giudicato nazionale e diritto comunitario* (2007) 4 *Il Foro italiano* 533.
[257] *See* the opinion of AG Tizzano, *Kapferer* (n 239), para. 72.
[258] The nexus between *res judicata* and legal certainty has been clear since *Eco Swiss China Time* (n 234), para. 46.
[259] *See* CJ, *Amministrazione dell'Economia e delle Finanze e Agenzia delle entrate v Fallimento Olimpiclub*, C-2/08, EU:C:2009:506, para. 22; CJ, *Asturcom Telecomunicaciones v Cristina Rodríguez Nogueira*, C-40/08, EU:C:2009:615, para. 35; CJ, *European Commission v Luxembourg*, C-526/08, EU:C:2010:379, para. 26; CJ, *ThyssenKrupp Nirosta v European Commission*, C-352/09 P, EU:C:2011:191, para. 123; CJ, *Artegodan v European Commission*, C-221/10 P, EU:C:2012:216, para. 86; CJ, *European Commission v Spain*, C-529/09, EU:C:2013:31, para. 64; CJ, *Impresa Pizzarotti v Comune di Bari and Others*, C-213/13, EU:C:2014:2067, para. 58; CJ, *Dragos¸ Constantin Târs¸ia v Statul român and Serviciul Public Comunitar Regim Permise de Conducere si Inmatriculare a Autovehiculelor*, C-69/14, EU:C:2015:662, para. 28; CJ, *Banco Primus v Jesús Gutiérrez García*, C-421/14, EU:C:2017:60, para. 46; CJ, *Apple and Pear Australia and Star Fruits Diffusion v EUIPO*, C-226/15 P, EU:C:2016:582, para. 51; CJ, *Telecom Italia*, C-34/19, EU:C:2020:148, para. 64; CJ, *CRPNPAC v Vueling Airlines*, joined cases C-370/17 and 37/18, EU:C:2020:260, para. 88; CJ, *FMS and Others v Országos Idegenrendészeti*

Against this backdrop, notwithstanding the frequent use of the above formula in the case law of the CJ, in *Lucchini* the principle of intangibility of *res judicata* was turned upside-down. At issue was whether Articles 107 and 108 TFEU precluded the application of Article 2909 of the Italian Civil Code because such rule prevented the recovery of State aid measures that were declared illegal due to a lack of notification to the Commission. The CJ, in its ruling, overturned the principle of intangibility implied in *res judicata*, observing that Article 2909 hindered the enforcement of EU law 'in so far as it would make it impossible to recover State aid that was granted in breach of Community law'.[260]

The core preliminary question submitted by the Italian Council of State was whether, 'in the light of the principle of the primacy of immediately applicable Community law requiring the recovery of aid . . . it [was] legally possible and compulsory for the national administrative authority to recover aid from a private recipient even though a final civil judgment has been delivered confirming the unconditional obligation to pay the aid in question'.[261] In response, the CJ recalled that, in the EU legal order, 'the jurisdiction of national courts is limited both in the field of State aid and as regards jurisdiction to declare Community acts invalid'.[262] With regard to State aid, it observed that national courts can be subject to disputes in respect of which they have to interpret and apply the concept of aid set forth in Article 107(1) TFEU, particularly with a view to determining whether a national measure, implemented without observing the preliminary examination procedure provided for in Article 108(3) TFEU, 'ought to have been subject to this procedure'.[263] On the contrary, it was observed that national courts do not have jurisdiction to decide upon the compatibility of State aid with the common market,[264] as this assessment falls within the exclusive competence of the Commission, which is subject to review by the EU Courts.[265] Based on these observations, the CJ went on in its reasoning to conclude that the application of Article 2909 of the Civil Code was precluded in so far as this rule prevents the recovery of State aid granted in breach of Community law which has been found to be incompatible with the common market in a decision of the Commission that has become final.[266]

The approach adopted by the CJ seems rooted in two rationales. The first rationale, also at the heart of AG Geelhoed's opinion in the case, is that the decision on the incompatibility and that on the duty to recover the aid are governed by the exclusive powers of the EU,[267] which 'a final judgment of a national civil court . . . cannot affect'[268] and are exercised by the Commission with its decision having, 'to put it bluntly',[269] value as *res judicata*. The Italian jurisdictions, therefore, 'also set aside the Commission's exclusive power, which is governed by Community law, to examine the aid measure in question for its compatibility

Fo"igazgatóság Dél-alföldi Regionális Igazgatóság and Országos Idegenrendészeti Fo"igazgatóság, joined cases C-924-925/19 PPU, EU:C:2020:367, para. 185.

260 *Lucchini* (n 232), para. 59.
261 *Lucchini* (n 232), para. 40.
262 *Lucchini* (n 232), para. 49.
263 *Lucchini* (n 232), para. 50.
264 *Lucchini* (n 232), para. 51.
265 *Lucchini* (n 232), para. 52.
266 *Lucchini* (n 232), paras 59–63.
267 *See* P. Nebbia, 'Do the Rules on State Aids Have a Life of Their Own? National Procedural Autonomy and Effectiveness in the Lucchini Case' (2008) *European Law Review* 427, 430.
268 Opinion of AG Geelhoed of 14 September 2006, *Lucchini*, EU:C:2006:576, para. 87.
269 A. Biondi, *Case Note*, 1465. *See* also B. Cortese, *L'incidenza del diritto comunitario sulle sentenze nazionali definitive: esclusività del sistema giurisdizionale comunitario e nuovi limiti al principio di autonomia procedurale degli Stati membri—Il caso Lucchini*, in F. Spitaleri (ed.), *L'incidenza del diritto comunitario e della CEDU sugli atti nazionali definitivi*, Milan, Giuffrè, 2009, 36–60, 46–47.

with the common market and impinges on the obligations to which Italy is subject under Community law when granting State aid'.[270] The second rationale provides that if it is true that the CJ, as stated above, was inspired by the AG's arguments, it is also true that the cornerstone of the judgment is not only the system of allocation of the competences between the Union and the national authorities, but also the application of the primacy principle, placed in an overarching position in respect to the principle of legal certainty. As for direct effect, there is no reference in *Lucchini* to the nature of the EU primary and secondary law at stake, be it directly effective or not. However, we may infer that the Court implicitly grounded its reasoning, and the duty to disapply resulting from it, in the direct effect of Articles 107 and 108 TFEU, as well as the Commission's decision in *Lucchini*.[271] If not, disapplication—we may assume—, in the Court's view, would end up being the result of primacy only, rather than of primacy and direct effect, which is not admissible.[272]

Against this background and in the light of the reconstruction made in the sections above, should *Lucchini* be hailed favourably? It should not since such a profound relativization of the *res judicata* principle generates an inadmissible *in malam partem* disapplication of EU law and ultimately challenges for good the principles of legal certainty and legitimate expectations.

In regard to State aid, three post-*Lucchini* decisions shall be mentioned: *(i) Commission v Slovak Republic*,[273] regarding the enforcement of Decision 2007/254[274] on a State aid granted by the Slovak Republic to a private company; *(ii) Klausner Holz*,[275] based on a request for a preliminary ruling submitted in the context of a dispute between a company and the Land Nordrhein-Westfalen with respect to the non-execution, by the Land, of certain supply contracts with Klausner Holz; and *(iii) Buonotourist*, whereby an Italian company attempted to rely on a final national judgment not to argue against the recovery of State aid found to be incompatible with the internal market, but as a factor for preventing the Commission from even identifying the aid.[276] Regarding the *Commission v Slovak* judgment, the CJ, on the one hand, confirmed the importance of *res judicata*,[277] while on the other, in contrast with the Commission, it clarified that the situation at issue was distinguishable from that in *Lucchini*, since, in *Commission v Slovak*, the judgment having acquired the force of *res judicata* 'precedes the decision whereby the Commission requires the recovery of the aid'.[278] Consequently, *Lucchini* could not be of direct relevance to this case.[279]

In *Klausner Holz* the Court held that the national judge must take into account two decisive factors to assess whether disapplication should come into play where consistent interpretation was not feasible. In the first place, it must be understood whether the principle of *res judicata*, as conceived under national law, precludes not only the review of the reasons

[270] Opinion of AG Geelhoed, *Lucchini* (n 269), para. 47.

[271] *See* CJ, *Prof. Alberto Campolongo*, joined cases 27/59 and 39/59, EU:C:1960:35.

[272] On this matter, *see* the reflections by R. Kovar, *L'incidence*, 203–208.

[273] CJ, *Commission v Slovak Republic*, C-507/08, EU:C:2010:802.

[274] Commission Decision 2007/254/EC of 7 June 2006 on State aid C 25/05 (ex NN 21/05) implemented by the Slovak Republic for Frucona Košice a.s. (OJ L 112, 30.4.2007, 14).

[275] CJ, *Klausner Holz Niedersachsen GmbH*, C-505/14, EU:C:2015:742, on which, *see* M. Breuer, *State Liability for Judicial Wrongs and Community Law: The Case of* Gerhard Köbler v Austria (2004) 29 *European Law Review* 243; C. D. Classen, *Österreichischer Rundfunk and Others* (2004) 41 *Common Market Law Review* 813. *See*, *ex multis*, H. Weiß, *Rechtskraftdurchbrechung bei (mutmaßlichem) Verstoß eines Vertrags gegen EU-Beihilferecht* (2016) 2 *Europäische Zeitschrift für Wirtschaftsrecht* 60.

[276] CJ, *Buonotourist*, C-586/18 P, EU:C:2020:152.

[277] *Commission v Slovak Republic* (n 273), paras 54 and 60.

[278] *Commission v Slovak Republic* (n 273), para. 57.

[279] *Commission v Slovak Republic* (n 273), para. 58.

upon which a final judgment has already been made, but also the possibility of addressing issues that could have been raised at the time of a prior dispute. If this were the case, the consequence would be to vest a decision of a national court with 'effects . . . which frustrate the application of EU law, in that they make it impossible for the national courts to satisfy their obligation to ensure compliance with the third sentence of Article 108(3) TFEU'.[280] In the second place, the national court should verify whether the principle of *res judicata* can deprive the *effet utile* of rules for which the Commission has exclusive jurisdiction in the evaluation of the compatibility of the aid with the internal market. The EU judges viewed this circumstance as having taken place in this case. Indeed, the CJ observed that:

> EU law precludes, in circumstances such as those at issue in the main proceedings, the application of a rule of national law enshrining the principle of *res judicata* from preventing a national court which has held that contracts forming the subject-matter of the dispute before it constitute State aid . . . from drawing all the consequences of that breach because of a national judicial decision which has become definitive, which court, without examining whether those contracts constitute State aid, has held that the contracts remain in force.[281]

With regards to the *Buonotourist* case, the GC held that the exclusive competence of EU institutions to verify if a State aid is compatible implies that it is not possible to rely on national *res judicata* to challenge the Commission's competence for adopting a decision on State aid.[282] The CJ confirmed this approach, explaining that the decision of a national court cannot prevent the Commission from exercising its exclusive jurisdiction.[283]

Outside the realm of State aid, after *Lucchini* followed the *Fallimento Olimpiclub* case,[284] which involved a reference for a preliminary ruling on the application of the principle of *res judicata* in a dispute regarding VAT, submitted in connection with litigation between Fallimento Olimpiclub Srl and the Italian tax administration, in relation to an incorrect application of EU VAT rules that were relied on before national courts. Here the CJ confirmed the core of the reasoning formulated in *Lucchini*. First, it stated that EU law does not require national courts to disapply their internal procedural rules conferring finality on a decision, even when this would remedy a violation of EU law, the procedural autonomy of Member States being at stake.

Second, by reaffirming the importance of the principles of equivalence and effectiveness, the CJ considered *res judicata* 'as meaning that, in tax disputes, where a final judgment in a given case concerns a fundamental issue common to other cases, it has binding authority as regards that issue, even if its findings were made in relation to a different tax period' and was not, in principle, compatible with the principle of effectiveness.[285]

As a matter of fact, where the final judicial decision is based on an interpretation of EU rules related to abusive VAT practices that are contrary to the EU legal order, 'those rules

[280] *Klausner Holz* (n 275), para. 42.

[281] *Klausner Holz* (n 275), para. 46.

[282] GC, *Buonotourist*, T-185/15, EU:T:2018:430, paras 188 and 191.

[283] *Buonotourist* (n 282), paras 92–95.

[284] *Fallimento Olimpiclub Srl* (n 259), on which, *see* D. Berlin, *De l'autorité relative de l'arrêt limitant l'autorité absolue* (2009) 4 *Revue des affaires européennes* 577; D. Poelzig, *Gemeinschaftsrechtlicher Begriff der Rechtskraft* (2009) 7 *Europäische Zeitschrift für Wirtschaftsrecht* 741; M. F. Orzan, *Ops . . . the ECJ Did It Again! The Relationship between the Principle of Effectiveness of EU Law and the Principle of Legal Certainty in the ECJ Case-by-Case Approach* (2010) 1 *European Law Reporter* 63; G. Vitale, *Il principio dell'autonomia procedurale in due recenti sentenze della Corte di giustizia: i casi* Olimpiclub e Asturcom (2010) 4 *Il Diritto dell'Unione europea* 727.

[285] *Fallimento Olimpiclub* (n 259), paras 26 and 32.

would continue to be misapplied for each new tax year, without it being possible to rectify the interpretation'.[286] In this respect, *Fallimento Olimpiclub*, which relates to the same provision of the Italian Civil Code as *Lucchini* (Article 2909), is a confirmation of the latter, though the contours of the two rulings differ: it involves, in fact, an external judgment, that is, the possibility to transpose in new proceedings a judgment resulting from a different proceeding. On the other hand, *Fallimento Olimpiclub* has potentially far-reaching implications since the fight against abusive practices in the field of VAT in the case at hand is not an area of EU exclusive competence. The approach has been confirmed in the recent *Cabinet de avocat UR* case, whereby the CJ suggested that the referring court should change the interpretation applied in the domestic proceedings in a way that is consistent with EU law and, in the event it should confirm that *res judicata* prevented it from doing so, affirmed that the national rule should be set aside as an excessive obstacle to the effectiveness of EU VAT law.[287]

Another sector, not falling under the exclusive competence of EU institutions, in which the CJ made the decision to shape and eventually soften the scope and impact of *res judicata*, by virtue of the twin principles of effectiveness and equivalence, is Directive 93/13 on unfair terms in consumer contracts. In *Finanmadrid* the CJ found that this directive precludes national legislation, such as the Spanish legislation at issue in the main proceedings, which does not permit the court ruling on the enforcement of an order for payment 'to assess of its own motion whether a term in a contract concluded between a seller or supplier and a consumer is unfair'. The EU judges argued that the unfairness resulted from the authority of *res judicata* granted to the decisions of court registrars who were competent to hear applications for such orders but not to assess the fairness of contractual terms.[288]

More recently, in the *Vueling* judgment, which resulted from a preliminary reference by the French regional court of Bobigny, the CJ mitigated the principle of *res judicata* with regard to the issuance of E-101 certificates by Vueling for its workers through the Spanish authorities, including the French workers who should have been subject to French social provisions. Vueling was convicted by the French courts for fraudulently arranging a labour scheme in breach of Regulation 1408/71.[289] However, the criminal court that convicted Vueling ruled on the case without making use of the procedure set forth in Article 84(a)3 of Regulation 1408/71, currently Article 76(6) of Regulation 883/2004. Therefore, the convictions acquired the force of *res judicata*. Under French law, the statements in the criminal judgment, once they become final, have a binding effect with respect to civil courts in determining the defendant's civil liability, in this case the employer vis-à-vis its French employees. As highlighted in the literature,[290] under the settled case law of the CJ, the case could have been resolved with a strict adherence to the principle of legal certainty, that is, to the principle of *res judicata*, with the result that the criminal conviction would deploy all its effects under national law, including in national civil proceedings. Instead, the CJ adopted the opposite stance and concluded that the criminal conviction, having *res judicata* force, cannot undermine the effectiveness of the E-101 certificates, that is, of Regulation 1408/71. According to the Court, thus, EU law precludes,

[286] *Fallimento Olimpiclub* (n 259), para. 30.

[287] *Cabinet de avocat UR* (n 130), para. 34.

[288] CJ, *Finanmadrid*, C-49/14, EU:C:2016:98, para. 55.

[289] Regulation (EEC) No. 1408/71 of the Council of 14 June 1971 on the application of social security schemes to employed persons and their families moving within the Community (OJ L 149, 5.7.1971, 2).

[290] *See* D. Sarmiento, *Primacy of EU law and res iudicata in national criminal proceedings, revisited and reversed. A comment on Vueling (C-370/17 and C-37/18)*, 8 April 2020, available at https://eulawlive.com/op-ed-primacy-of-eu-law-and-res-iudicata-in-national-criminal-proceedings-revisited-and-reversed-a-comment-on-vueling-c-370-17-and-c-37-18-by-daniel-sarmiento/.

> in a situation where an employer has, in the host Member State, received a criminal conviction based on a definitive finding of fraud made in breach of EU law, a civil court or tribunal of that Member State, bound by the principle of national law that a decision which has the authority of res judicata in criminal proceedings also has that authority in civil proceedings, from holding that employer to be liable, solely by reason of that criminal conviction, to pay damages intended to provide compensation to the workers or a pension fund of that Member State who claim to be affected by that employer's conduct.[291]

The *Vueling* judgment should be welcomed on the merits because it ensures that national authorities make use of the cooperation mechanisms under the Social Security coordination rules so that the procedures under Regulation 1408/71 will be followed more strictly. However, the ruling does not bring clarity to a crucial issue, that is, what would happen if the criminal court acquitted the accused who is in breach of EU law. In this respect, it could be affirmed that the effectiveness of EU law should not take precedence over the need to safeguard the rights of the acquitted person, precluding them from benefiting under civil or administrative rules of such an acquittal.

From the analysis of the case law of both the CJ and the GC, on the one hand, it can be drawn that normally the CJEU rules out that national legislation should be disapplied and, therefore, that the principle of *res judicata* should yield in favour of primacy. The EU judges, as a rule, tend to preclude the reopening of final national judgments that breach EU law: the rationale is, indeed, to let definitive judgments rest untouched.[292] On the other hand, if the *vis expansiva* of primacy and effectiveness is particularly far-reaching in those areas in which the EU holds exclusive competence, it can also prevail over the principle of *res judicata* in sectors where EU institutions do not hold exclusive competence. This means, looking ahead, that the relativization of *res judicata*, as embraced in *Lucchini*, is not an exception restricted to the peculiar features of State aid law, that is, to the centralized power detained by the European Commission in the field. Even if *Lucchini*, ultimately, did not 'open the door' to a thorough rethinking of *res judicata*, the opinion of those who consider the ruling one of the few judgments capable of demonstrating, in concrete terms, how a situation can arise where the effectiveness of EU law can only be ensured by a radical departure from national procedural law must be shared.[293]

As to the role of disapplication and direct effect, the case law is unclear. While a common thread in the jurisprudence is indeed the lack of references to direct effect, but not to disapplication, what can be inferred is that direct effect plays a role, as does disapplication, the latter being structurally attached to the former.[294] This is very problematic since the principles of legal certainty and legitimate expectations are heavily called into question precisely by a considerable relaxation of the *res judicata* principle. Direct effect, in fact, should not have come into play and consequently neither should have disapplication. From the standpoint of the judicial avenues foreseen at the national level, taking the Italian legal system as an example, in the light of the *Lucchini* and *Fallimento Olimpiclub* rulings, national judges should have referred the matter to the CJ in case of doubts regarding the scope or the internal effect of EU law, or, alternatively, should have turned to national constitutional courts. No direct effect was at play and consequently no disapplication should have had been triggered. In fact, differently from what has been written in the previous section, the solution

[291] *Vueling* (n 259), para. 98.
[292] *See*, amongst others, *Asturcom* (n 259), paras 35–40 and *Pizzarotti* (n 259), paras 53–64.
[293] R. Kovar, *L'incidence*, 242, wonders: '*concrètement comment peut se réaliser une situation où l'efficacité du droit communautaire ne peut être assurée qu'en se libérant du renvoi au droit procédural national?*'
[294] On disapplication as result of primacy and direct effect, *see* especially § 1 of Chapter V.

put forward therein regarding the possible limitation, *pro futuro*, of the CJ's preliminary ruling would not, upstream, be viable, since the rationale of *Lucchini* and similar judgments is precisely that of questioning a situation that has already crystallized over time. In short, the strand of case law from *Lucchini* onwards can hardly be justified and is in clear, irremediable conflict with the principles of legal certainty and legitimate expectations, which are safeguarded as general principles in both EU law and national legal orders.

11. 'Pathological' derogations from the duty to disapply

As written several times, most notably in the previous sections of this chapter, the well-known rule is that in the case of a conflict between national law and EU directly effective provisions, domestic authorities must disapply the former and apply the latter, unless the CJ allows them to derogate from such twofold duty, that is, disapplication of national law and application of EU law. To this end, the 'physiological' derogations illustrated in sections 6 and 7 shall be distinguished from a number of 'pathological' derogations that can be raised by domestic authorities, including governments and jurisdictions. More specifically, over the decades, several exceptions have been invoked by Member States' supreme/constitutional courts and were deemed applicable by them *in abstracto* or *in concreto* in the cases at hand. These are situations in which supreme/constitutional courts, often but not always alongside lower and appeals courts as well as the national governments participating in the proceedings before the CJ in the context of Article 267 TFEU, at various degrees and with more or less confrontational attitudes towards the EU legal order, aim at impeding the application of EU directly effective law. They do so by asserting, in open contrast with the jurisprudence of the CJ or irrespective of an express or implicit permission by the latter, that a core of constitutional supreme principles, often but not always connected to the protection of fundamental rights, cannot be encroached by the enforcement of EU law and, in case of direct effect, by the disapplication of domestic laws. Indeed, such attempts and doctrines are frequently tied to a biased conception of the national/constitutional identity clause enshrined in Article 4(2) TEU, which turns out to frequently act, in the eyes of domestic authorities, as a pathological, rather than physiological, exception to EU law, and have normally been at the heart of references for preliminary rulings to the CJ.[295] In most cases, it is the reasoning developed since *Internationale Handelsgesellshaft* by the CJ which is challenged, more or less explicitly: 'the law stemming from the Treaty, an independent source of law, cannot because of its very nature be overridden by rules of national law, however framed, without being deprived of its character as Community law and without the legal basis of the Community itself being called in question.'[296] A reasoning that was echoed in several other judgments, whereby the CJ observed that the validity of a Community/EU measure or its effect within a Member State 'cannot be affected by allegations that it runs counter to either fundamental rights as formulated by the Constitution of that State or the principles of a national constitutional structure'.[297]

Of course, it would be impossible to take into account all diversified situations in all Member States where supreme/constitutional courts rendered rulings which, while formally complying with EU law and the CJ's case law, are, in substance, less friendly towards EU law than they

[295] For bibliographical references on the use and misuse of such article, *see*, in this chapter, footnotes 147–148, § 7.

[296] CJ, *Internationale Handelsgesellschaft mbH v Einfuhr- und Vorratsstelle für Getreide und Futtermittel*, 11/70, EU:C:1970:114, para. 3.

[297] *Melloni* (n 349), paras 56–58; *Winner Wetten* (n 125), para. 61; *Asociația 'Forumul Judecătorilor din Romania'* (n 36), para. 245.

seem at first glance.[298] A well-known recent example is the *French Data Network* judgment rendered by the *Conseil d'Etat* in April 2021,[299] in which the highest French administrative court has shied away from the obligation to enforce the *La Quadrature du Net* preliminary ruling of October 2020.[300] In *La Quadrature du Net* the CJ, confirming and expanding the line of reasoning developed in *Tele2*, affirmed, *inter alia*, that Article 15(1) of Directive 2002/58 on privacy and electronic communications, as amended by Directive 2009/136/EC,[301] read in the light of Articles 7, 8, 11, and 52(1) of the Charter of Fundamental Rights, must be interpreted as precluding legislative measures which, for the purposes laid down in Article 15(1), provide, as a preventive measure, for the general and indiscriminate retention of traffic and location data. By contrast, the CJ clarified that Article 15(1) does not preclude legislative measures that 'allow, for the purposes of safeguarding national security, recourse to an instruction requiring providers of electronic communications services to retain, generally and indiscriminately, traffic and location data in situations where the Member State concerned is confronted with a serious threat to national security that is shown to be genuine and present or foreseeable'.[302] Several other conditions are also laid down by the CJ to allow a derogation from the prohibition of data retention, as well as from other obligations envisaged in Directive 2002/58.[303]

Against this background, in both the *La Quadrature du Net* and *French Data Network* cases the matter of direct effect and disapplication is implicitly considered, yet to be explicitly tackled is, more in general, the preclusion of national law stemming from the application of EU law. What the *Conseil d'Etat* does is relying on the rather strict derogation admitted by the CJ in its ruling in order to render legitimate the whole French data retention system in force at that time. It did so by referring several times to the notion of '*exigences constitutionnelles, qui ne bénéficierai[en]t pas, en droit de l'Union, d'une protection équivalente*'.[304] In this

[298] For a comprehensive recent survey, *see* A. Bobić, *The Jurisprudence of Constitutional Conflict in the European Union*, Oxford, Oxford University Press, 2022. On the place and mandate of Constitutional Courts in the EU, *see*, e.g., M. Claes, *The National Courts' Mandate in the European Constitution*, Oxford, Hart, 2006; G. Martinico, F. Fontanelli, *The Hidden Dialogue: When Judicial Competitors Collaborate* (2008) 8 *Global Jurist Issue* 1; M. Claes, M. de Visser, P. Popelier, C. Van de Heyning (eds.), *Constitutional Conversations in Europe: Actors, Topics and Procedures*, Cambridge-Oxford, Interesentia-Hart, 2012; J. Komárek, *The Place of Constitutional Courts in the EU* (2013) 9 *European Constitutional Law Review* 420; G. Martinico, *The 'Polemical' Spirit of European Constitutional Law: On the Importance of Conflicts in EU Law* (2015) 16 *German Law Journal* 1343; M. Dani (ed.), *Special Section 'Giurisdizione e ruolo delle corti costituzionali nel processo di integrazione europea'* (2019) 3 *Diritto pubblico comparato ed europeo* 715.

[299] *Conseil d'État, Assemblée*, 21/04/2021, 393099, on which *see e.g.* L. Azoulai, D. Ritleng, *L'État, c'est moi. Le Conseil d'État, la sécurité et la conservation des données* (2021) 2 *Revue trimestrielle de droit européen* 349; B. Bertrand, *L'arrêt French Data Network du Conseil d'Etat: un dialogue des juges en trompe l'œil*, in *Le Club des juristes*, 7 May 2021, available at https://www.leclubdesjuristes.com/archives-cdj/larret-french-data-network-du-conseil-detat-un-dialogue-des-juges-en-trompe-loeil-3538/; A. Turmo, *National Security as an Exception to EU Data Protection Standards: The Judgment of the Conseil d'État in French Data Network and Others* (2022) 59 *Common Market Law Review* 203.

[300] *La Quadrature du Net* (n 145), on which, *see* B. Bertrand, *Les enjeux de la surveillance numérique* (2021) 2 *Revue trimestrielle de droit européen* 175; I. Cameron, *Metadata Retention and National Security: Privacy International and La Quadrature du Net: Case C-623/17* (2021) 58 *Common Market Law Review* 1433; J. Sirinelli, *La protection des données de connexion par la Cour de justice: cartographie d'une jurisprudence européenne inédite* (2021) 2 *Revue trimestrielle de droit européen* 313; F.-X. Millet, *Le glissement jurisprudentiel en matière de données de connexion: l'expansion des compétences de l'Union et sa réception dans les États membres* (2023) 39 *Revue française de droit administratif* 606.

[301] CJ, *Tele2 Sverige and Watson and Others*, C-203/15 and C-698/15, EU:C:2016:970. *See* Directive 2009/136/EC of the European Parliament and of the Council of 25 November 2009 amending Directive 2002/22/EC on universal service and users' rights relating to electronic communications networks and services, Directive 2002/58/EC concerning the processing of personal data and the protection of privacy in the electronic communications sector and Regulation (EC) No. 2006/2004 on cooperation between national authorities responsible for the enforcement of consumer protection laws (OJ L 337, 18.12.2009, 11).

[302] *La Quadrature du Net* (n 145), para. 192.

[303] *La Quadrature du Net* (n 145), para. 168.

[304] *Conseil d'État, Assemblée*, 21/04/2021, 393099 (n 299), para. 5.

vein, the *Conseil d'Etat* seems to *de facto* merge the concept of '*exigences constitutionnelles*' with that of *identité constitutionnelle* employed by the *Conseil Constitutionnel* in its judgment of October 2021[305] and, by so doing, applies such reasoning to the very broad and undetermined objective of the protection of public order.

Leaving aside the matter of tense relationships between the CJ and constitutional/supreme courts and shifting the attention to situations of direct clashes, a well-known example is represented by the doctrine explicitly challenging the principle of primacy elaborated by the German Constitutional Court through a combination of the identity and *ultra vires* reviews. This has been designed by that Court originally in the *Maastricht* ruling,[306] confirmed in the *Lisbon*,[307] *Honeywell*,[308] and *OMT*,[309] decisions and applied for the first time, *in concreto*, in *Weiss*.[310]

[305] *Conseil constitutionnel*, Decision No. 2021-940 QPC, 15 October 2021, on which, *see* F.-X. Millet, *Mérites et démérites de l'élévation d'un principe indéterminé au rang de l'identité constitutionnelle de la France* (2022) 3 *Revue trimestrielle de droit européen* 333.

[306] German Federal Constitutional Court judgment of 12 October 1993 2 BvR 2134/92, 2 BvR 2159/92 Maastricht, on which, *see* V. Götz, *Das Maastricht-Urteil des Bundesverfassungsgerichts* (1993) 20 *Juristenzeitung* 1081; J. A. Frowein, *Das Maastricht-Urteil und die Grenzen der Verfassungsgerichtsbarkeit* (1994) 54 *Zeitschrift für ausländisches öffentliches Recht und Völkerrecht* 1; M. Herdegen, *Maastricht and the German Constitutional Court: constitutional restraints for an 'ever closer Union'* (1994) 31 *Common Market Law Review* 235; S. Hobe, *The German State in Europe after the Maastricht Decision of the German Constitutional Court*, in *German Yearbook of International Law*, vol. 37, 1994, 113–136; J. Wieland, *Germany in the European Union. The Maastricht Decision of the Bundesverfassungsgericht* (1994) 5 *European Journal of International Law* 259; U. Everling, *The Maastricht judgment of the German Federal Constitutional Court and its Significance for the Development of the European Union*, in *Yearbook of European Law*, vol. 14, 1995, 1–19; J. H. H. Weiler, *Does Europe Need a Constitution? Demos, Telos and the German Maastricht Decision* (1995) 1 *European Law Journal* 219.

[307] German Federal Constitutional Court judgment of 30 June 2009, 2 BvE 2/08 Treaty of Lisbon, on which, *see* R. Bieber, *An Association of Sovereign States*, (2009) 5 *European Constitutional Law Review* 391; D. Doukas, *The Verdict of the German Federal Constitutional Court on the Lisbon Treaty: Not Guilty but Don't Do it Again!*'(2009) 34 *European Law Review* 866; Editorial Comments, *Karlsruhe has spoken: 'Yes' to the Lisbon Treaty, but . . .* (2009) 46 *Common Market Law Review* 1023; D. Grimm, *Defending Sovereign Statehood Against Transforming the European Union into a State* (2009) 5 *European Constitutional Law Review* 353; D. Halberstam, C. Möllers, *The German Constitutional Court Says 'Ja zu Deutschland!'* (2009) 10 *German Law Journal* 1241; T. Lock, *Why the European Union is not a State* (2009) 5 *European Constitutional Law Review* 407; M. Nettesheim, *Ein Individualrecht auf Staatlichkeit? Die Lissabon-Entscheidung des BVerfG* (2009) 62 *Neue Juristische Wochenschrift* 2868; D. Thym, *In the Name of Sovereign Statehood: A Critical Introduction to the Lisbon judgment of the German Constitutional Court* (2009) 46 *Common Market Law Review* 1795; C. Schönberger, *Lisbon in Karlsruhe: Maastricht's Epigones at Sea* (2009) 10 *German Law Journal* 1201; J. H. H. Weiler, *Editorial. The 'Lisbon Urteil' and the Fast Food Culture* (2009) 20 *European Journal of International Law* 505; J. Ziller, *The German Constitutional Court's Friendliness Towards European Law: on the judgment of Bundesverfassungsgericht over the Ratification of the Treaty of Lisbon* (2010) 16 *European Public Law* 53; G. Beck, *The Lisbon Judgment of the German Constitutional Court, the Primacy of EU Law and the Problem of Kompetenz-Kompetenz: A Conflict between Right and Right in Which There is No Praetor* (2011) 17 *European Law Journal* 470.

[308] German Federal Constitutional Court judgment of 6 July 2010, 2 BvR 2661/06 *Honeywell*, on which, *see* C. Möllers, *Constitutional Review of European Acts Only Under Exceptional Circumstances* (2011) 7 *European Constitutional Law Review* 161.

[309] *See* German Federal Constitutional Court order of 14 January 2014, 2 BvR 2728/13, on which, *see* M. Kumm, *Rebel Without a Good Cause: Karlsruhe's Misguided Attempt to Draw the CJEU into a Game of 'Chicken' and What the CJEU Might do About It* (2014) 15 *German Law Journal* 203; I. Pernice, *A Difficult Partnership Between Courts: The First Preliminary Reference by the German Federal Constitutional Court to the CJEU* (2014) 21 *Maastricht Journal of European and Comparative Law* 3; M. Wendel, *Exceeding Judicial Competence in the Name of Democracy: The German Federal Constitutional Court's OMT Reference* (2014) 10 *European Constitutional Law Review* 263. *See* also the contributions in the Special Issue of *German Law Journal*, 2014, 108. For an analysis of the case and its aftermath, *see* F. Fabbrini, *After the OMT Case: The Supremacy of EU Law as the Guarantee of the Equality of the Member States* (2015) 16 *German Law Journal* 1003; M. Goldmann, *Constitutional Pluralism as Mutually Assured Discretion: The Court of Justice, the German Federal Constitutional Court, and the ECB* (2016) 23 *Maastricht Journal of European and Comparative Law* 119. *See* German Federal Constitutional Court judgment of 21 June 2016, 2 BvR 2728/13 OMT judgment, on which, *see* A. Pliakos, G. Anagnostaras, *Saving Face? The German Federal Constitutional Court Decides Gauweiler* (2017) 18 *German Law Journal* 213; M. Payandeh, *The OMT Judgment of the German Federal Constitutional Court* (2017) 13 *European Constitutional Law Review* 400.

[310] *See* BVerfG, Judgment of the Second Senate of 5 May 2020—2 BvR 859/15, on which, see P. Hilpold, *So Long Solange? The PSPP Judgment of the German Constitutional Court and the Conflict between the German and the*

The core of this twofold doctrine is that the German Constitutional Court has the capacity to review whether EU institutions respect the limit of their conferred competences and render inapplicable internally all legal acts adopted in violation of such boundaries, irrespective of whether the EU law at hand is directly effective or not. More specifically, the German Constitutional Court observed that the principle of democracy, embedded in the German Constitution, sets insurmountable limits for the expansion of the functions and competences of the EU. Most notably, in *Weiss*, with regard to the lawfulness of the ECB's Public Sector Purchase Programme and the previous *Weiss* judgment delivered by the CJ,[311] the German Constitutional Court called into question the CJ's interpretative monopoly in the interpretation of the proportionality principle, as well as the methodological approach which guided the EU judges in evaluating the interplay between economic and monetary policies, in the light of the principle of conferred powers. As a matter of fact, the German Constitutional Court subverted the rationale underlying Article 5 TEU, as such provision's content had been enlightened by the CJ over the decades, in order to preclude the application of EU law, including the duty to disapply conflicting domestic principles and provisions. This duty, however, was not expressly mentioned in the case at hand, as the doctrine of direct effect was outside the scope of the harsh dispute between the two courts.[312]

Another example of direct conflict exists in the ruling issued by the Czech Constitutional Court in the *Holubec* case concerning the scope of EU primary and secondary law on social security,[313] in which, for the first time, a few years before *Weiss*, a Member State's highest

European 'Popular Spirit' (2021) 23 *Cambridge Yearbook of European Legal Studies* 159–192; Editorial Comments, *Not Mastering the Treaties: The German Federal Constitutional Court's PSPP Judgment* (2020) 57 *Common Market Law Review* 965; A. Bobić, M. Dawson, *Making Sense of the 'Incomprehensible': The PSPP Judgment of the German Federal Constitutional Court* (2020) 57 *Common Market Law Review* 1953; F. Amtenbrink, R. Repasi, *The German Federal Constitutional Court's decision in Weiss: A Contextual Analysis* (2020) 45 *European Law Review* 757; F. Mayer, *The Ultra Vires Ruling: Deconstructing the German Federal Constitutional Court's PSPP Decision of 5 May 2020* (2020) 16 *European Constitutional Law Review* 733; D. U. Galetta, J. Ziller, *The Bundesverfassungsgericht's Glaring and Deliberate Breaches of EU law Based on 'Unintelligible' and 'Arbitrary' Grounds* (2021) 27 *European Public Law* 63; M. E. Vergara, G. V. Puig, *The Quiet Architect Finds its Voice: The Primacy of the Law of the European Union after Press Release No. 58/20 of the Court of Justice of the European Union* (2021) 27 *European Public Law* 673; G. Anagnostaras, *Activating Ultra Vires Review: The German Federal Constitutional Court Decides Weiss* (2021) 6 *European Papers* 801; P. Dermine, *The Ruling of the Bundesverfassungsgericht in PSPP—An Inquiry into its Repercussions on the Economic and Monetary Union* (2020) 16 *European Constitutional Law Review* 525; D. Sarmiento, J. H. H. Weiler, *The EU Judiciary After Weiss: Proposing A New Mixed Chamber of the Court of Justice*, 2 June 2020, available at https://verfassungsblog.de/the-eu-judiciary-after-weiss/; S. Poli, R. Cisotta, *The German Federal Constitutional Court's Exercise of Ultra Vires Review and the Possibility to Open an Infringement Action for the Commission* (2020) 21 *German Law Journal* 1078; F. C. Mayer, *To Boldly Go Where No Court Has Gone Before. The German Federal Constitutional Court's Ultra Vires Decision of May 5, 2020* (2020) 21 *German Law Journal* 1116; S. Biernat, *How Far Is It from Warsaw to Luxembourg and Karlsruhe: The Impact of the PSPP Judgment on Poland* (2020) 21 *German Law Journal* 1104; I. Feichtner, *The German Constitutional Court's* PSPP *Judgment: Impediment and Impetus for the Democratization of Europe* (2020) 21 *German Law Journal* 1090, 1097.

311 CJ, *Weiss and Others*, C-493/17, EU:C:2018:1000, on which, *see* A. Bobić, M. Dawson, *Quantitative Easing at the Court of Justice—Doing Whatever it Takes to Save the Euro: Weiss and Others* (2019) 56 *Common Market Law Review* 1005; F. Martucci, *Union économique et monétaire—Cour de justice, gde ch., 11 décembre 2018, Weiss e.a., aff. C-493/17, EU:C:2018:1000, Jurisprudence de la CJUE 2018* (2019) *Décisions et commentaires* 1033; M. Van der Sluis, *Similar, Therefore Different: Judicial Review of Another Unconventional Monetary Policy in* Weiss (2019) 46 *Legal Issues of Economic Integration* 263; E. Perillo, *De Karlsruhe au Kirchberg et retour: le long voyage, courageux mais prévisible, d´un tourmenté 'ultra vires Urteil'* (2020) 1 *Il Diritto dell'Unione Europea* 127; A. Pliakos, G. Anagnostaras, *Adjudicating Economics II: The Quantitative Easing Programme Declared Valid* (2020) 45 *European Law Review* 128.

312 For a recent comprehensive analysis on Germany and identity review, *see* M. Wendel, *The Fog of Identity and Judicial Contestation: Preventive and Defensive Constitutional Identity Review in Germany* (2021) 27 *European Public Law* 465.

313 *See* Pl. ÚS 5/12, *Holubec*, of 31 January 2012, on which, see G. Anagnostaras, *Activation of the Ultra Vires Review: The Slovak Pensions Judgment of the Czech Constitutional Court* (2012) 14 *German Law Journal* 959.

tribunal 'clearly and openly declared'[314] an EU act *ultra vires*. More specifically, the Czech Constitutional Court found the *Landtová* judgment of the CJ[315]—delivered in the context of a reference for a preliminary ruling raised by the Czech Supreme Administrative Court—not applicable within the national territory since EU judges, according to the Czech Constitutional Court, had wrongly interpreted Council Regulation (EEC) No. 1408/71 and, by so doing, stated, *inter alia*, that it precluded a national rule, such as that at issue in the main proceedings, 'which allows payment of a supplement to old age benefit solely to Czech nationals residing in the territory of the Czech Republic'.[316] The Czech Constitutional Court, while reasserting its commitment to the cooperation between Member States and EU institutions, also affirmed that the EU could not violate the basic principles of the Czech Constitution or transgress the competences transferred to it by the Czech state. In this vein, the Czech Constitutional Court established itself as the ultimate body exercising its *Kompetenz der Kompetenz* against the CJ and did so without considering the need to refer to the CJ pursuant to Article 267 TFEU. As occurred in the case of Germany, including in the *Weiss* saga, direct effect did not come into play in either the CJ's ruling or in the judgment delivered by the highest national court.

Since the focus of this section is on situations where direct effect plays a key role, the German and Czech cases will be left aside. In this framework, the first attempt to be mentioned consists in the counter-limits doctrine, as was conceived for the first time by the Italian Constitutional Court in *Frontini*,[317] mentioned occasionally in its jurisprudence, including in *Granital*,[318] recently explicitly evoked in the 2017 reference for a preliminary ruling in the *Taricco* saga and implicitly *de facto* applied in 2018 in the very same saga in the aftermath of the CJ's *Taricco II* judgment.[319] While the *Taricco I* and *II* cases were discussed in detail in section 9 of this chapter, here it is simply recalled that the counter-limits doctrine[320] means that EU law should not prevail over conflicting national law where its application results in a breach of the fundamental principles of the constitutional order and the inalienable rights of the individual, which is ultimately and solely a matter for the Italian Constitutional Court to assess. The trigger for the activation of the counter-limits doctrine is thus the directly effective character of the EU provision concerned, and its related ability to entail disapplication.

[314] In these terms M. Bobek, *Landtová, Holubec, and the Problem of an Uncooperative Court: Implications for the Preliminary Rulings Procedure* (2014) 10 *European Constitutional Law Review* 54, 55.

[315] *See* CJ, *Landtová*, C-399/09, EU:C:2011:415, on which, *see* L. Driguez, *Nouveaux États membres. L'attribution par la République tchèque d'une pension de retraite complémentaire à celle versée suivant la convention bilatérale de 1992 est acceptable, à moins qu'elle ne révèle une discrimination en raison de la nationalité* (2011) 8–9 August–Sept. *Europe* 23–24; A. Pliakos, *Le premier renvoi préjudiciel de la Cour constitutionnelle allemande à la CJUE: un pas en avant, deux pas en arrière?* (2014) 57 *Revue du marché commun et de l'Union européenne* 41; R. Král, *Questioning the Recent Challenge of the Czech Constitutional Court to the ECJ* (2013) 19 *European Public Law* 271; M. Faix, *Genesis eines mehrpoligen Justizkonflikts: Das Verfassungsgericht der Tschechischen Republik wertet ein EuGH-Urteil als Ultra-vires-Akt* (2012) 39 *Europäische Grundrechte-Zeitschrift* 597; R. Zbiral, *A Legal Revolution or Negligible Episode? Court of Justice Decision Proclaimed Ultra Vires* (2012) 49 *Common Market Law Review* 1475.

[316] *Landtová* (n 315), para. 54.

[317] Italian Constitutional Court, 18 December 1973 No. 183.

[318] Italian Constitutional Court, 5 June 1984, No. 70, para. 7. *See* also Italian Constitutional Court, 21 June 2010, No. 227, para. 7, and order, 26 January 2017, No. 24, para. 2.

[319] On the saga, *see* § 9 of this chapter.

[320] For references on the '*controlimiti*' doctrine, *see* footnote 203, § 9. An overview of the Italian Constitutional Court, also in the light of such doctrine, can be found, recently, in M. Cartabia, N. Lupo, *The Constitution of Italy: A Contextual Analysis*, Oxford, Hart, 2022, 37–39 and D. Tega, G. Repetto, G. Piccirilli, S. Ninatti (eds.), *Italian Constitutional Law in the European Context*, Milan, Wolters Kluwer, 2023, 149–164.

The second—again initiating in Italy—dialectical stance towards EU law, in particular EU directly effective provisions, is the dual preliminarity doctrine[321] which led the Italian Constitutional Court to mandate, in its 269/2017 ruling,[322] that domestic courts, when confronted with fundamental rights' issues raising problems of consistency with both the Italian Constitution and the EU Charter, should always submit questions of constitutionality rather than, or before, referring the matter to the CJ by virtue of Article 267 TFEU. This should occur irrespective of whether EU directly effective provisions are at stake (and disapplication is required). Furthermore, ruling 269/2017 prevents ordinary judges from referring to the CJ the same questions that had been previously submitted to the Italian Constitutional Court through the process of constitutional review. Such confrontational attitude vis-à-vis EU law has been softened in several judgments[323] to the extent that, nowadays *(i)* the prior referral to the Constitutional Court is deemed an option, and no longer an obligation; *(ii)* the subsequent reference to the CJ could also cover profiles that had been already tackled by the Constitutional Court; and *(iii)* the duty to disapply is reaffirmed in the presence of EU provisions endowed with direct effect. The latest jurisprudence, in substance, repositions the Constitutional Court in the frame of a cooperative and dialogical relationship with the CJ, especially through the use of Article 267 TFEU.[324] On the other hand, notwithstanding such evolution, uncertainties still remain today since, in some judgments,[325] the Italian Constitutional Court, although confronted with EU directly effective provisions safeguarding fundamental rights, rather than declaring the referrals of constitutional review by national courts inadmissible due to their duty to directly disapply domestic provisions

[321] For a general discussion of the rationale and limits of dual preliminarity in Italy, *see* M. Cartabia, *Taking Dialogue Seriously*, *Jean Monnet Working Paper*, December 2007, available at https://jeanmonnetprogram.org/paper/taking-dialogue-seriously-the-renewed-need-for-a-judicial-dialogue-at-the-time-of-constitutional-activism-in-the-european-union/; G. Martinico, *Multiple Loyalties and Dual Preliminarity: The Pains of Being a Judge in a Multilevel Legal Order* (2012) *International Journal of Constitutional Law* 871; G. Tesauro, P. De Pasquale, *La doppia pregiudizialità*, in F. Ferraro, C. Iannone (eds.), *Il rinvio pregiudiziale*, Turin, Giappichelli, 2020, 289–305. For some comparative remarks, *see* G. Martinico, *Dual Preliminarity in Comparative Law*, in D. Gallo, G. Piccirilli (eds.), *Dual Preliminarity through National, EU and Comparative Case Law*, Special Issue (2023) 15 *Italian Journal of Public Law* 120.

[322] Italian Constitutional Court, 14 December 2017, No. 269/2017.

[323] *See* also Constitutional Court, 23 January 2019, No. 20/2019, Constitutional Court, 20 February 2019, No. 63/2019, Constitutional Court, 6 March 2019, No. 112/2019, Constitutional Court, 6 March 2019, No. 117/2019; Constitutional Court, 30 July 2020, No. 182/2020. On ruling 269/2017 and its aftermath, *see* N. Lupo, *The Advantage of Having the 'First Word' in the Composite European Constitution* (2018) 10 *Italian Journal of Public Law* 186; D. Gallo, *Challenging*, 455–456; D. Gallo, *Efficacia diretta*; F. Donati, *I principi del primato e dell'effetto diretto del diritto dell'Unione in un sistema di tutele concorrenti dei diritti fondamentali* (2019) 2 *Federalismi.it* 104; N. Lupo, *Con quattro pronunce dei primi mesi del 2019 la Corte costituzionale completa il suo rientro nel sistema 'a rete' di tutela dei diritti in Europa* (2019) 14 *Federalismi.it* 1; G. Martinico, G. Repetto, *Fundamental Rights and Constitutional Duels in Europe: An Italian Perspective on Case 269/2017 of the Italian Constitutional Court and its Aftermath* (2019) 15 *European Constitutional Law Review* 731; A. Amato, *Disapplicazione giudiziale della legge e Carta di Nizza. Profili costituzionali*, Naples, Editoriale Scientifica, 2021, 150–178; D. Tega, *The Italian Constitutional Court in its Context: A Narrative* (2021) 17 *European Constitutional Law Review* 369; the contributions in D. Gallo, G. Piccirilli (eds.), *Dual Preliminarity*; L. Cecchetti, D. Gallo, *The Reception of the Narrative of a Europe of Judicial Cooperation in the Italian Jurisprudence and Legal Doctrine: Cooperative Federalism in the Making*, in A. Bailleux, E. Bernard, S. Jacquot, Q. Landenne (eds.), *Les récits judiciaires de l'Europe: Diffusion, réception et coproduction*, Brussels, Bruylant, 2023, 83–109; F. Medico, *Il doppio custode. Un modello per la giustizia costituzionale europea*, Bologna, Bologna University Press, 2023, 288–298.

[324] *See*, for instance, order Nos. 216 and 217 of November 2017 and judgments by the ICC 177 and 178 of 2023 regarding the European arrest warrant, which followed CJ, *E.D.L.*, C-699/21, EU:C:2023:295. On this matter, *see* C. Amalfitano, L. Cecchetti, *The ECJ's Approach to Dual Preliminarity 5 Years after the ITCC's Judgment No. 269/2017*, in D. Gallo, G. Piccirilli (eds.), *Dual Preliminarity*, 84.

[325] *See*, amongst others, Italian Constitutional Court, No. 54/2022. In the literature, *see* the recent account by G. Repetto, *Judgment No. 269/2017 and Dual Preliminarity in the Evolution of the Jurisprudence of the Italian Constitutional Court*, in D. Gallo, G. Piccirilli (eds.), *Dual Preliminarity*, 8.

conflicting with EU law endowed with direct effect, has decided to retain jurisdiction and annul those provisions itself.

The third unjustified derogation from the duty to disapply relates, once more, to Italy and is particularly illustrative of the short circuits that may stem from a wrongful interpretation of primacy, direct effect, and disapplication. The reference goes to the so-called seaside concessions, that is, the case of the twin decisions of 9 November 2021 issued by the Italian Council of State, which, at a plenary session, assessed the long-standing issue of compatibility of these concessions with EU law, challenging their *ex lege* reiterated prorogation without a tender procedure that was foreseen and then confirmed several times by the Italian legislator, as already remarked in section 1 of Chapter II, section 5 of Chapter III, and section 5 of this chapter.[326] However, in doing so, while acknowledging the primacy of EU law and the applicability of the so-called 'Bolkestein Directive', notably of Article 12,[327] which requires the execution of tenders for the allocation of expiring concessions rather than permitting automatic extensions, the Council of State did not immediately set aside the conflicting national law, but decided to adjust the temporary effects of its decision, postponing them to 31 December 2023. This was an unprecedented balancing instrument of the interests at stake and a surprising move taken by the Highest Administrative Court of Italy since the CJ had never been called upon to rule on the legitimacy of such judicial avenue and, thus, had never admitted that peculiar reasoning in a case where EU law has been systematically breached by Italian authorities. The Council of State chose this pattern because it was aware of the consequences arising from the disapplication of the Italian legislation, with regard to the protection of individual rights and with effects *in malam partem* towards the concessionaires, who would be subject, under the Italian legal framework, to criminal proceedings as a result of this disapplication.

In its judgment, the Council of State expressed the need to safeguard cornerstone principles of Italian law, guaranteed also at the EU law level, *in primis* those regarding legal certainty and legitimate expectations, and justified the postponement of the disapplication based on the CJ's well-known approach on the *ex nunc* effects of its own interpretative preliminary rulings pursuant to Article 267 TFEU—which is wrong, in any event, since, as has been noted in section 8 of this chapter, '*ex nunc*' does not mean '*pro futuro*'.[328]

[326] In the literature, *see* C. Burelli, *Le concessioni turistico-ricreative tra vincoli 'comunitari' e normativa italiana: criticità e prospettive* (2021) 2 *Il Diritto dell'Unione europea* 247; E. Cannizzaro, *Demanio marittimo: effetti in malam partem di direttive europee? In margine alle sentenze 17 e 18/2021 dell'Ad. Plen. del Consiglio di Stato*, 30 December 2021, available at https://www.giustiziainsieme.it/en/diritto-ue/2092-effetti-in-malam-partem-di-direttive-europee-in-margine-alle-sentenze-17-e-18-2021-dell-adunanza-plenaria-del-consiglio-di-stato-di-enzo-cannizzaro; A. Circolo, *L'epilogo della proroga ex lege delle concessioni balneari* (2021) 16 *Studi sull'integrazione europea* 573; F. Ferraro, *Diritto dell'Unione e concessioni demaniali: più luci o più ombre nelle sentenze gemelle dell'Adunanza Plenaria?* (2021) 46 *Diritto e Società* 359; R. Mastroianni, *L'Adunanza Plenaria del Consiglio di Stato e le concessioni balneari: due passi avanti e uno indietro?* (2022) 1 *Eurojus* 105; E. Chiti, *Le concessioni demaniali marittime e la Corte di Giustizia* (2023) 5 *Giornale di diritto amministrativo* 629; C. Curti Gialdino, *La sentenza della Corte di giustizia europea del 20 aprile 2023 in tema di concessioni balneari: spunti critici e proposte per chiudere una storia infinita* (2023) 2 *Ordine internazionale e diritti umani* 455; D. Diverio, *Nulla di nuovo*; G. Greco, *La Corte di giustizia*; G. Greco, *Il* suivi *della sentenza della Corte di giustizia sulle concessioni balneari (continua il braccio di ferro tra TAR Lecce e Consiglio di Stato)* (2023) 1 *Eurojus* 1; F. Liguori, *Efficacia diretta e primato europeo: condizioni, effetti e limiti di operatività nel settore delle concessioni demaniali maritime* (2023) 3 *Munus* 387; L. Lorenzoni, *The Doctrine of Dual Preliminarity in the Case Law of Italian Administrative Courts*, in D. Gallo, G. Piccirilli (eds.), *Dual Preliminarity*, 42, 4–51; A. Nato, *Le concessioni*; G. Parodi, *La proroga delle concessioni demaniali marittime tra disapplicazione e incidente di costituzionalità. Questioni aperte, opacità della giurisprudenza* (2023) 3 *DPCE online* 1607.

[327] Directive 2006/123/CE (OJ L 376, 27.12.2006, 36).

[328] On such effects, *see* § 7 of this chapter.

What is striking is the unjustified breaking of the nexus between primacy/direct effect and disapplication carried out by the Council of State. 'Unjustified' since derogations from the duty to immediately disapply cannot take place, as clarified above, outside an authorization to do so by the CJ based on EU rules and principles, as well as on its case law. On the merits of EU internal market and competition law, Italy was wrong in persisting in the prorogation of seaside concessions, as proved by the existence of a past infringement proceeding launched by the Commission[329] and the *Promoimpresa* judgment delivered by the CJ in 2016 about the Italian law on the same matter in force at the time.[330] Upstream, what the Council of State did was to admit inverse vertical direct effect with respect to a directive, which was invoked by a public authority directly in a dispute against an individual, while trying to safeguard the principles of legal certainty and legitimate expectations. This is why it could be argued that there were good grounds for a preliminary reference by the Council of State to urge the CJ to deal specifically with several core issues on the internal effect of directives in inverse vertical relationships. Indeed, an *in malam partem* disapplication, associated with the invocation of a rule of a directive by a public entity against a private entity, would seem to be hardly justifiable.[331] This is even more true when considering what will be clarified in section 5.1 of Chapter VI: it is one thing to admit a directives' direct effect in the context of disputes involving an individual against the State, with side effects for other individuals, or individuals against other individuals, while it is quite another to hold that the State can use the rules of a directive directly in a dispute against the individual, as in the case at hand before the Council of State. In any event, it is clear that, if the Council of State had considered the relevant EU law, beginning with Directive 2006/123, incapable of generating direct effects and/or entailing disapplication, the only possible solution would have been to refer the matter to the Italian Constitutional Court in order to avoid the infringement of the core principles of both the national and European legal orders, including the principles of legality, non-retroactivity in criminal law (which constitutes a corollary thereto), and legitimate expectations.[332]

The fourth attempt consists in the approach taken by the Austrian Constitutional Court in its judgment U 466/11,[333] inducing the Austrian Supreme Court of Justice to submit a preliminary reference to the CJ. In this respect, the CJ, in the *A. v B.* ruling,[334] dove into an

[329] *See* infringement procedure No. 2008/4908.

[330] CJ, *Promoimpresa srl and Others v Consorzio dei comuni della Sponda Bresciana del Lago di Garda e del Lago di Idro and Others*, C-458/14 and C-67/15, EU:C:2016:558, para. 57: 'Article 12(1) and (2) of Directive 2006/123/EC of the European Parliament and of the Council of 12 December 2006 on services in the internal market must be interpreted as precluding a national measure, such as that at issue in the main proceedings, which permits the automatic extension of existing authorisations of State-owned maritime and lakeside property for tourist and leisure-oriented business activities, without any selection procedure for potential candidates.'

[331] *See* also Council of State, judgment 2192 of 1 March 2023; Council of State, order of 6 September 2023 No. 8184. The CJ had the opportunity to deal with Italian seaside concessions in *Autorità Garante della Concorrenza e del Mercato* (n 82), whereby domestic law was found incompatible with EU law in the context of a preliminary reference originating from a dispute between two branches of the Italian public administration; for an analysis of this ruling and for a list of case-notes, *see* § 4 of this Chapter and § 5.1 of Chapter VI. For further developments, *see* CJ, *Società Italiana Imprese Balneari Srl v Comune di Rosignano Marittimo*, C-598/22, still pending before the CJ. For the latest scholarly developments in the aftermath of the CJ's ruling, *see* G. Greco, *Il* suivi, 1.

[332] On the limits of direct effect and *in malam partem* disapplication of national law, *see* §§ 3 and 5 of this chapter.

[333] *See* judgment of 14 March 2012.

[334] *See* CJ, *A v B*, C-112/13, EU:C:2014:2195, on which, *see* M. Kramme, *Kooperation, nein danke!—der EuGH untermauert seinen Führungsanspruch gegenüber den nationalen Verfassungsgerichten* (2014) 21 *Zeitschrift für Gemeinschaftsprivatrecht* 355; G. Martinico, *Il caso* A. c. B. *e il suo impatto sul rapporto fra Corti: un diritto per tre giudici* (2014) 4 *Quaderni costituzionali* 950; D. Paris, *Constitutional Courts as Guardians of EU Fundamental Rights? Centralised Judicial Review of Legislation and the Charter of Fundamental Rights of the EU* (2015) 11 *European Constitutional Law Review* 389; M. De Visser, *Juggling Centralized Constitutional Review and*

issue akin to that tackled by the Italian Constitutional Court in its 269/2017 judgment.[335] More specifically, the EU judges were asked if, in the case of rules of procedural law under which the ordinary courts are required to examine whether legislation is unconstitutional but are not empowered to strike down legislation—this being reserved for a specially organized constitutional court—, the principle of equivalence in the implementation of EU law means that, 'where legislation infringes Article 47 of the [Charter], the ordinary courts are also required, in the course of the proceedings, to request the constitutional court to strike down the legislation generally, and cannot simply refrain from applying that legislation in the particular case concerned'.[336] Indeed, since the Austrian Constitutional Court is deemed to have jurisdiction to review the constitutionality of national statutes also with respect to the provisions of the Charter, Austrian courts, while not being compelled to make a request to the CJ or disapply the conflicting national law, would be obliged to lodge an application with the Constitutional Court to seek a declaration of annulment of such law, regardless of the directly effective nature of the EU fundamental right at stake.[337] The CJ, fully aware of the impact that such type of centralized constitutionality review interlocutory procedure may have on the prolongation of the proceedings and on the uniformity in the enforcement of EU fundamental rights (due to the emergence of possible clashes between the case law of the CJ and the case law of the Constitutional Court), concluded that Article 267 TFEU must be interpreted as 'precluding national legislation, such as that at issue in the main proceedings . . . to the extent that the priority nature of that procedure prevents . . . all the other national courts or tribunals from exercising their right or fulfilling their obligation to refer questions to the Court of Justice for a preliminary ruling'.[338]

The fifth attempt concerns Denmark and is originally ingrained in the stance taken by the Supreme Court of Denmark in the reference for a preliminary ruling in the *Ajos* case,[339] in which it asked the CJ to assess whether the directly effective general principle of non-discrimination on grounds of age, as recognized from *Mangold* onwards,[340] read in light of Directive 2000/78 establishing a general framework for equal treatment in employment and occupation,[341] and the subsequent duty to disapply, should be weighed against the principles of legal certainty and the protection of legitimate expectations. In fact, in the opinion of the highest Danish court, such principles would be jeopardized by the horizontal application of the principle of non-discrimination. The CJ answered[342] by confirming its previous case law, most notably the *Ingeniφrforeningen i Danmark* ruling,[343] whereby, in respect of a vertical dispute, it had remarked that Articles 2 and 6(1) of Council Directive 2000/78 must be interpreted as

EU Primacy in the Domestic Enforcement of the Charter: A.v B (2015) 52 *Common Market Law Review* 1309; D. Düsterhaus, *Procedural Primacy and Effective Judicial Protection: A Trilogue* (2016) 23 *Maastricht Journal of European and Comparative Law* 317.

[335] On this point, *see* the reflections by G. Martinico, *Dual Preliminarity*, 128–132.
[336] *A v B* (n 334), para. 27.
[337] As clarified by the CJ in *A v B* (n 334), para. 25.
[338] *A v B* (n 334), para. 46.
[339] *See* SCDK, case No. 15/2014, *Dansk Industri acting for Ajos A/S v The estate left by A*, of 6 December 2016. ECJ.
[340] On the *Mangold* case, which has been already mentioned several times in the previous chapters, especially in § 3.1 of Chapter III, and the related doctrine on the combined application of fundamental rights and directives, *see* extensively Chapter VI, §§ 5.3–5.5.
[341] Council Directive 2000/78/EC of 27 November 2000 establishing a general framework for equal treatment in employment and occupation (OJ L 303, 2.12.2000, 16).
[342] CJ, *Dansk Industri*, C-441/14, EU:C:2016:278, para. 26.
[343] CJ, *Ingeniørforeningen i Danmark*, C-499/08, EU:C:2010:600.

precluding national legislation pursuant to which workers who are eligible for an old-age pension from their employer under a pension scheme which they have joined before attaining the age of 50 years cannot, on that ground alone, claim a severance allowance aimed at assisting workers with more than 12 years of service in the undertaking in finding new employment.[344]

Moreover, the CJ, by confirming its previous case law on the horizontality of fundamental rights[345] according to which a combined enforcement of directives and general principles of EU law is admissible in horizontal relationships, concluded that the Danish legislation, as it was interpreted by domestic courts, infringed EU law endowed with direct effects and must thus be disapplied, since 'the principles of legal certainty and the protection of legitimate expectations cannot alter that obligation', which would impair the full effectiveness of EU primary and secondary law.[346]

The Danish case is notable not only because the Danish Supreme Court referred matters to the CJ that it should have settled by its own motion, but above all because it never complied with the CJ's judgment. Indeed, in its 2016 decision adopted to implement the EU ruling, the Danish Supreme Court explicitly challenged the reasoning developed by the CJ and dismissed it, by observing that 'the question whether a rule of EU law can be given direct effect in Danish law, as required under EU law, turns first and foremost on the Law on accession by which Denmark acceded to the European Union'. Secondly, the Danish Supreme Court argued that the direct effect of EU law shall be assessed by the Supreme Court itself, relying on the Danish Law on accession, rather than by the CJ. Thirdly, the Danish Supreme Court affirmed that the source of the general principles of EU law could not be found in the Treaties and, thus, that general principles enshrined in Article 6(3) TEU do not produce direct effects in Denmark. Fourthly and lastly, it was concluded that a situation 'in which a principle at treaty level under EU law is to have direct effect (thereby creating obligations) and be allowed to take precedence over conflicting Danish law in a dispute between individuals, without the principle having any basis in a specific treaty provision, is not foreseen in the Law on accession'. Stated otherwise, the principle of non-discrimination on the grounds of age was deemed to be not 'directly applicable' by virtue of the Law on accession and, therefore, could not be relied on in horizontal relationships since such Law 'does not provide the legal basis to allow such principle . . . to take precedence' over domestic law on salaried employees in so far as the provision is contrary to the prohibition of discrimination. In fact, the Supreme Court 'would be acting outside the scope of its powers as a judicial authority if it were to disapply the provision in this situation'.[347] As a matter of fact, the violation of EU law on the part of Danish authorities persists today.[348]

[344] *Ingeniørforeningen i Danmark* (n 343), para. 49.

[345] *See* §§ 5.3–5.5 of Chapter VI.

[346] *Dansk Industri* (n 342), para. 42.

[347] Judgment of 6 December 2016, No. 15/2014, *DI acting for Ajos A/S v The estate left by A*, 45, 49, and 51.

[348] For a detailed analysis of the CJ's *Dansk Industri* judgment and on the saga concerning horizontality of fundamental rights in Denmark, *see* § 5.3 of Chapter VI. In the literature, *see* M. Benecke, *Altersdiskriminierung bei Entlassungsabfindung* (2016) 10 *Europäische Zeitschrift für Wirtschaftsrecht* 469; E. Dubout, *Grandeur et décadence de l'obligation d'interprétation conforme aux directives dans les litiges horizontaux* (2016) 22 *Revue des affaires européennes* 287; E. Gualco, L. Lourenço, *'Clash of Titans'. General Principles of EU Law: Balancing and Horizontal Direct Effect* (2016) 1 *European Papers* 643; M. Sprenger, *Kein Schutz des Vertrauens privater Arbeitgeber in die Anwendung altersdiskriminierender Gesetze* (2016) 4 *Europäische Zeitschrift für Arbeitsrecht* 460; E. Gualco, *'Clash of Titans 2.0'. From Conflicting EU General Principles to Conflicting Jurisdictional Authorities: The Court of Justice and the Danish Supreme Court in the Dansk Industri Case* (2017) 2 *European Papers* 223; S. Haket, *The Danish Supreme Court's Ajos judgment (Dansk Industri): Rejecting a Consistent Interpretation and Challenging the Effect*

The sixth attempt is set out in the Spanish Constitutional Tribunal's ruling delivered in the *Melloni* case,[349] as result of the CJ's judgment made in the context of a 2011 order for a preliminary ruling stemming from the Constitutional Tribunal.[350] The dispute originates from a European arrest warrant issued by the Italian authorities for the execution of a prison sentence handed down *in absentia* by Spanish courts against Mr. Melloni, who was hiding in Spain at that time. The request for a preliminary ruling concerned the interpretation and validity of Article 4a(1) of Council Framework Decision 2002/584/JHA on the European arrest warrant and the surrender procedures between Member States,[351] as amended by Council Framework Decision 2009/299/JHA.[352] In the request the CJ was also asked to verify whether a Member State may refuse to execute a European arrest warrant on the basis of Article 53 of the Charter on grounds of infringement of the fundamental rights of the person concerned guaranteed by the national Constitution. More particularly, the CJ was requested to rule on whether Article 53 allowed a Member State to make the surrender of a person convicted *in absentia* 'conditional upon the conviction being open to review in the requesting State, thus affording those rights a greater level of protection than that deriving from European Union law, in order to avoid an interpretation which restricts or adversely affects a fundamental right recognised by the Constitution of the first-mentioned Member State'.[353]

The judgment rendered by the CJ is straightforward and led to the rejection of the position expressed by the referring judge. Most notably, the CJ excluded that Article 53 gives

of a General Principle of EU Law in the Danish Legal Order (2017) 10 *Review of European Administrative Law* 135; M. R. Madsen, H. P. Olsen, U. Šadl, *Competing Supremacies and Clashing Institutional Rationalities: The Danish Supreme Court's Decision in the* Ajos *Case and the National Limits of Judicial Cooperation* (2017) 23 *European Law Journal* 140; U. Šadl, S. Mair, *Mutual disempowerment: case C-441/14 Dansk Industri, acting on behalf of Ajos A/S v Estate of Karsten Eigil Rasmussen and case no.15/2014 Dansk Industri (DI) acting for Ajos A/S v The Estate left by A* (2017) 13 *European Constitutional Law Review* 347; R. Holdgaard, D. Elkan, G. K. Schaldemose, *From Co-operation to Collision: the ECJ's Ajos Ruling and the Danish Supreme Court's Refusal to Comply* (2018) 55 *Common Market Law Review* 17; G. Zaccaroni, *Is the Horizontal Application of General Principles Ultra Vires? Dialogue and Conflict between Supreme European Courts in Dansk Industri* (2018) 9 *Federalismi.it* 1.

349 On CJ, *Stefano Melloni v Ministerio Fiscal*, C-399/11, EU:C:2013:107, *see* N. De Boer, *Addressing rights divergence under the Charter: Melloni* (2013) 50 *Common Market Law Review* 1083; M. De Visser, *Dealing with Divergences in Fundamental Rights Standards* (2013) 20 *Maastricht Journal of European and Comparative Law* 576; E. Dubout, *Le niveau de protection des droits fondamentaux dans l'Union européenne: unitarisme constitutif versus pluralisme constitutionnel. Réflexions autour de l'arrêt Melloni* (2013) 49 *Cahiers de droit européen* 293; P. Martín Rodríguez, *Crónica de una muerte anunciada: Comentario a la Sentencia del Tribunal de Justicia (Gran Sala) de 26 de febrero de 2013, Stefano Melloni, C-399/11* (2013) 30 *Revista General de Derecho Europeo* 1; V. Skouris, *Développements récents de la protection des droits fondamentaux dans l'Union européenne: les arrêts Melloni et Åkerberg Fransson* (2013) 2 *Il Diritto dell'Unione europea* 229; L. F. M. Besselink, *The Parameters of Constitutional Conflict after Melloni* (2014) 39 *European Law Review* 531; A. Torres Pérez, *Melloni in Three Acts: From Dialogue to Monologue* (2014) 10 *European Constitutional Law Review* 308; L. Bachmaier, *Más reflexiones sobre la sentencia Melloni: Primacía, diálogo y proteccíon de los derechos fundamentales en jucios in absentia en el derecho europeo* (2015) 56 *Revista española de Derecho Europeo* 153; K. Herzmann, *Das spanische Verfassungsgericht und der Fall Melloni* (2015) 42 *Europäische Grundrechte-Zeitschrift* 445; A. Pliakos, G. Anagnostaras, *Fundamental Rights and the New Battle over Legal and Judicial Supremay: Lessons from Melloni*, in *Yearbook of European Law*, vol. 34, 2015, 97–126.

350 *Tribunal Constitucional*, decision of 9 June 2011.

351 2002/584/JHA: Council Framework Decision of 13 June 2002 on the European arrest warrant and the surrender procedures between Member States—Statements made by certain Member States on the adoption of the Framework Decision (OJ L 190, 18.7.2002, 1).

352 Council Framework Decision 2009/299/JHA of 26 February 2009 amending Framework Decisions 2002/584/JHA, 2005/214/JHA, 2006/783/JHA, 2008/909/JHA, and 2008/947/JHA, thereby enhancing the procedural rights of persons and fostering the application of the principle of mutual recognition to decisions rendered in the absence of the person concerned at the trial (OJ L 81, 27.3.2009, 24).

353 *Melloni* (n 349), para. 26.

general authorization to a Member State to apply its constitutional law standard of protection of fundamental rights when it is 'higher than that deriving from the Charter' and, where necessary, 'to give it priority over the application of provisions of EU law', including both directly effective and non-directly effective norms.[354] Indeed, according to the CJ, Article 53 must be interpreted as not allowing a Member State to make the surrender of a person convicted *in absentia* conditional upon the conviction being open to review in the issuing Member State 'in order to avoid an adverse effect on the right to a fair trial and the rights of the defence guaranteed by its Constitution'.[355] In fact, a different interpretation of Article 53 'would undermine the principle of the primacy of EU law', allowing a Member State 'to disapply EU legal rules which are fully in compliance with the Charter',[356] and would thus question the uniformity of the standard of protection of fundamental rights as defined in Framework Decision 2009/299, by ultimately 'undermining the principles of mutual trust and recognition which that decision purports to uphold'.[357] The Spanish Constitutional Court, almost a year later, on the one hand, clarified that it ought to integrate the findings of the CJ with the doctrine established in its Declaration 1/2004,[358] whereby the compatibility between the Spanish Constitution and the unborn European Constitution was discussed and the Spanish version of the counter-limits doctrine had been evoked,[359] while on the other, affirmed that there are limits to the process of European integration that are not explicitly enshrined in the Constitution, including the compliance with fundamental rights. In this regard, therefore, the Spanish Constitutional Court concluded that the last word for recompositing the conflict between EU law and national legal orders shall always belong to itself.

In addition to the six diversified situations identified and described above, others shall be remembered. They deserve special attention since the reasoning drawn up by the authorities of Member States, including governments and constitutional/supreme courts, does not merely aim at derogating, in exceptional circumstances, from EU core constitutional legal principles, while reaffirming the general rule that EU law prevails over domestic legal systems. To the contrary, in all these situations a different narrative is submitted. A narrative that challenges, explicitly and for good, also on the basis of a distorted vision of national and constitutional identity, the true essence of EU law, that is the rationale implied in the principle of primacy, including when such principle engages with direct effect and, alongside the latter, entails the disapplication of national law. More specifically, the harsh approach adopted by the governments and constitutional/supreme courts marks the existence of a clash between EU law and national legal orders which is impossible to recompose. And this occurred, as is known, in a wide range of sectors, first and foremost with respect to the scope and extent of the EU rule of law principles,[360] especially in relation to the principles

[354] *Melloni* (n 349), para. 56.
[355] *Melloni* (n 349), para. 64.
[356] *Melloni* (n 349), para. 63.
[357] *Melloni* (n 349), para. 63.
[358] *See* the Spanish Constitutional Court declaration 1/2004 European Constitution, on which, *see* the comments by C. B. Schutte, *Tribunal Constitucional on the European Constitution. Declaration of 13 December 2004* (2005) 1 *European Constitutional Law Review* 281, and R. Alonso García, *The Spanish Constitution and the European Constitution: The Script for a Virtual Collision and Other Observations on the Principle of Primacy* (2005) 6 *German Law Journal* 1001.
[359] On this parallelism, *see* the observations by A. Torres Pérez, *Melloni*.
[360] On the rule of law crisis, from a legal perspective and with a focus on the confrontational dialogue between Member States' supreme/constitutional courts and the CJ, *see* K. Lenaerts, *Constitutional Relationships between Legal Orders and Courts within the European Union*, speech delivered at the Annual XXIX FIDE Congress, 4

of autonomy and independence of the judiciary, as they are safeguarded in Articles 2 and 19 TEU. In this context, Article 19 TEU, read in the light of Article 47 of the Charter, has been recognized as directly effective since the *Associação Sindical dos Juízes Portugueses* judgment and this confirms the importance of such recognition as a tool to address and counter the resistance of national authorities towards the application of EU law.

Leaving aside the arguments submitted by the governments of Member States, the analysis now turns to some of the most relevant rulings issued by Member States' supreme/constitutional courts in which EU law was waived in favour of core domestic principles embedded in national Constitutions. The national legal orders at stake are those of Hungary, Poland, and Romania. However, since direct effect was not even mentioned once, nor the duty to disapply, in the case of Hungary, brief remarks will now be made regarding this country, and thereafter attention will be devoted to the other two.

Reference[361] goes, first of all, to the 2016 judgment of the Hungarian Constitutional Court, whereby the latter interpreted the notion of constitutional identity as Hungary's

November 2021, whereby he asserted that 'it is no exaggeration to say that the Union foundations as a Union based on the rule of law are under threat and that the very survival of the European project in its current form is at stake', available at https://forumfws.eu/fide-opening-ceremony-koen-lenaerts-04112021-1-.pdf. *See* also, recently, F. Casolari, *Il rispetto della rule of law nell'ordinamento giuridico dell'Unione europea: un dramma in due atti* (2017) 1 *DPCE Online* 1; G. Delledonne, *L'omogeneità costituzionale degli ordinamenti composti*, Naples, Editoriale Scientifica, 2017, 252–269; A. Magen, L. Pech, *The rule of law and the European Union*, in C. May, A. Winchester (eds.), *Handbook on the rule of law*, Cheltenham, Edward Elgar, 2018, 235–256; D. Kochenov, *EU Law without the Rule of Law: Is the Veneration of Autonomy Worth It?*, in *Yearbook of European Law*, vol. 34, 2019, 74–96; D. Kochenov, P. Bárd, *The Last Soldier Standing? Courts vs Politicians and the Rule of Law Crisis in the New Member States of the EU*, in *European Yearbook of Constitutional Law*, vol. 1, 2019, 243–287; B. Bakó, *Judges Sitting on the Warsaw-Budapest Express Train: the Independence of Polish and Hungarian Judges before the CJEU* (2020) 26 *European Public Law* 587; D. Kochenov, *De facto Power Grab in Context: Upgrading Rule of Law in Europe in Populist Times*, in *Polish Yearbook of International Law*, vol. 40, 2020, 197–208; T. Drinóczi, A. Bień-Kacała, *Rule of law, Common Values, and Illiberal Constitutionalism: Poland and Hungary within the European Union*, Abingdon, Routledge, 2020; A. Torres Pérez, *From Portugal to Poland: the Court of Justice of the European Union as Watchdog of Judicial Independence* (2020) *27 Maastricht Journal of European and Comparative Law* 105; L. Pech, D. Kochenov, *Respect for the Rule of Law in the Case Law of the European Court of Justice: A Casebook Overview of Key Judgments since the Portuguese Judges Case*, Stockholm, SIEPS, 2021; C. Pinelli, *Respect for the Rule of Law as Embedded in Article 2 TEU and Protection of the Union's Financial Interests* (2021) 1 *Nuovi autoritarismi e democrazie. Diritto, istituzioni e società* 96; A. Baraggia, *The 'Conditionality' Regulation under the ECJ's Scrutiny: A Constitutional Analysis: Hungary v European Parliament (C-156/21) and Poland v European Parliament (C-157/21)* (2022) 47 *European Law Review* 687; G. de Búrca, *Poland and Hungary's EU Membership: on not Confronting Authoritarian Governments* (2022) 20 *International Journal of Constitutional Law* 13; V. Borger, *Constitutional Identity, the Rule of Law, and the Power of the Purse: the ECJ Approves the Conditionality Mechanism to Protect the Union Budget: Hungary and Poland v. Parliament and Council* (2022) 59 *Common Market Law Review* 1771; M. Fisicaro, *Protection of the Rule of Law and 'Competence Creep' Via the Budget: The Court of Justice on the Legality of the Conditionality Regulation: ECJ judgments of 16 February 2022, Cases C-156/21, Hungary v. Parliament and Council and C-157/21, Poland v. Parliament and Council* (2022) 18 *European Constitutional Law Review* 334; K. Podstawa, J. Gwizdak, *Judicial Independence: the EU's Prescription in the Making to the Polish (and Other) Maladies*, in F. Casarosa, M. Moraru (eds.), *The Practice of Judicial Interaction in the field of Fundamental Rights: The Added Value of the Charter of Fundamental Rights of the EU*, Cheltenham, Edward Elgar, 2022, 112–145; A. Circolo, *Il valore dello stato di diritto nell'Unione europea*, Naples, Editoriale Scientifica, 2023; D. Kochenov, *Restoring the Dialogical Rule of Law in the EU: Janus in the Mirror* (2024) 25 *Cambridge Yearbook of European Legal Studies* 1–16; C. Nagy, *The Rebellion of Constitutional Courts and the Normative Character of European Union Law* (2024) 73 *International and Comparative Law Quarterly* 65–101.

[361] On the violation of the rule of law in Hungarian constitutional law since the new 2011 Constitution, *see* M. Bánkuti, G. Halmai, K. L. Scheppele, *Hungary's Illiberal Turn: Disabling the Constitution* (2012) 23 *Journal of Democracy* 138; G. A. Tóth (ed.), *Constitution for a Disunited Nation: On Hungary's 2011 Fundamental Law*, Budapest-New York, Central European University Press, 2012; A. Vincze, M. Varju, *Hungary: The New Fundamental Law* (2012) 18 *European Public Law* 437; M. Volpi, *La nuova Costituzione ungherese: una democrazia dimezzata* (2012) 3 *Diritto pubblico comparato ed europeo* 1013; M. Dani, *The 'Partisan Constitution' and the Corrosion of European Constitutional Culture*, LEQS Paper, No. 68/2013; P. Sonnevend, A. Jakab, L. Csink, *The Constitution as an Instrument of Everyday Party Politics: The Basic Law of Hungary*, in A. Von Bogdandy,

self-identity and affirmed that it was not rooted in the Hungarian Fundamental Law, but in the very same concept of sovereignty. This means that such self-identity could only be 'acknowledged' by the Fundamental Law and, thus, should not be challenged by any international treaty, including the European treaties, whether the provisions contained therein are directly effective or not.[362] As a result, the Constitutional Court merged the identity review with sovereignty control and in this way found unconstitutional the obligation, imposed by the EU Council Decision (EU) 2015/1601,[363] establishing provisional measures in the area of international protection for the benefit of Italy and Greece, including the transfer of 1,294 persons to Hungary. The logic implied in the reasoning of the Constitutional Court is that the EU's powers must never question constitutional law principles of a Member State. As the conferral of powers to the EU by Member States was carried out by virtue of the national Constitution, in the opinion of the Constitutional Court, it is the latter that can define the boundaries of such powers and make it clear when the EU acts *ultra vires*, their actions lacking any binding force. The consequence, thus, was the violation of the primacy principle, as well as the infringement of the principle of sincere cooperation enshrined in Article 4(3) TEU.[364]

As to Poland, the loyal cooperation between EU institutions and the Polish authorities has been repeatedly placed in question by various decisions taken by the latter, including the Constitutional Tribunal.[365] Such decisions manifestly infringed EU core constitutional law by undermining the independence of the judiciary in that Member State through a number of domestic measures introduced over the years, amongst which, most recently, the revised law relating to the organization of the ordinary courts, the law on the Supreme Court, and some other laws of 20 December 2019. The Commission[366] and the CJ[367] have

P. Sonnevend (eds.), *Constitutional Crisis in the European Constitutional Area: Theory, Law and Politics in Hungary and Romania*, Oxford-Portland, Hart, 2015, 33–109; Z. Szente, F. Mandák, Z. Fejes (eds.), *Challenges and Pitfalls in the Recent Hungarian Constitutional Development: Discussing the New Fundamental Law of Hungary*, Paris, L'Harmattan, 2015. In the EU case law concerning the respect of (or lack thereof) the rule of law in Hungary, *see*, amongst others, CJ, *Commission v Hungary*, C-286/12, EU:C:2012:687; CJ, *Commission v Hungary*, C-66/18, EU:C:2020:792; CJ, *Commission v Hungary* (Transparency of Associations), C-78/18, EU:C:2020:476; CJ, *Hungary v Parliament*, C-650/18, EU:C:2021:426; CJ, C-156/21, *Hungary v Parliament and Council*, EU:C:2022:97. As observed by C. Nagy, *The Rebellion*, 95–96, the CJ acted to challenge Hungarian measures having an impact on the respect of the rule of law also through a reliance on EU law provisions which only indirectly relate to the enforcement of core EU values.

[362] *See* Hungarian Constitutional Court, decision 22/2016, paras 62–66, on which, *see* G. Halmai, *Abuse of Constitutional Identity. The Hungarian Constitutional Court on Interpretation of Article E (2) of the Fundamental Law* (2018) 43 *Review of Central and East European Law* 23 and N. Chronowski, B. Szentgáli-Tóth, A. Vincze, *Decision 22/2016. (XII. 5.) AB—Constitutional Self-identity of Hungary*, in F. Gárdos-Orosz, K. Zakariás (eds.), *The Main Lines of the Jurisprudence of the Hungarian Constitutional Court*, Baden-Baden, Nomos, 2022, 441–58.

[363] Council Decision (EU) 2015/1601 of 22 September 2015 establishing provisional measures in the area of international protection for the benefit of Italy and Greece (OJ L 248, 24.9.2015, 80).

[364] In similar terms, *see* Hungarian Constitutional Court, decision X/477/2021.

[365] *See*, *inter alia*, Polish Constitutional Tribunal, judgments of 14 July 2021 and of 7 October 2021.

[366] Recently, *see*, amongst others, the infringement proceedings launched by the Commission on 15 February 2023 and 8 June 2023, available, respectively, at https://ec.europa.eu/commission/presscorner/detail/en/ip_23_3134 and https://ec.europa.eu/commission/presscorner/detail/en/ip_23_842.

[367] *See* CJ, *A.B. and Others v Krajowa Rada Sądownictwa and Others*, C-824/18, EU:C:2021:153, paras 8, 109, and 112 and case law cited therein. *See* also CJ, order of 14 July 2021, *Commission v Poland*, C-204/21 R, EU:C:2021:593. *See*, on this point, also the order of 6 October 2021 in which the vice president of the Court rejected the request for *interim* measures made by the Republic of Poland. For further rulings, *see* CJ, order of 6 October 2021, *Republic of Poland v European Commission*, C-204/21 R-RAP, EU:C:2021:834; CJ, order of 20 November 2017, *Commission v Poland (Białowieża Forest)*, C-441/17 R, EU:C:2017:877; CJ, *Commission v Poland (Białowieża Forest)*, C-441/17, EU:C:2018:255; CJ, *Commission v Poland (Independence of the Supreme Court)*, C-619/18, EU:C:2019:531; CJ, *Commission v Poland (Independence of the lower courts)*, C-192/18,

found on many occasions that several EU provisions have been breached, including Articles 2, 4(3), 6(1), and 19(1) TEU, Article 267 TFEU, Articles 15(1), 20, 21(1), 47, and 52(1) of the Charter, as well as Articles 2(1)(2), 3(1)(a), and 9(1) of Council Directive 2000/78/EC of 27 November 2000 establishing a general framework for equal treatment in employment and occupation.[368] In particular, the conflict between the CJ and Poland[369] escalated in March of 2021 when the Grand Chamber delivered its judgment in the *A.B. and Others* case regarding the appointment of judges to the Polish Supreme Court. Through such judgment the CJ, confirming that the principles of primacy and direct effect are binding on all bodies of a Member State, imposed the duty upon the Supreme Administrative Court of Poland, that is, the referring judge, to set aside national laws,[370] such as the so-called Law on Supreme Court of Poland, and the jurisprudence of the Polish Constitutional Tribunal, since they violate, amongst others, Articles 1, 2, 4(3), and 19(1) TEU, Article 47 of the Charter, and Article 267 TFEU.[371] The *A.B. and Others* judgment must be read along with other numerous blunt positions taken by EU institutions, like the *Commission v Poland* ruling issued in July 2021 in the context of infringement proceedings on the establishment of the Polish Disciplinary Chamber.[372]

The adoption of several measures by the EU did not prevent the Polish Constitutional Tribunal from fully endorsing the stance taken by the Polish government and systematically voiced by it in the press over the years. In fact, in response to the *A. B. and Others* judgment, Poland's then Prime Minister, Mateusz Morawiecki, filed a request to the Constitutional Tribunal seeking an interpretation of several EU law provisions, starting with Articles 2 and 19 TEU. The final verdict was issued on 7 October 2021 with ruling K 3/21, one day after the CJ had dismissed Poland's request to cancel its injunction ordering the Member State to suspend a disciplinary regime for judges that Poland established in 2017. Some of the conclusions reached by the Constitutional Tribunal are unprecedented since they entirely call into question the constitutional pillars of the EU legal system, including the doctrines of primacy and direct effect. Firstly, it was ruled that Article 1 TEU, read in conjunction with Article 4(3) TEU, as well as with Articles 2 and 19(1) TEU, is incompatible with the Polish Constitution. Most notably, the Tribunal affirmed that the second subparagraph of Article 1 in which the TEU is described as marking 'a new stage in the process of creating an ever closer union among the peoples of Europe', by entrusting the CJ with new competences that go beyond

EU:C:2019:924; CJ, order of 8 April 2020, *Commission v Poland (Régime disciplinaire des juges)*, C-791/19 R, EU:C:2020:277, and CJ, *Commission v Poland (Régime disciplinaire des juges)*, C-791/19, EU:C:2021:596; CJ, order of 21 May 2021, *Czech Republic v Poland*, C-121/21 R, EU:C:2021:420; CJ, order of 20 September 2021, *Czech Republic v Poland*, EU:C:2021:752; CJ, *Poland v Parliament and Council*, C-157/21, EU:C:2022:98; CJ, *European Commission v Republic of Poland*, C-204/21, EU:C:2023:442.

[368] OJ 2000 L 303, 2.12.2000, 16.

[369] On such conflict, as well as on the violation of EU law by Polish authorities, *see*, recently, P. Bogdanowicz, M. Taborowski, *How to Save a Supreme Court in a Rule of Law Crisis: the Polish Experience* (2020) 16 *European Constitutional Law Review* 306; Editorial Comments, *Clear and Present Danger: Poland, the Rule of Law and Primacy* (2021) 58 *Common Market Law Review* 1635 and Editorial Comments, *The Polish Constitutional Court, Primacy, and Lawlessness* (2021) 46 *Common Market Law Review* 717; L. Pech, *Court of Justice protecting Polish Judges from Poland's Disciplinary 'Star Chamber': Commission v Poland (Interim Proceedings)* (2021) 58 *Common Market Law Review* 137; L. D. Spieker, *The Conflict over the Polish Disciplinary regime for Judges: An Acid Test for Judicial Independence, Union Values and the Primacy of EU law: Commission v Poland: Case C-791/19, Commission v Poland (Régime disciplinaire des juges)* (2022) 59 *Common Market Law Review* 777.

[370] *A. B. and Others* (n 367), paras 140–141.

[371] *A. B. and Others* (n 367), paras 140–150.

[372] The Chamber was the Polish institution responsible of reviewing decisions issued in disciplinary proceedings against judges, currently replaced by the Chamber of Professional Responsibility.

those conferred on the EU, breached Articles 2 and 8 of the Polish Constitution, according to which the Republic of Poland is a democratic State, and the Constitution is its supreme law. Secondly, the Tribunal held that that Articles 2 and 19(1) TEU were inconsistent with the Polish Constitution insofar as they allow lower national courts and the Polish Supreme Court to disapply the Constitution, to set aside the rulings of the Constitutional Tribunal, and to examine the legality of the procedure for the appointment of judges. Indeed, the Tribunal argued that by deriving a right to assess the organization of a Member State's judicial system from Article 19(1) TEU, the CJ has granted itself a new competence, which could not by any means be drawn from Article 2 TEU.

On 8 October 2021, the President of the European Commission, Ursula von der Leyen, responded to the Polish ruling with a statement vowing to employ all Treaty powers available to ensure the principle of primacy and, with the duty to disapply being at stake, also the principle of direct effect. In fact, von der Leyen held that '[a]ll rulings by the European Court of Justice are binding on all Member States' authorities, including national courts', that 'EU law has primacy over national law, including constitutional provisions' and that the EU 'will use all the powers' at its disposal 'to ensure this'.[373] In any case, already in April 2021, the Commission had begun an action for failure to fulfil obligations under Article 258 TFEU, which led to the judgment of 5 June 2023 by the CJ,[374] in which it was stated that the value of the rule of law is an integral part of the very identity of the European Union as a common legal order and that the review of respect by a Member State of such value, as well as of effective judicial protection and judicial independence, falls entirely within the competence of that Member State, unless, in exercising its power concerning the organization of justice, it does not comply with the obligations arising from EU law. As a matter of fact, Member States cannot disregard those obligations by relying on national provisions or case law, including constitutional provisions and case law. In this framework, the Court recalled

> that the second subparagraph of Article 19(1) TEU, interpreted in the light of Article 47 of the Charter, which imposes on the Member States a clear and precise obligation as to the result to be achieved and which is not subject to any condition . . . has direct effect, in accordance with the principle of primacy of EU law, which means that any provision, case-law or national practice contrary to those provisions of EU law, must be disapplied.[375]

As to Romania,[376] a very confrontational dialogue has taken place over the last few years between the CJ and the Romanian Constitutional Court. The first act of such dialogue is the *Asociația Forumul Judecătorilor din România* preliminary ruling delivered in May 2021, in which the CJ held that the principle of the primacy of EU law

> must be interpreted as precluding legislation of a Member State having constitutional status, as interpreted by the constitutional court of that Member State, according to which a lower court is not permitted to disapply of its own motion a national provision falling within the scope of Decision 2006/928/EC establishing a mechanism for cooperation and

[373] *See* Statement available at https://cyprus.representation.ec.europa.eu/news/statement-commission-president-von-der-leyen-2021-10-08_en.
[374] *Commission v Poland* (n 367).
[375] *Commission v Poland* (n 367), para. 78.
[376] For a general account, *see* B. Iancu, *Separation of Powers and the Rule of Law in Romania: The Crisis in Concepts and Contexts*, in A. Von Bogdandy, P. Sonnevend (eds.), *Constitutional Crisis*, 153–169.

> verification of progress in Romania to address specific benchmarks in the areas of judicial reform and the fight against corruption.

In the opinion of the CJ, then, the jurisprudence of the Romanian Constitutional Court was contrary to the above-mentioned decision and to the second subparagraph of Article 19(1) TEU.[377] The second act is judgment 390 of the Constitutional Court of Romania of 8 June 2021, whereby the latter, by excluding the primacy of EU law over the Romanian Constitution, albeit it being codified in its Article 148(2), affirmed that the CJ's *Asociația Forumul Judecătorilor din România* judgment was *ultra vires* insofar as it imposed the duty to disapply the domestic laws on judicial reforms in Romania.[378] The third act is the *Euro Box Promotion* preliminary ruling of December 2021, in which the CJ observed that the principle of primacy of EU law was to be interpreted as precluding national rules or a national practice under which

> national ordinary courts are bound by decisions of the national constitutional court and cannot, by virtue of that fact and without committing a disciplinary offence, disapply, on their own authority, the case-law established in those decisions, even though they are of the view, in the light of a judgment of the Court of Justice, that that case-law is contrary to the second subparagraph of Article 19(1) TEU, Article 325(1) TFEU or Decision 2006/928.[379]

The fourth act is the press release of the Constitutional Court, of December 2021, whereby it was held that the legal reasoning set forth by the CJ in *Euro Box Promotion* about the remedy of disapplication, was not enforceable in Romania. Thus, the Romanian courts should always comply with the case law of the Constitutional Court, rather with the case law of the CJ. Otherwise, Romanian judges would be subject to disciplinary measures for having disregarded rulings rendered by the Constitutional Court.[380]

The last act is represented by the *RS* ruling delivered by the CJ's Grand Chamber in 2022, already briefly examined above, whereby it was concluded that EU law precludes a national rule under which national courts have no jurisdiction to examine the conformity with EU law of national legislation which has been held to be constitutional by a judgment of the constitutional court of the Member State. As a matter of fact, the application of such a rule would undermine the principle of primacy and the effectiveness of the preliminary ruling mechanism.[381] As to direct effect, the CJ, first, recalled the existence of an obligation to disapply stemming from the joint application of the principles of primacy and direct effect,[382] then confirmed that both Article 19(1) TEU and the specific benchmarks in the areas of

[377] CJ, *Asociația 'Forumul Judecătorilor din România' and Others v Inspecția Judiciară and Others* (n 36), para. 252.

[378] *See RS* (n 3), on which, *see* A. Caiola, *Aller au fond des choses. Primauté du droit de l'Union européenne et indépendance des juges* (2022) 1 *Revue des affaires européennes* 165; D. Gallo, *Primato, identità nazionale e stato di diritto in Romania* (2022) 2 *Quaderni Costituzionali* 374; D. Călin, *Constitutional Courts cannot Build Brick Walls between the CJEU and National Judges Concerning the Rule of Law Values in Article 2 TEU: RS* (2023) 60 *Common Market Law Review* 819.

[379] *Euro Box Promotion* (n 3), para. 262. On this ruling, *see* D. Preßlein, *Der absolute Anwendungsvorrang des Unionsrechts als Garantie der Gleichheit der Mitgliedstaaten in der Europäischen Union?: Rs. C-357/19, C-379/19, C-547/19, C-811/19, und C-840/19* (2022) 4 *Europarecht* 688.

[380] *See* the press release available at https://www.ccr.ro/en/press-release-23-december-2021/.

[381] *RS* (n 3), paras 37, 46, 75, and 86.

[382] *RS* (n 3), para. 53.

judicial reform and the fight against corruption set out in the annex to Decision 2006/928[383] are endowed with direct effect,[384] and finally concluded that 'if it is not possible to interpret the national provisions in a manner consistent with .... Article 19(1) TEU or those benchmarks, the ordinary Romanian courts must disapply those national provisions of their own motion'.[385]

To conclude, in this section some spectacular cases, including the last three on Hungary, Poland, and Romania concerning the rule of law and the harsh rebellion vis-à-vis core principles of EU law, have been examined, taking primacy, direct effect, and disapplication as the privileged interpretive key for their assessment. They all involve the supreme and constitutional courts of Member States, and they often reached the CJ in the context of Article 267 TFEU.

That said, it shall be recalled that there are many other situations where the conflict between the CJ's case law and national judicial practices on core constitutional principles of EU law arose and the remedy provided by the internal legal order did not seem to be suitable for resolving the tense relationships between supranational and domestic judges without jeopardizing the EU legal order. This issue will not be addressed in this work: this is clearly not the place to carry out a thorough analysis to identify all the different kinds of exceptions related to the various legal systems and raised by the Member States' lower and highest courts and define their salient features.

[383] Commission Decision 2006/928/EC of 13 December 2006 establishing a mechanism for cooperation and verification of progress in Romania to address specific benchmarks in the areas of judicial reform and the fight against corruption (notified under document number C(2006) 6569) (OJ L 354, 14.12.2006, 56).

[384] *RS* (n 3), paras 56 and 58.

[385] *RS* (n 3), para. 59.

VI
CONTROVERSIAL HORIZONTAL DIRECT EFFECT

1. Framing the contentious matter of horizontal direct effect

Horizontal direct effect of EU law has been referred to on several occasions in the previous chapters, in particular when it has been reconstructed in its very essential elements, in the light of the CJ case law, and when it has been evoked alongside inverse vertical direct effect.[1] In this last respect and in view of the analysis made in this chapter, two reflections should be made. They are particularly useful where the case law on the prohibition of horizontal direct effect of directives is subject to criticism in the following sections 3–8. The first: the issue of horizontality differs from the issue of inverse vertical effect because, in the context of horizontal relationships, there is a balancing of interests that inevitably and necessarily leads to sacrificing the interests of a natural or legal person for the benefit of the interests of another individual, whereas, in inverse vertical relationships, it is the Member State that invokes an EU rule against the individual and, therefore, no prerogative for the private parties is safeguarded as a result of the application of EU law. The second: horizontality differs from inverse vertical effect also because the problems related to the estoppel doctrine that exist in the context of inverse vertical relationships do not arise in relation to inter-private disputes. In fact, whereas in inverse vertical relationships the State invokes an EU rule to seek the disapplication of its internal laws, in inter-private disputes the EU rule is invoked by the individual, against another individual, and not by the State. In short, the State would, *in concreto*, benefit from its own non-compliance only in the case of inverse vertical effect.[2] This is why, as explained in sections 2 and 8 of Chapter V, the admissibility (and practice) of inverse vertical direct effect should be handled with outmost care.

On the other hand, there is convergence of horizontal direct effect and inverse vertical direct effect because, as has been observed in section 3.3 of Chapter III, in both types of situations, the disapplication stemming from primacy and direct effect may have as its object both the private and the public measure, when the former is wholly or partly the consequence of the latter, or the private measure alone, when it is not the result of a public measure inducing the private actor to infringe EU law.

As for the structure of this chapter, some general considerations on the logic behind the attribution of horizontal direct effect to EU rules are expounded in section 2, where attention is devoted to primary law provisions, especially to the rules on freedoms of movement,

[1] *See*, respectively, § 3.2 of Chapter III and § 3 of Chapter V. All URLs for this chapter were last accessed on 30 April 2024.

[2] In the words of A. Arnull, *Annotation of Kolpinghuis* (1988) 13 *European Law Review* 42, 44, only in the context of inverse vertical direct effect does it occur that 'MS clearly cannot be allowed to have their cake by failing to implement directives and at the same time to eat it by enforcing them against private parties when it suits them'.

Direct Effect in EU Law. Daniele Gallo, Oxford University Press. © Daniele Gallo 2025. DOI: 10.1093/9780191925221.003.0007

as the most evolving facet of EU substantive law. In section 3 the underlying rationale of the prohibition of horizonal direct effect of directives is discussed and the stratagems devised by the EU courts to overcome this prohibition are identified, while, in section 4, the focus is on two of these stratagems, that is, the flexible interpretation of the concept of public authority and the State liability remedy. In sections 5–8 the focus is on three other stratagems, as they have been conceived by the CJ in its case law on the triangular/incidental effects of directives, the duty of consistent interpretation, and the joint application of directives with the EU Charter of Fundamental Rights and/or general principles of EU law.[3] Section 9 identifies, in systematic terms, the reasons why the prohibition of horizontal direct effect of directives should be overcome. Finally, section 10 is dedicated to a further contentious and neglected matter related to horizontality, that is, the internal effect of decisions foreseen in Article 288 TFEU.

As will be shown, the constant feature of EU case law, which emerges from the entire chapter, is the CJ's stubborn and prolonged reticence on problems concerning the horizontality of EU law, including its most problematic expression:[4] horizontal direct effect. This reticence exacerbates what has already been noted in other parts of this work about the perils of extreme argumentative minimalism and the lack of clarity in the jurisprudence of the CJ on the ever-evolving notion of direct effect. A jurisprudence, therefore, which is unsatisfactory from the point of view of legal certainty and the overall coherence of EU law. What defines the EU jurisprudence is, here as elsewhere, a repeated minimalism in dealing with issues that undoubtedly present a 'profound constitutional complexity'.[5] A complexity that should be dissolved by the CJ, at least in its salient features.

A final clarification: the matter of horizontality of international law in the EU legal system is addressed in section 4 of Chapter VII, to which reference is made.

2. Horizontal direct effect and the EU Treaties

As noted in section 3.1 of Chapter III, the rules contained in the European Treaties, in particular in the TFEU, where they are endowed with direct effect, by their very nature, being normally addressed to States, generate vertical direct effect. However, numerous provisions, such as those on the freedoms of movement, while naturally targeting public authorities as architects of unlawful discriminatory and/or protectionist policies, lack an explicit reference to those who are subject to the obligations envisaged therein, with a few exceptions, including Article 110 TFEU. Other rules, such as Articles 101 and 102 TFEU on competition law applicable to undertakings, impose direct obligations on private entities. Still others, such as Articles 107–109 TFEU on State aid, are addressed to Member States. Moreover, there are others which address both public bodies and private undertakings, for example

[3] On whether the case law is about general principles of EU law or other (unclear) types of principles, *see* further, § 5.3 of this chapter.

[4] For an interesting reconstruction of horizontality, which is not merely centred on horizontal direct effect, as the case of consistent interpretation clearly shows, *see* A. Hartkamp, *The Concept of (Direct and Indirect) Horizontal Effect of EU Law: The Terminology of European Law Scholars and of Private Law Scholars Compared*, in U. Bernitz, X. Groussot, F. Schulyok (eds.), *General Principles of EU Law and European Private Law*, Alphen aan den Rijn, Kluwer Law International, 2013, 189–197, 190–193; E. Frantziou, *The Horizontal Effect of Fundamental Rights in the European Union*, Oxford, Oxford University Press, 2019, 38–40 and 57–81.

[5] In these terms, on horizontality and the EU Charter, *see* P. Eeckhout, *EU Charter of Fundamental Rights and the Federal Question* (2002) 39 *Common Market Law Review* 945, 946.

Article 106 TFEU,[6] a provision establishing monopolies and entrusting, in its paragraph 2, certain undertakings holding special or exclusive rights, as well as public undertakings or private undertakings, with the provision of essential public services.

Over the years, the CJ, relying on the silence of the TFEU, has progressively broadened the personal scope of many of its provisions to include natural and legal persons, in addition to public authorities, unless those provisions were by their nature necessarily addressed only to the latter. This means that several rules that were already recognized as vertically directly effective are now considered capable of producing direct effect in horizontal situations, too. Thus, in spite of how they were originally conceived, such rules can be invoked nowadays by individuals against other individuals in disputes before national courts in order to obtain the disapplication of public and private statutes and conduct in conflict with EU law, or the disapplication of only[7] private statutes and conduct when they do not originate from the State's normative, administrative, or judicial behaviour.[8] In this vein, horizontality questions juridical categories of private law[9] and erodes the extent of private autonomy. Horizontality, in fact, means that EU law 'creates, modifies or extinguishes . . . subjective rights and obligations' in the context of inter-private relations, fully outside the realm of public law.[10]

The matter of EU primary law's horizontality recurs frequently in the EU jurisprudence, beginning with *Van Gend & Loos*, where it was stated that EU law 'not only imposes obligations on individuals but is also intended to confer upon them rights which become part of their legal heritage'.[11] The CJ was therefore ahead of its time already at the beginning of the sixties: in order to affirm the direct vertical effect of then-Article 12 of the EEC Treaty, now Article 30 TFEU, the Court recognized incidentally and not specifically vis-à-vis such provision that the Treaty can impose obligations upon individuals, as well as upon States. Indeed, that direct effect, in *Van Gend & Loos*, has a horizontal dimension appears to be a given, so much so that it is precisely from this circumstance that the Court has inferred that primary law rules, subject to certain conditions, may also give rise to direct effect vertically. Curiously and surprisingly, this is made clear in a case concerning a naturally vertical situation, such as the one covered by (the current) Article 30 TFEU, which is addressed, formally and substantially, to the States[12] and which, unlike the other key norms of the Treaties informing the European economic constitution, has never been recognized (and, in all likelihood, never will be) as a provision capable of producing horizontal direct effect.[13]

[6] On this norm as a *sui generis* and hybrid competition law provision, also in respect to its recipients, *see* J. L. Buendia Sierra, *Exclusive Rights and State Monopolies under EC Law: Article 86 (Formerly Article 90) of the EC Treaty*, Oxford, Oxford University Press, 1999, 131, and recently D. Gallo, *Public Services and EU Competition Law. Social Market Economy in Action*, London, Routledge, 2021, 131.

[7] *See* § 3.3 of Chapter III and § 2 of Chapter V.

[8] R. Schütze, *European Union Law*, 3rd ed., Oxford, Oxford University Press, 2021, 162, as recalled already in footnote 204, section 3.1 of Chapter III, distinguishes between the question of whether a rule can be invoked horizontally, given its effects in domestic proceedings, and 'the question of whether it also outlaws private party actions'.

[9] *See amplius* O. Gerstenberg, *Private Law and the New European Constitutional Settlement* (2004) 10 *European Law Journal* 766; A. Hartkamp, *European Law and National Private Law*, Oxford, Intersentia, 2016. *See* also the references included in footnotes 26–27 and 276 of this chapter.

[10] In these terms, *see* S. Walkila, *Horizontal Effect of Fundamental Rights in EU Law*, Groningen, Europa Law Publishing, 2016, 30.

[11] CJ, *NV Algemene Transport-en Expeditie Onderneming van Gend & Loos*, 26/62, EU:C:1963:1, 12. On *Van Gend & Loos*, *see* extensively Chapter I.

[12] Customs duties and charges having equivalent effect, of course, can only be levied by public authorities, as made clear by R. van Leuken, *Private Law and the Internal Market*, Cambridge, Intersentia, 2017, footnote 2, 39.

[13] *See* C. Barnard, *The Substantive Law of the EU. The Four Freedoms*, Oxford, Oxford University Press, 2022, 46, who, while noting that *Van Gend & Loos* established that Article 30 TFEU was (vertically) directly effective, reflected on what may happen 'if private parties are responsible for collecting the duties'. As recalled by Barnard, in

The revolutionary significance of *Van Gend & Loos*, therefore, lies not only in the fact that individuals are granted rights that they can exercise against the State, but also that the former can enforce them against other private parties. Indeed, the shift from a regime imbued with international law paradigms to a supranational one, in several respects closer to the constitutional law of States than to international law, already evident with the recognition of vertical direct effect, takes on even clearer contours in the perspective of horizontal direct effect.[14] Within this framework, the widening of the scope *ratione personae* of European law necessarily had to pass through a clearer and more generalized stance on the part of the CJ than had been done *en passant* in *Van Gend & Loos*. This has been the case since the mid-seventies.[15]

The fate of Article 157 TFEU, which enshrines the principle of equal pay for male and female workers, well demonstrates the extent to which the CJ's jurisprudence has evolved over time. Suffice it to recall that the CJ, in *Defrenne II*, on the application of the principle of non-discrimination to inter-individual relationships,[16] in particular in the context of subordinate employment relationships, in emphasizing the 'mandatory' nature of Article 141 TEC, now Article 157 TFEU, stressed that this prohibition of discrimination 'applies not only to the action of public authorities, but also extends to all agreements which are intended to regulate paid labour collectively, as well as to contracts between individuals'.[17] What clearly emerges is that the nature, public or private, of the employer is not diriment for the purposes of the applicability or inapplicability of Article 157 TFEU,[18] a norm that codifies the general principle of equal pay for men and women and which developed from an economic labour law-related standard to a fundamental right,[19] as explicitly asserted by the CJ several years after *Defrenne II*.[20]

The development of the EU case law on freedoms of movement is even more emblematic. Although the CJ did not explicitly refer to the recognition of horizontal direct effect, such recognition occurred for the first time in the *Walrave* case concerning Article 39 of

CJ, *Dubois v Garanor Exploitation*, C-16/94, EU:C:1995:268, para. 21, 'the Court said that Article 30 TFEU would still apply' since 'it made no difference whether the charge resulted from a unilateral measure adopted by the authorities or, as here, from a series of private contracts'. On the joint application of Articles 30 and 110 TFEU, with respect to an agreement concluded by various economic operators and then implemented by the legislator, *see* CJ, *Essent Netwerk Noord BV*, C-206/06, EU:C:2008:413, para. 45.

[14] For further observations on this issue, *see* A. Stone Sweet, *Constitutional Dialogues in the European Communities*, EUI WP RSC, 95/38, 1995.

[15] Accordingly, *see* E. Stein, *Lawyers, Judges, and the Making of a Transnational Constitution* (1981) 75 *American Journal of International Law* 1, 17–20.

[16] At the time Article 119 of the EEC Treaty. Amongst the first authors who focused on the provision's horizontal direct effect, *see* L. Daniele, *L'efficacia diretta delle disposizioni comunitarie in materia sociale*, in *Diritto comunitario e degli scambi internazionali*, 1991, 247.

[17] CJ, *Gabrielle Defrenne v Société anonyme belge de navigation aérienne Sabena*, 43/75, EU:C:1976:56, para. 39.

[18] For a harsh criticism of *Defrenne II*, which was allegedly based on a distorted and creative interpretation of Article 119 of the EEC Treaty, *see* C. A. Crisham, *Gabrielle Defrenne v Société anonyme belge de navigation aérienne Sabena* (1977) 14 *Common Market Law* 102, and E. Rasmussen, *On Law and Policy*, 29. For recent contextual analyses of the case, *see* S. O'Leary, *Defrenne II revisited*, in M. Poiares Maduro, L. Azoulai (eds.), *The Past and Future of EU Law: The Classics of EU Law Revisited on the 50th Anniversary of the Rome Treaty*, Oxford, Hart, 2010, 274–285 and D. Simon, *SABENA is Dead, Gabrielle Defrenne's Case is Still Alive: The Old Lady's Testament*, in M. Poiares Maduro, L. Azoulai (eds.), *The Past*, 265–273. In the same line of reasoning of *Defrenne II*, *see* CJ, *K and Others v Tesco Stores Ltd*, C-624/19, EU:C:2021:429.

[19] On this point, *see* S. Prechal, *Horizontal Direct Effect of the Charter of Fundamental Rights of the EU* (2020) 66 *Revista de Derecho Comunitario Europeo* 407, 411.

[20] According to the CJ, *Deutsche Telekom AG*, C-50/96, EU:C:2000:72, para. 56, Article 141 of the EC Treaty (now Article 157 TFEU) 'constitutes the expression of a fundamental human right'.

the EEC Treaty, now Article 45 TFEU, on free movement of workers, and Article 49 of the EEC Treaty, now Article 56 TFEU, on free movement of services, where the invocation of EU law was combined with the disapplication of one or more private law rules. In the ruling, the Court extended the application of these freedoms, also on the basis of Article 12 of the EEC Treaty, now Article 18 TFEU, to private operators, in particular to certain cycling associations, thereby undermining the assumption[21] that they could be enforced against State authorities alone. The EU judges clarified that the questions concerning the interpretation of Articles 18, 45, and 56 TFEU, in essence, 'relate to the applicability of the said provisions to legal relationships which do not come under public law',[22] that is, whether the prohibitions laid down therein also concern restrictions established by acts issued by private natural and legal persons or associations, and not only by State authorities. The CJ ruled in the affirmative, emphasizing, first, that the rules on fundamental freedoms 'have in common the prohibition, in their respective spheres of application, of any discrimination on grounds of nationality' and then that such prohibition 'does not only apply to the action of public authorities but extends likewise to rules of any other nature aimed at regulating in a collective manner gainful employment and the provision of services'.[23]

Such a change of perspective is justified by the objective of ruling out the possibility that certain activities may enjoy favourable treatment solely on account of the legal nature of the entity exercising them;[24] through such a functional criterion, the CJ focuses on the activity rather than on the entity performing it. In so doing, it ensures the effectiveness and useful effect of EU law, from an integrationist perspective, in order to prevent compliance with the TFEU from being circumvented by the emergence of loopholes resulting from a strict application of an institutional criterion.[25] The completion of the internal market, in fact, would not be pursued if private actors could create obstacles to trade similar to those maintained by public actors or obstacles that national governments could not create due to the intrinsic characteristics of the powers held by natural or legal persons. The recognition of horizontal direct effect is a natural consequence if we consider that the socio-economic transformations that have taken place in recent decades, produced by private intervention in welfare and, more generally, in the public sphere, as a result of the privatization and liberalization processes that continue to take place today,[26] like in the context of the sharing

[21] This assumption is particularly clear in the opinion of AG Mayras of 28 May 1974, *Reyners*, EU:C:1974:59, 661–665.

[22] CJ, *B.N.O. Walrave and L.J.N. Koch v Association Union cycliste internationale, Koninklijke Nederlandsche Wielren Unie and Federación Española Ciclismo*, 36/74, EU:C:1974:140, para. 13.

[23] *Walrave* (n 22), paras 16 and 17.

[24] As explained, with regard to both competition law and the freedoms of movement, by O. Odudu, *The Boundaries of EC Competition Law. The Scope of Article 81*, Oxford, Oxford University Press, 2006, 55–56.

[25] On the functional/institutional approach dichotomy, from the standpoint of freedoms of movement, *see amplius* D. Gallo, *I servizi di interesse economico generale. Stato, Mercato e Welfare nel diritto dell'Unione europea*, Milan, Giuffrè, 2010, 5–18.

[26] On the public/private divide in the spheres of the market and welfare, as well as on its partial erosion, not limited to a legal perspective, *see* C. Harlow, *Public and Private Law: Definition and without Distinction* (1980) 43 *Modern Law Review* 241; M. J. Horwitz, *History of the Public/Private Distinction* (1982) 130 *University of Pennsylvania Law Review* 1423; D. Kennedy, *Stages of the Decline of the Public/Private Distinction* (1982) 130 *University of Pennsylvania Law Review* 1349; C. D. Stone, *Corporate Vices and Corporate Virtues: Do Public/Private Distinctions Matter?* (1982) 130 *University of Pennsylvania Law Review* 1441; G. Borrie, *The Regulation of Public and Private Power* (1989) *Public Law* 552; C. Graham, T. Prosser, *Privatising Public Enterprises—Constitutions, the State and Regulation in Comparative Perspective*, Oxford, Oxford University Press, 1991; G. Majone, *Paradoxes of Privatization and Deregulation* (1994) 1 *Journal of European Public Policy* 54;

or on-demand economy, increasingly call into question the boundary between public and private in the economy and welfare. Without horizontality, some individuals' prerogatives would risk remaining without adequate protection for the 'simple' reason that the counterpart is a private entity.

After *Walrave*, the CJ, while continuing to refrain from using the expression 'horizontal direct effect,' recognized the applicability of freedoms of movement to restrictions imposed by private parties, that is, to inter-private disputes,[27] and acknowledged the existence of a

S. Strange, *The Retreat of the State. The Diffusion of Power in the World Economy*, Cambridge, Cambridge University Press, 1996; E. Schmidt-Aßman, *Öffentliches Recht und Privaterecht: Ihre Funktionen als wechselseitige Auffangordnungen*, in W. Hoffmann-Riem, E. Schmidt-Aßman (eds.), *Öffentliches Recht und Privatrecht als wechselseitige Auffangordnungen*, Baden-Baden, Nomos, 1996, 7–40; N. Bamforth, *The Public Law-Private Law Distinction: A Comparative and Philosophical Approach*, in P. Leyland, T. Woods (eds.), *Administrative Law Facing the Future: Old Constraints and New Horizons*, London, Blackstone, 1997, 136–159; P. Craig, *Public Law and Control over Private Power*, in M. Taggart (ed.), *The Province of Administrative Law*, Oxford, Oxford University Press, 1997, 196–216; S. Domberger, P. Jensen, *Contracting Out by the Public Sector: Theory, Evidence, Prospects* (1997) 13 *Oxford Review of Economic Policy* 67; G. Majone, *From Positive to the Regulatory State: Causes and Consequences of Changes in the Mode of Governance* (1997) 17 *Journal of Public Policy* 139; J. Baquero Cruz, *Free Movement and Private Autonomy* (1999) 24 *European Law Review* 603; J. Freeman, *The Private Role in Public Governance* (2000) 75 *New York University Law Review* 543; J. Freeman, *The Contracting State* (2000) 28 *Florida State University Law Review* 155; D. Oliver, *Common Values and the Public-Private Divide*, Cambridge, Cambridge University Press, 1999; J. Baquero Cruz, *Between Competition and Free Movement. The Economic Constitutional Law of the European Community*, Oxford, Oxford University Press, 2002; R. B. Hall, T. J. Biersteker (eds.), *The Emergence of Private Authority in Global Governance*, Cambridge, Cambridge University Press, 2002; C. Scott, *Private Regulation of the Public Sector: A Neglected Facet of Contemporary Governance* (2002) 29 *Journal of Law and Society* 56; J. Freeman, *Extending Public Law Norms through Privatization* (2003) 116 *Harvard Law Review* 1285; G. Napolitano, *Pubblico e privato nel diritto amministrativo*, Milan, Giuffrè, 2003; P. Drahos, *The Regulation of Public Goods* (2004) 7 *Journal of International Economic Law* 321; C. Crouch, *Capitalist Diversity and Change: Recombinant Governance and Institutional Entrepreneurs*, Oxford, Oxford University Press, 2005; T. Porter, *Private Production of Public Goods: Private and Public Norms in Global Governance*, in E. Grande, L. W. Pauly (eds.), *Complex Sovereignty: Reconstituting Political Authority in the Twenty-first*, Toronto, University of Toronto Press, 2005, 217–237; M. Rhodes, *'Varieties of Capitalism' and the Political Economy of European Welfare* (2005) 10 *New Political Economy* 363; S. Cassese, *Oltre lo Stato*, Rome-Bari, Laterza, 2006; N. Jansen, R. Michaels, *Private Law Beyond the State? Europeanization, Globalization, Privatization* (2006) 54 *American Journal of Comparative Law* 843; M. Freedland, J.-B. Auby (eds.), *The Public Law/Private Law Divide: une entente assez cordiale?*, Oxford, Oxford University Press, 2006; B. Hancké, M. Rhodes, M. Thatcher (eds.), *Beyond Varieties of Capitalism: Conflict, Contradictions and Complementaries in the European Economy*, Oxford, Oxford University Press, 2007; F. Cafaggi, H. Muir Watt (eds.), *The Regulatory Functions of European Private Law*, Cheltenham, Edward Elgar, 2007; M. Ruffert (ed.), *The Public-Private Law Divide: Potential for Transformation?*, London, British Institute of International and Comparative Law, 2009; W. Sauter, H. Schepel, *State and Market in European Union Law: The Public and Private Spheres of the Internal Market before the EU Courts*, Cambridge, Cambridge University Press 2009; F. I. Michelman, *Constitutions and the Public/Private Divide*, in M. Rosenfeld, A. Sajó (eds.), *The Oxford Handbook of Comparative Constitutional Law*, Oxford, Oxford University Press, 2012, 298–317.

[27] For a recent account, *see* R. van Leuken, *Private Law*, 64–100. On horizontality, including horizontal direct effect, and the freedoms of movement, *see*, amongst earlier works, S. Van den Bogaert, *Horizontality: The Court Attacks?*, in C. Barnard, J. Scott (eds.), *The Law of the Single Market—Unpacking the Premises*, Oxford, Oxford University Press, 2002, 123–152; P. Oliver, W.-H. Roth, *The Internal Market and the Four Freedoms* (2004) 41 *Common Market Law Review* 407, 421 and 426; H. Schepel, *The Constitution of Private Governance. Product Standards in the Regulation of Integrating Markets*, Oxford, Hart, 2005, 232–233; R. Lane, *The Internal Market and the Individual*, in N. N. Shuibhne (ed.), *Regulating the Internal Market*, Cheltenham, Edward Elgar, 2006, 245–276, 254 and 257; M. Poiares Maduro, *L'État-caméléon. Formes publique et privée de l'Homo Economicus*, in Y. Bot (ed.), *Mélanges en l'honneur de Philippe Léger. Le droit à la mesure de l'homme*, Paris, Pedone, 2006, 79–91; D. Gallo, *I servizi*, 5–86; G. Davies, *Freedom of Movement, Horizontal Effect, and Freedom of Contract* (2012) 20 *European Review of Private Law* 805; H. Schepel, *Constitutionalising the Market, Marketising the Constitution, and to Tell the Difference: On the Horizontal Application of the Free Movement Provisions in EU Law* (2012) 18 *European Law Journal* 177; H. Schepel, *Freedom of Contract in Free Movement Law: Balancing Rights and Principles* (2013) 21 *European Review of Private Law* 1211; S. Enchelmaier, *Horizontality: The Application of the Four Freedoms to Restrictions Imposed by Private Parties*, in P. Koutrakos, J. Snell (eds.), *Research Handbook on the Law of the EU's Internal Market*, Cheltenham, Edward Elgar, 2017, 54–81.

duty to disapply in a number of cases regarding workers,[28] services,[29] establishment,[30] and EU citizenship.[31]

The jurisprudence is, however, still problematic as to the legal foundations and rationale of the recognition of fundamental freedoms' horizontal direct effect, as well as to the generalization of such recognition in all freedoms of movement. The crux of the CJ's reasoning lies in the attainment of effectiveness/*effet utile* of EU law, which was already at the heart of *Walrave*.[32] Indeed, in order to ensure the enforcement of EU law, and thus to prevent the circumvention of the prohibitions enshrined in the treaties, it was necessary to extend these prohibitions to private actors as well. As held in *Bosman*, the abolition of obstacles to the freedoms of movement 'would be compromised if the abolition of State barriers could be neutralized by obstacles resulting from the exercise of their legal autonomy by associations or organizations not governed by public law'.[33] This reasoning seems even more appropriate when one considers the fundamental character of the freedoms of movement as it arises in the CJ's case law.[34]

Another strand of arguments in favour of horizontal direct effect raised by the CJ in its case law is imbued with considerations related to the respect of the principle of non-discrimination. The CJ was indeed aware that making the application or non-application of the provisions on freedoms of movement dependent on the public or private nature of the actor violating them undermines the equality between natural/legal persons. As a matter of fact, Articles 45, 49, and 56 TFEU operate precisely as *lex specialis* to Article 18 TFEU.[35] As observed in *Bosman*, since 'working conditions in the different Member States are sometimes governed by provisions laid down by law or regulation and sometimes by agreements and other acts concluded or adopted by private persons', if the scope of freedoms of movement were confined to acts of a public authority 'there would be a risk of creating inequality in its application'.[36] At the same time, however, it is still unclear whether the reference in *Walrave* and much of the subsequent case law to the circumstance that EU law applies likewise, in addition to the conduct of States, 'to rules of any other nature aimed at regulating in

[28] CJ, *Gaetano Donà v Mario Mantero*, 13/76, EU:C:1976:115; CJ, *S.r.l. Ufficio Henry van Ameyde v S.r.l. Ufficio centrale italiano di assistenza assicurativa automobilisti in circolazione internazionale (U.C.I.)*, 90/76, EU:C:1977:101; CJ, *Union royale belge des sociétés de football association ASBL e altri v Jean-Marc Bosman*, C-415/93, EU:C:1995:463; CJ, *Jyri Lehtonen and Castors Canada Dry Namur-Braine ASBL v Fédération royale belge des sociétés de basket-ball ASBL*, C-176/96, EU:C:2000:201; CJ, *Roman Angonese v Cassa di Risparmio di Bolzano SpA*, C-281/98, EU:C:2000:296; CJ, *Angelo Ferlini v Centre hospitalier de Luxembourg*, C-411/98, EU:C:2000:530; CJ, *Andrea Raccanelli v Max-Planck-Gesellschaft zur Förderung der Wissenschaften eV*, C-94/07, EU:C:2008:425; CJ, *Olympique Lyonnais SASP v Olivier Bernard and Newcastle UFC*, C-325/08, EU:C:2010:143; CJ, *Maurits Casteels v British Airways plc*, C-379/09, EU:C:2011:131; CJ, *Georges Erny v Daimler AG - Werk Wörth*, C-172/11, EU:C:2012:399.

[29] *Donà* (n 28); CJ, *Christelle Deliège v Ligue francophone de judo et disciplines associées ASBL, Ligue belge de judo ASBL, Union européenne de judo (C-51/96) and François Pacquée (C-191/97)*, joined cases C-51/96 and C-191/97, EU:C:2000:199; CJ, *J. C. J. Wouters, J. W. Savelbergh and Price Waterhouse Belastingadviseurs BV v Algemene Raad van de Nederlandse Orde van Advocaten*, C-309/99, EU:C:2002:98; CJ, *Laval un Partneri Ltd v Svenska Byggnadsarbetareförbundet, Svenska Byggnadsarbetareförbundets avdelning 1, Byggettan and Svenska Elektrikerförbundet*, C-341/05, EU:C:2007:809; CJ, *International Transport Workers' Federation and Finnish Seamen's Union v Viking Line ABP and OÜ Viking Line Eesti*, C-438/05, EU:C:2007:772.

[30] *Van Ameyde* (n 28); *Wouters* (n 29); *Viking* (n 29).

[31] CJ, *TopFit eV, Daniele Biffi v Deutscher Leichtathletikverband eV*, C-22/18, EU:C:2019:497.

[32] *Walrave* (n 22), para. 18.

[33] *Bosman* (n 28), para. 83.

[34] On this point, as well as on the variety of reasons underpinning the horizontal direct effect of freedoms of movement, *see* S. de Vries, R. van Mastrigt, *The Horizontal Direct Effect of the Four Freedoms: From a Hodgepodge of Cases to a Seamless Web of Judicial Protection in the EU Single Market?*, in U. Bernitz, X. Groussot, F. Schulyok (eds.), *General Principles*, 249–280, 264–266.

[35] *See*, e.g., *Walrave* (n 22), para. 32; *Raccanelli* (n 28), para. 45; *Angonese* (n 28), para. 35.

[36] *Bosman* (n 28), para. 84.

a collective manner'[37] the freedoms of movement, is to be understood as a genuine limitation on the generalization of the horizontal direct effect of the freedoms of movement with respect to workers, services, and establishment. If this were the case, the freedoms would be invocable in horizontal disputes and would impose the disapplication (frequently, in addition to public measures) of rules and measures adopted by private entities, including sports associations and other professional bodies, only if they were aimed at regulating in collective terms, albeit within a private framework, certain sectors of industry and the economy. Only bodies entrusted with the operation of private governance would be subject to obligations stemming from the freedoms of movement. Stated otherwise, only entities regulating gainful employment in a collective manner or aimed at regulating, collectively, the work of employees and self-employed persons (in the context of free movement of services and/or the right of establishment), should abide by the free movement provisions. For instance, a measure discriminating against Polish engineers, in terms of market access, taken by an AI company based in Portugal, would not fall within the scope of EU law, unlike a measure taken by the Portuguese Association of AI companies.[38]

In the light of the CJ's overall jurisprudence, uncertainty remains since the criterion used in *Walrave* and the other cases concerning sports and professional associations[39] disappeared in later rulings, where a different criterion leads the Court to capture within the rules on freedoms of movement behaviours and rules attributable to private actors. An example of this is the *Ferlini* case, in which the EU judges stated that Article 6 of the EC Treaty, now Article 18 TFEU, 'also applies in cases where a group or organisation such as the EHL [*Entente des Hôpitaux Luxembourgeois*—Luxembourg Hospitals Group] exercises a certain power over individuals and is in a position to impose on them conditions which adversely affect the exercise of the fundamental freedoms guaranteed under the Treaty'.[40] The precondition for the application of Article 18 TFEU, jointly with freedoms of movement, thus, is the position of dominance of the non-state actor. In other rulings, such as *Angonese*,[41] the CJ, while implicitly highlighting the dominance position exercised by a bank in respect of hiring personnel, disregarded the regulatory element and, in so doing, affirmed the horizontal effect of Articles 18 and 45 TFEU, while applying them 'equally to all agreements intended to regulate paid labour collectively, as *well as to contracts between individuals*'.[42]

In the last fifteen years, in cases like *Viking*, the CJ has echoed the approach first adopted in *Walrave* inasmuch as, after noting that Article 49 TFEU could be 'relied on by a private undertaking against a trade union or an association of trade unions',[43] clarified that in 'exercising their autonomous power to negotiate pay and conditions of employment with employers, trade unions participate in the drawing up of agreements seeking to regulate

[37] *Walrave* (n 22), para. 17.

[38] As brilliantly put by R. Schütze, *European Union Law*, 504.

[39] *See*, by way of example, *Donà* (n 28), para. 17; *Deliège* (n 29), para. 47.

[40] *Ferlini* (n 28), para. 50.

[41] On the relevance of the case and the twist made compared to previous case law, *see* E. J. Lohse, *Fundamental Freedoms and Private Actors—towards an 'Indirect Horizontal Effect'* (2007) 13 *European Public Law* 159, 166. *See* also R. Lane, N. N. Shuibhne, *Case C-281/98, Roman Angonese v. Cassa di Risparmio di Bolzano SpA, Judgment of 6 June 2000, not yet reported* (2000) 37 *Common Market Law Review* 1237. As noted by C. Barnard, *The Substantive Law*, 233–234, at the origins of *Angonese* is the *Clean Car* case (CJ, C-350/96, *Clean Car*, EU:C:1998:205), which, however, is rooted in a dispute between an Austrian private company, i.e. Clean Car Autoservice GmbH, and the Landeshauptmann von Wien (Prime Minister of Vienna Land), concerning the rejection of an application by Clean Car to register for a trade on the ground that it had appointed as manager a person who did not reside in Austria.

[42] *Angonese* (n 28), paras 34 and 36 (italics added).

[43] *Viking* (n 29), para. 61.

paid work collectively'.[44] However, notwithstanding the references to previous case law imbued with such a collective regulatory approach, it is one thing for collective interests to be regulated by an entity, but quite another for it to be done by trade unions, which, although participating in the drawing up of collective agreements, obviously do not have the power to define their content autonomously, that is, without the fundamental contribution of the associations representing employers. Through a collective action, trade unions can attempt to induce employers to shape as they wish and sign a certain collective agreement, but this is very different from the power to actually impose rules that could unduly restrict the internal market. In essence, the Court's reasoning seems to be inspired more by the concept of effectiveness of EU law, at the heart of *Defrenne II*, than by the logic implied in *Walrave*. This is demonstrated by a passage of the *Viking* judgment in which the CJ, after having recalled that the freedoms of movement would be endangered if bodies not governed by public law were excluded from the scope of EU law, concluded that 'such considerations must also apply to Article 43 EC [now Article 49 TFEU] which lays down a *fundamental* freedom'.[45]

As for EU citizenship, as pointed out in the literature,[46] the Court, in the *TopFit* judgment, has combined the collective regulatory approach with the dominance test in particular in relation to Articles 18 and 21 TFEU. The question asked by the German referring court was whether the rules of national sports associations were subject to the Treaty 'in the same way as they are subject to the rules of the State of origin'.[47] In this regard, the Court, after having recalled the criterion used from *Walrave* onwards,[48] observed that EU law shall apply also 'in cases where a group or organisation exercises a certain power over individuals and is in a position to impose on them conditions which adversely affect the exercise of the fundamental freedoms guaranteed under the Treaty'.[49]

With regard to capital rules, the question of their direct horizontal effect has so far not been clearly answered in the case law of the CJ, since the majority of rulings concern challenges to national laws on situations that are fully vertical, especially on taxation. However, it seems unlikely that the developments that have taken place in the area of the other freedoms cannot *a priori* also extend to Articles 63 TFEU *et seq.* in the absence of clear judgments to the contrary.[50]

As far as the free movement of goods is concerned, the issue is controversial.[51] The possible *de facto* equivalence between private individuals and public entities, in the field of goods, initially seems to have been envisaged in the *Iannelli* case, where the direct effect of Article 30 of the EEC Treaty, now Article 34 TFEU, was recognized in the context of a dispute between private individuals,[52] and then in the *Dansk Supermarked* judgment,[53] in which the CJ, with regard to the interpretation of Article 30 of the EEC Treaty and exclusive intellectual property rights, stated that 'it is impossible in any circumstances for agreements between

[44] *Viking* (n 29), para. 65; *see* also, in more explicit terms, the opinion of AG Maduro of 23 May 2007 in *Viking* (n 29), para. 43.

[45] *Viking* (n 29), para. 47 (italics added).

[46] See S. Prechal, *Horizontal Direct Effect*, 413–414 and F. Costamagna, *Diritti fondamentali e rapporti tra privati nell'ordinamento dell'Unione europea*, Turin, Giappichelli, 2022, 168–172.

[47] *TopFit* (n 31), para. 36.

[48] *TopFit* (n 31), para. 37.

[49] *TopFit* (n 31), para. 39.

[50] A different understanding is offered by C. Barnard, *The Substantive Law*, 523–524.

[51] The problem is well framed in D. Chalmers, G. Davies, G. Monti, *European Union*, 708–713.

[52] *See* R. Schütze, *European Union Law*, 161.

[53] CJ, *Dansk Supermarked A/S v A/S Imerco*, 58/80, EU:C:1981:17, on which, *see* the observations by M. Waelbroeck, *Les rapports entre les règles sur la libre circulation des marchandises et les règles de concurrence applicables aux entreprises dans la CEE*, in F. Capotorti, C.-D. Ehlermann, J.-A. Frowein (eds.), *Du droit international au droit de l'intégration*. Liber amicorum *Pierre Pescatore*, Baden-Baden, Nomos, 1987, 781–803, 785.

individuals to derogate from the mandatory provisions of the Treaty on the free movement of goods'.[54] In subsequent judgments this approach has not been confirmed, as proven by the fact that *Dansk Supermarked* is not generally cited by the CJ. Yet, in practice, as happened in the area of intellectual property rights,[55] Article 34 TFEU has been frequently applied to private conduct in breach of EU law. This occurred, however, on the grounds that the behaviour was attributed to State legislation.[56]

The *Delhaize* ruling on two preliminary references stemming from the *Tribunal de commerce de Bruxelles* and concerning the applicability of (now) Article 34 TFEU, raised in the context of a dispute between several private companies regarding the execution of a wine order, is emblematic. The CJ's statement that the rule may be relied on 'by individuals before the courts of the Member State in disputes against other individuals'[57] could be read in the light of AG Gulmann's opinion, whereby it was 'simply' held that the provision can be invoked in lawsuits between private individuals 'as the basis of a claim for a declaration of the legality under Community law of measures of public authorities'.[58] In particular, one of the two questions for a preliminary ruling is based on the fact that the respondent company argued, with regard to the lawfulness of the refusal to sell a product, that Article 34 TFEU applies only to measures of Member States that hinder trade and cannot be applied to relations between private undertakings. Gulmann observed that this argument was correct since the provision does not concern the conduct of undertakings, that is, it does not prohibit them from hindering the free movement of goods by conduct which they themselves decide upon.[59] In fact, the justification put forward by the company was that the Spanish legislation, in imposing the obligation to bottle the wine in the region of production as a condition for the use of the name of that region as a designation of origin, meant that wine in bulk could not be sold. In the opinion of Gulmann, the need for the individual to be able to assert rights arising from the rules on the free movement of goods also in horizontal disputes resulted from national law in breach of EU law as the source of the infringement of individual rights, rather from the conduct of the private party, who merely relied on domestic law.[60] According to Gulmann, therefore, it is one thing to admit the invocability of freedoms of movement by one private individual against another private individual, while it is quite another to recognize that such an invocability is a form of horizontal direct effect. However suggestive, this view clashes with this objection: if the disapplication of a private measure, as well as of a public measure, takes place (as we shall see within the framework of the Charter

[54] *Dansk Supermarked* (n 53), para. 17. For an early reflection on the horizontality of Article 34 TFEU *et seq*, *see* W. van Gerven, *The Recent Case-Law of the Court of Justice Concerning Articles 30 and 36 of the EEC Treaty* (1977) 14 *Common Market Law Review* 5.

[55] *See* D. T. Keeling, *Intellectual Property Rights in EU Law. Volume I—Free Movement and Competition Law*, Oxford, Oxford University Press, 2004, 176.

[56] As stressed by many, amongst whom, *see* R. Schütze, *European Union Law*, 504–505. Reference is made to the following judgments: CJ, *Commission v Ireland*, 249/81, EU:C:1982:402; CJ, *VZW Vereniging van Vlaamse Reisbureaus v VZW Sociale Dienst van de Plaatselijke en Gewestelijke Overheidsdiensten*, 311/85, EU:C:1987:418; CJ, *The Queen v Royal Pharmaceutical Society of Great Britain*, joined cases 266–267/87, EU:C:1989:205; CJ, *Apple and Pear Development Council*, 102/86, EU:C:1988:120; CJ, *Établissements Delhaize frères et Compagnie Le Lion SA v Promalvin SA and AGE Bodegas Unidas SA*, C-47/90, EU:C:1992:250; CJ, *Ruth Hünermund and Others v Landesapothekerkammer Baden-Württemberg*, C-292/92, EU:C:1993:932; CJ, *Commission v France*, C-265/95, EU:C:1997:595; CJ, *Eugen Schmidberger, Internationale Transporte und Planzüge v Republik Österreich*, C-112/00, EU:C:2003:333; CJ, *Sapod Audic v Eco-Emballages SA*, C-159/00, EU:C:2002:343; CJ, *Bundesverband der Arzneimittel-Importeure eV and Commission v Bayer AG*, joined cases C-2–3/01 P, EU:C:2004:2.

[57] *Delhaize* (n 56), para. 29.

[58] Opinion of AG Gulmann of 16 January 1992, *Delhaize*, EU:C:1992:9, para. 45.

[59] Opinion of AG Gulmann, *Delhaize* (n 58), para. 40.

[60] Opinion of AG Gulmann, *Delhaize* (n 58), para. 41.

of Fundamental Rights),[61] it does not seem to be possible to deny that in the *Delhaize* case, in addition to vertical direct effect, horizontal direct effect also plays a role *in concreto*.

The *Commission v France* and *Schmidberger* cases are also important since with these rulings the CJ, in respect to private actions, firstly, qualified the inaction of the public authorities in contrasting the conduct of private persons infringing the free movement of goods as a State measure within the meaning of Article 34 TFEU (*Commission v France*). Secondly, the Court provided a legal framework for the conduct of private persons who sought to exercise fundamental rights safeguarded by EU law, while restricting such freedom of movement (*Schmidberger*).[62] The question to ask is whether the attribution of a private action to the State is a sufficient reason to deny that the CJ has, *de facto*, admitted horizontal direct effect. Does it make sense to argue that such an effect has been ruled out if one considers that a private party, in the various disputes at stake, seeks the disapplication of a private measure?

As has already been observed,[63] disapplication, in vertical relationships, concerns only the conduct of the State, whereas, in horizontal relationships, it may concern, and frequently does, both a private and a public measure, where the former is a consequence of the latter. The focus on disapplication, that is, on the distinctive manifestation of primacy based on direct effect,[64] makes it possible to look at EU case law in different terms from how the doctrine usually relates to it.[65] Hence the conclusion that, while the CJ is reluctant to recognize horizontal direct effect in the area of goods unlike it does in the area(s) of persons, workers, services, and establishment, *de facto* and *in concreto*, the CJ admits horizontality and the duty to disapply in some cases concerning inter-private disputes, although not in express terms. On the other hand, the CJ, in *Sapod Audic*, has boldly rejected horizontal direct effect insofar as it has affirmed that a contractual obligation to affix the 'Green dot' recycling logo to packaging could not be regarded as a barrier to trade for the purposes of Article 34 TFEU 'since it was not imposed by a Member State but agreed between individuals'.[66]

Against this background, the *Fra.bo* ruling[67] confirms that there is still much uncertainty on the matter of Article 34 TFEU's horizontal direct effect. In fact, the case seems to return to the logic of *Iannelli* and *Dansk Supermarked* since, not only *de facto*, as in some of the previous judgments, but also *de jure*, there seem to be clear openings towards the recognition of horizontal direct effect.[68] The judgment concerns the issue of the legality, under Article 34 TFEU, of certain technical standards decided by the German Association for Gas and Water, a non-profit certifying body governed by private law, whose main objective, according to its statutes, is the promotion of the gas and water sectors. The question was whether the Association, in setting standards, was bound by Article 28 of the EC Treaty, now Article 34 TFEU. The EU judges, while observing that the body was recognized as a public-benefit entity, given that its activities were aimed at disinterestedly helping the community in the material, spiritual, or moral spheres—therefore not at defending the interests of manufacturers in the sector—, dwelled on the fact that it was not financed by public authorities and, above all, noted that

[61] For a comparison *see* some comparative observations beyond freedoms of movement, most notably the Charter, *see* §§ 5-3 and 5.4 of Chapter VI, for instance in respect to the *Cresco* judgment.

[62] For a comprehensive account of these two cases, *see* C. Krenn, *A Missing Piece in the Horizontal Effect 'Jigsaw': Horizontal Direct Effect and the Free Movement of Goods* (2012) 49 *Common Market Law Review* 177.

[63] *See* § 3.3 of Chapter III, § 2 of Chapter V and § 1 of this chapter.

[64] *See* § 1 of Chapter V.

[65] Amongst textbooks where a clear denial of rules on goods' horizontal direct effect has been inferred from the CJ's case law, *see* C. Barnard, *The Substantive Law*, 75–76.

[66] *Sapod Audic* (n 56), para. 74.

[67] CJ, *Fra.bo SpA*, C-171/11, EU:C:2012:453.

[68] On this point, *see* the reflections by R. Schütze, *European Union Law*, 506.

Germany 'has no decisive influence' over its standardization and certification activities.[69] In particular, the Court emphatically pointed out that it was the only body in Germany that had the power under German law to regulate the entry onto the German market of products such as the copper fittings at issue in the main proceedings.[70] Against this background, the CJ affirmed that Article 34 TFEU must be interpreted as meaning that it applies to standardization and certification activities of a private law body, 'where the national legislation considers the products certified by that body to be compliant with national law and that has the effect of restricting the marketing of products which are not certified by that body'.[71]

In spite of the absence of a clear stance on the issue of the horizontality of Article 34 TFEU,[72] as well as of specific references to the case law concerning the other free movement rules,[73] it seems fair to say that the approach adopted by the EU courts, albeit quite cautious[74] and based on the regulatory criterion,[75] marks a significant change of perspective.[76] Such change has in the assertion of a new criterion the dividing line between admission and rejection of horizontality, that is, the production of effects giving rise to privately made restrictions on the free movement of goods 'in the same manner as do measures imposed by the State'.[77] Therefore, in the understanding of the CJ, the type of effects resulting from a behaviour, be it public or private, would be the only true parameter for the applicability of Article 34 TFEU to private parties. This means that if such actors have the power to do what legislators or the administrations normally do, including restricting and/or dissuading other private parties from engaging in cross-border contractual relations, horizontality shall be asserted.[78] The extent of this change, however, seems to be quite limited since *Fra.bo* represents an isolated case and no realignment with the jurisprudence on the other fundamental freedoms has been made by the CJ so far.

On the basis of what has been written to date about the principle of non-discrimination codified in Articles 18 and 157 TFEU, in the rules on freedoms of movement (to different degrees), and less manifestly in Article 21 TFEU, it emerges that the CJ has used, also jointly, several criteria to justify the horizontal application of EU primary law provisions and the related duty to disapply: *(i)* the recognition of core provisions of EU law as codified general

[69] *Fra.bo* (n 67), para. 24.

[70] *Fra.bo* (n 67), paras 14, 28, and 31.

[71] *Fra.bo* (n 67), para. 32.

[72] As remarked by P. Oliver, *L'article 34 TFUE peut-il avoir un effet direct horizontal? Réflexions sur l'arrêt* Fra. bo? (2014) 1 *Cahiers de droit européen* 77, 81, the direct horizontal effect of Article 34 TFEU has never been explicitly admitted in the judgment.

[73] H. Van Harten, T. Nauta, *Towards Horizontal Direct Effect of the Free Movement of Goods? Comment on* Fra. bo (2013) 38 *European Law Review* 677, 693, observed that the CJ, in this matter, deliberately and systematically avoids referring to its previous jurisprudence.

[74] Differently from the clear openings made by AG Trstenjak in his opinion of 28 March 2012, *Fra.bo*, EU:C:2012:176, paras 44 and 46–49.

[75] On such criterion, and its limits, *see* the analysis carried out above in this §, with regard to the other freedoms of movement.

[76] In these terms, *see*, with different nuances, N. N. Shuibhne, *The Treaty is Coming to Get You* (2012) 37 *European Law Review* 367; W.-H. Roth, *Die 'horizontale' Anwendbarkeit der Warenverkehrsfreiheit (Art. 34 AEUV)* (2013) 12 *Europäische Wirtschafts- und Sprachakademie* 16, 20; H. Van Harten, T. Nauta, *Towards Horizontal Direct Effect*, 677, according to whom 'a new era is dawning in which the obligations placed on private individuals within the internal market are continually growing'; H. Schepel, *Annotation of Fra.bo* (2013) 9 *European Review of Contract Law* 186; R. van Leuken, *Direct Horizontal Effect of the Fundamental Freedoms*, in A. Hartkamp, C. H. Sieburgh, L. A. D. Keus, J. S. Kortmann, M. H. Wissink (eds.), *The Influence of EU Law on National Private Law*, Deventer, Kluwer, 2013, 73–94, 86–89; and R. van Leuken, *Private Law*, 128–129. *Contra*, R. van Gestel, H.-W. Micklitz, *European Integration through Standardization: How Judicial Review is Breaking Down the Club House of Private Standardization Bodies* (2013) 50 *Common Market Law Review* 145, 159–160; P. Oliver, *L'article 34 TFUE*, 94–95, who refers to '*effet direct vertical étendu*'.

[77] *Fra.bo* (n 67), para. 26.

[78] *See* the observations in D. Chalmers, G. Davies, G. Monti, *European Union*, 711.

principles of EU law, notably fundamental rights, including above all the prohibition of discrimination; *(ii)* the collective regulation criterion; *(iii)* the dominance test; and *(iv)* the equivalence test between private and State-made restrictions envisaged for the first and only time in *Fra.bo*. The diversity of these criteria and their intermittent relevance, thus, render unclear which situations may be covered by horizontal direct effect, just as it is unclear what the legal basis for such horizontality is. Cases such as *Viking* and *Laval* further complicate matters since none of the above-mentioned criteria seems to be applicable. Moreover, in these rulings, the major critical issues do not seem to concern the acceptance *per se* of the horizontality of free movement rules in disputes between trade unions and companies, where the position of strength, for different reasons, seems to be held by both the boycotting trade unions and the employers exercising their private autonomy even in defiance of social justice objectives. Rather, the criticisms vis-à-vis *Viking* and *Laval* relate mainly to the CJ's strict reasoning on the general interest justifications and the principle of proportionality.[79]

At the risk of oversimplifying the reading of the EU jurisprudence, the recurring legal basis for the attribution of horizontality is, as highlighted by the CJ since *Walrave* and *Defrenne II*, the respect of the principle of effectiveness/*effet utile* of EU law, often, but not always, in combination with arguments related to non-discrimination and equality. As to the criterion of the regulation of collective interests, which was frequently used by the CJ, it is problematic because it gives rise to a dichotomy between individual private actions, which tend to be excluded from horizontality, and regulatory collective private actions, which are instead covered by EU law. This dichotomy is conceptually and operationally difficult to justify. Indeed, how does one place activities that are on the borderline between these two categories? Consider a measure jointly adopted by some private German universities which discriminates against law graduates from Spain. Once it is accepted that the freedoms of movement impose obligations on private actors, limiting it to private actions which have a regulatory character would imply that horizontality depends on the characteristics and the legal status of the actors, rather than on the concrete activities performed by them. In this vein, an institutional, rather than functional, criterion would apply, with all the consequences in terms of legal uncertainty and discrimination amongst companies and individuals.

Ultimately, the CJ, by recognizing, asymmetrically and through a case-by-case approach, the horizontal direct effect of the rules on fundamental freedoms, in addition to other primary rules, has been able to strengthen the protection of those individual economic rights that these rules are intended to safeguard, thus giving them the status of fundamental rights. In this sense, horizontality ensures a more advanced protection of individual rights, as occurs *mutatis mutandis* in Member States due to the jurisprudence of their constitutional courts. There is a difference, however: whereas the application by domestic courts of the *mittelbare Drittwirkung* doctrine[80] to fundamental rights in inter-private relations served

[79] Amongst critical appraisals on *Viking* and *Laval*, *see*, *inter alia*, B. Bercusson, *The Trade Union Movement and the European Union: Judgement Day* (2007) 13 *European Law Journal* 279; J. Malmberg, T. Sigeman, *Industrial Actions and EU Economic Freedoms: The Autonomous Collective Bargaining Model Curtailed by the European Court of Justice* (2008) 45 *Common Market Law Review* 1115.; S. Sciarra, *Solidarity and Conflict. European Social Law in Crisis*, Cambridge, Cambridge University Press, 2019, 91–117. For a different perspective, *see* L. Azoulai, *The Court of Justice and the Social Market Economy: the Emergence of an Ideal and the Conditions for its Realization* (2008) 57 *Common Market Law Review* 1335; C. Barnard, *Viking and Laval: An Introduction* (2008) 10 *Cambridge Yearbook of European Legal Studies* 463–492; S. Weatherill, Viking *and* Laval: *The EU Internal Market Perspective*, in M. Freedland, J. Prassl (eds.), Viking, Laval *and Beyond*, Oxford, Oxford University Press, 2014, 23–39.

[80] *See* the *Lüth-Urteil* judgment of the German Constitutional Court of 15 January 1958 (1 BvR 400/51). *See*, more recently, on the *mittelbare Drittwirkung* doctrine from the standpoint of EU law R. Streinz, S. Leible, *Die unmittelbare Drittwirkung der Grundfreiheiten* (2000) 11 *Europäische Zeitschrift für Wirtschaftsrecht* 259 and, amongst monographs, L. C. Kroemer, *Drittwirkung der Grundrechte. Die Unterscheidung zwischen Staat und*

as a means of safeguarding national constitutional values generally different from the protection of economic interests, the attribution of horizontal direct effect in the EU context to Articles 45, 49, and 56 TFEU (with the limitations and nuances mentioned above) aims at the realization and refinement of the founding economic values and principles of the intra-EU market, in line with the ordoliberal *Zeitgeist* underpinning the EU's legal system.[81] It is precisely due to the *ordo*liberal, rather than *neo*liberal, 'soul' of the EU legal order that horizontality has been affirmed by the CJ. In fact, the application of the freedoms of movement to entities other than the State means that the law, with its conforming function (*'funzione conformatrice'*),[82] has found a space that was previously inaccessible. The result is the (partial) reformulation of the relationship between EU law and private autonomy,[83] the most obvious manifestation of which is the restriction of the latter in favour of the expansion of the scope of intervention of EU rules. In this sense, the recognition of horizontal direct effect to internal market provisions aims ultimately to respond to market failures and create a situation of greater competition between private operators. Horizontality ensures that the 'extension of party autonomy across borders'[84] occurs in a balanced manner and is not questioned in favour of one party over another; in other words, it makes it possible to relativize the idea that the market is always able to regulate itself and that private autonomy is *per se* untouchable.[85] In this framework, it is one thing to consider that a private actor may legitimately invoke EU market rules against another private actor, and quite another to consider that such invocability must necessarily lead the court hearing the case to uphold the position expressed by the plaintiff. Indeed, if the CJ was right in admitting the reliance by a company on freedoms of services and establishment in the *Viking* and *Laval* cases, the approach taken by the Court raises problems where the general interest justifications put forward by the trade unions have been dismissed.

For what concerns the CJ's stance on the rules on capital, whose horizontal direct effect has never been explicitly either confirmed or denied by the CJ, and the rules on goods, whose possible horizontal direct effect is still doubtful, the dissonance with the case law on Articles 45, 49, and 56 TFEU does not seem justifiable.[86] First, there is no reason why the rationale guiding the case law on workers, services, and establishment, inspired by ensuring the effectiveness of EU law, should be different from that guiding the case law on goods and capital. Secondly, there is no reason why measures of private origin, regulatory or otherwise, and agreements between private parties, if detrimental to the free market, can be challenged before a court under some rules on freedom of movement, but not others. The existence of divergences of interpretation in the area of fundamental freedoms must be circumscribed as much as possible, moreover, in view of the need to respond in the best manner possible to

Gesellschaft als staatstheoretische Bedingung der Drittwirkungsproblematik, Tübingen, Mohr Siebeck, 2024. *See* also H. C. Nipperdey, *Grundrechte und Privatrecht*, in H. C. Nipperdey, *Festschrift für Erich Molitor*, Munich, Beck, 1962; C.-W. Canaris, *Grundrechte und Privatrecht* (1984) 184 *Archiv für die civilistische Praxis* 201. On such doctrine and EU fundamental rights, *see* § 5.3 of this chapter.

[81] On such issue, *see* J. Suerbaum, *Die Schutzpflichtdimension der Gemeinschaftsgrundrechte* (2003) 3 *Europarecht* 390.

[82] *See* N. Irti, *L'ordine giuridico del mercato*, Rome-Bari, Laterza, 2001, 54–59.

[83] On the evolving relations between freedoms of movement and private autonomy, *see* J. Baquero Cruz, *Free Movement*, 603–620.

[84] S. Grundmann, *The Structure of European Contract Law* (2019) 27 *European Review of Private Law* 505, 510.

[85] *Contra* G. Davies, *Freedom*, 813; M. Safjan, P. Mikłaszewicz, *Horizontal Effect of the General Principles of EU law in the Sphere of Private Law* (2010) 18 *European Review of Private Law* 475, 485.

[86] Generally, on the principal problems concerning the emergence of assonances and divergences amongst freedoms of movement, *see* M. Poiares Maduro, *Harmony and Dissonance in Free Movement*, in *Cambridge Yearbook of European Legal Studies*, vol.4, 2001, 315.

the socio-economic changes brought about by private intervention in sectors once subject to State domestic jurisdiction, also as a result of the privatization and liberalization processes. Thirdly, the variable-geometry recognition of the horizontal direct effect, on the one hand, does not ensure legal certainty and, on the other, risks calling into question the overall coherence (and therefore uniformity) of the system. Fourthly and finally, it is unclear why restrictions on the free movement of capital and goods caused by private parties, according to the Court, could only be subject to the scrutiny of national courts in the context of disputes concerning Articles 101 and 102 TFEU, unlike what the Court itself stated with regard to other freedoms of movement, for example in *Wouters*, where the combined application of antitrust law and the right of establishment was conducted.[87]

In conclusion, what is certain is that, as far as the matter of freedoms of movement's horizontality is concerned, the CJ's jurisprudence lacks a solid line of argumentation, including in relation to the criteria justifying a prevalence of economic freedoms over fundamental rights or vice versa. This mirrors the whole problematic legal discourse on the scope and practicability of the doctrine of direct effect developed in the Court's rather ambiguous case law.

3. Overview on the CJ's unsatisfactory techniques to get around the no horizontal direct effect rule for directives (NHDE)

An examination of established EU case law shows that a directive can never entail direct effect in inter-private disputes and thus cannot be invoked and enforced by an individual against another individual on its own before a national court.[88] Thus, a directive cannot trigger the disapplication of incompatible national law, nor of the private measure originating from the latter, in the context of inter-individual relations.[89] This has been reiterated throughout the case law, including in the very recent *Gabel Industria Tessile* ruling.[90]

Obligations on national/legal persons may, on the other hand, be indirectly imposed on the basis of other sources of EU law that are addressed to both individuals and States. In this connection, it is one thing for the other source to be a regulation,[91] whose direct effect is usually beyond doubt, and quite another for it to be a different provision whose direct effect is doubtful, as in the case of the Charter of Fundamental Rights.[92] Furthermore, obligations contained in directives may be indirectly imposed if the disapplication of national law, in horizontal relationships, is decided by a judge (or a branch of the administration) on the basis of domestic law, and therefore not as a result of EU rules. EU rules, in fact, can only lead to setting aside national law if they are granted direct effect.[93] A direct effect that, as anticipated in section 3.1 of Chapter III and previously observed, at least on paper,[94] shall not

[87] This point is highlighted, amongst others, by R. van Leuken, *Private Law*, 129.

[88] On inverse vertical direct effect, *see* §§ 5–7 of Chapter V.

[89] For brief introductory remarks, *see* § 3.1 of Chapter III.

[90] CJ, *Gabel Industria Tessile*, C-316/22, EU:C:2024:301, para. 22. *See* also, amongst recent judgments, CJ, *Sambre & Biesme*, joined cases C-383–384/21, EU:C:2022:1022, para. 36.

[91] With reference to sources other than directives, a special case is that of rules concerning private persons that can be applied because of a reference by an EU regulation. In these situations, the directive is relevant not as such but only in order to supplement the rules contained in an act which has general application, is binding in its entirety, and is directly effective/applicable in all Member States. *See* CJ, *Viamex Agrar Handels GmbH (C-37/06) and Zuchtvieh-Kontor GmbH (ZVK) (C-58/06) v Hauptzollamt Hamburg-Jonas*, joined cases C-37/06 and C-58/06, EU:C:2008:18. On this topic, *see* L. Daniele, *Diritto dell'Unione europea*, 8th ed., Milan, Giuffrè, 2022, 304–305.

[92] On the joint application of directives and fundamental rights, *see* extensively § 5.3–5.5 of this chapter.

[93] *See*, recently, *Gabel Industria Tessile* (n 90), paras 23–25. For some observations on the case, *see* § 1 of Chapter V.

[94] For the reasons why such inexistence is 'on paper', *see* the following §§.

come into play when the applicability of directives in horizontal disputes is at stake. In this regard, it has already been pointed out that the existence of a power of disapplication, on the basis of national rather than EU law, outside direct effect,[95] is not surprising, as the CJ is concerned about the effectiveness of EU law, that is, about the removal, in the domestic legal order, of the inconsistencies with EU law. As clarified in section 1 of Chapter V, such situations can occur if there exists an antinomy within the domestic legal order and the judge, or the administration, opts for setting aside, amongst conflicting national provisions, the one not in compliance with EU law and consequently applies the domestic rule which is, instead, compatible with EU norms, most notably with an EU directive, including in a horizontal situation.

Against this background, the *Marshall I* and *Faccini Dori* judgments are the first in which the horizontal direct effect of directives was explicitly excluded. In both it was stated that a directive 'cannot of itself impose obligations on an individual'.[96] In *Marshall I*, concerning Directive 76/207 on the implementation of the principle of equal treatment for men and women as regards access to employment, vocational training and promotion, and working conditions,[97] it was written that, according to Article 189 of the EEC Treaty, now Article 288 TFEU, 'the binding nature of a directive, which constitutes the basis for the possibility of relying on the directive before a national court, exists only in relation to "each Member State to which it is addressed"'.[98] In *Faccini Dori*, on Directive 85/577 for the protection of consumers in the case of contracts negotiated away from business premises,[99] it was better clarified why, according to the EU judges, direct effect is only vertical for directives: to extend the case law on direct effect to the sphere of inter-individual relations would mean recognizing 'a power in the Community to enact obligations for individuals with immediate effect, whereas it has competence to do so only where it is empowered to adopt regulations'.[100] The CJ raised a constitutional argument related to the repartition of competences enshrined in the Treaties. Such argument has inspired the subsequent case law,[101] in which it has consistently been held that, even if clear, precise, and unconditional, a provision of a directive does not allow the national court to disapply a provision of its domestic law that is contrary to it if, by so doing, an additional obligation would be imposed on an individual.[102]

[95] The power to disapply shall not be confused with the duty to disapply. *See* § 1 of Chapter V.

[96] *See* CJ, *Marshall v Southampton and South-West Hampshire Area Health Authority* (*Marshall I*), C-152/84, EU:C:1986:84, para. 48 and CJ, *Paola Faccini Dori v Recreb Srl*, C-91/92, EU:C:1994:292, para. 20.

[97] Council Directive 76/207/EEC of 9 February 1976 on the implementation of the principle of equal treatment for men and women as regards access to employment, vocational training and promotion, and working conditions (OJ L 39 14.2.1976, 40).

[98] See *Marshall I* (n 96), para. 48.

[99] Council Directive 85/577/EEC of 20 December 1985 to protect the consumer in respect of contracts negotiated away from business premises (OJ L 372 31.12.1985, 31).

[100] *Faccini Dori* (n 96), para. 24.

[101] *See*, amongst many others, CJ, *Pfeiffer*, C-397-403/01, EU:C:2004:584, paras 108–109; CJ, *El Corte Inglés SA v Cristina Blázquez Rivero*, C-192/94, EU:C:1996:88, para. 17; CJ, *Portgás—Sociedade de Produção e Distribuição de Gás SA v Ministério da Agricultura, do Mar, do Ambiente e do Ordenamento do Território*, C-425/12, EU:C:2013:829, para. 22; CJ, *Dansk Industri (DI), acting on behalf of Ajos A/S v Estate of Karsten Eigil Rasmussen*, C-441/14, EU:C:2016:278, para. 30; CJ, *Elaine Farrell*, C-413/15, EU:C:2017:492, para. 31; CJ, *David Smith v Patrick Meade and Others*, C-122/17, EU:C:2018:631, para. 42; CJ, *Criminal proceedings against Daniel Adam Popławski* (*Popławski* II), C-573/17, EU:C:2019:530, para. 66; CJ, *Cresco Investigation GmbH v Markus Achatzi*, C-193/17, EU:C:2019:43, para. 72; CJ, *Thelen Technopark*, C-261/20, EU:C:2022:33, para. 32.

[102] On this point, *see* CJ, *Criminal proceedings against Silvio Berlusconi (C-387/02), Sergio Adelchi (C-391/02) and Marcello Dell'Utri and Others (C-403/02)*, C-387/02, C-391/02, and C-403/02, EU:C:2005:270, paras 72–73; CJ, *Arcor AG & Co. KG (C-152/07), Communication Services TELE2 GmbH (C-153/07) and Firma 01051 Telekom GmbH (C-154/07) v Bundesrepublik Deutschland*, joined cases C-152–154/07, EU:C:2008:426, paras 35–44; CJ, *OSA—Ochranný svaz autorský pro práva k dílům hudebním o.s. v Léčebné lázně Mariánské Lázně a.s*, C-351/12, EU:C:2014:110, paras 46–47; *Popławski II* (n 101), para. 67; *Thelen Technopark* (n 101), para. 32.

As already noted in section 5 of Chapter V in relation to inverse vertical effect, the crux of the case law lies in the fact that directives are designed, in EU law, as legal sources binding upon the Member States and not individuals. They are not acts of general application, but rather indirect normative sources for natural and legal persons. According to the CJ, in order to create direct obligations, an intervention by the State is always necessary. Article 288 TFEU cannot be interpreted in the sense of 'making it say' what could not be allowed following an interpretation, not only literal,[103] but in line with its spirit and purposes. Admitting the invocability of directives against individuals would be a sign of inadmissible judicial activism[104] that would lead to subverting the underlying rationale of Article 288 TFEU rooted in a clear distinction between directives and regulations.[105] In short, the recognition of horizontal direct effect would imply recognizing 'a power in the Union to enact obligations for individuals with immediate effect' which is vested with the Union only through the enactment of regulations.[106]

The CJ has also used the estoppel principle[107] to support the prohibition of horizontal direct effect. In *Faccini Dori*, it affirmed that the case law on direct effect of directives seeks to prevent 'the State from taking advantage of its own failure to comply with Union law'.[108] Indeed, in the view of the Court, the estoppel doctrine enables the conferral of rights to individuals in vertical situations as it aims to prevent the Member States from benefiting from their failure, which would result from a non-implementation of a directive or its delayed transposition. Consequently, the recognition of horizontal direct effect shall be excluded because individuals cannot be held liable for the Member States' failures.[109]

A closely related reason implied in the prohibition of horizontal direct effect of directives stems from the circumstance that the private individual against whom a directive is invoked cannot be subject to specific, additional obligations because it is not up to them to implement it. In particular, at the heart of the Court's approach is the protection of legitimate expectations, whereby natural and legal persons cannot be charged with a given act of commission or omission contrary to the directive if they have acted in accordance with one or more rules of national law in force at the time.[110] The CJ has held that 'the principle of legal certainty prevents directives from creating obligations for individuals'[111] because the recognition of horizontal direct effect would cause insecurity towards individuals who should be able to rely on national law.[112] Natural and legal persons, therefore, would be impaired should an obligation not deriving from national law be imposed on them.[113]

[103] D. Curtin, *The Province of Government: Delimiting the Direct Effect of Directives in the Common Law Context* (1990) 15 *European Law Review* 195, observed that the CJ relied on a literal interpretation of Article 288 TFEU.
[104] As noted by C. A. Varner, *The Effectiveness of European Community Law with Specific Regard to Directives: The Critical Step Not Taken by the European Court of Justice* (2001) 22 *Michigan Journal of International Law* 457, 476: 'the argument is that if the court continues to pursue judicial activism, it will lose all credibility and Member States will not respect its decisions at all.'
[105] As observed by K. Lenaerts, J. A. Gutiérrez-Fons, *Les méthodes*, 13, '*un des exemples les plus célèbres où la Cour s'est servie de l'interprétation littérale pour fonder son appréciation est la jurisprudence concernant l'absence d'effet direct horizontal des directives*'.
[106] *Faccini Dori* (n 96), para. 24.
[107] *See* also § 3.1 of Chapter III.
[108] *Faccini Dori* (n 96), para. 22.
[109] *See* S. Prechal, *Directives in EC Law*, 2nd ed., Oxford, Oxford University Press, 2005, 223.
[110] *See* CJ, *Wells*, C-201/02, EU:C:2004:12, para. 56.
[111] *Wells* (n 110), para. 56.
[112] *See* S. Prechal, *Directives*, 257.
[113] As noted by S. Prechal, *Directives*, 257.

On the other hand, the problems raised by the prohibition of horizontal direct effect cannot be neglected. They are significant and apt to undermine both the effectiveness of EU law and the adequate protection of individuals who are affected by the poor compliance record of Member States towards the implementation of EU directives. In this framework, the CJ attempted to balance the pursuance of these two goals with the respect of its own case law through several alternative mechanisms, referred to by the Court in its rulings, immediately after denying, explicitly or implicitly, directives' horizontal direct effect: the action for damages against the State; a broad understanding of the concept of the State; the remedy of consistent interpretation; the distinction between inadmissible horizontal direct effect, on the one hand, and, admissible negative repercussions for third (private) parties resulting from directives' incidental/triangular effect, on the other; and the joint application of directives with general principles of EU law and/or the Charter of Fundamental Rights. While the first and second remedies will be tackled in the following section, the third and fourth will be carefully examined in sections 5–6. Section 6 will be devoted to an overall critical appraisal of the directives' lack of horizontality. Overall, sections 5–6 will challenge the idea that a directive can never be invoked in such a manner as to affect the legal position of another individual.[114] That which is challenged, therefore, is the very exclusion of directives' horizontal direct effect.

4. Inconclusive responses to the NHDE rule: stretching the notion of public authority and reliance on the State liability remedy

With regard to the principle of State liability for loss and damage caused to individuals as a result of breaches of EU law (for which the State can be held responsible), including of directives, as is known, such action 'is inherent in the system of the treaties on which the EU is based'.[115] It is, therefore, a remedy at the disposal of the individual to obtain redress due to the non-implementation or the delayed or incorrect implementation of a directive by the authorities of a Member State[116] which caused the damages suffered by a private party.[117] However, the State liability remedy, while being a key means of rights' protection, is a different avenue from direct effect, as is clear from EU case law.[118] It is one thing to guarantee an individual the enjoyment of a right deriving from an EU rule, in particular through the disapplication of the illegitimate national rule, but quite another to grant them compensation on the assumption that a breach by the State has materialized. Compensation does not generally allow the individual to fully enjoy their rights, that is, to be restored to the subjective legal situation they enjoyed before the breach of EU law.

As to the other mechanism developed by the CJ to bypass the prohibition of horizontal direct effect for directives, that is, the notion of *public* authority 'covered' by vertical direct effect, there is no doubt that the broad and functional interpretation of what is to be

[114] In these terms, *see* the opinion of AG Spuznar of 15 July 2021, *Thelen Technopark*, EU:C:2021:620, para. 24.

[115] *See*, *inter alia*, CJ, *Kantarev*, C-571/16, EU:C:2018:807, para. 92.

[116] *See* the observations by AG Lenz, opinion of 9 February 1994, *Paola Faccini Dori v Recreb Srl*, C-91/92, EU:C:1994:45, para. 38.

[117] For a brief account on the interplay between direct effect and the State liability remedy, *see* § 3.3 of Chapter III and § 3 of Chapter IV.

[118] *See*, recently, *Thelen Technopark* (n 101), paras 43–48.

considered 'State', from the *Marshall I* judgment onwards,[119] allows some drawbacks to be overcome. According to the CJ, it is sufficient, in order for the respondent body to be held liable under EU law, that it is a private entity acting under the State's authority or control, for example an undertaking entrusted with the provision of a public service,[120] irrespective 'of the capacity in which [it] is acting, whether employer or public authority'.[121] A reading of the EU jurisprudence shows that bodies holding 'indirect public power' shall also be included in the concept of State.[122] According to the CJ, in fact, such flexibility in the definition of 'public' is 'necessary to prevent the State from taking advantage of its own failure to comply with Community law'.[123] In *Foster*[124] it was stated, in its 'famous' paragraph 18, that there are two conditions for a rule of a directive to be deemed enforceable against private individuals: *(i)* they must be entities subject to the authority or control of the State and *(ii)* they must have special powers exceeding the limits of those resulting from the normal rules that apply to relations between individuals.[125] In the same vein, in the ruling it was observed, in paragraph 20, that a body,

> whatever its legal form, which has been made responsible, pursuant to a measure adopted by the State, for providing a public service under the control of the State and has for that purpose powers beyond those which result from the normal rules applicable in relations between individuals is included in any event among the bodies against which the provisions of a directive capable of having direct effect may be relied upon.[126]

As for the more or less conjunctive nature of the two conditions, after years of ambiguity since the *Foster* case and in subsequent cases where the requirement of State control had been the only one employed by the Court,[127] the exclusion of the need for such cumulation was clearly asserted in the *Farrell* ruling,[128] following, in this way, the approach proposed by AG Sharpston[129] and consequently confirming the expansive scope of EU case law. As a matter of fact, *Farrell* served to clarify *Foster* whereby the CJ stated that individuals can rely on EU directives 'against organisations or bodies which are subject to the authority or control of the State or have special powers beyond those which result from the normal rules

[119] *See*, *ex multis*, *Farrell* (n 101); CJ, *Vasil Ivanov Georgiev v Tehnicheski universitet - Sofia, filial Plovdiv*, joined cases C-250/09 and C-268/09, EU:C:2010:699; CJ, *Rosa María Gavieiro Gavieiro (C-444/09) and Ana María Iglesias Torres (C-456/09) v Consellería de Educación e Ordenación Universitaria de la Xunta de Galicia*, joined cases C-444/09 and C-456/09, EU:C:2010:819; CJ, *Portgás* (n 101); CJ, *OSA––Ochranný svaz autorský pro práva k dílům hudebním o.s. v Léčebné lázně Mariánské Lázně a.s.*, C-351/12, EU:C:2014:110.

[120] *Portgás* (n 101).

[121] *Marshall I* (n 96), para. 49.

[122] In these terms, *see* the opinion by AG Lenz, *Faccini Dori* (n 116), para. 34.

[123] *Marshall I* (n 96), para. 49; *see* also, amongst others, CJ, *Gavieiro* (n 119), para. 82.

[124] *See* also CJ, *Renato Collino and Luisella Chiappero v Telecom Italia SpA*, C-343/98, EU:C:2000:23, para. 23. On the nature of the regulatory powers under scrutiny by the courts in *Foster* and subsequent case law, *see*, in the abundant literature, D. Curtin, *The Province*; E. Szyszczak, *Case C-188/89, Foster and Others v British Gas plc* (1990) 27 *Common Market Law Review* 859; A. Albors-Llorens, *The Direct Effect of EU Directives: Fresh Controversy or a Storm in a teacup?* (2014) 39 *European Law Review* 850.

[125] CJ, *A. Foster and Others v British Gas plc*, C-188/89, EU:C:1990:313, para. 18.

[126] *Foster* (n 125), para. 20. *See* also *Smith* (n 101), para. 45; CJ, *Pensions-Sicherungs-Verein*, C-168/18, EU:C:2019:1128, para. 48; CJ, *Y*, C-636/19, EU:C:2021:885, para. 60.

[127] *See*, for instance, CJ, *Commission v Austria*, C-205/98, EU:C:2000:493 and CJ, *Andrea Vassallo*, Case C-180/04, EU:C:2006:518.

[128] On this judgment, *see* A. Sanchez-Graells, *Interesting Clarification (and Broadening) of the Foster Test on 'Emanation of the State' for Purposes of Direct Effect of EU Directives (C-413/15)*, in *How to Crack a Nut. A Blog on European Law*, 10 October 2017, available at http://www.howtocrackanut.com/blog/2017/10/10/interesting-clarification-of-the-foster-test-on-emanation-of-the-state-for-purposes-of-direct-effect-of-eu-directives-c-41315.

[129] Opinion of AG Sharpston of 22 June 2017, *Farrell* (n 101), EU:C:2017:492.

applicable to relations between individuals'.[130] Accordingly, the conditions that the body concerned must be subject to the authority or control of the State and must possess special powers 'cannot be conjunctive'.[131]

In any event, the CJ's reasoning continues to be problematic upstream because, as several cases show,[132] the respondent bodies, while public in nature, in a more or less broad sense, cannot be held liable for failing to comply with the transposition of directives invoked against them.[133] That is to say, to a large extent, the logic of estoppel, at least in its strictest and most literal version, which lies at the heart of the prohibition of directives' horizontal direct effect,[134] seems to fall away and, therefore, the contours of the rationale underlying this prohibition appear, from this point of view, unclear.

5. Disguised forms of horizontal direct effect

5.1 Triangular/incidental effects

A further avenue used by the CJ to *de facto* overcome the prohibition of horizontal direct effect of directives, while continuing to confirm it on paper, is the recognition of so-called triangular and incidental effects. A survey of the ambiguous EU jurisprudence rendered pursuant to Article 267 TFEU[135] allows three situations to be identified.

[130] *Farrell* (n 101), para. 33. *See* also, most recently, *Gabel Industria Tessile* (n 90), para. 26.

[131] *Farrell* (n 101), para. 28.

[132] As noted in *Editorial Comments. Horizontal direct effect—A Law of Diminishing Coherence?* (2006) 1 *Common Market Law Review* 1, 3, in respect to *Foster* (n 125). The same problems arise for several other judgments, such as *Collino* (n 124), para. 23, and CJ, *Rieser Internationale Transporte GmbH v Autobahnen- und Schnellstraßen-Finanzierungs-AG (Asfinag)*, C-157/02, EU:C:2004:76, paras 22–28.

[133] On this matter, *see* R. Scarborough, *Directives and the Doctrine of Direct Effect: A Critique of* Marshall v. Southampton Area Health Authority (1992) 1992 *University of Chicago Legal Forum* 315, 324–327; W. van Gerven, *The Horizontal Effect of Directive Provisions Revisited – The Reality of Catchwords*, in D. Curtin, T. Heukels (eds.), *Institutional Dynamics of European Integration. Essays in Honour of Henry G. Schermers*, The Hague, Martinus Nijhoff, 1994, 337–353, 343; P. Manin, *L'invocabilité des directives: quelques interrogations* (1990) 26 *Revue trimestrielle de droit européen* 669, 691; G. Betlem, *Medium Hard Law—Still No Horizontal Direct Effect of European Community Directives after* Faccini Dori (1994–1995) 1 *Columbia Journal of European Law* 469, 484; A. Dashwood, *From Van Duyn to Mangold via Marshall: Reducing Direct Effect to Absurdity?*, in *Cambridge Yearbook of European Legal Studies*, vol. 9, 2007, 81–109, 88–89; F. Costamagna, *Diritti fondamentali*, 35. *See* the opinion of van Gerven of 26 January 1993, *Marshall v Southampton and South West Hampshire Area Health Authority (Marshall II)*, C-271/91, EU:C:1993:30, para. 12.

[134] In favour 'of discarding estoppel altogether', *see* the comments by G. Betlem, *Medium*, 485. More generally, on the limits of the estoppel doctrine, *see* G. Winter, *The Directive: Problems of Construction and Directions for Reform*, in G. Winter, *Sources and Categories of European Union Law*, Baden-Baden, Nomos, 1996, 487–506, 503.

[135] Tough criticism has been raised, amongst others, by D. Colgan, *Triangular Situations: The Coup de Grâce for the Denial of Horizontal Direct Effect of Community Directives* (2002) 8 *European Public Law* 545; M. Dougan, *When Worlds Collide! Competing Visions of the Relationship between Direct Effect and Supremacy* (2007) 44 *Common Market Law Review* 931, 957–963; E. Dubout, *L'invocabilité d'éviction des directives dans les litiges horizontaux. Le 'bateau ivre' a-t il sombré?* (2010) 46 *Revue trimestrielle de droit européen* 277; R. Schütze, *Direct Effects and Indirect Effects of Union Law*, in R. Schütze, T. Tridimas (eds.), *Oxford Principles of European Union Law: The European Union Legal Order: Volume I*, Oxford, Oxford University Press, 2018, 265–299, 281–283; L. Squintani, J. Lindeboom, *The Normative Impact of Invoking Directives: Casting Light on Direct Effect and the Elusive Distinction between Obligations and Mere Adverse Repercussions*, in *Yearbook of European Law*, vol. 38, 2019, 18–72. *See* also the critical appraisal by C. W. A., Timmermans, *Community Directives Revisited*, in *Yearbook of European Law*, vol. 17, 1997, 1–28, 16–23; C. Hilson, T. Downes, *Making Sense of Rights: Community Rights in EC Law* (1999) 24 *European Law Review* 121; M. Dougan, *The Disguised Vertical Direct Effect of Directives?* (2000) 59 *Cambridge Law Journal* 586; M. Lenz, D. S. Tynes, L. Young, *Horizontal What? Back to Basics* (2000) 25 *European Law Review* 509; S. Weatherill, *Breach of Directives and Breach of Contract* (2001) 26 *European Law Review* 177; T. Tridimas, *Black, White, and Shades of Grey: Horizontality of Directives Revisited*, in *Yearbook of European Law*, vol. 21, 2002, 327–354.

The first two have been the focus of scholars' attention since the early nineties and differ depending on whether the dispute, at the domestic level, formally arises between an individual and the State or between private individuals. In particular, the EU judges consider that the provisions of a directive can be invoked, in the context of so-called triangular relationships, by the individual against the State, with side effects[136] against natural and legal persons who have relied over time on domestic law (first situation), or they can be invoked, as an 'exception of illegality' or 'incidental plea',[137] in disputes between private individuals (second situation). At the heart of both strands of cases is the request by a private individual before a national court to disapply an internal rule incompatible with a directive which, in turn, triggered an illegitimate private behaviour. In addition to these two situations, there is a third on, which has been described and investigated already in sections 3.1 and 5 of Chapter III, as well as section 4 of Chapter 5, from the standpoint of its comparison with inverse vertical direct efect. This situation differs from the other two since the dispute, at the domestic level, is between two public subjects, that is, between the public plaintiff invoking the rule of a directive and the defendant, as a distinct branch of the State, which has allegedly incorrectly enforced this rule (third situation).

Based on the case law, it can be said that in the first strand of rulings (private vs. State/triangular relations) the consequences of a vertical dispute between a private party and the State affect the legal situation of a third private party. This would include the following judgments: *Fratelli Costanzo*,[138] *Busseni*,[139] *Wells*,[140] *Bernáldez*,[141] *Pafitis*,[142] *Arcor*,[143] *WWF*,[144] *Kraaijeveld*,[145] *Landelijke Vereniging tot Behoud van de Waddenzee and Nederlandse Vereniging tot Bescherming van Vogels*,[146] *Linster*,[147] *Smith & Nephew*,[148] *Daihatsu*,[149] *Santex*,[150] *Portgás*,[151] and *Infraestruturas de Portugal SA*.[152] In the second strand (private vs. private), the non-compliance with directives requiring Member States to notify to the Commission new technical regulations or measures impacting the internal market has the

[136] In the literature the expression 'incidental effects' was used for the first time by A. Arnull, *Editorial. The Incidental Effect of Directives* (1999) 24 *European Law Review* 1. S. Prechal, *Directives*, 261, refers to 'horizontal side effects'. *See* also K. Lackhoff, H. Nyssens, *Direct Effect of Directives in Triangular Situations* (1998) 23 *European Law Review* 397; R. Král, *Questioning the Limits of Invocability of EU Directives in Triangular Situations*' (2010) 16 *European Public Law* 239. For a recent detailed survey, *see* L. Cecchetti, *L'efficacia diretta delle direttive negli ordinamenti nazionali, oggi: questioni ancora aperte alla vigilia del 50° anniversario della sentenza* van Duyn (2023) 3 *Eurojus* 151.

[137] In these terms, *see* S. Prechal, *Van Duyn and the nature of Directives*, in P. Craig, R. Schütze (eds.), *Landmark Cases in EU Law*, Oxford, Hart.

[138] CJ, *Fratelli Costanzo SpA v Comune di Milano*, 103/88, EU:C:1989:256.

[139] CJ, *Acciaierie and Ferriere Busseni SpA*, C-221/88, EU:C:1990:84.

[140] *Wells* (n 110).

[141] CJ, *Criminal proceedings against Rafael Ruiz Bernáldez*, C-129/94, EU:C:1996:143.

[142] CJ, *Panagis Pafitis and Others v Trapeza Kentrikis Ellados A.E. and Others*, C-441/93, EU:C:1996:92.

[143] *Arcor* (n 102).

[144] CJ, *World Wildlife Fund (WWF) and Others v Autonome Provinz Bozen and Others*, C-435/97, EU:C:1999:418.

[145] CJ, *Aannemersbedrijf P.K. Kraaijeveld BV e.a. v Gedeputeerde Staten van Zuid-Holland*, C-72/95, EU:C:1996:404.

[146] CJ, *Landelijke Vereniging tot Behoud van de Waddenzee and Nederlandse Vereniging tot Bescherming van Vogels v Staatssecretaris van Landbouw, Natuurbeheer en Visserij*, C-127/02, EU:C:2004:482.

[147] CJ, C-287/98, *Grand Duchy of Luxemburg v Berthe Linster, Aloyse Linster and Yvonne Linster*, EU:C:2000:3.

[148] CJ, *The Queen v The Medicines Control Agency, ex parte Smith & Nephew Pharmaceuticals Ltd and Primecrown Ltd v The Medicine Control Agency*, C-201/94, EU:C:1996:432.

[149] CJ, *Verband deutscher Daihatsu-Händler eV*, C-97/96, EU:C:1997:581.

[150] CJ, *Santex SpA*, C-327/00, EU:C:2003:109.

[151] *Portgás* (n 101).

[152] CJ, *Infraestruturas de Portugal, SA and Futrifer Indústrias Ferroviárias, SA v Toscca—Equipamentos em Madeira Lda*, C-66/22, EU:C:2023:1016, on whose peculiarities, *see* extensively § 5 of Chapter V.

effect of rendering them inapplicable in a dispute between private parties.[153] This would include the following judgments: *Cia Security International*,[154] *Österreichische Unilever*,[155] *Unilever*,[156] *Lemmens*,[157] *Smith*,[158] and *Airbnb*.[159]

As regards the first strand, the *Fratelli Costanzo* case is illustrative in that the application by the municipality of Milan of Council Directive 71/305/EEC of 26 July 1971 concerning the co-ordination of procedures for the award of public works contracts, hitherto unimplemented,[160] resulted in the exclusion of an offer which complied with national law but not with the directive, submitted by the company Fratelli Costanzo SpA in a call for tenders, and, consequently, in the award of that contract to a competing undertaking whose tender followed, instead, the procedure laid down in Article 29(5) of the directive. In short, in triangular relationships, the individual invokes the directive against the State with the consequence that the position of other interested private parties is compromised. In *Wells* it was affirmed that an individual could submit a claim based directly on a directive against a public authority, despite the emergence of consequences which are detrimental to another individual. The CJ has admitted that, under certain circumstances, 'mere adverse repercussions on the rights of third parties, even if the repercussions are certain, do not justify preventing an individual from invoking the provisions of a directive against the Member State concerned'.[161] The *cul de sac* which arises in this type of situation is that there will always be a private party whose interests are injured: the subject-owner of prerogatives safeguarded by the application of the directive or the subject-owner of prerogatives safeguarded by the application of the national rule (which is contrary to the directive).

As to the second strand of case law, the *Cia Security International* and *Unilever* cases, which have been already analyzed in Chapters IV and V, are useful to understand what the horizontal implications of the cases consist of.[162] At the heart of the two rulings is the interpretation of Council Directive 83/189/EEC of 28 March 1983 laying down a procedure for

[153] As noted by AG Spuznar in his opinion in *Thelen Technopark* (n 114), footnote 9, the directives concerned (which lie at the core of *Cia Security International*, *Unilever* and *Lemmens*) include: Council Directive 83/189/EEC of 28 March 1983 laying down a procedure for the provision of information in the field of technical standards and regulations (OJ 1983 L 109, 8), subsequently Directive 98/34/EC of the European Parliament and of the Council of 22 June 1998 laying down a procedure for the provision of information in the field of technical standards and regulations (OJ 1998 L 204, 37), and, finally, Directive (EU) 2015/1535 of the European Parliament and of the Council of 9 September 2015 laying down a procedure for the provision of information in the field of technical regulations and of rules on information society services (codification) (OJ 2015 L 241, 1); Directive 2000/31/EC of the European Parliament and of the Council of 8 June 2000 on certain legal aspects of information society services, in particular electronic commerce, in the Internal Market (Directive on electronic commerce) (OJ 2000 L 178, 1). In addition to these directives, it shall be recalled that in CJ, *Österreichische Unilever*, C-77/97, EU:C:1999:30, and *Smith* (n 101), the application of Council Directive 76/768/EEC of 27 July 1976 on the approximation of the laws of the Member States relating to cosmetic products (OJ 1976 L 262, 169) and Third Council Directive 90/232/EEC of 14 May 1990 on the approximation of the laws of the Member States relating to insurance against civil liability in respect of the use of motor vehicles (OJ 1990 L 129, 33) were, respectively, assessed.

[154] CJ, *CIA Security International SA v Signalson SA and Securitel SPRL*, C-194/94, EU:C:1996:172, para. 48.

[155] *Österreichische Unilever* (n 153), paras 33–37, whereby the matter of incidental effect was not even mentioned.

[156] CJ, *Unilever Italia SpA v Central Food SpA*, C-443/98, EU:C:2000:496, paras 44 and 50–51.

[157] CJ, *Lemmens*, C-226/97, EU:C:1998:296, paras 32–38.

[158] *Smith* (n 101), paras 50–57, whereby the duty of disapplication, in the light of the EU directive, has been excluded.

[159] CJ, *Airbnb Ireland UC*, C-390/18, EU:C:2019:1112, paras 88–100.

[160] Council Directive 71/305/EEC of 26 July 1971 concerning the co-ordination of procedures for the award of public works contracts (OJ L 185 1.08.1985, 5), now repealed and replaced by Council Directive 93/37/EEC of 14 June 1993 concerning the coordination of procedures for the award of public works contracts (OJ L 199 54 21.4.1994).

[161] *Wells* (n 110), para. 57.

[162] In fact, as stressed by R. Schütze, *European Union Law*, 102: 'what else was this but horizontal direct effect?'

the provision of information in the field of technical standards and regulations, that is, of a directive that subjects States to a notification and control procedure, prescribing obligations that the national authorities must comply with even during the so-called standstill phase.[163] In theory, the directive does not directly affect the regulation of inter-individual relations, with a view to guaranteeing the effectiveness of EU law.[164] However, from the point of view of the individual, a problem does exist because the directive precludes the application of a national regulation or measure issued (in violation of the technical standards required by EU law, or) without being notified to the Commission. The result of this preclusion is that those who have complied with the new non-notified obligations introduced in the domestic law cannot, according to the CJ, invoke them against those who have continued to comply with the old national ones. In these cases, the dispute is formally between private parties, not between a private party and the State as is the case in triangular relationships (first strand of case law).

In substantive terms, however, it may be argued that the triangular dimension exists also in the second strand of case law since the action of an individual, albeit directed against another individual, is aimed at challenging the conduct assumed by the State, which is therefore involved as a 'legal outsider'[165] and, for this reason, connotes, through an element of verticality, a dispute involving two private parties. *Mutatis mutandis*, the reasoning developed in *Cia Security International* and *Unilever* is reiterated in *Airbnb*, with reference to the obligation laid down in Article 3(4) of Directive 2000/31/EC of the European Parliament and of the Council of 8 June 2000 on certain legal aspects of information society services, in particular electronic commerce, in the internal market. In the case, in fact, it was observed that Article 3(4)(b) of Directive 2000/31 must be interpreted as meaning that, in criminal proceedings with an ancillary civil action, individuals may oppose the application to them of measures of a Member State restricting the freedom to provide an information society service which those individuals provide from another Member State 'where those measures were not notified in accordance with that provision'.[166] Thus, a Member State's failure to fulfil its obligation to make such notification in respect to a service provided by an operator established on the territory of another Member State renders the measure unenforceable against individuals.[167] As emphasized by the CJ, 'as was the case in relation to the technical rules not notified in a number of previous judgments', which can be traced back to the second strand of case law referred to above, 'the fact that a non-notified measure restricting the freedom to provide information society services is unenforceable may be relied on, not only in criminal proceedings . . . but also in a dispute between individuals'.[168] The novelty of the ruling, therefore, lies in the transposition of the reasoning on technical standards to a different case, which is in turn applicable to numerous other situations concerning different areas of EU law, in particular restrictive measures adopted at the national level as an exception to freedoms of movement—in this case, of services.

The third situation is very rare, as has been mentioned in other chapters,[169] and recently clearly arises in the *Autorità Garante della Concorrenza e del Mercato* judgment of April

[163] On the duty of standstill and directives, *see* § 3.1 of Chapter III.
[164] *See CIA Security International* (n 154), para. 40 and *Unilever* (n 156), paras 44, 50–51.
[165] D. Colgan, *Triangular Situations*, 547.
[166] *Airbnb Ireland* (n 159), para. 100.
[167] *Airbnb Ireland* (n 159), para. 96.
[168] *Airbnb Ireland* (n 159), para. 97.
[169] *See* especially § 4 of Chapter V, relating to the case law beyond *Autorità Garante della Concorrenza e del Mercato*. *See* also § 11 of Chapter V.

2023. In that case the domestic dispute was between two public entities, that is, a horizontal dispute involving only the State, *rectius*, two of its branches, and not private parties.[170] The CJ, in a preliminary ruling stemming from a request by the Regional Administrative Court of Lecce—which originated from a dispute between the Italian Competition Authority and the municipality of Ginosa—, attributed direct effect to Article 12 of Directive 2006/123/EC of the European Parliament and of the Council of 12 December 2006 on services in the internal market and, in so doing, in line with the previous *Promoimpresa* ruling,[171] imposed an obligation on Member States to apply an impartial and transparent selection procedure to potential candidates wishing to obtain seaside concessions, while prohibiting the automatic renewal of such concessions for the occupation of the maritime domain. The *Autorità Garante della Concorrenza e del Mercato* decision cannot be subsumed under inverse vertical direct effect either, as some scholars have argued, since it is not an EU rule invoked by the State against an individual.[172] Nor can it be subsumed into the jurisprudential strand on incidental effects, *à la Cia Security International* and *Unilever*, since it is not an EU norm invoked by an individual against another individual. It cannot be traced back to a triangular situation either, since it is not an EU rule invoked by the individual against the State with detrimental effects for another individual, but by a public entity against another public entity, with possible detrimental effects for the current private contractor and, on the other hand, possibly beneficial effects for future potential tender candidates. It is, therefore, a peculiar situation and is also different from the one under consideration in the ruling of 9 November 2021 delivered by the Italian Council of State, which, as recalled in section 11 of Chapter V, recognized the direct effect of Article 12 of Directive 2006/123/EC in a dispute where such provision was invoked by a municipality against a concessionaire—whose request for prorogation was rejected by the former—rather than by a public body against another branch of the State.[173]

That being said, it is easy to understand that the subdivision made above, although useful in reconstructive terms, is not in itself fully satisfactory since a clear-cut boundary between these three strands of case law, from the point of view of the legal effects of directives on

[170] On this point, for an interesting case note, *see* A. Nato, *Le concessioni balneari, tra mercato interno, armonizzazione e tutela della proprietà: primato, effetto diretto e disapplicazione nella causa Autorità garante della Concorrenza e del Mercato c. Comune di Ginosa* (2023) 2 *Eurojus* 22.

[171] On such ruling, as well as on the intricacies of the 'seaside concessions saga' in Italy, *see* the literature cited in footnotes 81 and 326, respectively, §§ 4 and 11 of Chapter V.

[172] As recalled in § 4 of Chapter V, the Italian Council of State was called to rule upon the national regulation of seaside concessions in the judgment Nos. 17 and 18 of 9 November 2021 concerning a dispute between the municipality of Lecce and a contractor, and in the ruling No. 2192 of 1 March 2023 about a dispute between two public bodies, notably the Italian Competition Authority and the municipality of Manduria. *See* also the preliminary reference by the Council of State No. 8010 of 15 September 2022, that led to the ongoing preliminary ruling procedure of CJ, *Società Italiana Imprese Balneari Srl v Comune di Rosignano Marittimo*, C-598/22, and the order No. 8184 of 6 September 2023, which both concerned the dispute between a private company and the municipality of Rosignano Marittimo.

[173] As for this case, in the Italian literature there are those who argue that at stake was a situation of inverse vertical direct effect E. Cannizzaro, *Demanio marittimo: effetti in malam partem di direttive europee? In margine alle sentenze 17 e 18/2021 dell'Ad. Plen. del Consiglio di Stato*, 30 December 2021, available at https://www.giustiziainsieme.it/en/diritto-ue/2092-effetti-in-malam-partem-di-direttive-europee-in-margine-alle-sentenze-17-e-18-2021-dell-adunanza-plenaria-del-consiglio-di-stato-di-enzo-cannizzaro; F. Ferraro, *Diritto dell'Unione e concessioni demaniali: più luci o più ombre nelle sentenze gemelle dell'Adunanza Plenaria?* (2021) 46 *Diritto e Società* 359; G. Greco, *La Corte di giustizia ritorna sulle concessioni balneari precisandone le regole: problemi superatie problemi ancora aperti in sede di applicazione nazionale del diritto UE* (2023) 14 *Federalismi.it*, 125, while others exclude this relying on the inexistence of obligations stemming directly from Directive 2006/123/EC R. Mastroianni, *L'Adunanza Plenaria del Consiglio di Stato e le concessioni balneari: due passi avanti e uno indietro?* (2022) 1 *Eurojus* 105 and A. Circolo, *Un 'approdo' per le concessioni balneari: l'Adunanza plenaria nega la proroga automatica delle concessioni*, in *Quaderni AISDUE 2021*, Naples, Editoriale Scientifica, 2022, 155–164).

individuals, cannot be drawn. The identification of the effects is not made possible by the Court's very succinct line of reasoning. In this context, the decisive problem, for all of the above cases, is to grasp what the distinction between a non-admissible horizontal direct effect and an admissible indirect imposition of burdens for individuals in atypical inter-private situations consists of, taking into account the two recurring elements of EU case law. The first is that the original defect, in the perspective of EU law, lies in the non-implementation or inadequate implementation of a directive by the State.[174] The second consists in the recognition of the directive as an act which is, on one hand, suitable to entail indirectly negative effects for individuals as result of the application of EU law and, on the other, is unable to directly prescribe obligations for the latter. Two consequences originate from the jurisprudence of the CJ. The first is the unenforceability against private parties, according to the Court, by the State or the individual (depending on the nature of the dispute), of national legislation in conflict with the directive. The second consequence is the occurrence of adverse repercussions for the individual who has acted in accordance with domestic law and who, on the basis of that law, has benefited, could benefit, or could have benefited, knowingly or unknowingly, from the national authorities' failure to transpose the directive.[175]

The distinction between permissible and impermissible consequences for natural and legal persons[176] is first clearly identified only in the *Wells* judgment, then reaffirmed in *Arcor* and finally made explicit in *Unilever*. The Court's reasoning hinges on the observation that the provisions of a directive regulating the legal positions of private individuals cannot be invoked (not only by the State against an individual, but also) by an individual against another individual, and thus, *per se*, cannot introduce obligations vis-à-vis the latter, operating as a parameter for the legality of the (disapplied) internal rules. However, the CJ makes it clear in its case law that a directive is by no means *per se* irrelevant in horizontal relationships. In *Wells*, on the interpretation of Council Directive 85/337/EEC of 27 June 1985 on the assessment of the impact of certain public and private projects on the environment, with reference to the granting of a new concession for the exploitation of a quarry without a prior environmental impact assessment having been carried out, the CJ observed that relations between private parties could be affected by the directive only indirectly where its rules lead to 'mere negative repercussions on the rights of third parties'.[177] The fact that mining operations had to be interrupted in order to await the outcomes of the assessment, as a result of the late fulfilment of the obligations imposed on the State, did not preclude the directive from being enforced against the quarry owners.[178]

Most recently, the CJ rendered its judgment in *Infraestruturas de Portugal SA*, which has been already examined with regard to the possible admissibility of inverse vertical direct effect of directives. In this case, the CJ did not explicitly refer to its previous case law on the triangular effects of directives. Nonetheless, the Court, in respect to the interpretation of one of the facultative grounds for exclusion enshrined in the first subparagraph of Article 57(4) of Directive 2014/24/EU, admitted that in a dispute between a private party, invoking Directive 2014/24/EU, and the State-owned company managing the Portuguese rail and

[174] As highlighted by S. Amadeo, *L'efficacia 'obiettiva' delle direttive comunitarie ed i suoi riflessi nei confronti dei privati. Riflessioni a margine delle sentenze sui casi* Linster *e* Unilever' (2001) 1 *Il Diritto dell'Unione europea* 95, 114–115, who underscores the presence of a convergence between *Fratelli Costanzo* and *Uniliver*.

[175] This is clear above all in the following two cases in which the CJ has denied directives' horizontal direct effect, as observed by L. Squintani, J. Lindeboom, *The Normative Impact*, 27: *El Corte Inglés* (n 101) and *Pfeiffer* (n 101).

[176] *See* C. W. A., Timmermans, *Community*, 16–20.

[177] *Wells* (n 110), para. 57.

[178] *Wells* (n 110), para. 57.

road infrastructure, negative repercussions for this latter undertaking could be deemed legitimate. This is so given that Portugal infringed the directive for not having transposed internally the facultative grounds for exclusion. The plaintiff in the case, who was seeking to be awarded the public contract, could then invoke a directive against the State, even if other companies may be affected by the application of such directive.

In the *Unilever* case, which, as said, was entrenched in a domestic dispute between two private companies, the reasoning is even clearer: if a directive, in addition to not creating obligations for individuals, 'does not in any way define the substantive scope of the legal rule on the basis of which the national court must decide the case before it',[179] the individual may rely on it, even in horizontal relationships, before a court, even though its application affects third parties.

In *Autorità Garante della Concorrenza e del Mercato*, the CJ, while not reflecting at all on the relationship between this case and the two strands mentioned above, in affirming the direct effect of Article 12 of Directive 2006/123/EC in the context of a reference for a preliminary ruling made by a national court called upon to settle a dispute between two public bodies, implicitly recognized that in the case the effects produced on private third-party litigants were to be deemed 'mere repercussions', by analogy with what had been established in the other two strands of case law. That is to say, it would not be a question of the invocation, by a public subject against another public body, of rules of a directive imposing obligations on the individual, but 'only' of obligations imposed on States for the benefit of potential private candidates. That the invocation of this directive by one public body against another results, indirectly, in the creation of detrimental effects for a private party is not seen by the Court as a decisive obstacle to trigger disapplication.

Against this background, in the literature, four viewpoints have been detected to justify EU case law on incidental effects or triangular relationships without calling into question the rule of the prohibition of the horizontal direct effect of directives. First of all, it has been said that since the problem of horizontality normally arises in the context of cases concerning directives entailing exclusionary, not substitutive, effects, and since this type of effect has not been traced back by several Advocates General and scholars to direct effect,[180] the Court's case law would not be such as to challenge the axiom of non-horizontality. According to some scholars, if this were the case and, therefore, the principle of primacy did not act in combination with direct effect, problems of consistency with the prohibition of horizontal direct effect could not even logically arise.[181] In particular, AG Saggio, in his opinion in *Océano*, first emphasized that the task of national courts as EU courts[182] implies that they must always guarantee the primacy of European law over domestic law. Subsequently, the AG clarified that the exclusion of inconsistent national provisions serves to prevent the harmonizing action of EU directives from being undermined by unilateral (commissive and omissive) conduct of the Member States. The decisive assertion is the following: the exclusionary effect deriving from the application of EU directives can achieve its results on the condition that it is realized 'whenever the national rule comes into consideration for the

[179] *Unilever* (n 156), para. 51. *See* also the opinion by AG Spuznar, *Thelen Technopark* (n 114), para. 49.
[180] *See* extensively Chapter IV.
[181] On this matter, *see* the considerations by A. Dashwood, *From* Van Duyn, 101–104; M. Dougan, *When Worlds Collide!*, 949–953; T. Tridimas, *Black*, 343–346; G. Di Federico, *Il recepimento delle direttive nella giurisprudenza della Corte di Giustizia*, in Di Federico, G., Odone, C. (ed.), *Il recepimento delle direttive dell'Unione europea nella prospettiva delle regioni italiane. Modelli e soluzioni*, Naples, Editoriale Scientifica, 2010, 1–68, 55.
[182] On national courts as ordinary courts of EU law, *see* § 4 of Chapter II.

purpose of resolving a dispute, irrespective of the public or private status of the parties concerned'.[183] Such an approach aimed at asserting a duty to disapply outside direct effect, however, cannot be accepted. As written in Chapter IV and recalled in both section 1 of Chapter V and in this section, since the duty to disapply is always a result of primacy and direct effect, the exclusionary effect, that is, disapplication, shall be considered a form of direct effect.

The second avenue to bypass the prohibition of horizontal direct effect of directives consists in arguing that if the rules are contained in a 'private law directive', that is, in a directive aimed at regulating inter-individual relations, like in *Faccini Dori*, the prohibition of horizontal direct effect shall apply so that only alternative remedies, such as consistent interpretation or the State liability doctrine, could play a role.[184] If, on the other hand, at stake is a 'public law directive',[185] that is, a directive intended not so much to directly govern inter-individual relations but rather to regulate vertical relations between individuals and States, imposing obligations on the latter, as in *Cia Security International* and *Unilever*, the provisions contained therein could be invoked in legal proceedings (also) against private parties (incidental effect) or against them in the context of a dispute against the State (triangular relations). This reconstruction on the case law has led authors to focus on the personal and material scope of directives, with the result that a directive could be invoked and applied also in horizontal disputes in order to seek disapplication of a conflicting national law, as well as of the resulting behaviour by the private party, in case the public measure is the source of the infringement of the directive and the directive does not impose direct obligations on the individuals.[186] As a specification of such theory, one author in particular, by applying his reasoning on direct effect of EU fundamental freedoms[187] also to directives, proposed shifting from prohibiting horizontal direct effect to prohibiting giving effect to directives when their personal scope includes actions by private parties. Unimplemented directives which do not cover such actions could thus be invoked in horizontal situations when that to be challenged is the legality of State actions.[188]

The problem with both these reconstructions is that they do not guarantee sufficient legal certainty. Indeed, there are many doubts as to whether it is possible to identify the boundary between directives aimed at regulating the legal situation of natural and legal persons, and essentially impose obligations on them, on the one hand, and, on the other, directives that instead regulate the behaviour of States. It seems even more difficult to identify, upstream and in systematic terms, those directives which include in their scope actions of private parties. Indeed, in many sectors, such as environmental law, directives generally contain provisions that, while being exclusively aimed at creating obligations for Member States, 'are nevertheless clearly capable of resulting in the imposition of direct obligations upon individuals if they were to be invoked before a national court'.[189] Admitting the application of

[183] Opinion of AG Saggio of 16 December 1999, Océano, EU:C:1999:620, para. 37. The approach taken by the AG is neither endorsed nor discussed in the judgment: CJ, *Océano Grupo Editorial SA v Rocío Murciano Quintero and Salvat Editores SA v José M. Sánchez Alcón Prades, José Luis Copano Badillo, Mohammed Berroane and Emilio Viñas Feliú*, C-240-244/98, EU:C:2000:346.

[184] This point is raised, with regard to *Océano* (n 183), by J. Stuyck, *Case Note on* Océano Grupo, in *Common Market Law Review*, 2001, 728, 735.

[185] A. Dashwood, *From* Van Duyn, 98.

[186] *See* J. H. Jans, M. J. M. Verhoeven, *Europeanisation via Consistent Interpretation and Direct Effect*, in Jans, J. H., Prechal, S., Widdershoven, R. J. G. M. (eds.), *Europeanisation of Public Law*, 2nd ed., Groningen, Europa Law Publishing, 2015, 71–132, 117 and M. Dougan, *The Disguised Vertical Direct Effect of Directives?* (2000) 59 *Cambridge Law Journal* 586, 601–605.

[187] *See* R. Schütze, *Direct Effects*, 283. *See* § 2 of this chapter.

[188] R. Schütze, *Direct Effects*, 283.

[189] L. Squintani, J. Lindeboom, *The Normative Impact*, 46.

such directives in inter-individual disputes serves necessarily to challenge the prohibition of horizontal direct effect.

The third course to circumvent the prohibition of horizontal direct effect of directives is to consider that the effect created by these acts is indeed direct but vertical in nature[190]—an atypical vertical direct effect, of course. As noted by Jans and Verhoeven, it could be said that 'vertical direct effect has clearly horizontal effects'.[191] Ensuring that individuals can invoke the rules of directives against other individuals, claiming non-compliance by the State, would also reinforce the liability regime envisaged for the national authorities as responsible bodies for the violation of the EU act.[192] This solution is based, therefore, on the fact that in triangular relationships the dispute is between private individuals and the State, whereas, when the dispute is between private individuals, there is, in any case, a breach of State origin at the roots of the incidental effect for individuals.[193] In other words, even when the dispute is between private individuals, it is always the State which has breached the directive, the position of the private party being 'assimilated entirely to that of the defaulting Member State'.[194] As Dougan put it, the rationale seems to be that 'not only the guilty public authority but also an opportunistic passer-by should be prevented from taking advantage of the Member State's substantive breach of Community law'.[195]

If, in theory, the approach last described by Dougan would make it possible to bypass, on a strictly formal level, the prohibition of horizontal direct effect, in practice it does not seem possible to affirm a substantial difference between horizontal direct effect, on the one hand, and, on the other, the effects generated on individuals incidentally or in the context of triangular relationships.[196] This holds especially true if the driver of the CJ case law is the distinction between obligations on individuals (not admissible) and mere repercussions on the latter (admissible), as a result of the application of EU directives. Moreover, as noted by the very same proponent of this theory, the individual who has not actively breached the directive will 'suffer' from the enforcement of the directive to the benefit of their opponent, while the party who has actively infringed a directive would take advantage of the prohibition of horizontal direct effect, although more 'culpable'.[197]

The fourth and last possible way to get around the prohibition of horizontal direct effect is offered by the 'normative impact theory', which consists in verifying whether the invocation of a directive before a national court leads to a change of the rules applicable in the case concerned. If it does, it would be the imposition of an obligation which is contrary, as such, to the rule of the prohibition of horizontality; if it does not, it would be a mere adverse repercussion for individuals, as such, different from direct obligations and admissible according to EU law.[198] In this vein, it might be said that this theory is the specification of the CJ's case law, whereby it was stated, as previously recalled, that a directive could apply in horizontal relationships only if it 'does not define the substantive content of the legal rule on the basis

[190] *See* M. Dougan, *The Disguised*, 586. R. Král, *Questioning the Limits*, 240, speaks of 'direct vertical invocation'.
[191] J. H. Jans, M. J. M. Verhoeven, *Europeanization*, 111.
[192] M. Dougan, *The Disguised*, 610–611.
[193] D. Colgan, *Triangular Situations*, 556–557. *See* also, in a similar vein, R. Mastroianni, *Direttive non attuate, rimedi alternativi e principio di uguaglianza (Commento all'art. 189 Trattato CE)* (1998) 1 *Il diritto dell'Unione Europea* 95 and P. J. Slot *Case C-194/94, CIA Security International SA v. Signalson SA and Securitel SPRL* (1996) 33 *Common Market Law Review* 1035, 1049.
[194] M. Dougan, *The Disguised*, 607.
[195] M. Dougan, *The Disguised*, 607.
[196] This is the stance taken by AG Maduro in his opinion of 23 May 2007, *Viking*, EU:C:2007:292, para. 40.
[197] *See* M. Dougan, *The Disguised*, 608–609. For a critique, *see* L. Squintani, J. Lindeboom, *The Normative Impact*, 44.
[198] *See* L. Squintani, J. Lindeboom, *The Normative Impact*, 71.

of which the national court was to decide the dispute before it'.[199] In fact, invoking a norm of an unimplemented directive could be possible, for an individual, if such invocation affects a norm different from the one imposing an obligation upon the other individual. In such a situation, a mere adverse repercussion, rather than an obligation, arises. This theory, however, raises a similar criticism to the one put forward in relation to the second avenue examined above: the lack of legal certainty concerning the applicable norms. In the end, the normative impact theory seems to be biased by a case-by-case approach, whose concrete functioning would inevitably depend upon the factual background and the scope of the preliminary references stemming from national courts.

Ultimately, what is certain is that when it is the State that invokes a directive vis-à-vis a private party, the risks of being confronted with a hypothesis of inverse vertical direct effect are significant, although at stake there are, in principle, 'mere adverse repercussions' rather than obligations directly imposed on the individual. Situations such as those under the *Fratelli Costanzo/Wells* and *Cia Security International/Unilever* schemes, in which the invocation is by the private party against the State or another private party, respectively, are potentially less problematic, where, of course, the directive concerned is not used to enforce duties against individuals. But, as has been seen, the boundaries between 'private law directives' and 'public law directives', as well as between 'obligations' and 'mere adverse repercussions', are fuzzy and difficult to track.

5.2 The expansion of consistent interpretation

The duty of consistent interpretation, that is, the so-called '*invocabilité d'interprétation*',[200] requires all authorities in all Member States to interpret national law, 'to the greatest extent possible, in the light of the text and the purpose' of EU law in order to achieve the results sought by the latter.[201] In this respect, the CJ has observed that domestic judges cannot claim that it is impossible for them to interpret a provision of national law in a manner that is in compliance with EU law merely because that provision has consistently been interpreted in contrast with EU law.[202] In fact, the obligation of consistent interpretation requires national courts to change or at least not follow established case law, even that of a higher court, if the case law is incompatible with EU law.[203] Rather than disapplication, in fact, at the core of these situations lies the interpretation of domestic law, *rectius*, a different way of interpreting national law that leads a judge (or the administration) to not apply previous domestic case law (or administrative practice).

[199] *See Unilever* (n 156), para. 51; *Smith* (n 101), para. 53. *See* the opinion of AG Szpunar, *Thelen Technopark* (n 114), para. 49.

[200] This is the term used in the French-speaking literature; *see*, for instance, F. Martucci, *Droit de l'Union européenne*, 3rd ed., Paris, Dalloz, 2021, 839 and 842.

[201] *See*, amongst others, CJ, *Pupino*, C-105/03, EU:C:2005:386, para. 43; CJ, *Lopes Da Silva*, C 42/11, EU:C:2012:517, para. 54; CJ, *Ognyanov*, C-554/14, EU:C:2016:835, para. 59; *Popławski II* (n 101), 73. In § 4 of Chapter IV, consistent interpretation and direct effect, most notably the consequences of disapplication, were discussed in the context of exclusionary direct effect, where consistent interpretation may intervene once disapplication has already taken place and normative *lacunae* materialize. It has been seen that consistent interpretation comes to the aid of national courts, grappling with regulatory gaps, so that through such remedy one or more further domestic rules, read in the light of EU law, may be identified to regulate the dispute, after the disapplication of that part of national law in conflict with EU law has occurred as a result of the doctrines of primacy and direct effect.

[202] *See* CJ, *Max-Planck-Gesellschaft zur Förderung der Wissenschaften*, C-684/16, EU:C:2018:874, para. 60.

[203] In this vein, see *Dansk Industri* (n 101), para. 33.

Before dwelling on the interplay between consistent interpretation, directives, and horizontality, some preliminary remarks shall be made on the relationship between such interpretive avenue and directives. As is well-known, *von Colson*, concerning the interpretation of Council Directive 76/207 on the implementation of the principle of equal treatment for men and women as regards access to employment, vocational training and promotion, and working conditions, is the first judgment in which the CJ, inspired by some of its considerations already made in *Haaga*,[204] *Bonsignore*,[205] and *Mazzalai*,[206] distinctly determined the existence of an obligation of consistent interpretation incumbent on the national authorities[207]—an obligation imposed 'from above',[208] that is, by EU law, not by domestic legal orders.

In *von Colson* many of the elements that would later become recurring features in EU jurisprudence were specified. In the ruling and in the subsequent case law, it was stated that the obligation of consistent interpretation, valid for all authorities of the Member States, 'including, for matters within their jurisdiction, the courts', derives from Article 4(3) TEU[209] and requires them to 'achieve the results' set forth by the directive, thus complying with Article 288 TFEU.[210] In particular, with regard to Article 4(3) TEU, starting with *Wagner Miret*,[211] the idea was affirmed that any national court, when interpreting and applying domestic law, 'must presume that the State had the intention of fulfilling entirely the obligations arising from the directive concerned'.[212] Moreover, with *Pfeiffer*, on the one hand, the EU courts made it clear that the instrument of consistent interpretation is 'inherent in the system of the Treaty',[213] while on the other, they held that consistent interpretation, in addition to being necessary for the effectiveness of EU law, is indispensable for the individual to benefit from adequate judicial protection,[214] which constitutes, as has already been demonstrated, the *noyau dur* of the principle of effective judicial protection.[215] In fact, it could be maintained that, just as primacy is a manifestation of effectiveness, consistent interpretation is the means by which respect for primacy is normally and physiologically enforced in Member States' courts,[216] ensuring that national legislation is 'freed' of its '*venin anticommunautaire*'

[204] CJ, *Friedrich Haaga GmbH*, 32/74, EU:C:1974:116.

[205] CJ, *Carmelo Angelo Bonsignore v Oberstadtdirektor der Stadt Köln*, 67/74, EU:C:1975:34.

[206] CJ, *Impresa costruzioni comm. Quirino Mazzalai v Ferrovia del Renon*, 111/75, EU:C:1976:68. On this case law, *see* K. A. Bettermann, *Die Verfassungskonforme Auslegung*, Heidelberg, C.F. Müller, 1986; S. Prechal, *Directives*, 181–183; G. Pistorio, *Interpretazione e giudici. Il caso dell'interpretazione conforme al diritto dell'Unione europea*, Naples, Editoriale scientifica, 2012, 111–113; D. Simon, *La panacée de l'interprétation conforme: injection homéopathique ou thérapie palliative?*, in M. T. D'Alessio, V. Placco, V. Kronenberger (eds.), *De Rome à Lisbonne: les juridictions de l'Union européenne à la croisée des chemins. Mélanges en l'honneur de Paolo Mengozzi*, Brussels, Bruylant, 2013, 279–300, 279–281.

[207] CJ, *von Colson*, 14/83, EU:C:1984:153, para. 26. *See*, amongst subsequent judgments, CJ, *Marleasing*, C-106/89, EU:C:1990:395, para. 8 and *Pfeiffer* (n 101), paras 113–114.

[208] '*Dall'alto*', as written by G. Gaja, *L'esigenza di interpretare le norme nazionali in conformità con il diritto comunitario*, in S. P. Panunzio, E. Sciso (eds.), *Le riforme istituzionali e la partecipazione dell'Italia all'Unione europea*, Milan, Giuffrè, 2002, 133–143, 134.

[209] *von Colson* (n 207), para. 26. *See* also, for instance, *Marleasing* (n 207), para. 8.

[210] *von Colson* (n 207), para. 26.

[211] CJ, *Wagner Miret*, C-334/92, EU:C:1993:945.

[212] *Wagner Miret* (n 211), para. 20. From *Mau* onwards (CJ, *Mau*, C-160/01, EU:C:2003:280), it has been affirmed that the national courts must ensure 'the full effectiveness of the Community rules when determining the dispute before it' (para. 34).

[213] *Pfeiffer* (n 101). *See* also CJ, *Adeneler*, C-212/04, EU:C:2006:443, para. 109, and CJ, *Impact v Minister for Agriculture and Food*, C-268/06, EU:C:2008:223, para. 99.

[214] *See* S. Drake, *Twenty Years after* Von Colson: *The Impact of 'Indirect Effect' on the Protection of the Individual's Community Rights* (2005) 30 *European Law Review* 329, 332–335.

[215] On the ties between effectiveness and effective judicial protection, *see* § 2 of Chapter III.

[216] *See* also E. Cannizzaro, *Interpretazione conforme fra tecniche ed effetti normativi*, in A. Bernardi (ed.), *L'interpretazione conforme al diritto dell'Unione europea*, Naples, Editoriale Scientifica, 2015, 3–16, 16.

and that, in this way, '*la guerre des droits n'aura pas lieu*'.[217] As a matter of fact, in *Poplawski II* the principle of primacy was seen as the principal trigger and justification of consistent interpretation,[218] and this was explicitly confirmed and reiterated *in Thelen Technopark*.[219]

Regardless of whether the disputes concerned are vertical or horizontal, 'all provisions of national law',[220] including those of a constitutional nature,[221] must be subject to consistent interpretation and, as can be seen from the *Marleasing* judgment[222] onwards, the exegesis on national law must 'cover' the provisions both before and after the entry into force of the directive. Moreover, the CJ, despite an obscure passage in the *Kolpinghuis* judgment,[223] has clarified that the duty of consistent interpretation does not affect non-transposed directives that have already entered into force and whose transposition deadline has not yet expired.[224] In fact, the EU courts are now clear in concluding that, up to the deadline, 'Member States cannot be faulted for not having transposed the directive into their internal legal order before expiry of that period'.[225] On the other hand, what could be said is that anticipatory effects would be realized in voluntary, not obligatory terms, and would in any case be based on Article 4(3) TEU alone, not also on Article 288 TFEU.[226] In this vein, the CJ affirmed several times in numerous judgments concerning the effectiveness of directives, starting with *Inter-Environnement Wallonie*,[227] that even if the Member States are not obliged to enact measures transposing a directive before the expiry of the deadline, they must nevertheless refrain from adopting provisions that might seriously jeopardize the result prescribed by the directive. It follows that, from the date on which a directive has entered into force, domestic courts 'must refrain as far as possible from interpreting domestic law in a manner which might seriously compromise, after the period for transposition has expired, attainment of the objective pursued by that directive'.[228] However, the boundaries between the negative duty to abstain and the positive duty of interpretation are not always clear, so much so that, in practice, it is not uncommon for national courts to interpret domestic law in a manner consistent with a directive, pending the deadline for implementation.[229]

An acquired fact is that consistent interpretation can operate in the presence of EU rules with or without direct effect. In the latter case, consistent interpretation is the only viable means to ensure the immediate enforcement of EU law since disapplication is not a feasible option. Conversely, where the EU law at stake is directly effective, consistent interpretation is

[217] D. Simon, *La panacée*, 282. See also the intriguing reflections by F. Munari, *Gli effetti del diritto dell'Unione europea sul sistema interno delle fonti* (2013) 4 *Il Diritto dell'Unione europea* 725.

[218] *Popławski II* (n 101), para. 57.

[219] *Thelen Technopark* (n 101), paras 26–27.

[220] *See*, *ex multis*, *Marleasing* (n 207), para. 8; CJ, *Annalisa Carbonari*, C-131/97, EU:C:1999:98, para. 49.

[221] *See* explicitly CJ, *Angelidaki*, joined cases C-378–380/07, EU:C:2009:250, paras 206–207.

[222] *Marleasing* (n 207), paras 6–13.

[223] *See* CJ, *Criminal proceedings against Kolpinghuis Nijmegen BV*, 80/86, EU:C:1987:431, para. 15: 'the third question concerning the limits which Community law might impose on the obligation or power of the national court to interpret the rules of its national law in the light of the directive, it makes no difference whether or not the period prescribed for implementation has expired.'

[224] *Contra see* opinion of AG Kokott of 18 May 2004, *Wippel*, C-313/02, EU:C:2004:308, para. 60, whose reasoning was further refined in opinion of AG of Kokott 27 October 2005, *Adeneler*, C-212/04, EU:C:2005:654 paras 47–49 and 53, taken up and developed by AG Tizzano, opinion of 22 November 2005, *Mangold*, EU:C:2005:420, paras 114–120, and confirmed by AG Trstenjak, opinion of 21 October 2008, *VTA-VAB NV*, C-261/07, EU:C:2008:581, paras 52–53 and 62. In the literature *see* C. W. A. Timmermans, *Directives*, 535–537.

[225] CJ, *Inter-Environnement Wallonie ASBL* (*Inter-Environnement Wallonie I*), 129/96, EU:C:1997:628, para. 43.

[226] *See* M. Klamert, *Judicial Implementation of Directives and Anticipatory Indirect Effect: Connecting the Dots* (2006) 43 *Common Market Law Review* 1251.

[227] *See Inter-Environnement Wallonie I* (n 225), paras 35–50.

[228] *Inter-Environnement Wallonie I* (n 225), para. 45.

[229] *See*, for instance, as for Italian jurisdictions, Cassazione penale, sezione III, 4 February 2013, No. 5486.

a remedy that shall take place in the first instance as an alternative to (the far more intrusive remedy of) disapplication. In this vein, disapplication is a key, yet residual, type of remedy. Although there is no proper hierarchical order in the exercise of one or the other remedy, the national court will be led first to use consistent interpretation and only thereafter[230] disapplication.[231] In the literature, in fact, the complementary relationship between direct effect and consistent interpretation is frequently highlighted.[232] A proof of such complementarity is *NE*, whereby it was affirmed that

> the principle of primacy places the national court which is called upon within the exercise of its jurisdiction to apply provisions of EU law under a duty, *where it is unable to interpret national legislation in compliance with the requirements of EU law*, to give full effect to the requirements of that law in the dispute before it, *if necessary disapplying of its own motion any national legislation or practice.*[233]

Going back to the matter of horizontality, the CJ has repeatedly held that a national court applying the provisions of domestic law adopted for the purpose of transposing obligations laid down by a directive, including when confronted with disputes between private individuals, is required 'to consider the whole body of rules of national law and to interpret them, so far as possible, in the light of the wording and purpose of the directive in order to achieve an outcome consistent with the objective pursued by that directive'.[234] In situations of this kind, due to the prohibition against horizontal direct effect, a hermeneutical indirect avenue is the only one that can be used in accordance especially with EU directives and thus guarantee their correct and effective enforcement. 'Especially', but not only, because some of the considerations valid for directives also arise in relation to acts of the former third pillar, as confirmed by the famous *Pupino* case concerning Framework Decision 2001/220/JHA on the standing of victims in criminal proceedings,[235] and by the *Popławski II* judgment[236] concerning Framework Decision 2002/584/JHA.[237] In this connection, the CJ is clear in declaring that consistent interpretation is to be realized also with regard to these types of acts, which are binding and are not endowed with direct effect.[238]

Undoubtedly, the most controversial profile of the CJ's case law that really strikes the interpreter and lies at the heart of the present study is the use of consistent interpretation in situations concerning directives and their application in horizontal relationships. The well-known *Marleasing* case, already mentioned several times, regarding the interpretation of Article 11 of First Council Directive 68/151/EEC of 9 March 1968 on coordination of safeguards which, for the protection of the interests of members and others, are required by

[230] *See* CJ, *Maribel Dominguez*, C-282/10, EU:C:2012:33, para. 23; CJ, *Amia SpA*, C-97/11, EU:C:2012:306, para. 27.

[231] For further considerations, *see*, *ex multis*, V. Bouhier, *La généralisation du caractère préalable de l'obligation d'interprétation conforme* (2012) 2 *Revue des affaires européennes* 433.

[232] On such matter, *see* L. Daniele, *Vingt-cinq ans d'interprétation conforme: un principe encore en quete de définition?* (2008) 4 *Revue des Affaires Europeennes* 705, 709 and 714, who refers to '*alternative complémentaire*'.

[233] *NE*, para. 37 (italics added). *See* also *Dansk Industri* (n 101), para. 43.

[234] *Thelen Technopark* (n 101), para. 27. *See, inter alia*, CJ, *Association de médiation sociale v Union locale des syndicats CGT and Others*, C-176/12, EU:C:2014:2, para. 38, and CJ, *Faber*, C-497/13, EU:C:2015:357, para. 33.

[235] Council Framework Decision of 15 March 2001 on the standing of victims in criminal proceedings (OJ L 82, 22.3.2001, 1).

[236] *Popławski II* (n 101).

[237] Council Framework Decision of 13 June 2002 on the European arrest warrant and the surrender procedures between Member States—Statements made by certain Member States on the adoption of the Framework Decision (OJ L 190, 18.7.2002, 1).

[238] *Popławski II* (n 101), para. 43.

Member States of companies within the meaning of the second paragraph of Article 58 of the Treaty, with a view to making such safeguards equivalent throughout the Community,[239] is the first in which the CJ transferred, albeit only incidentally, at the level of inter-individual relations, the reasoning formulated up to that time at the level of individual–State relations when direct effect does not come into play. The same logic has inspired subsequent case law. *Océano*,[240] *Pfeiffer*, and *Centrosteel*,[241] among others, crystallize a trend—that has never been questioned by the CJ up to this point—whose main characteristic is that it guarantees the application of directives even to disputes between individuals, that is, 'directives that are not (or not correctly) transposed are ultimately allowed to have at least partial "horizontal effects"' (*'in definitiva alle direttive non (o non correttamente) trasposte di esplicare almeno in parte "effetti orizzontali"'*).[242]

The approach adopted with regard to directives and horizontal relationships has been used *mutatis mutandis* in respect to inverse vertical effect,[243] insofar as consistent interpretation does not lead to a determination or aggravation of the individual's criminal liability.[244] There are, however, also those who consider that the same limitation should extend to areas other than criminal law.[245] For example, AG van Gerven, in his opinion in the *Marleasing* case, after observing that the interpretation of national law in conformity with a directive 'cannot result in criminal liability unless such liability has been introduced by the national legislation implementing the directive', emphasized that a directive, in itself, also cannot 'introduce a civil penalty, such as nullity, in national law'.[246] At present, it does not seem that the CJ has leaned in this direction.

Does the circumstance that a directive applies, by means of interpretation, in the context of horizontal relationships, imply that the EU case law, as pointed out in the literature, is tantamount to a '*de facto* horizontal direct effect'[247] of directives? Such question requires a twofold response on the nature of the frontiers between direct effect/disapplication and consistent interpretation. On one hand, there is a clear dividing line between these two realms of EU law, as made clear by the CJ, insofar as consistent interpretation, unlike direct effect, is subject to two limitations. Firstly, a *contra legem* interpretation of national law cannot be justified,[248] regardless of whether there is established case law in the domestic courts,

[239] OJ L 65, 14.3.1968, 8.

[240] *Océano* (n 183), on which, *see*, for critical-contextual appraisal on horizontality, F. Nicola, E. Tichadou, Océano Grupo: *A Transatlantic Victory for the Consumer and a Missed Opportunity for European Law*, in F. Nicola, B. Davies (eds.), *EU Law Stories. Contextual and Critical Histories of European Jurisprudence*, Cambridge, Cambridge University Press, 2017, 369–390.

[241] CJ, *Centrosteel Srl*, C-456/98, EU:C:2000:402.

[242] A. Tizzano, *La tutela dei privati nei confronti degli Stati membri dell'Unione europea* (1995) 4 *Il Foro Italiano* 14, 21.

[243] *See Kolpinghuis* (n 223), paras 12–14. *See* also CJ, *Hans Markus Kofoed v Skatteministeriet*, C-321/05, EU:C:2007:408, para. 45; CJ, *Volker und Markus Schecke GbR (C-92/09), Hartmut Eifert (C-93/09)*, joined cases C-92–93/09, EU:C:2010:662, para. 34. On the scope and limits of the prohibition of inverse vertical direct effect, *see* §§ 3–5 and 8–9 of Chapter V.

[244] According to T. Hartley, *The Foundations of European Union Law*, 7th ed., Oxford, Oxford University Press, 2010, 239 and K. Sawyer, *The Principle of 'interprétation conforme': How Far Can or Should National Courts Go When Interpreting National Legislation Consistently with European Community Law* (2007) 28 *Statute Law Review* 165, 179, inverse vertical direct effect is prohibited only in the field of criminal law.

[245] Along these lines, *see* P. Craig, *Directives: Direct Effect, Indirect Effect and the Construction of National Legislation* (1997) 22 *European Law Review* 519, 524–528. *See* the opinion by AG Gerven of 12 July 1990, *Marleasing*, EU:C:1990:310, para. 8; *contra*, *see* the opinions by AG Jacobs of 13 December 1989, *G. Vessoso and G. Zanetti*, joined cases C-206–207/88, EU:C:1989:644, paras 24–26, and AG Jacobs of 16 March 2000, *Centrosteel*, C-456/98, EU:C:2000:137, para. 35.

[246] Opinion by AG van Gerven, *Marleasing* (n 245), para. 8.

[247] S. Prechal, *Directives*, 211.

[248] *See*, in the abundant case law, *Impact* (n 213), para. 100, and CJ, *Sumal, S.L. v Mercedes Benz Trucks España, S.L*, C-882/19, EU:C:2021:800, para. 72.

including higher courts, or established administrative practices, including those undertaken by important regulatory bodies, that are contrary to EU law.[249] As remarked by AG Elmer in *Arcaro*, the principle of consistent interpretation, which must be applied '"as far as possible", to interpret national legal provisions in a manner consistent with Community law',[250] cannot lead to an actual reformulation of those provisions because that would generate, in essence, their disapplication, with the consequence that, in the case of directives and inter-individual relations, the interpretation would surreptitiously take the form of a direct imposition of specific obligations on natural and legal persons.[251] The second limit to the duty of consistent interpretation requires that the interpretation not violate general principles of EU law, in particular, those of legal certainty and legitimate expectations.[252] These limits manifestly do not apply to direct effect and the resulting duty of disapplication, since the latter necessarily leads, in horizontal disputes, to a favourable application of EU law for some private parties and to a disruption of the existing regulatory fabric at the cost of undermining the prerogatives of those who have relied, up to the time of application of EU law, on that regulatory fabric.[253]

On the other hand, in answering the questions posed above as to whether the prohibition of horizontal direct effects of directives has been fictitiously overcome by the CJ in its case law, there is no doubt that the boundaries between disapplication and interpretation have blurred considerably over the years. In a number of national cases that have come before the CJ by virtue of Article 267 TFEU, the domestic court, in choosing the applicable law that was 'as close as possible'[254] to EU law, reduced the scope of one rule in favour of another, to the point of discarding it. By way of example, in *Dominguez* the CJ pointed out, very clearly, the path to be followed by the national judge, who was required to favour such an expansive interpretation of 'accident at work' as to extend the application of paid annual leave also to accidents occurring on the way between the worker's home and the workplace.[255] The internal legislation remained, of course, intact; however, there is no doubt that the CJ required the referring court, through a real *revirement* of the latter's case law, to extend the national provisions' scope and boundaries out of all proportion in order to ensure the effectiveness of EU law.

The blurring between direct effect and consistent interpretation is obvious in *King*, with regard to the applicability of Directive 2003/88/EC to horizontal relations between a worker and their employer. Such clarity can be easily inferred from the reading of the operative

[249] *See Popławski II* (n 101), paras 78–79. On this matter, *see* R. Kovar, *L'interprétation des droits nationaux en conformité avec le droit communautaire*, in I. Boev (ed.), *La France, l'Europe et le Monde. Mélanges en l'honneur de Jean Charpentier*, Paris, Pedone, 2009, 381–394.

[250] Opinion of AG Elmer of 14 March 1996, *Arcaro*, EU:C:1996:107, para. 39.

[251] Recently, in the contentious *Corneli* case (GC, *Francesca Corneli v European Central Bank*, T-502/19, EU:T:2022:627), about the matter of interaction between EU and national law in the field of banking supervision stemming from the situation of financial stress in which Banca Carige found itself in the course of 2017 and 2018, the GC, while considerably expanding the limit of *contra legem*, rendered a 'strict and formalistic approach towards the duty of conform interpretation', as remarked by D. Sarmiento, *Setting the limits of implementation of national law by EU Institutions: the Corneli v ECB case (T-502/19)*, 22 October 2022, available at https://eulawlive.com/op-ed-setting-the-limits-of-implementation-of-national-law-by-eu-institutions-the-corneli-v-ecb-case-t-502-19-by-daniel-sarmiento/.

[252] *See* CJ, *Hein*, C-385/17, EU:C:2018:1018, para. 51; *Popławski II* (n 101), paras 74 and 76–79; *Thelen Technopark* (n 101), para. 28.

[253] On the extent of disapplication, as well as on the possible derogations from such duty, *see* extensively § 3.3 of Chapter III and §§ 2, 6-11 of Chapter V.

[254] On the relevance of such expression in the CJ case law, *see* M. Amstutz, *In-Between Worlds:* Marleasing *and the Emergence of Interlegality in Legal Reasoning* (2005) 11 *European Law Journal* 766, 771–773.

[255] *Dominguez* (n 230), para. 44.

part of the judgment, whereby it was written that EU law must be interpreted as meaning that, 'in the case of a dispute between a worker and his employer as to whether the worker is entitled to paid annual leave', it precludes both the worker 'having to take his leave first before establishing whether he has the right to be paid in respect of that leave' and 'national provisions or practices that prevent a worker from carrying over and, where appropriate, accumulating, until termination of his employment relationship, paid annual leave rights not exercised in respect of several consecutive reference periods because his employer refused to remunerate that leave'. Such reasoning appears to be inspired more by direct effect than by consistent interpretation. As a matter of fact, in contrast with AG Trstenjak's position,[256] the conclusion reached by the Court, in substance, formally rests on the hermeneutic criterion, but, in practice, leads the referring court to disapply several provisions of UK legislation before the EU courts, starting with Article 13(9) of the Working Time Regulations 1998, which provides that: 'Leave to which a worker is entitled under this regulation may be taken in instalments, but (a) it may only be taken in the leave year in respect of which it is due, and (b) it may not be replaced by a payment in lieu except where the worker's employment is terminated.'[257] Hence, *de facto* disapplication, or *contra legem* interpretation, rather than consistent interpretation strictly speaking.

The reflections above confirm the similarities between consistent interpretation and direct effect, which relate to the deeper nature of a remedy that requires the interpreter to fill a rule with content belonging to an external legal order and, in this vein, seems to be a symptom of a conceptual reversal. This reversal affects the very logic underlying the classic techniques of systematic interpretation.[258] From this point of view, consistent interpretation tends to be placed on the borderline between normative production activity and interpretation activity.[259] The European norm becomes a parameter and produces effects, indirectly, on the national legal system, through one or more provisions that are, in fact, included in that system.[260] Consistent interpretation is, thus, a form of disguised disapplication, that is, a remedy that, rather than imposing a certain hermeneutical reconstruction, determines a 'manipulative'[261] and '*abrogans*'[262] interpretation of national law.[263] Consistent interpretation has a '*nature ambivalente*'[264] and is an '*object quelque peu mystérieux*'[265] because it oscillates between functioning as a teleological method of

[256] Opinion of AG Trstenjak of 8 September 2011, *Maribel Dominguez v Centre informatique du Centre Ouest Atlantique and Préfet de la région Centre*, C-282/10, EU:C:2011:559, paras 169, 175, 182.

[257] CJ, *Conley King v The Sash Window Workshop Ltd and Richard Dollar*, C-214/16, EU:C:2017:914, para. 11.

[258] As observed by E. Cannizzaro, *Interpretazione conforme*, 5.

[259] S. Prechal, *Directives*, 210, refers to 'remedial interpretation'.

[260] *See* the analysis by G. Betlem, *The Doctrine of Consistent Interpretation—Managing Legal Uncertainty* (2002) 22 *Oxford Journal of Legal Studies* 397, and G. Pistorio, *Interpretazione*, 111–113.

[261] '*Interpretazione manipolativa*', in the words of L. Daniele, *Novità in tema di efficacia delle direttive comunitarie (nota a Corte giust. CE 13.11.1990, causa C-106/89)* (1992) 4 *Il Foro italiano* 173, 178.

[262] R. Caranta, *Intorno al problema dell'individuazione delle posizioni giuridiche soggettive del cittadino comunitario* (1994) 4 *Rivista italiana di diritto pubblico comunitario* 992.

[263] On the overlap between consistent interpretation and direct effect, *see* G. Betlem, *The Doctrine*; S. Amadeo, *Norme comunitarie, posizioni giuridiche soggettive e giudizi interni*, Milan, Giuffrè, 2002, 211 and 225; D. Simon, *La directive*, 96; O. Porchia, *La dinamica dei rapporti tra norme interne e dell'Unione nel dialogo tra giudici nazionali e Corte di giustizia* (2013) 1 *Studi sull'integrazione europea* 71, 83; G. de Búrca, *Giving Effect to European Community Directives* (1992) 55 *Modern Law Review* 215, 223; O. Pallotta, *Effetto orizzontale delle direttive? Solo se indiretto* (2005) 1 *Diritto pubblico comparato ed europeo* 505, 509; A. Arnull, A. Dashwood, M. Dougan, M. Ross, E. Spaventa, D. Wyatt, *Wyatt and Dashwood's European Union Law*, 6th ed., London, Sweet & Maxwell, 2011, 239–244; R. Mastroianni, G. Strozzi, *Diritto dell'Unione europea: Parte istituzionale*, 8th ed., Turin, Giappichelli, 2019, 308–313.

[264] L. Daniele, *Vingt-cinq*, 705.

[265] L. Daniele, *Vingt-cinq*, 705.

interpretation, on the one hand, and, on the other, as a manifestation of the primacy of EU law over national law, that is, between a purely interpretative dimension and a different dimension rooted in the principle of effectiveness. In this framework, the results brought about by consistent interpretation often 'are not very different from those brought about by the pure and simple assertion of direct effect',[266] so that the distinction between directly and non-directly effective directives is, today, less decisive. Such a deviation from the traditional concept of interpretation, whereby the national court is guided *de facto* by the CJ towards the interpretation of domestic legal systems as well as the concrete results to be achieved[267] and, in doing so, is obliged to adopt a creative interpretation of national law, is evident in the whole case law of the CJ, not only in those rulings concerning directives and horizontal relationships.

If one takes the perspective of exclusionary direct effect, in particular, the overlap between consistent interpretation and the doctrine of direct effect becomes very clear.[268] In fact, in both situations that which is to be enforced is national law, not EU law. What the doctrine points out regarding the differences between direct effect and consistent interpretation, where the former implies the application of EU law while the latter of national law,[269] holds true only for substitutive direct effect.[270]

Ultimately, if the only perspective is the effectiveness of unimplemented directives, the advantages of the hermeneutic method are manifold. One stands out above all: the application of the directive is irrespective of the degree of unconditionality of its rules and of the type of disputes at stake, vertical or horizontal.[271] However, there are serious risks arising from a massive and random use of the hermeneutic criterion in terms of legal certainty and uniform application, in all Member States, of EU law. Indeed, as discussed in the previous sections, if the prohibition of horizontal direct effect, in practice, is breached by the CJ itself in many of its judgments, why not retrace its steps and admit horizontal direct effect?[272] The CJ's approach, also with respect to consistent interpretation, seems contradictory and apt to undermine the principles of legal certainty and legitimate expectations.[273] Furthermore, an indefinite and broad expansion of consistent interpretation is likely to challenge another core principle of law, rooted in both EU and national legal orders: the separation between legislative and judicial powers.[274]

[266] G. Tesauro, *Diritto dell'Unione europea*, 4th ed., edited by P. De Pasquale, F. Ferraro, vol. I, Naples, Editoriale Scientifica, 2023, 279: '*non sono molto diversi da quelli che si realizzerebbero con l'affermazione pura e semplice dell'effetto diretto*.'

[267] *See*, amongst many rulings, CJ, *AES-3C Maritza East 1 EOOD*, C-124/12, EU:C:2013:488.

[268] Y. Galmot, J.-C. Bonichot, *La Cour de Justice des Communautés européennes et la transposition des directives en droit national* (1988) 1 *Revue française de droit administratif* 1, 20–23 and G. Betlem, *The Doctrine*, 398.

[269] Insofar as only through the hermeneutic instrument would the rule of the directive be '*transfusée*' into the domestic legal system, as noted by Y. Galmot, J.-C. Bonichot, *La Cour*, 20.

[270] On this point, *see* A. Tancredi, *Il ruolo dell'interpretazione conforme al diritto dell'Unione europea fra disapplicazione ed efficacia diretta*, in *Quaderni del Consiglio superiore della magistratura*, Rome, 2010, 1, 14, whereby consistent interpretation is deemed *de facto* equivalent to exclusionary effect.

[271] As noted by L. Daniele, *Novità*, 178.

[272] On the inconsistencies underpinning the CJ case law, *see* S. Prechal, *Directives*, 211; A. Alì, *Some Reflections on the Principle of Consistent Interpretation through the Case Law of the European Court of Justice*, in N. Boschiero, T. Scovazzi, C. Pitea, C. Ragni (eds.), *International Courts and the Development of International Law*, The Hague, Martinus Nijhoff, 2013, 881–895.

[273] In more general terms, on the unsatisfactory case law of the CJ concerning the prohibition of horizontal direct effect, *see* § 5.5 of this chapter.

[274] The term 'judicial creativity' is employed by S. Prechal, *Directives*, 214.

5.3 The joint application with the general principles and/or the Charter: a convoluted relationship of mutual assistance until the *Mangold-Kücükdeveci-Dansk Industri* trio

The following sections are devoted to the matter of the horizontal direct effect of fundamental rights in the EU legal order.[275] At stake, therefore, is not the applicability, by way of interpretation, of fundamental rights in disputes between private parties, that is, the indirect effect of general principles of EU law and/or the Charter of Fundamental Rights.[276] On the contrary, at the heart of the analysis is the horizontal direct effect of both these sources of EU law, and the related duty to disapply. A connected question is whether and to what extent it can be said that through the *Mangold/Kücükdeveci/Dansk Industri* doctrine, which has crystallized over the years in relation to the principle of non-discrimination on grounds of age and beyond, the prohibition of horizontal direct effect of directives is, today, circumvented, as seen with reference to the other remedies investigated in the previous sections. A further question is whether the jurisprudence of the CJ is satisfactory or problematic, as is the jurisprudence, examined in the preceding sections, in which the Court, while bypassing the prohibition of direct horizontal effect of directives, *de facto* confirms their horizontality. If this is problematic, would it not be preferable, even in that respect, to admit *apertis verbis* the horizontal direct effect of directives?[277]

The answer to those questions is by no means straightforward. In short, today, there is uncertainty, though not as to 'if' horizontal direct effect can be attributed, but about when, why, and how horizontal direct effect can be associated with general principles of EU law and the Charter. This uncertainty is *per se* troublesome because, as has been already noted regarding economic freedoms[278] and claimed by several scholars,[279] horizontal direct

[275] Horizontal direct effect of fundamental rights is rooted in the so-called *unmittelbare Drittwirkung*, which was already mentioned in § 2 of this chapter. Besides the authors cited in § 2 and amongst key studies beyond EU law, *see* A. Barak, *Constitutional Human Rights and Private Law* (1996) 3 *Revue of Constitutional Studies* 220; A. Clapham, *Human Rights in the Private Sphere*, 2nd ed., Oxford, Oxford University Press, 1996; A. Clapham, *The Human Rights Obligations of Non-State Actors*, Oxford, Oxford University Press, 2006; J. H. Knox, *Horizontal Human Rights Law* (2008) 102 *American Journal of International Law* 1; G. Tubner, *Transnational Fundamental Rights: Horizontal Effect?* (2011) 40 *Rechtsfilosofie & Rechtstheorie* 191.

[276] An excellent analysis of the different types of horizontality, not limited to direct effect and the EU case law, is carried out by E. Frantziou, *The Horizontal Effect of Fundamental Rights*, 38–40 and 57–81. For a comparative law account, *see* M. Tushnet, *State Action, Social Welfare Rights, and the Judicial Role: Some Comparative Observations* (2002) 3 *Chicago Journal of International Law* 435; D. Oliver, J. Fedtke (eds.), *Human Rights and the Private Sphere: A Comparative Study*, New York, Routledge-Cavendish, 2007. For private/contract law perspectives and the phenomenon of the so-called 'constitutionalisation of private law relationships', *see* H. Schepel, *The Enforcement of EC Law in Contractual Relations: Case Studies in How Not to 'Constitutionalize' Private Law* (2004) 18 *European Review of Private Law* 661; A. Colombi Ciacchi, *The Constitutionalization of European Contract Law: Judicial Convergence and Social Justice* (2006) 2 *European Review of Contract Law* 167; A. Sajó, R. Uitz (eds.), *The Constitution in Private Relations: Expanding Constitutionalism*, The Hague, Eleven International Publishing, 2005; T. Barkhuysen, S. Lindenberg (eds.), *Constitutionalisation of Private Law*, The Hague, Martinus Nijhoff, 2006; M. Kumm, *Who is Afraid of the Total Constitution? Constitutional Rights as Principles and the Constitutionalization of Private Law* (2006) 7 *German Law Journal* 341; E. Navarretta, *Costituzione, Europa e diritto privato. Effettività e Drittwirkung ripensando la complessità giuridica*, Turin, Giappichelli, 2017; A. Zoppini, *Il diritto privato e i suoi confini*, Bologna, Il Mulino, 2020.

[277] For some introductory considerations on the interplay between general principles of EU law and the Charter, as well as on the internal effect of the latter, including on the rights/principles divide enshrined in its Article 52(5), *see* § 3.1 of Chapter III.

[278] *See* § 2 of this chapter.

[279] *See*, recently, the study by L. Cecchetti, *Unravelling Horizontal Direct Effect in EU Law: The Case of the Fundamental Right to Paid Annual Leave between 'Myth' and 'Practice'*, in *Yearbook of European Law*, vol. 42, 2024, 42–83.

effect greatly affects the relationship between private autonomy and fundamental rights,[280] thereby having an impact on the deepest foundations of the EU legal order.[281]

Against this background, just as it is not a foregone and trivial conclusion that primary norms on economic freedoms are interpreted in the sense of imposing obligations also on private actors, in the same way it is not a foregone and trivial conclusion that the same can happen in relation to fundamental rights, which for decades have permeated the CJ case law as an interpretative aid to primary or secondary EU law and/or an instrument of protection of the individual against public, not private, entities.[282] Moreover, as noted by Frantziou, 'traditional conceptions of constitutional theory have generally associated the application of fundamental rights with State obligations'.[283]

The point of departure for any analysis on the horizontality of fundamental rights can only be the *Defrenne II* ruling, which concerns a primary law provision entrenched in the European Treaties, at the time Article 119 of the EEC Treaty, now Article 157 TFEU, that is also enforceable in horizontal disputes, as noted in section 2 of this chapter. This provision, according to the CJ, codifies the principle of equal pay between men and women,[284] which is a clear manifestation of the general principle of non-discrimination enshrined in Article 21 of the Charter of Fundamental Rights. Moreover, the *Defrenne II* judgment was implicitly inspired[285] by the CJ's choice, made a year and a half earlier in *Walrave*, to apply the rules on freedom of movement to inter-private relationships.

The rationale, as seen with regard to the freedoms of movement, is to ensure the effectiveness of EU law and the effective judicial protection of individuals, which would be both called into question if the breach stemming in whole or in part from the conduct of private persons were not covered by EU law. This is particularly serious nowadays due to the increasing involvement[286] of such actors in the exercise of activities that were once the sole responsibility of States. Denying that the respect for fundamental rights, as supreme values safeguarded by Article 6(3) TEU,[287] could materialize, upstream, at the level of horizontal

[280] P. Craig, *The Lisbon Treaty: Law, Politics, and Treaty Reforms*, Oxford, Oxford University Press, 2010, 208.

[281] E. Muir, *Of Ages in—and Edges of—EU Law* (2011) 48 *Common Market Law Review* 39.

[282] For a legal and historical account about the original rationale of the general principles, *see* C. Amalfitano, *General Principles of EU Law and the Protection of Fundamental Rights*, Cheltenham, Edward Elgar, 2018, 18; K. Lenaerts, J. A. Gutiérrez-Fons, *The Constitutional Allocation of Powers* (2010) 47 *Common Market Law Review* 1629, 1639; R. Schütze, *European Union Law*, 488.

[283] E. Frantziou, *The Horizontal Effect of Fundamental Rights*, 1. For an international law perspective, *see* C. Tomuschat, *Human Rights: between Idealism and Realism*, Oxford, Oxford University Press, 2008, 84.

[284] For early works that predicted the horizontal direct effect of general principles, even before the adoption of the Charter, *see* A. Arnull, *The General Principles of EEC Law and the Individual*, Leicester, Leicester University Press, 1990; P. Oliver, *General Principles of Community Law and Horizontal Effect* (1993) 4 *Europäische Zeitschrift für Wirtschaftsrecht* 393.

[285] 'Implicitly' since in *Defrenne II* there are no references to *Walrave*.

[286] As observed by S. Prechal, *Horizontal Direct Effect*, 418, 'there is an important shift of power to the private sector. In such a context, the need for an adequate and different protection of fundamental rights has changed too. Horizontal direct effect of fundamental rights is one of the possible means to realize such a protection.' On the erosion of the public/private divide, from the standpoint of the Charter's horizontality, *see* M. Safjan, P. Mikłaszewicz, *Horizontal Effect*; E. Frantziou, *The Horizontal Effect of the Charter of Fundamental Rights of the EU: Rediscovering the Reasons for Horizontality* (2015) 21 *European Law Journal* 657, 674–675; D. Leczykiewicz, *Horizontal Effect of Fundamental Rights: In Search of Social Justice or Private Autonomy in EU Law?*, in U. Bernitz, X. Groussot, F. Schulyok (eds.), *General principles*, 171–186; C. Sieburgh, *General Principles and the Charter in Private Law Relationships: Constructive and Critical Input from Private Law*, in U. Bernitz, X. Groussot, F. Schulyok (eds.), *General principles*, 233–247, 233–238; M. Fornasier, *The Impact of EU Fundamental Rights on Private Relationships: Direct or Indirect Effect?* (2015) 23 *European Review of Private Law* 29; S. Walkila, *Horizontal Effect*, 132 and 198–202. *See* also the reflections in § 2 of this chapter, as well as the authors cited therein.

[287] On fundamental rights, EU values, and Article 6(3) TEU, *see* E. Muir, *Of Ages*, 57–59 and E. Spaventa, *The Horizontal Application of Fundamental Rights as General Principles of Union Law*, in A. Arnull, A. Dashwood, M. Dougan, M. Ross, E. Spaventa, D. Wyatt, *Wyatt and Dashwood's European Union Law*, 6th ed., London, Sweet & Maxwell, 2011, 199–218, 208–209.

relations, would constitute a dangerous aporia in the EU legal order. Additionally, to argue, as AG Trstenjak[288] did, that the horizontality of the Charter should be ruled out because its Article 51(1) shall be enforced only against EU institutions and Member States, and because Article 52(1) allows exceptions to be invoked only by States, is a purely formalistic argument[289] and, as such, inadmissible. Moreover, Trstenjak's reasoning is not in line with the *travaux préparatoires* of the Charter and its Explanations, from which it in no way emerges that the drafters' intention was to exclude private individuals from its personal scope.[290]

The recognition of fundamental rights' horizontal direct effect, in this sense, is inherent in the development of the European integration process. Excluding such a recognition is at odds with that process.[291] Moreover, the fact that in many constitutional orders a prohibition, such as, for example, that of discriminating between men and women and of establishing different wages, is not necessarily applicable to inter-private, in addition to State–individual, relations, is not conclusive. On the one hand, it is true that the non-horizontal applicability of the right of non-discrimination in the workplace pursuant to some domestic legal orders is justified on the grounds of respect for private autonomy.[292] On the other hand, however, bringing these situations within the scope of EU law is precisely a legitimate expression of its autonomy from Member States. As stated in *Association de médiation sociale*, 'the fundamental rights guaranteed in the legal order of the European Union are applicable in all situations governed by European Union law'.[293] In this respect, the circumstance that in the same judgment, after such statement, the CJ, while recognizing the direct effect of Article 21, excluded the horizontal direct effect of Article 27, reveals the degree of complexity underpinning the matter of fundamental rights' horizontality.[294]

The first[295] application of general principles in horizontal relationships dates back to the *Mangold* judgment on the interpretation of Article 6 of Directive 2000/78/EC establishing a general framework for equal treatment in employment and occupation.[296] With regard to the preliminary reference raised by the *Arbeitsgericht München* (Germany) in the context of a dispute between two private parties concerning a fixed-term employment contract, the CJ departed from the consideration that that directive 'does not itself lay down the principle of equal treatment in the field of employment and occupation'.[297] Next, it stated that the

[288] See the opinion of AG Trstenjak, *Dominguez* (n 256).

[289] On this point, *see* E. Frantziou, *The Horizontal Effect of Fundamental Rights*, 83.

[290] As noted by F. Costamagna, *Diritti fondamentali*, 81–85. On the *travaux préparatoires* of the Charter, *see*, recently, S. Lattanzi, *I 'travaux préparatoires' del diritto dell'Unione Europea: tassonomia, ruolo e funzioni*, Padua, Cedam, 2022, 83–88.

[291] For a harsh criticism to the recognition of horizontal direct effect of general principles of EU law, seen as a distortion of the ideals and goals of the European process of integration, *see* Danish Supreme Court, *Dansk Industri*, 15/2014, acting on behalf of Ajos A/Sv. Estate of A, 42 (https://domstol.dk/media/2udgvvvb/judgment-15-2014.pdf). In the literature, *see* the authors cited in footnote 348, § 11, Chapter V.

[292] As remarked by R. Schütze, *European Union Law*, 488–489.

[293] CJ, *Association de médiation* (n 234), para. 42.

[294] In the same vein, *see* the observations by C. Murphy, *Using the EU Charter of Fundamental Rights against Private Parties after* Association de Médiation Sociale (2014) 2 *European Human Rights Law Review* 170.

[295] The CJ expanded its jurisdiction over the protection of fundamental rights also through horizontal direct effect. On such phenomenon, *see* J. Coppel, A. O'Neill, *The European Court of Justice: Taking Rights Seriously* (1992) 29 *Common Market Law Review* 669.

[296] On *Mangold* and horizontality, *see*, amongst others, G. Thüsing, *Europarechtlicher Gleichbehandlungsgrundsatz als Bindung des Arbeitgebers?* (2005) 26 *Zeitschrift für Wirtschaftsrecht* 2149; A. Junker, *Der EuGH zum Arbeitsrecht: Betriebsübergang, Gleichbehandlung und Bestandsschutz* (2006) 17 *Europäische Zeitschrift für Wirtschaftsrecht* 524; D. Schiek, *The ECJ Decision in Mangold: A Further Twist on Effects of Directives and Constitutional Relevance of Community Equality Legislation* (2006) 35 *Industrial Law Journal* 329; A. Von Oettingen, D. Rabenschlag, *Europäische Richtlinien und allgemeiner Gleichheitssatz im innerstaatlichen Recht - Anmerkungen anlässlich des Mangold-Urteils des EuGH* (2006) 9 *Zeitschrift für Europarechtliche Studien* 363.

[297] CJ, *Werner Mangold v Rüdiger Helm*, C-144/04, EU:C:2005:709, para. 74.

principle of non-discrimination on grounds of age,[298] as codified 'in various international instruments and in the constitutional traditions common to the Member States', must be regarded as 'a general principle of Community law'.[299] This is the reason why compliance with that principle does not depend, as such, on the deadline for transposition of a directive, which in the case had not yet expired. Hence, the national court shall ensure 'the legal protection which individuals derive from the rules of Community law and . . . that those rules are fully effective, setting aside any provision of national law which may conflict with that law', irrespective of the horizontal nature of the dispute.[300] General principles, thus, are recognized, albeit in a hasty manner, as a source of rights and obligations for individuals. The tone is assertive, lacking an in-depth theoretical elaboration to support the granting of horizontal direct effect to these principles,[301] as demonstrated by the type of judgments cited by the CJ, including *Simmenthal*, which concern disputes that are clearly vertical in nature and, therefore, with no analogy with the *Mangold* case.[302]

The approach outlined in *Mangold*, after a number of rulings distancing themselves from it in relation to other principles within and beyond social law, that is, the principle of non-discrimination on grounds of sickness[303] and the principle of equality of shareholders,[304] is specified and confirmed, again with regard to the principle of non-discrimination on grounds of age, as a manifestation of the principle of equality before the law,[305] in *Kücükdeveci*[306] and

[298] On whether the principle of non-discrimination on the basis of age could be deemed a general principle of EU law at that time is a contentious matter. The answer seems to be negative since, at least when the Court ruled in the *Mangold* and *Kücükdeveci* cases, only for a handful of States did the principle have constitutional status, as explained by M. Dougan, *In Defence of* Mangold?, in A. Arnull, A. Dashwood, M. Dougan, M. Ross, E. Spaventa, D. Wyatt, *Wyatt and Dashwood's European Union Law*, 221 and G. Thüsing, S. Horler, *Case C-555/07, Seda Kücükdeveci v. Swedex, Judgment of the Court (Grand Chamber) of 19 January 2010* (2010) 47 *Common Market Law Review* 1161, 1170. On the impact of *Mangold* on the legal status of the principle of non-discrimination in EU law, *see* E. Muir, *Enhancing the Effects of EC Law on National Labour Markets: The* Mangold *Case* (2006) 31 *European Law Review* 879; G. Di Federico, *Le discriminazioni in base all'età nella più recente giurisprudenza della Corte di Giustizia: da* Mangold *a* Georgiev *. . . e oltre* (2011) 6 *Studi sull'integrazione europea* 585. On the different layers of the principle of non-discrimination as a general principle of EU law before the '*Mangold* revolution', *see* C. Favilli, *La non discriminazione nell'Unione europea*, Bologna, Il Mulino, 2008.

[299] *Mangold* (n 297), paras 74–75.

[300] *Mangold* (n 297), para. 78.

[301] The Court's reasoning on the subject is, in truth, rather hasty, as stressed in the opinion of AG Mazák of 15 February 2007, *Félix Palacios de la Villa v Cortefiel Servicios SA*, C-411/05, EU:C:2007:106, paras 87–97 and 132–138. Instead, an in-depth analysis is performed by AG Tizzano in his opinion, *Mangold* (n 224), paras 106–109, whereby the attribution of horizontal direct effect is openly challenged. A very harsh position has been taken by the former President of the Federal Republic of Germany, Roman Herzog, who raised several concerns about *Mangold* in R. Herzog, *Stop the European Court of Justice, Frankfurter Allgemeine Zeitung* 8 September 2008, on which, *see* the critical appraisal by O. Pollicino, *La Corte di giustizia riconosce l'efficacia diretta orizzontale dei principi generali ma non delle direttive* (2016) 3 *Quaderni costituzionali* 597, 598.

[302] These are the following judgments: CJ, *Amministrazione delle Finanze dello Stato v Simmenthal SpA*, 106/77, EU:C:1978:49 and CJ, *Solred SA v Administración General del Estado*, C-347/96, EU:C:1998:87, both cited in para. 77, as well as CJ, *Ángel Rodríguez Caballero*, C-442/00, EU:C:2002:752, cited in para. 75. For some insightful considerations in this respect, *see* F. Costamagna, *Diritti fondamentali*, 62.

[303] *See* CJ, *Chacón Navas*, C-13/05, EU:C:2006:456.

[304] *See* CJ, *Audiolux*, C-101/08, EU:C:2009:626.

[305] In these terms, *see* the opinion by AG Tizzano, *Mangold* (n 224), paras 84 and 101, and the opinion by AG Sharpston of 30 November 2006, *Maria-Luise Lindorfer*, C-227/04 P, EU:C:2006:748, paras 52–58. Other principles are encompassed in the scope of the principle of equality before the law enshrined in the Charter, most notably in Article 20, such as the principle of integration of persons with disabilities pursuant to its Article 26, as clarified by the CJ in CJ, *Wolfgang Glatzel v Freistaat Bayern*, 356/12, EU:C:2014:350, paras 74–86.

[306] On *Kücükdeveci* and horizontality, *see*, amongst others, S. Lorenzon, *La Corte di giustizia e il riconoscimento degli effetti diretti orizzontali delle direttive comunitarie: il caso* Kücükdeveci (2010) 2 *Quaderni costituzionali* 430; S. Peers, *Supremacy, Equality and Human Rights: Comment on* Kucukdeveci (C-555/07) (2010) 35 *European Law Review* 849; T. Roes, *Case Note—Case C-555/07, Seda Kücükdeveci v Swedex GmbH & Co. KG (2009–2010)* (2010) 15 *Columbia Journal of European Law* 497; D. Schiek, *Constitutional Principles and Horizontal Effect:* Kücükdeveci *Revisited* (2010) 1 *European Labour Law Journal* 368; G. Thüsing, S. Horler, *Case C-555/07*, 1161.

Dansk Industri.[307] These decisions, although in line with the core of the reasoning developed in *Mangold*, mark a significant evolution. Indeed, whereas in *Mangold*, as regards the source of the duty to disapply, there is ambivalence[308] between the role attributed to the directive and that of the general principle, in *Kücükdeveci*[309] the directive plays an important function but one that is entirely instrumental to the effectiveness of the general principle.[310] Indeed, the Court observed that the directive gives 'specific expression' to the principle of non-discrimination on grounds of age.[311] Again in contrast to *Mangold*, in *Kücükdeveci* the CJ expressly made the connection between such principle and Article 21 of the Charter,[312] although the link between the latter provision and Directive 2000/78/EC is absent. The same attitude is reiterated in *Dansk Industri*. The common thread, therefore, is that in all three judgments the recognition of horizontal direct effect to the general principle does not, as in *Defrenne II*, pass through an EU primary norm, but through a directive which specifies its content and scope, regardless of whether the deadline for the transposition has expired (*Mangold*) or not (*Kücükdeveci* and *Dansk Industri*).[313] With reference to *Dansk Industri* in particular, in the operative part, unlike both *Mangold* and *Kücükdeveci*, the Court was clear in affirming the horizontal direct effect of the principle of non-discrimination on grounds of age, since it observed, referring to *Association de médiation sociale*, that it 'confers on private persons an individual right which they may invoke as such and which, even in disputes between private persons, requires the national courts to disapply national provisions',[314] notably provisions which deprive an employee of entitlement to a severance allowance 'where the employee is entitled to claim an old-age pension from the employer under a pension scheme which the employee joined before reaching the age of 50, regardless of whether the employee chooses to remain on the employment market or take his retirement'.[315] Moreover, in *Dansk Industri*, for the first time, the nexus is made explicit not only between the general principle of non-discrimination on the basis of age and Article 21 of the Charter, but also between that provision (rather than 'simply' the general principle) and Directive 2000/78/EC, as a factor of concretization of the former by the latter.[316]

[307] On the reception of the *Mangold-Kücükdeveci* logic by the CJ in *Dansk Industri*, *see* the authors cited in footnote 348, § 11, Chapter V.

[308] As convincingly argued by F. Fontanelli, *General Principles of the EU and a Glimpse of Solidarity in the Aftermath of* Mangold *and* Kücükdeveci (2011) 17 *European Public Law* 225, 228.

[309] In this regard, on the departure of *Kücükdeveci* from *Mangold*, *see* M. De Mol, Kücükdeveci: Mangold *Revisited—Horizontal Direct Effect of a General Principle of EU Law* (2011) 7 *European Constitutional Law Review* 293 and M. De Mol, *The Novel Approach of the CJEU on the Horizontal Direct Effect of the EU Principle of Non-Discrimination* (2011) 18 *Maastricht Journal of European and Comparative Law* 109.

[310] Similarly *see* E. Muir, *Of Ages*, 53.

[311] CJ, *Seda Kücükdeveci v Swedex GmbH & Co. KG*, C-555/07, EU:C:2010:21, para. 21.

[312] As noted by N. Lazzerini, *Effetti diretti orizzontali dei principi generali . . . ma non delle direttive che li esprimono? La sentenza della Corte di giustizia nel caso* Kücükdeveci (2010) 2 *Rivista di diritto internazionale* 443, 448; K. Lenaerts, J. A. Gutiérrez-Fons, *The Constitutional Allocation*, 1655–1660. In this connection, A. Bailleux, *La Cour de justice, la Charte des droits fondamentaux et l'intensité normative des droits sociaux* (2014) 2 *Revue de Droit Social* 294, recalled that, at the time of the *Mangold* case, the Charter did not yet have binding force, unlike *Kücükdeveci*. *See* also the observations by AG Cruz Villalón of 19 May 2011, *Prigge*, C-447/09, EU:C:2011:321, para. 26, where it was stated that the principle of non-discrimination on the basis of age 'has been enshrined in the "Lisbon Charter" and it is therefore from this source that the possibilities and limitations of the principle's usefulness must flow'.

[313] E. Spaventa, *The Horizontal Application*, 208–209, wrote that 'general principles are applicable whenever the situation falls within the scope of Union law, regardless of whether the trigger is the treaty or a directive, and regardless of whether the litigation is vertical or horizontal'.

[314] *Dansk Industri* (n 101), para. 36 (italics added).

[315] *Dansk Industri* (n 101), para. 27.

[316] *Dansk Industri* (n 101), para. 22.

A further recurring element in the three judgments, as well as in the case law regarding the horizontality of general principles, is the lack of express references to the doctrine of direct effect, including the test for the assessment of its premises. Conversely, a reference is made to the duty of disapplication stemming from the general principle, to the extent that some scholars have wondered whether such a duty was the product[317] of primacy and direct effect or of primacy alone.[318] In this regard, as has been written several times in the course of this work about the duty to disapply as a consequence stemming always from primacy and direct effect, the fact that there is a lack of both an express reference to direct effect and of an enquiry into its core conditions simply means that direct effect is presumed.[319] And, in any case, if it were only primacy that caused disapplication, rather than direct effect and primacy, what need would the Court have had to use the general principle of non-discrimination rather than 'only' the directive? In fact, such reconstruction, proposed by AG Bot in *Kücükdeveci*, according to whom the exclusionary effect would take the form of 'disconnecting the horizontal direct effect of directives from the right to plead them to exclude contrary national law in proceedings between private parties',[320] is rejected by the CJ,[321] whose minimalism in this area raises doubts and complicates matters, as it does in many others.[322]

In the same period of, or shortly after, *Mangold-Kücükdeveci-Dansk Industri*,[323] horizontal direct effect was excluded in all rulings on social law-related matters different from those connected to the principle of non-discrimination: the *Dominguez, Fenoll*,[324] *Sobczyszyn*,[325] and *King*[326] rulings concerning paid annual leave, and the *Association de médiation sociale* judgment, which relates to the right to information and consultation within the undertaking, as has already been mentioned several times. In these five decisions about inter-private disputes, no horizontal direct effect was recognized, either expressly or otherwise.[327] In *Association de médiation sociale* the reason lies in the qualification, within the meaning of Article 52(5) of the Charter, as a 'principle' rather than as a 'right,' of the prerogative, asserted by an employee, to information and consultation within an undertaking

[317] On the interplay between direct effect and primacy in the field, *see* E. Muir, *Of Ages*, 42–47.

[318] On the 'supremacy' of primacy over direct effect in and beyond *Kücükdeveci* G. Di Federico, *La sentenza* Kücükdeveci *e la* vexata quaestio *degli effetti diretti (orizzontali) delle direttive* (2010) 29 *Rivista italiana di diritto del lavoro* 1002; S. Peers, *Supremacy*; P. Cabral, R. Neves, *General Principles of EU Law and Horizontal Direct Effect* (2011) 17 *European Public Law* 437, 450–451.

[319] *See* also § 4 of Chapter II.

[320] Opinion of AG Bot of 7 July 2009, *Seda Kücükdeveci v Swedex GmbH & Co. KG*, C-555/07, EU:C:2009:429, para. 63.

[321] *See* S. Prechal, *Competence Creep and General Principles of Law* (2010) 3 *Review of European and Administrative Law* 5, 17, E. Muir, *Of Ages*, 56 and A. Wiesbrock, *Case Note—C-555/07*, Kücükdeveci v Swedex, *Judgment of the Court (Grand Chamber) of 19 January* (2010) *11 German Law Journal* 539, 544, who argue that the CJ in the *Mangold/Kücükdeveci/Dansk Industri* saga has regarded the principle of non-discrimination on the basis of age as a directly effective principle endowed with exclusionary effects.

[322] The matter of horizontal direct effect is wrongfully 'ignored' according to *Common Market Law Review, Editorial Comments. Horizontal direct effect*, 7–8; *contra, see* R. C. Tobler, *Putting* Mangold *in Perspective: In Response to Editorial Comments, Horizontal Direct Effect—A Law of Diminishing Coherence?* (2007) 44 *Common Market Law Review* 1177.

[323] On the potential for the attribution of horizontal direct effect originating from the principle of non-discrimination on the basis of age, *see* T. Tridimas, *Horizontal Effect of General Principles: Bold Rulings and Fine Distinctions*, in U. Bernitz, X. Groussot, F. Schulyok (eds.), *General principles*, 213–232, 232.

[324] CJ, *Gérard Fenoll*, C-316/13, EU:C:2015:200, on which, *see* M. Bell, *Mark, Disability, Rehabilitation and the Status of Worker in EU Law:* Fenoll (2016) 53 *Common Market Law Review* 197.

[325] CJ, *Alicja Sobczyszyn v Szkoła Podstawowa w Rzeplinie*, C-178/15, EU:C:2016:502.

[326] *King* (n 257).

[327] M. Bobek, *Why is it Better to Treat Every Provision of EU Directives as Having Horizontal Direct Effect?* (2023) 39 *International Journal of Comparative Labour Law and Industrial Relations* 211, 214, refers also to CJ, *Edward Cussens and Others v T. G. Brosman*, C-251/16, EU:C:2017:881, but this ruling seems to concern the application of the general principle of the prohibition of abuse of law in the field of taxation in vertical relationships.

established within European territory. The Court does not believe that this prerogative may be relied on by an individual against another individual in order to request the disapplication of a national rule which excludes workers with assisted contracts 'from the calculation of staff numbers in the undertaking when determining the legal thresholds for setting up bodies representing staff'.[328] A different reading is not justified by the existence of Article 27 of the Charter since, according to the CJ, it incorporates a principle and cannot, therefore, generate direct effect, either vertical or (*a fortiori*) horizontal. In this regard, it could be argued that such principle shall be deemed as a general principle of EU law when the CJ finds that the margin of discretion left to the States in the choice of measures aimed at pursuing the objectives of their social policies 'cannot have the effect of frustrating the implementation of a fundamental principle of European Union law or of a provision of that law'.[329] On the other hand, the objection is that, had the Court wished to make such equivalence, it would have stated so expressly, as it did in relation to other principles, for instance, in *Kücükdeveci* and *Glatzel*.[330] In any case, whether or not the principle enshrined in Article 27 of the Charter is a *general* principle, for the purposes of this analysis, is not decisive. What is of interest to emphasize here is that the CJ, while admitting that Article 3(1) of Directive 2002/14, invoked by the applicant in the main proceedings, was sufficiently precise and unconditional, excluded direct effect since the directive could not be applied to a horizontal dispute and Article 27 of the Charter could not 'come to the rescue', as was the case in *Mangold* and *Kücükdeveci*. The only solution available to the individual to circumvent the constraints stemming from the prohibition of directives' horizontal direct effect, considering the lack of direct effect of Article 27 of the Charter and regardless of the qualification of the principle codified therein as a general principle, thus, was the remedy of consistent interpretation.[331]

In short, *Association de médiation sociale* is of particular interest for three reasons. Firstly, the CJ reiterated the idea that directives cannot produce horizontal direct effects. Secondly, with reference to the relationship between general principles and the Charter, on one hand, it reiterated the idea that the former can be codified in the latter, as for the principle of non-discrimination and Article 21 of the Charter, while on the other hand it left unsettled the issue about the nature of Article 27 as a norm codifying a general principle and the possible disconnection between a general principle and direct effect. Thirdly, the Court emphasized that the direct (vertical and horizontal) effect of a principle (general or not) codified in a rule of the Charter can be considered unconditional only if it takes place through a right and not a principle within the meaning of Article 52(5) of the Charter,[332] as will be extensively clarified further in this section.

As to *Dominguez* and *Fenoll*, the CJ, similarly to how it ruled with respect to the right to information and consultation within the undertaking in *Association de médiation sociale*, did not expressly state that the right to paid annual leave is a general principle of EU law.[333]

[328] *Association de médiation sociale* (n 234), para. 29.
[329] *Association de médiation sociale* (n 234), para. 27.
[330] *Kücükdeveci* (n 311), para. 22 and *Glatzel* (n 305), para. 43, whereby the CJ has recognized and denied the direct effect of the Charter, respectively.
[331] For further insights on this issue, *see* F. Bestagno, *Validità e interpretazione degli atti dell'UE alla luce della Carta: conferme e sviluppi nella giurisprudenza della Corte in tema di dati personali* (2015) 1 *Il Diritto dell'Unione europea* 21.
[332] *See* the analysis by D. Dittert, *Droits fondamentaux européens: vers un effet direct horizontal généralisé?* (2014) 20 *Revue des affaires européennes* 177, 179.
[333] On this silence, in critical terms, *see* N. Lazzerini, *Gli effetti diretti orizzontali dei diritti fondamentali in materia sociale: la sentenza* Dominguez *della Corte di giustizia e la strada del silenzio* (2012) 3 *Rivista di diritto internazionale* 455.

Moreover, there are asymmetries between the two rulings. In the first place, while in *Dominguez* no reference is made to Article 31(2) of the Charter, according to which every worker 'has the right to limitation of maximum working hours, to daily and weekly rest periods and to an annual period of paid leave',[334] in *Fenoll* a reference to this provision is made. In the second place, while in *Dominguez* there is a reference to the right to paid annual leave as a 'particularly important principle', this is absent in *Fenoll*. Thirdly, while in *Dominguez* the CJ merely dealt with the applicability of consistent interpretation to a horizontal dispute, in *Fenoll* it explicitly observed that the Charter, and thus Article 31(2), was not applicable *ratione temporis* because, as AG Mengozzi pointed out,[335] Mr. Fenoll's claim to his annual leave was not applicable in the present case since it related 'to a period before the date of entry into force of the Lisbon Treaty and, therefore, before the date from which the Charter acquired the same legal value as the Treaties, pursuant to Article 6(1) of the EU Treaty'.[336] The joint examination of *Dominguez* and *Fenoll* brings forth, also in relation to Article 31(2) of the Charter, the pronounced self-restraint on the part of the CJ in respect to direct effect, both vertical and horizontal, of the Charter and of general principles. Indeed, while Article 31(2) of the Charter is not invoked in *Dominguez* and is not *ratione temporis* applicable in *Fenoll*, *quid* of the application of general principles and the matter of horizontal direct effect?

The *Sobczyszyn* and *King* judgments, on the one hand, allow us to delve deeper into the issue and sketch out some answers but, on the other hand, complicate matters further. Both are part of a jurisprudential trend, which began with *KHS* and continued with *Neidel*,[337] concerning Article 7 of Directive 2003/88 and Article 31(2) of the Charter. In *KHS*, the Court saw no problems of compatibility between domestic and EU law, whereas in *Neidel* the dispute involved public servants. Therefore, only the *Sobczyszyn* and *King* cases, which concern disputes between private parties initiated after the Charter's entry into force, are relevant. In both of them, not only was Article 31(2) mentioned, but it was also affirmed that the provision enshrines the right to paid annual leave and that it shall be regarded as a 'particularly important principle of EU social law'.[338] Again, as remarked in *Association de médiation sociale*, *Dominguez*, and *Fenoll*, the first doubt is the meaning of this second expression: is a 'particularly important principle of EU social law' a general principle of EU law? The second doubt is whether we are in the realm of 'rights', as AG Tanchev argued in his opinion in the *King* case,[339] or of 'principles', as referred to in Article 52(5) of the Charter. The Court did not dwell on the point, that is, it did not clarify whether the right to paid annual leave is a general principle that is directly effective and whether this direct effect is horizontal as well as vertical. Once again, the CJ is silent on central issues of EU law. It could be said that since in both cases it was a matter of consistent interpretation, and consequently disapplication did not arise, there was no need for the doctrine of direct effect to play a role.[340] But why not say so explicitly? The answer is simple, but not necessarily wrong, and applies not only

[334] In *Dominguez* (n 230), the CJ focused only on Directive 2003/88/CE, and not on Article 31(2) of the Charter, from the standpoint of both consistent interpretation (paras 23–31) and the State liability remedy (para. 43). For a strong criticism, *see* extensively L. Pech, *Between Judicial Minimalism and Avoidance: The Court of Justice's Sidestepping of Fundamental Constitutional Issues in* Römer *and* Dominguez (2012) 49 *Common Market Law Review* 1841.

[335] Opinion of AG Mengozzi of 12 January 2014, *Fenoll*, EU:C:2014:1753, paras 48–61.

[336] *Fenoll* (n 324), para. 46.

[337] CJ, *KHS AG v Winfried Schulte*, C-214/10, EU:C:2011:761; CJ, *Neidel*, C-337/10, EU:C:2012:263.

[338] *Sobczyszyn* (n 325), para. 19; *King* (n 257), para. 32.

[339] Opinion of AG Tanchev of 8 June 2017, *King*, EU:C:2017:439, para. 96.

[340] Opinion of AG Tanchev, *King* (n 339), para. 58.

to *Sobczysyn* and *King*, but to all the above-mentioned judgments rendered at the same time as *Kücükdeveci* and *Dansk Industri*: until then the preliminary references did not contain any explicit reference to the possible horizontal direct effect of the Charter, in particular of Article 31(2) of the Charter.[341]

5.4 ... and after

In the *post-Mangold-Kücükdeveci-Dansk Industri* era, the CJ changed its approach and explicitly attributed to the Charter the capacity to produce horizontal direct effects. Although not directly solicited by the referring courts through the preliminary reference proceedings, it did so in relation to the principle of non-discrimination on the grounds of religion[342] codified in Article 21 of the Charter (*IR*),[343] read together with its Article 47 (*Egenberger*).[344] It also did so in other cases concerning the Charter, with respect to Article 21 (*Cresco*)[345] about non-discrimination on the grounds of religion and to Article 31(2) (*Bauer, Max-Planck*)[346] about the right to paid annual leave,[347] at the request of the referring court. In the very recent *K.L.* ruling, the CJ, for the first time in such clear terms, building its reasoning also on *Egenberger*,[348] in spite of any related questions raised by the referring court, affirmed that Article 47, independently[349] from Article 21, is able to be directly invoked and applied in

[341] *See* the compelling account by L. Cecchetti, *Unravelling*.

[342] On freedom of religion within EU law, from the standpoint of horizontality, first and foremost with regard to *IR*, *Egenberger*, and *Cresco*, *see* S. Polo, R. José, *Estado y confesiones religiosas en el Derecho de la Unión Europea: la repercusión del artículo 17 del Tratado de Funcionamiento de la Unión Europea en la jurisprudencia del TJUE* (2018) 46 *Revista General de Derecho Europeo* 270; A. Colombi Ciacchi, *The Direct Horizontal Effect of EU Fundamental Rights* (2019) 15 *European Constitutional Law Review* 294; M. Klein, *Das Recht der Kirchen im Tauziehen zwischen Luxemburg und Karlsruhe—Das kirchliche Arbeitsrecht als Machtprobe?*, (2019) 54 *Europarecht* 338; S. Röß, *Die europäische Gesetzgebungskompetenz in Fragen religionsbezogener Einstellungsvoraussetzungen: der Fall Egenberger* (2022) 25 *Zeitschrift für Europarechtliche Studien* 607; M. Van den Brink, *When can Religious Employers Discriminate? The Scope of the Religious Ethos Exemption in EU Law* (2022) 1 *European Law Open* 89.

[343] CJ, *IR v JQ*, C-68/17, EU:C:2018:696, paras 68–70.

[344] CJ, *Vera Egenberger v Evangelisches Werk für Diakonie und Entwicklung e.V*, C-414/16, EU:C:2018:257, paras 47, 76, and 78.

[345] *Cresco* (n 101), paras 76 and 89.

[346] CJ, *Pensions-Sicherungs-Verein VVaG v Günther Bauer*, C-168/18, EU:C:2019:1128, paras 84–86; *Max-Planck* (n 202), paras 74–81. *See* also, for a case within the realm of consistent interpretation rather than direct effect, CJ, *Federación de Servicios de Comisiones Obreras (CCOO)*, C-55/18, EU:C:2019:402, paras 60–71, whereby Article 31(2) was invoked in a case concerning 'the right of every worker to a limitation of maximum working hours and to daily and weekly rest periods'.

[347] On the developments brought about by *Bauer* and/or *Max-Planck see*, *ex multis*, beyond the blogsphere, S. de Vries, *The Bauer et al. and Max Planck judgments and EU Citizens' Fundamental Rights: An Outlook for Harmony* (2019) 3 *European Equality Law Review* 16; S. Sciarra, *Diritti sociali fondamentali nazionali e europei. A proposito di diritto alle ferie retribuite* (2019) 10 *Federalismi.it* 1; R. Palladino, *Diritti, principi ed effetto diretto orizzontale delle disposizioni (in materia sociale) della Carta dei diritti fondamentali dell'Unione europea* (2019) 1 *Il Diritto dell'Unione europea* 175; M. A. Panascì, *The RIght to Paid Annual Leave as an EU Fundamental Social Right. Comment on Bauer et al.: Joined Cases C-569/16 and C-570/16 Stadt Wuppertal v Maria Elisabeth Bauer and Volker Willmeroth v Martina Broßonn, EU:C:2018:871* (2019) 26 *Maastricht Journal of European and Comparative Law* 441; L. He, *Une protection remarquable du droit au repos et au loisir: Commentaire de l'arrêt CJUE 6 nov. 2018, aff. C-684/16, Société Max-Planck c/M. Shimizu* (2019) 55 *Revue trimestrielle de droit européenne* 651; D. Leczykiewicz, *The Judgment in* Bauer *and the Effect of the EU Charter of Fundamental Rights in Horizontal Situations* (2020) 16 *European Review of Contract Law* 323; E. Muir, *The Horizontal Effects of Charter Rights Given Expression to in EU Legislation, from* Mangold *to* Bauer (2019) 12 *Review of European Administrative Law* 185; K. Lenaerts, *The Horizontal Application of the Charter* (2020) 4 *Quaderni costituzionali* 633; R. Krause, *Horizontal Effect of the EU Charter of Fundamental Rights: Bauer and Willmeroth, MPG* (2021) 58 *Common Market Law Review* 1173.

[348] CJ, *K.L. v X sp. z o.o.*, C-715/20, EU:C:2024:139, para. 80.

[349] On the necessary joint application of Article 47 and other rights safeguarded in the Charter, *see* the opinion of 30 March 2023 of AG Pitruzzella, *K.L.*, EU:C:2023:281, whereby it was affirmed that the horizontal direct effect of

horizontal situations.[350] In the background is, if only implicitly, the statement contained in recital 6 of the Preamble to the Charter, according to which the enjoyment of fundamental rights 'entails responsibilities and duties with regard to other persons, to the human community and to future generations'.

The above cases, with the exception of *K.L.*, which is examined further in this section, have four common threads. The first: unlike the uncertainties in the previous case law, it is not decisive for a principle codified in the Charter to be considered directly effective, vertically and horizontally, that it be defined as a general principle of EU law. Proof of this is that, in *Bauer* and *Max-Planck*, the directly effective right to paid annual leave is never qualified as a general principle, being instead considered an 'essential principle of EU social law'.[351] The second: unlike the minimalism of the previous case law, the issue of the horizontality of fundamental rights is directly addressed, albeit to differing degrees, in all the judgments. The third: just as it is stated that the principles codified in the Charter are 'mandatory in nature',[352] it is also declared that the rules contained therein are to be considered sufficient in themselves to be applied by the judiciary in the case at hand[353] and this occurs by references to precision and/or unconditionality of EU law, or without reference to any of the conditions embodied in the test of direct effect.[354] Fourthly, and finally: despite the self-sufficiency of the Charter's provisions, the latter are always applied in conjunction with secondary law, namely Article 4(2) of Directive 2000/78/EC (*Egenberger, IR*), Articles 1 and 2(2) of the same directive (*Cresco*), and Article 7 of Directive 2003/88 (*Bauer, Max-Planck*). The Charter, thus, contains sufficiently accomplished rules but, in order to exert its legal effects in national legal systems, must necessarily be enforced in conjunction with other EU rules. This is a real conundrum that brings to light the lack of clarity on the identification of the source of horizontal direct

Article 47 'has always been recognised in combination with other rights enforceable against a private individual' since such joint application 'is required by the same regulatory structure of Article 47: it recognises the right to an effective remedy for everyone "whose rights and freedoms guaranteed by the law of the Union" are violated' (para. 98). Thus, the enforceability of Article 47 in inter-private relationships 'presupposes that the private individual concerned is the holder of a right or a freedom, guaranteed by the law of the Union, on which he or she may rely in legal proceedings' (para. 99).

350 *K.L.* (n 348), para. 82: 'The national court hearing a dispute between individuals is required, where it is not possible for it to interpret the applicable national law in a way which is consistent with that clause, to ensure, within its jurisdiction, the judicial protection which individuals derive from Article 47 of the Charter and to guarantee the full effectiveness of that article by disapplying, in so far as necessary, any contrary provision of national law'. On the implications of *K.L.* for the horizontal direct effect of the Charter, *see* L. Cecchetti, *Something new under the Sun: The direct effect of directives plus Article 47 Charter in horizontal situations in the K.L. judgment, BlogDUE*, 24 April 2024, available at https://www.aisdue.eu/lorenzo-cecchetti-something-new-under-the-sun-the-direct-effect-of-directives-plus-article-47-charter-in-horizontal-situations-in-the-k-l-judgment/; J. Gundel, *EuGH: Gleichbehandlung befristeter undunbefristeter Arbeitsverhältnisse bei Kündigung* (2024) 14 *Neue Juristische Wochenschrift* 949; D. Sarmiento, S. Iglesias Sanchez, *Insight: Is Direct Effect Morphing into Something Different?*, Madrid, EU Law Live, 4 March 2024, available at https://eulawlive.com/insight-is-direct-effect-morphing-into-something-different-by-daniel-sarmiento-and-sara-iglesias-sanchez/; F. Van Reempts, *The Effectiveness of Directives in Horizontal Situations: the Charter Unchained? (K.L. v. X)*, EU Law Live, 5 March 2024, available at https://eulawlive.com/op-ed-the-effectiveness-of-directives-in-horizontal-situations-the-charter-unchained-k-l-v-x-by-fien-van-reempts/.

351 *Bauer* (n 346), para. 49; *Max-Planck* (n 202), para. 69.

352 *IR* (n 343), para. 69; *Egenberber* (n 344), paras 76–77; *Cresco* (n 101), paras 76–77; *Bauer* (n 346), para. 83; *Max-Planck* (n 202), paras 45 and 72.

353 As observed by A. Bogg, M. Ford, *Article 31*, in S. Peers, T. Hervey, J. Kenner, A. Ward (eds.), *The EU Charter of Fundamental Rights: A Commentary*, 2nd ed., Oxford, Hart, 2021, 875–922, 895.

354 Doubts about the meaning of direct effect of the Charter's provisions, being 'mandatory in nature', are expressed by M. Bobek, *Institutional Report. National Courts and the Enforcement of EU Law*, in M. Botman, J. Rijpma (eds.), *National Courts and the Enforcement of EU Law: The Pivotal Role of National Courts in the EU Legal Order. The XXIX FIDE Congress Publications*, Vol. 1, The Hague, Eleven International Publishing, 2020, 61–89, 66–67.

effect. Moreover, there is a divergence concerning the relationship between the Charter and the directives which further complicates matters: in *Egenberger* it is written that the directive 'is a specific expression' of the principle of non-discrimination enshrined in (Article 21, not Article 47, of) the Charter,[355] in *IR* and *Cresco* there is no mention of this, while in *Bauer* and *Max-Planck* the unconditional nature of the right to a period of paid annual leave is deemed as 'not needing to be given concrete expression by the provisions of EU or national law, which are only required to specify the exact duration of annual leave and, where appropriate, certain conditions for the exercise of that right'.[356] In this vein, to be reiterated is the idea expressed by the CJ in its case law on the vertical direct effect of EU sources other than the Charter: unconditionality, as a constitutive factor of direct effect, can be realized even in the presence of a certain margin of discretion, that is, even when the adoption of measures aimed at better specifying the content of the EU rule, and at making it enforceable, is deemed necessary.[357] In any case, regardless of whether the concretization is complete or partial, it is undeniable that in the case law there is a transfusion of both the principle of non-discrimination and the right to paid annual leave in Articles 21 and 31(2) of the Charter, respectively.

The jurisprudence subsequent to *Bauer* and *Max-Planck* includes, in particular, two strands and one important judgment, that is, the *K.L.* case, previously mentioned. The first strand[358] *(i)* relates to Article 31(2) of the Charter[359] with respect to the multiple prerogatives composing the right to paid annual leave invoked by an employee against a private company. The second strand *(ii)* concerns disputes between employees and employers on the prohibition of manifestation, in the workplace, of religious (and philosophical or political) beliefs, including through wearing of an item of religious clothing, and with particular reference to the prohibition of Islamic headscarves[360] envisaged in the internal rules of the companies.[361] The *K.L.* ruling *(iii)* is on the interpretation of clause 4 of the framework

[355] *Egenberger* (n 344), para. 47. In most other languages the term is 'concretization': for instance, '*concretizza*', '*konkretisiert*', '*concrétise*', respectively, in Italian, German, and French.

[356] *Bauer* (n 346), para. 85; *Max-Planck* (n 202), para. 74.

[357] *See* § 5 of Chapter III.

[358] *Hein* (n 252); CJ, *Terveys- ja sosiaalialan neuvottelujärjestö (TSN) ry v Hyvinvointialan liitto ry and Auto- ja Kuljetusalan Työntekijäliitto AKT ry v Satamaoperaattorit ry*, joined cases C-609/17 and C-610/17, EU:C:2019:981; CJ, *QH v Varhoven kasatsionen sad na Republika Bulgaria and CV v Iccrea Banca SpA*, joined cases C-762/18 and C-37/19, EU:C:2020:504; CJ, *WD v job-medium GmbH*, C-233/20, EU:C:2021:960, CJ, *DS v Koch Personaldienstleistungen GmbH*, C-514/20, EU:C:2022:19; CJ, *XP and AR*, joined cases C-518/20 and C-727/20, EU:C:2022:707; CJ, *LB v TO*, C-120/21, EU:C:2022:718; CJ, *Keolis Agen*, joined cases C-271–275/22, EU:C:2023:834.

[359] *See*, recently, as to the first strand, L. Cecchetti, *Unravelling*, 63–64.

[360] *See* CJ, *Achbita*, C-157/15, EU:C:2017:203; CJ, *Bougnaoui*, C-188/15, EU:C:2017:204, both regarding the prohibition of Islamic headscarves. *See* also CJ, *Wabe*, joined cases C-804/18 and C-341/19, EU:C:2021:594; CJ, *L.F.*, C-344/20, EU:C:2022:774, relating to disputes on the duties imposed by private companies to its employees from refraining to manifest in the workplace, in particular through their clothing, their religious, philosophical, or political beliefs. For a recent case involving a public administration, *see* CJ, *OP*, C-148/22, EU:C:2023:924, on which, *see* E. Howard, *The Court of Justice and headscarves at work: discretion in EU anti-discrimination law: a dangerous precedent (Case C-148/22 OP v Commune d'Ans)*, EU Law Live, 5 December 2023, available at https://eulawlive.com/op-ed-the-court-of-justice-and-headscarves-at-work-discretion-in-eu-anti-discrimination-law-a-dangerous-precedent-case-c-148-22-op-v-commune-dans-by-erica-howard/#.

[361] As to the second strand, with regard to the matter of horizontality, *see* F. Costamagna, *Diritti fondamentali*, 198–216. For analyses mainly focused on the substantive law profiles of the case law, i.e. the scope and extent of freedom of religion in the workplace, *see* S. Hennette-Vauchez, *Equality and the Market: The Unhappy Fate of Religious Discrimination in Europe.* Bougnaoui, Achbita (2017) 13 *European Constitutional Law Review* 749; E. Howard, *Islamic Headscarvers and the CJEU:* Achbita *and* Bougnaoui (2017) 24 *Maastricht Journal of European and Comparative Law* 351; L. Salvadego, *Il divieto per i dipendenti di imprese private di esibire simboli religiosi all'esame della Corte di giustizia dell'Unione europea* (2017) 4 *Rivista di diritto internazionale* 808; E. Cloots, *Safe Harbour or Open Sea for Corporate Headscarf Bans?* (2018) 55 *Common Market Law Review* 602; R. Xenidis, *The Polysemy of Anti-discrimination Law: The Interpretation Architecture of the Framework Employment Directive at*

agreement on fixed-term work concluded on 18 March 1999, which is annexed to Council Directive 1999/70/EC of 28 June 1999 concerning the framework agreement on fixed-term work concluded by ETUC, UNICE, and CEEP,[362] and the interpretation of Article 47 of the Charter. The request was made in proceedings between K.L., a worker who was dismissed, and the former employer, that is, a private company governed by Polish law, on the termination of the fixed-term employment contract between the two parties to the dispute. The incompatibility with Articles 21 and 30 of the Charter was also raised by the referring court, but the Court dismissed such request as it found that, 'when adopting legislation specifying and giving specific expression to the employment conditions which are governed, *inter alia*, by clause 4 of the framework agreement, a Member State implements EU law', and, for this reason, it is the compliance with the right to an effective remedy enshrined in Article 47 of the Charter which must be assessed.[363]

In relation to the first strand *(i)*, four principal features can be highlighted. First: partially in line with the trend which emerged in part of the previous case law (*Bauer* and *Max-Planck*), the principles codified in the Charter, which are applicable in horizontal relationships and are the source of the duty of disapplication, are not defined as 'general principles of EU law', regressing to 'particularly important principle[s] of EU social law' in almost all cases.[364] A regression, however, that does not seem to entail practical consequences in terms of their internal effect given that, in *Keolis Agen*, the CJ explicitly observed that 'the right to paid annual leave is, as a principle of EU social law, not only particularly important, but is also expressly laid down in Article 31(2) of the Charter, which Article 6(1) TEU recognizes as having the same legal value as the Treaties'.[365] Second: direct effect is neither mentioned nor is the issue of the Charter's horizontality directly addressed in any of the cases, in line with older case law. Third: even with this *caveat*, the Charter and directives, in particular Article 7 of Directive 2003/88, are applied together.[366] In this sense, the joint application of these two sources of EU law continues to be the trigger for the duty to disapply. Fourth: in contrast to the silence of *IR* and *Cresco* and to the approach taken in *Bauer* and *Max-Planck*, but in line with *Egenberger*, in almost all cases,[367] significantly in all the most recent ones, it is expressly stated that the directive 'gives concrete expression' to the Charter or that it 'implements the principle' enshrined therein,[368] enabling the Charter to achieve that degree of completeness which allows it to be enforced in the case at hand, even in horizontal disputes.[369]

the Court of Justice (2021) 58 *Common Market Law Review* 1659; I. Anrò, F. Croci, *I simboli religiosi di fronte alla Corte di giustizia: sviluppi recenti e prospettive*, in A. Negri, G. Ragone, M. Toscano, L. P. Vanoni (eds.), *I simboli religiosi nella società contemporanea*, Turin, Giappichelli, 2022, 5–28; E. Howard, *Headscarves and the CJEU: Protecting Fundamental Rights and Pandering to Prejudice, the CJEU Does Both* (2022) 29 *Maastricht Journal of European and Comparative Law* 245.

[362] OJ 1999 L 175, 43.
[363] *K.L.* (n 348), para. 77.
[364] *Hein* (n 252), para. 22; *WD* (n 358), para. 24; *DS* (n 358), para. 23; *XP and AR* (n 358), para. 24; *LB* (n 358), para. 33. 'Almost' since in neither *TSN* (n 358), nor *Iccrea Banca* (n 358), are there references to 'principles'.
[365] *Keolis Agen* (n 358), para. 21.
[366] Except for *TSN* (n 358), paras 32–55, whereby the CJ reflected separately on the directive and the Charter, in line with the reasoning developed by the referring court.
[367] *See WD* (n 358), para. 25 (where the sentence in English—not in the other languages—is slightly different: 'Article 7(1) of Directive 2003/88 reflects and *gives effect* to the fundamental right to an annual period of paid leave, enshrined in Article 31(2) of the Charter') (italics added); *DS* (n 358), para. 23; *XP and AR* (n 358), para. 24; *LB* (n 358), para. 33. There is no reference to such effect of concretization in *Hein* (n 252), *TSN* (n 358), and *Iccrea Banca* (n 358).
[368] *Keolis Agen* (n 358), para. 22.
[369] This reasoning, therefore, lies far away from the praise for a constitutional law approach to fundamental rights' horizontality aimed at regarding the Charter as the true source of enforceable rights for the individuals

With reference to the second strand *(ii)*, the picture is more complicated. There are three significant divergences and two common elements. The first divergence is that, while in *Achbita*, *Wabe*, and *LF*, Articles 10 and 21 of the Charter were both invoked by the applicant and are mentioned by the CJ, in *Bougnaoui* there is only a reference to Article 10 and, consequently, there is no reference to either Article 21 or to the principle of non-discrimination. The second divergence relates to the role played by Article 16: in *Wabe* and *LF* the norm is relied on by the Court to justify the employer's choice to prevent the employee from wearing the veil and the Court examined this matter in depth; in *Achbita* there is a mere reference to that provision; in *Bougnaoui* it is not even mentioned.[370] The third difference is that, while in *Achbita*, *Wabe*, and *LF* the CJ concluded that private rules governing labour relationships are compatible with Directive 2000/78/EC, in *Bougnaoui* the conclusion is the opposite. More notably, in *Achbita*[371] it was written that Article 2(2)(a) of Directive 2000/78/EC must be interpreted as meaning that 'the prohibition on wearing an Islamic headscarf, which arises from an internal rule of a private undertaking prohibiting the visible wearing of any political, philosophical or religious sign in the workplace, does not constitute direct discrimination based on religion or belief within the meaning of that directive'.[372] In *Wabe* it was affirmed that Articles 1 and 2(2)(a) of Directive 2000/78/EC must be interpreted as meaning that

> an internal rule of an undertaking, prohibiting workers from wearing any visible sign of political, philosophical or religious beliefs in the workplace, does not constitute, with regard to workers who observe certain clothing rules based on religious precepts, direct discrimination on the grounds of religion or belief, for the purpose of that directive, provided that that rule is applied in a general and undifferentiated way.[373]

In *LF* it was concluded that Article 2(2)(a) of Directive 2000/78 must be interpreted as meaning that

> a provision of an undertaking's terms of employment which prohibits workers from manifesting, through words, through clothing, or in any other way, their religious or philosophical beliefs, whatever those beliefs may be, does not constitute, with regard to workers who intend to exercise their freedom of religion and conscience through the visible wearing of a sign or an item of clothing with religious connotations, direct discrimination 'on the [ground] of religion or belief' for the purposes of that directive, provided that that provision is applied in a general and undifferentiated way.

In *Bougnaoui*, instead, it was observed that Article 4(1) of Directive 2000/78/EC must be interpreted as meaning that 'the willingness of an employer to take account of the wishes of

set out in part of the literature; *see*, for instance, E. Frantziou, *(Most of) the Charter of Fundamental Rights is Horizontally Applicable. ECJ 6 November 2018, Joined Cases C-569/16 and C-570/16, Bauer et al* (2019) 15 *European Constitutional Law Review* 306.

[370] *Wabe* (n 360), paras 40–41, 63, 67, 83–84; *Achbita* (n 360), para. 38.

[371] For a strong criticism on the alleged ideological neutrality of *Achbita* (and *Bougnanoui*), *see* J. H. H. Weiler, *Je Suis Achbita* (2017) 28 *European Journal of International Law* 989 and Z. Adams, J. Olusegun Adenitire, *Ideological Neutrality in the Workplace* (2018) 81 *Modern Law Review* 337.

[372] *Achbita* (n 360), para. 49.

[373] *Wabe* (n 360), operative part of the judgment.

a customer no longer to have the services of that employer provided by a worker wearing an Islamic headscarf cannot be considered a genuine and determining occupational requirement within the meaning of that provision'.[374]

As for the common threads underpinning the second strand of rulings, first of all, in the operative parts of *Achbita*, *Wabe*, and *LF*, which are all favourable to the employer, and of *Bougnaoui*, which is not, the focus is exclusively on the directive and no reference is made to the Charter. Additionally, except for a fleeting reference to the inter-individual nature of the dispute, in none of the cases is there the slightest reasoning on the horizontal direct effect of EU law. This is probably because, as noted above, the preliminary references do not contain any. The problem is that, if with regard to *Achbita*, *Wabe*, and *LF*, lacking disapplication, such minimalism is understandable since in practice no disapplication of private conduct took place, in the case of *Bougnaoui* it is hardly clear why the issue was not addressed by the CJ, given that the decision taken by the employer must be set aside and this occurs on the basis 'only' of the directive.

With respect to *K.L. (iii)*, on the one hand, the ruling has several features in common with the *IR*, *Egenberger*, *Cresco*, *Bauer*, and *Max-Planck* cases since the matter of horizontal direct effect is openly tackled and the Charter, most notably its Article 47, was deemed 'sufficient in itself' so as 'to confer on individuals a right on which they may rely as such'.[375] On the other hand, the reasoning of the CJ is different, in its *structure*, from the first strand of rulings, discussed above, concerning Article 31(2) of the Charter. Indeed, the Court neither referred to the ability of Directive 1999/70/EC to give concrete expression to Article 47 of the Charter nor led back the duty of disapplication to Article 47 and Directive 1999/70/EC, read jointly. Furthermore, the Court seems to dissociate the long examination of EU secondary law carried out in paras 50–76, which are mainly aimed at affirming the direct effect of Article 4(1) of the framework agreement annexed to the directive,[376] from the very short part of the judgment, contained in paras 77–82, about Article 47. As a matter of fact, the source of disapplication, at first glance, seems to be Article 47 since, in the operative part of the judgment, it is held that 'the national court hearing a dispute between individuals is required . . . to ensure, within its jurisdiction, the judicial protection which individuals derive from Article 47 of the Charter of Fundamental Rights of the European Union and to guarantee the full effectiveness of that article by disapplying, in so far as necessary, any contrary provision of national law'.[377] However, the Court's statement builds upon two previous assertions. One comes immediately before, whereby it is clarified, in the very same paragraph 83, that clause 4 of the framework agreement on fixed-term work 'must be interpreted as precluding national legislation according to which an employer is not required to state, in writing, the reasons for the termination of a fixed-term employment contract with a notice period, although it is bound by such an obligation in the event of termination of an employment contract of indefinite duration'. The other assertion is in para. 79, which reads as follows: 'it must be held that the difference in treatment introduced by the applicable national law, *as established in paragraph 56 of the present judgment*, undermines the fundamental right to an effective remedy enshrined in Article 47 of the Charter'. What triggers the breach of Article 47, thus the duty of disapplication, is the breach of Directive 1999/70/EC in so far as para. 56 is the key part of the judgment fully devoted to the directive. More specifically, in para. 56 it was stated that

374 *Bougnanoui* (n 360), operative part of the judgment.
375 For instance, *see K.L.* (n 348), para. 80.
376 *K.L.* (n 348), paras 44–45.
377 *K.L.* (n 348), para. 83.

> national legislation such as that at issue in the main proceedings establishes a difference in treatment involving less favourable treatment of fixed-term workers as opposed to permanent workers, arising from the fact that the latter are not subject to the limitation in question concerning the provision of information on the reasons justifying the dismissal.

Hence, *in substance*, the breach of the directive is the true reason for the conflict between EU law and the Polish legal order, as well as for the obligation imposed upon national authorities to set aside Article 30(4) of the Polish Labour Code.

In short and to summarize, while several uncertainties emerge in the light of the two strands described above, some tentative answers should be given all the same. First: can we once and for all affirm that the attribution of direct effect, vertical or horizontal, is independent of the qualification of a principle as a general principle of EU law? *Probably* yes. Second: does Article 16 of the Charter have direct effect and, if so, can it also be enforced in horizontal disputes?[378] *Probably* yes. Third, what is the real basis of the duty to disapply generated by the recognition of horizontal direct effect? The Court, on the one hand, in the case law on Article 31(2) of the Charter, wrote that the concretization of the Charter is achieved by means of the directive, while on the other hand, precisely because of this concretization, it concludes that the rules of the Charter are 'mandatory and unconditional',[379] self-sufficient, and consequently apt to be applicable in a horizontal situation. In this vein, the Charter, like the general principles in *Mangold*, *Kücükdeveci*, and *Dansk Industri*, is deemed as the source of disapplication, while the directive is its normative parameter.[380] But how is it possible for a provision to be, at the same time, concretized by another rule and autonomously able to govern a given case?[381] As written above and on several occasions, one answer could be that unconditionality need not be absolute to trigger the doctrine of direct effect and consequently disapplication, since EU unconditional law requires *naturaliter* further concretization.[382] There is no doubt that this is so. However, it is one thing to say that there is a need for a specification of particular operational profiles of a given provision, but quite another to say that one rule shall be concretized, that is, filled with content, by another. The true counter-objection is that a clear boundary between these two situations is difficul to draw. The confusion, upstream, therefore, is difficult to overcome. Moreover, as not every provision of a directive 'will make it into a Charter-guaranteed right', there remains the problem of the lack of predictability of this process of concretization, the problem, that is, of the prerequisites for

[378] Article 16 has been examined in the literature (S. Weatherill, *Use and Abuse of the EU's Charter of Fundamental Rights: On the Improper Veneration of 'freedom of contract'* (2014) 10 *European Review of Contract Law* 167) for other reasons than its internal effect, as the case of T. Lock, *Article 16*, in M. Kellerbauer, M. Klamert, J. Tomkin (eds.), *The EU Treaties and the Charter of Fundamental Rights. A Commentary*, Oxford, Oxford University Press, 2019, 2147–2148.

[379] In the most recent ruling on Article 31(2) of the Charter, i.e. *Keolis Agen* (n 358), para. 23, the CJ employed both terms.

[380] As explained by K. Lenaerts, J. A. Gutiérrez-Fons, *The Constitutional Allocation*, 1647, and M. De Mol, Kücükdeveci, 300.

[381] On the complexities and inconsistencies of such approach, before and after the two strands examined above, *see* T. Tridimas, *Horizontal Effect of General Principles*, 232; E. Muir, *The Fundamental Rights Implications of EU Legislation: Some Constitutional Challenges* (2014) 51 *Common Market Law Review* 219; E. Gualco, L. Lourenço, *'Clash of Titans'. General Principles of EU Law: Balancing and Horizontal Direct Effect* (2016) 1 *European Papers* 643, 649; F. Fontanelli, *You Can Teach a New Court* Mangold *Tricks—The Horizontal Effect of the Charter Right to Paid Annual Leave*, in *EU Law Analysis*, 11 November, 2018; R. Mastroianni, G. Strozzi, *Diritto*, 314–316 and R. Schütze, *European Union Law*, 109, according to whom 'the court remained ambivalent about whether the general principle was violated *because* the directive had been violated' (italics in the original).

[382] On the meaning and extent of unconditionality, *see* § 5 of Chapter III.

this to happen.[383] The *K.L.* ruling only apparently seems to make a step towards a definitive emancipation of the Charter, in terms of its horizontal direct effect, from directives. The opposite is *probably* true: national law is inconsistent and must be disapplied due to a breach of the rights stemming from the directive, which is, albeit not explicitly and formally, both the ultimate source of disapplication and parameter of legality of national law. The fourth intertwined uncertainty: must the rules of a directive be directly effective in order for their joint application with the Charter to be realized? As a matter of fact, even though this has been recognized by the CJ in only a few judgments,[384] the answer seems to be affirmative, *probably*. The fifth and last uncertainty: how do we evaluate *Bougnaoui* in so far as there seems no doubt that a directive was directly applied in a dispute between private individuals? *Probably*, it must be evaluated in the sense that horizontal direct effect has been implicitly affirmed.

The doubts expressed so far and the suggested answers confirm that the CJ's entire reasoning on fundamental rights foreseen in the Charter and directives reveals a troublesome relationship of mutual assistance between these two sources of law: the former provides the directive with horizontality, while the latter, either explicitly or implicitly, gives concrete expression to the Charter.[385] To explain this, Lenaerts,[386] in a writing coeval with *Bauer/Max-Planck*, builds his arguments on the 'essence test' enshrined in Article 52(1) of the Charter, whereby it is stated that 'any limitation on the exercise of the rights and freedoms recognised by this Charter must . . . respect the essence of those rights and freedoms'.[387] This way, Lenaerts relies on a test created to assess the admissibility of a derogation from a fundamental right and uses it to verify whether a rule of the Charter has direct effect and can be successfully invoked in a horizontal dispute. According to him, a distinction may be drawn between two types of situations: *(i)* when the essence of a fundamental right enshrined in the Charter can produce horizontal direct effect but its 'non-essential elements may not', the directive comes into play and shall necessarily give concrete expression to the Charter's provision; *(ii)* when, in addition to the essence of a fundamental right, its non-essential elements are also sufficiently unconditional, the directive shall not apply and a concretization by means of different rules than those in the Charter is not necessary. Lenaerts takes *Bauer* as an example, recalling that in the case the CJ did not explicitly 'use' the directive to fill with content Article 31(2) of the Charter. Moreover, in *Bauer* there is a reference to the infringement of 'the very substance' of the right to paid annual leave or of 'his corresponding right to payment of an allowance in lieu of leave not taken upon termination of the employment relationship' as a reason for triggering the disapplication of national law.[388] Such a reference manifestly mirrors the 'essence' criterion enshrined in Article 52(1) of the Charter. Yet, as

[383] The sentence above in the text is borrowed from M. Bobek, *Why is it Better*, 215; *see* also opinion of AG Bobek of 25 July 2018, *Cresco*, EU:C:2018:614, paras 139–145.

[384] *See Bauer* (n 346), paras 70–75; *Max-Planck* (n 202), paras 63–69.

[385] In the same vein *see* E. Muir, *The Horizontal Effects*, 205–212; R. Xenidis, *The Polysemy Of Anti-Discrimination Law: The Interpretation Architecture Of The Framework Employment Directive At the Court of Justice* (2021) 58 *Common Market Law Review* 1649, 1681. Doubts about the tenability of such scheme were raised, before the *post-Bauer/Max-Planck*, by N. Lazzerini, *(Some of) the Fundamental Rights Granted by the Charter may be a Source of Obligations for Private Parties:* AMS (2014) 51 *Common Market Law Review* 907, 921–922, and, more recently, by E. Frantziou, *(Most of) the Charter of Fundamental Rights*, 314–319.

[386] K. Lenaerts, *Limits on Limitations: The Essence of Fundamental Rights in the EU*, in *German Law Journal*, 2019, 779, 788–792.

[387] On such test, *see* C. Antpöhler, J. Dickschen, S. Hentrei, M. Kottmann, M. Smrkolj, A. von Bogdandy, *Reverse* Solange*—Protecting the Essence of Fundamental Rights against EU Member States* (2012) 49 *Common Market Law Review* 489 and M. Brkan, *The Concept of Essence of Fundamental Rights in the EU Legal Order: Peeling the Onion to its Core* (2018) 14 *European Constitutional Law Review* 332.

[388] *Bauer* (n 346), paras 49–50.

remarked in the literature, the fact that in *Bauer* there isn't an express indication that Article 7 of Directive 2003/88 gives concrete expression to the Charter does not mean that, in reality, this does not happen. The contrary is true, as may be easily inferred from the numerous referrals to the directive throughout the judgment whereby the Court repeatedly states that Article 31(2) reflects what is said in the directive, for instance where it was affirmed that 'the right to annual leave constitutes only one of two aspects of the right to paid annual leave as an essential principle of EU social law reflected in Article 7 of Directive 93/104 and Article 7 of Directive 2003/88, now expressly enshrined as a fundamental right in Article 31(2) of the Charter'.[389] Put differently, as was also observed by AG Bot in his opinion in *TSN*, the very meaning of the 'essence' of Article 31(2), that is, of its hard core 'of minimum protection', is laid down in secondary law, notably in Article 7 of Directive 2003/88.[390] As remarked in the literature, 'there is therefore little doubt that the Court felt it necessary both to draw from the content of the directive to decide on the substance of the fundamental right in the Charter, and to justify its approach to the joint reading of the two layers of norms'.[391] Moreover, on the one hand, it seems problematic, in practice very difficult, to draw a clear dividing line between the essence of a right and its non-essential elements. On the other hand, if in *Bauer* the 'essence test' is implicitly referred to by the Court, the same cannot be said about all other judgments, *in primis* those concerning Articles 21 and 47 of the Charter, which are not related to social rights.[392]

The added value of the Charter, therefore, in both the case law after *Bauer* and in this very same ruling, appears to be merely instrumental, not only in 'activating' the field of application of EU law under its Article 51(1), but in bypassing the prohibition of horizontality.[393] Actually, the approach of the CJ rests on a blatant *fictio iuris*,[394] aimed at *de facto* infringing the prohibition of the directives' horizontality rather than 'simply' overcoming it, making it liable to create legal uncertainty among legal practitioners, citizens, and businesses. It is a prohibition that no longer seems to have any justification. *Mutatis mutandis*, as seen with respect to the recognition of direct effect of general principles of EU law in vertical relationships,[395] direct effect is *in concreto* attached to the (more) detailed provisions which give expression to the principle or to the Charter, although the latter are, *on paper*, the source of disapplication.

5.5 Realm and justification of fundamental rights' horizontal direct effect

On a more general level, four further problems emerge from the analysis of EU case law performed in the previous sections. First, although the case law on the horizontality of

[389] *Bauer* (n 346), para. 58.
[390] Opinion of AG Bot of 4 June 2019, *TSN*, joined cases C-609–610/17, EU:C:2019:459, para. 112.
[391] E. Muir, *The Horizontal Effects*, 209–211. For a more general *critique* of Lenaerts' proposal, *see* T. Tridimas, G. Gentile, *The Essence of Rights: An Unreliable Boundary?* (2019) 20 *German Law Journal* 794; *see Bauer* (n 346), para. 83.
[392] E. Muir, *The Horizontal Effects*, 211.
[393] On this matter, *see Association de médiation sociale* (n 234), para. 43 and *Bauer* (n 346), para. 53. *See* N. Lazzerini, *La Carta dei diritti fondamentali dell'Unione europea. I limiti di applicazione*, Milan, Franco Angeli, 2018, 183–269.
[394] Similarly *see* M. Condinanzi, *L'invocabilità della Carta dei diritti fondamentali dell'Unione europea nei rapporti orizzontali*, in C. Amalfitano, M. D'Amico, S. Leone (eds.), *La Carta dei diritti fondamentali dell'Unione Europa nel sistema integrato di tutela*, Turin, Giappichelli, 2022, 125–146, 139.
[395] *See* §§ 3.1-3.2 and 4 of Chapter III.

fundamental rights to date concerns only some workers' prerogatives in the context of horizontal disputes, in relation to Articles 21, 31(2), and 47[396] of the Charter, as remarked by Prechal, there are many other Charter provisions, not only related to social rights, that may be interpreted as imposing obligations upon individuals and triggering a duty to disapply public and private measures.[397] The reasoning of the CJ, if initially centred on the principle of non-discrimination, now goes beyond its material scope. Indeed, there seems to be no particular reason why horizontality cannot be allowed in areas that have little to do not only with non-discrimination, as was the case for the right to paid annual leave, but also with social law.[398] One example is the digital sector:[399] it is probably only a matter of time before the CJ applies the Charter in horizontal relations and possibly imposes the disapplication of conflicting national laws, and/or of conflicting measures of private origin in relation to a number of provisions of the Charter, such as, for example, Articles 7 and 8, respectively, on the respect for private and family life and the protection of personal data. That which has already happened regarding the enforcement of the Charter in vertical relationships, in respect of which the CJ has progressively extended the recognition of direct effect to several of its provisions, may also happen in horizontal relationships.

Secondly, the *Thelen Technopark* judgment casts doubt on whether the *Mangold/Bauer* scheme is also applicable to directives *and Treaty provisions*, not only to directives and Charter provisions. The points raised by the German Federal Court of Justice, in essence, concerned the legal consequences of the incompatibility with Article 15 of Directive 2006/123/EC with national legislation that fixed minimum fees for the services offered by architects and engineers and established the nullity of contracts derogating from those minimum fees. In particular, the CJ was asked whether the domestic provisions were to be considered discriminatory and, as such, subject to disapplication with regard to a dispute between private individuals, and, in the alternative, whether they infringed Article 49 TFEU or other general principles of EU law. In summary, the Court focused on the first preliminary question, confirming the prohibition of horizontal direct effect of directives. The second preliminary question, relating to Article 49, was considered inadmissible, since the reference did not indicate any element from which the cross-border nature of the dispute could be inferred. The disapplication on the basis of Article 16 of the Charter—or even the Charter itself—was never mentioned in the judgment. In this respect, it should be noted, from one side, that the choice made by the CJ, and the rejection of AG Spuznar's interpretive reconstruction,[400] was certainly understandable from the perspective of the EU courts and the prohibition of horizontal direct effect envisaged in their case law since the application by analogy of the *Mangold* logic to directives and Treaty provisions other than the Charter would *de facto* lead to directives applying systematically in horizontal disputes. This is

[396] In this vein, *see* K. Lenaerts, J. A. Gutiérrez-Fons, *The Place of the Charter in the European Legal Space*, in S. Peers, T. Hervey, J. Kenner, A. Ward (eds.), *The EU Charter*, 1711–1734, 1719 and S. Prechal, *Horizontal Direct Effect*, 419.

[397] S. Prechal, *Horizontal Direct Effect*, 419: 'This is not only true for rights such as respect for private and family life, freedom of expression and information and freedom to conduct a business, which includes freedom of contract, but might also include provisions like the right to the integrity of the person, prohibition of torture and inhuman or degrading treatment and prohibition of slavery.'

[398] *See* the reflections by S. Peers, *Supremacy*, 856–857; M. De Mol, Kücükdeveci, 303; T. Papadopoulos, *Criticizing the Horizontal Direct Effect of the EU General Principle of Equality* (2019) 4 *European Human Rights Law Review* 437, 446.

[399] On this point, *see* the analysis by E. Frantziou, *The Horizontal Effect of Fundamental Rights*, 109–113. *See* also some brief remarks in D. Gallo, *Un droit opposable à Internet en vertu des obligations de service publique européennes?*, in F.-X. Millet (ed.), *Le constitutionnalisme numérique*, Brussels, Bruylant, forthcoming, 2025.

[400] *See* the opinion of AG Spuznar, *Thelen Technopark* (n 114), paras 34, 36, 42, 47, and 114.

especially true when it comes to rules, such as Article 49, that lie at the heart of the internal market.[401] From the other side, this very circumstance makes the inconsistency of the CJ case law on the prohibition of horizontal direct effect of directives quite obvious. As a matter of fact, it is unclear why the *Mangold* scheme cannot also apply to Treaty rules, rather than only to the Charter. Indeed, a careful reading of *Thelen Technopark* reveals that the non-application of this scheme would seem to depend more on the purely internal nature of the situation at hand than on the rejection *per se* of AG Spuznar's reasoning, with the consequence that, if the situation concerned had a cross-border dimension, the CJ could have taken a different course.[402]

Thirdly, as already written in section 3.1 of Chapter III, the question remains today about the soundness of the *summa divisio* 'rights'-'principles', within the meaning of Article 52(5) of the Charter and with regard to their internal effect, most notably as per the justiciability of social rights. In particular, the qualification of norms containing principles as directly effective provisions seems to have to be excluded *prima facie*, in the light of the text of Articles 51(1) and 52(5) of the Charter, already recalled in section 3.1 of Chapter III, as also specified in the Explanations relating to the Charter, as well as in the CJ jurisprudence. Indeed, substitutive effect, which presupposes that the rule is directly effective, that is, self-sufficient, in the sense of conferring a right (subjective direct effect) in a sufficiently complete manner so as to replace (via disapplication) national law, is certainly to be ruled out. However, the discourse is different if the standpoint is that of exclusionary effect and if direct effect is seen as a combination of two or more precepts.

In fact, on a closer reading of the Charter, there is no reason why it should be denied, almost ontologically, that a 'principle' can give rise to exclusionary direct effect. 'Principles' can be directly invoked and enforced and act as parameters of legality of national law if they are read in systematic terms with other EU provisions of primary or secondary law and, in this way, can entail direct effect. There seems to be no difference between the notion of 'parameter of legality', pursuant to exclusionary direct effect, and the control on legality foreseen in Article 52(5) of the Charter, which is undertaken 'only' when acts implementing the Charter's principles 'are interpreted or reviewed'.[403] Reference is made not only to Articles 25, 26, and 37—with respect to which the (cryptic) Explanations to the Charter clarify that they incorporate 'principles'—but also to all the other norms, not referred to in the aforementioned Explanations, contained in Chapter IV on Solidarity, on which there is no clear position on the part of the CJ, with the sole exception of Article 27, as restrictively interpreted—regarding its scope—in *Association de médiation sociale*.

Against this backdrop, when a provision, of primary law or more likely of secondary law, provides for the concrete filling and enforcement of what is recognized by a given norm-'right' or by a norm-'principle' of the Charter, completeness is achieved all the same, although supplemented by a further provision. As occurs with 'rights', directives can thus 'give specific expression to the content and objectives determined by the principle'.[404] This approach, inspired by the need to ensure as much as possible the useful effect of the Charter,[405]

[401] As also supported by B. de Witte, *The Thelen Technopark Berlin judgment: the Court of Justice sticks to its guns on the horizontal effect of directives*, REALaw.blog, 6 May 2022, available at https://realaw.blog/?p=1195.

[402] As suggested by J. Lindeboom, *Thelen Technopark and the Legal Effects of the Services Directive in Purely Internal and Horizontal Disputes* (2022) 7 *European Papers* 305, 310, and 318–321.

[403] *See* the Explanations to the Charter.

[404] Opinion of AG Cruz Villalón of 18 July 2013, *Association de médiation sociale v Union locale des syndicats CGT and Others*, C-176/12, EU:C:2013:491, para. 56.

[405] On this point *see*, *inter alia*, S. Iglesias Sanchez, *The Court and the Charter: the Impact of the Entry into Force of the Lisbon Treaty on the ECJ's Approach to Fundamental Rights* (2012) 49 *Common Market Law Review* 1565

originates, first of all, from a comparative argument: in the constitutional systems of many Member States, 'rights', in particular (but not only) those of a social nature,[406] are in any case justiciable, that is, enforceable most notably by the judge, in the sense of acting as a parameter of legality of national law. This is a *conditional* justiciability insofar as it is ensured by the presence (and enforcement) of other provisions that serve as a means for the enforcement of fundamental rights, but is still a form of direct invocability, that is, direct effect.[407] Moreover, to the objection that if 'principles' were to be considered as having direct effect, in practice, all programmatic norms would be considered equally because such an effect would be the result of their combination with other, more detailed, EU provisions, it could be answered that, in the case of the Charter, at the heart of their precept is an individual advantage/interest. An advantage/interest that is directly attributed in the case of 'rights' and, in the case of 'principles', arises from the application of the norm-parameter of legality. Put differently, and to give an example, Article 4(3) TEU is and remains a programmatic norm because it aims to govern relations between States and the Union, it being devoid, in this perspective, of the characteristics underpinning the Charter. The distinction would seem to be whether the concretization, carried out by a further norm, *rectius*, as Cruz Villalón pointed out in *Association de médiation sociale*, by an 'implementing act',[408] aims at safeguarding individual prerogatives: *(i)* this is the case of the Charter and the effect is direct; *(ii)* this is not the case of Article 4(3) TEU, nor of other EU provisions, and the effect is not direct.

In the knowledge that what has been written is not supported to date by the case law of the CJ, as proven by the *Association de médiation sociale* ruling, from the observations made so far it follows that, on closer inspection, the rights/principles dichotomy seems to be quite useless should there be further EU provisions/acts concretizing the Charter. The rule becomes, thanks to this concretization, a precept 'without qualification', as observed by AG Tanchev in his opinion in *King* on Article 31(2).[409] This conclusion could apply to many of the rules of the Charter, not only those safeguarding social rights, as shown by the case of Article 31(2), but also others, including Article 36 on access to services of general economic interest,[410] Article 37 on environmental protection, or Article 38 on consumer protection.

Fourthly, a still puzzling crucial issue, not exclusively related to the matter of direct effect of the Charter/general principles and directives, regards the legal basis for, and justification of, the recognition of fundamental rights' horizontal direct effect. In this regard, there are those who believe that such recognition is a matter of social justice and shall be thus connected, in redistributive terms, to the protection of the weaker party as this objective is spelled out in Article 3(3) TEU.[411] Or, rather, linked to the position of supremacy of a party,

and L. Weitzel, *La Charte des droits fondamentaux de l'Union européenne, avancée ou régression?*, in L. Weitzel, *L'Europe des droits fondamentaux. Mélanges en hommage à Albert Weitzel*, Paris, Pedone, 2013, 225–250. *See* also CJ, *Opinion 2/13, Accession of the European Union to the European Convention for the Protection of Human Rights and Fundamental Freedoms*, EU:C:2014:2454, paras 167–169.

406 For instance, rights which relate to the protection of the environment.

407 On such matter, *see* § 3.1 of Chapter III.

408 *See* the reflections in the opinion of AG Cruz Villalón, *Association de médiation sociale* (n 404), paras 57–71.

409 Opinion of AG Tanchev, *King* (n 339), para. 2.

410 On the internal effect of such provision, *see* D. Gallo, *I servizi*, 822–826; A. Arena, *Art. 36. Accesso ai servizi d'interesse economico generale*, in R. Mastroianni, O. Pollicino, S. Allegrezza, F. Pappalardo, O. Razzolini (eds.), *Carta dei diritti fondamentali dell'Unione europea*, Milan, Giuffrè, 2017, 680–691; D. Gallo, *Article 36 of the Charter and Access to Public Services: Scope, Extent and Limits of a* sui generis *Provision* (2018) 5 *E-PÚBLICA* 51.

411 'The Union shall establish an internal market. It shall work for the sustainable development of Europe based on balanced economic growth and price stability, a highly competitive social market economy, aiming at full employment and social progress, and a high level of protection and improvement of the quality of the environment [. . .] It shall combat social exclusion and discrimination, and shall promote social justice and protection, equality between women and men, solidarity between generations and protection of the rights of the child.' On

against whom the EU norm is invoked, over the other party invoking it.[412] In this regard, the fact that horizontal direct effect, as has already been observed, was granted especially to (social) rights, like those contained in Chapter IV of the Charter, imbued with a low degree of justiciability, is not surprising. Indeed, horizontal direct effect serves as a means for those who are in a situation of subordination to challenge private power and authority. However, an approach that would create a structural link between horizontality and such need of re-balancing (between the employee and the private employer), while applicable to labour disputes, may be considered discriminatory with respect to other types of disputes. Consider, for example, a dispute between two competing companies: should horizontal direct effect be rejected due to a lack of an imbalance of powers between the two operators? If this were the case, developments in the case law concerning the internal effect of the Charter other than those about social rights could hardly occur. A different reasoning might lead one to argue that the regulatory approach developed by the CJ regarding the freedoms of movement[413] would also be applicable, by analogy, to fundamental rights.[414] The objection, however, is twofold: on the one hand, it has already been seen that, as the CJ affirmed in the *Angonese* case, the regulatory function of the private party is not always a precondition for admitting horizontal direct effect, since it was written in the judgment that the prohibition of discrimination shall apply 'equally to all agreements intended to regulate paid labour collectively, as well as to contracts between individuals'.[415] And, as pointed out in the literature,[416] the same argument can be made in relation to fundamental rights: in *Bauer*, for example, the CJ was clear in observing that a private party action may fall within the scope of application of Article 31(2) of the Charter, the individuals being 'directly required to comply with' the latter and creating with this rule, in addition to a right on the part of the employee, also a 'corresponding obligation on the employer'.[417] On the other hand, limiting horizontal direct effect to situations imbued with such a regulatory dimension entails an excessive and unjustified compression of fundamental rights. Furthermore, some might argue that the recognition of horizontal direct effect to fundamental rights would irretrievably harm private autonomy[418] with potentially exacerbating consequences for the free market.[419] This view, however, does not seem to take into account either the new facets underpinning the process of European integration beyond economic goals nor the need for the EU to intercept situations otherwise excluded from the scope of EU law given the growing role of the private sector in the welfare and strategic sectors of the Member States. In short, the basis of horizontal direct effect, as

the ties between such provision and the internal effect of fundamental rights, *see* the opposing arguments by O. Gerstenberg, *Fundamental Rights and Democratic Sovereignty in the EU: The Role of the Charter of Fundamental Rights of the EU (CFREU) in Regulating the European Social Market Economy*, in *Yearbook of European Law*, vol. 39, 2020, 199–227, 199–200, and F. Costamagna, *Diritti fondamentali*, 178. For a commentary, *see* M. Klamert, *Article 3 TEU*, in M. Kellerbauer, M. Klamert, J. Tomkin (eds.), *The EU Treaties*, 31–34.

412 O. Gerstenberg, *Fundamental Rights*, 223–225.
413 *See* § 2 of this chapter.
414 *See* the account by F. Costamagna, *Diritti fondamentali*, 168–173.
415 *Angonese* (n 28), paras 34 and 36.
416 R. Schütze, *European Union Law*, 490–491.
417 *Bauer* (n 346), paras 87 and 90.
418 On the limits of horizontality, as well as on the risks of banalization for the comprehension of fundamental rights stemming from its recognition, from the standpoint of constitutional adjudication and private law, *see* M. Tushnet, *State Action*, 79 and, in more general terms, A. Barak, *Constitutional Human Rights*; *see* also the contributions in D. Friedmann, D. Barak-Erez (eds.), *Human Rights in Private Law*, Oxford, Hart, 2001; S. Besson, *Comment humaniser le droit privé sans commodifier les droits de l'homme?*, in F. Werro (ed.), *Droit civil et Convention européenne des droits de l'homme*, Zurich, Schulthess, 2006, 1–51.
419 In this direction, *see* extensively O. Gerstenberg, *Private Law*; D. Leczykiewicz, *Horizontal Effect*; D. Leczykiewicz, *Horizontal Application of the Charter of Fundamental Rights* (2013) 38 *European Law Review* 479; M. Safjan, P. Miklaszewicz, *Horizontal Effect*.

regards the protection of fundamental rights, also in their relationship with directives, is the same as that examined in section 2 of this chapter: the effectiveness of EU law, to be ensured through an extensive and teleological interpretation of both primary and secondary provisions.

In conclusion, on this section: when the provisions of a directive are sufficiently unambiguous, it is difficult to understand why we should persist with the idea that they cannot entail horizontal direct effect. This seems even more so if one considers that such effect was granted to general principles, like that of non-discrimination on the basis of age, whose actual 'generality' across Member States is doubtful and whose contours are 'nebulous'.[420] Moreover, the fact that the internal horizontal effect produced by directives is mediated by the principles and rules of the Charter does not make the approach adopted by the CJ any less problematic than that taken with regard to incidental/triangular effects and consistent interpretation: in all these cases there is a misuse of the prohibition of horizontal direct effect of directives, with the consequences that this entails in terms of legal certainty and legitimate expectations.[421] In view of the constitutional relevance of the issue related to the horizontality of fundamental rights, the purely casuistic and ultimately 'particularistic' approach of the CJ, 'limited to a specific right and dispute', is such as to question the very legitimacy of its jurisprudence.[422]

6. The unbearable lightness of the NHDE rule and the way forward

In the light of the considerations made so far concerning the nature of the remedies developed by the CJ to bypass the prohibition of horizontal direct effect of directives, as well as their shortcomings, we shall now take stock of the reasons why, on a more general level, the reasoning of the Court is not defensible, as pointed out, with different gradations, by some Advocates General[423] and by the majority[424] of scholars.[425] These criticisms are often in

[420] The term is borrowed from O. Pollicino, *La Corte*, 598 ('*nebulosi*'). On such matter, *see* E. Gualco, L. Lourenço, *'Clash of Titans'*, 651–652, and T. Papadopoulos, *Criticizing*, 446–447. On legal certainty and legitimate expectations, *see* next §.

[421] *See* also *Common Market Law Review, Editorial Comments. The Scope of Application of the General Principles of Union Law: An Ever Expanding Union?* (2010) 47 *Common Market Law Review* 1589.

[422] E. Frantziou, *The Horizontal Effect of Fundamental Rights*, 3, who also supports 'a shift towards an understanding of rights in the Union as public goods, rather than as interests in the effective application of the Treaties' (4) or 'a doctrinal tool in the application of EU law' (57), and regards the CJ case law as 'a law of diminishing legitimacy' (113). *See* also extensively E. Frantziou, *The Horizontal Effect of the Charter: Towards an Understanding of Horizontality as a Structural Constitutional Principle?* (2020) 22 *Cambridge Yearbook of European Legal Studies* 208–232.

[423] *See* the opinion of AG Lenz, *Faccini Dori* (n 116), paras 43–73; opinion of AG van Gerven, *Marshall II* (n 133), para. 12; opinion of AG Jacobs of 27 January 1994, *Nicole Vaneetveld v Le Foyer SA and Le Foyer SA v Fédération des Mutualités Socialistes et Syndicales de la Province de Liège*, C-316/93, EU:C:1994:32, paras 15 and 31, whereby it was stated that 'it might well be conducive to greater legal certainty, and to a more coherent system, if the provisions of a directive were held in appropriate circumstances to be directly enforceable against individuals'.

[424] Amongst those who advocated in favour of the prohibition of the horizontal direct effect of directives, *see* R. Baratta, *Norme contenute in direttive comunitarie inattuate e loro opponibilità ai singoli* (1989) 2 *Rivista di diritto internazionale* 253, 266–281, and P. V. Figueroa Regueiro, *Invocability of Substitution and Invocability of Exclusion: Bringing Legal Realism to the Current Developments of the Case-Law of 'Horizontal' Direct Effect of Directives, Jean Monnet Working Paper 7/02*, 2002, available at http://www.jeanmonnetprogram.org/archive/papers/02/020701.pdf.

[425] In addition to the authors already cited in the previous §§ about specific aspects and with a focus on one or more of the Court's expedients to circumvent the prohibition of horizontal direct effect, *see* H. G. Schermers, *Indirect Obligations. Four Questions in respect of EEC—Obligations Arising from Rights or Obligations of*

practice shared by national courts.[426] What is certain is that the EU jurisprudence on horizontality and directives is, to date, a minefield, studded with alternative solutions and argumentative palliatives that undermine the principle of legal certainty and the related principle of legitimate expectations.[427] Moreover, the Court's reluctance to provide clear guidelines for national courts when they have to cope with directives in horizontal situations means that they are left alone in interpreting and applying case law that certainly does not shine for argumentative clarity.[428] What the Court increasingly does today to ensure legal certainty, that is, relying on the possible disapplication of national law on the basis of other domestic rules that are suitable to enforce the unimplemented directives, is not sufficient and cannot solve once and for all the problems underpinning the prohibition of horizontal direct effect of directives.[429]

The first critical remark regarding the CJ's case law lies in the negative implications for the effectiveness of directives and their uniform enforcement in national legal orders.[430] Preventing the explicit recognition of horizontal direct effect of directives, outside of the convoluted contrivances outlined in the previous sections, prevents them from expressing their normative potential and adequately regulating situations that risk, in this way, not being subject to EU law.

Others (1977) 24 *Netherlands International Law Review* 260; J. Easson, *Can Directives Impose Obligations on Individuals?* (1979) 4 *European Law Review* 77; P. Pescatore, *L'effet des directives*; C. W. A. Timmermans, *Directives*; R. Barents, *Some Remarks on the 'Horizontal' Effect of Directives*, in D. O'Keeffe, H. G. Schermers (eds.), *Essays*, 97–104; F. Capelli, *Le direttive comunitarie*, Milan, Giuffrè, 1983, 432 and 441; D. Wyatt, *The Direct Effect of Community Social Law—Not Forgetting Directives* (1983) 8 *European Law Review* 241; A. Arnull, *The Direct Effect of Directives: Grasping the Nettle* (1986) 35 *International and Comparative Law Quarterly* 939; P. Manin, *L'invocabilité*; F. Emmert, *Horizontale Drittwirkung von Richtlinien? Lieber ein Ende mit Schrecken als ein Schrecken ohne Ende!* (1992) 3 *Europäisches Wirtschafts und Steuerrecht* 56; F. Emmert, M. Pereira de Azevedo, *L'effet horizontal des directives. La jurisprudence de la CJCE: un bateau ivre?* (1993) 29 *Revue trimestrielle de droit européen* 503; F. Schockweiler, *Effets des directives non transposées en droit national à l'égard des particuliers*, in M. Pérez González (ed.), *Hacia un nuevo orden internacional y europeo—Estudios en homenaje al Profesor Don Manuel Diez de Velasco*, Madrid, Tecnos, 1993, 1201–1220; T. Tridimas, *Horizontal Effect of Directives: A Missed Opportunity* (1994) 10 *European Law Review* 621; W. van Gerven, *The Horizontal Effect of Directive Provisions*; D. Kinley, *Direct Effect of Directives: Stuck on Vertical Hold* (1995) 1 *European Public Law* 79; P. Craig, *Directives: Direct Effect, Indirect Effect and the Construction of National Legislation* (1997) 22 *European Law Review* 519; C. W. A. Timmermans, *Community Directives*; R. Mastroianni, *On the Distinction Between Vertical and Horizontal Direct Effects of Community Directives: What Role for the Principle of Equality?* (1999) 5 *European Public Law* 417; M. Lenz, D. Sif Tynes, L. Young, *Horizontal What? Back to Basics* (2000) 25 *European Law Review* 509; C. A. Varner, *The Effectiveness*; S. Weatherill, *Breach*; T. Tridimas, *Black*; P. Craig, *The Legal Effect of Directives: Policy, Rules and Exceptions* (2009) 34 *European Law Review* 349, whereby it was affirmed that 'the rationales for the core rule that Directives do not have horizontal direct effect based on the Treaty text, legal certainty and the Regulations/Directives divide are unconvincing' (390); S. Prechal, *Directives*, 211, 261–270; F. Becker, A. Campbell, *The Direct Effect of European Directives: Towards the Final Act?* (2007) 13 *Columbia Journal of European Law* 401; G. Di Federico, *Il recepimento*, 51–56; C. Haguenau-Moizard, *Pour la reconnaissance d'un effet direct horizontal aux directives* (2011) 550 *Revue du Marché Commun de l'Union européenne* 454; M. Bobek, *The Effects of EU Law in the National Legal Systems*, in C. Barnard, S. Peers (eds.), *European Union Law*, 3rd ed., Oxford, Oxford University Press, 2020, 154–189, 154–156; D. Gallo, *L'efficacia diretta del diritto dell'Unione europea negli ordinamenti nazionali. Evoluzione di una dottrina ancora controversa*, Milan, Giuffrè, 2018, 275–350; D. Gallo, *La* vexata *quaestio dell'efficacia interna delle direttive: l'insostenibile leggerezza del divieto di effetti diretti orizzontali*, in E. Moavero Milanesi, G. Piccirilli (eds.), *Attuare il diritto dell'Unione europea in Italia*, Bari, Caucci, 2018, 17; M. Bobek, *Why is it Better*.

[426] As observed by L. Daniele, *Diritto*, 302.

[427] M. Dougan, *When Worlds Collide!*, 963: 'to search for a theoretically respectable, watertight descriptive account of the fractured, fumbling case law on the direct effect of directives is a task fit only for masochists.'

[428] According to T. Papadopoulos, *Criticizing*, 447 and L. Pech, *Between Judicial Minimalism and Avoidance*, 24, the CJ should have provided guiding criteria to counter legal uncertainty.

[429] On the ever-increasing key role exercised by such reasoning, *see Gabel Industria Tessile* (n 90), paras 23–25, on which, *see* § 1 of Chapter V and the brief reference in § 3 of this chapter.

[430] S. Prechal, *Directives*, 258.

The second critical remark relates to the idea that the attribution of horizontal direct effect would lead the CJ to distort the meaning of Article 288 TFEU, as a result of dangerous judicial activism, since the addressees of the rule are only the States. Such belief does not take into account two circumstances. Firstly, as already remarked by AG Jacobs in *Vaneetveld*, Article 288 TFEU does not explicitly deny that rules of directives can be invoked against private parties.[431] Secondly, a wide variety of doctrines and principles are the result of a jurisprudential development that has gone far beyond the literal text of EU law, as has been recalled several times in this work.[432] The same vertical direct effect of directives rests on a break from a literal interpretation of Article 288(3) TFEU.[433] As a matter of fact, a genuine understanding of *Van Gend & Loos* should lead to a denial of direct effect of directives since any rights or obligations foreseen therein are, as stated in that judgment, 'qualified by any reservation on the part of states which would make its implementation conditional upon a positive legislative measure enacted under national law'.[434] To hold that the rationale behind the denial of the direct horizontal effect of directives is ultimately a political one[435] and that the issue of directives' horizontality should be framed within the scope and limits of Article 5 TEU[436] seems to reiterate the core of the narrative according to which the EU legal order has unduly extended its material and personal scope over the decades. In fact, the attribution of vertical direct effect to directives makes perfect sense since, as written in section 3.1 of Chapter III, it is the consequence of an evolution, that is, of the increasingly detailed nature of these acts, several of which are not so different in substance from regulations,[437] as well as of a jurisprudential development that has driven the CJ to recognize that such an attribution is indispensable to ensure the effectiveness of EU law and the full protection of the rights that stem from it.

The third critical remark pertains to the argument that horizontal direct effect shall not be granted to directives because their provisions tend to be vaguer than those contained in EU primary sources, as well as in other secondary legal acts,[438] with the result that legal certainty would be breached should they apply in horizontal disputes since they are 'binding, as to the result to be achieved' and require national implementing measures. In this respect, three points shall be raised. First, when rules of an unimplemented directive are sufficiently complete and, for this reason, are given direct effect, the difference with other sources of EU law disappears. Secondly, even other rules of primary or secondary law, recognized as directly effective by the Court, often require in practice the adoption of further measures

[431] Opinion of AG Jacobs, *Vaneetveld* (n 423), para. 20.

[432] J. Bengoetxea, *The Legal Reasoning of the European Court of Justice*, Oxford, Oxford University Press, 1993, 237–238: 'in order to affirm vertical direct effect of directives the Court has gone beyond the wording of Article 288 whilst in order to deny horizontal direct effect of directives it has chosen to interpret the article in a narrow way'; J. Coppel, *Rights, Duties and the End of* Marshall (1994) 57 *Modern Law Review* 859, 863; P. Craig, *Directives*, 520: 'the formalist mode of treaty interpretation . . . does not sit comfortably with the more purposive approach' related to rules different than Article 288 TFEU.

[433] As discussed in § 3.1 of Chapter III.

[434] CJ, *NV Algemene Transport- en Expeditie Onderneming van Gend & Loos v Netherlands Inland Revenue Administration*, 26/62, EU:C:1963:1, 13.

[435] On this point *see* G. Gaja, *Reviewing Bengoetxea—Survey of Books* (1994) 92 *Michigan Law Review* 1971.

[436] In any case, the opposition of governments to the recognition of horizontal direct effect emerges clearly in the *Faccini Dori* case, where all intervening countries addressed such recognition with criticism.

[437] See § 7 of Chapter III on the relationship between direct effect and direct applicability from the standpoint of the similarities and divergences between regulations and directives.

[438] R. Valladares, Francovich: *Light at the End of the Marshall Tunnel*, in *The University of Miami Yearbook of International Law*, vol. 3, 1995, 1–52, 24: the attribution of horizontal direct effect to primary law sources rather than to directives 'results in absurdities'.

by the State in order to apply domestically.[439] Moreover, the Court itself, in *Ratti*, pointed out that directives could produce similar effects to regulations since they are mandatory acts too. Thus, there is no ontological distinction between the competence to enact one or the other type of act. Thirdly, admitting the enforceability against an individual of an obligation contained in a directive would not erase the differences between a regulation and a directive, given that the direct effect of a directive is realized only in the event of non-transposition or incorrect transposition and in any case after the expiry of the time-limit for its implementation.[440]

A fourth critical remark is that the prohibition of horizontal direct effect entails discrimination between different categories of individuals,[441] as illustrated by that set forth in EU law textbooks about labour law disputes: a directive could be invoked by employees against the State, when the latter is their employer, but not against another private party, when the latter does not fulfil the *Marshall I*, *Foster*, and *Farrell* criteria, examined above in section 4. Given the same legal situation, only those who wish to assert their claim against public entities (understood in the broad sense) will be able to do so. Conversely, those who wish to do so against private natural or legal persons will be precluded from this, creating an 'intermittent' direct effect, since 'at the same time and in entirely similar circumstances, the same directive is or is not directly effective depending on the subject against whom it is invoked'.[442] The public or private nature of an entity becomes, therefore, the dividing line of whether to ensure the protection of individual prerogatives.

A fifth critical remark is that, while the inequality described above should be allowed only during the period prescribed for transposition, one of the principal aims of directives is that comparable conditions should apply after that period has expired. Moreover, as observed by AG Lenz, if those disparities were to be maintained, 'it would go against the stated aim of the approximation of legislation'.[443] Legal harmonization, therefore, would be called into question.[444] This circumstance is in itself serious if one considers that the CJ's expansive interpretation of the concept of 'State' exacerbates the discrimination between employees of entities exercising a certain activity in one country and employees of entities exercising the same activity in another country. This is due to the different legal nature of the entity and depending on the greater or lesser interventionism of the State in the market, welfare, and general interest sectors.[445]

A sixth critical remark is that Article 297 TFEU, as is well-known, since the amendments introduced by the Treaty of Maastricht, requires the publication in the EU *Official Journal* of directives 'which are addressed to all Member States',[446] confirming that they

[439] The argument above would in principle apply not only against horizontal direct effect but also against the vertical direct effect of directives, as well as of EU law as a whole, as noted by P. Craig, *Directives*, 524.

[440] *See*, *inter alia*, T. Tridimas, *Horizontal Effect of Directives*, 631. *See* also the account by R. Schütze, *The Morphology of Legislative Power in the European Community: Legal Instruments and the Federal Division of Powers*, in *Yearbook of European Law*, vol. 25, 2006, 25, 91–151.

[441] *See*, among many others, N. Green, *Directives, Equity and the Protection of Individual Rights* (1984) 9 *European Law Review* 295; A. Arnull, *The Direct Effect of Directives*, 946.

[442] L. Daniele, *La Corte di giustizia conferma l'efficacia diretta 'intermittente' delle direttive comunitarie* (1995) 1 *Il Foro italiano* 38–42: '*in uno stesso momento e in circostanze del tutto simili, la medesima direttiva è o non è direttamente efficace a seconda del soggetto nei cui confronti è invocata*.'

[443] Opinion of AG Lenz, *Faccini Dori* (n 116), para. 52.

[444] Opinion of AG Lenz, *Faccini Dori* (n 116), para. 52.

[445] W. van Gerven, *The Horizontal Effect*, 349.

[446] As for 'other directives', they 'shall take effect upon' the notification to 'those to whom they are addressed' (Article 297(2) TFEU).

have the same normative value as regulations.[447] This implies that directives, just like regulations, can be known by individuals, not only as holders of prerogatives recognized therein but also, in certain cases, as addressees of obligations arising therefrom, and not only by virtue of a 'purely declaratory' act, their publication having, instead, a 'constitutive' effect.[448]

A final and key critical remark is that if it is true that the protection of legitimate expectations guides the reasoning of the CJ in its jurisprudence against the recognition of horizontal direct effect of directives, this principle, in addition to being relevant from the point of view of the person who behaves in accordance with national rules contrary to EU law, is also relevant from the point of view of the person who complies with an EU directive that has not yet been transposed into national law (despite the fact that the transposition deadline has passed) or that has been transposed incorrectly and who is a party to a dispute with another private individual.[449] Attributing horizontal direct effect to a directive would ensure that the persons invoking it are able to protect their prerogatives arising from its implementation and thus avoid putting their legal position indefinitely at the discretion of a non-complying State. The paradox resulting from the prohibition of horizontal direct effect of directives is that the one who acts in conformity with a directive is at a disadvantage compared to the one who acts contrary to that directive, but in conformity with national law—a law that, in any case, must be amended to ensure conformity with the EU legal system.[450] A paradox that, on the other hand, does not occur in the hypothesis of inverse vertical direct effect. The prohibition of the latter, in the case of directives, is always justified[451] on the grounds that, where this type of relationship is involved, the State relies on EU law in order to come into conflict with the individual interest, to take advantage from its own wrongdoing and to seek the disapplication of its *own* national law. It is a different situation from what occurs in horizontal relationships, where two individual countervailing interests are at stake, one of which must be sacrificed, and the estoppel doctrine plays no role. Such divergences also illustrate why, should the *Infraestruturas de Portugal SA* ruling be confirmed by the CJ in its jurisprudence—leading to an explicit admissibility of directives' vertical direct effect—, there seems no reason why, *a fortiori*, horizontal direct effect could not also be recognized, just as inverse vertical direct effect has been asserted in that case. However, whereas the recognition of horizontal direct effect to directives would mark a positive evolution, the possible confirmation of *Infraestruturas de Portugal SA* would cristallyze a negative evolution, considering the peculiarities of inverse vertical direct effect.

[447] On this point, *see* R. Baratta, *Quali prospettive in tema di effetti c.d. orizzontali di norme di direttive inattuate?* (1994) 3 *Rivista di diritto internazionale* 487, 488–489.

[448] *See* opinion of AG Lenz, *Faccini Dori* (n 116), paras 63–64 and 73, who argued that, at that time, 'the basic condition for a burden imposed on the citizen by legislative measures is their constitutive publication in an official organ. That condition is not fulfilled by directives adopted on the basis of the EEC Treaty. The usage of publishing directives in the Official Journal of the European Communities as measures whose publication is not a condition for their applicability does not remedy that situation. Publication in the Official Journal of the European Communities is purely declaratory and is not a condition for directives to take effect' (para. 64).

[449] *See* S. Prechal, *Directives*, 257. On such principle and horizontal direct effect of directive, *see* also T. Tridimas, *General Principles*, 244.

[450] As remarked by L. Squintani, J. Lindeboom, *The Normative Impact*, 25, 'in the ordinary state of the law individuals ought to be able to enforce the rights they would have been granted, had the State correctly implemented the respective directive.'

[451] This justification holds true notwithstanding the very recent opposite stance that the CJ seems to have taken, albeit only implicitly, in *Infraestruturas de Portugal SA* (n 152), as clarified especially in § 5 of Chapter V.

The desire for an explicit and reasoned case law overruling[452] the express denial of horizontal direct effect of directives stems from the need to ensure that the legitimate expectations of individuals vis-à-vis the EU system, and not only those vis-à-vis the national system, are duly taken into account.[453] The argument about the need to protect the claims of the individual, even from the perspective of the person who has acted in full conformity with EU law rather than with the (unlawful) national rule, makes it possible to understand why affirming the horizontal direct effect of directives provides individuals with greater guarantees than those deriving from the current EU case law. In fact, although it cannot be said that the enforceability against individuals of obligations contained in unimplemented directives is devoid of any problems, in particular from the point of view of legal certainty and legitimate expectations, for those who behave in compliance with national law but not with the directive, the discourse changes if the perspective is that of the balancing of interests. Indeed, there is the interest of the individual who has relied on domestic law (and the need to protect the prerogatives attached thereto). The degree of protection to be afforded to that interest, furthermore, depends on a number of factors, first and foremost on the attitude, more or less negligent or 'captious', driving the individual's actions and which led the other party to rely on the unimplemented directive.[454]

There is, on the other hand, a second interest that deserves to be safeguarded. Against the interest(s) of those who have acted on the basis of national law (contrary to EU law) there is the interest of individuals in exercising the rights granted to them by the directive. It cannot be neglected that such interest identifies with the interest of the EU system as a whole, also represented by the elimination of disparities and inequities amongst individuals as a result of the divergent enforcement of EU law in Member States. To always let the interest of the individual who has acted in accordance with a national law which conflicts with an EU law prevail is not the best solution. On the contrary, it may well be claimed that the interest of the person invoking EU law, that is, a source superior to national law, should prevail over the interest of the person invoking a national rule which is in contrast with EU law. If the perspective is that of balancing opposing individual interests, only the attribution of horizontal direct effect to clear, precise, and unconditional rules of directives[455] could ensure, at the same time, legal certainty, the protection of legitimate expectations, and the effectiveness of EU law.[456] Such a solution would ensure greater linearity in a jurisprudence[457] that is increasingly inclined to recognize direct effect both as to directives, in its vertical dimension, and to other sources of EU law, in vertical and horizontal terms,[458]

[452] On the overruling technique(s), including the 'reconsideration' of the previous case law, *see* extensively D. Sarmiento, *The 'Overruling Technique' at the Court of Justice of the European Union*, in D. Gallo, L. Cecchetti (eds.), *The Preliminary Ruling*, 107, 110–114, as well as the observations made in § 2 of Chapter II.

[453] Amongst others, *see* P. Craig, *The Legal Effect*, 367–369 and S. Weatherill, *Breach*.

[454] See the remarks by AG Jacobs, *Vaneetveld* (n 423), para. 34.

[455] On the flaws implied in such test, *see* § 4 of Chapter III.

[456] The fact that, in some cases, such as *Wells* (n 110), paras 65–70, the EU courts held that it was up to the State and fell within its procedural autonomy to verify, in compliance with the principles of equivalence and effectiveness, that there were adequate means to address the problems of legal certainty generated by the application of the directive and the consequent infringement of the individual's prerogatives, contributes to mitigating, not resolving, the problems identified in the text above.

[457] According to W. van Gerven, *The Horizontal Effect*, 348, maintaining the prohibition of horizontal direct effect would inevitably result in 'inconsistencies and inequalities' in the case law.

[458] P. Craig, G. de Búrca, *EU Law: Text, Cases, and Materials*, 7th ed., 2020, 205, ironically, wrote that 'the meaning of legal certainty', which is one of the reasons of the prohibition of horizontal direct effect, 'is unclear since the ECJ has provided no elaboration or plausible explanation for why it prohibits the horizontal direct effect of directives'.

such as the rules on freedoms of movement or the general principles of EU law, with respect to which the attribution of horizontal direct effect is no less problematic than that concerning directives. Admitting such effect for directives, which are written sources published in the EU *Official Journal*,[459] would allow the individual to be informed, take cognizance of them, and be ultimately aware of their prerogatives and obligations to a greater extent than when the CJ extends the application of abstract non-written sources of law to inter-individual relations.[460]

The CJ, in over-extending the notion of public measure and systematically relying on a multiplicity of techniques and alternative remedies, has complicated and continues to further complicate matters in relation to such a peculiar normative source as the directive.[461] As observed by AG Bobek in his opinion in the *Cresco* ruling, 'the persistence in formally denying horizontal direct effect to directives while moving heaven and earth to ensure that that restriction has no practical consequences whatsoever . . . appears increasingly questionable'.[462] If a Treaty amendment of Article 288(3) TFEU removing the reference to the Member States alone as addressees of directives[463] could solve the problems outlined above, a change of case law, in the absence of a change in primary law, would be possible and desirable. A proof in this regard could be seen in the unexpected twist undertaken by the CJ in the *Infraestruturas de Portugal SA* ruling with regard to directives' inverse vertical direct effect. A twist that may mark the beginning of a velvet revolution, in case the Court should decide, in its future jurisprudence, to uphold the reasoning developed therein, as has been already remarked several times in this work. Indeed, as mentioned above, Article 288(3) TFEU does not expressly exclude that obligations may be imposed on natural and legal persons. That, then, the turmoil in the case law serves to justify not a strengthening of the judicial protection of individuals but, to the contrary, a weakening thereof, is no longer defensible. Moreover, the fact that the denial of horizontal direct effect, by depriving individuals of the possibility of invoking EU law against other individuals, ultimately undermines the effectiveness of EU law, should thus induce the Court to finally change its approach.[464]

[459] On the inherent problems of predictability and judicial creativity connected to the Charter, *see* the opinion of AG Bobek, *Cresco* (n 383), para. 141, and F. Costamagna, *Diritti fondamentali*, 84–85.

[460] On the breach of legal certainty and legitimate expectations originating from the horizontal direct effect of unclear general principles and on the transformation of State liability in individual responsibility, *see* E. Spaventa, *The Horizontal Application*, 216.

[461] *See* M. Bobek, *The Effect*, 151: 'the original rule is that EU law provisions generally are capable of direct effect. The exception to this rule is that in certain types of legal relationships, in particular in horizontal relationships, a directive or a decision is precluded from becoming directly effective. However, the subsequent case law of the Court has created further exceptions to the latter exception, thus somewhat silently reaffirming the original rule, in a number of ways'; S. Rodin, *Les effets horizontaux du droit de l'Union européenne*, in A. Tizzano, A. Rosas, R. S. De Lapuerta, K. Lenaerts, J. Kokott (eds.), *La Cour de justice de L'Union européenne sous la présidence de Vassilios Skouris (2003–2015)*. Liber amicorum *Vassilios Skouris*, Brussels, Bruylant, 2015, 491–50, 498: the CJ, in the elaboration of alternatives to the horizontal direct effect of directives, '*a dû adopter une créativité interprétative plus importante que celle qui aurait été demandée pour reconnaître simplement l'effet direct horizontal*'.

[462] Opinion of AG Bobek, *Cresco* (n 343), para. 145; *contra*, explicitly, A. Dashwood, *From Van Duyn*, 82.

[463] In this vein, *see* S. Prechal, *Van Duyn*.

[464] From a legal theory perspective, *see* the fascinating works by J. Van der Valt on the nexus between horizontality and sovereignty. In his opinion, the rights stemming from the Constitution(s) should be invoked in both vertical and horizontal situations since the Constitution is the backbone of national sovereignty. The reluctance on the part of the CJ to accept directives' horizontal direct effect might be seen in the profound nature of the EU, seen as a type of international, not *sovereign*, organization. At the same time, the horizontalization of the fundamental freedoms, as observed in § 2 of this chapter, can be considered a significant advancement of the process of European integration. *See* J. Van der Valt, *The Horizontal Effect Revolution and the Question of Sovereignty*, Berlin-Boston, De Gruyter, 2014.

7. Horizontality and decisions: a variable-geometry mysterious liaison

As already mentioned, it is rare to find in-depth studies on the internal effect of decisions.[465] Even rarer is the literature that has dealt with the recognition of horizontal direct effect in relation to these acts. Moreover, the jurisprudence is scarce. While section 3.1 of Chapter III is devoted to decisions' direct effect mainly in vertical relationships, this section is about their horizontal direct effect.

As for decisions addressed towards natural and legal persons,[466] there is no doubt that they can produce horizontal direct effects insofar as their rules not only confer individual rights but also impose obligations on specific natural and legal persons, that is, the addressee(s) of the decision. Obviously, for this to happen, the rules of the decision must have the well-known characteristics of direct effect, first and foremost the unconditionality of the obligation. Moreover, a decision addressed to a private party may be binding also for other parties, which means that it can have horizontal direct effect in disputes not specifically related to the actual recipient of the act. This can be inferred from Article 263(4) TFEU, which refers to decisions that are addressed to one person but may be of 'direct and individual concern' to others.[467]

Decisions addressed towards States, on the contrary, as the case law stands, are directly effective only in vertical relationships. The prerogatives they create, in the hands of natural and legal persons, in the view of the Court, cannot be enforced against other private persons beyond consistent interpretation.[468] Underlying this approach is the same reasoning that the CJ follows with regard to directives: individuals are to be protected against the non-fulfilment of the State and the latter must be sanctioned since it cannot benefit from that non-fulfilment. *Carp*,[469] in fact, dealt with Decision 1999/93/EC on the procedure for attesting the conformity of construction products pursuant to Article 20(2) of Directive 89/106, with regard to doors, windows, shutters, blinds, gates, and related accessories,[470] as already recalled in section 3.1 of Chapter III. In this case, the Court, after stating that that decision constituted an act of general application and that it was binding only on the Member States, affirmed that the considerations inspiring the case law on directives 'apply *mutatis mutandis*' to the possibility of relying on decisions against an individual.[471] In this vein, if the reasoning that led the CJ to exclude the horizontal direct effect of decisions is the same as that guiding its jurisprudence on directives, the objections, developed above with regard to directives, also apply to decisions.[472]

[465] *See* § 3.1 of Chapter III, also for references, including R. Schütze, *Direct Effects*, 276, and F. Cherubini, *Decisions under the Law of European Union: 'You May Be Six People, but I Love You'*, in *Yearbook of European Law*, vol. 41, 2022, 117–161, 27–34.

[466] *See* A. Barav, *Applicabilité directe*, in A. Barav, C. Philip, C. Boutayeb (eds.), *Dictionnaire juridique des Communautés européennes*, Paris, Pedone, 1993, 104–180, 106; P. Craig, G. de Búrca, *EU Law*, 200; *see* also the reflections by AG Trstenjak of 29 March 2007, *Carp Snc*, C-80/06, EU:C:2007:200, para. 58.

[467] R. Schütze, *Direct Effects*, 276.

[468] *See* GC, *Federazione nazionale delle cooperative della pesca (Federcoopesca)*, T-312/14, EU:T:2015:472, para. 60.

[469] CJ, *Carp Snc di L. Moleri e V Corsi v Ecorad Srl*, C-80/06, EU:C:2007:327, on which, *see* D. Simon, *Absence d'effet direct horizontal des directives et des décisions adressées aux États membres* (2007) *Europe Août-Septembre* 10.

[470] Council Directive 89/106/EEC of 21 December 1988 on the approximation of laws, regulations and administrative provisions of the Member States relating to construction products (OJ L 040, 11/02/1989, 12).

[471] *Carp* (n 469), para. 21.

[472] *See* the previous §§ of this chapter.

Moreover, two further considerations militate in favour of decisions' horizontal direct effect. The first is that in *Carp* the decision under scrutiny was based, upstream, on a directive. In other words, the CJ seems to derive the non-horizontality of the decision from the non-horizontality of the directive. It could be argued, therefore, that if the link to a directive was not present, the result would be different. The second is that decisions, even those addressed to the generality of States, are mandatory in all their elements, unlike, precisely, directives: despite the undoubted similarities, there is no full equivalence between the two acts, and this could culminate in the recognition of horizontal direct effect in respect of decisions to a more decisive extent than has been argued in respect of directives.

As regards decisions, which are also provided for in Article 288(4) TFEU, without specific addressees, that is, substantially legislative acts of a general nature, the CJ has not yet expressed a clear position. In any event, should such decision be deemed to have direct effect, not only vertical direct effect would be possible, but also horizontal direct effect, as is the case for regulations due to their general scope. There are no specific reasons for denying such effect. Moreover, *Carp* cannot serve as a precedent against the recognition of horizontal direct effect because in this ruling the addressees were the generality of States, not individuals.[473]

In short, in line with the observations made in the preceding sections in other respects, here, too, there is a need for a clear statement of position by the CJ, hopefully as 'inclusive' as possible, on the scope and effectiveness of decisions, taking into account the different categories of acts falling within the object and purpose of Article 288(4) TFEU.

[473] As stressed by U. Villani, *Istituzioni di diritto dell'Unione europea*, 6th ed., Bari, Cacucci, 2020, 328.

VII
UNSTEADY 'EXTERNAL' DIRECT EFFECT

1. Incorporation and direct effect of international law in the EU legal order: setting the scene

This chapter deals with the direct effect of international law,[1] or lack thereof, within the EU legal order. As a matter of fact, it deals with a partially different topic than the direct effect of EU law within national legal orders, which is at the core of the volume. The topic is only *partially* different since international law is a source of EU law.[2] As a matter of fact, investigating the direct effect of international law within the EU legal order also means investigating the direct effect of international law within the legal orders of the EU Member States because the national authorities are bound to respect EU law 'via Community law in Member State law'.[3]

[1] On the effects of international law in domestic legal orders at large, with a particular focus on judicial enforcement, direct effect, and self-executing treaties, *see*, in the abundant literature, in addition to those authors cited in footnotes 129 and 142 of § 4, Chapter II, about monism and dualism, H. Mosler, *L'application du droit international public par les tribunaux nationaux*, in *Recueil des Cours*, vol. 91, 1957, 619–709; J. J. Paust, *Self-Executing Treaties* (1988) 82 *American Journal International Law* 760; A. Bleckmann, *Begriff und Kriterien der innerstaatlichen Anwendbarkeit völkerrechtlicher Verträge*, Berlin, Duncker & Humblot, 1970; A. Koller, *Die unmittelbare Anwendbarkeit völkerrechtlicher Verträge und des EWG-Vertrages im innerstaatlichen Bereich*, Bern, Stämpfli, 1971; M. J. M. Verhoeven, *La notion*; J. Velu, *Les effets directs des instruments internationaux en matière de droits de l'homme*, Brussels, Swinnen, 1981; F. G. Jacobs, S. Roberts (eds.), *The Effect of Treaties in Domestic Law*, London, Sweet & Maxwell, 1987; E. Jiménez de Aréchaga, *Self-Executing Provisions of International Law*, in K. Hailbronner, G. Resse, T. Stein (eds.), *Staat und Völkerrechtsordnung: Festschrift für Karl Doehring*, Berlin, Springer, 1989, 409–419; T. Buergenthal, *Self-Executing and Non-Self-Executing Treaties in National and International Law*, in *Recueil des Cours*, vol. 235, 1992, 303–400; B. Conforti, *International Law and the Role of Domestic Legal Systems*, The Hague, Martinus Nijhoff, 1993; J. H. Jackson, *Status of Treaties in Domestic Legal Systems: A Policy Analysis* (1992) 86 *American Journal of International Law* 310; G. Buchs, *Die unmittelbare Anwendbarkeit völkerrechtlicher Vertragsbestimmungen am Beispiel der Rechtsprechung der Gerichte Deutschlands, Österreichs, der Schweiz und der Vereinigten Staaten von Amerika*, Baden-Baden, Nomos, 1993; M. Fitzmaurice, C. Flinterman (eds.), *Interactions between International and Municipal Law: A Comparative Case Law Study*, The Hague, TMC Asser Instituut, 1993; P. M. Eisemann (ed.), *The Integration of International and European Community Law into the National Legal Order*, The Hague, Kluwer, 1996; J. M. Henckaerts, *Self-Executing Treaties and the Impact of International Law on National Legal Systems: Research Guide* (1998) 26 *International Journal of Legal Information* 56; P. E. Holzer, *Die Ermittlung der innerstaatlichen Anwendbarkeit völkerrechtlicher Vertragsbestimmungen*, Zurich, Schulthess, 1999; H. Charlesworth, *The Fluid State: International Law and National Legal Systems*, Sydney, Federation Press, 2005; D. B. Hollis, M. R. Blakeslee, L.B. Ederington (eds.), *National Treaty Law and Practice*, Leiden, Martinus Nijhoff, 2005; K. Kaiser, *Treaties, Direct Applicability*, in *Max Planck Encyclopedia of Public International Law*, 2013; D. Sloss, *Self-Executing Treaties and Domestic Judicial Remedies* (2004) 98 *American Society of International Law Proceedings* 346; A. Nollkaemperer, *National Courts and the International Rule of Law*, Oxford, Oxford University Press, 2011; M. Oesch, *Direct Effect of International Agreements*, in T. Cottier, K. Nadakavukaren Schefer (eds.), *Elgar Encyclopedia of International Economic Law*, Cheltenham, Edward Elgar, 2017, 277–279; R. Baratta, *L'effetto diretto delle disposizioni internazionali* self-executing, in G. Palmisano (ed.), *Il diritto internazionale ed europeo nei giudizi interni*. Atti del XXIV Convegno SIDI di Roma, 5–6 June 2019, 2020, 75–111. All URLs for this chapter were last accessed on 30 April 2024.

[2] More specifically, international agreements concluded by the EU (either alone or with Member States) are regarded as acts of the EU institutions; *see*, e.g., CJ, *S. Z. Sevince v Staatssecretaris van Justitie*, C-192/89, EU:C:1990:322, para. 10.

[3] A. Peters, *The Position of International Law within the European Community Legal Order*, in *German Yearbook of International Law*, vol. 40, 1997, 9–77, 19.

Direct Effect in EU Law. Daniele Gallo, Oxford University Press. © Daniele Gallo 2025. DOI: 10.1093/9780191925221.003.0008

The purpose of this chapter is to understand whether and, if so, how international law can generate direct effect, that is, how the doctrine of direct effect informs the relationship between international law and EU law, rather than between the latter and the legal systems of the Member States. The direct effect referred to is that produced, within the EU legal order, by international treaties to which the Union is a party either exclusively or jointly with the Member States,[4] by decisions adopted by the bodies established by those agreements, as well as by general international law.[5]

The subject of this chapter, therefore, is neither the possible direct effect of the EU 'legislative instruments implementing' the agreements concluded by the EU,[6] nor the legal status of the rules and principles of international law in the EU legal system,[7] except for a few sporadic references contained in this section. Nor is it the indirect effect of those rules and principles.[8]

[4] Generally, on mixed agreements, including on their effects, *see*, amongst others, D. O'Keeffe, H. G. Schermers (eds.), *Mixed Agreements*, The Hague, Kluwer, 1983; M. J. F. M. Dolmans, *Problems of Mixed Agreements*, The Hague, TMC Asser Press, 1985; K. D. Stein, *Der gemischte Vertrag im Recht der Außenbeziehungen der Europäischen Wirtschaftsgemeinschaft*, Berlin, Duncker and Humblot, 1986; J. H. J. Bourgeois, J.-L. Dewost, M. A. Gaiffe (eds.), *La Communauté et les accords mixtes. Quelles perspectives?*, Brussels, Presses interuniversitaires européennes, 1997; A. Rosas, *Mixed Union: Mixed Agreements*, in M. Koskenniemi (ed.), *International Law Aspects of the European Union*, The Hague, Kluwer, 1998, 125–148; J. Heliskoski, *Mixed Agreements as a Technique for Organizing the International Relations of the European Community and its Member States*, The Hague, Kluwer, 2001; E. Neframi, *Les accords mixtes de la Communauté européenne: aspects communautaires et internationaux*, Brussels, Bruylant, 2007; M. Cremona, *Defending the Community Interest: the Duties of Cooperation and Compliance*, in M. Cremona, B. de Witte (eds.), *EU Foreign Relations Law: Constitutional Fundamentals*, Oxford, Hart, 2008, 125–169; C. Hillion, *Tous pour un, un pour tous! Coherence in the External Relations of the Union*, in M. Cremona (ed.), *Developments in EU External Relations Law*, Oxford, Oxford University Press, 2008, 10–36; R. Holdgaard, *External Relations Law of the European Community. Legal Reasoning and Legal Discourses*, The Hague, Kluwer, 2008, 156–63; C. Hillion, P. Koutrakos (eds.), *Mixed Agreements Revisited*, Oxford, Hart, 2010; M. Cremona, *Member States as Trustees of the Union Interest: Participating in International Agreements on Behalf of the EU*, in A. Arnull, C. Barnard, M. Dougan, E. Spaventa (eds.), *A Constitutional Order of States—Essays in Honour of Alan Dashwood*, Oxford, Oxford University Press, 2010, 435-457; E. Baroncini, S. Cafaro, N. Criseide, *Le relazioni esterne dell'Unione Europea*, Turin, Giappichelli, 2012, 75-89; P. Eeckhout, *EU External Relations Law*, 2nd ed., Oxford, Oxford University Press, 2012, 212–266; M. Cremona, A. Thies, *The European Court of Justice and External Relations Law: Constitutional Challenges*, Oxford, Hart, 2014; J. Heliskoski, *Mixed Agreements: The EU Law Fundamentals*, in R. Schütze, T. Tridimas (eds.), *Oxford Principles*, 1174–1207; M. Chamon, *Constitutional Limits to the Political Choice for Mixity*, in E. Neframi, M. Gatti (eds.), *Constitutional Issues of EU External Relations Law*, Baden-Baden, Nomos, 2018, 137–166; B. Van Vooren, R. A. Wessel, *EU External Relations Law: Text, Cases and Materials*, Oxford, Oxford University Press, 2014; M. Chamon, I. Govaere (eds.), *EU External Relations Post-Lisbon: The Law and Practice of Facultative Mixity*, Leiden, Martinus Nijhoff, 2020; J. Wouters, F. Hoffmeister, G. De Baere, T. Ramopoulos, *The Law of EU External Relations: Cases, Materials, and Commentary on the EU as an International Legal Actor*, 3rd ed., Oxford, Oxford University Press, 2021, 101–127, 105, and 124–126; N. Levrat, Y. Kaspiarovich, C. Kaddous, R. A. Wessel (eds.), *The EU and its Member States' Joint Participation in International Agreements*, Oxford, Hart, 2022.

[5] On the quite subtle differences between customary law and general principles of international law, both encompassed in the broad notion of general international law, *see* I. Brownlie, *Principles of Public International Law*, 9th ed., Oxford, Oxford University Press, 2019, 6–12 and 15–18. In this chapter, most notably in § 2.4, the focus will be on customary law since this is the term normally used by the CJ.

[6] Expression borrowed from M. Mendez, *The Legal Effects of EU Agreements*, Oxford, Oxford University Press, 2013, XX. On the need to differentiate EU measures implementing the international agreement and the agreement itself, *see* T. Hartley, *International Agreements and the Community Legal System: Some Recent Developments* (1983) 3 *European Law* 383, 390–391.

[7] On the status and ranking of international agreements within the EU legal order, *see*, *ex multis*, J. Wouters, P. A. Nollkaemper, E. de Wet, *The Europeanisation of International Law—The Status of International Law in the EU and its Member States*, The Hague, TMC Asser Press, 2008; A. Rosas, *The Status in EU Law of International Agreements Concluded by EU Member States* (2011) 34 *Fordham International Law Journal* 1304; E. Cannizzaro, P. Palchetti, R. A. Wessel (eds.), *International Law as Law of the European Union*, The Hague, Martinus Nijhoff, 2012; E. Neframi, *Status and Enforceability of EU International Agreements within the Domestic Legal Systems of the Member States:* Kupferberg, in G. Butler, R. A. Wessel (eds.), *EU External Relations Law: The Cases in Context*, Oxford, Hart 2022, 155–165.

[8] Amongst contributions specifically devoted to this matter, *see* F. Casolari, *Giving Indirect Effect to International Law within the EU Legal Order: the Doctrine of Consistent Interpretation*, in E. Cannizzaro, P. Palchetti, R. A. Wessel, *International Law*, 395–415.

Moreover, in order to better delineate and grasp the contours of the doctrine of direct effect, the focus is, first, on the evaluation of EU case law carried out in sections 2–4 of this chapter, including a few judgments on customary law, and secondly, on the similarities and divergences between 'internal direct effect', that is, EU law's direct effect within national legal orders as examined in the previous chapters, and 'external direct effect', that is, international law's direct effect within the EU legal order (section 5).[9] In doing so, some brief considerations are made on the pros and cons of the limping process of externalization of direct effect that began in the seventies and is now slowing down. Finally, section 6 is dedicated to the increasing practice of precluding external direct effect in the text of the international agreements concluded by the EU.

The starting point for testing the operability of external direct effect in the light of the CJEU case law is that neither the TEU nor the TFEU stipulate what the effects of international law are in EU law, just as they do not explain what the effects of EU law are within national legal orders . Instead, references to the observance of international law by the EU and its Member States are made in Articles 21(1) TEU,[10] 3(5) TEU,[11] and 216(2) TFEU. In particular, Article 216(2) TFEU provides that 'agreements concluded by the Union are binding upon the institutions of the Union and on its Member States'. In this respect, there is a limit to the entry of such agreements into the EU legal order. Indeed, in the event of a conflict between the international agreement and EU primary law (TEU, TFEU, Protocols, Charter of Fundamental Rights, general principles), it is primary law that prevails, as confirmed by Article 218(11) TFEU, which allows the CJ to issue a (binding) opinion on the compatibility of a negotiated agreement with EU primary law.[12] It could not be otherwise since EU law is not classic international law, as has already been explained,[13] and, for this reason, the legal status of its constitutional backbone cannot be 'simply' governed by international rules and principles on the conflict of treaties and the internal law of international organizations.[14] On the other hand, international agreements are above EU legislation and thus pre-empt inconsistent EU secondary acts. As held by the CJ, 'where international agreements are concluded by the European Union they are binding upon its institutions and, *consequently*, they prevail over acts of the European Union'.[15] This is the reason why the question of the direct effect

[9] Both terms are borrowed from P. Eeckhout, *EU External Relations*, 229–230.

[10] '1. The Union's action on the international scene shall be guided by the principles which have inspired its own creation, development and enlargement, and which it seeks to advance in the wider world: democracy, the rule of law, the universality and indivisibility of human rights and fundamental freedoms, respect for human dignity, the principles of equality and solidarity, and respect for the principles of the United Nations Charter and international law.'

[11] '5. In its relations with the wider world, the Union shall uphold and promote its values and interests and contribute to the protection of its citizens. It shall contribute to peace, security, the sustainable development of the Earth, solidarity and mutual respect among peoples, free and fair trade, eradication of poverty and the protection of human rights, in particular the rights of the child, as well as to the strict observance and the development of international law, including respect for the principles of the United Nations Charter.'

[12] '11. A Member State, the European Parliament, the Council or the Commission may obtain the opinion of the Court of Justice as to whether an agreement envisaged is compatible with the Treaties. Where the opinion of the Court is adverse, the agreement envisaged may not enter into force unless it is amended or the Treaties are revised.' For an example of an opinion that found the draft agreement incompatible with EU law, *see* CJ, *France v Commission*, C-327/91, EU:C:1994:305.

[13] See §§ 2.2, 2.4, and 3 of Chapter I, as well as § 4 of Chapter II.

[14] In this vein, *see* A. Peters, *The Position*, 11.

[15] *See* CJ, *Air Transport Association of America and Others v Secretary of State for Energy and Climate Change*, C-366/10, EU:C:2011:864, para. 50 (italics added). *See* also, amongst many others, CJ, *Commission v Germany*, C-61/94, EU:C:1996:313, para. 52; CJ, *Yassin Abdullah Kadi and Al Barakaat International Foundation v Council of the European Union and Commission of the European Communities*, C-402/05 P and C-415/05 P, EU:C:2008:461.

of international agreements becomes vital: if a provision of an international agreement is not considered by the CJEU to be directly effective, the 'validity' of an EU act, according to the Court, 'cannot be affected' by that provision.[16] The denial of direct effect, consequently, breaches the judicial protection of those, be they individuals (Article 267 TFEU on the validity of EU law or Article 263(4) TFEU) or Member States (Article 263(2) TFEU), who are affected by the EU's failure to comply with its international obligations under the agreement concluded with a Third Country (or other international organizations). Likewise, lacking direct effect, the national rule, which comes into play in domestic proceedings and/or interpretive preliminary ruling proceedings and is in conflict with international law, in the opinion of the CJEU, cannot be disapplied. The denial of direct effect thus affects individuals' prerogatives when at stake are proceedings before domestic courts and/or interpretative preliminary rulings proceedings. Overall, if the doctrine of direct effect is deemed by the Court the trigger for challenging, not only national law, but also EU secondary law, yet such direct effect is often neglected *in concreto*, the applicants' prerogatives before national courts or EU jurisdictions would be greatly curtailed.[17] Additionally, direct effect is not only relevant from the point of view of safeguarding individual prerogatives associated with natural and legal persons, but also from the point of view of compliance with the agreement, that is, its proper enforcement.

Against this backdrop, there are reasons for which the CJEU has frequently denied the direct effect of international agreements and, in this regard, softened the monistic facet of EU law.[18] This practice will be discussed in detail in the following sections.

At this stage, a closely connected matter shall be examined: the incorporation of international agreements in the EU legal order.[19] Indeed, logically, the analysis as to how international agreements penetrate EU law precedes the analysis as to their effects in the context of (national and EU) judicial proceedings concerning the validity of EU secondary law or the compatibility of domestic law. Given that the European Treaties do not contain any decisive indication regarding either their effects or their incorporation, the main problem remains: whether international agreements, in order to bind the EU institutions and Member States, must necessarily be transfused into EU law by means of further acts of secondary legislation.

In the literature, most authors consider EU law to be monist because, as the CJ has stated since *Haegeman II*,[20] provisions of EU international agreements 'form an integral part of Community law' from their coming into force.[21] This would therefore imply an automatic

[16] CJ, *International Fruit Company*, joined cases 21–24/72, EU:C:1972:115, para. 28. For a criticism on considering direct effect as a precondition for challenging EU secondary law *see* sections 3 and 5 of this chapter.

[17] In this vein, *see* N. Ghazaryan, *Who Are the 'Gatekeepers'? In Continuation of the Debate on the Direct Applicability and the Direct Effect of EU International Agreements*, in *Yearbook of European Law*, vol. 37, 2018, 27–74, 40, who also wrote that international agreements devoid of direct effect are 'toothless as far as their enforcement in national courts is concerned'.

[18] As observed by R. Schütze, *On 'Middle Ground'. The European Union and Public International Law*, in R. Schütze, *Foreign Affairs and the EU Constitution*. Selected essays, Cambridge, Cambridge University Press, 2014, 47–90, 51, the doctrine of direct effect represents 'a yardstick for the actual openness of a legal system: it is a *chiffre* for the intensity of its monist creed'.

[19] 'Incorporation' is a recurring term in the literature. Among the first to use it, *see* F. Casolari, *L'incorporazione del diritto internazionale nell'ordinamento dell'Unione Europea*, Milan, Giuffrè, 2008. *See*, more recently, M. Mendez, *The Legal Effects*, 62.

[20] The ruling has been delivered in the context of a preliminary ruling procedure on both interpretation and validity concerning the Association Agreement with Greece of 1961. CJ, *R. & V. Haegeman v Belgian State* (*Haegeman II*), 181-73, EU:C:1974:41, has been confirmed in the case law: two examples are CJ, *Kupferberg*, 104/81, EU:C:1982:362, para. 13 and CJ, *Brita*, C-386/08, EU:C:2010:91, para. 39.

[21] *Haegeman II* (n 20), para. 5.

entry of international agreements into the EU legal order,[22] and of decisions taken by bodies established by these agreements as they are 'directly linked to the agreement which they implement'.[23]

A minority of authors believe, on the other hand, that the EU legal system is not, in truth, monist, but dualist, because integration into the EU legal system would take place by means of acts of transposition of secondary law.[24] Underlying this reconstruction is, again, *Haegeman II*, where the CJ wrote that the Association Agreement with Greece is 'an act of one of the institutions of the Community'.[25] *Haegeman II*, therefore, following this reasoning, should be interpreted as meaning that the agreement can only become part of EU law by means of a further act adopted by the EU institutions, most notably by the decision of the Council to conclude the agreement with the Third Country, that is, Greece in the case at hand. Moreover, the circumstance that in *Haegeman II* reference is made to the fact that the provisions of the agreement, rather than the agreement itself, are incorporated into the EU legal order, would seem to imply that this incorporation passes through acts of implementation. In the words of Jan Klabbers, 'otherwise, why not simply say that the agreement is an integral part of Community law? Why make a distinction between the agreement and its provisions?'[26]

In this framework, two objections can be raised against the 'dualists'. First: as Klabbers himself pointed out,[27] the *Haegeman II* judgment 'attach[es] relevance to the moment of entry into force *of the agreement*', rather than to the decision to adopt or approve it. Second: it is the CJ itself which clarified that the nature of the act that approved the international agreement 'cannot affect whether it is recognized as having direct effect'.[28] Therefore, further confirmation that the agreement is directly incorporated into EU law, without the need for measures of transposition, also comes from the irrelevance of these measures in terms of the agreement's legal effects. Despite a certain ambivalence in the CJEU's reasoning,[29] an interpretation in the sense that the EU way of incorporating international agreements is monist seems thus preferable *prima facie*. Nonetheless, there is no doubt that, in practice, it is the Council's decision that enables the international agreement to produce legal effects at both the level of international law and EU law. Without the

[22] *See, inter alia*, K. Lenaerts, *Direct Applicability and Direct Effect of International Law in the EU Legal Order*, in I. Govaere, E. Lannon, P. van Elsuwege, S. Adam (eds.), *The European Union in the World. Essays in Honour of Marc Maresceau*, The Hague, Martinus Nijhoff, 2013, 45–64; M. Mendez, *The Legal Effects*, 63; P. Eeckhout, *The Integration of Public International Law in EU Law. Analytical and Normative Questions*, in P. Eeckhout, M. López Escudero (eds.), *The European Union's External Action in Times of Crisis*, Oxford, Hart, 2019, 189–204; B. de Witte, *Direct Effect, Primacy and the Nature of the Legal Order*, in P. Craig, G. De Búrca (eds.), *The Evolution of EU Law*, 3rd ed., Oxford, Oxford University Press, 2021, 187–227, 199. M. Mendez, *The Legal Effects*, 17–37, carried out a survey on the characteristics of treaty incorporation, also in the light of the comparison among EU Member States. On monism and mixed agreements, *see* S. Gáspár-Szilágyi, *EU Member State Enforcement of 'Mixed' Agreements and Access to Justice: Rethinking Direct Effect* (2013) 40 *Legal Issues of Economic Integration* 163; R. Schütze, *Federalism and Foreign Affairs: Mixity as an (Inter)national Phenomenon*, in C. Hillion, P. Koutrakos (eds.), *Mixed Agreements*, 57–86.

[23] In these terms, *see* CJ, *Deutsche Shell AG*, C-188/91, EU:C:1993:24, para. 17.

[24] T. Hartley, *International Agreements*, 383; J. Klabbers, *International Law in Community Law: The Law and Politics of Direct Effect*, in *Yearbook of European Law*, vol. 21, 2001, 263–298, 293.

[25] *Haegeman II* (n 20), para. 4 and *Brita* (n 20), para. 39.

[26] J. Klabbers, *International Law*, 276.

[27] J. Klabbers, *International Law*, 276.

[28] CJ, *Ioannis Katsivardas*, C-160/09, EU:C:2010:29, para. 34. *See* also the opinion of AG Saggio of 25 February 1999, *Portugal v Council*, C-149/96, EU:C:1999:92, para. 20.

[29] As noted by K. Lenaerts, P. Van Nuffel, T. Corthaut, *EU Constitutional Law*, Oxford, Oxford University Press, 2021, 695–712, 695. K. Lenaerts, *Direct Applicability*, 45: 'the incorporation of public international law into EU law follows, *to some extent*, a "monist approach" (italics added).'

Council's decision, the international agreement could not be incorporated into EU law. In this sense, the EU seems to present also the traits of a dualist legal order.[30] EU law, therefore, is a middle ground between monism and dualism and this very same fact, as noted in the literature, starting with A. von Bogdandy,[31] calls for a release from this diatribe.[32] Moreover, as A. Peters made clear, the question whether a provision of an international agreement concluded by the EU has direct effect 'must be distinguished from the prior question of how rules of international law are integrated into the internal [EU] order and acquire the formal status of a source of law'.[33] As a matter of fact, even in dualist systems direct effect could be recognized. In such a case, the possibility of invoking a rule of international law is admitted albeit rooted (and justified) in domestic law.[34] In any event, as noted, once again, by Peters, the fact that two opposing arguments can be made regarding the nexus between direct effect either with monism or with dualism 'demonstrates that it is analytically preferable to distinguish the mode of incorporating international law and the question of direct effect.'[35]

The focus, as regards both the adaptation to international agreements and their effects, must therefore be turned to the practice of case law, in the awareness that it is up to the CJEU to identify the prerequisites and avenues of reception and legal effects, that is, to fill the legal vacuum underpinning EU primary law under both profiles: incorporation and direct effect (or lack thereof). The Court has, in fact, 'monopolized' both matters,[36] acting as 'gatekeeper'[37] with respect to the entry of international law into EU law and the determination of its effects.

[30] As is recognized by P. Eeckhout, who supports the view that EU law is a monist legal system towards international agreements, 'legally there is no need for any act of transformation beyond the Council's decision to conclude [the agreement].' *See* P. Eeckhout, *The Domestic Legal Status of the WTO Agreement: Interconnecting Legal Systems* (1997) 34 *Common Market Law Review* 11, 25.

[31] As mentioned already in § 4 of Chapter II with regard, more generally, to the effects of international law beyond the EU legal order.

[32] For a definition of these concepts when international agreements in the EU legal order are at stake, *see* A. Peters, *The Position*, 18: 'in the monist model, international law and domestic law are only different elements of one universal body of law, so that—strictly speaking—the question of how to incorporate international law into domestic law does not arise. According to the dualist conception, international law and domestic law are two separate legal systems because they have different sources, different contents, and different subjects.'

[33] A. Peters, *The Position*, 48. *See* also N. Ghazaryan, *Who are the Gatekeepers*, 39, who noted that 'monism and dualism denote the process of the incorporation of a treaty into a domestic legal order. From this perspective, caution is required against conflating the issues of direct effect or "invocability of a treaty provision" with the classification of the system as monist or dualist'. In respect to the WTO, AG Maduro observed that 'the fact that WTO law cannot be relied upon before a court does not mean that it does not form part of the Community legal system' (opinion of AG Maduro of 20 February 2008, *FIAMM*, joined cases C-120-121/06 P, EU:C:2008:98, para. 37). *Contra see* J. Klabbers, *International Law*, 263: 'starkly put: if the Court finds treaty provisions, or other rules of international law, to be directly effective, then it will treat those rules as being part of Community law; if the Court thinks these rules are not directly effective, then they will not enter the Community legal order.'

[34] In this vein, *see* P. Eeckhout, *The Domestic Legal Status*, 28–29. *Contra* R. Kovar, *Les Accords liant les Communautés Européennes et l'ordre juridique communautaire: à propos d'une jurisprudence récente de la Cour de Justice* (1974) 17 *Revue du Marché Commun* 345, 352.

[35] A. Peters, *The Position*, 49.

[36] In these terms, with regard to direct effect of international law, *see* R. Schütze, *On 'Middle Ground'*, 51.

[37] On such role, with regard to both the reception and legal effects, *see* F. Snyder, *The Gatekeepers: The European Courts and WTO Law* (2013) 50 *Common Market Law Review* 313; J. Klabbers, *International Law*, 296; M. Cremona, *External Relations and External Competence of the European Union: The Emergence of an Integrated Policy*, in P. Craig, G. de Búrca (eds.), 215–268, 234; I. Hadjiyianni, *The CJEU as the gatekeeper of International Law: The Cases of WTO Law and the Aarhus Convention* (2021) 70 *International & Comparative Law Quarterly* 895, 897; F. C. Mayer, *European Law as a Door Opener for Public International Law?*, in J. M. Thouvenin, C. Tomuschat (eds.), *Droit International et Diversité des Cultures Juridiques—International Law and Diversity of Legal Cultures*, Paris: Pédone, 2008, 241–255, spoke of 'door opener', as reported by B. Van Vooren, R. A. Wessel, *EU External Relations*, 218.

The rationale for the above-described centralization is to ensure uniformity[38] in the EU legal order[39] and among the Member States.[40] Obviously, the choice of the type of reception of international agreements that is deemed necessary, once made, as was the case in *Haegeman II*,[41] with regard to a specific agreement, from then on applies to all agreements concluded by the Union. In this regard, the CJEU found 'no difference'[42] between agreements concluded by the Community/EU alone,[43] by the Community/EU and the Member States,[44] or only by the Member States.[45] With respect to the latter agreements, they include the General Agreement on Tariffs and Trade (GATT) of 1947, no longer in force, and the 1951 UN Geneva Convention and Protocol relating to the Status of Refugees and other relevant treaties of 1967, still in force. As to the GATT, the agreement was considered binding by the CJEU because the Community had assumed 'the competence previously exercised by the Member State in the field to which the agreement applie[d]'.[46] As for the UN Convention and the Protocol on the Status of Refugees, these are agreements with binding force for the EU, as well as for the States, since the TFEU is the source of the EU competence in this area by virtue of the express reference to both agreements in Article 78(1) TFEU.

Regarding the recognition or denial of direct effect, in the absence of provisions in the agreement or in a subsequent Council's decision, the CJEU has to decide on a case-by-case basis.[47] Hence, the dangers stemming from a wavering attitude by the Court and the absence of certain guidelines in the conceptualization of the legal effects of international agreements, resulting in the many doubts that the EU jurisprudence on the 'externalization' of direct effect[48] continues to raise.[49]

Now, while these questions are at the heart of the analysis carried out in the following sections, one issue must be addressed here, before resuming its examination in section 5: the relationship between direct effect and direct applicability.

Since claiming that international agreements are incorporated in the EU legal system from their entry into force means something different than asserting direct effect, the key question is whether all international agreements are directly applicable, as if they were *mutatis mutandis* EU (external) regulations.[50]

[38] *See* the opinion of AG Trabucchi of 14 January 1976, *Bresciani*, 87/75, EU:C:1976:3, 148. On uniformity and the principle of equality, *see* F. Casolari, *The Acknowledgment of the Direct Effect of EU International Agreements: Does Legal Equality Still Matter?*, in L.S. Rossi, F. Casolari (eds.), *The Principle of Equality in EU Law*, Heidelberg, Springer, 2017, 83–129.

[39] *See Kupferberg* (n 20), para. 14: 'it is for the Court, within the framework of its jurisdiction in interpreting the provisions of agreements, to ensure their uniform application throughout the Community.'

[40] On international agreements and the principle of uniformity from the standpoint of Member States, *see* the opinion of AG Mayras of 25 October 1972, *International Fruit Company*, EU:C:1972:89, 1234.

[41] *See* the analysis above on the lack of clarity underpinning such choice.

[42] A. Peters, *The Position*, 21.

[43] e.g. *Kupferberg* (n 20).

[44] e.g. CJ, *Meryem Demirel*, 12/86, EU:C:1987:400.

[45] e.g. *International Fruit Company* (n 16). On the specificities of these agreements, *see* R. Schütze, *On 'Middle Ground'*, 61–76.

[46] K. Lenaerts, P. Van Nuffel, T. Corthaut, *EU Constitutional Law*, 695, who also wrote that 'since the competence in connection with the application of that agreement was conferred on the Community by the EC Treaty and the Community itself subsequently took part in the tariff negotiations'. *See International Fruit Company* (n 16), paras 10–17, whose core reflections have been reiterated in the subsequent case law, such as CJ, *Peralta*, C-379/92, EU:C:1994:296, para. 16.

[47] As confirmed by the CJ in CJ, *Portugal v Council*, C-149/96, EU:C:1999:574, para. 34.

[48] The term is borrowed from N. Ghazaryan, *Who are the Gatekeepers*, 29.

[49] On the diversity of interpretative methods related to the interplay between international law and EU law, and on the lack of clarity in the case law of the CJEU, *see*, most recently, R. Dunbar, *Learning from Failure in 'an Integral Part' of EU Law: Interpretation of International Treaties in the CJEU* (2024) 1 *European Law Open* 1.

[50] R. Schütze, *Direct Effects and Indirect Effects of Union Law*, in R. Schütze, T. Tridimas (eds.), *Oxford Principles*, 265–299, 286.

Claiming that all international agreements are directly applicable necessarily presupposes that direct applicability[51] and direct effect are regarded as distinct categories. In fact, if the assumption is that international agreements are *per se* directly applicable, should direct applicability and direct effect be considered equivalent, the conclusion would be that all international agreements, *insofar* as they are directly applicable, are also, consequently, directly effective. However, this assertion is unfounded and at odds with the case law, which is often reluctant to attribute direct effect to international agreements, especially multilateral agreements. Indeed, only some international agreements, subject to certain conditions indicated by the CJEU, contain directly effective rules, as will be observed at length in the following sections. This is why a reconstruction that holds all international agreements to be directly applicable can only consider the notion of direct applicability to be different from that of direct effect, which is *only a possible* feature of those agreements. Among those who hold, on the one hand, that direct effect and direct applicability are not the same thing,[52] and, on the other, that direct effect is a possible, rather than inevitable, attribute of international agreements,[53] there are those who write that direct applicability 'only makes [international agreements] capable of having direct effects'.[54] Direct applicability would therefore be the precondition for direct effect.

In this book the perspective is different. In line with AG Tesauro's opinion in *Yousfi*,[55] direct effect and direct applicability have, in practice, the same meaning when it comes to international agreements,[56] as was argued also with reference to internal direct effect in section 7 of Chapter III. This is because once a rule of an international agreement is sufficiently unconditional to regulate the case, then it is necessarily also clear and precise, that is, directly effective, and directly applicable. Proof of this is that the CJEU, in much of its case law, uses the terms to indicate the same concept, as it often does about internal direct effect.[57] For example, the overlap is clear in the *Demirel*[58] and *Kziber*[59] judgments, whereby it was noted that a provision of an agreement concluded by the Community with non-Member third-parties should be considered 'directly applicable' where it involves 'a clear and precise obligation which is not subject, in its implementation or effects, to the adoption of any subsequent measure'.[60]

There are, thus, two takeaways from all this. The first: direct applicability is different from the concept of reception and integration of international agreements into the EU legal

[51] Both R. A. Wessel, *Reconsidering the Relationship between International and EU law: Towards a Content-Based Approach?*, in E. Cannizzaro, P. Palchetti, R. A. Wessel, *International Law*, 7–33, and A. Nollkaemper, *The Direct Effect of Public International Law*, in J. M. Prinssen, A. Schrauwen (eds.), *Direct Effect: Rethinking a Classic of EC Legal Doctrine*, Groningen, European Law Publishing, 2002, 156–180, 160–161, quite surprisingly, referred to 'validity' rather than to 'direct applicability'.

[52] Expressly in these terms, *see* F. Castillo de la Torre, *The Status of GATT in EC Law,* Revisited, in *Journal of World Trade.* Revisited, 1995, 35, 53, I. Cheyne, *International Agreements and the European Community Legal System* (1994) 19 *European Law Review* 581; A. Rosas, *EU Law*, 12.

[53] N. Ghazaryan, *Who are the Gatekeepers*, 40, first wrote that 'all agreements concluded by the EU are directly applicable' and then noted that international agreements devoid of direct effect are 'toothless as far as their enforcement in national courts is concerned'. K. Lenaerts, *Direct Applicability*, 45, considered direct effect and direct applicability as 'two different, albeit intertwined, concepts'.

[54] R. Schütze, *Direct Effects*, 275.

[55] *See* the opinion of AG Tesauro of 23 February 1994, *Zoubir Yousfi*, C-58/93, EU:C:1994:63, para. 4.

[56] Accordingly, *see* A. Peters, *The Position*, 158.

[57] *See* extensively § 7 of Chapter III.

[58] *Demirel* (n 44).

[59] CJ, *Office national de l'emploi (Onem) v Bahia Kziber*, C-18/90, EU:C:1991:36.

[60] *Demirel* (n 44), para. 14 and *Kziber* (n 59), para. 15. *See* also, amongst many others, CJ, *Asda Stores*, C-372/06, EU:C:2007:787, para. 82.

order.[61] The second: direct applicability and direct effect mean the same thing in practice. When an international agreement, following the decision of the Council concluding it, enters into force for the Union and is valid in international law, that is, it is binding on third States that have ratified it together with the Union, as well as for the Union and its Member States, some of its rules, or all of them, may be considered directly applicable/effective, provided that they are sufficiently complete in their scope and content.

Against this background, there is a starting point from which to proceed to examine, in the following section, the case law of the CJEU. In the literature it has been observed that 'the paradox of the extension of [direct effect] to international agreements lies in the fact that the doctrine helped to "define" the EU legal order "in opposition to international law", largely due to reversing the presumption that international treaties were not capable of having direct effect'.[62] Therefore, direct effect, on the one hand, is a doctrine that, as has already been pointed out in section 1 of Chapter I, although known to international law at the time of *Van Gend & Loos*, represents the means to free EU law from standard international legal categories, with the consequence that a real presumption of direct effect is asserted. On the other hand, direct effect is used by the CJEU as a means to exploit the potential of EU international agreements, and decisions of international organizations,[63] from the point of view of their enforceability and justiciability before both national and EU courts. In this respect, precisely because EU law is a legal order different from international law, the external direct effect cannot be investigated using, to the letter, the same logic that applies to internal direct effect. The fact that internal direct effect is the rule rather than the exception, that its establishment originates in EU law rather than in national law, and that the interpretation for its detection is objective rather than subjective, requires us to look at external direct effect somewhat differently from the *Van Gend & Loos* doctrine.[64] This look allows us to understand the extent to which external direct effect has unclear contours and is characterized by a development on a non-linear course. Indeed, the potential inherent in international agreements is only partially grasped by the CJEU in its case law. Much depends on the type of judicial proceedings in which international law is at stake and on the type of international agreement, bilateral or multilateral, at the heart of such proceedings. Additionally, one should not underestimate the contribution to these uncertainties stemming from the CJEU's tendency, as will be highlighted in the sections that follow—already noted with respect to internal direct effect—towards argumentative minimalism and the—at times—barely comprehensible and foreseeable application of rules and principles of interpretation that the Court itself uses in its jurisprudence.

2. The unclear judicial trajectories of 'external' direct effect

The great majority of case law of the GC and CJ on the matter of direct effect and international law relates to international agreements.

Regardless of whether the agreements are concluded by the Community/Union alone, by the Community/Union with the Member States, or, as in the case of the GATT or the UN

[61] *Contra*, A. Rosas, *EU Law and National Law: A Common Legal System*, AEL working paper, 2024, available at https://cadmus.eui.eu/handle/1814/76744, 12, observed that the Council's decision renders the international agreement directly applicable within the EU legal system.

[62] N. Ghazaryan, *Who are the Gatekeepers*, 29.

[63] The CJ is more reluctant to so the same vis-à-vis general international law, as observed in § 2.4 of this chapter.

[64] *See* also §§ 2.2, 2.4, and 3 of Chapter I and § 4 of Chapter II.

Convention and Protocol on the Status of Refugees, only by the Member States, individuals, in both preliminary rulings on interpretation and validity as well as in actions for annulment, can challenge domestic law (also via preliminary references on interpretation before the CJ under Article 267 TFEU) or EU law (preliminary references on validity before the CJ under Article 267 TFEU and actions for annulment before the GC under Article 263(4) TFEU). The case law also covers international agreements invoked under Article 263(2) TFEU before the CJ by States against EU acts.

As to the nature of the agreements, it is possible to identify three types.[65] While some, like the WTO Agreement(s), are multilateral, others—the majority—are bilateral: (*i*) trade agreements; (*ii*) association, cooperation, and partnership agreements; and (*iii*) non-trade related agreements. Excluded from agreements that are relevant, or contentious, in terms of direct effect, are all new-generation[66] free trade agreements,[67] some association, partnership and cooperation agreements,[68] some protocols establishing dispute settlement mechanisms mainly related to trade,[69] and the agreements related to both the AFSJ[70] and the CFSP,[71] because they explicitly deny, frequently in their general and final provisions,[72] that their provisions have direct effect. The same holds true for the EU–UK Trade and Cooperation Agreement of 2021.[73] In most of these cases the preclusion of direct effect is also included in

[65] For a systematization of all EU agreements, from the standpoint of their legal effects, *see* M. Mendez, *The Legal Effects*, 107–286; N. Zipperle, *EU International Agreements. An Analysis of Direct Effect and Judicial Review Pre- and Post-Lisbon*, Cham, Springer, 2017, 9–62.

[66] *See*, *inter alia*, the account by A. Semertzi, *The Preclusion of Direct Effect in the Recently Concluded EU Free Trade Agreements* (2014) 51 *Common Market Law Review* 1125; G. Van der Loo, P. Van Elsuwege, R. Petrov, *The EU-Ukraine Association Agreement: Assessment of an Innovative Legal Instrument*, EUI LAW working paper, 2014, available at https://cadmus.eui.eu/handle/1814/32031; A. Van Waeyenberge, P. Pecho, *Free Trade Agreements after the Treaty of Lisbon in the Light of the Case Law of the Court of Justice of the European Union* (2014) 20 *European Law Journal* 749; D. Thym, *The Missing Link: Direct Effect, CETA/TTIP and Investor-State-Dispute Settlement*, 4 January 2015, available at https://verfassungsblog.de/en-verhinderte-rechtsanwendung-deutsche-gerichte-cetatiip-und-investor-staat-streitigkeiten-2/; V. Stoynov, *The Direct Effect of EU Bilateral Trade Agreements Such as the TTIP in the Light of the Jurisprudence of the CJEU* (2017) 9 *Amsterdam Law Forum* 42; S. Poli, *La diretta invocabilità degli accordi internazionali*, in M. E. Bartoloni, S. Poli (eds.), *L'azione esterna dell'Unione europea*, Naples, Editoriale Scientifica, 2021, 93–97; C. H. L., Labus, *L'esclusione dell'effetto diretto negli accordi internazionali dell'Unione: riflessioni alla luce della prassi recente*, in S. Poli, S. Marinai (eds.), *L'Unione europea sulla scena internazionale: sfide e trasformazioni sul piano interno ed esterno. Atti del V Convegno AISDUE di Pisa*, Naples, Editoriale Scientifica, forthcoming, 2025.

[67] *See*, e.g., Article 30(6) of the Comprehensive Economic and Trade Agreement (CETA) between Canada, of the one part, and the European Union and its Member States, of the other part, of 2017: 'Nothing in this Agreement shall be construed as conferring rights or imposing obligations on persons other than those created between the Parties under public international law, nor as permitting this Agreement to be directly invoked in the domestic legal systems of the Parties.'

[68] *See*, e.g., all annexes to the Association Agreement between the European Union and the European Atomic Energy Community and their Member States, of the one part, and Georgia, of the other part, of 2014.

[69] *See*, e.g., Article 18(2) of the Protocol between the European Union and the Republic of Tunisia establishing a Dispute Settlement Mechanism applicable to disputes under the trade provisions of the Euro-Mediterranean Agreement establishing an association between the European Community and its Member States, of the one part, and the Republic of Tunisia, of the other part, of 2010.

[70] e.g. Article 21(1) of the Agreement between the EU and the United States of America on the processing and transfer of Financial Messaging Data from the European Union to the United States for purposes of the Terrorist Finance Tracking Program.

[71] e.g. surreptitiously, Article 24 of the Agreement between the EU and the Democratic Republic of the Congo on the status and activities of the European Union police mission in the Democratic Republic of the Congo: 'the purpose of the privileges and immunities as provided for in this Agreement are not to benefit individuals but to ensure the efficient performance of the EU Mission/operation.' *See* R. Schütze, *European Union Law*, 187.

[72] The preclusion may also be provided in other provisions of the agreement, as noted by A. Semertzi, *The preclusion*, 1129.

[73] 'Nothing in this Agreement or any supplementing agreement shall be construed as conferring rights or imposing obligations on persons other than those created between the Parties under public international law, nor as permitting this Agreement or any supplementing agreement to be directly invoked in the domestic legal systems

the Council decisions by which the agreement is concluded.[74] Moreover, in very few cases, while the text of the agreement identifies the area in which direct effect is excluded, especially in respect to the provision of services, the Council decision contains a general preclusion, which affects the agreement as a whole with no further specifications.[75] Conversely, there are no Council decisions which preclude direct effect independently from the text of the agreement.[76]

Overall, from the analysis of the approximately 100 cases about the direct effect (or lack thereof) of international law in the EU legal order,[77] it can be inferred, as will be shown in sections 2–4, that while many bilateral agreements have been found to comprise directly effective provisions, the contrary holds true for the great majority of multilateral treaties, such as the GATT 1947, the WTO agreements, including GATT 1994, the United Nations Convention on the Law of the Sea (UNCLOS), the European Convention on the Protection of Animals Kept for Farming Purposes, and the Aarhus Convention on Access to Information, Public Participation in Decision-making and Access to Justice in Environmental Matters.[78] Multilateral treaties found to have direct effect are rare and include the Yaounde/Lomé/Cotonou agreements between the EU and African, Caribbean, and Pacific countries[79] and the Montreal Convention for the Unification of Certain Rules for International Carriage by Air.[80]

As to the judicial enforceability of decisions of bodies of international organizations established by EU international agreements, the rulings that are relevant from the point of view of direct effect are less frequent.[81] They are issued by the CJEU in preliminary (interpretation and validity) and annulment proceedings, with individuals or States as plaintiffs.

With regard to customary law,[82] the question has arisen in a few cases, three in particular: the *Racke* preliminary ruling, concerning the validity of Council Regulation (EEC) No. 3300/91 of 11 November 1991[83] suspending the trade concessions provided

of the Parties.' *See* C. Eckes, P. Leino-Sandberg, *The EU-UK Trade and Cooperation Agreement—Exceptional Circumstances or a new Paradigm for EU External Relations* (2021) 84 *Modern Law Review* 164, 191–192.

[74] e.g. Article 5 of the Council Decision 2016/838/EU of 23 May 2016 on the conclusion, on behalf of the European Union, of the Association Agreement between the European Union and the European Atomic Energy Community and their Member States, of the one part, and Georgia, of the other part, of 2016. For some more examples, *see* N. Ghazaryan, *Who are the Gatekeepers*, 64–65.

[75] *See* A. Semertzi, *The preclusion*, 1131–1135, who refers to the Association Agreement with Ukraine, the Association Agreement with Korea, and the Association Agreement between the European Union and Central America.

[76] But *see* Article 4 of the Proposal for a Council Decision on the signing and provisional application of the Economic Partnership Agreement with Eastern African Community, as observed by F. Casolari, *The Acknowledgment*, 107–108. On the importance of the clauses precluding direct effect, as well as of the Council decisions, for a comprehensive analysis of direct effect of international agreements imbued with both legal and political features, *see* § 9 of this chapter.

[77] For a very recent survey, *see* C. H. L. Labus, *L'esclusione*.

[78] On the case law about all such conventions but the European Convention on the Protection of Animals Kept for Farming Purposes (on which CJ, *Compassion in World Farming*, C-1/96, EU:C:1998:113, paras 32–34), *see* §§ 2–4 of this chapter.

[79] *See*, e.g. CJ, *Chiquita Italia*, C-469/93, EU:C:1995:435.

[80] *See*, e.g. *International Air Transport Association* (n 15).

[81] As is the case of both the reports issued by the World Trade Organization (WTO)'s Dispute Settlement Body (DSB) and the recommendations rendered by the Aarhus Convention Compliance Committee (ACCC). Some references will be made in this § and the following §§. For a comparison of the two types of decisions, *see* I. Hadjiyianni, *The CJEU*.

[82] *See* § 2.4 of this chapter.

[83] Council Regulation (EEC) No. 3300/91 of 11 November 1991 suspending the trade concessions provided for by the Cooperation Agreement between the European Economic Community and the Socialist Federal Republic of Yugoslavia, OJ L 315, 15.11.1991, 1.

for in the Cooperation Agreement between the EEC and the Socialist Federal Republic of Yugoslavia;[84] *Opel Austria*, concerning the annulment of Council Regulation (EC) No. 3697/93 of 20 December 1993[85] withdrawing tariff concessions pursuant to Articles 23(2) and 27(3)(a) of the Free Trade Agreement between the Community and Austria (General Motors Austria);[86] and *Air Transport Association of America*, with respect to the validity of Directive 2008/101/EC of the European Parliament and of the Council of 19 November 2008 amending Directive 2003/87/EC[87] so as to include aviation activities in the scheme for greenhouse gas emission allowance trading within the Community.[88]

2.1 The international agreements in the pre-WTO era

The first case in which the CJEU had occasion to reflect on the nature, directly effective or not, of provisions of an international agreement, is *International Fruit Company*,[89] concerning the compatibility of certain Commission regulations with Article XI (prohibition of quantitative restrictions) of the GATT. The case, therefore, relates to the role of direct effect when an individual wishes to invoke an international agreement to challenge an EU measure. The case has four main features, which are also at the heart of many, though not all, subsequent rulings on the legal effects of international agreements, especially when it comes to preliminary rulings on validity or annulment proceedings. Firstly, direct effect is seen as a precondition for challenging EU acts. The reasons why it is so, differently from what occurs in internal direct effect, however, are not provided by the CJ. Secondly, the CJ clearly links direct effect to the existence of a right arising from the international agreement insofar as the latter can only be invoked, and lead to the invalidity of an EU act, if the provision contained therein is 'capable of conferring on Community nationals rights which they can invoke in court'.[90] Thirdly, the interpretation to be used to make such assessment must take into account, not only the 'terms', but also the 'general scheme' of the GATT.[91] Fourthly, several factors—that will be mentioned in the subsequent case law on the WTO—are identified by the CJ and preclude, in the opinion of the Court, the recognition of direct effect of Article XI of the GATT. They all serve to highlight the flexible character of the agreement, resulting from the fact that it 'is based on the principle of negotiations undertaken on the basis of "reciprocal and mutually advantageous arrangements"'.[92] Proof of this includes the provisions 'conferring the possibility of derogation, the measures to be taken when confronted with exceptional difficulties and the settlement of conflicts between the contracting parties'.[93] In this respect, by dwelling on Article XXIII of the GATT, the CJ made it clear that the Contracting Parties can adopt

[84] CJ, *Racke*, C-162/96, EU:C:1998:293.

[85] Council Regulation (EC) No. 3697/93 of 20 December 1993 withdrawing tariff concessions in accordance with Article 23 (2) and Article 27 (3) (a) of the Free Trade Agreement between the Community and Austria (General Motors Austria), OJ L 343, 31.12.1993, 1.

[86] GC, *Opel Austria*, T-115/94, EU:T:1997:3.

[87] Directive 2008/101/EC of the European Parliament and of the Council of 19 November 2008 amending Directive 2003/87/EC so as to include aviation activities in the scheme for greenhouse gas emission allowance trading within the Community (Text with EEA relevance), OJ L 8, 13.1.2009, 3.

[88] *Air Transport Association of America* (n 15).

[89] On the case, *see* also the brief remarks made in § 1 of this chapter.

[90] *International Fruit Company* (n 16), para. 27.

[91] *International Fruit Company* (n 16), para. 27.

[92] *International Fruit Company* (n 16), para. 20.

[93] *International Fruit Company* (n 16), para. 21.

> written recommendations or proposals which are to be 'given sympathetic consideration', investigations possibly followed by recommendations, consultations between or decisions of the contracting parties, including that of authorizing certain contracting parties to suspend the application to any others of any obligations or concessions under the General Agreement and, finally, in the event of such suspension, the power of the party concerned to withdraw from that agreement.[94]

Significantly, the test of direct effect, examined in the preceding chapters with respect to rules of EU law and its infiltration in national legal orders, gives way to considerations centred exclusively on the dimension, political in the broad sense, of the GATT. This is the premise at the origins of the CJ's approach formulated in its subsequent WTO jurisprudence, about the problem of the separation of judicial and executive powers when an international agreement is at stake.

The reasoning developed in *International Fruit Company* is endorsed by the CJ, albeit in less plain terms, again with reference to the GATT, in this case Article II (schedule of concessions), and again in the context of a preliminary ruling on validity, in the *Schlüter* judgment. In fact, there remains the identification of a structural link between direct effect and the conferral of a right and also the reliance on a systematic and teleological interpretation of the agreement.[95]

Some two years after the *International Fruit Company/Schlüter* duo, the direct effect of (a rule of) an international agreement was recognized by the CJ in the *Bresciani* case.[96] This is the first case[97] in which the CJ extended the application of the doctrine of internal direct effect to the external dimension of the relationship between EU law and international law. It was a question submitted by the Tribunal of Genoa for a preliminary ruling so that the CJ could directly rule on the effects, direct or otherwise, of the Association Agreement between the European Economic Community and the African States and Madagascar associated with that Community (Convention of Yaoundé). The extension of direct effect to international law is performed by the CJ in a bland manner, as evidenced by the absence in the judgment of any reference to *Van Gend & Loos*. Indeed, in *Bresciani* it was 'simply' stated that 'Article 2 (1) of the Yaoundé Convention of 1963 confers on Community citizens the right, which the national courts of the Community must protect, not to pay to a Member State a charge having an effect equivalent to customs duties'.[98] The approach of the CJ has five distinctive features. First: the object of the domestic proceedings, unlike in *International Fruit Company* and *Schlüter*, was a challenge to national legislation, in this case, Italian legislation. At stake there were no EU law provisions. Second: the interpretation of Article 2(1) of the Yaoundé Convention was systematic and teleological, in line with the type of interpretation made by the CJ on internal direct effect, whereby it was written that 'regard must simultaneously be paid to the spirit, the general scheme and the wording of the Convention',[99] as well as with part of the reasoning carried out in *International Fruit Company*. Third: an

[94] *International Fruit Company* (n 16), para. 25.
[95] CJ, *Schlüter*, 9/73, EU:C:1973:110, paras 27–30.
[96] CJ, *Conceria Daniele Bresciani v Amministrazione Italiana delle Finanze*, 87/75, EU:C:1976:18.
[97] A. von Bogdandy, M. Smrkolj, *European Union Law and International Law*, in *Max Planck Encyclopedia of Public International Law*, February 2011, available at https://opil.ouplaw.com/display/10.1093/law:epil/9780199231690/law-9780199231690-e620?rskey=jIgrVs&result=3&prd=OPIL, para. 11, noted that at the time the CJ was generous in attributing direct effect to international agreements.
[98] *Bresciani* (n 96), para. 26.
[99] *Bresciani* (n 96), para. 16.

assessment, although rather superficial, was made as to the existence of an individual right deriving from Article 2(1). Indeed, the conferral of that right was the backbone of the CJ's thinking on direct effect, as already made clear in both *International Fruit Company* and *Schlüter*. Fourth: attention was drawn to several provisions of the EEC Treaty, including Article 13 on customs duties and charges having equivalent effect, which are reflected and referred to in the Convention.[100] Fifth: the fact that, as the CJ argued, there is an 'imbalance between the obligations assumed by the Community towards the Associated States, which is inherent in the special nature of the Convention', did not imply that its provisions were deprived of direct effect.[101]

In the aftermath of *Bresciani*, although the referring courts or the parties had explicitly mentioned the matter of direct effect, the CJ decided not to explicitly deal with such issue. This occurred in *Nederlandse Spoorwegen*[102] and, especially, in *Polydor*. *Polydor* is about the interpretation of Articles 14 and 23 of the Agreement concluded on 22 July 1972 between the European Economic Community and the Portuguese Republic.[103] Here the Court, seized pursuant to Article 267 TFEU by the Court of Appeal of England and Wales, excluded the application of the exhaustion doctrine of industrial and intellectual property rights to that Agreement. This stance was taken despite the fact that direct effect was at the heart of the submissions of the parties, the intervening States, the Commission, and the referral by the UK Court, and despite the similarities of some of the Agreement's provisions to those of the EEC Treaty.[104] The Court did so also highlighting that the Agreement, differently from the EEC Treaty, does not aim at establishing a domestic market. No reference is made anywhere in the judgment to the possible enforceability of Articles 14 and 23 and/or to the conferral of rights originating from those provisions.

The approach adopted by the CJ in *Polydor* could be explained as follows: if the Court had recognized direct effect for rules with characteristics similar to directly effective EU rules, in a dispute between private companies concerning the alleged infringement of copyright, it would have had to admit direct effect in horizontal disputes.[105] An issue, that of horizontal direct effect, which was very problematic and unexplored at the time.[106]

Polydor is followed by an abundant case law, beginning with a preliminary ruling related to the interpretation of another Association Agreement. This is the *Pabst* case,[107] in which the CJ, with respect to a reference stemming from the *Finanzgericht* of Hamburg on the interpretation of Article 53(1) of the Agreement establishing an Association between the European Economic Community and Greece, stated that that provision 'precludes a national system of relief from providing more favorable tax treatment for domestic spirits than for those imported from Greece'.[108] The reasoning of the Court revolves around six

[100] *Bresciani* (n 96), paras 6–7, 15, 17, 19, 21–22, 25.

[101] *Bresciani* (n 96), para. 23.

[102] CJ, *Nederlandse Spoorwegen*, 38/75, EU:C:1975:154.

[103] CJ, *Polydor*, 270/80, EU:C:1982:43.

[104] The existence of similarities between EU directly effective provisions and provisions of international organizations does not necessarily imply that the latter are directly effective as well, as noted by R. Schütze, *European Union Law*, 186. This depends on the nature of the agreement, as a whole, rather than on the specific provision(s) at hand. *See* also J. Boulouis, *Le droit des Communautés européennes dans ses rapports avec le droit international général*, in *Recueil des cours*, vol. 235, 1992, 13–79, 77.

[105] As remarked by M. Mendez, *The Legal Effects*, 99.

[106] As it is today, and still remains unresolved in systematic terms with respect to international agreements, as well as to other sources of EU law. On international agreements' horizontal direct effect, *see* § 4 of this chapter; on other sources, *see* extensively § 3.2 of Chapter III and the whole of Chapter VI.

[107] CJ, *Pabst*, 17/81, EU:C:1982:129.

[108] *Pabst* (n 107), 27.

firm points, some of which confirmed the previous case law, especially *Bresciani*, while others marked an evolution. First: the CJ focused on an interpretation related to the 'objective' and 'nature' of the Association Agreement, in line with the teleological interpretation employed in *Bresciani*.[109] Second: the reasoning on the direct effect of Article 53(1) builds upon the directly effective character of Article 95 of the EEC Treaty, currently Article 114 TFEU. Even though, unlike the Yaoundé Convention in *Bresciani*, the Association Agreement with Greece did not include express references to Community law provisions, the CJ highlighted the similarity between Article 53(1) of the Association Agreement and Article 95 of the EEC Treaty inasmuch as the former provision 'fulfil[led], within the framework of the Association Agreement', the same function of the latter, forming part of a group of provisions the purpose of which was to introduce, in the Greek legal system, several measures 'for the gradual adjustment to the requirements of Community law'.[110] Third: unlike *Bresciani*, there is no reference to the conferral of an individual right. Here began, from this case onwards, the Court's wavering attitude regarding the conferral of rights, in some cases explicitly associated with direct effect, in others not even referred to. Fourth: there appears, for the first time in relation to the direct effect of international agreements, the well-known, and controversial,[111] test on direct effect insofar as Article 53(1) was considered a provision containing 'a clear and precise obligation which is not subject, in its implementation or effects, to the adoption of any subsequent measure'.[112] A test which has two seemingly overlapping elements[113] and seems to revolve only around the condition of unconditionality. Fifth: the CJ referred to direct applicability rather than to direct effect for both Article 95 of the EEC Treaty and Article 53(1) of the Association Agreement. On the relationship between direct effect and direct applicability, too, the Court is ambiguous, as it will be in later rulings. Sixth: the CJ affirmed that 'all measures conflicting' with Article 53(1) had 'to be abolished'. The remedy of disapplication, here like in most of the subsequent case law, has no relevance, unlike in the EU case law on internal direct effect, as is well known.

The *Kupferberg* case concerns a preliminary question raised by the *Bundesfinanzhof* on the interpretation of Article 21 of the Agreement of 1972 between the EEC and the Portuguese Republic. At stake was a challenge against a national tax law. The case is particularly important because the CJ, for the first time, focused its analysis, and the answer to the questions posed by the referring judge, on the direct effect of Article 21, recognizing it in opposition to the intervening States and AG Rozès.[114] As seen in relation to *Pabst*, the judgment, on the one hand, stands in continuity with the previous case law, while on the other it is the origin of six developments, which would go on to guide subsequent case law. Continuity is discernible for three reasons. First of all, reference is made to the ability of Article 21 to produce direct effect because of its precise and unconditional nature.[115] Secondly, in addition to the notion of direct effect, that of direct applicability is employed, with identical meaning.[116] Thirdly, interpretation is systematic, contextual, and teleological. The CJ considers that attention

[109] *Pabst* (n 107), 27.
[110] *Pabst* (n 107), para. 26.
[111] *See* § 4 of Chapter III.
[112] *Pabst* (n 107), para. 26.
[113] Accordingly, *see* A. Van Waeyenberge, P. Pecho, *Free Trade*, 754, who noted that there is no difference between 'clarity' and 'precision' and that the case law is generally not clear.
[114] On this matter, *see* the reflections by P. Eeckhout, *EU External Relations*, 336.
[115] *Kupferberg* (n 20) paras 10 and 23.
[116] *Kupferberg* (n 20), para. 21.

must be paid to the 'subject-matter',[117] 'purpose',[118] 'nature',[119] 'structure',[120] 'object',[121] and 'context'[122] of the Agreement.

On the other hand, as anticipated, there are six developments stemming from *Kupferberg*. The first: for the first time, the CJ emphasized the need for a uniform interpretation of the Agreement. In fact, it is written in the judgment that it is for the Court, 'within the framework of its jurisdiction in interpreting the provisions of agreements, to ensure their uniform application throughout the Community'.[123] In this sense, the Court made it clear that it is for the Court, in the absence of express indications in the Agreement as to its legal effects, to regulate the latter.[124] The second: for the first time, the existence of a 'special institutional framework for consultations and negotiations *inter se* in relation to the implementation of the agreement' is not sufficient in itself to exclude 'any judicial application of that agreement',[125] thus also its direct effect. At the same time, the recognition of direct effect 'does not adversely affect the powers' conferred by the agreement on bodies, such as the joint committees provided for in the Agreement with Portugal, which can make recommendations and take decisions.[126] The third: not even the existence of derogations in the Agreement that allow the Parties to derogate from some of its rules 'in specific circumstances and as a general rule after consideration in the Joint Committee in the presence of both Parties' is 'sufficient in itself' to preclude the direct effect of some of the Agreement's provisions.[127] The fourth: for the first time, the CJ is confronted with the risks associated with the lack of reciprocity in the implementation of the Agreement, should direct effect be affirmed by the CJ but denied by the courts of the States Parties.[128] The fifth: like *Pabst*, but unlike *Bresciani*, there are no references in *Kupferberg* to the conferral of rights as a precondition for direct effect. The sixth development: the CJ, once clarifying that the test for direct effect is to be made only if there are no clear indications, one way or the other, in the agreement, envisaged a 'two-stage test'.[129] The first step takes the form of a global 'policy' assessment of the agreement,[130] by means of an interpretation, as seen above, related to the intention of the Contracting Parties and the purposes of the agreement.[131] The second step aims to investigate the nature of the specific provision whose direct effect is at issue.[132]

Two strands of judgments can be identified in the subsequent case law—but prior to the jurisprudence related to the WTO agreements—to which a specific analysis is devoted later in this section. The first strand *(i)*, concerning association, partnership, and cooperation agreements as well as the GATT, is characterized by a confirmation of the reasoning and arguments developed in the CJEU's previous case law. With a few exceptions, such as some interpretive preliminary rulings of the early eighties about the effects of the GATT in which

[117] *Kupferberg* (n 20), para. 18.
[118] *Kupferberg* (n 20), para. 23.
[119] *Kupferberg* (n 20), para. 22.
[120] *Kupferberg* (n 20), para. 22.
[121] *Kupferberg* (n 20), para. 23.
[122] *Kupferberg* (n 20), para. 23.
[123] *Kupferberg* (n 20), para. 14.
[124] *Kupferberg* (n 20), para. 17.
[125] *Kupferberg* (n 20), para. 20.
[126] *Kupferberg* (n 20), para. 19.
[127] *Kupferberg* (n 20), para. 21.
[128] *Kupferberg* (n 20), para. 18.
[129] In these terms, *see* R. Schütze, *On 'Middle Ground'*, 51.
[130] R. Schütze, *On 'Middle Ground'*, 52, referred to a 'policy test' in relation to the intention of the parties.
[131] *Kupferberg* (n 20), paras 11–22.
[132] *Kupferberg* (n 20), paras 23–27.

no reference was made to the doctrine of direct effect,[133] the CJEU, in more or less incidental terms,[134] often[135] but not always[136] reiterating the direct effect/conferral of a right nexus, on the one hand systematically recognizes direct effect to partnership, cooperation, and association agreements,[137] frequently overlapping it with direct applicability,[138] on the other hand, in an equally systematic manner denies it with respect to the GATT.[139]

There are three developments in the pre-WTO strand of rulings. The first is the *Sevince* judgment,[140] and the subsequent rulings that refer to it,[141] where it was stated that the provisions contained in the decisions of the Council for the conclusion of the agreement can have direct effect if they 'satisfy the same conditions as those applicable to the provisions of the Agreement'.[142] The reasoning used with regard to international agreements is therefore extended to the decisions of the entities established by those agreements, including dispute settlement bodies.

The second development lies in the *Germany v Council* judgment, in which, for the first time, the CJ had to reflect on direct effect, international agreements, and the challenging of EU law by a Member State pursuant to Article 263 TFEU (rather than a request for a preliminary ruling pursuant to Article 267 TFEU). At stake was the request for annulment by Germany of Title IV and Article 21(2) of Council Regulation (EEC) No. 404/93 of 13 February 1993 on the common organization of the market in bananas[143] in the light of the GATT. The Court concluded that the direct effect of the international agreement was a condition, not only to challenge Member States' legislation, as stated in the previous case law, but also to allow a Member State to request the legality review of EU acts. The critical points, still today, also considering the reiteration of this approach in subsequent case law, are precisely these two: firstly, is it acceptable to make the recognition of direct effect a condition for an annulment action under Article 263 TFEU? Secondly, is it acceptable, for the CJ, to deny, by virtue of an interpretation regarding the 'spirit' and 'general scheme' of the agreement, such recognition based on a narrow conception of direct effect, where the conferral of a right is its *condicio sine qua non*?[144]

According to the CJ, with reference to the GATT, both the denial of a conferral of a right and the flexibility underpinning the agreement's obligations based on the principle of negotiations and on reciprocal arrangements 'preclude the Court from taking provisions of GATT into consideration to assess the lawfulness of a regulation in an action brought by a Member

[133] *See* CJ, *SIOT*, 266/81, EU:C:1983:77; CJ, *Singer and Geigy*, joined cases 290–291/81, EU:C:1983:79. More recently, *see* CJ, *Commission v Germany* (n 15), on which, see the observations by S. Gáspár-Szilágyi, *The 'Primacy' and 'Direct Effect' of EU International Agreements* (2015) 21 *European Public Law* 343, 363.

[134] For cases containing a mere reliance on previous direct effect, *see* CJ, *Hallouzi-Choho*, C-126/95, EU:C:1996:368; CJ, *Kus*, C-237/91, EU:C:1992:527. For cases where, albeit direct effect is not even mentioned, there is a reference to a preclusion of national law, *see* CJ, *Administration des Douanes et Droits Indirects v Léopold Legros and Others*, C-163/90, EU:C:1992:326, paras 22–27.

[135] e.g. *Demirel* (n 44), para. 24.

[136] e.g. CJ, *Deutscher Handballbund*, C-438/00, EU:C:2003:255.

[137] e.g. *Demirel* (n 44), para. 14; *Hallouzi-Choho* (n 134), paras 19–20; *Kziber* (n 59), paras. 15–23; CJ, *Zoubir Yousfi v Belgian State*, C-58/93, EU:C:1994:160, paras 16–19; CJ, *Pissouri*, C-432/92, EU:C:1994:277, paras 23–27; CJ, *Krid*, C-103/94, EU:C:1995:97, paras 21–24.

[138] e.g. *Sevince* (n 2), para. 26.

[139] CJ, *Germany v Council*, C-280/93, EU:C:1994:367, paras 103–112; *Chiquita Italia* (n 79), paras 26–29.

[140] *Sevince* (n 2), para. 14.

[141] e.g. CJ, *Eroglu*, C-355/93, EU:C:1994:369, paras 11 and 17.

[142] *Sevince* (n 2), para. 14.

[143] Council Regulation (EEC) No. 404/93 of 13 February 1993 on the common organization of the market in bananas, OJ L 47, 25.2.1993, 1.

[144] On the dissociation between internal direct effect and Article 263 TFEU or Article 267 TFEU (on validity of EU secondary law), *see* § 1 of Chapter II.

State under the first paragraph of Article 173 of the Treaty [currently Article 263 TFEU]'.[145] Referring to the detailed analysis in the following section, as well as in section 1 of Chapter II, it must be here anticipated that the CJ's reconstruction is problematic and presents several serious loopholes. On the one hand, it is difficult to understand why direct effect, which is not a prerequisite for challenging EU secondary law under Article 267 TFEU or Article 263 TFEU in the light of EU primary law, should instead be such a prerequisite where the legal basis for the challenge is an international agreement. On the other hand, even if it were to be accepted that direct effect is a necessary condition, it is difficult to understand why direct effect should be interpreted narrowly rather than broadly, whereby 'broadly' means encompassing legality review in the absence of a conferral of a right stemming from an international agreement.[146]

The third development is that the direct effect test described above, consisting of a first stage centred on the agreement as a whole and a second stage related to the specific provision(s) of the agreement, while it is often replicated, in some cases it is carried out in inverted terms.[147] Thus, the CJ happened to reason first about the specific provision and then about the agreement as a whole, with the consequence, evidently, of distorting the test. Indeed, as pointed out by F. G. Jacobs, 'it seems that it would make little sense to analyze the provision and conclude that it is apt to have direct effect, but then to deny that conclusion on the ground that the agreement as a whole is not apt to have such effect'.[148] In this respect, the reading of the judgments in which the CJ chooses to invert the phases of the test makes it clear that the reasoning on the object and purpose of the agreement supports and confirms the crucial reasoning on clarity, precision, and unconditionality since the CJ, after verifying the presence of these conditions, regularly asks whether what it found 'is not contradicted by consideration of the purpose and the nature of the Agreement' of which the provision at stake 'forms part'.[149] Conversely, the test is not reversed, and thus the first step is the one related to the agreement as a whole, as far as the GATT is concerned. More specifically, the Court focuses only on the overall analysis of the agreement, thus going no further than this first step, since none of its rules can be considered directly effective. Once the analysis on the first step has been concluded in negative terms, the analysis on the second step becomes unnecessary.

The second strand of rulings consists of the only two exceptions, labelled by Eeckhout as 'implementation principle',[150] to the rule that the GATT cannot be directly invoked before a court to challenge an EU act: the *Fediol*[151] and *Nakajima* cases.[152] Referring to section 3 of this chapter on the deeper nature, extent, and unexpressed potential of these rulings, as well as their relationship with broad direct effect, here we merely recall, in a nutshell, what they consist of. According to the *Fediol* doctrine, the CJEU can review the legality of a Community/EU measure in the light of the GATT if the former refers to a precise provision of the latter. According to the *Nakajima* doctrine, such review can be conducted if the Community/EU legislature intends to implement a particular GATT obligation.[153] In this

[145] *Germany v Council* (n 139), para. 109.
[146] *See* § 3 of this chapter.
[147] *See*, for instance, *Kziber* (n 59), paras 15–29.
[148] F. G. Jacobs, *Direct Effect and Interpretation of International Agreements in the Recent Case Law of the European Court of Justice*, in A. Dashwood, M. Maresceau (eds.), *Law and Practice of EU External Relations*, Cambridge, Cambridge University Press, 2008, 13–33, 32.
[149] Amongst others, *see* CJ, *Nour Eddline El-Yassini, v Secretary of State for Home Department*, C-416/96, EU:C:1999:107, para. 28.
[150] P. Eeckhout, *The Integration*, 189–204.
[151] CJ, *Fédération de l'industrie de l'huilerie de la CEE (Fediol)*, 70/87, EU:C:1989:254.
[152] CJ, *Nakajima*, C-69/89, EU:C:1991:186.
[153] For an early ruling following the two doctrines, *see Germany v Council* (n 139), para. 111. On *Fediol* and *Nakajima* and their aftermath, *see* F. Castillo de la Torre, *Anti-dumping Policy and Private Interest* (1992) 17

connection, while it could be said that formally it is not direct effect because the CJEU says so—although *de facto* this is open to criticism as will be shown below in section 3—, it is not indirect effect because Community/EU law, instead of being subject to a consistent interpretation in the light of the GATT, is possibly reviewed and annulled.

2.2 The WTO agreements

The systematic denial of the direct effect of the GATT 1947 is confirmed by the CJEU in its jurisprudence concerning the challenge of both national law (in the context of preliminary rulings proceedings on interpretation pursuant to Article 267 TFEU)[154] and EU law (preliminary rulings proceedings on validity pursuant to Article 267 TFEU and annulment proceedings pursuant to Article 263 TFEU)[155] on the basis of the WTO agreements, to which both Member States and the EU are parties, as is well known. Such denial goes through the use of the direct effect test, which, as occurred in the context of the GATT 1947, follows the original trend, that is, first, the assessment on the nature and the broad logic of the agreement, secondly, if the first step is successfully met, the evaluation of its specific provisions.[156] This second step, however, has never been taken by the CJEU. The twofold circumstance that the WTO regime has a more developed institutional structure and a more advanced dispute settlement system, characterized by 'many compulsory elements',[157] does not lead the CJ and the GC to attribute direct effect to WTO agreements[158] and to

European Law Review 346; A. González, N. Luis, *Nuevos desarrollos en la aplicación del GATT* (1992) 19 *Revista de Instituciones Europeas* 195; P. Egli, J. Kokott, *Portuguese Republic v Council of the European Union (Judgment). Case C-149/96* (2000) 94 *American Journal of International Law* 740; S. Peers, *WTO Dispute Settlement and Community Law* (2001) 26 *European Law* Review 605; G. A. Zonnekeyn, *The Latest on Indirect Effect of WTO Law in the EC Legal Order: The Nakajima Case Law Misjudged?* (2001) 4 *Journal of International Economic Law* 597; G. A. Zonnekeyn, *The ECJ's Petrotub Judgment: Towards a Revival of the 'Nakajima Doctrine'?* (2003) 30 *Legal Issues of Economic Integration* 249; J. F. Delile, *A propos de l'arrêt* Vereniging Milieudefensie: *la seconde naissance de l'invocabilité* Nakajima (2012) 48 *Cahiers de droit européen* 687; S. Gáspár-Szilágyi, *The relationship between EU law and international Agreements: Restricting the Application of the* Fediol *and* Nakajima *Exceptions in* Vereniging Milieudefensie (2015) 52 *Common Market Law Review* 1059; K. Stoyanov, *Three Decades of the 'Nakajima' Doctrine in EU Law: Where Are We Now?* (2021) 24 *Journal of International Economic Law* 724; T. Perišin, E. Antonakin, *Judicial Review of EU Measures in the Light of WTO Rules:* Fediol *and* Nakajima, in G. Butler, R. A. Wessel (eds.), *EU External Relations*, 183–193.

[154] e.g. *Chiquita Italia* (n 79).

[155] As for preliminary rulings on validity, *see*, amongst others, CJ, *Omega Air*, joined cases C-27/00 and C-122/00, EU:C:2002:161. As for judgments *ex* Article 263 TFEU *see*, amongst others, *Portugal v Council* (n 47).

[156] e.g. CJ, *C & J Clark International*, joined cases C-659/13 and C-34/14, EU:C:2016:74, para. 84.

[157] The term is borrowed from S. Gáspár-Szilágyi, *EU Member State Enforcement*, 170.

[158] On the lack of direct effect of WTO agreements, *see*, *inter alia*, *Portugal v Council* (n 47), paras 34–52; CJ, *Parfums Christian Dior and Others*, joined cases C-300/98 and C-392/98, EU:C:2000:688, paras 41–44; CJ, *Netherlands v European Parliament and Council*, C-377/98, EU:C:2001:523, para. 52; *Omega Air* (n 155), paras 89–97. For further reading, *see*, in the huge literature, amongst those who have a supporting view of the CJ's approach, E. L. M. Volker, *The Direct Effect of International Agreements in the Community's Legal Order* (1983) 10 *Legal Issues of Economic Integration* 131; P. Eeckhout, *The Domestic Legal Status*; J. Trachtman, *Bananas, Direct Effect and Compliance* (1999) 10 *European Journal of International Law* 655; A. Rosas, *Case Annotation on Case C-149/96, Portugal v Council, judgment of the Full Court of 23 November 1999* (2000) 37 *Common Market Law Review* 797; A. Rosas, *Implementation and Enforcement of WTO Dispute Settlement Findings: An EU Perspective* (2001) 4 *Journal of International Economic Law* 131; P. Mengozzi, *Les droits et les intérets des entreprises, le droit de l'OMC et les prérogatives de l'Union européenne: vers une doctrine communautaire des 'political questions'* (2005) 9 *Revue du droit de l'Union européenne* 229; A. Antoniadis, *The European Union and WTO Law: A Nexus of Reactive, Coactive, and Proactive Approaches* (2007) 6 *World Trade Review* 45; A. Arcuri, S. Poli, *What Price for the Community Enforcement of WTO Law?*, EUI Working Papers, Law 2010/01, 2010, available at https://cadmus.eui.eu/handle/1814/13534; P. Eeckhout, *EU External Relations Law*, 343–365; M. Mendez, *The Legal Effects*, 202–249; P. Eeckhout, *The Application of International Law by the Court of Justice of the European Union*, in C. A.

the decisions of the Dispute Settlement Body (DSB), which cannot be distinguished from the WTO rules that are interpreted in the DSB's reports.[159] Such an effect, from *Portugal v Council* onwards, is excluded. In *Portugal v Council*, more specifically, it is written that the WTO agreements by their nature and structure 'are not in principle among the rules in the light of which the Court is to review the legality of measures adopted by the [Union] institutions'.[160] Additionally, in the very same judgment, as stated with respect to the GATT 1947, the CJ clarified[161] that the only exceptions, also with respect to the WTO, are those outlined in *Fediol* and *Nakajima*. Furthermore, these exceptions are interpreted by the CJ in a very restrictive manner,[162] given that, in practice, while *Fediol* has never been successfully applied so far, the *Nakajima* doctrine has been applied (only) in respect of the anti-dumping regulation adopted to comply with the obligations of Article VI of the GATT and the GATT Anti-Dumping Code adopted for the implementation of that Article.[163]

At the core of the reluctance of the CJEU to attribute direct effect to the WTO agreements lies its political character. Indeed, the CJEU's reasoning, in respect to such agreements, confirms and develops the previous case law regarding the GATT 1947 by holding

Bradley (ed.), *The Oxford Handbook of Comparative*, 79–98. Criticism is made by many others, amongst whom, *see* E.-U. Petersmann, *Proposals for a New Constitution for the European Union: Building-Blocks for a Constitutional Theory and Constitutional Law of the EU* (1995) 32 *Common Market Law Review* 1123; J. M. Beneyto, *The EU and the WTO. Direct Effect of the New Dispute Settlement System?* (1996) 10 *Europäische Zeitschrift für Wirtschaftsrecht* 295; M. Bronckers, P. Kuijper, *WTO Law in the European Court of Justice* (2000) 37 *Common Market Law Review* 1313; S. Griller, *Judicial Enforceability of WTO Law in the European Union: Annotation to Case C-149/96, Portugal v Council* (2000) 3 *Journal of International Economic Law* 441; S. Peers, *Fundamental Right or Political Whim? WTO Law and the European Court of Justice*, in G. de Búrca, J. Scott (eds.), *The EU and the WTO: Legal and Constitutional Aspects*, Oxford, Hart, 2001, 111–130; A. Ott, *Der EuGH and das WTO Recht: Die Entdeckung der politischen Gegenseitigkeit—altes Phänomen oder neuer Ansatz* (2003) 3 *Europarecht* 504; M. Bronckers, *The Effect of the WTO in the European Court Litigation* (2005) 40 *Texas International Law Review* 443; D. De Mey, *Recent Developments on the Invocability of WTO Law in the EC: A Wave of Mutilation* (2006) 11 *European Foreign Affairs Review* 63; M. Bronckers, *The Relationship of the EC Courts with Other International Tribunals: Non-Committal, Respectful or Submissive?* (2007) 44 *Common Market Law Review* 601; M. Bronckers, *The Domestic Law Effect of the WTO in the EU—A Dialogue with Jacques Bourgeois*, in I. Govaere, R. Quick, M. Bronckers (eds.), *Trade and Competition Law in the EU and Beyond*, Cheltenham, Edward Elgar, 2011, 240–256.

[159] As foreseen in *FIAMM* (n 33), paras 128–129. On the lack of direct effect of the DSB's decisions, *see* GC, *Fruchthandelsgesellschaft Chemnitz*, T-254/97, EU:T:1999:178, paras 28–30; CJ, *Atlanta*, C-104/97 P, EU:C:1999:498, para. 20; CJ, *Van Parys*, C-377/02, EU:C:2005:121, paras 38–48; GC, *Cordis Obst*, T-18/99, EU:T:2001:95, paras 44–60; GC, *Bocchi Food Trade International GmbH*, T-30/99, EU:T:2001:96, para 49–65; GC, *T. Port GmbH*, T-52/99, EU:T:2001:97, paras 44–60; GC, *Internationale Fruchtimport Gesellschaft Weichert*, joined cases T-64-65/01, EU:T:2004:37, paras 139–142. In the literature, *see* N. Lavranos, *Die Rechtswirkung von WTO panel reports im Europäischen Gemeinschaftsrecht sowie im deutschen Verfassungsrecht* (1999) 34 *Europarecht* 289–308; G. A. Zonnekeyn, *The Legal Status of WTO Panel Reports in the EC Legal Order. Some Reflections on the Opinion of Advocate General Mischo in the Atlanta Case* (1999) 2 *Journal of International Economic Law* 713; G.A. Zonnekeyn, *The Status of Adopted Panel and Appellate Body Reports in the European Court of Justice and the European Court of First Instance* (2000) 34 *Journal of World Trade* 93; S. Peers, *W.T.O. Dispute Settlement and Community Law* (2001) 26 *European Law Review* 605; A. Rosas, *Implementation and Enforcement of WTO Dispute Settlement Findings: An EU Perspective* (2001) 4 *Journal of International Economic Law* 131; M. Bronckers, *From 'Direct Effect' to 'Muted Dialogue': Recent Developments in the European Courts' Case Law on the WTO and Beyond* (2008) 11 *Journal of International Economic Law* 885; A. Tancredi, *On the Absence of Direct Effect of the WTO Dispute Settlement Body's Decisions in the EU Legal Order*, in E. Cannizzaro, P. Palchetti, R. A. Wessel (eds.), *International law*, 249–268; M. Q. Zang, *Shall We Talk? Judicial Communication between the CJEU and WTO Dispute Settlement* (2017) 28 *European Journal of International Law* 273; I. Hadjiyianni, *The CJEU.*

[160] *Portugal v Council* (n 47), para. 47.

[161] *Portugal v Council* (n 47), para. 49.

[162] For some bibliographical references on the two doctrines, *see* footnote 153 in this §.

[163] CJ, *Petrotub SA and Republica SA v Council of the European Union*, C-76/00 P, EU:C:2003:4, paras 52–63. The application of the *Fediol-Nakajima* doctrines has been explicitly excluded in the great majority of judgments, amongst which: CJ, *Biret*, 93/02 P, EU:C:2003:517, para. 53; *Van Parys* (n 159), paras 41–54; *FIAMM* (n 33), para. 112; CJ, *Ikea Wholesale Ltd*, C-351/04, EU:C:2007:547, paras 29–35; CJ, *Commission v Armenal*, C-21/14 P, EU:C:2015:494, paras 40–41; CJ, *Rotho Blaas*, C-207/17, EU:C:2018:840, paras 42–57.

that the test of direct effect is ultimately political[164] since at its heart lie two closely interconnected principles: the separation of powers[165] and the institutional balance.[166] As observed by AG Ćapeta in her opinion in *KaiKai*, 'the reason for refusing, in principle, to recognise the direct effect of WTO law was not to deprive individuals of the possibility of relying on international agreements in court, but rather was aimed at allowing the EU institutions a political margin of manoeuvre'.[167]

In short, if the CJEU, in the case of actions for annulment under Article 263 TFEU and preliminary rulings on validity under Article 267 TFEU, and the national courts, in the case of domestic proceedings and/or interpretative preliminary rulings proceedings, had full freedom in reviewing the legality of EU law or national laws, respectively, the other institutional actors responsible for the EU's international policy, above all the Council and the Commission, would be considerably limited in the exercise of their competences and, upstream, of their discretion.[168] This could have a particularly negative impact if in the other WTO Contracting States direct effect was not admitted, as is in fact the case of US and Japan, amongst others. In other words, the CJ denied the direct effect of a complex multilateral legal system like the WTO to preserve the political discretion of the EU institutions in charge of steering the EU's trade external relations. As written in the literature, the CJEU chooses not to take over tasks that should be carried out, with great political flexibility, by other institutions.[169] A flexibility that allows the EU 'every latitude to resolve disputes with trading partners within the WTO framework'[170] through negotiation.[171] This flexibility, moreover, is less significant in the context of bilateral trade agreements, which frequently—as seen in the previous section—contain provisions identical or similar to those of the EU.[172] The *Fediol* and *Nakajima* exceptions do not call into question such reasoning because they are considered by the CJEU to be the result of the EU legislator's intention to limit its discretion as far as the application of WTO rules is concerned. This is the reason why the Court could review the legality of an EU measure and the measures taken to implement it in the light of the WTO agreements.[173]

[164] J. Klabbers, *International Law*, 264: international law's direct effect is 'inherently political'. *See*, for a global law perspective, T. Cottier, *A Theory*.

[165] On this point, *see* R. Schütze, *European Union Law*, 187. As affirmed by Oesch, *Direct Effect* 278, the matter 'boils down to the issue of separation of powers among the branches of government and, in particular, the proper role of courts in external trade relations'. *See* also T. Cottier, K. N. Schefer, *The Relationship between World Trade Organization Law, National and Regional* (1998) 1 *Journal of International Economic Law* 83, 120–122.

[166] On the EU, the principle of institutional balance, and international law, *see* the critical remarks by P. Eeckhout, *Judicial Enforcement of WTO Law in the European Union—Some Further Reflections* (2002) 5 *Journal of International Economic Law* 110; A. Tancredi, *EC Practice in the WTO: How Wide is the 'Scope for Manoeuvre'?* (2004) 15 *European Journal of International Law* 933; M. Bronckers, P. Kuijper, *WTO Law*, 1317–1323; A. Tancredi, *On the Absence.* On the denial of direct effect based on a number of arguments and allegations regarding the relationships between EU institutions, *see*, e.g. *Kupferberger* (n 20), paras 16–17. In general, on EU external relations law and the importance of balance of competences in the EU institutional framework, *see* C. Hillion, *Conferral, Cooperation and Balance in the Institutional Framework of EU External Action*, in M. Cremona (ed.), *Structural Principles in EU External Relations law*, Oxford, Hart, 2018, 117–174.

[167] Opinion of AG Ćapeta of 13 July 2023, *KaiKai*, C-328/21 P, EU:C:2023:576, para. 62.

[168] On the matter of States' discretionary power, *see* I. Hadjiyianni, *The CJEU*, 927.

[169] *See* P. Eeckhout, *The Integration*, 375–378.

[170] K. Lenaerts, P. Van Nuffel, T. Corthaut, *EU Constitutional Law*, 701.

[171] On this matter, *see* C. Dordi, *The Direct Effect of the Agreements Concluded by the EU: Some Inconsistencies in ECJ Case Law?* in C. Dordi (ed.), *The Absence of Direct effect of WTO in the EC and in other Countries*, Turin, Giappichelli, 2010, 1–11, 2–3. In this regard, A. von Bogdandy, M. Smrkolj, *European Union*, para. 26, wrote that at the origins of the denial of direct effect by the CJ lies, along with the lack of reciprocity, 'the negotiability of WTO obligations'.

[172] This point is stressed by P. Eeckhout, *The integration*, 196.

[173] *See* also *Commission v Armenal* (n 163), para. 40.

In this sense, reciprocity, which was already the focus of *International Fruit Company*,[174] has become the key of the Court's approach. Indeed, the starting point from which the EU judges move is that 'some of the contracting parties, which are among the Community's most important trading partners, have concluded from the subject-matter and purpose of the WTO agreements that they are not among the rules applicable by their judicial organs when reviewing the legality of their rules of domestic law'.[175]

While the CJ recalls in *Portugal v Council*, citing paragraph 18 of the *Kupferberg* ruling, that lack of reciprocity is not *per se* associated with lack of direct effect,[176] it also clarifies that, when it comes to WTO agreements, which are based on 'reciprocal and mutually advantageous arrangements', the lack of reciprocity 'may lead to disuniform application of the WTO rules'.[177] Hence, 'to accept that the role of ensuring that Community law complies with those rules devolves directly on the Community judicature would deprive the legislative or executive organs of the Community of the scope for manoeuvre enjoyed by their counterparts in the Community's trading partners'.[178]

The logic behind the CJEU's denial of direct effect is political, then, because in so doing it safeguards the allocation of powers and does not subvert the institutional balance underlying the external policies of the EU. On the other hand, there is a further rationale, which is also imbued with political connotations: the preservation of EU law when international law is at stake.[179] In other words, it is no coincidence that the recognition of direct effect, with respect to international agreements, is the rule when a measure of a Member State is challenged as opposed to when an EU act is challenged, as the WTO case law demonstrates.[180] This is an asymmetry that gives rise to perplexity and will be investigated more in detail, alongside the pros and cons of the CJEU's approach, in section 6.

2.3 International agreements, trade and non-trade related, beyond the WTO

The EU case law on the WTO, which is particularly restrictive regarding the recognition of direct effect, has not affected the generally favourable attitude of the CJEU towards the direct effect of bilateral trade agreements, as well as of partnership, cooperation, and association agreements, including the decisions of the bodies established therein. In numerous judgments the Court, reiterating the approach taken in its earlier case law, does indeed recognize direct effect[181] and does so often on the basis of an inverted test, so much so that the rule, also confirmed by more recent practice, seems to be as follows: the test is, first, on the specific provision(s) whose direct effect is in question, then on the agreement, as a whole. An example is the *Simutenkov* case,[182] concerning a reference for a preliminary ruling on the

[174] *International Fruit Company* (n 16), para. 21.
[175] *Portugal v Council* (n 47), para. 43.
[176] *Portugal v Council* (n 47), para. 44.
[177] *Portugal v Council* (n 47), para. 45.
[178] *Portugal v Council* (n 47), para. 46
[179] For a critical appraisal, *see* G. Bebr, *Agreements Concluded by the Community and Their Possible Direct Effect: From International Fruit Company to Kupferberg* (1983) 20 *Common Market Law Review* 35, 46.
[180] In the opinion of A. von Bogdandy, M. Smrkolj, *European Union*, para. 12, 'the policy dimension becomes apparent in the fact that the ECJ is more prone to attributing direct effect to an international agreement if the legality of a Member State measure is in question'.
[181] But *see* other judgments, such as *Asda* (n 60), para. 91.
[182] CJ, *Igor Simutenkov*, C-265/03, EU:C:2005:213. On the case and horizontal direct effect, *see* § 6.

interpretation of Article 23(1) of the Partnership and Cooperation Agreement establishing a partnership between the European Communities and their Member States, on the one side, and the Russian Federation, on the other, of June 1994.

Under challenge in *Simutenkov* were several Spanish sporting rules which limited the number of players from non-Member countries who could be fielded in national competitions. With the ruling, the CJ considered a priority to first verify compliance with the classic conditions regarding the clarity, precision, and unconditionality of Article 23, and then shifted the analysis to the agreement and found confirmation of the assessment made in relation to the specific provision(s) concerned. As already observed in relation to the pre-WTO era, this second part of the analysis on direct effect seems to be merely an aid for supporting the findings of the first part.[183]

The CJ, first of all, held that Article 23(1) of the Community–Russia Partnership Agreement 'lays down, in clear, precise and unconditional terms, a prohibition precluding any Member State from discriminating, on grounds of nationality, against Russian workers, vis-à-vis their own nationals, so far as their conditions of employment, remuneration and dismissal are concerned'.[184] As a matter of fact, the rule provides for a precise obligation of result and, 'by its nature, can be relied on by an individual before a national court as a basis for requesting that court to disapply discriminatory provisions without any further implementing measures being required to that end'.[185] Moreover, the CJ deemed that a certain margin of appreciation underlying the unconditionality inherent in Article 23(1) would not *per se* preclude the recognition of direct effect.[186] Subsequently, the CJ noted that the attribution of direct effect cannot be refuted by the nature and purpose of the Agreement. Indeed, Article 1 provides that the purpose 'is to establish a partnership between the parties with a view to promoting, *inter alia*, the development between them of close political relations, trade and harmonious economic relations, political and economic freedoms, and the achievement of gradual integration between the Russian Federation and a wider area of cooperation in Europe'.[187] The Court observed that the fact that the agreement merely establishes a partnership between the parties, 'without providing for an association or future accession of the Russian Federation to the Communities, is not such as to prevent certain of its provisions from having direct effect'[188] The Court was careful not to cite previous judgments in which the test was the original one, that is, first the analysis of the agreement and then that of the specific provision, preferring other judgments in which the order of the assessment was the opposite, including *Gloszczuk* and *Wählergruppe Gemeinsam*.[189]

Beyond the WTO and the partnership, cooperation, and association Agreements, the EU jurisprudence is characterized by a progressive closure to the recognition of direct effect and/or to the transposition of the *Fediol-Nakijma*-style legality review in non-trade-related areas. The most illustrative cases are the following:[190] (a) *Intertanko*, concerning the UNCLOS;[191] (b) *Brown Bear*,[192] *Vereniging Milieudefensie and Stichting Stop*

[183] *Simutenkov* (n 182), paras 21–29.
[184] *Simutenkov* (n 182), para. 22.
[185] *Simutenkov* (n 182), para. 23.
[186] *Simutenkov* (n 182), para. 24. On this point, *see* the remarks by C. Dordi, *The Direct Effect*, 6.
[187] *Simutenkov* (n 182), para. 27.
[188] *Simutenkov* (n 182), para. 28.
[189] *Simutenkov* (n 182), para. 21. *See* CJ, *Gloszczuk*, C-63/99, EU:C:2001:488, paras 30–38, and CJ, *Wählergruppe Gemeinsam*, C-171/01, EU:C:2003:260, paras 54–67.
[190] *See* the overview in M. Mendez, *The Legal Effects*, 250–286.
[191] CJ, *Intertanko*, C-308/06, EU:C:2008:312.
[192] CJ, *Lesoochranárske zoskupenie VLK* (*Brown Bear*), C-240/09, EU:C:2011:125.

Luchtverontreiniging Utrecht,[193] *ClientEarth*,[194] *Protect Natur-, Arten- und Landschaftsschutz Umweltorganisation*,[195] *North East Pylon Pressure Campaign Ltd*,[196] *LB*,[197] and *Societatea Civilă Profesională de Avocați Plopeanu & Ionescu*[198]concerning the Aarhus Convention; (c) *Air Transport Association of America*, on the Air Transport Agreement between the European Community and the United States (the so-called 'Open Skies Agreement') and the Kyoto Protocol; and (d) *SCF*[199] and *Recorded Artists Actors Performers Ltd*[200] on the 1996 World Intellectual Property Organization (WIPO) Performances and Phonograms Treaty (WPPT), as well as *KaiKai*[201] on the Paris Convention for the Protection of Industrial Property and the Patent Cooperation Treaty (PTC).

In the case of *Intertanko*,[202] a preliminary reference was made by the High Court of Justice of England and Wales on the validity of Articles 4 and 5 of Directive 2005/35/EC on ship-source pollution and the introduction of penalties for infringements under UNCLOS,[203] to which the Community, now the EU, was a party.[204] The reference was made in proceedings brought by a number of associations, including the International Association of Independent Tanker Owners (Intertanko), against the Secretary of State for Transport. The salient aspects of the ruling, from the point of view of UNCLOS' direct effect, are three. First, the review of legality under Article 267 TFEU presupposes that the provisions of UNCLOS are directly effective. Second, the test on direct effect first covers the agreement in its entirety, taking into account its nature and logic as 'disclosed in particular by its aim, preamble and terms',[205] and then the specific provision(s) that the applicants intend to invoke before the national court. Thus, it is the original test that is applied, rather than the inverted test used in part of the case law. Third, the enquiry as to clarity, precision, and unconditionality is inextricably linked to the conferral of a right stemming from the UNCLOS. Indeed, the CJ stated, at first, that it can examine the validity of Community legislation in

[193] CJ, *Vereniging Milieudefensie and Stichting Stop Luchtverontreiniging Utrecht*, joined cases C-401–403/12 P, EU:C:2015:4.

[194] CJ, *ClientEarth*, C-602/13 P, EU:C:2015:486.

[195] CJ, *Protect Natur-, Arten- und Landschaftsschutz Umweltorganisation*, C-664/15, EU:C:2017:987.

[196] CJ, *North East Pylon Pressure Campaign Limited*, C-470/16, EU:C:2018:185.

[197] CJ, *LB*, C-826/18, EU:C:2021:7.

[198] CJ, *Societatea Civilă Profesională de Avocați Plopeanu & Ionescu*, C-252/22, EU:C:2024:13, paras 76–78.

[199] CJ, *SCF*, C-135/10, EU:C:2012:140.

[200] CJ, *Recorded Artists Actors Performers Ltd*, C-265/19, EU:C:2020:677.

[201] CJ, *KaiKai*, C-382/21 P, EU:C:2024:172.

[202] *See, ex multis*, E. Denza, *A Note on Intertanko* (2008) 33 *European Law Review* 870; J. González Giménez, *Régimen comunitario de la contaminación por descargas procedentes de buques: la relación con las normas internacionales y la sentencia del TJCE sobre el asunto* Intertanko (2009) 13 *Revista de Derecho Comunitario Europeo* 915; J. Makowiak, *Spécificité de l'ordre juridique communautaire et pragmatisme de la Cour: ou comment lutter efficacement contre les pollutions maritimes* (2009) 3 *Revue trimestrielle de droit européen* 402; S. Vezzani, *Pacta sunt servanda? La sentenza della Corte di giustizia nell'affare Intertanko (caso C-308/06) e l'adattamento dell'ordinamento comunitario al diritto internazionale pattizio* (2009) 1 *Studi sull'integrazione europea* 233.

[203] Directive 2005/35/EC of the European Parliament and of the Council of 7 September 2005 on ship-source pollution and on the introduction of penalties for infringements, OJ L 255, 30.9.2005, 11.

[204] The claimants in the domestic proceedings also claimed that the legality of the directive had to be assessed in the light of the International Convention for the Prevention of Pollution from Ships (MARPOL). The CJ responded in these terms: 'It is true that all the Member States of the Community are parties to Marpol 73/78. Nevertheless, in the absence of a full transfer of the powers previously exercised by the Member States to the Community, the latter cannot, simply because all those States are parties to Marpol 73/78, be bound by the rules set out therein, which it has not itself approved. Since the Community is not bound by Marpol 73/78, the mere fact that Directive 2005/35 has the objective of incorporating certain rules set out in that Convention into Community law is likewise not sufficient for it to be incumbent upon the Court to review the directive's legality in the light of the Convention' (paras 49–50).

[205] *Intertanko* (n 191), para. 54.

the light of an international treaty 'only where the nature and the broad logic of the latter do not preclude this and, in addition, the treaty's provisions appear, as regards their content, to be unconditional and sufficiently precise'.[206] Afterwards, the Court, while recognizing that 'certain provisions of UNCLOS, such as Articles 17, 110(3) and 111(8), appear to attach rights to ships',[207] noted that it does not follow from this that those rights are 'conferred on the individuals linked to those ships, such as their owners, because a ship's international legal status is dependent on the flag State and not on the fact that it belongs to certain natural or legal persons'.[208] The Court, therefore, curiously draws a dividing line between natural persons and legal persons, the former being the only ones that should be taken into account regarding the attribution of direct effect. In so doing, the CJ excludes direct effect precisely because 'UNCLOS does not establish rules intended to apply directly and immediately to individuals and to confer on them rights or freedoms enforceable against States'.[209] The entire reasoning, however, seems to be centred on the enquiry into the agreement as a whole, given the statement of the CJ that 'it follows that the nature and the broad logic of UNCLOS prevent the Court from being able to assess the validity of a Community measure in the light of that Convention'.[210]

As to the Aarhus Convention,[211] the CJ denied, for the first time, the direct effect of some of its provisions, although not of the agreement in its entirety, in *Brown Bear*. This case concerned an environmental association's request to be a 'party' to the administrative proceedings relating to the granting of derogations to the system of protection for species such as the brown bear, access to protected countryside areas, or the use of chemical substances in such areas. More specifically, in its interpretive preliminary ruling, the Court denied that Article 9(3) was directly effective and could then be invoked to challenge a decision to derogate from a system of environmental protection, such as that put in place by the Council Directive 92/43/EEC of 21 May 1992[212] on the conservation of natural habitats and of wild fauna and flora ('the Habitats Directive'),[213] as confirmed in *Vereniging Milieudefensie and Stichting Stop Luchtverontreiniging Utrecht*,[214] as well as in *Protect Natur, Arten- und Landschaftsschutz Umweltorganisation*,[215] *North East Pylon Pressure Campaign Ltd*,[216] and *LB*.[217] In other rulings, other provisions were deemed deprived of direct effect, such as Articles 4(1) and (4)(c)

[206] *Intertanko* (n 191), para. 45.
[207] *Intertanko* (n 191), para. 61.
[208] *Intertanko* (n 191), para. 62.
[209] *Intertanko* (n 191), para. 64.
[210] *Intertanko* (n 191), para. 65.
[211] *See* E. Chiti, *EU Administrative Law in an International Perspective*, in C. Harlow, P. Leino, G. della Cananea (eds.), *Research Handbook of EU Administrative Law*, Cheltenham, Edward Elgar, 2017, 545–571; L. Ankersmit, *An Incoherent Approach Towards Aarhus and CETA: The Commission and External Oversight Mechanisms*, in I. Govaere, S. Garben (eds.), *The Interface between EU and International Law: Contemporary Reflections*, Chicago, Hart, 2019, 321–340; H. Schoukens, *Access to Justice before EU Courts in Environmental Cases against the Backdrop of the Aarhus Convention: Balancing Pathological Stubbornness and Cognitive Dissonance?*, in C. Voigt (ed.), *International Judicial Practice on the Environment: Questions of Legitimacy*, Cambridge, Cambridge University Press, 2019, 74–118; G. de Búrca, C. Kilpatrick, J. Scott, *Questioning the EU's 'Principled Openness' to International Law: An Examination of the Court's Reception of the Aarhus Convention and the Convention on the Rights of Persons with Disabilities*, in M. Claes, E. Vos (eds.), *Making Sense of European Union law*, Oxford, Hart, 2022, 3–18.
[212] Council Directive 92/43/EEC of 21 May 1992 on the conservation of natural habitats and of wild fauna and flora, OJ L 206, 22.7.1992, 7.
[213] *Brown Bear* (n 192), para. 52.
[214] *Vereniging Milieudefensie and Stichting Stop Luchtverontreiniging Utrecht* (n 193), para. 55.
[215] *Protect Natur, Arten- und Landschaftsschutz Umweltorganisation* (n 195), para. 45.
[216] *North East Pylon Pressure Campaign Ltd* (n 196), para. 52.
[217] *LB* (n 197), para. 69.

(*ClientEarth*),[218] Article 9(2) (*LB*),[219] Article 9(4) (*North East Pylon Pressure Campaign Ltd*[220]), and Article 9(5).[221]

The *Brown Bear* ruling, whose argumentative core is often transposed in later case law, complicates matters when it comes to identifying the main elements for specifying the content and extent of direct effect. First of all, references to the conferral of a right as a precondition for the legality review disappear altogether. Moreover, the CJ, while moving from the assumption enshrined in many previous judgments, according to which direct effect—*rectius*, in the CJ's wording, direct applicability—[222] exists if a provision 'contains a clear and precise obligation which is not subject, in its implementation or effects, to the adoption of any subsequent measure', 'regard being had to its wording and to the purpose and nature of the agreement',[223] completely overlooked this second aspect. Arguably, this is because, once unconditionality has been ruled out on the grounds that 'only members of the public who meet the criteria, if any, laid down by national law are entitled to exercise the rights provided for in Article 9(3)' and, thus, serving 'a subsequent measure', there is not even any need to reason about the agreement as a whole.[224] The problem with this approach is that it does not give due consideration to the fact that, unlike many other multilateral agreements, such as the WTO, the Aarhus Convention is not based on reciprocal and mutually beneficial agreements. Nor is due consideration given to the fact that the Convention is 'the expression of a human right to the environment'.[225] It is a Convention, therefore, which has little to do with the WTO and which, nevertheless, the CJ considers in the same way as the latter, although the reasoning relates only to the individual provisions rather than to the agreement as a whole. But there is more. Not only has the Convention, to date, been held to lack direct effect, with reference to some of its most innovative provisions for the protection of the subjective prerogatives connected with the protection of the environment. The CJ has also excluded, without further elaboration, in a number of cases, that the *Fediol* and *Nakajima* doctrines could be used in connection with the Aarhus Convention. It did so by emphasizing, in this respect, the peculiarities of the WTO and the special, unexplained, exclusive connection of both doctrines to the latter agreement.[226]

With regard to the Open Skies Agreement and the Kyoto Protocol, the most notable case is the *Air Transport Association of America* judgment,[227] which involved a reference for a preliminary ruling relating to some provisions of some international agreements which the applicants (Air Transport Association of America, American Airlines Inc., Continental Airlines Inc., and United Airlines Inc.) relied upon to challenge both a measure adopted by the UK and the validity of Directive 2008/101/EC,[228] inasmuch as the latter includes aviation in the scheme for greenhouse gas emission allowance trading under Directive 2003/87. The CJ, first of all, remarked that the EU is bound by Article 2(2) of the Kyoto Protocol

[218] *ClientEarth* (n 194), para. 40.
[219] *LB* (n 197), para. 52.
[220] *North East Pylon Pressure Campaign Ltd* (n 196), para. 52.
[221] *Societatea Civilă Profesională de Avocați Plopeanu & Ionescu* (n 198), paras 76–78.
[222] On the merging of these two concepts in respect to international law, *see* §§ 1 and 2 of this chapter.
[223] *Brown Bear* (n 192), para. 44.
[224] *Intertanko* (n 191), para. 45.
[225] Opinion of AG Jääskinen of 8 May 2014, *Vereniging Milieudefensie and Stichting Stop Luchtverontreiniging Utrecht*, EU:C:2014:310, paras 88–89.
[226] e.g. *ClientEarth* (n 194), para. 38.
[227] *See* also § 2.4 of this chapter on the case and customary law.
[228] Directive 2008/101/EC of the European Parliament and of the Council of 19 November 2008 amending Directive 2003/87/EC so as to include aviation activities in the scheme for greenhouse gas emission allowance trading within the Community, OJ L 8, 13.1.2009, 3.

and Articles 7, 11(2)(c), and 15(3) of the Open Skies Agreement, but not by the Convention on International Civil Aviation (the so-called 'Chicago Convention') since 'the powers previously exercised by the Member States in the field of application of the Chicago Convention have not to date been assumed in their entirety by the EU'.[229] Secondly, the Court referred to the test on direct effect in order to verify whether a legality review can be made and did so by reaffirming the classic two-stage assessment on the 'nature and the broad logic' of the agreement and, subsequently, 'where the nature and the broad logic of the treaty in question permit the validity of the act of European Union law to be reviewed in the light of the provisions of that treaty', on the characteristics of the provision(s) of the agreement. In this respect, the question to be asked is whether clarity, precision, and unconditionality are fulfilled.[230] As for the Open Skies Agreement, the CJ's answer was affirmative because it contains rules which are 'designed to apply directly and immediately to airlines and thereby to confer upon them rights and freedoms' and the nature and the broad logic of the agreement do not preclude such conferral.[231] At the core of the reasoning, therefore, lies the attribution of rights, which should be inferable from the agreement as a whole and from the specific provisions that are invoked before the judiciary.

As for the Kyoto Protocol, following the same type of (and order in the) assessment, the CJ instead[232] denied direct effect of the provision at hand, that is, Article 2(2). According to the Court, an interpretation of the objectives of the Kyoto Protocol leads to the conclusion that the latter allows certain Contracting Parties which are undergoing the process of transition to a market economy a certain degree of flexibility in the implementation of their commitments. Moreover, the Conference of the Parties, established by the Framework Convention, 'is responsible for approving appropriate and effective procedures and mechanisms to determine and to address cases of non-compliance with the provisions of the protocol'.[233] This means that the Parties to the Protocol 'may comply with their obligations in the manner and at the speed upon which they agree'.[234] From this flows a significant degree of flexibility left to the domestic authorities. In particular, as far as Article 2(2) of the Kyoto Protocol is concerned, it provides that the Parties thereto must limit their emissions of certain greenhouse gases from aviation bunker fuels thanks to cooperation with the International Civil Aviation Organization (ICAO). Hence, in the opinion of the Court, that provision, as regards its content, 'cannot in any event be considered to be unconditional and sufficiently precise so as to confer on individuals the right to rely on it in legal proceedings in order to contest the validity of Directive 2008/101'.[235]

As for the case law on intellectual property rights, the reasoning on the effects of the WPPT was briefly developed in *SCF* in respect to its Article 23(1). That provision requires the Contracting Parties 'to adopt, in accordance with their legal systems, the measures necessary to ensure the application'[236] of the Agreement on Trade-Related Aspects of Intellectual Property Rights (TRIPS), that is, of a WTO agreement whose direct effect had already been excluded.[237] Hence, direct effect was denied by the CJ since the provisions of the WPPT,

[229] *Air Transport Association of America* (n 15), para. 71.
[230] *Intertanko* (n 191), paras 53–55.
[231] *Intertanko* (n 191), para. 84.
[232] *Intertanko* (n 191), paras 73–78.
[233] *Intertanko* (n 191), para. 75.
[234] *Intertanko* (n 191), para. 76.
[235] *Intertanko* (n 191), para. 77.
[236] *SCF* (n 199), para. 47.
[237] *SCF* (n 199), paras 45–48.

being subject to the adoption of subsequent measures, were 'not such as to create rights for individuals which they may rely on before the courts by virtue of that law'.[238] As regards *Recorded Artists Actors Performers Ltd*, the CJ observed that private parties, such as performers or their collecting societies, could not rely directly on Article 15(3) of the WPPT due to its lack of unconditionality.[239] Finally, in *KaiKai* the CJ, differently from AG Ćapeta,[240] on one hand, simply[241] reiterated the approach taken in *SCF* inasmuch as it held that 'the rules set out in Article 4 of the Paris Convention must be regarded as producing the same effects as those produced by the TRIPs Agreement'[242] and, for this reason, due to the lack of direct effect of the TRIPs Agreement, considered Article 4 unable 'to create rights upon which individuals may rely directly before the courts by virtue of EU law'.[243] On the other hand, the Court excluded the applicability of the *Fediol* and *Nakajima* exceptions—enabling 'private individuals [to] rely directly on the provisions of the WTO Agreements before the Courts of the European Union'—to the case at hand.[244] It did so noting that it is not possible either to find in EU law any express reference to Article 4 of the Paris Convention[245] nor to infer from any EU law specific provisions regarding the 'legislature's intention'[246] 'to implement into EU law a particular obligation stemming from the WTO Agreements'.[247] From all this flows the consequence that direct effect shall not be asserted.[248]

There are four considerations to be made in the light of *SCF*, *Recorded Artists Actors Performers Ltd*, and *KaiKai*. Firstly, the conferral of rights returns to be a pillar of the CJ's reasoning on the direct effect of international agreements. Secondly, the test on direct effect seems to consist exclusively of the enquiry into its premises, rather than the purpose and nature of the agreement. Thirdly, unconditionality plays a key role, *de facto* absorbing the other two on clarity and precision. Lastly, from the *KaiKai* judgment it may be inferred that the two *Fediol* and *Nakajima* doctrines, if applicable, are a form of direct effect rather than an exception to the latter and an unusual form of legality review, or indirect effect.[249]

2.4 Customary law

Finally, leaving aside international agreements, and the decisions of the bodies established by these agreements, it must be understood whether and if so to what extent general international law can be invoked by individuals, States, and EU institutions to challenge EU law.[250]

[238] *SCF* (n 199), para. 48.
[239] *Recorded Artists Actors Performers Ltd* (n 200), para. 87.
[240] Opinion of AG Ćapeta, *KaiKai* (n 167).
[241] On the problematic self-restraint of the CJ in the case *see* D. Sarmiento, S. Iglesias Sanchez, *Insight: Is Direct Effect Morphing into Something Different?*, Madrid, EU Law Live, 4 March 2024, available at https://eulawlive.com/insight-is-direct-effect-morphing-into-something-different-by-daniel-sarmiento-and-sara-iglesias-sanchez/.
[242] *KaiKai* (n 201), para. 62.
[243] *KaiKai* (n 201), para. 63.
[244] *KaiKai* (n 201), para. 64.
[245] *KaiKai* (n 201), para. 65.
[246] *KaiKai* (n 201), para. 67.
[247] *KaiKai* (n 201), para. 66.
[248] *KaiKai* (n 201), para. 68. On this point, *see* the analysis by L. Lonardo, *The Will of the Legislator and the Direct Effect of EU International Agreements (Case C 382/21 P KaiKai Company)*, EU Law Live, 2 May 2024, available at https://eulawlive.com/op-ed-the-will-of-the-legislator-and-the-direct-effect-of-eu-international-agreements-case-c%E2%80%91382-21-p-kaikai-company-by-luigi-lonardo/.
[249] On the interplay between direct effect and the *Fediol* and *Nakajima* doctrines, *see* § 3 of this chapter.
[250] Amongst those who support the view that customary law can entail direct effect according to the EU case law, *see* J. Wouters, D. Van Eeckhoutte, *Giving Effect to Customary International Law through European Community*

The question arises, of course, because the EU must comply with customary law in addition to international agreements.

In this regard, it was recalled in section 1 that the question has arisen in a few cases, notably in *Racke*, *Opel Austria*, and *Air Transport Association of America*, all concerning the matter of compatibility of EU secondary law with customary law raised in preliminary rulings proceedings on validity (*Racke* and *Air Transport Association of America*) and annulment proceedings (*Opel Austria*). The red thread is that customary law is invoked by the plaintiffs to challenge EU law by virtue of direct effect. For example, in the *Racke* case, the analysis of the validity of the contested Council Regulation (EEC) No. 3300/91 in the light of customary law emerged 'incidentally' in a dispute in which the company Racke argued that the preferential rates of customs duties resulting from Article 22 of the Cooperation Agreement between the European Economic Community and the Socialist Federal Republic of Yugoslavia should be applied. According to the Commission, the CJ had no jurisdiction because the preliminary reference concerned the validity of the contested regulation based on customary law 'alone',[251] in particular on the principles governing the termination of treaties and their suspension.

The CJ boldly rejected this (poorly elaborated) argument and did so, implicitly, on the basis of the idea that there is no difference between international agreements and customary law, as to their possible invocation in the courts.[252] The CJ noted that Article 22(4) of the Contested Regulation is 'capable of conferring rights to preferential customs treatment directly upon individuals',[253] as is also confirmed by the purpose and nature of the Cooperation Agreement with Yugoslavia of which Article 22(4) is a part. It then wondered whether,[254] when invoking preferential customs treatment under Article 22(4), Racke may challenge the validity, under the rules of customary law, of the contested Regulation suspending the trade concessions granted under that agreement from 15 November 1991, because of a fundamental change of circumstances.

The answer given by the CJ is that this can occur in a situation where the plaintiff 'is incidentally challenging the validity of a Community regulation under those rules in order to rely upon rights which it derives directly from an agreement of the Community with a non-member country'.[255] This is the reason, according to the Court, why the case 'does not . . . concern the direct effect of those rules'.[256] At the same time, however, the CJ, in order to allow individuals to rely upon rights originating from international agreements, affirmed that an individual can invoke, 'in order to challenge the validity of the suspending regulation, obligations deriving from rules of customary international law which govern the termination

Law, in J. M. Prinssen, A. Schrauwen (eds.), *Direct Effect*, 181–234; A. von Bogdandy, M. Smrkolj, *European Union*, paras 45–51; R. Schütze, *On 'Middle Ground'*, 59–60; R. Dunbar, *The Application*, 580. For similar thoughts, and also for some clarifications about the specificities of the direct effect test vis-à-vis customary law, *see* N. A. J. Croquet, *The Import of International Customary Law into the EU Legal Order: The Adequacy of a Direct Effect Analysis* (2013) 15 *Cambridge Yearbook of European Legal Studies* 47–81. For a contextualization of customary law's direct effect in the light of the international legal regime, *see* A. T. Müller, *The Direct Effect of Customary International Law*, in F. Lusa Bordin, A. T. Müller, F. Pascual-Vives (eds.), *The European Union and Customary International Law*, Cambridge, Cambridge University Press, 2022, 210–239.

[251] *Racke* (n 84), para. 25.
[252] *Racke* (n 84), paras 26–27.
[253] *Racke* (n 84), para. 30
[254] *Racke* (n 84), para. 37.
[255] *Racke* (n 84), para. 47.
[256] *Racke* (n 84), para. 47.

and suspension of treaty relations'.[257] This is quite an argumentative short-circuit: to rely on rights enshrined in agreements and challenge an EU act, the plaintiff invokes the compliance with obligations which are part of customary law. In this connection, the Court believes that such 'judicial review'[258] must be limited to the matter of whether, by adopting the suspending Regulation, 'the Council made manifest errors of assessment concerning the conditions for applying customary rules'.[259] Notwithstanding the Court's assumption that direct effect does not come into play, the question arises as to how this invocation, which is instrumental to reliance on international agreements, differs in practice from the direct effect doctrine itself. There seems to be no difference at all, upon a closer look. The fact that the direct effect test is not performed, of course, depends on the assumption from which the CJ moves, but also on what has already been observed in sections 3.1 of Chapter III and 5.5 of Chapter VI regarding the direct effect of general principles of EU law: in the case of unwritten principles/rules, the test tends to be naturally devoid of utility.

Opel Austria neither contradicts nor confirms *Racke*. In the case the GC ruled on an action *ex* Article 260(4) TFEU seeking the annulment of Council Regulation (EC) No. 3697/93 withdrawing tariff concessions in accordance with Article 23(2) and Article 27(3) (a) of the Free Trade Agreement between the Community and Austria (General Motors Austria). The annulment was sought on the ground that the Council allegedly infringed the public international law principle of good faith, as a key rule of customary law binding on the Community,[260] a few days before the European Economic Agreement (EEA) Agreement entered into force. The GC, rather than affirming explicitly that the principle of good faith is directly effective and/or can be relied upon to challenge an EU act, noted that such principle 'is the corollary in public international law of the principle of protection of legitimate expectations which, according to the caselaw, forms part of the Community legal order'.[261] Hence, any economic operator to whom an institution has given justified hopes 'may rely on the principle of protection of legitimate expectations'[262] and can do so on the basis of a general principle of EU law. The fact that an EU principle, which includes a customary rule of international law, is invoked, rather than that rule expressly, in no way means that the latter is not endowed with direct effect and that therefore its breach cannot be a ground for challenging EU law. Arguably, however, it could be said that doubts remain.

The doubts above seem to be definitively overcome by the aforementioned *Air Transport Association of America* judgment, where the CJ, regarding several customary international maritime and air law principles which were invoked by some private parties to challenge the validity of Directive 2008/101/EC, affirmed that they can be relied upon by natural and legal persons.[263] And this is possible, according to the Court, 'even though the principles at issue appear only to have the effect of creating obligations between States'.[264]

On closer inspection, *Air Transport Association of America*, in which no direct effect test was carried out, is a confirmation of *Racke*, in the sense argued above, where the Court, while clarifying that a rule of customary law does not have 'the same degree of precision as a provision of an international agreement', concludes that 'judicial review must necessarily

[257] *Racke* (n 84), para. 51.
[258] *Racke* (n 84), para. 52.
[259] *Racke* (n 84), para. 52.
[260] *Racke* (n 84), para. 90.
[261] *Opel Austria* (n 86), para. 93.
[262] *Opel Austria* (n 86), para. 94.
[263] *Air Transport Association of America* (n 15), paras 107–110.
[264] *Air Transport Association of America* (n 15), para. 109.

be limited to the question whether, in adopting the act in question, the institutions of the European Union made manifest errors of assessment concerning the conditions for applying' customary law.[265] Here there are no rules of the agreement, as in *Racke*, which stand between the customary rule and the claimant as to its invocability. There is legality review and, therefore, direct effect. This holds true although there is no conferral of a right. In fact, as written in respect to internal direct effect in Chapter IV and observed in-depth in the following section, there is no reason why direct effect should be understood only in its narrow meaning. To the contrary, a broad-objective direct effect, on the one hand, is consistent with what the CJ affirms in its jurisprudence, and, on the other, preserves the useful effect of a doctrine aimed at allowing individuals to assert their prerogatives before the courts and EU law to be properly enforced.

3. The blurred boundaries between (broad) direct effect, legality review, and the *Fediol-Nakajima* doctrine(s)

In Chapter IV it was argued that direct effect, when it comes to the relationship between EU law and domestic legal orders, must be interpreted broadly. Thus, it has a second dimension in addition to the subjective and narrow one rooted in the *Van Gend & Loos* judgment. This dimension is objective insofar as the (explicit or implicit) conferral of a right is not a *condicio sine qua non* for the recognition of direct effect. Such a conception of direct effect, which is independent from the conferral of a right as one of its core characteristics, by now, seems to have been acquired by the CJEU in its case law.

As for the external direct effect, things are more complicated for four reasons. Firstly, at stake is the challenge of not only national measures, in respect of which direct effect is often recognized, but also of EU measures. In this regard, it has been seen that the CJEU's approach to direct effect is restrictive to the extent that the possibility for individuals and States to challenge EU acts based on international agreements is systematically denied, especially vis-à-vis the GATT/WTO agreements. This challenge, when there are EU provisions at stake, is not aimed at disapplication, but rather at annulment, through a preliminary ruling on validity *ex* Article 267 TFEU or by virtue of Article 263 TFEU. In the second place, the CJEU, frequently, regardless of the judicial proceeding concerned, seems to consider the conferral of a right a necessary condition of direct effect. Thus, the Court often endorses narrow direct effect rather than broad direct effect. Thirdly, on the one hand, narrow direct effect is generally[266] considered the prerequisite for challenging EU acts,[267] while on the other hand, the Court admits, with the *Fediol* and *Nakajima* doctrines, that legality review is independent of direct effect. Fourth, beyond the intention to implement an international obligation or the specific referral to the latter in EU law, it is not easy to understand why legality review in

[265] *Air Transport Association of America* (n 15), para. 110.

[266] But *see*, in respect to customary law, *Racke* (n 84), para. 54: 'Even if, as the Council maintains, the CBD contains provisions which do not have direct effect, in the sense that they do not create rights which individuals can rely on directly before the courts, that fact does not preclude review by the courts of compliance with the obligations incumbent on the Community as a party to that agreement.'

[267] *See*, amongst others, *Germany v Council* (n 139), para. 109; CJ, *The Queen, on the application of International Air Transport Association and European Low Fares Airline Association v Department for Transport*, C-344/04, EU:C:2006:10, para. 39; *Intertanko* (n 191), para. 45; *FIAMM* (n 33), para. 110; *Air Transport Association of America* (n 15), para. 54; *SCF* (n 199), para. 46; CJ, *Z*, C-363/12, EU:C:2014:159, para. 86; CJ, *Ordre des barreaux francophones et germanophone and others*, C-543/14, EU:C:2016:605, para. 49.

the *Fediol* and *Nakajima* doctrines differs from direct effect when the challenge to EU law is at stake, as these two doctrines have nothing to do with a purely interpretative approach, as would be the case with consistent interpretation. The reference is to what the Court stated in *Nakajima* whereby it was held that the applicant was 'not relying on ... direct effect' since natural and legal persons, in the context of Article 263 TFEU, 'in fact question ... in an incidental manner ... the applicability' of EU law 'by invoking one of the grounds for review of legality' referred to in that article.[268]

The proposal put forward in this volume is based on three criticisms of EU case law. Criticism number one: direct effect shall not be understood as a condition for a legality review under Article 263 TFEU and Article 267 TFEU,[269] as recently confirmed by the CJ in *Changmao Biochemical Engineering*[270] and *KaiKai*.[271] It shall not when it comes to invoking EU primary law to challenge EU secondary law, as explained in section 1 of Chapter II, and also when it comes to investigating the legal effects of international law within the EU in order to challenge an EU act.[272] Direct effect serves to challenge national law in order to entail its disapplication. It does not concern the annulment of EU provisions. To this end, the instrument available to individuals and States is the legality review provided for in Articles 263 and 267 TFEU, in view of the specific procedural conditions laid down in those two articles, which are particularly strict, as is well known, with regard to the direct and individual concern of Article 263 TFEU.[273] Thus, the CJ adopts a quite incomprehensible approach when it either explicitly states or implicitly suggests that direct effect is a prerequisite for performing legality review under Articles 263 and 267 TFEU. The truth is that direct effect should not be such a prerequisite, just as is not in relation to infringement actions pursuant to Articles 258–260 TFEU, whereby the matter of direct effect is never examined by the CJ.[274]

Criticism number two: in any case, if one wanted to draw direct effect into the scope of the legality review of EU acts, the existence of an ontological difference between direct effect and legality review must be excluded. At stake is the invocability of a norm, its justiciability, that is, the ability of an external provision (of international law) to govern the case in place of a provision of EU law. *Fediol* and *Nakajima* are, as has been anticipated, very far from indirect effect. In concrete terms, they act similarly to how the doctrine of direct effect operates.[275] The boundaries between such doctrines and direct effect seem to be thin to the point of disappearing in *KaiKai*, whereby, *immediately* after having denied *their* application in relation to Article 4 of the Paris Convention, the Court wrote: '[i]t *follows* that the rules set out in Article 4 of the Paris Convention do not have direct effect and, accordingly,

[268] *Nakajima* (n 152), para. 28.

[269] For a different opinion, mainly based on the need to ensure legal certainty and avoid divergences in EU judicial protection, *see*, amongst many others, A. Peters, *The Position*, 66–71; P. Eeckhout, *EU External Relations*, 295; P. Koutrakos, *EU International Relations Law*, 2nd ed., Oxford, Hart, 2015, 255.

[270] CJ, *Changmao Biochemical Engineering*, C-123/21P, EU:C:2023:708, paras 70–71.

[271] *KaiKai* (n 201), para. 63.

[272] As far as international law is concerned, *see*, in the same vein, O. Jacot-Guillamord, *Droit communtaituaire et droit international public*, Geneva, *Librairie de l'université Georg*, 1979, 226; R. Dunbar, *The Application*, 572.

[273] A. Peters, *The Position*, 68: 'The procedural prerequisites for launching an action (in particular the question of standing) are one issue; the capacity to make a legal argument based on an international agreement is a different issue which relates to substance.'

[274] P. Eeckhout, *The Domestic Legal Status*, 45.

[275] P. Eeckhout, *The Domestic Legal Status*, 42, observed that '[W]hether one calls that type of effect direct or indirect, it is clear that, in theory at least, it involves more than mere consistent interpretation.' *See* also P. Eeckhout, *Judicial enforcement*, 104 and I. Hadjiyianni, *The CJEU*, 901, who spoke of a 'narrow exception' 'akin to direct effect'.

are not such as to create, for individuals, rights on which they may directly rely by virtue of EU law.'[276] Legality review and direct effect mean the same thing. In this sense, to hold that direct effect is a prerequisite for the legality review of EU acts cannot be shared, upstream, because, in practice, the plaintiff directly invokes a rule within the realm of both direct effect and legality review and because the effects of legality review and direct effect are the same.

Criticism number three: to exclude direct effect, as the CJEU generally[277] does, and consequently the legality review of EU law, on the ground that the provisions of international law do not confer rights on individuals is to follow a narrow conception of direct effect, which cannot be justified[278] either as regards internal direct effect, as has been shown, or as regards external direct effect. A view centred on the conferral of a right as a structural element of direct effect unduly constricts effective judicial protection and the private (fair) enforcement of the law. The enquiry into direct effect, understood in the broad sense, as done by the CJ with respect to customary law,[279] is an enquiry into legality review, when one is within the external direct effect. This is an enquiry on the unconditionality of an international norm, that is, on its capacity to be invoked by an applicant, individual, or State,[280] before a judge and enforced by the latter to govern the dispute.[281] In Oesch's words,

> a norm of international law is directly effective when it can be invoked by a private party in proceedings before domestic authorities. Direct effect can have a twofold purpose: (1) a treaty norm, which is granted direct effect, might allow individuals to derive rights therefrom; and/or (2) it might serve as a basis to challenge the legality of an existing (conflicting) domestic legal act.[282]

As observed by Peters, 'as a matter of consistency and legal stringency, we do not need a specific concept (other than justiciability) reserved to applicability of international treaties'.[283]

It flows from the above reflections that the restrictive approach of the CJEU regarding the recognition of direct effect, for example with respect to the GATT and WTO, the Aarhus Convention, and the Kyoto Protocol, does not seem to rest on a sufficiently solid reconstruction of direct effect. In any event, the true reason for the denial of direct effect, when the challenge of EU acts is at stake, seems to be another. Indeed, it lies in the political dimension of external direct effect, especially with reference to the GATT and WTO. This will be investigated in more detail in sections 5–6.

276 *KaiKai* (n 201), para. 68 (italics added).

277 *See* § 2 of this chapter on the jurisprudence, beginning with *International Fruit Company* (n 16).

278 For a categorization of the different forms of invocability, *see* A. Peters, *The Position*, 43.

279 *See* § 4 of this chapter.

280 As demonstrated in § 3.2 of Chapter III and § 4 of Chapter V, the direct effect doctrine can be relied on also by the State.

281 *Contra* J. Klabbers, *International Law*, 265; A. Antoniadis, *The* Chiquita *and* Van Parys *Judgments: Rules, Exceptions and the Law* (2005) 32 *Legal Issues of Economic Integration* 460.

282 M. Oesch, *Direct Effect*, 277.

283 A. Peters, *The Position*, 44, who also observed: 'Therefore, I shall define "direct effect" as follows: A provision in an international treaty has direct effect whenever courts are entitled and bound to apply the rule without having to wait for any executory legislation. This is the case when two conditions are fulfilled: the Contracting Parties must have intended the rule to be applicable by the judiciary, and the rule must be, by its contents, suited to give rise to concrete legal consequences. In the purely domestic context (within the national legal order), the fulfillment of these conditions makes national laws "justiciable".'

4. Horizontal direct effect of international law?

The question of the horizontal direct effect of international law has not yet been explicitly answered by the CJEU.[284] The issue, moreover, has so far only arisen with reference to international agreements. The CJEU, for decades, has neither denied nor asserted the capacity of international agreements to generate direct effects in inter-individual relations.[285] The first case in which this capacity was discussed and implicitly granted is *Deutscher Handballbund*, where the CJ admitted that international agreements may be invoked by private parties against other private parties, not only against the States and the EU.

The problem at hand was whether Article 38(1) of the Association Agreement with Slovakia establishing the movement of workers applied to a rule laid down by a (private) sports federation. The question is always the same when it comes to horizontality: are certain rules—of EU law when the framework is that of internal direct effect, of international law when the framework is that of external direct effect—capable of creating obligations vis-à-vis private entities?

In response, the CJ relied on the prohibition of discrimination enshrined in the EC Treaty, in particular Article 48, now Article 45 TFEU, as well as on the *Bosman* judgment, in which it was stated that working conditions in the different Member States are governed 'sometimes by laws or regulations and sometimes by agreements and other acts concluded or adopted by private persons'. Limiting the application of the freedoms of movement to acts of public authority would create 'inequality' in their application.[286] At the heart of the Court's reasoning, therefore, was the comparison with EU law, as has been done in some of its previous case law on the applicability of international law in vertical relationships.[287] The Court, while noting that association agreements, such as the one with Poland of 1991, do not establish a principle of full freedom of movement for third-country workers within the Community, unlike the EC Treaty, stated that certain provisions of those agreements, such as Article 38(1) of the Association Agreement with Slovakia, establishing 'the right to equal treatment as regards working conditions', have the same scope as their counterparts in the EC Treaty. It follows that the approach adopted by the Court in respect of Community law, in particular with regard to its direct effect in horizontal situations, 'can be transposed' to the association agreements, including the association agreement with Slovakia.[288] Although the Court did not expressly recognize the horizontal direct effect, there is no doubt about the direct application of an international rule in disputes between private parties made by the Court in this case.

Confirmation of the possible horizontal direct effect of international agreements comes from the *Simutenkov* case, already cited and discussed in section 2.3 of this chapter with regard to the extent of the direct effect test. In the judgment, concerning Article 23(1) of the Agreement on Partnership and Cooperation with the Russian Federation, the CJ first acknowledged that such a provision, 'very similar' to Article 38(1) of the Association Agreement with Slovakia,[289] has direct effect and then, without expressly mentioning the horizontal character of direct effect, considered Article 23(1) to be applicable in the present

[284] According to R. Schütze, *European Union Law*, 188, the CJ 'evaded' the problem.
[285] *See*, e.g. *Polydor* (n 103).
[286] *Deutscher Handballbund* (n 136), para. 32.
[287] *See* § 2 of this chapter.
[288] *Deutscher Handballbund* (n 140), para. 50.
[289] *Simutenkov* (n 182), para. 34.

case.[290] The Court does in relation to the external direct effect what it often does in relation to the horizontal internal direct effect of Treaty provisions, as has already been seen: it applies the rule to disputes between private parties, without expressly providing its reasoning with regard to horizontal direct effect.

5. Comparing 'external' and 'internal' direct effect

This section aims to investigate, on the basis of what has been written so far, the most distinctive aspects of the direct effect of international law, including the pros and cons of its recognition. This will be done through a comparison with the doctrine of internal direct effect, which has been discussed in previous chapters. There are some similarities *(i)*, some divergences *(ii)*, and some halfway features *(iii)*.

(i) As to similarities, first of all, the jurisprudence on both internal and external direct effect is unsteady and ambiguous. The confusion, exacerbated by the different approaches and terminologies used in the literature,[291] is mainly the result of the CJEU's steady argumentative minimalism. This ambiguity, confusion, and self-restraint affect many aspects, including the following: the relationship between direct effect and direct applicability; the narrow or broad conception of direct effect and the role of the conferral of rights in the direct effect test; the order of the two steps of the test, the one focusing on the nature and purpose of the agreement and the other on its specific provisions; and the interplay between direct effect and challenges to EU law in proceedings under Articles 263 and 267 TFEU (on validity of EU secondary law).

Secondly, notwithstanding what is written in some of the literature, as can be seen from several judgments of the CJEU, just as internal direct effect and direct applicability are identical concepts, in practice, there is also no difference between external direct effect and direct applicability, both being related to the justiciability of a norm. The matter of incorporation of international law into EU law,[292] in fact, does not relate to the direct applicability of the agreement; it has to do, rather, with its immediate transposition within the EU legal order.

Thirdly, the direct effect test is neither mentioned nor carried out when dealing with unwritten rules. This holds true for both general principles of EU law and customary law.

Fourthly, in the context of both internal and external direct effect, direct effect can be recognized also when the rule is imbued with a certain margin of appreciation.

Fifthly, as to the test for direct effect, both internal and external, the dividing line between clarity and precision is neither clear nor precise. Indeed, there does not appear to be one. Moreover, it can be inferred from the case law that unconditionality, at the heart of the case law on internal direct effect, is also the core of the reasoning of the CJEU on external direct effect.

(ii) Regarding the specifics of the external direct effect, and thus the differences with the internal direct effect, first of all, the centrality of the political dimension, *lato sensu*, of the external direct effect is evident. Politics means separation of powers and institutional balance

[290] *Simutenkov* (n 182), paras 29, 33–34.

[291] *See* A. Peters, *The Position*, 42, with regard to both the EU case law and the literature: '[T]he problem of direct effect of international agreements concluded by the Community in Community and Member State law suffers from a considerable degree of confusion.' *See* also J. Klabbers, *International Law*, 263, according to whom, 'there is nothing "natural"' about external direct effect.

[292] On the unclear boundaries between monism and dualism in the field *see* § 1 of this chapter.

within the Union. Separation of powers means the allocation of legislative, executive, and judicial competences amongst EU institutions in the realm of external relations. In short, with internal direct effect the disapplication made by the judge, or by the administration, which results from the application of directly effective EU law, limits the perimeter of the legislative power to the benefit of the expansion of EU law, its effectiveness, and penetration into national legal systems. Within external direct effect and when such doctrine is an instrument for challenging a national law, the discourse is partly similar and partly different. It is similar because the EU agreement, that is, an act of the Union, is enforced in the place of the national law with which it conflicts. It is different because the recognition of external direct effect gives private applicants and judges the opportunity to enforce the agreement in a diffuse manner, thereby eroding the discretion of the EU institutions in charge of steering the external relations of the EU. On the other hand, when the external direct effect aims at challenging EU law, rather than national law, the CJEU is reluctant to admit direct effect because it tends to preserve its own legal order, that is, its autonomy. This seems to be the reason for the CJEU's particularly restrictive approach towards challenging EU law, as opposed to the expansionism of EU jurisprudence concerning the recognition of internal direct effect.

Secondly, while the remedy of disapplication is a recurring element of EU case law regarding internal direct effect, insofar as the CJEU explicitly refers to a duty to set aside a national law which conflicts with EU law, within external direct effect such a remedy is not systematically referred to, not even in interpretative preliminary rulings, where at the origins of domestic proceedings is national, rather than EU, law.

Thirdly, whereas, *outside the realm of international agreements*, in proceedings under Articles 263 and 267 (on the validity of EU secondary law) TFEU when EU primary law is the parameter of legality, the review of EU secondary law is independent of direct effect, within external direct effect, generally, direct effect is considered by the CJEU as a precondition for the annulment of EU secondary law under those two provisions. A direct effect that, while, in principle, should be distinguished, in the opinion of the Court, from the legality review underpinning the *Fediol/Nakajima* doctrines, in practice, does not seem to be so different from the latter.

Fourthly, while in internal direct effect the test, if it is carried out at all, has only one step, that of checking for clarity/precision and unconditionality, in external direct effect, with reference to international agreements and decisions of international bodies, there are two steps, in an order that changes repeatedly in the EU case law for apparently no reason. One stage concerns the conditions just mentioned, another the agreement, investigated in its entirety. Hence, the consequence that identical rules may generate direct effect, if they are part of EU primary or secondary law, and an effect that is not direct, if they are contained in international agreements or in decisions of international bodies.

(iii) With regard to the points that are partially in common, first, the interpretation of the rule, EU in the case of internal direct effect, international in the case of external direct effect, relates, for both, to its nature, logic, and purpose. However, in the case of external direct effect, in line with international law subjective methods of interpretation, the focus is also considerably on the intention of the Contracting Parties.[293] Secondly, while horizontal direct effect is recognized with respect to both the relationship between EU law and domestic legal orders and the relationship between international and EU law, the case law, despite

[293] On the importance of subjective interpretation, *see* M. Prek, S. Lefèvre, *La dimension 'subjective' de l'invocabilité des accords internationaux*, in E. Neframi, M. Gatti (eds.), *Constitutional issues*, 231–255.

uncertainties, is much clearer in relation to internal direct effect than to external direct effect. Thirdly, while the CJEU has traditionally been at the heart of the doctrine of direct effect, both external and internal, because centralizing the assessment on direct effect ensures legal uniformity, nowadays, on such matter there isn't full convergence between internal and external direct effect. Indeed, as anticipated above and will be further explained in the next section, there is a significant recent trend, especially in international agreements related to trade, characterized by a preclusion of direct effect in the text of such agreements, advocated by both the Commission and the Council, with the consequence that the role of the CJEU as 'gatekeeper' is being weakened with respect to external direct effect.

6. The diminishing role of the CJEU as a 'gatekeeper' in the conceptualization and practice of 'external' direct effect

A few brief concluding considerations should be made on the pros and cons of recognizing the direct effect of international law, as well as on the role of the CJEU in this respect, *today*.

The recognition of international agreements' external direct effect, and their decentralized direct invocability, can affect the institutional balance, the reciprocal relationships with Third Countries partners, and the uniform application of those agreements in domestic legal systems. It is, therefore, understandable that the EU jurisdictions are cautious in using the doctrine of direct effect with respect to international law. Acting cautiously, however, does not mean systematically, and increasingly, denying the prerequisites of legality review. This denial by the CJEU occurred especially when EU law was at stake. The Court has based its reasoning on the assumption that direct effect, in its narrow dimension, is the precondition for challenging EU acts. A reconstruction that has been subject to criticism in this chapter. In any case, even if it were to be considered that EU acts could be challenged only on the basis of the recognition of international agreements' direct effect, the constant denial of external direct effect leading to the denial of legality review regarding such acts is such as to challenge the two rationales underpinning *Van Gend & Loos* and its progeny. Firstly, just as internal direct effect allows applicants to act as private enforcers of EU law, the legality review through external direct effect guarantees the enforcement of the principle *pacta sunt servanda*, as codified in Article 26 of the Vienna Convention on the Law of Treaties. Direct effect, thus, is instrumental to the enforcement of international law by which the EU is bound.[294] Secondly, the recognition of external direct effect for the purpose of challenging EU acts is closely related to the effective judicial protection of States' interests, and of natural and legal persons' rights, as safeguarded in EU law and explicitly held in the *Les Verts* ruling.[295] Such interests and rights are questioned if, notwithstanding the existence of a breach of a sufficiently clear, precise, and unconditional international law provision by an EU act, the latter cannot be subject to legality review due to a narrow interpretation of direct.[296]

To date, the jurisprudential practice is unclear, characterized by multiple uncertainties and criticalities, as described and detailed above. Most importantly, there has been a major

[294] On the efficiency of, and compliance with, international law through direct effect, *see* J. Bello, *The WTO Dispute Settlement Understanding: Less is More* (1996) 90 *American Journal of International Law* 416; M. Mendez, *The Legal Effects*, 107–113; A. Nollkaemper, *The Duality of Direct Effect of International Law* (2014) 25 *European Journal of International Law* 105, 118.

[295] CJ, *Parti écologiste 'Les Verts' v European Parliament*, 294/83, EU:C:1986:166, para. 23.

[296] A. Tancredi, *On the Absence*, 267–268.

evolution of the role of the CJEU and the other EU institutions regarding the direct effect of international agreements. Ever since the 1970s, the CJEU assumed the function of a gatekeeper deciding on direct effect of international agreements since back then it was unusual to regulate their legal effects directly in one or more of their provisions.

In recent years, however, there has been a trend emerging with the Commission, as negotiator, and the Council, willing to take matters into their own hands. Indeed, the EU negotiating teams have started the practice of advocating for the insertion of clauses precluding effect directly in the text of EU free trade or association/cooperation agreements. Indeed, the preclusion of direct effect is nowadays a recurring feature of many EU international agreements, especially, but not only, trade related. This creates inconsistencies between recent agreements containing such clauses and others, mainly old partnership, cooperation, and association agreements whose rules have been deemed directly effective by the CJEU. The asymmetry arising between the recognition of direct effect to the EC Partnership and Cooperation Agreement with the Russian Federation of 1994 made in the oft-cited *Simutenkov* case, on the one hand, and, on the other hand, the EU-Ukraine Association Agreement, which denies such recognition,[297] is a key demonstration of the side-effects stemming from the current trend occurring in the EU external action policies. Possibly, in the case of a Council decision denying direct effect to an EU agreement that does not expressly preclude direct effect or, as happened in some association agreements,[298] that precludes such effect only to some of its provisions, the CJEU, theoretically, may decide to proceed with the annulment of the EU act pursuant to Articles 263 or 267 TFEU based on the characteristics of the agreement as a whole and its provisions.[299] Indeed, as the CJ has affirmed in *Ioannis Katsivardas* and as has been noted by AG Saggio in his opinion, the Council's decision cannot challenge what is stated in the agreement. In fact, 'the Council may not, by an act of secondary legislation, limit the Court's jurisdiction, nor decide to rule out the jurisdiction of national courts to apply' EU agreements.[300] The possibility of the CJEU challenging the Council's choice of direct effect preclusion, however, risks being a solution only on paper since it has already been shown to what extent both the GC and the CJ are reluctant, in the present times, more than before, to recognize the direct effect of international agreements, trade and non-trade related.

Overall, the current practice of the Commission and the Council of precluding direct effect through the insertion of clauses in international agreements is apt to challenge the principle of effective judicial protection and shows once and for all what has been already remarked in this chapter: the choice on the recognition of the external direct effect—torn between respect of the autonomy of the EU legal order and compliance with international law—is ultimately political.[301] Hence, it comes as no surprise that the EU institutions in charge of the EU external action have taken the lead in this field.

In light of the above, one has to wonder what role the CJEU may assume in the future. One thing is certain: the position of the CJEU as a gatekeeper has shrunk dramatically regarding bilateral trade agreements. Against this background, on the one hand, one might hope that, in the long run, the CJEU will resolve the numerous doubts about the scope and extent of

[297] *See* § 2.3 of this chapter.
[298] On these agreements *see* footnote 75, § 2 of this chapter.
[299] For further reflections *see* F. Casolari, *The Acknowledgment*, 119–124.
[300] *Ioannis Katsivardas* (n 28), para. 34, and opinion of AG Saggio, *Portugal v Council* (n 28), para. 20.
[301] In such explicit terms, *see* the opinion of AG Colomer of 23 January 2007, *Merck Genéricos*, C-431/05, EU:C:2007:48, para. 79, who noted that the arguments rejecting direct effect of international agreements 'belong rather to the political than the legal sphere.'

external direct effect identified in the sections above in order to enhance legal certainty. On the other hand, the hope is that the EU will fully grasp the potential inherent in such doctrine, following, in this regard, the expansionist approach adopted in its jurisprudence on internal direct effect. This is, however, an unrealistic hope, at least in the short term since it is seems unlikely that the Court will return to a more favourable approach towards external direct effect in the near future. A more modest, yet perhaps realistic, proposal is that the CJEU, instead of interpreting the doctrine of direct effect in an unduly restrictive manner, where it is willing—as is unfortunately often the case—to deny the invocability of EU agreements, and the review of legality that follows from them, when a challenge to an EU act is at stake, should do so without bringing up the doctrine of direct effect. Rather than relying on a contorted interpretation of direct effect that is filled with loopholes, the CJEU should build its reasoning *apertis verbis* on policy considerations related to the principle of EU institutional balance, most notably on the respect for the role of the Commission and the Council in the exercise of EU external action. As a matter of fact, the denial of external direct effect, and the legality review of EU law that goes with it, should always be handled with care, especially when there is a high risk that it could be improperly used to pursue goals that, while being politically legitimate, have little to do with EU law and its proper enforcement.

CONCLUSION

RETHINKING DIRECT EFFECT IN TIMES OF JUDICIAL ARGUMENTATIVE MINIMALISM: A PROPOSAL

Throughout its seven chapters, this volume makes the following ten intertwined arguments.

1) The test on clarity, precision, and unconditionality is no longer a pillar in the conceptualization and practice of direct effect, as can be inferred from the EU case law, where the CJEU applies the three criteria vaguely and in a shifting, evanescent manner, without steady guiding principles. This is testified, first and foremost, by the Court's jurisprudence on fundamental rights since a reference to the conditions of direct effect and/or the test itself is lacking.
2) Clarity and precision are absorbed in the premise of unconditionality, and, for this reason, the latter is the only true core element and *condicio sine qua non* of the test on direct effect. In other words, if a norm is clear/precise, it is not necessarily unconditional, while if a norm is unconditional, it is inevitably clear/precise. If there is no need for the adoption of a further internal legal act to make the EU provision enforceable, then the obligation contained therein, due to its unconditional character, is also *in re ipsa* clear/precise.
3) If unconditionality means that a norm is self-sufficient since it does not require an additional act of transposition, unconditionality equals direct applicability. Moreover, since direct applicability/unconditionality, by absorbing the conditions of clarity and precision, is the only premise of the test on direct effect, direct effect and direct applicability, albeit conceptually distinct, end up being, in practice, the same thing rather than 'simply' closely connected. As a matter of fact, an analysis of EU and national case law shows that direct effect and direct applicability often merge: what really matters is whether an EU provision is justiciable, that is, applicable to the dispute at issue. This implies that, aside from issues of terminology, direct applicability not only is a feature of regulations but also of other EU legal sources, including directives, under the guise of their unconditional character. Indeed, there are no significant differences between the effects of regulations and unimplemented directives when national acts are not needed. Just as the direct effect/applicability of regulations does not *a priori* exclude that some of their provisions should be implemented at the domestic level via further acts, other EU legal sources, both primary and secondary, although not defined as directly applicable by the Treaties or the CJEU, may contain obligations which, being unconditional, in order to be enforced, do not require the adoption of additional measures.
4) Direct effect is a broad notion, not necessarily associated with either the conferral of rights or substitutive effects. Hence, direct effect has two facets: aside from a

Direct Effect in EU Law. Daniele Gallo, Oxford University Press. © Daniele Gallo 2025. DOI: 10.1093/9780191925221.003.0009

subjective substitutive form of direct effect, there exists an objective exclusionary manifestation of direct effect, whereby a directly effective EU provision entails the disapplication of national law, without either conferring immediately an individual right or replacing the domestic norm in governing the case at hand. Insofar as direct effect is intended in broad terms, it coincides with the concept of justiciability. Furthermore, if subjective substitutive direct effect and objective exclusionary direct effect seem to be two theoretical boxes with limited practicability, choosing between broad or narrow direct effect is very important *in concreto* since it affects whether and how individuals are entitled to invoke (and rely on) EU law, and thus to request disapplication. Indeed, advocating for a broad understanding of direct effect has evident practical implications since it expands the scope of intervention of a doctrine of EU law as key as it is direct effect.

5) The duty to disapply is always the result of both primacy *and* direct effect, never primacy alone, otherwise the principle of conferral would be infringed. Direct effect ensures that the EU principle of conferral and the related principle of subsidiarity are not called into question by a generalized, unrestrained use of the principle of primacy. Justifying disapplication on the basis of only the primacy principle is likely to undermine the logic implied in the relationship between the EU legal order and domestic legal systems. It would entail a blank proxy to the EU capable of undermining the fertile relationship between EU law and domestic legal systems, as well as the mutual cooperation between EU institutions and Member States' authorities. Against this background, direct effect continues to be an essential doctrine capable of shaping, in its interaction with primacy, in proto-federalist terms, a legal order that, albeit juridically mature and unique in its kind, is not a federal union. In this sense, direct effect acts as a filter and trigger for ensuring the enforcement of EU law through the remedy of disapplication. Conversely, as recently stated by the CJEU, albeit in quite unclear terms, domestic authorities, on the basis of national, rather than EU, law, have the discretion to set aside pieces of legislation that are in contrast with non-EU directly effective provisions. Such situations can surely occur if there is an antinomy within the domestic legal order and either the judge, or the administration, confronted with conflicting national provisions of equal standing essentially regulating the same issue, decides to set aside a national law not in compliance with EU law and consequently applies another domestic rule which is compatible with EU norms. Moreover, if the antinomy arises between an EU-friendly superior domestic norm, such as a statute passed by the national parliament, and an inferior norm, like a national regulation passed by the executive, which stands in contrast to EU law, the problem is easily solved in terms of hierarchy of norms.
6) A paramount quality of direct effect, along with unconditionality, is the attribution of an advantage resulting from the application of EU law and the subsequent disapplication of national law. Alternatively, lacking such an advantage for any of the private parties involved in the dispute, in order for direct effect to be asserted, the application of EU law should, at least, not worsen, for all said parties, the condition they were in before EU law was enforced. In other words, the disapplication stemming from EU directly effective provisions cannot be detrimental for all private parties to the dispute, that is, only *in malam partem*, with the result that the admissibility, and practice, of inverse vertical direct effect shall be handled with outmost care. The prohibition of inverse vertical direct effect concerns especially directives as well as decisions that are addressed only at States. As for regulations and those decisions

that are not only addressed at States, the enforcement of unconditional provisions enshrined therein should not be subject to the same limitations on inverse vertical direct effect which are viable for the other EU provisions, as they are directly applicable acts of general application published in the *Official Journal* of the EU. Indeed, once enacted, both regulations and decisions immediately replace the conflicting domestic provisions. Hence, they provide natural and legal persons with clear guidance on the rules to comply with: the principles of legal certainty and legitimate expectations are consequently respected. As for EU primary law, instead, in inverse vertical situations direct effect can be asserted and the duty to disapply should occur on the sole condition that the CJEU limits *ratione temporis* the effects of its preliminary ruling rendered under Article 267 TFEU in which it offers an interpretation of EU law that, until that moment, was not foreseeable. This implies that such interpretation neither would have retroactive effects *ex tunc*, nor would it apply *ex nunc* from that very same judgment issued by the Court. In those situations, in fact, the interpretation of EU law should be prospective/*pro futuro*. Therefore, through the principle of primacy, domestic authorities would be obliged to modify the national legal order accordingly and, also through the principle of direct effect, would be required to disapply, for all new cases, the conflicting domestic rule(s). Indeed, the content of the doctrine of direct effect cannot be reconstructed without putting it in context in the light of the consequences stemming from disapplication. In this vein, direct effect is not *ex se* a predetermined and fixed quality of the EU provision. Contextualizing direct effect means thus taking into consideration the implications for the individuals deriving from the enforcement of EU law in the domestic legal system.

7) There are physiological derogations from the obligation to immediately disapply a domestic provision conflicting with EU directly effective provisions in so far as they are admitted by the CJEU; otherwise, they would be considered pathological, that is, in breach of EU law. Legitimate derogations can be advocated first and foremost when the replacement of a national provision by an EU norm harms individual rights and/or questions the national identities clause enshrined in Article 4(2) TEU, as ultimately interpreted by the CJEU.
8) Recognizing directives' horizontal direct effect is a more suitable route than the judiciary-based stratagems designed by the CJEU to bypass its prohibition. The principal, though not only, reason for this recognition is the protection of legitimate expectations. In fact, such principle, in addition to being relevant from the point of view of the person who conducts oneself in accordance with national rules contrary to EU law, is also relevant from the point of view of the person who complies with an EU directive that has not been transposed into national law, notwithstanding the expiration of the transposition deadline (or it has been wrongfully transposed). The paradox resulting from the prohibition of horizontal direct effect of directives is that the party who acts in conformity with a directive is at a disadvantage compared to the party who acts contrary to that directive, but in conformity with national law. This is a paradox that does not occur in the case of inverse vertical direct effect, whose prohibition, with respect to directives, can never be overcome on the grounds that, where this type of relationship is involved, the State relies on EU law and comes into conflict with individual interests so as to take advantage of its wrongdoing and seek the disapplication of its *own* law. Hence, inverse vertical situations are different from horizontal relationships. In the latter two individual countervailing interests are affected, one of which must be sacrificed, and the estoppel doctrine plays no role since

at stake are two private parties confronting each other (rather than the State against an individual or a legal person). To always let the interest of the individual who has acted in accordance with a national provision which conflicts with an a directive prevail is not the best solution. On the contrary, it may well be claimed that the interest of the person invoking a directive, that is, a source superior to domestic law, should normally prevail over the interest of the person invoking a national rule that infringes EU law.

9) The narrow conception of international law's direct effect within the EU legal order advocated by the CJEU, imbued with connotations related to the conferral of rights, is justified mainly in political, not legal, terms. So is the choice to rule out that the *Fediol/Nakajima* doctrines constitute a form of direct effect, albeit being both a means of legality review which have little in common with indirect effect/consistent interpretation. The appreciation of direct effect as a precondition for challenging EU acts is also political. As for the latter issue, more specifically, the CJEU has been increasingly denying the possibility for individuals, companies, and States to challenge EU measures by virtue of international law, so as not to subvert the institutional balance and the separation of powers between the judiciary, on the one hand, and both the legislature and the executive, on the other, in the management of EU external policies. However, this approach builds upon considerations that have little to do with the profound characteristics of direct effect. In any case, the role of the CJEU as gatekeeper for the judicial review of international agreements in the EU legal order is destined to significantly diminish due to the current practice of the EU and its partners—related not only to free trade agreements—to include in the text of the agreements clauses that explicitly preclude their direct effect in the EU, as well as in the legal orders of Member States.

10) Direct effect is a naturally dynamic concept, as are the legal categories of jurisprudential origin, through which ever-developing social phenomena are legally framed. Direct effect has evolved into a broader legal category than it was at the outset of the process of European legal integration. Such a change of perspective should be understood, voiced, and systematized by the CJEU. As a matter of fact, even though—from *Van Gend & Loos* onwards—several constitutive and recurring elements have consolidated over the decades, an *originalist* understanding of the *Van Gend & Loos* doctrine is misleading since it overlooks the transformation that occurred in this domain and gave rise to a constant fulfilment, refinement, and partial reshaping of direct effect. In this context, the jurisprudence of the CJEU does not provide sufficient legal certainty as to the content, scope, limits, and consequences of direct effect. It is often vague, imprecise, unpredictable, too minimalist, and, at times, inconsistent. This form of judicial self-restraint is as problematic as judicial activism. When at issue are fundamental principles from which other principles, rules of reason, and legal taxonomies are derived, judges should use their best efforts to understand legal concepts and establish the relevant/applicable legal framework so as to fill gaps that may arise and avoid the risk of incoherent application of the law. Moreover, argumentative minimalism and lack of clarity, most notably with regard to the constitutional principles of EU law, run the risk of undermining the spirit and purpose of the process of European integration, especially in a time like ours, when new forms of populism, sovereigntism, and anti-Europeanism are on the rise. Indeed, to avoid the departure of national courts from EU constitutional law, as interpreted by the EU judges, and to try to mitigate as much as possible the judicial (confrontational) activism of national

> courts, the CJEU should go back to doing what it boldly did over a long period of time since the sixties and seventies.

In the light of the above, it is vital that the CJEU exercise its interpretive monopoly on the *ifs*, *whens*, and *hows* of direct effect by reasserting its constitutional role in shaping the *primus inter pares* principle *par excellence*: direct effect. The attempts outlined in the seven chapters of this volume aimed precisely at identifying solutions to strengthen the ability of direct effect to pursue its twofold purpose: safeguarding individuals' rights and ensuring the (private) correct enforcement of EU law.

Bibliography

1. Textbooks, monographs, edited volumes, journals special issues, and conference proceedings

Adam, R., Tizzano, A., *Manuale di diritto dell'Unione europea*, 2nd ed., Turin, Giappichelli, 2017

Adam, R., Tizzano, A., *Lineamenti di diritto dell'Unione europea*, 5th ed., Turin, Giappichelli, 2022

Alabrune F. (ed.), *Mélanges en l'honneur de Jean-Pierre Puissochet – L'Etat souverain dans le monde d'aujourd'hui*, Paris, Pedone, 2008

Alberti, J., De Cristofaro, G. (eds.), *Il rinvio pregiudiziale come strumento di sviluppo degli ordinamenti*, Pisa, Pacini, 2023

Alexy, R., *A Theory of Constitutional Rights* (translated by Rivers, J.), Oxford, Oxford University Press, 2002

Alter, K. J., *Establishing the Supremacy of European Law. The Making of an International Rule of Law in Europe*, Oxford, Oxford University Press, 2001

Alter, K. J., *The European Court's Political Power*, Oxford, Oxford University Press, 2009

Amadeo, S., *Norme comunitarie, posizioni giuridiche soggettive e giudizi interni*, Milan, Giuffrè, 2002

Amalfitano, C., Condinanzi, M., *Unione europea: fonti, adattamento e rapporti tra ordinamenti*, Turin, Giappichelli, 2015

Amalfitano, C., (ed.), *Primato del diritto dell'Unione europea e controlimiti alla prova della 'saga Taricco'*, Milan, Giuffrè, 2018

Amalfitano, C., *General Principles of EU Law and the Protection of Fundamental Rights*, Cheltenham, Edward Elgar, 2018

Amalfitano, C., D'Amico, M., Leone, S. (eds.), *La Carta dei diritti fondamentali dell'Unione Europa nel sistema integrato di tutela*, Turin, Giappichelli, 2022

Amato, A., *Disapplicazione giudiziale della legge e Carta di Nizza. Profili costituzionali*, Naples, Editoriale Scientifica, 2021

Ambtenbrink, F., Davies, G., Kochenov, D., Lindeboom, J. (eds.) *The Internal Market and the Future of European Integration. Essays in Honour of Laurence W. Gormley*, Cambridge, Cambridge University Press, 2019

Amrhein Hofmann, C., *Monismus und Dualismus in den Volkerrechtslehren*, Berlin, Duncker & Humblot Gmbh, 2003

Andenas, M. (ed.), *Article 177 References to the European Court—Policy and Practice*, London, Butterworths, 1994

Anderson, D., Demetriou, M., *References to the European Court*, 2nd ed., London, Sweet & Maxwell, 2002

Annoni, A., Forlati, S., Franzina, P. (eds.), *Il diritto internazionale come sistema di valori*, Naples, Jovene, 2021

Anzilotti, D., *Il diritto internazionale nei diritti interni*, Naples, ESI, 1905

Anzilotti, D., *Cours de droit international*, Paris, Sirey, 1929

Arnold, R., Colcelli, V. (eds.), *Europeanization through Private Law Instruments*, Regensburg, Schnell & Steiner, 2015

Arnull, A., *The General Principles of EEC Law and the Individual*, Leicester, Leicester University Press, 1990

Arnull, A., *The European Union and its Court of Justice*, Oxford, Oxford University Press, 1999

Arnull, A., Barnard, C., Dougan, M., Spaventa, E. (eds.), *A Constitutional Order of States—Essays in Honour of Alan Dashwood*, Oxford, Oxford University Press, 2010

Arnull, A., Dashwood, A., Dougan, M., Ross, M., Spaventa, E., Wyatt, D., *Wyatt and Dashwood's European Union Law*, 6th ed., London, Sweet & Maxwell, 2011

Arzoz Santisteban, X., *La garantía constitucional del deber de reenvío prejudicial*, Madrid, Centro de Estudios Políticos y Constitucionales, 2020

Aust, H. P., Nolte, G. (eds.), *The Interpretation of International Law by Domestic Courts: Uniformity, Diversity, Convergence*, Oxford, Oxford University Press, 2016

Avbelj, M., Komárek, J. (eds.), *Constitutional Pluralism in the European Union and Beyond*, Oxford, Hart, 2012

Avbelj, M., Fontanelli, F., Martinico, G. (eds.), Kadi *on Trial: A multifaceted Analysis of the* Kadi *Judgment*, Abindgon, Routledge, 2014

Azoulai, L. (ed.), *The Question of Competence in the European Union*, Oxford, Oxford University Press, 2014

Bailleux, A., Bernard, E., Jacquot, S., Landenne, Q. (eds.), *Les récits judiciaires de l'Europe: Diffusion, réception et coproduction*, Brussels, Bruylant, 2023

Baquero Cruz, J., *Between Competition and Free Movement: The Economic Constitutional Law of the European Community*, Oxford, Oxford University Press, 2002

Barav, A., Vandersanden, G., *Contentieux Communautaire*, Paris, Pedone, 1977

Barav, A., *La fonction communautaire du juge national*, Strasbourg, Université R. Schuman, 1983

Barav, A., Philip, C., Boutayeb, C. (eds.), in *Dictionnaire juridique des Communautés européennes*, Paris, Pedone, 1993

Barav, A., *Études sur le renvoi préjudicial dans le droit de l'Union européenne*, Brussels, Bruylant, 2010

Barbieri, S., *Il rinvio pregiudiziale tra giudici ordinari e Corte costituzionale*, Naples, Jovene, 2023

Barents, R., *The Autonomy of Community Law*, Alphen aan den Rijn, Kluwer Law International, 2004

Barkhuysen, T., Lindenberg, S. (eds.), *Constitutionalisation of Private Law*, The Hague, Martinus Nijhoff, 2006

Barnard, C., Scott, J. (eds.), *The Law of the Single Market—Unpacking the Premises*, Oxford, Oxford University Press, 2002

Barnard, C. (ed.), *The Fundamentals of EU Law Revisited. Assessing the Impact of the Constitutional Debate*, Oxford, Oxford University Press, 2007

Barnard, C., Peers, S. (eds.), *European Union Law*, 3rd ed., Oxford, Oxford University Press, 2020

Barnard, C., *The Substantive Law of the EU. The Four Freedoms*, 7th ed., Oxford, Oxford University Press, 2022

Baroncini, E., Cafaro, S., Criseide, N., *Le relazioni esterne dell'Unione Europea*, Turin, Giappichelli, 2012

Bartoloni, M. E., *Ambito d'Applicazione del Diritto dell'Unione Europea e Ordinamenti Nazionali*, Naples, Editoriale Scientifica, 2018

Bartoloni, M. E., Poli, S. (eds.), *L'azione esterna dell'Unione europea*, Naples, Editoriale Scientifica, 2021

Bast, J., *Grundbegriffe der Handlungsformen der EU: entwickelt am Beschluss als praxisgenerierter Handlungsform des Unions- und Gemeinschaftsrechts*, Heidelberg, Springer, 2006

Bebr, G., *Development of Judicial Control of the European Communities*, The Hague, Martinus Nijhoff, 1981

Beck, G., *The Legal Reasoning of the Court of Justice of the EU*, Oxford, Hart, 2012

Bengoetxea, J., *The Legal Reasoning of the European Court of Justice*, Oxford, Oxford University Press, 1993

Bernardi, A. (ed.), *L'interpretazione conforme al diritto dell'Unione europea*, Naples, Editoriale Scientifica, 2015

Bernardi, A., Cupelli, C. (eds.), *Il caso* Taricco *e il dialogo tra le corti*, Naples, Jovene, 2017

Bernitz, U., Nergelius, J., Cardner, C. (eds.), *General Principles of EC Law in a Process of Development*, Alphen aan de Rijn, Kluwer Law International, 2008

Bernitz, U., Groussot, X., Schulyok, F. (eds.), *General Principles of EU law and European Private Law*, Alphen aan den Rijn, Kluwer Law International, 2013

Bertrand, B., Sirinelli, J., *Droit du contentieux de l'Union européenne*, Paris, LGDJ, 2022

Bettermann, K. A., *Die verfassungskonforme Auslegung*, Heidelberg, C.F. Müller, 1986

Beukers, T. W. B., Van Harten, H. J., Prechal, S. (eds.), *Het recht van de Europese Unie in 50 klassieke arresten*, The Hague, Boom Juridische Uitgevers, 2010

Biavati, P., *Diritto processuale dell'Unione europea*, 5th ed., Milan, Giuffrè, 2015
Bieber, R., Nickel, D. (eds.), *Das Europa der Zweiten Generation: Gedächtnisschrift für Christoph Sasse*, Baden-Baden, Nomos, 1981
Bin, R., *Atti normativi e norme programmatiche*, Milan, Giuffrè, 1988
Biondi, A., Farley, M., *The Right to Damages in European Law*, Austin (Texas), Wolters Kluwer, 2009
Blanquet, M., Isaac, G., *Droit général de l'Union européenne*, 10th ed., Paris, Dalloz, 2012
Blanquet, M., *Droit général de l'Union européenne*, 11th ed., Paris, Sirey, 2018
Bleckmann, A., *Begriff und Kriterien der innerstaatlichen Anwendbarkeit völkerrechtlicher Verträge*, Berlin, Duncker & Humblot, 1970
Blumann, C., Dubouis, L., *Droit institutionnel de l'Union européenne*, 6th ed., Paris, Lexis Nexis, 2016
Bobek, M., Adams-Prassl, J. (eds.), *The EU Charter of Fundamental Rights in the Member States*, Oxford, Hart, 2020
Bobić, A., *The Jurisprudence of Constitutional Conflict in the European Union*, Oxford, Oxford University Press, 2022
Boev, I. (ed.), *La France, l'Europe et le Monde. Mélanges en l'honneur de Jean Charpentier*, Paris, Pedone, 2009
Bolognese, M., *Il giudicato nazionale nel diritto dell'Unione europea e della CEDU*, Naples, Editoriale Scientifica, 2023
Boschiero, N., Scovazzi, T., Pitea, C., Ragni, C. (eds.), *International Courts and the Development of International Law*, The Hague, Martinus Nijhoff, 2013
Bot Y. (ed.), *Mélanges en l'honneur de Philippe Léger. Le droit à la mesure de l'homme*, Paris, Pedone, 2006
Botman, M., Rijpma, J. (eds.), *National Courts and the Enforcement of EU Law: The Pivotal Role of National Courts in the EU Legal Order. The XXIX FIDE Congress Publications*, Vol. 1, The Hague, Eleven International Publishing, 2020
Bougorgue-Larsen, L. (ed.), *La Charte des droits fondamentaux saisie par les juges en Europe*, Paris, Pedone, 2017
Boulouis, J., *Le droit des Communautés européennes dans ses rapports avec le droit international général*, in *Recueil des cours*, vol. 235, 1992, 13–79
Bourgeois, J. H. J., Dewost, J.-L., Gaiffe, M. A. (eds.), *La Communauté et les accords mixtes: Quelles perspectives?*, Brussels, Presses interuniversitaires européennes, 1997
Bradley, C. A. (ed.), *The Oxford Handbook of Comparative Foreign Relations Law*, Oxford, Oxford University Press, 2019
Braibant, G., *La Charte des droits fondamentaux de l'Union européenne*, Paris, Éditions du Seuil, 2001
Brealey, M., Hoskins, M., *Remedies in EC Law*, 2nd ed., London, Sweet & Maxwell, 1998
Broberg, M., Fenger, N., *Preliminary References to the European Court of Justice*, 3rd ed., Oxford, Oxford University Press, 2021
Brownlie, I., *Principles of public international law*, 9th ed., Oxford, Oxford University Press, 2019
Buchs, G., *Die unmittelbare Anwendbarkeit völkerrechtlicher Vertragsbestimmungen am Beispiel der Rechtsprechung der Gerichte Deutschlands, Österreichs, der Schweiz und der Vereinigten Staaten von Amerika*, Baden-Baden, Nomos, 1993
Buendia Sierra, J. L., *Exclusive Rights and State Monopolies under EC law: Article 86 (Formerly Article 90) of the EC Treaty*, Oxford, Oxford University Press, 1999
Buergenthal, T., *Self-Executing and Non-Self-Executing Treaties in National and International Law*, in *Recueil des Cours*, vol. 235, 1992, 303–400
Butler, G., Wessel, R. A. (eds.), *EU External Relations Law: The Cases in Context*, Oxford, Hart, 2022
Cafaggi, F., Muir Watt, H. (eds.), *The Regulatory Functions of European Private Law*, Cheltenham, Edward Elgar, 2007
Caiger, A., Floudas, D. A. (eds.), *1996 Onwards: Lowering the Barriers Further*, Chichester, Chancery Law, 1996
Calliess, C., Van Der Schyff, G. (eds.), *Constitutional Identity in a Europe of Multilevel Constitutionalism*, Cambridge, Cambridge University Press, 2019
Campbell, A. I. K., Voyatzi, M. (eds.), *Essays in the Honour of Lord Mackenzie-Stuart*, Trenton, New Jersey, 1996

Cannizzaro, E., *Il diritto dell'integrazione europea*, 4th ed., Turin, Giappichelli, 2022
Cannizzaro, E., Palchetti, P., Wessel, R. A. (eds.), *International Law as Law of the European Union*, The Hague, Martinus Nijhoff, 2012
Capelli, F., *Le direttive comunitarie*, Milan, Giuffrè, 1983
Capotorti, F., Ehlermann, C., Frowein, J.-A. (eds.), *Du droit international au droit de l'intégration.* Liber amicorum *Pierre Pescatore*, Baden-Baden, Nomos, 1987
Cappelletti, M., Seccombe, M., Weiler, J. H. H. (eds.), *Integration through Law: Europe and the American Federal Experience*, Berlin-New York, New York: Walter de Gruyter and Co., 1986, I
Carbone, S. M., *Organi comunitari, controllo di legittimità e soggetti privati*, Padua, Cedam, 1973
Carbone, S. M., *Principio di effettività e diritto comunitario*, Naples, Editoriale Scientifica, 2010
Cardonnel, P., Rosas, A., Wahl, N. (eds.), *Constitutionalising the EU Judicial System-Essays in Honour of Pernilla Lindh*, Oxford, Oxford University Press, 2012
Cartabia, M., *Principi inviolabili e integrazione europea*, Milan, Giuffrè, 1995
Cartabia, M., Lupo, N., *The Constitution of Italy: A Contextual Analysis*, Oxford, Hart, 2022
Caruso, F., Medico, F., Morrone, A. (eds.), *Granital* Revisited?, Bologna, Bononia University Press, 2020
Casarosa, F., Moraru, M. (eds.), *The Practice of Judicial Interaction in the Field of Fundamental Rights: The Added Value of the Charter of Fundamental Rights of the EU*, Cheltenham, Edward Elgar, 2022
Casolari, F., *L'incorporazione del diritto internazionale nell'ordinamento dell'Unione Europea*, Milan, Giuffrè, 2008
Cassese, S., *Oltre lo Stato*, Rome-Bari, Laterza, 2006
Cassese, S. (ed.), *Dizionario di diritto pubblico*, vol. III, Milan, Giuffrè, 2006
Catalano, N., *La Comunità economica europea e l'EURATOM*, Milano, 1959
Catalano, N., *Manuel de droit des Communautés européennes*, Brussels, Bruylant, 2024
Chalmers, D., Arnull, A. (eds.), *Oxford Handbook of European Union Law*, Oxford, Oxford University Press, 2015
Chalmers, D., Davies, G., Monti, G., *European Union Law. Cases and Materials*, 4th ed., Cambridge, Cambridge University Press, 2019
Chamon, M., Govaere, I. (eds.), *EU External Relations Post-Lisbon: The Law and Practice of Facultative Mixity*, Leiden, Martinus Nijhoff, 2020
Charlesworth, H., *The Fluid State: International Law and National Legal Systems*, Sydney, Federation Press, 2005
Chiocchetti, P., Allemand, F. (eds.), *Competitiveness and Solidarity in the European Union. Interdisciplinary Perspectives*, Abingdon, Routledge, 2019
Christianos, V. (ed.), *Evolution récente du droit judiciaire communautaire*, European Institute of Public Administration, Maastricht, Vol. I, 1994
Cimiotta, E., *L'ambito soggettivo di efficacia delle sentenze pregiudiziali della Corte di giustizia dell'Unione europea. L'efficacia nei confronti dei giudici diversi dal giudice del rinvio*, Turin, Giappichelli, 2023
Circolo, A., *Il valore dello stato di diritto nell'Unione europea*, Naples, Editoriale Scientifica, 2023
Claes, M., *The National Courts' Mandate in the European Constitution*, Oxford, Hart, 2006
Claes, M., De Visser, M., Popelier, P., Van de Heyning, C. (eds.), *Constitutional Conversations in Europe: Actors, Topics, and Procedures*, Cambridge-Oxford, Intersentia-Hart, 2012
Claes, M., Vos, E. (eds.), *Making sense of European Union law*, Oxford, Hart, 2022
Clapham, A., *Human Rights in the Private Sphere*, 2nd ed., Oxford, Oxford University Press, 1996
Clapham, A., *The Human Rights Obligations of Non-State Actors*, Oxford, Oxford University Press, 2006
Clément-Wilz, L. (ed.), *Le rôle politique de la Cour de justice de l'Union européenne*, Brussels, Bruylant, 2018
Cohen Jonathan, G., Constantinesco, V., Michel, V. (eds.), *Chemins d'Europe—Mélanges en l'honneur de Jean Paul Jacqué*, Paris, Pedone, 2010
Colneric, N., Edward, D., Puissochet, J.-P., Colomer, D. R. (eds.), *Une communauté de droit—Festschrift für G.C. Rodríguez Iglesias*, Berlin, Berliner Wissenschafts-Verlag, 2003
Condinanzi, M., Mastroianni, R., *Il contenzioso dell'Unione europea*, Turin, Giappichelli, 2009

Conforti, B., *International Law and the Role of Domestic Legal Systems*, The Hague, Martinus Nijhoff, 1993

Constantinesco, L.-J., *Actes officiels du Congrès international d'études sur la Communauté européenne du charbon et de l'acier*, II, Milan, Giuffrè, 1958

Constantinesco, L.-J., *Traité de droit comparé*, I, Paris, LGDJ, 1972

Constantinesco, L.-J., *L'applicabilité directe dans le droit de la CEE*, Brussels, Bruylant, 2006

Correra, A., *Natura ed effetti delle sentenze pregiudiziali della Corte di giustizia*, Naples, Editoriale Scientifica, 2023

Costa, O., Magnette, P. (eds.), *Une Europe des élites? Réflexions sur la fracture démocratique de l'Union européenne*, Brussels, Bruylant, 2007

Costamagna, F., *Diritti fondamentali e rapporti tra privati nell'ordinamento dell'Unione europea*, Turin, Giappichelli, 2022

Cottier, T., Nadakavukaren Schefer, K. (eds.), *Elgar Encyclopedia of International Economic Law*, Cheltenham, Edward Elgar, 2017

Cozzi, A.-O., *Diritti e principi sociali nella Carta dei diritti fondamentali dell'Unione Europea—Profili costituzionali*, Naples, Jovene, 2017

Craig, P., *The Lisbon Treaty: Law, Politics, and Treaty Reforms*, Oxford, Oxford University Press, 2010

Craig, P., *EU Administrative Law*, 3rd ed., Oxford, Oxford University Press, 2018

Craig, P., De Búrca, G., *EU Law. Text, Cases, and Materials*, 7th ed., Oxford, Oxford University Press, 2020

Craig, P., De Búrca, G. (eds.), *The Evolution of EU Law*, 3rd ed., Oxford, Oxford University Press, 2021

Craig, P., Schütze, R. (eds.), *Landmark Cases in EU Law*, Oxford, Hart, 2025, forthcoming

Cremona, M. (ed.), *Developments in EU External Relations Law*, Oxford, Oxford University Press, 2008

Cremona, M. (ed.), *Structural Principles in EU External Relations Law*, Oxford, Hart, 2018

Cremona, M., De Witte, B. (eds.), *EU Foreign Relations Law: Constitutional Fundamentals*, Leiden, Kluwer, 2008

Cremona, M., Thies, A., *The European Court of Justice and External Relations Law: Constitutional Challenges*, Oxford, Hart, 2014

Crisafulli, V., *La Costituzione e le sue disposizioni di principio*, Milan, Giuffrè, 1952

Crouch, C., *Capitalist Diversity and Change: Recombinant Governance and Institutional Entrepreneurs*, Oxford, Oxford University Press, 2005

Curtin, D., Heukels, T. (eds.), *Institutional Dynamics of European Integration. Essays in Honour of Henry G. Schermers*, The Hague, Martinus Nijhoff, 1994

D'Agnone, G., *L'interpretazione soggettiva nella giurisprudenza della Corte di giustizia dell'Unione europea*, Turin, Giappichelli, 2020

D'Alessandro, E., *Il procedimento pregiudiziale interpretativo dinanzi alla Corte di giustizia: oggetto ed efficacia della pronuncia*, Turin, Giappichelli, 2012

D'Alessio, M. T., Placco, V., Kronenberger, V. (eds.), *De Rome à Lisbonne: les juridictions de l'Union européenne à la croisée des chemins. Mélanges en l'honneur de Paolo Mengozzi*, Brussels, Bruylant, 2013

D'Andrea, L., Moschella, G., Ruggeri, A., Saitta, A. (eds.), *La Carta dei diritti dell'Unione europea e le altre Carte (ascendenze culturali e mutue implicazioni)*, Turin, Giappichelli, 2016

Daniele, L., *Diritto dell'Unione europe*, 8th ed., Milan, Giuffrè, 2022

Dashwood, A., Maresceau M. (eds.), *Law and Practice of EU External Relations*, Cambridge, Cambridge University Press, 2008

Dauser, M., *Das Vorabentscheidungsverfahren nach Artikel 177 EG-Vertrag*, Munich, C. H. Beck, 1995

Dawson, M., De Witte, B., Muir, E. (eds.), *Judicial Activism at the European Court of Justice*, Cheltenham, Edward Elgar, 2015

De Búrca, G., Scott, J. (eds.), *The EU and the WTO: Legal and Constitutional Aspects*, Oxford, Hart, 2001

De Búrca, G. (ed.), *EU Law and the Welfare State: In Search of Solidarity*, Oxford, Oxford University Press, 2005

De Visser, M., *Constitutional Review in Europe. A Comparative Analysis*, Oxford, Hart, 2014.

De Walsche, A., Lévy, A. (eds.), *Promenades au sein du droit européen. Mélanges en hommage à Georges Vandersanden*, Brussels, Bruylant, 2008

De Witte, B., Mayoral, J. A., Jaremba, U., Wind, M., Podstawa, K. (eds.), *National Courts and EU Law: New Issues, Theories and Methods*, Cheltenham, Edward Elgar, 2016

De Zwaan, J., Nelissen, F. A., Jans, J. H., Blockmans, S. (eds.), *The European Union: An Ongoing Process of Integration*, The Hague, TMC Asser Press, 2004

Degan, V. D., *L'interprétation des accords en droit international*, The Hague, Martinus Nijhoff, 1963

Delledonne, G., *L'omogeneità costituzionale degli ordinamenti composti*, Naples, Editoriale Scientifica, 2017

Di Federico, G., *L'identità nazionale degli Stati membri nel diritto dell'Unione europea. Natura e portata dell'art. 4, par. 2, TUE*, Naples, Editoriale Scientifica, 2017

Di Federico, G. (ed.), *Ordinamento giudiziario. Uffici giudiziari, CSM e governo della magistratura*, Bologna, Bononia University Press, 2019

Di Federico, G., Odone, C. (ed.), *Il recepimento delle direttive dell'Unione europea nella prospettiva delle regioni italiane. Modelli e soluzioni*, Naples, Editoriale Scientifica, 2010

Dickson, J., Eleftheriadis, P. (eds.), *Philosophical Foundations of European Union Law*, Oxford, Oxford University Press, 2012

Dolmans, M. J. F. M., *Problems of Mixed Agreements*, The Hague, TMC Asser Press, 1985

Dordi, C. (ed.), *The Absence of Direct Effect of WTO in the EC and in Other Countries*, Turin, Giappichelli, 2010

Dougan, M., *National Remedies before the Court of Justice: Issues of Harmonisation and Differentiation*, Oxford, Oxford University Press, 2004

Drinóczi, T., Bień-Kacała, A., *Rule of Law, Common Values, and Illiberal Constitutionalism: Poland and Hungary within the European Union*, Abingdon, Routledge, 2020

Dubout, E., *Droit constitutionnel de l'Union européenne*, 2nd ed., Brussels, Bruylant, 2021

Edward, D., Lane, R., *Edward and Lane on European Union Law*, Cheltenham, Edward Elgar, 2014

Eeckhout, P., *EU External Relations Law*, 2nd ed., Oxford, Oxford University Press, 2012

Eeckhout, P., López Escudero, M. (eds.), *The European Union's External Action in Times of Crisis*, Oxford, Hart, 2019

Ehmke, H., Kaiser, J. H., Kewenig, W. A., Meessen, K. M., Rüfner, W. (eds.), *Festschrift für Ulrich Scheuner zum 70. Geburtstag*, Berlin, Duncker & Humblot, 1973

Eisemann, P. M. (ed.), *The Integration of International and European Community Law into the National Legal Order*, The Hague, Kluwer, 1996

Ellingsen, H. K., *Standing to Enforce European Union Law before National Courts*, Oxford, Hart, 2021

Emiliou, N., *The Principle of Proportionality in European Law: A Comparative Study*, Alphen aan de Rijn, Kluwer Law International, 1996

Faraguna, P., *Ai confini della Costituzione. Principi supremi e identità costituzionale*, Milan, Franco Angeli, 2015

Faraguna, P., Fasone, C., Piccirilli, G. (eds.), *Constitutional Adjudication in Europe between Unity and Pluralism*, Special Issue (2018) 10 *Italian Journal of Public Law*

Favilli, C., *La non discriminazione nell'Unione europea*, Bologna, Il Mulino, 2008

Ferrajoli, L., *Diritti fondamentali. Un dibattito teorico*, Rome-Bari, Laterza, 2001

Ferraro, F., *La responsabilità risarcitoria degli Stati per violazione del diritto dell'Unione*, Milan, Giuffrè, 2008

Ferraro, F., Iannone, C. (eds.), *Il rinvio pregiudiziale*, Turin, Giappichelli, 2020

Fitzmaurice, M., Flinterman, C. (eds.), *Interactions between International and Municipal Law: A Comparative Case Law Study*, The Hague, TMC Asser Instituut, 1993

Focarelli, C., *Introduzione storica al diritto internazionale*, Milan, Giuffrè, 2021

Frantziou, E., *The Horizontal Effect of Fundamental Rights in the European Union*, Oxford, Oxford University Press, 2019

Franzen, M., Gallner, I., Oetker, H. (eds.), *Kommentar zum europäischen Arbeitsrecht*, 4th ed., Munich, Beck, 2024

Fredman, S., *Human Rights Transformed. Positive Rights and Positive Duties*, Oxford, Oxford University Press, 2008

Freedland, M., Auby, J.-B. (eds.), *The Public Law/Private Law Divide: une entente assez cordiale?*, Oxford, Oxford University Press, 2006

Freedland, M., Prassl, J. (eds.), Viking, Laval *and Beyond*, Oxford, Oxford University Press, 2014

Friedmann, D., Barak-Erez, D. (eds.), *Human Rights in Private Law*, Oxford, Hart, 2001

Fritz, V., *Juges et avocats généraux de la Cour de Justice de l'Union européenne (1952-1972: une approche biographique de l'histoire d'une révolution juridique*, Frankfurt, Klostermann, 2018

Galetta, D. U., *Procedural Autonomy of EU Member States: Paradise Lost? A Study on the 'Functionalized Procedural Competence' of EU Member States*, Heidelberg, Springer, 2009

Gallo, D., *I servizi di interesse economico generale. Stato, Mercato e Welfare nel diritto dell'Unione europea*, Milan, Giuffrè, 2010

Gallo, D., *L'efficacia diretta del diritto dell'Unione europea negli ordinamenti nazionali. Evoluzione di una dottrina ancora controversa*, Milan, Giuffrè, 2018

Gallo, D., *Public Services and EU Competition Law. Social Market Economy in Action*, Abingdon, Routledge, 2021

Gallo, D., Piccirilli, G. (eds.), *Dual Preliminarity through National, EU and Comparative Case Law*, Special Issue (2023) 15 *Italian Journal of Public Law*

Gallo, D., Cecchetti L. (eds.), *The Preliminary Ruling Procedure, Today: Revisiting Article 267 TFEU's Constitutional Backbone*, Special Issue (2023) 15 *European Journal of Legal Studies*

Gallo, D., Mastroianni, R., Nicola, F., Cecchetti, L. (eds.), *The Italian Influence on European Law: Judges and Advocates General* (1952–2000), Oxford, Hart, forthcoming

Ganhof van der Meersch, W., *L'ordre juridique des Communautés européennes et le droit international*, Alphen aan den Rijn, Sijthoff & Noordhoff, 1979

Gárdos-Orosz, F., Zakariás, K. (eds.), *The Main Lines of the Jurisprudence of the Hungarian Constitutional Court*, Baden-Baden, Nomos, 2022

Giliker, P. (ed.), *Research Handbook on EU Tort Law*, Cheltenham, Edward Elgar, 2017

Goldstein, L. F., *Constituting Federal Sovereignty: The European Union in Comparative Context*, Baltimore, The Johns Hopkins University Press, 2001

Gordon, M. (ed.), *A Companion to International History 1900 - 2001. Blackwell companions to history*, Oxford, Blackwell, 2007

Gordon, R., Moffatt, R., *EU Law in Judicial Review*, 2nd ed., Oxford, Oxford University Press, 2014

Govaere, I., Quick, R., Bronckers, M. (eds.), *Trade and Competition Law in the EU and Beyond*, Cheltenham, Edward Elgar, 2011

Govaere, I., Lannon, E., Van Elsuwege, P., Adam, S. (eds.), *The European Union in the World. Essays in Honour of Marc Maresceau*, The Hague, Martinus Nijhoff, 2013

Govaere, I., Garben, S. (eds.), *The Interface between EU and International Law: Contemporary Reflections*, Chicago, Hart, 2019

Gragl, P., *Legal Monism: Law, Philosophy, and Politics*, Oxford, Oxford University Press, 2018

Graham, C., Prosser, T., *Privatising Public Enterprises—Constitutions, the State and Regulation in Comparative Perspective*, Oxford, Oxford University Press, 1991

Grande, E., Pauly, L. W. (eds.), *Complex Sovereignty: Reconstituting Political Authority in the Twenty-first*, Toronto, University of Toronto Press, 2005

Graziadei, M., Iannone, C., Nascimbene, B., Salvato, L., Vincenti, E. (eds.), *Il diritto europeo e il giudice nazionale*, Rome, SSM, 2023

Grossi, P., *A History of European law*, New York, John Wiley & Sons, 2010

Groussot, X., *General Principles of Community Law*, Groningen, Europa Law Publishing, 2006

Guastaferro, B., *Legalità sovranazionale e legalità costituzionale. Tensioni costitutive e giunture ordinamentali*, Turin, Giappichelli, 2013

Hailbronner, K., Resse, G., Stein, T. (eds.), *Staat und Völkerrechtsordnung. Festschrift für Karl Doehring*, Berlin, Springer, 1989

Hall, R. B., Biersteker, T. J. (eds.), *The Emergence of Private Authority in Global Governance*, Cambridge, Cambridge University Press, 2002

Hallstein, W., *Communautés Européennes*, Luxembourg, 1964

Hallstein, W., Schlochauer, H. J. (eds.), *Zur Integration Europas. Festschrift für Carl Friedrich Ophüls aus Anlass seines siebzigsten Geburtstages*, Karlsruhe, Verlag CF Müller, 1965

Haltern, U., Weiler, J. H. H. (eds.), *Europe. The New Legal Realism*, Copenhagen, Djøf Forlag, 2010
Hamilton, A.; Madison, J.; Jay, J., *The Federalist*, 1787/1788, 187
Hancké, B., Rhodes, M., Thatcher, M. (eds.), *Beyond Varieties of Capitalism: Conflict, Contradictions and Complementaries in the European Economy* , Oxford, Oxford University Press, 2007
Harlow, C., Leino, P., della Cananea, G. (eds.), *Research Handbook of EU Administrative Law*, Cheltenham, Edward Elgar, 2017
Hartkamp, A., Sieburgh, C. H., Keus, L. A. D., Kortmann, J. S., Wissink, M. H. (eds.), *The Influence of EU Law on National Private Law*, Deventer, Kluwer, 2013
Hartkamp, A., *European Law and National Private Law*, Oxford, Intersentia, 2016
Hartley, T., *The Foundations of European Union Law*, 7th ed., Oxford, Oxford University Press, 2010
Hay, P., *Federalism and Supranational Organizations*, Urbana, University of Illinois Press, 1966
Heliskoski, J., *Mixed Agreements as a Technique for Organizing the International Relations of the European Community and its Member States*, The Hague, Kluwer, 2001
Hervey, T., Kenner, J. (eds.), *Economic and Social Rights under the EU Charter of Fundamental Rights. A Legal Perspective*, Oxford, Hart, 2003
Herzog, T., *A Short History of European Law: the Last Two and a Half Millennia*, Cambridge (Mass.), Harvard University Press, 2018
Higgins, R., *Problems & Process: International Law and How We Use It*, Oxford, Clarendon Press, 1995
Hillion, C., Koutrakos, P. (eds.), *Mixed Agreements Revisited*, Oxford, Hart, 2010
Hoffmann-Riem, W., Schmidt-Aßman, E. (eds.), *Öffentliches Recht und Privatrecht als wechselseitige Auffangordnungen*, Baden-Baden, Nomos, 1996
Hofstötter, B., *Non-Compliance of National Courts: Remedies in European Community Law and Beyond*, The Hague, TM.C. Asser Press, 2005
Holdgaard, R., *External Relations Law of the European Community. Legal Reasoning and Legal Discourses*, The Hague, Kluwer, 2008
Hollis, D. B., Blakeslee, M. R., Ederington, L. B. (eds.), *National Treaty Law and Practice*, Leiden, Martinus Nijhoff, 2005
Holzer, P. E., *Die Ermittlung der innerstaatlichen Anwendbarkeit völkerrechtlicher Vertragsbestimmungen*, Zurich, Schulthess, 1999
Hoskins, M., Robinson, W. (eds.), *A True European. Essays for Judge David Edward*, Oxford, Oxford University Press, 2004
Iannone, C., Ferraro, F. (eds.), *Il rinvio pregiudiziale*, Turin, Giappichelli, 2020
Irti, N., *L'ordine giuridico del mercato*, Rome-Bari, Laterza, 2001
Isaac, G., *Droit communautaire général*, 3rd ed., Paris, Dalloz, 1990
Isaac, G., *L'effet direct du droit Communautaire*, Répertoire européen Dalloz, 1997, 1
Jacobs, F. G., Roberts, S. (eds.), *The Effect of Treaties in Domestic Law*, London, Sweet & Maxwell, 1987
Jacot-Guillamord, O., *Droit communtaituaire et droit international public*, Geneva, *Librairie de l'université Georg*, 1979
Jakab, A., Kochenov, D., *The Enforcement of EU Law and Values: Ensuring Member States' Compliance* , Oxford, Oxford University Press, 2017
Jans, J. H., Prechal, S., Widdershoven, R. J. G. M. (eds.), *Europeanisation of Public Law*, 2nd ed., Groningen, Europa Law Publishing, 2015
Jareborg, N. (ed.), *Towards Universal Law—Trends in National, European and International Lawmaking*, Iustus Forlag, 1995
Keeling, D. T., *Intellectual Property Rights in EU Law. Volume I—Free Movement and Competition Law*, Oxford, Oxford University Press, 2004
Keller, H., *Rezeption des Völkerrechts*, Berlin, Springer, 2003
Kellerbauer, M., Klamert, M., Tomkin, J. (eds.), *The EU Treaties and the Charter of Fundamental Rights. A Commentary*, Oxford, Oxford University Press, 2019
Kelsen, H., *Les rapports de système entre le droit interne et le droit international public*, in *Recueil des Cours*, vol. 14, 1926, 226–331
Kilpatrick, C., Novitz, T., Skidmore, P. (eds.), *The Future of Remedies in Europe*, Oxford, Oxford University Press, 2000
Kilpatrick, C., Scott, J. (eds.), *New Legal Approaches to Studying the Court of Justice*, Oxford, Oxford University Press, 2020

Kjeldgaard-Pedersen, A., *The International Legal Personality of the Individual*, Oxford, Oxford University Press, 2018

Koller, A., *Die unmittelbare Anwendbarkeit völkerrechtlicher Verträge und des EWG-Vertrages im innerstaatlichen Bereich*, Bern, Stämpfli, 1971

Koskenniemi, M. (ed.), *International Law Aspects of the European Union*, The Hague, Kluwer, 1998

Koutrakos, P., *EU International Relations Law*, 2nd ed., Oxford, Hart, 2015

Koutrakos, P., Snell, J. (eds.), *Research Handbook on the Law of the EU's Internal Market*, Cheltenham, Edward Elgar, 2017

Kovács, C., *Die temporale Wirkung von Urteilen des EuGH im Vorabentscheidungsverfahren*, Baden-Baden, Nomos, 2015

Kovar, R., *La contribution de la Cour de justice à l'édification de l'ordre juridique communautaire. Cours général de droit communautaire*, in *Recueil des cours de l'Académie de droit européen*, The Hague, Martinus Nijhoff, 1995, 15–122

Kovar, R., *Itinéraire d'un juriste européen*, Brussels, Bruylant, 2010

Krisch, N., *Beyond Constitutionalism: The Pluralist Structure of Postnational Law*, Oxford, Oxford University Press, 2013

Kroemer, L. C., *Drittwirkung der Grundrechte: Die Unterscheidung zwischen Staat und Gesellschaft als staatstheoretische Bedingung der Drittwirkungsproblematik*, Tübingen, Mohr Siebeck, 2024

Krommendijk, J., *National Courts and Preliminary References to the Court of Justice*, Elgar, Cheltenham, 2021

Lacchi, C., *Preliminary References to the Court of Justice of the European Union and Effective Judicial Protection*, Brussels, Larcier, 2020

Lasser, M., *Judicial Deliberations: A Comparative Analysis of Judicial Transparency and Legitimacy*, 2nd ed., Oxford, Oxford University Press, 2009

Lattanzi, S., *I 'travaux préparatoires' del diritto dell'Unione Europea: tassonomia, ruolo e funzioni*, Padua, Cedam, 2022

Lauterpacht, H., *The Development of International Law by the International Court*, London, Stevens, 1958

Lazowski, A., Blockmans, S. (eds.), *Research Handbook in EU Institutional Law*, Cheltenham, Edward Elgar, 2016

Lazzerini, N., *La Carta dei diritti fondamentali dell'Unione europea. I limiti di applicazione*, Milan, Franco Angeli, 2018

Leanza, U., Tizzano, A., Vassalli di Dachenhausen, T., Mastroianni, R., De Pasquale, P., Ciccone, R. (Organising Committee), *Scritti in onore di Giuseppe Tesauro*, Naples, Editoriale Scientifica, 2014

Lecourt, R., *L'Europe des juges*, Brussels, Bruylant, 1976

Lenaerts, K., *Le juge et la Constitution aux États-Unis d'Amérique et dans l'ordre juridique européen*, Brussels, Bruylant, 1988

Lenaerts, K., Gutiérrez-Fons, J. A., *Les méthodes d'interprétation de la Cour de justice de l'Union européenne*, Brussels, Bruylant, 2020

Lenaerts, K., Van Nuffel, P., Corthaut, T., *EU Constitutional Law*, Oxford, Oxford University Press, 2021

Lenaerts, K., *Constitutional Relationships between Legal Orders and Courts within the European Union*, speech delivered at the Annual XXIX FIDE Congress, 4 November 2021, available at //efaidnbmnnnibpcajpcglclefindmkaj/https://forumfws.eu/fide-opening-ceremony-koen-lenaerts-04112021-1-.pdf

Lenaerts, K., Gutman, K., Nowak, J. T., *EU Procedural Law*, 2nd ed., Oxford, Oxford University Press, 2023

Levrat, N., Kaspiarovich, Y., Kaddous, C., Wessel, R. A. (eds.), *The EU and its Member States' Joint Participation in International Agreements*, Oxford, Hart, 2022

Leyland, P., Woods, T. (eds.), *Administrative Law Facing the Future: Old Constraints and New Horizons*, London, Blackstone, 1997

Lindeboom, J., Wessel R. A. (eds.), *The Autonomy of EU Law, Legal Theory and European Integration*, Special Issue (2023) 8 *European Papers* 1247

Lonbay, J., Biondi, A. (eds.), *Remedies for Breach of EC Law*, London, Wiley, 1997

Louis, J.-V., *Le droit de la CEE*, vol. 10 (*La Cour de Justice, Les actes des institutions*), 2nd ed., Brussels, Bruylant, 1993

Ludlow, N. P., *The European Community and the crises of the 1960s: negotiating the Gaullist challenge*, London, Routledge, 2006

Lusa Bordin, F., Müller, A. T., Pascual-Vives, F. (eds.), *The European Union and Customary International Law*, Cambridge, Cambridge University Press, 2022

Luzzatto, R., *La diretta applicabilità del diritto comunitario*, Milan, Giuffrè, 1983

MacCormick, N., Summers, R. S. (eds.), *Interpreting Precedents—A Comparative Study*, London, Routledge, 1997

Mancaleoni, A. M., Poillot, E. (eds.), *National Judges and the Case Law of the Court of Justice of the European Union*, Rome, Roma Tre Press, 2021

Mancini, F., *Democracy and Constitutionalism in the EU*, Oxford, Oxford University Press, 2000

Mangenot, M. (ed.), *Un légiste de Vichy à la Communauté européenne. Maurice Lagrange: une biographie professionnelle*, dossier, Civitas Europa n. 50, 2023, 101–120

Martucci, F., *Droit de l'Union européenne*, 3rd ed., Paris, Dalloz, 2021

Mason, H. L., *The European Coal and Steel Community: Experiment in Supranationalism*, The Hague, Martinus Nijhoff, 1955

Mastroianni, R., Pollicino, O., Allegrezza, S., Pappalardo, F., Razzolini, O. (eds.), *Carta dei diritti fondamentali dell'Unione europea*, Milan, Giuffrè, 2017

Mastroianni, R., Strozzi, G., *Diritto dell'Unione europea: Parte istituzionale*, 8th ed., Turin, Giappichelli, 2019

May, C., Winchester, A. (eds.), *Handbook on the Rule of Law*, Cheltenham, Edward Elgar, 2018

Medico, F., *Il doppio custode. Un modello per la giustizia costituzionale europea*, Bologna, Bologna University Press, 2023

Mégret, J., Louis, J. V., Vignes, D., Waelbroeck, W. (eds.), *Commentaire Mégret. Le droit de la Communauté économique européenne*, 2nd ed., vol. X, Brussels, Bruylant, 1993

Mendez, M., *The Legal Effects of EU Agreements*, Oxford, Oxford University Press, 2013

Mestre, C. (ed.), *Europe(s), droit(s) européen(s), Une passion d'universitaire*, Brussels, Bruylant, 2015

Meyer, J. (ed.), *Charta der Grundrechte der Europäischen Union*, 4th ed., Baden-Baden, Nomos, 2014

Micklitz, H.-W., De Witte, B. (eds.), *The European Court of Justice and the Autonomy of the Member States*, Oxford, Intersentia, 2012

Millet, F.-X., *L'Union européenne et l'identité constitutionnelle des Etats membres*, Paris, LGDJ, 2013

Millet, F.-X. (ed.), *Le constitutionnalisme numérique*, Brussels, Bruylant, forthcoming, 2025

Moavero Milanesi, E., Piccirilli, G. (eds.), *Attuare il diritto dell'Unione europea in Italia. Un bilancio a 5 anni dall'entrata in vigore della legge n. 234 del 2012*, Bari, Cacucci, 2018

Monaco, R., *Primi lineamenti di diritto pubblico europeo*, Milan, Giuffrè, 1962

Mosler, H., *L'application du droit international public par les tribunaux nationaux*, in *Recueil des Cours*, vol. 91, 1957, 619–709

Naomé, C., *Le renvoi préjudiciel en droit de l'Union*, 2nd ed., Brussels, Bruylant, 2010

Napolitano, G., *Pubblico e privato nel diritto amministrativo*, Milan, Giuffrè, 2003

Navarretta, E., Costituzione, *Europa e diritto privato. Effettività e Drittwirkung ripensando la complessità giuridica*, Turin, Giappichelli, 2017

Neframi, E., *Les accords mixtes de la Communauté européenne: aspects communautaires et internationaux*, Brussels, Bruylant, 2007

Neframi, E. (ed.), *Renvoi préjudiciel et marge d'appréciation du juge national*, Brussels, Bruylant, 2015

Neframi, E., Gatti, M. (eds.), *Constitutional Issues of EU External Relations Law*, Baden-Baden, Nomos, 2018

Negri, A., Ragone, G., Toscano, M., Vanoni, L. P. (eds.), *I simboli religiosi nella società contemporanea*, Turin, Giappichelli, 2022

Neville Brown, L., Jacobs, F. G., *The Court of Justice of the European Communities*, London, Sweet & Maxwell, 1977

Newhouse, J., *30 juin 1965: crise à Bruxelles*, Paris, Dalloz, 1969

Nicola, F., Davies, B. (eds.), *EU Law Stories. Contextual and Critical Histories of European Jurisprudence*, Cambridge, Cambridge University Press, 2017

Nijman, J., Nollkaemper, A. (eds.), *New Perspectives on the Divide between International and National Law*, Oxford, Oxford University Press, 2007

Nikoilaidis, K., Howse, R. (eds.), *The Federal Vision: Legitimacy and Levels of Governance in the United States and the European Union*, Oxford, Oxford University Press, 2002

Nipperdey, H. C., *Festschrift für Erich Molitor*, Munich, Beck, 1962

Nollkaemper, A., *National Courts and the International Rule of Law*, Oxford, Oxford University Press, 2011

Nollkaemper, A., Reinisch, A., Janik, R., Simlinger, F., *International Law in Domestic Courts. A Casebook*, Oxford, Oxford University Press, 2018

Nollkaemper, A., Reinisch, A., *Oxford Reports on International Law in Domestic Courts*, available at https://opil.ouplaw.com/page/212

O'Keeffe, D., Schermers, H. G. (eds.), *Essays in European Law and Integration*, Deventer, Kluwer, 1982

O'Keeffe, D., Schermers, H. G. (eds.), *Mixed Agreements*, The Hague, Kluwer, 1983

Odudu, O., *The Boundaries of EC Competition Law. The Scope of Article 81*, Oxford, Oxford University Press, 2006

Oliver, D., *Common Values and the Public-Private Divide*, Cambridge, Cambridge University Press, 1999

Oliver, D., Fedtke, J. (eds.), *Human Rights and the Private Sphere: A Comparative Study*, New York, Routledge-Cavendish, 2007

Pace, L. F., *La natura giuridica dell'Unione europea*, Bari, Cacucci, 2021

Palmisano, G. (ed.), *Il diritto internazionale ed europeo nei giudizi interni.* Atti del XXIV Convegno SIDI di Roma, 5-6 June 2019, Naples, Editoriale Scientifica, 2020

Panunzio, S. P., Sciso, E. (eds.), *Le riforme istituzionali e la partecipazione dell'Italia all'Unione europea*, Milan, Giuffrè, 2002

Paulussen, C., Takacs, T., Lazic, V., Van Rompuy, B. (eds.), *Fundamental Rights in International and European Law*, The Hague, TMC Asser Press, 2015

Pavone, T., *The Ghostwriters: Lawyers and the Politics Behind the Judicial Construction of Europe*, Cambridge, Cambridge University Press, 2022

Peers, S., Hervey, T., Kenner, J., Ward, A. (eds.), *The EU Charter of Fundamental Rights: A Commentary*, Oxford, Hart, 2021

Pellet, A., *Les fondements juridiques internationaux du droit communautaire*, in *Recueil des cours de l'Académie de droit européen*, The Hague, Martinus Nijhoff, 1997, V, 2, 193–271

Pérez González, M. (ed.), *Hacia un nuevo orden internacional y europeo—Estudios en homenaje al Profesor Don Manuel Diez de Velasco*, Madrid, Tecnos, 1993

Pertek, J., *Coopération entre juges nationaux et Cour de justice de l'UE. Le renvoi préjudiciel*, Brussels, Bruylant, 2013

Pertek, J., *Le renvoi préjudiciel. Droit, liberté ou obligation de coopération des juridictions nationales avec la CJUE*, 2nd ed., Brussels, Bruylant, 2021

Pescatore, P., *The Law of Integration: Emergence of a New Phenomenon in International Relations*, The Hague, Martinus Nijhoff, 1974

Pescatore, P., *L'ordre juridique des Communautés européennes*, Liège, Presses universitaires de Liège, 1975

Pescatore, P., *L'effet des directives communautaires—une tentative de démythification*, in *Recueil Dalloz-Sirey*, XXV, 1980, 171–176

Pescatore, P., *Le droit de l'intégration*, Brussels, Bruylant, 2005

Peters, A., Sparks, T., *The Individual in International Law. History and Theory*, Oxford, Oxford University Press, 2024

Petrlik, D., Bobek, M., Passer, J. M., Masson, A. (eds.), *Évolution des rapports entre les orders juridiques de l'Union européenne, international et nationaux: Liber amicorum Jiří Malenovský*, Brussels, Bruylant, 2020

Phelan, W., *Great Judgments of the European Court of Justice. Rethinking the Landmark Decisions of the Foundational Period*, Cambridge, Cambridge University Press, 2020

Pino, G., *Il costituzionalismo dei diritti*, Bologna, Il Mulino, 2017

Pistorio, G., *Interpretazione e giudici. Il caso dell'interpretazione conforme al diritto dell'Unione europea*, Naples, Editoriale Scientifica, 2012

Piva, P., *Giudice nazionale e diritto dell'Unione europea. L'efficacia diretta e il primato*, Naples, Editoriale Scientifica, 2008

Piva, P., *Il principio di effettività della tutela giurisprudenziale del diritto dell'Unione europea*, Naples, Editoriale Scientifica, 2012

Plant, R., *Modern political thought*, Oxford, Basil Blackwell, 1991

Plouvier, L., *Le dècisions de la Cour de Justice des Communautés Européennes et leur effects Juridiques*, Brussels, Bruylant, 1975

Poiares Maduro, M., *We the Court. The European Court of Justice and the European Economic Constitution*, Oxford, Oxford University Press, 1998

Poiares Maduro, M., Azoulai, L. (eds.), *The Past and Future of EU Law: The Classics of EU Law Revisited on the 50th Anniversary of the Rome Treaty*, Oxford, Hart, 2010

Póltorak, N., *European Union Rights in National Courts*, Alphen aan den Rijn, Kluwer Law International, 2015

Prechal, S., *Directives in EC Law*, 2nd ed., Oxford, Oxford University Press, 2005

Prechal, S., Van Roermund, B. (eds.), *The Coherence of EU Law. The Search for Unity in Divergent Concepts*, Oxford, Oxford University Press, 2008

Prinssen, J. M., Schrauwen, A. (eds.), *Direct Effect: Rethinking a Classic of EC Legal Doctrine*, Groningen, European Law Publishing, 2002

Quadri, R., Monaco, R., Trabucchi, A. (eds.), *Trattato istitutivo della Comunità economica europea. Commentario*, Milan, Giuffrè, 1965

Rask Madsen, M., Nicola, F., Vauchez, A., *Researching the European Court of Justice. Methodological Shifts and Law's Embeddedness*, Cambridge, Cambridge University Press, 2022

Rasmussen, H., *On Law and Policy in the European Court of Justice: A Comparative Study in Judicial Policymaking*, The Hague, Martinus Nijhoff, 1986

Rawls, J., *Political Liberalism*, New York, Columbia University Press, 1993

Reich, N., *'System der subjektiven öffentlichen Rechte' in the Union: A European Constitution for Citizens of Bits and Pieces*, in *Recueil des cours de l'Académie de droit européen*, 1998, 157–236

Robert, J., *Sur une égalité des droits devant la Communauté économique européenne des ressortissants des Etats membres avec ces Etats eux-mêmes*, in *Recueil Sirey*, 1963

Romito, A. M., *La tutela giurisdizionale nell'Unione europea tra effettività del sistema e garanzie individuali*, Bari, Cacucci, 2015

Rondu, J., *L'individu, sujet du droit de l'Union européenne*, Brussels, Bruylant, 2020

Rosas, A., Levits, E., Bot, Y. (eds.), *The Court of Justice and the Construction of Europe: Analyses and Perspectives on Sixty Years of Case-law*, Berlin, Springer, 2013

Rosas, A., Armati, L., *EU Constitutional Law: An Introduction*, 3rd ed., Oxford, Hart, 2018

Rosenfeld, M., Sajó, A. (eds.), *The Oxford Handbook of Comparative Constitutional Law*, Oxford, Oxford University Press, 2012

Rossi, L. S. (eds.), *Carta dei diritti fondamentali e Costituzione dell'Unione europea*, Milan, Giuffré, 2002

Rossi, L. S., Casolari, F. (eds.), *The Principle of Equality in EU Law*, Heidelberg, Springer, 2017

Rousseau, C. (ed.), *Le droit international demain*, Neuchâtel, Edition Ides et Calendes, 1974

Roux, J., *Droit général de l'Union européenne*, 10th ed., Paris, LexisNexis, 2016

Rubenfeld, J., *Freedom and Time—A Theory of Constitutional Self-Government*, New Heaven, Yale University Press, 2001

Ruffert, M., *Subjektive Rechte im Umweltrecht der Europäischen Gemeinschaft. Unter besonderer Berücksichtigung ihrer prozessualen Durchsetzung*, Heidelberg, University of Heidelberg (dissertation), 1996

Ruffert, M. (ed.), *The Public-Private Law Divide: Potential for Transformation?*, London, British Institute of International and Comparative Law, 2009

Sajó, A., Uitz, R. (eds.), *The Constitution in Private Relations: Expanding Constitutionalism*, The Hague, Eleven International Publishing, 2005

Sarmiento, D., *Poder judicial e integración europea*, Madrid, Civitas, 2004

Sarmiento, D., *El Derecho de la Unión europea*, 4th ed., Madrid, Marcial Pons, 2022

Sauregger, S., Terpan, F., *The Court of Justice of the European Union and the Politics of Law*, London, Palgrave, 2016

Sauter, W., Schepel, H., *State and Market in European Union Law: The Public and Private Spheres of the Internal Market before the EU Courts*, Cambridge, Cambridge University Press, 2009

Schepel, H., *The Constitution of Private Governance. Product Standards in the Regulation of Integrating Markets*, Oxford, Hart, 2005

Schepisi, C. (ed.), *L'impatto del diritto dell'Unione europea sul processo amministrativo*, Naples, Editoriale Scientifica, 2013

Schütze, R., *From Dual to Cooperative Federalism: The Changing Structure of European Law*, Oxford, Oxford University Press, 2009

Schütze, R. (ed.), *Foreign Affairs and the EU Constitution*. Selected essays, Cambridge, Cambridge University Press, 2014

Schütze, R., *European Constitutional Law*, Cambridge, Cambridge University Press, 2016

Schütze, R., Tridimas, T., *Oxford Principles of European Union Law: The European Union Legal Order: Volume I*, Oxford, Oxford University Press, 2018

Schütze, R., *European Union Law*, 3rd ed., Oxford, Oxford University Press, 2021

Schwarze, J., *European Administrative Law*, London, Sweet & Maxwell, 2006

Sciarra, S., *Solidarity and Conflict. European Social Law in Crisis*, Cambridge, Cambridge University Press, 2019

Sen, A., *Resources, Values and Development*, Cambridge (Mass.), Harvard University Press, 1984

Sen, A., *Development as Freedom*, New York, Oxford University Press, 1999

Sereni, P. A., *Diritto internazionale*, II, Milan, Giuffrè, 1960

Shuibhne, N. N. (ed.), *Regulating the Internal Market*, Cheltenham, Edward Elgar, 2006

Shuibhne, N. N., *EU Citizenship Law*, Oxford, Oxford University Press, 2023

Siedentopf, H., Ziller, J. (eds.), *Making European Policies Work: The Implementation of Community Legislation in the Member States*, London, Sage, 1988, I

Simon, D., *L'interprétation judiciaire des traités d'organisations internationales (Morphologie des conventions et fonction juridictionnelle)*, Paris, Pedone, 1981

Simon, D., *La directive européenne*, Paris, Pedone, 1997

Simon, D., *Le système juridique communautaire*, Paris, Puf, 1997

Sperduti, G., *La CECA, ente sopranazionale*, Padua, Cedam, 1960

Spitaleri, F. (ed.), *L'incidenza del diritto comunitario e della CEDU sugli atti nazionali definitivi*, Milan, Giuffrè, 2009

Stein, K. D., *Der gemischte Vertrag im Recht der Außenbeziehungen der Europäischen Wirtschaftsgemeinschaft*, Berlin, Duncker & Humblot, 1986

Steiner, E. (ed.), *Comparing the Prospective Effect of Judicial Rulings Across Jurisdictions*, Heidelberg, Springer, 2015

Stone Sweet, A., *The Judicial Construction of Europe*, Oxford, Oxford University Press, 2004

Strange, S., *The Retreat of the State. The Diffusion of Power in the World Economy*, Cambridge, Cambridge University Press, 1996

Szente, Z., Mandák, F., Fejes, Z. (eds.), *Challenges and Pitfalls in the Recent Hungarian Constitutional Development: Discussing the New Fundamental Law of Hungary*, Paris, L'Harmattan, 2015

Taggart, M. (ed.), *The Province of Administrative Law*, Oxford, Oxford University Press, 1997

Tega, D., Repetto, G., Piccirilli, G., Ninatti, S. (eds.), *Italian Constitutional Law in the European Context*, Milan, Wolters Kluwer, 2023

Tesauro, G., *Diritto dell'Unione europea*, 7th ed., Padua, Cedam, 2012

Tesauro, G., *Diritto dell'Unione europea*, 4th ed., edited by De Pasquale, P., Ferraro, F., vol. I, Naples, Editoriale Scientifica, 2023

Thorson, B., *Individual Rights in EU Law*, Berlin, Springer, 2016

Thouvenin, J. M., Tomuschat, C. (eds.), *Droit International et Diversité des Cultures Juridiques – International Law and Diversity of Legal Cultures*, Paris, Pédone, 2008

Tizzano, A., *I* 'grands arrêts' *della giurisprudenza dell'Unione europea*, Turin, Giappichelli, 2012

Tizzano, A., Kokott, J., Prechal, S. (Organising Committee), *50ème anniversaire de l'arrêt Van Gend en Loos: 1963-2013: actes du colloque*, Luxembourg, 13 mai 2013, https://curia.europa.eu/jcms/jcms/P_95693/en/

Tizzano, A. (ed.), *Trattati dell'Unione europea. Commentario*, 2nd ed., Milan, Giuffrè, 2014

Tizzano, A., Rosas, A., De Lapuerta, R. S., Lenaerts, K., Kokott, J. (eds.), *La Cour de justice de L'Union européenne sous la présidence de Vassilios Skouris (2003-2015).* Liber amicorum *Vassilios Skouris*, Brussels, Bruylant, 2015

Tomuschat, C., *International Law Ensuring the Survival of Mankind on the Eve of a New Century: General Course on Public International Law*, in *Recueil des Cours*, vol. 281, 1999, 9–438

Tomuschat, C., *Human Rights: between Idealism and Realism*, Oxford, Oxford University Press, 2008

Tóth, G. A. (ed.), *Constitution for a Disunited Nation: On Hungary's 2011 Fundamental Law*, Budapest-New York, Central European University Press, 2012

Tridimas, T., *The General Principles of EU Law*, 2nd ed., Oxford, Oxford University Press, 2006

Triepel, H., *Völkerrecht und Landesrecht*, Leipzig, C. L. Hirschfeld, 1899

Tufano, M. L. (ed.), *Cantiere Europa—Le riforme istituzionali dell'Europa*, Naples, Editoriale Scientifica, 2004

Tuori, K., *European Constitutionalism*, Cambridge, Cambridge University Press, 2015

Turmo, A., *L'autorité de la chose jugée en droit de l'Union européenne*, Brussels, Bruylant, 2017

Turmo, A., Res Judicata *in European Union Law*, Madrid, EU Law Live Press, 2023

Van der Valt, J., *The Horizontal Effect Revolution and the Question of Sovereignty*, Berlin-Boston, De Gruyter, 2014

Van Leuken, R., *Private Law and the Internal Market*, Cambridge, Intersentia, 2017

Van Vooren, B., Wessel, R. A., *EU External Relations Law: Text, Cases and Materials*, Oxford, Oxford University Press, 2014

Vandersanden, G., *Renvoi préjudiciel en droit européen*, Brussels, Bruylant, 2013

Vauchez, A., De Witte, B. (eds.), *Lawyering Europe: European Law as a Transnational Social Field*, Oxford, Oxford University Press, 2013

Vauchez, A., *Brokering Europe. Euro-Lawyers and the Making of a Transnational Polity*, Cambridge, Cambridge University Press, 2015

Velu, J., *Les effets directs des instruments internationaux en matière de droits de l'homme*, Brussels, Swinnen, 1981

Verdross, A., *Die Verfassung der Völkerrechtsgemeinschaft*, Berlin, Springer, 1926

Verdú, P. L., *Curso de Derecho Político*, Vol. II, Madrid, Tecnos, 1977

Viganò, F., *La proporzionalità della pena. Principi di diritto penale e costituzionale*, Turin, Giappichelli, 2021.

Villani, U., *Istituzioni di diritto dell'Unione europea*, 6th ed., Bari, Cacucci, 2020

Vitale, G., *Diritto processuale nazionale e diritto dell'Unione europea, L'autonomia procedurale degli Stati membri in settori a diverso livello di 'europeizzazione'*, Catania, Ed.it, 2010

Voigt, C. (ed.), *International Judicial Practice on the Environment: Questions of Legitimacy*, Cambridge, Cambridge University Press, 2019

Von Bogdandy, A., Mavroidis, P. C., Mény, Y. (eds.), *European Integration and International Co-ordination*, Alphen aan den Rijn, Kluwer Law International, 2002

Von Bogdandy, A., *I principi fondamentali dell'Unione europea*, Naples, Editoriale Scientifica, 2011

Von Bogdandy, A., Sonnevend, P. (eds.), *Constitutional Crisis in the European Constitutional Area: Theory, Law and Politics in Hungary and Romania*, Oxford-Portland, Hart, 2015

Von Gerber, C. F., *Grundzüge eines Systems des deutschen Staatsrechts*, Leipzig, Nabu Press, 1865

Von Jhering, R., *Der Zweck im Recht*, Leipzig, Druck und Verlag Von Breitkopf & Härtel, 1877

Waelbroeck, M., *Traités internationaux et juridictions internes dans les pays du Marché commun*, Brussels, Bruylant, 1969

Waelbroeck, M., Velu, J. (eds.), *Les recours des individus devant les instances nationales en cas de violation du droit européen*, Brussels, Larcier, 1978

Walker, N. (ed.), *Sovereignty in Transition*, Oxford, Hart, 2003

Walkila, S., *Horizontal Effect of Fundamental Rights in EU Law*, Groningen, Europa Law Publishing, 2016

Ward, A., *Judicial Review and the Rights of Private Parties in EU Law*, Oxford, Oxford University Press, 2007

Weatherill, S., *Cases and Materials on EU Law*, Oxford, Oxford University Press, 2014

Weiler, J. H. H., *The Constitution of Europe: 'Do the New Clothes Have an Emperor?' and Other Essays on European Integration*, Oxford, Oxford University Press, 1999

Weitzel, L., *L'Europe des droits fondamentaux. Mélanges en hommage à Albert Weitzel*, Paris, Pedone, 2013

Werro, F. (ed.), *Droit civil et Convention européenne des droits de l'homme*, Zurich, Schulthess, 2006

Wessel, R. A., Blockmans, S. (eds.), *Between Autonomy and Dependence: The EU Legal Order Under the Influence of International Organizations*, The Hague, Martinus Nijhoff, 2013

Wiklund, O. (ed.), *Judicial Discretion in European Perspective*, Stockholm, Kluwer Law International, 2003

Winter, G., *Sources and Categories of European Union Law*, Baden-Baden, Nomos, 1996

Wohlfahrt, C., *Die Vermutung unmittelbarer Wirkung des Unionsrechts. Ein Plädoyer für die Aufgabe der Kriterien hinreichender Genauigkeit und Unbedingtheit*, Heidelberg, Springer, 2016

Wouters, J., Nollkaemper, A., De Wet, E., *The Europeanisation of International Law - The Status of International Law in the EU and its Member States*, The Hague, Asser Press, 2008

Wouters, J., Hoffmeister, F., De Baere, G., Ramopoulos, T., *The Law of EU External Relations: Cases, Materials, and Commentary on the EU as an international Legal Actor*, 3rd ed., Oxford, Oxford University Press, 2021

Zimmermann, R., *Roman Law, Contemporary Law, European Law: The Civilian Tradition Today*, Oxford, Oxford University Press, 2001

Zipperle, N., *EU International Agreements. An Analysis of Direct Effect and Judicial Review Pre- and Post-Lisbon*, Cham, Springer, 2017

Zoppini, A., *Il diritto privato e i suoi confini*, Bologna, Il Mulino, 2020

2. Journals articles, contributions in journals special issues, encyclopaedia and commentaries entries

Accetto, M., Zleptnig, S., *The Principle of Effectiveness: Rethinking its Role in Community Law* (2005) 11 *European Public Law* 375

Adams, Z., Olusegun Adenitire, J., *Ideological Neutrality in the Workplace* (2018) 81 *Modern Law Review* 337

Adinolfi, A., *La rilevanza della Carta dei diritti fondamentali nella giurisprudenza interna: qualche riflessione per un tentativo di ricostruzione sistematica* (2018) 1 *Studi sull'integrazione europea* 29

Adobati, E., *La sentenza di un giudice nazionale passata in giudicato non può più essere rimessa in discussione anche se viola il diritto comunitario* (2006) 1 *Diritto comunitario e degli scambi internazionali* 83

Albors-Llorens, A., *The Direct Effect of EU Directives: Fresh Controversy or a Storm in a Teacup?* (2014) 39 *European Law Review* 850

Alland, D., *L'applicabilité directe du droit international considerée du point de vue de l'office du juge: des habits neufs pour une nouvelle dame?* (1998) 2 *Revue générale de droit international public* 203

Allott, P., *Preliminary Rulings—Another Infant Disease* (2000) 5 *European Law Review* 538

Alonso García, R., *The Spanish Constitution and the European Constitution: The Script for a Virtual Collision and Other Observations on the Principle of Primacy* (2005) 6 *German Law Journal* 1001

Amadeo, S., *L'efficacia 'obiettiva' delle direttive comunitarie ed i suoi riflessi nei confronti dei privati. Riflessioni a margine delle sentenze sui casi Linster e Unilever* (2001) 1 *Il Diritto dell'Unione europea* 95

Amalfitano, C., *Il ruolo dell'art. 325 TFUE nella sentenza Taricco e le sue ricadute sul rispetto del principio di legalità penale* (2016) *forumcostituzionale.it*, 5 October 2016, 9 available at https://www.forumcostituzionale.it/wordpress/wp-content/uploads/2016/06/amalfitano.pdf

Amalfitano, C., *Il diritto non scritto nell'accertamento dei diritti fondamentali dopo la riforma di Lisbona* (2016) 1 *Il diritto dell'Unione europea* 21

Amalfitano, C., *La vicenda Taricco e il dialogo (?) tra giudici nazionali e Corte di giustizia* (2018) 1 *Il Diritto dell'Unione europea* 153

Amalfitano, C., Cecchetti, L., *The ECJ's Approach to Dual Preliminarity 5 Years after the ITCC's Judgment No. 269/2017*, in Gallo, D., Piccirilli, G. (eds.), *Dual Preliminarity through National, EU and Comparative Case Law*, Special Issue (2023) 15 *Italian Journal of Public Law* 84

Amstutz, M., *In-Between Worlds: Marleasing and the Emergence of Interlegality in Legal Reasoning* (2005) 11 *European Law Journal* 766

Amtenbrink, F., Repasi, R., *The German Federal Constitutional Court's decision in Weiss: A contextual analysis* (2020) 45 *European Law Review* 757

Anagnostaras, G., *Activation of the Ultra Vires Review: The Slovak Pensions Judgment of the Czech Constitutional Court* (2012) 14 *German Law Journal* 959

Anagnostaras, G., *Activating Ultra Vires Review: The German Federal Constitutional Court Decides Weiss* (2021) 6 *European Papers* 801

Anderson, P., *The European Coup* (2020) 42 *London Review of Books* 24

Antoniadis, A., *The Chiquita and Van Parys Judgments: Rules, Exceptions and the Law* (2005) 32 *Legal Issues of Economic Integration* 460

Antoniadis, A., *The European Union and WTO Law: A Nexus of Reactive, Coactive, and Proactive Approaches* (2007) 6 *World Trade Review* 45

Antpöhler, C., Dickschen, J., Hentrei, S., Kottmann, M., Smrkolj, M., Von Bogdandy, A., Reverse Solange–*Protecting the essence of fundamental rights against EU Member States* (2012) 49 *Common Market Law Review* 489

Arangio-Ruiz, G., *Dualism Revisited: International Law and Interindividual Law* (2003) 86 *Rivista di Diritto Internazionale* 909

Arena, A., *Exercise of EU Competences and Pre-emption of Member States' Powers in the Internal and the External Sphere: Towards 'Grand Unification'?* (2016) 35 *Yearbook of European Law* 28–105

Arena, A., *From an Unpaid Electricity Bill to the Primacy of EU Law: Gian Galeazzo Stendardi and the Making of Costa v. ENEL* (2019) 30 *European Journal of International Law* 101

Arena, A., Rosanò, A., *Nicola Catalano (1910-1984): padre del rinvio pregiudiziale d'interpretazione e apostolo del primato del Diritto Comunitario* (2024) 1 *Eurojus* 89

Arnull, A., *The Direct Effect of Directives: Grasping the Nettle* (1986) 35 *International and Comparative Law Quarterly* 939

Arnull, A., *Annotation of Kolpinghuis* (1988) 13 *European Law Review* 42

Arnull, A., *The Use and Abuse of Article 177 ECC* (1989) 52 *Modern Law Review* 622

Arnull, A., *Editorial. The Incidental Effect of Directives* (1999) 24 *European Law Review* 1

Arnull, A., *The Principle of Effective Judicial Protection in EU Law: An Unruly Horse?* (2011) 36 *European Law Review* 51

Arnull, A., *European Union Law and the Contra Legem Principle* (2022) 47 *European Law Review* 291

Atripaldi, V., *Leale cooperazione comunitaria ed obbligo degli Stati al riesame degli atti amministrativi definitivi contrari al diritto comunitario* (2004) 4 *Diritto pubblico comparato ed europeo* 883

Azoulai, L., *Le rôle constitutionnel de la Cour de justice des Communautés européennes tel qu'il se dégage de sa jurisprudence* (2008) 1 *Revue trimestrielle de droit européen* 29

Azoulai, L., *The Court of Justice and the Social Market Economy: the Emergence of an Ideal and the Conditions for its Realization* (2008) 57 *Common Market Law Review* 1335

Azoulai, L., Ritleng, D., *L'État, c'est moi. Le Conseil d'État, la sécurité et la conservation des données* (2021) 2 *Revue trimestrielle de droit européen* 349

Bachmaier, L., *Más reflexiones sobre la sentencia Melloni: Primacía, diálogo y proteccíon de los derechos fundamentales en jucios in absentia en el derecho europeo* (2015) 56 *Revista española de Derecho Europeo* 153

Bailleux, J., *Michel Gaudet a law entrepreneur: the role of the legal service of the European executives in the invention of EC Law* (2013) 50 *Common Market Law Review* 359

Bailleux, A., *La Cour de justice, la Charte des droits fondamentaux et l'intensité normative des droits sociaux* (2014) 2 *Revue de Droit Social* 281

Bakó, B., *Judges sitting on the Warsaw-Budapest express train: the Independence of Polish and Hungarian judges before the CJEU* (2020) 26 *European Public Law* 587

Balladore Pallieri, G., *Le Comunità europee e gli ordinamenti interni degli Stati membri* (1961) 1 *Diritto internazionale* 3

Bánkuti, M., Halmai, G., Scheppele, K. L., *Hungary's Illiberal Turn: Disabling the Constitution* (2012) 23 *Journal of Democracy* 138

Baquero Cruz, J., *Free Movement and Private Autonomy* (1999) 24 *European Law Review* 603

Baraggia, A., *The 'Conditionality' Regulation under the ECJ's Scrutiny: A Constitutional Analysis: Hungary v European Parliament (C-156/21) and Poland v European Parliament (C-157/21)* (2022) 47 *European Law Review* 687

Barak, A., *Constitutional Human Rights and Private Law* (1996) 3 *Revue of Constitutional Studies* 220

Baratta, R., *Norme contenute in direttive comunitarie inattuate e loro opponibilità ai singoli* (1989) 2 *Rivista di diritto internazionale* 253

Baratta, R., *Quali prospettive in tema di effetti c.d. orizzontali di norme di direttive inattuate?* (1994) 3 *Rivista di diritto internazionale* 487

Baratta, R., *National Courts as 'Guardians' and 'Ordinary Courts' of EU Law: Opinion 1/09 of the ECJ* (2011) 38 *Legal Issues of Economic Integration* 297

Barber, M., *Legal Pluralism in the European Union* (2006) 12 *European Law Journal* 306

Barnard, C., *Viking and Laval: An Introduction* (2008) 10 *Cambridge Yearbook of European Legal Studies* 463–492

Barnard, C., *Are Social 'Rights' Rights?* (2020) 11 *European Labour Law Journal* 351

Bastos, F. B., *Derivative Illegality in European Composite Administrative Procedures* (2018) 55 *Common Market Law Review* 101

Baudenbacher, C., *The Implementation of Decisions of the ECJ and of the EFTA Court in Member States' Domestic Legal Orders* (2005) 40 *Texas International Law Journal* 383

Bebr, G., *Les dispositions de droit communautaire directement applicables: développement d'une notion communautaire* (1970) 1 *Cahiers de droit européen* 3

Bebr, G., *Directly Applicable Provisions of Community Law: The Development of a Community Concept* (1970) 19 *International and Comparative Law Quarterly* 257

Bebr, G., *Preliminary Rulings of the Court of Justice: Their Authority and Temporal Effect* (1981) 18 *Common Market Law Review* 475

Bebr, G., *Agreements Concluded by the Community and Their Possible Direct Effect: From International Fruit Company to Kupferberg* (1983) 20 *Common Market Law Review* 35

Beck, G., *The Lisbon Judgment of the German Constitutional Court, the Primacy of EU Law and the Problem of Kompetenz-Kompetenz: A Conflict between Right and Right in Which There is No Praetor* (2011) 17 *European Law Journal* 470

Becker, F., Campbell, A., *The Direct Effect of European Directives: Towards the Final Act?* (2007) 13 *Columbia Journal of European Law* 401

Bell, M., *Mark, Disability, Rehabilitation and the Status of Worker in EU Law: Fenoll* (2016) 53 *Common Market Law Review* 197

Bello, J., *The WTO Dispute Settlement Understanding: Less Is More* (1996) 90 *American Journal of International Law* 416

Benecke, M., *Altersdiskriminierung bei Entlassungsabfindung* (2016) 10 *Europäische Zeitschrift für Wirtschaftsrecht* 469

Beneyto, J. M., *The EU and the WTO. Direct Effect of the New Dispute Settlement System?* (1996) 10 *Europäische Zeitschrift für Wirtschaftsrecht* 295

Benvenisti, E., Downs, G. W., *The Premises, Assumptions, and Implications of Van Gend en Loos: Viewed from the Perspectives of Democracy and Legitimacy of International Institutions* (2014) 25 *European Journal of International Law* 85

Bercusson, B., *The Trade Union Movement and the European Union: Judgement Day* (2007) 13 *European Law Journal* 279

Berlin, D., *De l'autorité relative de l'arrêt limitant l'autorité absolue* (2009) 4 *Revue des affaires européennes* 577

Bertrand, B., *Les enjeux de la surveillance numérique* (2021) 2 *Revue trimestrielle de droit européen* 175

Besselink, L. F. M., *The Parameters of Constitutional Conflict after Melloni* (2014) 39 *European Law Review* 531

Besselink, L. F. M., *The Persistence of a Contested Concept: Reflections on Ten Years Constitutional Identity in EU Law* (2021) 27 *European Public Law* 597

Bestagno, F., *Validità e interpretazione degli atti dell'UE alla luce della Carta: conferme e sviluppi nella giurisprudenza della Corte in tema di dati personali* (2015) 1 *Il Diritto dell'Unione europea* 21

Betlem, G., *Medium Hard Law—Still No Horizontal Direct Effect of European Community Directives after Faccini Dori* (1994–1995) 1 *Columbia Journal of European Law* 469–484

Betlem, G., *The Doctrine of Consistent Interpretation—Managing Legal Uncertainty* (2002) 22 *Oxford Journal of Legal Studies* 397

Beukers, T., *Case C-409/06, Winner Wetten GmbH v. Bürgermeisterin der Stadt Bergheim, Judgment of the Court (Grand Chamber) of 8 September 2010* (2011) 48 *Common Market Law Review* 1985

Biavati, P., *La sentenza Lucchini: il giudicato nazionale cede al diritto comunitario* (2007) 5 *Rassegna tributaria* 1591

Bieber, R., *An Association of Sovereign States* (2009) 5 *European Constitutional Law Review* 391

Biernat, S., *How Far is it from Warsaw to Luxembourg and Karlsruhe: The Impact of the PSPP Judgment on Poland* (2020) 21 *German Law Journal* 1104

Bignami, F., *Rethinking the Legal Foundation of the European Constitutional Order: The Lessons of the New Historical Research* (2013) 28 *American University International Law Review* 1311

Bin, R., *Taricco, una sentenza sbagliata: come venirne fuori?* (2016) *Diritto penale contemporaneo* 4 July 2016

Biondi, A., *The European Court of Justice and Certain National Procedural Limitations: Not Such a Tough Relationship* (1999) 36 *Common Market Law Review* 1271

Biondi, A., *Ministero dell'Industria, del Commercio e dell'Artigianato v. Lucchini SpA* (2008) 45 *Common Market Law Review* 1459

Biondi, A., Mastroianni, R., *Annotation of Berlusconi* (2006) 43 *Common Market Law Review* 553

Bleckmann, A., *Self-Executing Treaty Provisions, Encyclopedia of Public International Law*, IV, 2000, 374

Bobek, M., *Landtová, Holubec, and the Problem of an Uncooperative Court: Implications for the Preliminary Rulings Procedure* (2014) 10 *European Constitutional Law Review* 5

Bobek, M., *Why is it Better to Treat Every Provision of EU Directives as Having Horizontal Direct Effect?* (2023) 39 *International Journal of Comparative Labour Law and Industrial Relations* 211

Bobić, A., Dawson, M., *Quantitative Easing at the Court of Justice—Doing Whatever it Takes to Save the Euro: Weiss and Others* (2019) 56 *Common Market Law Review* 1005

Bobić, A., Dawson, M., *Making Sense of the 'Incomprehensible': The PSPP Judgment of the German Federal Constitutional Court* (2020) 57 *Common Market Law Review* 1953

Boch, L., *European Community Law in National Courts: A Continuing Contradiction* (1992) 5 *Leiden Journal of International Law* 171

Boerger, A., Rasmussen, M., *The Making of European Law: Exploring the Life and Work of Michel Gaudet* (2017) 57 *American Journal of Legal History* 51

Bogdanowicz, P., Taborowski, M., *How to Save a Supreme Court in a Rule of Law Crisis: the Polish Experience* (2020) 16 *European Constitutional Law Review* 306

Bogg, A., Ford, M., *Article 31*, in Peers, S., Hervey, T., Kenner, J., Ward, A., *The EU Charter of Fundamental Rights: A Commentary*, 2nd ed. Oxford, Hart, 2021, 875–922

Bonelli, M., *The Taricco Saga and the Consolidation of Judicial Dialogue in the European Union* (2018) 25 *Maastricht Journal of European and Comparative Law* 357

Bonelli, M., *National Identity and European Integration Beyond 'Limited Fields'* (2021) 27 *European Public Law* 537

Borger, V., *Constitutional Identity, The Rule of Law, and the Power of the Purse: The ECJ Approves the Conditionality Mechanism to Protect the Union Budget: Hungary and Poland v. Parliament and Council* (2022) 59 *Common Market Law Review* 1771

Borowsky, M., *Artikel 51—Anwendungsbereich*, in Meyer, J. (ed.), *Charta der Grundrechte der Europäischen Union*, 5th ed., Baden-Baden, Nomos, 2014, 743–760

Borrie, G., *The Regulation of Public and Private Power* (1989) *Public Law* 552

Bouhier, V., *La généralisation du caractère préalable de l'obligation d'interprétation conforme* (2012) 2 *Revue des affaires européennes* 433

Boulouis, J., *A propos de la fonction normative de la jurisprudence. Remarques sur l'oeuvre jurisprudentielle de la Cour de justice des Communautés européennes* (1999) 1 *Recueil d'Etudes, Droit communautaire et droit français* 99–111

Breuer, M., *State Liability for Judicial Wrongs and Community Law: The Case of Gerhard Köbler v. Austria* (2004) 29 *European Law Review* 243

Bridge, J., *Procedural Aspects of the Enforcement of European Community Law through the Legal Systems of the Member States* (1984) 9 *European Law Review* 28

Bříza, P., *Lucchini SpA—Is There Anything Left of res judicata Principle?* (2008) 27 *Civil Justice Quarterly* 40

Brkan, M., *The Concept of Essence of Fundamental Rights in the EU Legal Order: Peeling the Onion to its Core* (2018) 14 *European Constitutional Law Review* 332

Broberg, M., Fenger, N., *If You Love Somebody Set Them Free: On the Court of Justice's Revision of The Acte Clair Doctrine* (2022) 59 *Common Market Law Review* 711

Bronckers, M., Kuijper, P., *WTO Law in the European Court of Justice* (2000) 37 *Common Market Law Review* 1313

Bronckers, M., *The Effect of the WTO in the European Court Litigation* (2005) 40 *Texas International Law Review* 443

Bronckers, M., *The Relationship of the EC Courts with Other International Tribunals: Non-Committal, Respectful or Submissive?* (2007) 44 *Common Market Law Review* 60

Bronckers, M., *From 'Direct Effect' to 'Muted Dialogue': Recent Developments in the European Courts' Case Law on the WTO and Beyond* (2008) 11 *Journal of International Economic Law* 885

Broussy, E., Donnat, F., Lambert, C., *Stabilité des situations juridiques et droit communautaire* (2006) *L'actualité juridique. Droit administratif* 2275–2776

Burelli, C., *Le concessioni turistico-ricreative tra vincoli 'comunitari' e normativa italiana: criticità e prospettive* (2021) 2 *Il Diritto dell'Unione europea* 247

Buxbaum, R. M., Riesenfeld, S. A., N. V. *Algemene Transport - En Expeditie Onderneming van Gend & Loos v. Administration Fiscale Néerlandaise: A Pioneering Decision of the Court of Justice of the European Communities* (1964) 12 *American Journal of Comparative Law* 152

Cabral, P., Neves, R., *General Principles of EU Law and Horizontal Direct Effect* (2011) 17 *European Public Law* 437

Caianiello, M., *Processo penale e prescrizione nel quadro della giurisprudenza europea. Dialogo tra sistemi o conflitto identitario?* (2017) *Diritto penale contemporaneo* 24 February 2017

Caiola, A., *Aller au fond des choses. Primauté du droit de l'Union européenne et indépendance des juges* (2022) 1 *Revue des affaires européennes* 165

Călin, D., *Constitutional Courts cannot Build Brick Walls between the CJEU and National Judges Concerning the Rule of Law Values in Article 2 TEU: RS* (2023) 60 *Common Market Law Review* 819

Calliess, C., *Zur unmittelbaren Wirkung der EG-Richtlinie über die Umweltverträglichkeitsprüfung und ihrer Umsetzung im deutschen Immissionsschutzrecht* (1996) 9 *Neue Zeitschrift für Verwaltungsrecht* 339

Cameron, I., *Metadata Retention and National Security: Privacy International and La Quadrature du Net: Case C-623/17* (2021) 58 *Common Market Law Review* 1433

Canaris, C.-W., *Grundrechte und Privatrecht* (1984) 184 *Archiv für die civilistische Praxis* 201

Cannizzaro, E., *Demanio marittimo: effetti in malam partem di direttive europee? In margine alle sentenze 17 e 18/2021 dell'Ad. Plen. del Consiglio di Stato* (2021), *giustiziainsieme.it*, 30 December 2021, https://www.giustiziainsieme.it/en/diritto-ue/2092-effetti-in-malam-partem-di-direttive-europee-in-margine-alle-sentenze-17-e-18-2021-dell-adunanza-plenaria-del-consiglio-di-stato-di-enzo-cannizzaro

Capotorti, F., *Il diritto comunitario dal punto di vista del giudice nazionale* (1977) 13 *Rivista di diritto internazionale privato e processuale* 497

Caranta, R., *Intorno al problema dell'individuazione delle posizioni giuridiche soggettive del cittadino comunitario* (1994) 4 *Rivista italiana di diritto pubblico comunitario* 981

Caranta, R., *Judicial Protection against Member States: A New* Jus Commune *Takes Shape* (1995) 32 *Common Market Law Review* 703

Caranta, R., *Case Note on Kühne* (2005) 42 *Common Market Law Review* 179

Caruso, D., *The Missing View of the Cathedral: The Private Law Paradigm of European Legal Integration* (2002) 8 *European Law Journal* 3

Casolari, F., *Il rispetto della rule of law nell'ordinamento giuridico dell'Unione europea: un dramma in due atti* (2017) 1 *DPCE Online* 1

Castillo de la Torre, F., *Anti-dumping Policy and Private Interest* (1992) 17 *European Law Review* 346
Castillo de la Torre, F., *The Status of GATT in EC Law*, Revisited (1995) 29 *Journal of World Trade* 35
Catalano, N., *L'inserimento diretto delle disposizioni contenute nel Trattato istitutivo della Comunità economica europea negli ordinamenti giuridici degli Stati membri* (1963) 5 *Il Foro padano* 33
Cecchetti, L., *Gli strumenti del giudizio di eguaglianza della Corte di giustizia alla prova del divieto di discriminazione sulla base della religione: il caso Cresco Investigation* (2020) 2 *Il Diritto dell'Unione europea* 317
Cecchetti, L., *L'efficacia diretta delle direttive negli ordinamenti nazionali, oggi: questioni ancora aperte alla vigilia del 50° anniversario della sentenza van Duyn* (2023) 3 *Eurojus* 151
Cecchetti, L., Gallo, D., *The Unwritten Exceptions to the Duty to Refer after Consorzio Italian Management II: 'CILFIT Strategy' 2.0 and its Loopholes* (2022) 15 *Review of European Administrative Law* 29
Cecchetti, L., *The Scope* Ratione Temporis *of the Interpretive Rulings of the ECJ: Should the Temporal Limitation Still be a Strict Derogation from Retroactive Effects?*, in Gallo, D., Cecchetti, L. (eds.), *The Preliminary Ruling Procedure,* Today: *Revisiting Article 267 TFEU's Constitutional Backbone*, Special Issue (2023) 15 *European Journal of Legal Studies* 71
Cecchetti, L., *Unravelling Horizontal Direct Effect in EU law: The Case of the Fundamental RIght to Paid Annual Leave between 'Myth' and 'Practice'* (2024) 42 *Yearbook of European Law* 42–83
Chalmers, D., Barroso, L., *What Van Gend en Loos Stands for* (2014) 12 *International Journal of Constitutional Law* 105
Cherubini, F., *Decisions under the Law of European Union: 'You May Be Six People, but I Love You'* (2022) 41 *Yearbook of European Law* 117–161
Chevalier, M., *Commentaire d'arrêt* (1963) 1 *Gazette du Palais* 1
Cheyne, I., *International Agreements and the European Community Legal System* (1994) 19 *European Law Review* 581
Chiti, E., *Le concessioni demaniali marittime e la Corte di Giustizia* (2023) 5 *Giornale di diritto amministrativo* 629
Circolo, A., *L'epilogo della proroga ex lege delle concessioni balneari* (2021) 16 *Studi sull'integrazione europea* 573
Claes, M., *National Identity and the Protection of Fundamental Rights* (2021) 27 *European Public Law* 517
Classen, C. D., *Österreichischer Rundfunk and Others* (2004) 41 *Common Market Law Review* 813
Clément-Wilz, L., *L'office du juge interne pour moduler les effets de l'annulation d'un acte contraire au droit de l'Union. Reflexions sur l'arrêt Association France Nature Environnement du Conseil d'Etat français* (2017) 2 *European Papers* 259
Cloots, E., *Safe Harbour or Open Sea for Corporate Headscarf Bans?* (2018) 55 *Common Market Law Review* 602
Cohen, A., *Constitutionalism without Constitution: Transnational Elites between Political Mobilization and Legal Expertise in the Making of a Constitution for Europe (1940s–1960s)* (2007) 32 *Law and Society Inquiry* 109
Cohen, J. C., *The European Preliminary Reference and U.S. Supreme Court Review of State Court Judgments: A Study in Comparative Judicial Federalism* (1996) 44 *American Journal of Comparative Law* 421
Colgan, D., *Triangular Situations: The Coup de Grâce for the Denial of Horizontal Direct Effect of Community Directives* (2002) 8 *European Public Law* 545
Colombi Ciacchi, A., *The Constitutionalization of European Contract Law: Judicial Convergence and Social Justice* (2006) 2 *European Review of Contract Law* 167
Colombi Ciacchi, A., *The Direct Horizontal Effect of EU Fundamental Rights* (2019) 15 *European Constitutional Law Review* 294
Common Market Law Review, Editorial Comments. The EU Charter of Fundamental Rights still under discussion (2001) 1 *Common Market Law Review* 3
Common Market Law Review, Editorial Comments. Horizontal Direct Effect—A Law of Diminishing Coherence (2006) 1 *Common Market Law Review* 1
Common Market Law Review, Editorial Comments. The Scope of Application of the General Principles of Union Law: An Ever Expanding Union? (2010) 47 *Common Market Law Review* 1589

Common Market Law Review, Editorial Comments. Karlsruhe has Spoken: 'Yes' to the Lisbon Treaty, but... (2009) 46 *Common Market Law Review* 1023

Common Market Law Review, Editorial Comments. Not Mastering the Treaties: The German Federal Constitutional Court's PSPP Judgment (2020) 57 *Common Market Law Review* 965

Common Market Law Review, Editorial Comments. The Polish Constitutional Court, Primacy, and Lawlessness (2021) 46 *Common Market Law Review* 717

Common Market Law Review, Editorial Comments. Clear and Present Danger: Poland, the Rule of Law and Primacy (2021) 58 *Common Market Law Review* 1635

Consolo, C., *La sentenza Lucchini della Corte di Giustizia: quale possibile adattamento degli ordinamenti processuali interni e in specie del nostro?* (2008) 63 *Rivista di diritto processuale* 225

Contaldi, G., *Effetto diretto e primato*, in Cassese, S. (ed.), *Dizionario di diritto pubblico*, vol. III, Milan, Giuffrè, 2006, 2124

Coppel, J., O'Neill, A., *The European Court of Justice: Taking Rights Seriously?* (1992) 29 *Common Market Law Review* 669

Coppel, J., Rights, *Duties and the End of Marshall* (1994) 57 *Modern Law Review* 859

Corrias, L. D. A., *Populism in a Constitutional Key: Constituent Power, Popular Sovereignty and Constitutional Identity* (2016) 12 *European Constitutional Law Review* 6

Cortese, B., *A la recherche d'un parcours d'autoconstitution de l'ordre juridique interindividuel européen: essai d'une lecture pluraliste 50 ans après Van Gend en Loos et Costa* contre *ENEL* (2015) 2 *Il Diritto dell'Unione europea* 271

Cottier, T., Nadakavukaren Schefer, K., *The Relationship between World Trade Organization Law, National and Regional* (1998) 1 *Journal of International Economic Law* 83

Coutron, L., *Retour fataliste aux fondements de l'invocabilité des directives* (2015) 51 *Revue trimestrielle de droit européen* 39

Craig, P., *Once upon a Time in the West: Direct Effect and the Federalization of EEC Law* (1992) 12 *Oxford Journal of Legal Studies* 453

Craig, P., *Francovich, Remedies and the Scope of Damages Liability* (1993) 109 *Law Quarterly Review* 595

Craig, P., *Directives: Direct Effect, Indirect Effect and the Construction of National Legislation* (1997) 22 *European Law Review* 519

Craig, P., *The Legal Effect of Directives: Policy, Rules and Exceptions* (2009) 34 *European Law Review* 349

Craig, P., *The ECJ and Ultra Vires Action: A Conceptual Analysis* (2011) 48 *Common Market Law Review* 395

Crisham, C. A., *Gabrielle Defrenne v. Société anonyme belge de navigation aérienne Sabena* (1977) 14 *Common Market Law Review* 102

Curti Gialdino, C., *La sentenza della Corte di giustizia europea del 20 aprile 2023 in tema di concessioni balneari: spunti critici e proposte per chiudere una storia infinita* (2023) 2 *Ordine internazionale e diritti umani* 455

Curtin, D., *The Province of Government: Delimiting the Direct Effect of Directives in the Common Law Context* (1990) 15 *European Law Review* 195

Curtin, D., *Directives: The Effectiveness of Judicial Protection of Individual Rights* (1990) 27 *Common Market Law Review* 709

Croquet, N. A. J., *The Import of International Customary Law into the EU Legal Order: The Adequacy of a Direct Effect Analysis* (2013) 15 *Cambridge Yearbook of European Legal Studies* 47–81

Dal Farra, T., *L'invocabilité des directives communautaires devant le juge national de la légalité* (1992) 28 *Revue trimestrielle de droit européen* 631

Dani, M., *Special Section 'Giurisdizione e ruolo delle corti costituzionali nel processo di integrazione europea'* (2019) 3 *Diritto pubblico comparato ed europeo* 715

Daniele, L., *L'efficacia diretta delle disposizioni comunitarie in materia sociale* (1991) 30 *Diritto comunitario e degli scambi internazionali* 247

Daniele, L., *La Corte di giustizia conferma l'efficacia diretta "intermittente" delle direttive comunitarie* (1995) 1 *Il Foro italiano* 38–42

Daniele, L., *Novità in tema di efficacia delle direttive comunitarie (nota a Corte giust. CE 13.11.1990, causa C-106/89)* (1992) 4 *Il Foro italiano* 173–178

Daniele, L., *Vingt-cinq ans d'interprétation conforme: un principe encore en quete de définition?* (2008) 4 *Revue des Affaires Europeennes* 705

Dashwood, A., *From Van Duyn to Mangold via Marshall: Reducing Direct Effect to Absurdity?* (2007) 9 *Cambridge Yearbook of European Legal Studies* 81–109

Davies, B., Rasmussen, M., *Towards a New History of European Law* (2012) 21 *Contemporary European History* 305

Davies, G., *Freedom of Movement, Horizontal Effect, and Freedom of Contract* (2012) 20 *European Review of Private Law* 3

De Boer, N., *Addressing Rights Divergence under the Charter: Melloni* (2013) 50 *Common Market Law Review* 1083

De Búrca, G., *Giving Effect to European Community Directives* (1992) 55 *Modern Law Review* 215

De Búrca, G., *The European Court of Justice and the International Legal Order after Kadi* (2009) 51 *Harvard International Law Journal* 1

De Búrca, G., *After the EU Charter of Fundamental Rights: The Court of Justice as a Human Rights Adjudicator?* (2013) 20 *Maastricht Journal of European and Comparative Law* 168

De Búrca, G., *Poland and Hungary's EU: On Not Confronting Authoritarian Governments* (2022) 20 *International Journal of Constitutional Law* 13

De Mey, D., *Recent Developments on the Invocability of WTO Law in the EC: A Wave of Mutilation* (2006) 11 *European Foreign Affairs Review* 63

De Mol, M., *Kücükdeveci: Mangold Revisited—Horizontal Direct Effect of a General Principle of EU Law* (2011) 7 *European Constitutional Law Review* 293

De Mol, M., *The Novel Approach of the CJEU on the Horizontal Direct Effect of the EU Principle of Non-Discrimination* (2011) 18 *Maastricht Journal of European and Comparative Law* 109

De Pasquale, P., *Art. 5 TUE*, in Tizzano, A. (ed.), *Trattati dell'Unione europea.* 2nd ed., Milan, Giuffrè, 2014, 50–54

De Pretis, D., *'Illegittimità comunitaria" dell'atto amministrativo definitivo, certezza del diritto e potere di riesame* (2004) 10 *Giornale di diritto amministrativo* 725

De Visser, M., *Dealing with Divergences in Fundamental Rights Standards* (2013) 20 *Maastricht Journal of European and Comparative Law* 576

De Visser, M., *Juggling Centralized Constitutional Review and EU Primacy in the Domestic Enforcement of the Charter: A.v. B.* (2015) 52 *Common Market Law Review* 1309

De Vries, S., *The Bauer et al. and Max Planck Judgments and EU Citizens' Fundamental Rights: An Outlook for Harmony* (2019) 3 *European Equality Law Review* 16

De Witte, B., *Article 4(2) TEU as a Protection of Institutional Diversity of the Member States* (2021) 27 *European Public Law* 559

De Witte, B., *Retour à Costa. La primauté du droit communautaire à la lumiere du droit international* (1984) 20 *Revue trimestrielle de droit européen* 425

De Witte, B., *European Union Law: How Autonomous is its Legal Order?* (2010) 65 *Zeitschrift fur öffentliches Recht* 14

De Witte, B., *Relire van Gend en Loos* (2012) 17 *Il Diritto dell'Unione europea* 513

Delicostopoulos, J. S., *Towards European Procedural Primacy in National Legal Systems* (2003) 9 *European Law Journal* 599

Delile, J. F., *A propos de l'arrêt Vereniging Milieudefensie: la seconde naissance de l'invocabilité Nakajima* (2012) 48 *Cahiers de droit européen* 687

Denza, E., *A note on Intertanko* (2008) 33 *European Law Review* 870

Dermine, P., *The Ruling of the Bundesverfassungsgericht in PSPP—An Inquiry into its Repercussions on the Economic and Monetary Union* (2020) 16 *European Constitutional Law Review* 525

Di Federico, G., *La sentenza Kücükdeveci e la* vexata quaestio *degli effetti diretti (orizzontali) delle direttive* (2010) 29 *Rivista italiana di diritto del lavoro* 1002

Di Federico, G., *Le discriminazioni in base all'età nella più recente giurisprudenza della Corte di Giustizia: da Mangold a Georgiev... e oltre* (2011) 6 *Studi sull'integrazione europea* 585

Di Federico, G., *The Potential of Article 4(2) TEU in the Solution of Constitutional Clashes Based on Alleged Violations of National Identity and the Quest for Adequate (Judicial) Standards* (2019) 25 *European Public Law* 347

Dickson, J., *Directives in EU Legal Systems: Whose Norms are They Anyway?* (2011) 17 *European Law Journal* 190

Dittert, D., *Droits fondamentaux européens: vers un effet direct horizontal généralisé?* (2014) 20 *Revue des affaires européennes* 177

Domberger, S., Jensen, P., *Contracting Out by the Public Sector: Theory, Evidence, Prospects* (1997) 13 *Oxford Review of Economic Policy* 67

Donati, F., *I principi del primato e dell'effetto diretto del diritto dell'Unione in un sistema di tutele concorrenti dei diritti fondamentali* (2019) 2 *Federalismi.it* 104

Donner, A. M., *National Law and the Case Law of the Court of Justice of the European Community* (1963) 1 *Common Market Law Review* 8

Dougan, M., *The Disguised Vertical Direct Effect of Directives?* (2000) 59 *Cambridge Law Journal* 586

Dougan, M., *Case C-443/98, Unilever Italia v. Central Food* (2001) 38 *Common Market Law Review* 1503

Dougan, M., *The Francovich Right to Reparation: Reshaping the Contours of Community Remedial Competence* (2006) 12 *European Public Law* 103

Dougan, M., *When Worlds Collide! Competing Visions of the Relationship between Direct Effect and Supremacy* (2007) 44 *Common Market Law Review* 931

Dougan, M., *Primacy and the Remedy of Disapplication* (2019) 56 *Common Market Law Review* 1459

Dougan, M., *The Primacy of Union Law over Incompatible National Measures: Beyond Disapplication and Towards a Remedy of Nullity* (2022) 59 *Common Market Law Review* 1301

Doukas, D., *The Verdict of the German Federal Constitutional Court on the Lisbon Treaty: Not Guilty but Don't Do it Again!* (2009) 34 *European Law Review* 866

Drahos, P., *The Regulation of Public Goods* (2004) 7 *Journal of International Economic Law* 321

Drake, S., *Twenty Years after Von Colson: The Impact of 'Indirect Effect' on the Protection of the Individual's Community Rights* (2005) 30 *European Law Review* 329

Driguez, L., *Nouveaux États membres. L'attribution par la République tchèque d'une pension de retraite complémentaire à celle versée suivant la convention bilatérale de 1992 est acceptable, à moins qu'elle ne révèle une discrimination en raison de la nationalité* (2011) 8–9 August–Sept. *Europe* 23–24

Dubout, E., *L'invocabilité d'éviction des directives dans les litiges horizontaux. Le «bateau ivre» a-t-il sombré?* (2010) 46 *Revue trimestrielle de droit européen* 277

Dubout, E., *Le niveau de protection des droits fondamentaux dans l'Union européenne: unitarisme constitutif versus pluralisme constitutionnel. Réflexions autour de l'arrêt Melloni* (2013) 49 *Cahiers de droit européen* 293

Dubout, E., *Principes, droits et devoirs dans la Charte des droits fondamentaux de l'Union européenne* (2014) 50 *Revue trimestrielle de droit européen* 409

Dubout, E., *Grandeur et décadence de l'obligation d'interprétation conforme aux directives dans les litiges horizontaux* (2016) 22 *Revue des affaires européennes* 287

Dumon, F., *La notion de 'disposition directement applicable' en droit européen* (1968) 4 *Cahiers de droit européen* 369

Dunbar, R., *The Application of International Law in the Court of Justice of the European Union: Proportionality Rising* (2021) 22 *German Law Journal* 557–566

Dunbar, R., *Learning from Failure in 'an Integral Part' of EU Law: Interpretation of International Treaties in the CJEU* (2024) 1 *European Law Open* 1

Durante, F., *Giudizio pregiudiziale, rapporti tra ordinamenti e principio di effettività nella recente giurisprudenza della Corte di giustizia delle Comunità europee* (1963) 46 *Rivista di diritto internazionale* 415

Düsterhaus, D., *Procedural Primacy and Effective Judicial Protection: A Trilogue* (2016) 23 *Maastricht Journal of European and Comparative Law* 317

Düsterhaus, D., *Eppur si muove! The Past, Present and (possible) Future of Temporal Limitations in the Preliminary Reference Procedure* (2017) 36 *Yearbook of European Law* 237–274

Easson, J., *Can Directives Impose Obligations on Individuals?* (1979) 4 *European Law Review* 77

Eckes, C., Leino-Sandberg, P., *The EU-UK Trade and Cooperation Agreement—Exceptional Circumstances or a New Paradigm for EU External Relations?* (2021) 84 *Modern Law Review* 164

Eeckhout, P., *The Domestic Legal Status of the WTO Agreement: Interconnecting Legal Systems* (1997) 34 *Common Market Law Review* 11

Eeckhout, P., *EU Charter of Fundamental Rights and the Federal Question* (2002) 39 *Common Market Law Review* 945

Eeckhout, P., *Judicial Enforcement of WTO Law in the European Union—Some Further Reflections* (2002) 5 *Journal of International Economic Law* 110

Egan, M., *Towards a New History of European Law: New Wine in Old Bottles* (2013) 28 *American University International Law Review* 1223

Egli, P., Kokott, J., *Portuguese Republic v. Council of the European Union (Judgment). Case C-149/96* (2000) 94 *American Journal of International Law* 740

Ehle, D., *Van Gend & Loos* (1963) 16 *Neue Juristische Wochenschrift* 974

Eilmansberger, T., *The Relationship between Rights and Remedies in EC Law: In Search of the Missing Link* (2004) 41 *Common Market Law Review* 1199

Eleftheriadis, P., *The Direct Effect of Community Law: Conceptual Issues* (1996) 16 *Yearbook of European Law* 205–221

Emmert, F., *Horizontale Drittwirkung von Richtlinien? Lieber ein Ende mit Schrecken als ein Schrecken ohne Ende!* (1992) 3 *Europäisches Wirtschafts und Steuerrecht* 56

Emmert, F., Pereira de Azevedo, M., *L'effet horizontal des directives – La jurisprudence de la CJCE: un bateau ivre?* (1993) 29 *Revue trimestrielle de droit européen* 503

Epiney, A., *Unmittelbare Anwendbarkeit und Objektive Wirkung von Richtlinien* (1996) 111 *Deutsches Verwaltungsblatt* 409

Erpelding, M., *International Law and the European Court of Justice: The Politics of Avoiding History* (2020) 22 *Journal of the History of International Law* 446

Everling, U., *The Maastricht Judgment of the German Federal Constitutional Court and its Significance for the Development of the European Union* (1995) 14 *Yearbook of European Law* 1–19

Fabbrini, F., *After the OMT Case: The Supremacy of EU Law as the Guarantee of the Equality of the Member States* (2015) 16 *German Law Journal* 1003

Fabbrini, F., Sajó, A., *The Dangers of Constitutional Identity* (2019) 25 *European Law Journal* 457

Faix, M., *Genesis eines mehrpoligen Justizkonflikts: Das Verfassungsgericht der Tschechischen Republik wertet ein EuGH-Urteil als Ultra-vires-Akt* (2012) 39 *Europäische Grundrechte-Zeitschrift* 597

Faraguna, P., *Constitutional Identity in the EU—A Shield or a Sword?* (2018) 19 *German Law Journal* 1617

Faraguna, P., *Unamendability and Constitutional Identity in the Italian Constitutional Experience* (2019) 21 *European Journal of Law Reform* 329

Faraguna, P., *On the Identity Clause and its Abuses: 'Back to the Treaty'* (2021) 27 *European Public Law* 411

Fasone, C., Gallo, D., Wouters, J., *Re-connecting Authority and Democratic Legitimacy in the EU: Introductory Remarks* (2020) 5 *European Papers* 175

Feichtner, I., *The German Constitutional Court's PSPP Judgment: Impediment and Impetus for the Democratization of Europe* (2020) 21 *German Law Journal* 1090

Ferraro, F., *Diritto dell'Unione e concessioni demaniali: più luci o più ombre nelle sentenze gemelle dell'Adunanza Plenaria?* (2021) 46 *Diritto e Società* 359

Fisicaro, M., *Protection of the Rule of Law and 'Competence Creep' via the Budget: The Court of Justice on the Legality of the Conditionality Regulation: ECJ Judgments of 16 February 2022, Cases C-156/21, Hungary v. Parliament and Council and C-157/21, Poland v. Parliament and Council* (2022) 18 *European Constitutional Law Review* 334

Fontana, E., *Qualche osservazione in margine al caso Lucchini. Un tentativo di spiegazione* (2008) 22 *Diritto del commercio internazionale* 193

Fontanelli, F., *General Principles of the EU and a Glimpse of Solidarity in the Aftermath of Mangold and Kücükdeveci* (2011) 17 *European Public Law* 225

Fontanelli, F., *National Measures and the Application of the EU Charter of Fundamental Rights—Does curia.eu Know iura.eu?* (2014) 14 *Human Rights Law Review* 231

Fornasier, M., *The Impact of EU Fundamental Rights on Private Relationships: Direct or Indirect Effect?* (2015) 23 *European Review of Private Law* 29

Frantziou, E., *The Horizontal Effect of the Charter of Fundamental Rights of the EU: Rediscovering the Reasons for Horizontality* (2015) 21 *European Law Journal* 657

Frantziou, E., *(Most of) the Charter of Fundamental Rights is Horizontally Applicable. ECJ 6 November 2018, Joined Cases C-569/16 and C-570/16, Bauer et al.* (2019) 15 *European Constitutional Law Review* 306

Frantziou, E., *The Horizontal Effect of the Charter: Towards an Understanding of Horizontality as a Structural Constitutional Principle?* (2020) 22 *Cambridge Yearbook of European Legal Studies* 208–232

Freeman, J., *The Contracting State* (2000) 28 *Florida State University Law Review* 155

Freeman, J., *The Private Role in Public Governance* (2000) 75 *New York University Law Review* 543

Freeman, J., *Extending Public Law Norms through Privatization* (2003) 116 *Harvard Law Review* 1285

Fromage, D., *National Constitutional Identity and Its Regional Dimension Post-Lisbon as Part of a General Trend Towards Multilevel Governance within the EU* (2021) 27 *European Public Law* 497

Fromage, D., De Witte, B., *National Constitutional Identity Ten Years on: State of Play and Future Perspectives* (2021) 27 *European Public Law* 411

Frowein, J. A., *Das Maastricht-Urteil und die Grenzen der Verfassungsgerichtsbarkeit* (1994) 54 *Zeitschrift für ausländisches öffentliches Recht und Völkerrecht* 1

Gaja, G., *Reviewing Bengoetxea—Survey of Books* (1994) 92 *Michigan Law Review* 1971

Galetta, D. U., Ziller, J., *The Bundesverfassungsgericht's glaring and deliberate breaches of EU law based on 'unintelligible' and 'arbitrary' grounds* (2021) 27 *European Public Law* 63

Gallo, D., *Controlimiti, identità nazionale e i rapporti di forza tra primato ed effetto diretto nella saga Taricco* (2017) 2 *Il Diritto dell'Unione europea* 249

Gallo, D., *La Corte costituzionale chiude la 'saga Taricco': tra riserva di legge, opposizione de facto del controlimite e implicita negazione dell'effetto diretto* (2017) 2 *European Papers* 885

Gallo, D., *Article 36 of the Charter and Access to Public Services: Scope, Extent and Limits of a Sui Generis Provision* (2018) 5 *E-PÚBLICA* 51

Gallo, D., *Challenging EU Constitutional Law: The Italian Constitutional Court's New Stance on Direct Effect and the Preliminary Reference Procedure* (2019) 25 *European Law Journal* 434

Gallo, D., *Effetto diretto del diritto dell'Unione europea e disapplicazione, oggi* (2019) 1 *Osservatorio sulle Fonti* 1

Gallo, D., *Efficacia diretta del diritto UE, procedimento pregiudiziale e Corte costituzionale: una lettura congiunta delle sentenze n. 269/2017 e 115/2018* (2019) 1 *Rivista AIC* 219

Gallo, D., *L'effetto diretto quale dottrina fondante dell'ordinamento dell'Unione Europea* (2020) 3 *Rivista internazionale di filosofia del diritto* 537

Gallo, D., Cecchetti, L., *La prassi regolatoria e giurisprudenziale italiana in materia di self-cleaning è compatibile con il diritto dell'Unione Europea?* (2021) 2 *Rivista della Regolazione dei Mercati* 244

Gallo, D., *Primato, identità nazionale e stato di diritto in Romania* (2022) 2 *Quaderni Costituzionali* 374

Gallo, D., *Rethinking Direct Effect and its Evolution: A Proposal* (2022) 1 *European Law Open* 576

Gallo, D., *Assegni di natalità e maternità nella recente sentenza della Corte di giustizia: riflessioni 'a caldo'* (2023) 1 *Eurojus* 1

Gallo, D., Cecchetti, L., *Introduction: Article 267 TFEU,* today, in Gallo, D., Cecchetti L. (eds.), The Preliminary Ruling Procedure, Today: Revisiting Article 267 TFEU's Constitutional Backbone, Special Issue (2023) 15 *European Journal of Legal Studies* 1

Galmot, Y., Bonichot, J.-C., *La Cour de Justice des Communautés européennes et la transposition des directives en droit national* (1988) 1 *Revue française de droit administratif* 1

Gáspár-Szilágyi, S., *EU Member State Enforcement of 'Mixed' Agreements and Access to Justice: Rethinking Direct Effect* (2013) 40 *Legal Issues of Economic Integration* 163

Gáspár-Szilágyi, S., *The 'Primacy' and 'Direct Effect' of EU International Agreements* (2015) 21 *European Public Law* 343

Gáspár-Szilágyi, S., *The Relationship between EU Law and International Agreements: Restricting the Application of the Fediol and Nakajima Exceptions in Vereniging Milieudefensie* (2015) 52 *Common Market Law Review* 1059

Gattinara, G., *Il ruolo comunitario delle amministrazioni nazionali alla luce della sentenza Kühne & Heitz* (2004) 4 *Diritto comunitario e degli scambi internazionali* 489

Gattini, A., *Joined Cases C-402/05 P & 415/05 P, Yassin Abdullah Kadi, Al Barakaat International Foundation v. Council and Commission, Judgment of the Grand Chamber of 3 September 2008* (2009) 46 *Common Market Law Review* 213

Gentile, G., *Inter-Environnement Expanded: Another Brick Out of the Wall of EU Law Supremacy?* (2017) 2 *European Papers* 321

Gerstenberg, O., *Private Law and the New European Constitutional Settlement* (2004) 10 *European Law Journal* 766

Gerstenberg, O., *The Justiciability of Socio-economic Rights, European Solidarity, and the Role of the Court of Justice of the EU* (2014) 33 *Yearbook of European Law* 245–276

Gerstenberg, O., *Fundamental Rights and Democratic Sovereignty in the EU: The Role of the Charter of Fundamental Rights of the EU (CFREU) in Regulating the European Social Market Economy* (2020) 39 *Yearbook of European Law* 199–227

Ghazaryan, N., *Who Are the 'Gatekeepers'? In Continuation of the Debate on the Direct Applicability and the Direct Effect of EU International Agreements* (2018) 37 *Yearbook of European Law* 27–74

Ghera, F., *Pregiudiziale comunitaria, pregiudiziale costituzionale e valore di precedente delle sentenze interpretative della Corte di giustizia* (2000) 4 *Giurisprudenza costituzionale* 1193

Giannini, M. S., *Stato Sociale: una nozione inutile* (1977) 42 *Il Politico* 205

Goldmann, M., *Constitutional Pluralism as Mutually Assured Discretion: The Court of Justice, the German Federal Constitutional Court, and the ECB* (2016) 23 *Maastricht Journal of European and Comparative Law* 119

Goldsmith, L., *A Charter of Rights, Freedoms and Principles* (2001) 38 *Common Market Law Review* 1201

González Giménez, J., *Régimen comunitario de la contaminación por descargas procedentes de buques: la relación con las normas internacionales y la sentencia del TJCE sobre el asunto Intertanko* (2009) 13 *Revista de Derecho Comunitario Europeo* 915

González, A., Luis, N., *Nuevos desarrollos en la aplicación del GATT* (1992) 19 *Revista de Instituciones Europeas* 195

Gori, P., *Una pietra miliare nell'affermazione del diritto europeo* (1963) 4 *Giurisprudenza italiana* 49

Gori, P., *Retrospettiva sulla genesi dei principi dell'applicabilità diretta e della preminenza del diritto comunitario: le sentenze Costa c. Enel e Van Gend & Loos* (2014) 4 *Diritto comunitario e degli scambi internazionali* 653

Götz, V., *Das Maastricht-Urteil des Bundesverfassungsgerichts* (1993) 20 *Juristenzeitung* 1081

Granger, M.-P., *National Applications of Francovich and the Construction of a European Administrative Ius Commune* (2007) 32 *European Law Review* 157

Greco, G., *La Corte di giustizia ritorna sulle concessioni balneari precisandone le regole: problemi superati e problemi ancora aperti in sede di applicazione nazionale del diritto UE* (2023) 14 *Federalismi.it* 125

Greco, G., *Il suivi della sentenza della Corte di giustizia sulle concessioni balneari (continua il braccio di ferro tra TAR Lecce e Consiglio di Stato)* (2023) 1 *Eurojus* 1

Green, N., *Directives, Equity and the Protection of Individual Rights* (1984) 9 *European Law Review* 295

Griller, S., *Judicial Enforceability of WTO Law in the European Union: Annotation to Case C-149/96, Portugal v Council* (2000) 3 *Journal of International Economic Law* 441

Grimm, D., *Defending Sovereign Statehood against Transforming the European Union into a State* (2009) 5 *European Constitutional Law Review* 353

Groussot, X. and Minssen, T., *Res Judicata in the Court of Justice Case-Law: Balancing Legal Certainty with Legality?* (2007) 3 *European Constitutional Law Review* 385

Grundmann, S., *The Structure of European Contract Law* (2019) 27 *European Review of Private Law* 505

Gualco, E., Lourenço, L., *'Clash of Titans'. General Principles of EU Law: Balancing and Horizontal Direct Effect* (2016) 1 *European Papers* 643

Gualco, E., *'Clash of Titans 2.0'. From Conflicting EU General Principles to Conflicting Jurisdictional Authorities: The Court of Justice and the Danish Supreme Court in the 'Dansk Industri Case'* (2017) 2 *European Papers* 223

Guastaferro, B., *Beyond the Exceptionalism of Constitutional Conflicts: The Ordinary Functions of the Identity Clause* (2012) 31 *Yearbook of European Law* 263–318

Guðmundsdóttir, D., *A Renewed Emphasis on the Charter's Distinction between Rights and Principles: Is a Doctrine of Judicial Restraint More Appropriate?* (2015) 52 *Common Market Law Review* 685

Gundel, J., *EuGH: Gleichbehandlung befristeter und unbefristeter Arbeitsverhältnisse bei Kündigung. Anmerkung zu EuGH (Große Kammer) Urteil vom 20.2.2024 – C-715/20* (2024) 14 *Neue Juristische Wochenschrift* 949

Hadjiyianni, I., *The CJEU as the Gatekeeper of International Law: The Cases of WTO Law and the Aarhus Convention* (2021) 70 *International & Comparative Law Quarterly* 895

Haguenau-Moizard, C., *Pour la reconnaissance d'un effet direct horizontal aux directives* (2011) 550 *Revue du Marché Commun de l'Union européenne* 454

Haket, S., *The Danish Supreme Court's Ajos judgment (Dansk Industri): Rejecting a Consistent Interpretation and Challenging the Effect of a General Principle of EU Law in the Danish Legal Order* (2017) 10 *Review of European Administrative Law* 135

Halberstam, D., Möllers, C., *The German Constitutional Court Says 'Ja zu Deutschland!'* (2009) 10 *German Law Journal* 1241

Halmai, G., *Abuse of Constitutional Identity. The Hungarian Constitutional Court on Interpretation of Article E (2)* of the Fundamental Law (2018) 43 *Review of Central and East European Law* 23

Hancox, E., *The Relationship between the Charter and General Principles: Looking Back and Looking Forward* (2022) 24 *Cambridge Yearbook of European Legal Studies* 233–257

Harbo, T.-I., *The function of the Proportionality Principle in EU Law* (2010) 16 *European Law Journal* 159

Harlow, C., *Public and Private Law: Definition and without Distinction* (1980) 43 *Modern Law Review* 241

Harlow, C., *Francovich and the Problem of the Disobedient State* (1996) 2 *European Law Journal* 199

Hartley, T., *Direct Applicability and the Failure to Repeal Incompatible National Legislation* (1975) 1 *European Law Review* 53

Hartley, T., *The Effects in National Law of Judgments of the European Court* (1980) 5 *European Law Review* 366

Hartley, T., *International Agreements and the Community Legal System: Some Recent Developments* (1983) 3 *European Law* 383

Hartley, T., *The European Court, Judicial Objectivity and the Constitution of the EU* (1996) 112 *Law Quarterly Review* 95

Hay, P., *Federal Jurisdiction of the Common Market* (1963) 12 *American Journal of Comparative Law* 21

Hay, P., *Van Gend & Loos* (1963) 12 *American Journal of Comparative Law* 404

He, L., *Une protection remarquable du droit au repos et au loisir: Commentaire de l'arrêt CJUE 6 nov. 2018, aff. C-684/16, Société Max-Planck c/ M. Shimizu* (2019) 55 *Revue trimestrielle de droit européenne* 651

Henckaerts, J. M., *Self-Executing Treaties and the Impact of International Law on National Legal Systems: Research Guide* (1998) 26 *International Journal of Legal Information* 56

Héraud, G., *Nature juridique de la Communauté Européenne d'après le projet de Statut du 10 mars 1953* (1953) 69 *Revue du Droit Public et de la Science Politique en France et à l'Etranger* 581

Herdegen, M., *Maastricht and the German Constitutional Court: Constitutional Restraints for an 'Ever Closer Union'* (1994) 31 *Common Market Law Review* 235

Herzmann, K., *Das spanische Verfassungsgericht und der Fall Melloni* (2015) 42 *Europäische Grundrechte-Zeitschrift* 445

Herzog, R., *Stop the European Court of Justice, Frankfurter Allgemeine Zeitung* 8 September 2008

Hilpold, P., *So Long Solange? The PSPP Judgment of the German Constitutional Court and the Conflict between the German and the European 'Popular Spirit'* (2021) 23 *Cambridge Yearbook of European Legal Studies* 159–192

Hilson, C., *Rights and Principles in EU Law: A Distinction without Foundation?* (2008) 15 *Maastricht Journal of European and Comparative Law* 193

Hilson, C., Downes, T., *Making Sense of Rights: Community Rights in EC Law* (1999) 24 *European Law Review* 121

Himsworth, C. M. G., *Things Fall Apart: The Harmonisation of Community Judicial Procedural Protection Revisited* (1997) 22 *European Law Review* 291

Hobe, S., *The German State in Europe after the Maastricht Decision of the German Constitutional Court* (1994) 37 *German Yearbook of International Law* 113–136

Hohfeld, W. N., *Some Fundamental Legal Conceptions as Applied in Judicial Reasoning* (1913) 23 *Yale Law Journal* 16

Hohfeld, W. N., *Fundamental Legal Conceptions as Applied in Judicial Reasoning* (1917) 26 *Yale Law Journal* 710

Holdgaard, R., Elkan, D., Schaldemose, G. K., *From Co-operation to Collision: The ECJ's Ajos Ruling and the Danish Supreme Court's Refusal to Comply* (2018) 55 *Common Market Law Review* 17

Horwitz, M. J., *History of the Public/Private Distinction* (1982) 130 *University of Pennsylvania Law Review* 1423

Hoskins, M., *Tilting the Balance: Supremacy and National Procedural Rules* (1996) 21 *European Law Review* 365

Howard, E., *Islamic Headscarves and the CJEU: Achbita and Bougnaoui* (2017) 24 *Maastricht Journal of European and Comparative Law* 351

Howard E., *Headscarves and the CJEU: Protecting Fundamental Rights and Pandering to Prejudice, the CJEU Does Both* (2022) 29 *Maastricht Journal of European and Comparative Law* 245

Huglo, J.-H., *Primauté du droit communautaire et autorité de la chose jugée par les juridictions nationales* (2007) 53 *Gazette du Palais* 18

Iglesias Sánchez, S., *The Court and the Charter: The Impact of the Entry into Force of the Lisbon Treaty on the ECJ's Approach to Fundamental rights* (2012) 49 *Common Market Law Review* 1565

Jackson, J. H., *Status of Treaties in Domestic Legal Systems: A Policy Analysis* (1992) 86 *American Journal of International Law* 310

Jaenicke, G., *Die Europäische Gemeinschaft für Kohle und Stahl – Struktur und Funktionen ihrer Organe* (1952) 13 *Zeitschrift für ausländisches öffentliches Recht und Völkerrecht* 727

Jansen, N., Michaels, R., *Private Law Beyond the State? Europeanization, Globalization, Privatization* (2006) 54 *American Journal of Comparative Law* 843

Jeantet, F.-C., *Droit communautaire et juridictions internes* (1963) 147–148 *Le Barreau de France* 25

Jeantet, F.-C., *Originalité d'interprétation du traité de Rome* (1966) 1 *La Semaine juridique* 1987

Joliet, R., *La protection juridictionnelle des particuliers contre les manquements étatiques* (1994) 10 *Revue Française de Droit Administratif* 647

Junker, A., *Der EuGH zum Arbeitsrecht: Betriebsübergang, Gleichbehandlung und Bestandsschutz* (2006) 17 *Europäische Zeitschrift für Wirtschaftsrecht* 524

Kaiser, K., *Treaties, Direct Applicability*, in *Max Planck Encyclopedia of Public International Law*, Oxford, Oxford University Press, 2013

Kakouris, C. N., *Do the Member States Possess Judicial Procedural 'Autonomy'?* (1997) 34 *Common Market Law Review* 1389

Kendrick, J. M., *Modifying Procedural Autonomy: Better Protection for Community Rights* (2000) 8 *European Review of Private Law* 565

Kennedy, D., *Stages of the Decline of the Public/Private Distinction* (1982) 130 *University of Pennsylvania Law Review* 1349

Kinley, D., *Direct Effect of Directives: Stuck on Vertical Hold* (1995) 1 *European Public Law* 79

Klabbers, J., *International Law in Community Law: The Law and Politics of Direct Effect* (2001) 21 *Yearbook of European Law* 263–298

Klamert, M., *Judicial Implementation of Directives and Anticipatory Indirect Effect: Connecting the Dots* (2006) 43 *Common Market Law Review* 1251

Klein, M., *Das Recht der Kirchen im Tauziehen zwischen Luxemburg und Karlsruhe - Das kirchliche Arbeitsrecht als Machtprobe?* (2019) 54 *Europarecht* 338

Knox, J. H., *Horizontal Human Rights Law* (2008) 102 *American Journal of International Law* 1

Kochenov, D., Bárd, P., *The Last Soldier Standing? Courts vs Politicians and the Rule of Law Crisis in the New Member States of the EU* (2019) 1 *European Yearbook of Constitutional Law* 243–287

Kochenov, D., *EU Law without the Rule of Law: Is the Veneration of Autonomy Worth It?* (2019) 34 *Yearbook of European Law* 74–96

Kochenov, D., *De Facto Power Grab in Context: Upgrading Rule of Law in Europe in Populist Times* (2020) 40 *Polish Yearbook of International Law* 197–208

Kochenov, D., *Restoring the Dialogical Rule of Law in the EU: Janus in the Mirror* (2024) 25 *Cambridge Yearbook of European Legal Studies* 1–16

Komárek, J., *In the Courts We Trust? On the Need for Hierarchy and Differentiation in the Preliminary Ruling Procedure* (2007) 32 *European Law Review* 467

Komárek, J., *Precedent and Judicial Lawmaking in Supreme Courts: The Court of Justice Compared to the US Supreme Court and the French Cour de Cassation* (2009) 11 *Cambridge Yearbook of European Legal Studies* 399–433

Komárek, J., *The Place of Constitutional Courts in the EU* (2013) 9 *European Constitutional Law Review* 420

Kornezov, A., *Res judicata of National Judgments Incompatible with EU Law: Time for a Major Rethink?* (2014) 50 *Common Market Law Review* 809

Kovar, R., *L'application directe du droit communautaire* (1973) 100 *Journal du droit international* 279

Kovar, R., *Les Accords liant les Communautés Européennes et l'ordre juridique communautaire: à propos d'une jurisprudence récente de la Cour de Justice* (1974) 17 *Revue du Marché Commun* 345

Král, R., *Questioning the Limits of Invocability of EU Directives in 'Triangular Situations'* (2010) 16 *European Public Law* 239

Král, R., *Questioning the Recent Challenge of the Czech Constitutional Court to the ECJ* (2013) 19 *European Public Law* 271

Kramme, M., *Kooperation, nein danke!—der EuGH untermauert seinen Führungsanspruch gegenüber den nationalen Verfassungsgerichten* (2014) 21 *Zeitschrift für Gemeinschaftsprivatrecht* 355

Krause, R., *Horizontal Effect of the EU Charter of Fundamental Rights: Bauer and Willmeroth, MPG* (2021) 58 *Common Market Law Review* 1173

Krenn, C., *A Missing Piece in the Horizontal Effect 'Jigsaw': Horizontal Direct Effect and the Free Movement of Goods* (2012) 49 *Common Market Law Review* 177

Krommendijk, J., *Principled Silence or Mere Silence on Principles? The Role of the EU Charter's Principles in the Case Law of the Court of Justice* (2015) 11 *European Constitutional Law Review* 321

Kumm, M., *Who is Afraid of the Total Constitution? Constitutional Rights as Principles and the Constitutionalization of Private Law* (2006) 7 *German Law Journal* 341

Kumm, M., *Rebel Without a Good Cause: Karlsruhe's Misguided Attempt to Draw the CJEU into a Game of 'Chicken' and What the CJEU Might do About It* (2014) 15 *German Law Journal* 203

Kunz, J. L., *Supra-national Organs* (1952) 46 *American Journal of International Law* 697

La Pergola, A., *Il giudice costituzionale italiano di fronte al primato e all'effetto diretto del diritto comunitario: note su un incontro di studio* (2003) 4 *Giurisprudenza costituzionale* 2419

Lackhoff, K., Nyssens, H., *Direct Effect of Directives in Triangular Situations* (1998) 23 *European Law Review* 397

Lagrange, M., *La Cour de justice de la Commanauté éuropéenne du carbon et de l'acier* (1954) 70 *Revue du droit public et de la science politique en France et à l'étranger* 417

Lagrange, M., *L'organisation, le fonctionnement et le rôle de la Cour de justice des Communautés européennes* (1963) 13–14 *Bulletin de l'Association des juristes européens* 10

Lagrange, M., *The Court of Justice as a factor in European Integration* (1966–1967) 15 *American Journal of Comparative Law* 709

Lane, R., Shuibhne, N. N., *Case C-281/98, Roman Angonese v. Cassa di Risparmio di Bolzano SpA, Judgment of 6 June 2000, not yet reported* (2000) 37 *Common Market Law Review* 1237

Lanotte, M., *La proporzionalità della sanzione: un principio ritrovato? Note a margine della sentenza NE*, Serie Speciale (2023) 17 *Quaderni AISDUE* 367

Lavranos, N., *Die Rechtswirkung von WTO panel reports im Europäischen Gemeinschaftsrecht sowie im deutschen Verfassungsrecht* (1999) 34 *Europarecht* 289–308

Lazzerini, N., *Effetti diretti orizzontali dei principi generali... ma non delle direttive che li esprimono? La sentenza della Corte di giustizia nel caso Kücükdeveci* (2010) 2 *Rivista di diritto internazionale* 443

Lazzerini, N., *Gli effetti diretti orizzontali dei diritti fondamentali in materia sociale: la sentenza Dominguez della Corte di giustizia e la strada del silenzio* (2012) 3 *Rivista di diritto internazionale* 455

Lazzerini, N., *(Some of) the fundamental rights granted by the Charter may be a source of obligations for private parties: AMS* (2014) 51 *Common Market Law Review* 907

Lecourt, R., *L'Europe dans le prétoire, Le Monde*, 23 February 1963

Leczykiewicz, D., *Horizontal Application of the Charter of Fundamental Rights* (2013) 38 *European Law Review* 479

Leczykiewicz, D., *The Judgment in Bauer and the Effect of the EU Charter of Fundamental Rights in Horizontal Situations* (2020) 16 *European Review of Contract Law* 323

Lenaerts, K., *L'égalité de traitement en droit Communautaire* (1991) 1-2 *Cahiers de droit européen* 3

Lenaerts, K., *Federalism: Essential Concepts in Evolution – The Case of the European Union* (1998) 21 *Fordham International Law Journal* 746

Lenaerts, K., Corthaut, T., *Of Birds and Hedges: The Role of Primacy in Invoking Norms of EU Law* (2006) 31 *European Law Review* 287

Lenaerts, K., *Interpretation and the Court of Justice: A Basis for Comparative Reflection* (2007) 41 *International Lawyer* 1011

Lenaerts, K., Gutiérrez-Fons, J. A., *The Constitutional Allocation of Powers* (2010) 47 *Common Market Law Review* 1629

Lenaerts, K., *Some Thoughts on the State of the European Union as a Rights-Based Legal Order* (2015) 1 *Il Diritto dell'Unione europea* 5

Lenaerts, K., *Limits on Limitations: The Essence of Fundamental Rights in the EU* (2019) 20 *German Law Journal* 779

Lenaerts, K., *The Horizontal Application of the Charter* (2020) 4 *Quaderni costituzionali* 633

Lenaerts, K., J.-A. Gutiérrez-Fons, Adam, S., *Exploring the Autonomy of the European Union Legal Order* (2021) 1 *Zeitschrift für ausländisches öffentliches Recht und Völkerrecht* 47

Lenz, M., Sif Tynes, D., Young, L., *Horizontal What? Back to Basics* (2000) 25 *European Law Review* 509

Liguori, F., *Efficacia diretta e primato europeo: condizioni, effetti e limiti di operatività nel settore delle concessioni demaniali marittime* (2023) 3 *Munus* 387

Lindeboom, J., *The Autonomy of EU Law: A Hartian View* (2021) 13 *European Journal of Legal Studies* 37

Lindeboom, J., *Thelen Technopark and the Legal Effects of the Services Directive in Purely Internal and Horizontal Disputes* (2022) 7 *European Papers* 305

Lock, T., *Why the European Union is not a State* (2009) 5 *European Constitutional Law Review* 407

Lock, T., *Is Private Enforcement of EU Law through State Liability a Myth? An Assessment 20 years after Francovich* (2012) 49 *Common Market Law Review* 1675

Lock, T., *Are There Exceptions to a Member State's Duty to Comply with the Requirements of a Directive?: Inter-Environnement Wallonie* (2013) 50 *Common Market Law Review* 217

Lock, T., *Rights and Principles in the EU Charter of Fundamental Rights* (2019) 56 *Common Market Law Review* 1201

Lock, T., *Article 16*, in Kellerbauer, M., Klamert, M., Tomkin, J. (eds.), *The EU Treaties and the Charter of Fundamental Rights. A Commentary*, Oxford, Oxford University Press, 2019, 2147–2148

Lock, T., *Article 51 CFR*, in Kellerbauer, M., Klamert, M., Tomkin, J. (eds.), *The EU Treaties and the Charter of Fundamental Rights. A Commentary*, Oxford, Oxford University Press, 2019, 2241–2246

Lock, T., *Article 52*, in Kellerbauer, M., Klamert, M., Tomkin, J. (eds.), *The EU Treaties and the Charter of Fundamental Rights. A Commentary*, Oxford, Oxford University Press, 2019, 2248–2260

Lock, T., Martin, D., *Article 47 CFEU*, in Kellerbauer, M., Klamert, M., Tomkin, J. (eds.), *The EU Treaties and the Charter of Fundamental Rights. A Commentary*, Oxford, Oxford University Press, 2019, 2214–2225

Lohse, E. J., *Fundamental Freedoms and Private Actors – towards an 'Indirect Horizontal Effect'* (2007) 13 *European Public Law* 159

Lorenzon, S., *La Corte di giustizia e il riconoscimento degli effetti diretti orizzontali delle direttive comunitarie: il caso Kücükdeveci* (2010) 2 *Quaderni costituzionali* 430

Lorenzoni, L., *The Doctrine of Dual Preliminarity in the Case Law of Italian Administrative Courts*, in Gallo, D., Piccirilli, G. (eds.), Dual Preliminarity through National, EU and Comparative Case Law, Special Issue (2023) 15 *Italian Journal of Public Law* 42

Luciani, M., *Il brusco risveglio. I controlimiti e la fine mancata della storia costituzionale* (2016) 1 *Rivista AIC* 13

Ludwigs, M., *Der Schutz der Rechtskraft im Gemeinschaftsrecht* (2006) 47 *Zeitschrift für Rechtsvergleichung*, internationales Privatrecht und Europarecht 191

Lupo, E., *La primauté del diritto dell'UE e l'ordinamento penale nazionale. Riflessioni sulla sentenza Taricco* (2016) 2 *Diritto penale contemporaneo* 217

Lupo, N., *The Advantage of Having the 'First Word' in the Composite European Constitution* (2018) 10 *Italian Journal of Public Law* 186

Lupo, N., *Con quattro pronunce dei primi mesi del 2019 la Corte costituzionale completa il suo rientro nel sistema 'a rete' di tutela dei diritti in Europa* (2019) 14 *Federalismi.it* 1

MacCormick, N., *Beyond the Sovereign State* (1993) 56 *Modern Law Review* 1

Maciejewski, T., Theilen, J., *Temporal Aspects of the Interaction between National Law and EU Law: Reintroducing the Protection of Legitimate Expectations* (2017) 42 *European Law Review* 707

Madsen, M. R., Olsen, H. P., Šadl, U., *Competing Supremacies and Clashing Institutional Rationalities: The Danish Supreme Court's Decision in the Ajos Case and the National Limits of Judicial Cooperation* (2017) 23 *European Law Journal* 140

Maher, I., *National Courts as European Community Courts* (1994) 14 *Legal Studies* 226

Majone, G., *Paradoxes of Privatization and Deregulation* (1994) 1 *Journal of European Public Policy* 54

Majone, G., *From Positive to the Regulatory State: Causes and Consequences of Changes in the Mode of Governance* (1997) 17 *Journal of Public Policy* 139

Makowiak, J., *Spécificité de l'ordre juridique communautaire et pragmatisme de la Cour: ou comment lutter efficacement contre les pollutions maritimes* (2009) 3 *Revue trimestrielle de droit européen* 402

Malmberg, J., Sigeman, T., *Industrial Actions and EU Economic Freedoms: The Autonomous Collective Bargaining Model Curtailed by the European Court of Justice* (2008) 45 *Common Market Law Review* 1115

Mancini, F., Keeling, D., *Democracy and the European Court of Justice* (1994) 57 *Modern Law Review* 175

Manes, V., *Some Lessons from the Taricco Saga* (2018) 9 *New Journal of European Criminal Law* 12

Manfredi, M., *Enhancing Economic and Social Rights within the Internal Market through Recognition of the Horizontal Effects of the European Charter of Fundamental Rights* (2021) 6 *European Papers* 293

Manin, P., *L'invocabilité des directives: quelques interrogations* (1990) 26 *Revue trimestrielle de droit européen* 669

Manin, P., *De l'utilisation des directives communautaires par les personnes physiques ou morales* (1994) 4 *L'Actualité juridique. Droit administratif* 259–269

Marsh, N. S., *Some Reflections on Legal Integration in Europe* (1963) 12 *International and Comparative Law Quarterly* 1411

Martín Rodríguez, P., *Crónica de una muerte anunciada: Comentario a la Sentencia del Tribunal de Justicia* (Gran Sala) de 26 de febrero de 2013, *Stefano Melloni, C-399/11* (2013) 30 *Revista General de Derecho Europeo* 1

Martines, F., *Direct Effect of International Agreements of the European Union* (2014) 25 *European Journal of International Law* 12

Martinico, G., *Le sentenze interpretative della Corte di giustizia come fonte di produzione normativa* (2004) 9 *Rivista di diritto costituzionale* 249

Martinico, G., Fontanelli, F., *The Hidden Dialogue: When Judicial Competitors Collaborate* (2008) 8 *Global Jurist Issue* 1

Martinico, G., *Multiple Loyalties and Dual Preliminarity: The Pains of being a Judge in a Multilevel Legal Order* (2012) 10 *International Journal of Constitutional Law* 871

Martinico, G., *Il caso A. c. B. e il suo impatto sul rapporto fra Corti: un diritto per tre giudici* (2014) 4 *Quaderni costituzionali* 950

Martinico, G., *The 'Polemical' Spirit of European Constitutional Law: On the Importance of Conflicts in EU Law* (2015) 16 *German Law Journal* 1343

Martinico, G., Repetto, G., *Fundamental Rights and Constitutional Duels in Europe: An Italian Perspective on Case 269/2017 of the Italian Constitutional Court and Its Aftermath* (2019) 15 *European Constitutional Law Review* 731

Martinico, G., *Taming National Identity: A Systematic Understanding of Article 4.2 TUE* (2021) 27 *European Public Law* 447

Martinico, G., *Dual Preliminarity in Comparative Law*, in Gallo, D., Piccirilli, G. (eds.), Dual Preliminarity through National, EU and Comparative Case Law, Special Issue (2023) 15 *Italian Journal of Public Law* 120

Martinico, G., *Retracing Old (Scholarly) Path. The* Erga Omnes *Effects of the Interpretative Preliminary Rulings*, in Gallo, D., Cecchetti, L. (eds.), The Preliminary Ruling Procedure, *Today*: Revisiting Article 267 TFEU's Constitutional Backbone, Special Issue (2023) 15 *European Journal of Legal Studies* 37

Martucci, F., *Union économique et monétaire - Cour de justice, gde ch., 11 décembre 2018, Weiss e.a., aff. C-493/17, ECLI:EU:C:2018:1000, Jurisprudence de la CJUE 2018* (2019) *Décisions et commentaires* 1033

Martucci, F., *Les principes de sécurité juridique et de confiance légitime dans la jurisprudence de la Cour de justice de l'Union européenne* (2020) 5 *Titre VII – Les Nouveaux Cahiers du Counseil constitutionnel* 70–78

Mastroianni, R., *Direttive non attuate, rimedi alternativi e principio di uguaglianza (Commento all'art. 189 Trattato CE)* (1998) 1 *Il diritto dell'Unione Europea* 81

Mastroianni, R., *On the Distinction between Vertical and Horizontal Direct Effects of Community Directives: What Role for the Principle of Equality?* (1999) 5 *European Public Law* 417

Mastroianni, R., *Supremazia del diritto dell'Unione e 'controlimiti' costituzionali* (2016) *Diritto penale contemporaneo* 7 November 2016

Mastroianni, R., *L'Adunanza Plenaria del Consiglio di Stato e le concessioni balneari: due passi avanti e uno indietro?* (2022) 1 *Eurojus* 105

Mattli, W., Slaughter, A.-M., *Revisiting the European Court of Justice* (1998) 52 *International Organization* 177–209

Mayer, F. C., *The ultra vires ruling: Deconstructing the German Federal Constitutional Court's PSPP decision of 5 May 2020* (2020) 16 *European Constitutional Law Review* 733

Mayer, F. C., *To Boldly Go Where No Court Has Gone Before. The German Federal Constitutional Court's Ultra Vires Decision of May 5, 2020* (2020) 21 *German Law Journal* 1116

Mengozzi, P., *Les droits et les intérêts des entreprises, le droit de l'OMC et les prérogatives de l'Union européenne: vers une doctrine communautaire des 'political questions'* (2005) 9 *Revue du droit de l'Union européenne* 229

Mengozzi, P., *Quelques réflexions sur les origines de l'arrêt Van Gend en Loos* (2013) 4 *Il Diritto dell'Unione Europea* 679

Mertens de Wilmars, J., *L'efficacité des différentes techniques nationales de protection juridique contre les violations du droit communautaire par les autorités nationales et les particuliers* (1982) 18 *Cahiers de Droit Européen* 379

Miasik, D., Szwarc, M., *Primacy and Direct Effect—Still Together: Popławski II* (2021) 58 *Common Market Law Review* 571

Migliazza, A., *Ordinamento comunitario e ordinamenti nazionali* (1963) 4 *Rivista di diritto processuale* 651

Millet, F.-X., *Successfully Articulating National Constitutional Identity Claims: Strait is the Gate and Narrow is the Way* (2021) 27 *European Public Law* 571

Millet, F.-X., *Cilfit Still Fits* (2022) 18 *European Constitutional Law Review* 533

Millet, F.-X., *Mérites et démérites de l'élévation d'un principe indéterminé au rang de l'identité constitutionnelle de la France* (2022) 3 *Revue trimestrielle de droit européen* 333

Millet, F.-X., *Le glissement jurisprudentiel en matière de données de connexion: l'expansion des compétences de l'Union et sa réception dans les États membres* (2023) 39 *Revue française de droit administratif* 606

Millet, F.-X., *How to Enforce 'Mild' Obligations under EU Law? Proceduralising the Weak Duty to Refer as a Strong Duty to State Reasons*, in Gallo, D., Cecchetti L. (eds.), The Preliminary Ruling Procedure, Today: Revisiting Article 267 *TFEU's Constitutional Backbone*, Special Issue (2023) 15 *European Journal of Legal Studies* 7

Mitsilegas, V., *Judicial Dialogue in Three Silences. Unpacking Taricco* (2018) 9 *New Journal of European Criminal Law* 38

Möllers, C., *Constitutional Review of European Acts Only Under Exceptional Circumstances* (2011) 7 *European Constitutional Law Review* 161

Montaldo, S., *Handle with Care! The Direct Effect of the Requirement of Proportionality of Sanctions and the Remedy of Disapplication: NE v. Bezirkshauptmannschaft Hartberg-Fürstenfeld* (2023) 60 *Common Market Law Review* 863

Morelli, G., *Appunti sulla CECA* (1954) 1 *Rivista di diritto internazionale* 3

Morelli, G., *Stati e individui nelle organizzazioni internazionali* (1957) 1 *Rivista di diritto internazionale* 3

Mosler, E. H., *Der Vertrag über die Europäische Gemeinschaft für Kohle und Stahl* (1951-52) 14 *Zeitschrift für ausländisches öffentliches Recht und Völkerrecht* 8

Muir, E., *Enhancing the Effects of EC Law on National Labour Markets: The Mangold Case* (2006) 31 *European Law Review* 879

Muir, E., *Of Ages in—and Edges of—EU Law* (2011) 48 *Common Market Law Review* 39

Muir, E., *The Fundamental Rights Implications of EU Legislation: Some Constitutional Challenges* (2014) 51 *Common Market Law Review* 219

Muir, E., *The Horizontal Effects of Charter Rights Given Expression to in EU Legislation, from Mangold to Bauer* (2019) 12 *Review of European Administrative Law* 205

Munari, F., *Gli effetti del diritto dell'Unione europea sul sistema interno delle fonti* (2013) 4 *Il Diritto dell'Unione europea* 725

Murillo de la Cueva, P. L., *Normas programáticas, estatutos y autonomía comunitaria* (1984) 1 *Revista de Derecho Político* 7

Murphy, C., *Using the EU Charter of Fundamental Rights against Private Parties after Association de Médiation Sociale* (2014) 2 *European Human Rights Law Review* 170

Nagy, C., *The Rebellion of Constitutional Courts and the Normative Character of European Union Law* (2024) 73 *International and Comparative Law Quarterly* 65–101

Nato, A., *Le concessioni balneari, tra mercato interno, armonizzazione e tutela della proprietà: primato, effetto diretto e disapplicazione nella causa Autorità garante della Concorrenza e del Mercato c. Comune di Ginosa* (2023) 2 *Eurojus* 22

Nebbia, P., *Do the Rules on State Aids Have a Life of Their Own? National Procedural Autonomy and Effectiveness in the Lucchini Case* (2008) 33 *European Law Review* 427

Neill QC, P., *The European Court of Justice: A Case Study in Judicial Activism* (1995) *European Policy Forum/ Frankfurter Institut—Stiftung Marktwirtschaft und Politik, London, European Policy Forum* 1

Nettesheim, M., *Ein Individualrecht auf Staatlichkeit? Die Lissabon-Entscheidung des BVerfG* (2009) 62 *Neue Juristische Wochenschrift* 2868

Nicola, F., *Luxemburg Judicial Style with or without the UK* (2017) 41 *Fordham International Law* 1504

Nicola, F., Fasone, C., Gallo, D., *Comparing the Effects of US Unconstitutionality and EU's Preliminary Interpretative Rulings: Disapplication, Resistance and Coordination Procedures*, in Gallo, D., Cecchetti L. (eds.), The Preliminary Ruling Procedure, Today: Revisiting Article 267 TFEU's Constitutional Backbone, Special Issue (2023) 15 *European Journal of Legal Studies* 147

Nollkaemper, A., *The Duality of Direct Effect of International Law* (2014) 25 *European Journal of International Law* 105

Oliver, P., *General Principles of Community Law and Horizontal Effect* (1993) 4 *Europäische Zeitschrift für Wirtschaftsrecht* 393

Oliver, P., *L'article 34 TFUE peut-il avoir un effet direct horizontal? Réflexions sur l'arrêt Fra.bo?* (2014) 1 *Cahiers de droit européen* 77

Oliver, P., Roth, W.-H., *The Internal Market and the Four Freedoms* (2004) 41 *Common Market Law Review* 407

Orzan, M. F., *Ops...the ECJ Did It Again! The Relationship between the Principle of Effectiveness of EU Law and the Principle of Legal Certainty in the ECJ Case-by-Case Approach* (2010) 1 *European Law Reporter* 63

Ott, A., *Der EuGH and das WTO Recht: Die Entdeckung der politischen Gegenseitigkeit—altes Phänomen oder neuer Ansatz?* (2003) 3 *Europarecht* 504

Palladino, R., *Diritti, principi ed effetto diretto orizzontale delle disposizioni (in materia sociale) della Carta dei diritti fondamentali dell'Unione europea* (2019) 1 *Il Diritto dell'Unione europea* 175

Pallotta, O., *Effetto orizzontale delle direttive? Solo se indiretto* (2005) 1 *Diritto pubblico comparato ed europeo* 505

Panascì, M. A., *The Right to Paid Annual Leave as an EU Fundamental Social Right. Comment on Bauer et al.: Joined Cases C-569/16 and C-570/16 Stadt Wuppertal v. Maria Elisabeth Bauer and Volker Willmeroth v. Martina Broßonn, EU:C:2018:871* (2019) 26 *Maastricht Journal of European and Comparative Law* 441

Pani, F., *L'obbligo (flessibile) di rinvio pregiudiziale e i possibili fattori di un suo irrigidimento. Riflessioni in margine alla sentenza Association France Nature Environnement* (2017) 2 *European Papers* 384

Papadopoulos, T., *Criticizing the Horizontal Direct Effect of the EU General Principle of Equality* (2019) 4 *European Human Rights Law Review* 437

Paris, D., *Constitutional Courts as Guardians of EU Fundamental Rights? Centralised Judicial Review of Legislation and the Charter of Fundamental Rights of the EU* (2015) 11 *European Constitutional Law Review* 389

Paris, D., *Limiting the 'Counter-Limit': National Constitutional Courts and the Scope of the Primacy of EU Law*, in Faraguna, P., Fasone, C., Piccirilli, G. (eds.), Constitutional Adjudication in Europe between unity and Pluralism, in *Italian Journal of Public Law*, 2018, 206

Parodi, G., *La proroga delle concessioni demaniali marittime tra disapplicazione e incidente di costituzionalità. Questioni aperte, opacità della giurisprudenza* (2023) 3 *DPCE online* 1607

Paust, J. J., *Self-Executing Treaties* (1988) 82 *American Journal International Law* 760

Payandeh, M., *The OMT Judgment of the German Federal Constitutional Court* (2017) 13 *European Constitutional Law Review* 400

Pech, L., *Between Judicial Minimalism and Avoidance: The Court of Justice's Sidestepping of Fundamental Constitutional Issues in Römer and Dominguez* (2012) 49 *Common Market Law Review* 1841

Pech, L., *Court of Justice protecting Polish judges from Poland's Disciplinary 'Star Chamber': Commission v. Poland (Interim Proceedings)* (2021) 58 *Common Market Law Review* 137

Pech, L., Kochenov, D., *Respect for the Rule of Law in the Case Law of the European Court of Justice: A Casebook Overview of Key Judgments since the Portuguese Judges Case* (2021) 3 *SIEPS*

Pechstein, M., *Die Anerkennung der Rein Objektiven Unmittelbaren Richtlinienwirkung* (1996) 7 *Europäisches Wirtschafts- und Steuerrecht* 261

Peerbux-Beaugendre, Z., *Une administration ne peut invoquer le principe de la force de chose définitivement jugée pour refuser de réexaminer une décision dont une interprétation préjudicielle ultérieure a révélé la contrariété avec le droit communautaire. Commentaire de l'arrêt de la CJCE du 13 janvier 2004* (2004) 8 *Revue du droit de l'Union européenne* 559

Peers, S., *W.T.O. Dispute Settlement and Community Law* (2001) 26 *European Law Review* 605

Peers, S., *Supremacy, Equality and Human Rights: Comment on Kucukdeveci (C-555/07)* (2010) 35 *European Law Review* 849

Pepy, A., *Le rôle de la Cour de justice des Communautés européennes dans l'application de l'article 177 du Traité de Rome* (1966) 2 *Cahiers de droit européen* 459

Perillo, E., *De Karlsruhe au Kirchberg et retour: le long voyage, courageux mais prévisible, d´un tourmenté 'ultra vires Urteil'* (2020) 1 *Il Diritto dell'Unione europea* 127

Pernice, I., *A Difficult Partnership between Courts: The First Preliminary Reference by the German Federal Constitutional Court to the CJEU* (2014) 21 *Maastricht Journal of European and Comparative Law* 3

Peroni, G., *Il diritto comunitario prevale sul giudicato sostanziale* (2008) 22 *Diritto del commercio internazionale* 221

Perrin, A., *Droit européen et droit communautaire: Que reste-t-il de l'autonomie procédurale des états membres?* (2008) 124 *Revue de droit public* 789

Pescatore, P., *International Law and Community Law—A Comparative Analysis* (1970) 7 *Common Market Law Review* 167

Pescatore, P., *Rôle et chance du droit et des juges dans la construction de l'Europe* (1974) 26 *Revue internationale de droit comparé* 5

Pescatore, P., *The Doctrine of 'Direct Effect': An Infant Disease of Community Law* (1983) 8 *European Law Review* 155

Pescatore, P., *Robert Lecourt (1908-2004)* (2005) 3 *Revue trimestrielle de droit européen* 589

Pesce, C., *Il principio dell'effetto utile e la tutela dei diritti nella giurisprudenza dell'Unione* (2014) 2 *Studi sull'integrazione europea* 359

Petersmann, E.-U., *Proposals for a New Constitution for the European Union: Building-Blocks for a constitutional theory and constitutional law of the EU* (1995) 32 *Common Market Law Review* 1123

Peters, A., *The Position of International Law within the European Community Legal Order* (1997) 40 *German Yearbook of International Law* 9–77

Phelan, W., *The Troika: The Interlocking Roles of Commission v. Luxembourg and Belgium, Van Gend en Loos and Costa v. ENEL in the Creation of the European Legal Order* (2015) 21 *European Law Journal* 116

Phelan, W., *Supremacy, Direct Effect, and Dairy Products in the Early History of European law* (2016) 14 *International Journal of Constitutional Law* 6

Phelan, W., *The Revolutionary Doctrines of European Law and the Legal Philosophy of Robert Lecourt* (2017) 28 *European Journal of International Law* 935

Piccirilli, G., *The 'Taricco Saga': the Italian Constitutional Court Continues its European Journey* (2018) 14 *European Constitutional Law Review* 814

Pinelli, C., *Respect for the Rule of Law as Embedded in Article 2 TEU and Protection of the Union's Financial Interests* (2021) 1 *Nuovi autoritarismi e democrazie. Diritto, istituzioni e società* 96

Plaza Martin, C., *Furthering the Effectiveness of EC Directives and the Judicial Protection of Individual Rights Thereunder* (1994) 43 *International and Comparative Law Quarterly* 26

Pliakos, A., *Le premier renvoi préjudiciel de la Cour constitutionnelle allemande à la CJUE: un pas en avant, deux pas en arrière?* (2014) 57 *Revue du marché commun et de l'Union européenne* 41

Pliakos, A., Anagnostaras, G., *Fundamental Rights and the New Battle over Legal and Judicial Supremay: Lessons from Melloni* (2015) 34 *Yearbook of European Law* 97–126

Pliakos, A., Anagnostaras, G., *Saving Face? The German Federal Constitutional Court Decides Gauweiler* (2017) 18 *German Law Journal* 213

Pliakos, A., Anagnostaras, G., *Adjudicating Economics II: The Quantitative Easing Programme Declared Valid* (2020) 45 *European Law Review* 128

Poelzig, D., *Gemeinschaftsrechtlicher Begriff der Rechtskraft* (2009) 7 *Europäische Zeitschrift für Wirtschaftsrecht* 741

Poiares Maduro, M., *Harmony and Dissonance in Free Movement* (2001) 4 *Cambridge Yearbook of European Legal Studies* 315 –341

Poiares Maduro, M., *Interpreting European Law: Judicial Adjudication in a Context of Constitutional Pluralism* (2007) 1 *European Journal of Legal Studies* 137

Poli, S., Cisotta, R., *The German Federal Constitutional Court's Exercise of Ultra Vires Review and the Possibility to Open an Infringement Action for the Commission* (2020) 21 *German Law Journal* 1078

Pollicino, O., *La Corte di giustizia riconosce l'efficacia diretta orizzontale dei principi generali ma non delle direttive* (2016) 3 *Quaderni costituzionali* 597

Polo, S., José, R., *Estado y confesiones religiosas en el Derecho de la Unión Europea: la repercusión del artículo 17 del Tratado de Funcionamiento de la Unión Europea en la jurisprudencia del TJUE* (2018) *46 Revista General de Derecho Europeo* 270

Porchia, O., *La dinamica dei rapporti tra norme interne e dell'Unione nel dialogo tra giudici nazionali e Corte di giustizia* (2013) 1 *Studi sull'integrazione europea* 71

Prechal, S., *Community Law in National Courts: The Lessons from Van Schijndel* (1998) *35 Common Market Law Review* 681

Prechal, S., *Does Direct Effect Still Matter?* (2000) 37 *Common Market Law Review* 1047

Prechal, S., Hancher, L., *Individual Environmental Rights: Conceptual Pollution in EU Environmental Law?* (2002) 2 *Yearbook of European Environmental Law* 89–115

Prechal, S., *Member State Liability and Direct Effect: What's the Difference after All?* (2006) 17 *European Business Law Review* 299

Prechal, S., *National Courts in EU Judicial Structures* (2006) 25 *Yearbook of European Law* 429–450

Prechal, S., *Competence Creep and General Principles of Law* (2010) 3 *Review of European and Administrative Law* 5

Prechal, S., *Horizontal Direct Effect of the Charter of Fundamental Rights of the EU* (2020) 66 *Revista de Derecho Comunitario Europeo* 407

Prek, M., Lefèvre, S., *The Eu Courts as 'National Courts': National Law in the EU Judicial Process* (2017) 54 *Common Market Law Review* 369

Preßlein, D., *Der absolute Anwendungsvorrang des Unionsrechts als Garantie der Gleichheit der Mitgliedstaaten in der Europäischen Union?: Rs. C-357/19, C-379/19, C-547/19, C-811/19, und C-840/19* (2022) 4 *Europarecht* 688

Rasmussen, M., *The Origins of a Legal Revolution—The Early History of the European Court of Justice* (2008) 14 *Journal of European Integration History* 77–98

Rasmussen, M., *Establishing a Constitutional Practice of European Law: The History of the Legal Service of the European Executive (1952–65)* (2012) 21 *Contemporary European History* 375

Rasmussen, M., *Revolutionizing European law: A History of the Van Gend en Loos Judgment* (2014) 12 *International Journal of Constitutional Law* 136

Rasmussen, M., *How to enforce European law? A New History of the Battle over the Direct effect of Directives 1958-1987* (2017) 23 *European Law Journal* 290

Rasmussen, M., Martinsen, D. S., *EU Constitutionalisation Revisited: Redressing a Central Assumption in European Studies* (2019) 25 *European Law Journal* 1

Rauchegger, C., *National Constitutional Rights and the Primacy of EU Law: M.A.S.* (2018) 55 *Common Market Law Review* 1521

Reich, N., *A European Constitution for Citizens: Reflections on the Rethinking of Union and Community Law* (1997) 3 *European Law Journal* 131

Reich, N., *Horizontal Liability in EC Law: Hybridization of Remedies for Compensation in case of Breaches of EC Rights* (2007) 44 *Common Market Law Review* 705

Repetto, G., *Judgment No. 269/2017 and Dual Preliminarity in the Evolution of the Jurisprudence of the Italian Constitutional Court*, in Gallo, D., Piccirilli, G. (eds.), Dual Preliminarity through National, EU and Comparative Case Law, Special Issue (2023) 15 *Italian Journal of Public Law* 8

Rhodes, M., *'Varieties of Capitalism' and the Political Economy of European Welfare States* (2005) 10 *New Political Economy* 363

Rigaux, F., *Van Gend & Loos* (1963) 12 *Journal des tribunaux* 190

Robin-Olivier, S., *La contribution de la Charte des droits fondamentaux à la protection des droits sociaux dans l'Union européenne: un premier bilan après Lisbonne* (2013) 1 *Journal européen des droits de l'homme* 109

Robin-Olivier, S., *The Evolution of Direct Effect in the EU: Stocktaking, Problems, Projections* (2014) 12 *International Journal of Constitutional Law* 165

Rodin, S., *La valeur des précédents dans la jurisprudence de la Cour* (2017) 4 *Il Diritto dell'Unione Europea* 661

Rodriguez Iglesias, R., *Sui limiti dell'autonomia procedimentale e processuale degli Stati membri nell'applicazione del diritto comunitario* (2001) 1 *Rivista italiana di diritto pubblico comunitario* 5–28

Roes, T., *Case Note—Case C-555/07, Seda Kücükdeveci v Swedex GmbH & Co. KG* (2010) 15 *Columbia Journal of European Law* 497

Ronzitti, N., *L'art. 12 del Trattato istitutivo della CEE ed i rapporti tra ordinamento comunitario ed ordinamento degli Stati membri* (1964) 4 *Il Foro italiano* 98

Rosas, A., *Case Annotation on Case C-149/96, Portugal v Council, Judgment of the Full Court of 23 November 1999* (2000) 37 *Common Market Law Review* 797

Rosas, A., *Implementation and Enforcement of WTO Dispute Settlement Findings: An EU Perspective* (2001) 4 *Journal of International Economic Law* 131

Rosas, A., *The Status in EU Law of International Agreements Concluded by EU Member States* (2011) 34 *Fordham International Law Journal* 1304

Rosenfeld, M., *Comparing Constitutional Review by the European Court of Justice and the U.S. Supreme Court* (2006) 4 *International Journal of Constitutional Law* 618

Ross, M., *Beyond Francovich* (1993) 56 *Modern Law Review* 55

Ross, M., *Effectiveness in the European Legal Order(s): Beyond Supremacy to Constitutional Proportionality?* (2006) 31 *European Law Review* 476

Rossi, L. S., *'Same Legal Value as the Treaties'? Rank, Primacy, and Direct Effects of the EU Charter of Fundamental Rights* (2017) 18 *German Law Journal* 771

Rossi, L. S., *Effetti diretti delle norme dell'Unione europea ed invocabilità di esclusione: i problemi aperti dalla seconda sentenza Popławski*, in *Giustizia Insieme*, 3 February 2021, https://www.giustiziainsieme.it/it/diritto-ue/1517-effetti-diretti-delle-norme-dell-unione-europea-ed-invocabilita-di-esclusione-i-problemi-aperti-dalla-seconda-sentenza-poplawski

Röß, S., *Die europäische Gesetzgebungskompetenz in Fragen religionsbezogener Einstellungsvoraussetzungen: der Fall Egenberger* (2022) 25 *Zeitschrift für Europarechtliche Studien* 607

Roth, W.-H., *Die 'horizontale' Anwendbarkeit der Warenverkehrsfreiheit (Art. 34 AEUV)* (2013) 12 *Europäische Wirtschafts- und Sprachakademie* 16

Ruffert, M., *Rights and Remedies in European Community Law: A Comparative View* (1997) 34 *Common Market Law Review* 307

Sabau, P., Ramón, J., *La sentencia del TJUE de 22 de enero de 2019 en el asunto Cresco Investigation GmbH: una nueva muestra de la irrelevancia del art. 17 del Tratado de Funcionamiento de la Unión Europea* (2020) 49 *Revista General de Derecho Europeo* 242

Šadl, U., Hink, S., *Precedent in the Sui Generis Legal Order: A Mine Run Approach* (2014) 20 *European Law Journal* 544

Šadl, U., Mair, S., *Mutual disempowerment: case C-441/14 Dansk Industri, acting on behalf of Ajos A/S v Estate of Karsten Eigil Rasmussen and case no.15/2014 Dansk Industri (DI) acting for Ajos A/S v The Estate left by A* (2017) 13 *European Constitutional Law Review* 347

Safjan, M., Mikłaszewicz, P., *Horizontal Effect of the General Principles of EU law in the Sphere of Private Law* (2010) 18 *European Review of Private Law* 475

Safjan, M., D. Dusterhaus, *A Union of Effective Judicial Protection: Addressing a Multi-Level Challenge through the Lens of Article 47 CFREU* (2014) 33 *Yearbook of European Law* 3–40

Salvadego, L., *Il divieto per i dipendenti di imprese private di esibire simboli religiosi all'esame della Corte di giustizia dell'Unione europea* (2017) 4 *Rivista di diritto internazionale* 808

Sarmiento, D., *El Derecho de la Unión europea: medio siglo de historia. Comentario a la celebración del 50 aniversario de la sentencia Van Gend en Loos* (2013) 10 *Unión Europea Aranzadi* 37

Sarmiento, D., *Who's Afraid of the Charter? The Court of Justice, National Courts and the New Framework of Fundamental Rights Protection in Europe* (2013) 50 *Common Market Law Review* 1267

Sarmiento, D., *The 'Overruling Technique' at the Court of Justice of the European Union*, in Gallo, D., Cecchetti L. (eds.), The Preliminary Ruling Procedure, Today: Revisiting Article 267 TFEU's Constitutional Backbone, Special Issue (2023) 15 *European Journal of Legal Studies* 107

Sauter, W., *Proportionality in EU Law: A Balancing Act?* (2013) 15 *Cambridge Yearbook of European Legal Studies* 439–466

Sawyer, K., *The Principle of 'interprétation conforme': How Far Can or Should National Courts Go when Interpreting National Legislation Consistently with European Community Law?* (2007) 28 *Statute Law Review* 165

Scaccia, G., *The Lesson Learned from the Taricco Saga: Judicial Nationalism and the Constitutional Review of E.U. Law* (2020) 35 *American University International Law Review* 821

Scarborough, R., *Directives and the Doctrine of Direct Effect: A Critique of Marshall v. Southampton Area Health Authority* (1992) 1992 *University of Chicago Legal Forum* 315

Schepel, H., *The Enforcement of EC Law in Contractual Relations: Case Studies in How Not to 'Constitutionalize' Private Law* (2004) 18 *European Review of Private Law* 661

Schepel, H., *Constitutionalising the Market, Marketising the Constitution, and to Tell the Difference: On the Horizontal Application of the Free Movement Provisions in EU Law* (2012) 18 *European Law Journal* 177

Schepel, H., *Annotation of Fra.bo* (2013) 9 *European Review of Contract Law* 186
Schepel, H., *Freedom of Contract in Free Movement Law: Balancing Rights and Principles* (2013) 21 *European Review of Private Law* 1211
Schermers, H. G., *Indirect Obligations. Four Questions in respect of EEC—Obligations Arising from Rights or Obligations of Others* (1977) 24 *Netherlands International Law Review* 260
Schermers, H. G., *No Direct Effect for Directives* (1997) 3 *European Public Law* 527
Scherzberg, A., *Die Innerstaatlichen Wirkungen von EG-Richtlinien* (1993) 15 *Juristische Ausbildung* 225
Schiek, D., *The ECJ Decision in Mangold: A Further Twist on Effects of Directives and Constitutional Relevance of Community Equality Legislation* (2006) 35 *Industrial Law Journal* 329
Schiek, D., *Constitutional Principles and Horizontal Effect: Kücükdeveci Revisited* (2010) 1 *European Labour Law Journal* 368
Scholtes, J., *Abusing Constitutional Identity* (2021) 22 *German Law Journal* 534
Schönberger, C., *Lisbon in Karlsruhe: Maastricht's Epigones at Sea* (2009) 10 *German Law Journal* 1201
Schubert, C., Art 51 CGR, in Franze, M., Gallner, I., Oetker, H. (eds.), Kommentar zum europäischen Arbeitsrecht, 4th ed., Munich, Beck, 2024
Schutte, C. B., *Tribunal Constitucional on the European Constitution. Declaration of 13 December 2004* (2005) 1 *European Constitutional Law Review* 281
Schütze, R., *The Morphology of Legislative Power in the European Community: Legal Instruments and the Federal Division of Powers* (2006) 25 *Yearbook of European Law* 91-151
Schütze, R., *On 'Federal' Ground: The European Union as an (Inter)national Phenomenon* (2009) 46 *Common Market Law Review* 1069
Schütze, R., *Three 'Bills of Rights' for the European Union* (2011) 30 *Yearbook of European Law* 131–158
Schütze, R., *Conclusion: Article 267 TFEU and EU Federalism*, in Gallo, D., Cecchetti L. (eds.), The Preliminary Ruling Procedure, *Today*: Revisiting Article 267 TFEU's Constitutional Backbone, Special Issue (2023) 15 *European Journal of Legal Studies* 221
Sciarra, S., *Diritti sociali fondamentali nazionali e europei. A proposito di diritto alle ferie retribuite* (2019) 10 *Federalismi.it* 1
Scoditti, E., *Giudicato nazionale e diritto comunitario* (2007) 4 *Il Foro italiano* 533
Scott, C., *Private Regulation of the Public Sector: A Neglected Facet of Contemporary Governance* (2002) 29 *Journal of Law and Society* 56
Sebba, I., *The Doctrine of Direct Effect: A Malignant Disease of Community Law* (1995) 22 *Legal Issues of Economic Integration* 35
Semertzi, A., *The Preclusion of Direct Effect in the Recently Concluded EU Free Trade Agreements* (2014) 51 *Common Market Law Review* 1125
Shuibhne, N. N., *The Treaty is Coming to Get You* (2012) 37 *European Law Review* 367
Simon, D., *Obligation de réexamen d'une décision administrative définitive. L'autorité d'un arrêt préjudiciel en interprétation postérieur à une décision administrative devenue définitive impose la prise en compte de la demande de retrait de celle-ci* (2004) *Europe Mars* 14
Simon, D., *Absence d'effet direct horizontal des directives et des décisions adressées aux États membres* (2007) *Europe Août-Septembre* 10
Simon, D., *Retour au mythe du gouvernement des juges?* (2006) *JurisClasseur Europe*, February, 1
Simoncini, M., *Different Shades of Legal Standing and the Right to Judicial Protection of Private Parties in the Banking Union: Trasta Komercbanka* (2020) 57 *Common Market Law Review* 1867
Sirinelli, J., *La protection des données de connexion par la Cour de justice: cartographie d'une jurisprudence européenne inédite* (2021) 2 *Revue trimestrielle de droit européen* 313
Skouris, V., *Développements récents de la protection des droits fondamentaux dans l'Union européenne: les arrêts Melloni et Åkerberg Fransson* (2013) 2 *Il Diritto dell'Unione europea* 229
Sloss, D., *Self-Executing Treaties and Domestic Judicial Remedies* (2004) 98 *American Society of International Law Proceedings* 346
Slot, P. J., *Case C-194/94, CIA Security International SA v. Signalson SA and Securitel SPRL* (1996) 33 *Common Market Law Review* 1035

Slynn, G., *The Court of Justice of the European Communities* (1984) 33 *International and Comparative Law Quarterly* 409

Snyder, F., *The Effectiveness of European Community Law. Institutions, Processes, Tools and Techniques* (1993) 56 *Modern Law Review* 19

Snyder, F., *The Gatekeepers: The European Courts and WTO Law* (2013) 50 *Common Market Law Review* 313

Sowery, K., *Reconciling Primacy and Environmental Protection: Association France Nature Environnement* (2017) 54 *Common Market Law Review* 1

Spieker, L. D., *Framing and Managing Constitutional Identity Conflicts: How to Stabilize the Modus Vivendi between the Court of Justice and National Constitutional Courts* (2020) 57 *Common Market Law Review* 361

Spieker, L. D., *The Conflict over the Polish Disciplinary Regime for Judges: An Acid Test for Judicial Independence, Union Values and the Primacy of EU Law: Commission v. Poland: Case C-791/19, Commission v. Poland (Régime disciplinaire des juges)* (2022) 59 *Common Market Law Review* 777

Sprenger, M., *Kein Schutz des Vertrauens privater Arbeitgeber in die Anwendung altersdiskriminierender Gesetze* (2016) 4 *Europäische Zeitschrift für Arbeitsrecht* 460

Squintani, L., Lindeboom, J., *The Normative Impact of Invoking Directives: Casting Light on Direct Effect and the Elusive Distinction between Obligations and Mere Adverse Repercussions* (2019) 38 *Yearbook of European Law* 18–72

Stein, E., *Lawyers, Judges, and the Making of a Transnational Constitution* (1981) 75 *American Journal of International Law* 1

Steiner, J., *Direct Applicability in EEC Law—A Chameleon Concept* (1982) 98 *Law Quarterly Review* 229

Steiner, J., *From Direct Effects to Francovich: Shifting Means of Enforcement of Community Law* (1993) 18 *European Law Review* 2

Stone, C. D., *Corporate Vices and Corporate Virtues: Do Public/Private Distinctions Matter?* (1982) 130 *University of Pennsylvania Law Review* 1441

Stoyanov, K., *Three Decades of the 'Nakajima' Doctrine in EU Law: Where Are We Now?* (2021) 24 *Journal of International Economic Law* 724

Stoynov, V., *The Direct Effect of EU Bilateral Trade Agreements Such as the TTIP in the Light of the Jurisprudence of the CJEU* (2017) 9 *Amsterdam Law Forum* 42

Streinz, R., Leible, S., *Die unmittelbare Drittwirkung der Grundfreiheiten* (2000) 11 *Europäische Zeitschrift für Wirtschaftsrecht* 459

Stuyck, J., *Case Note on Océano Grupo* (2001) 38 *Common Market Law Review* 728

Suerbaum, J., *Die Schutzpflichtdimension der Gemeinschaftsgrundrechte* (2003) 3 *Europarecht* 390

Szyszczak, E., *Case C-188/89, Foster and Others v. British Gas plc* (1990) 27 *Common Market Law Review* 859

Szyszczak, E., *Making Europe More Relevant to Its Citizens: Effective Judicial Process* (1996) 21 *European Law Review* 351

Talberg, J., *Supranational Influence in EU Enforcement: The ECJ and the Principle of State Liability* (2000) 7 *Journal of European Public Policy* 104

Tancredi, A., *EC Practice in the WTO: How Wide is the 'Scope for Manoeuvre'?* (2004) 15 *European Journal of International Law* 933

Tash, A. P., *Remedies for European Community Law Claims in Member State Courts: Toward a European Standard* (1993) 31 *Columbia Journal of Transnational Law* 377

Tega, D., *The Italian Constitutional Court in its Context: A Narrative* (2021) 17 *European Constitutional Law Review* 369

Temple Lang, J., *The Development by the Court of Justice of the Duties of Cooperation of National Authorities and Community Institutions Under Article 10 EC* (2007) 31 *Fordham International Law Journal* 1483

Tesauro, G., *The Effectiveness of Judicial Protection and Cooperation between the Court of Justice and National Courts* (1993) 13 *Yearbook of European Union Law* 1–17

Tesauro, G., *Alcune riflessioni sul ruolo della Corte di giustizia nell'evoluzione dell'Unione europea* (2013) 3 *Il Diritto dell'Unione europea* 483

Thüsing, G., *Europarechtlicher Gleichbehandlungsgrundsatz als Bindung des Arbeitgebers?* (2005) 26 *Zeitschrift für Wirtschaftsrecht* 2149

Thüsing, G., Horler, S., *Case C-555/07, Seda Kücükdeveci v. Swedex, Judgment of the Court (Grand Chamber) of 19 January 2010* (2010) 47 *Common Market Law Review* 1161–1170

Thym, D., *In the Name of Sovereign Statehood: A Critical Introduction to the Lisbon Judgment of the German Constitutional Court* (2009) 46 *Common Market Law Review* 1795

Timmermans, C. W. A., *Directives: Their Effect within the National Legal Systems* (1979) 16 *Common Market Law Review* 533

Timmermans, C. W. A., *Community Directives Revisited* (1997) 17 *Yearbook of European Law* 1–28

Tizzano, A., *La tutela dei privati nei confronti degli Stati membri dell'Unione europea* (1995) 4 *Il Foro italiano* 14

Tizzano, A., *Dall'unità nazionale all'integrazione sopranazionale* (2012) 3 *Il Diritto dell'Unione europea* 621

Tobler, R. C., *Putting Mangold in Perspective: In Response to Editorial Comments, Horizontal Direct Effect—A Law of Diminishing Coherence?* (2007) 44 *Common Market Law Review* 1177

Torres Pérez, A., *Melloni in Three Acts: From Dialogue to Monologue* (2014) 10 *European Constitutional Law Review* 308

Torres Pérez, A., *From Portugal to Poland: the Court of Justice of the European Union as watchdog of judicial independence* (2020) 27 *Maastricht Journal of European and Comparative Law* 105

Toth, A. G., *The Authority of Judgments of the European Court of Justice: Binding Force and Legal Effects* (1984) 4 *Yearbook of European Law* 1–77

Trabucchi, A., *Un nuovo diritto* (1963) 1 *Rivista di diritto civile* 259

Trabucchi, A., *L'effet erga omnes des décision préjudicielles rendues par la Cour de justice des Communautés européennes* (1974) 10 *Revue trimestrielle de droit européen* 56

Trachtman, J., *Bananas, Direct Effect and Compliance* (1999) 10 *European Journal of International Law* 655

Tridimas, T., *Horizontal Effect of Directives: A Missed Opportunity* (1994) 10 *European Law Review* 621

Tridimas, T., *The Court of Justice and Judicial Activism* (1996) 21 *European Law Review* 21

Tridimas, T., *Black, White, and Shades of Grey: Horizontality of Directives Revisited* (2002) 21 *Yearbook of European Law* 327–354

Tridimas, T., *Constitutional Review of Member State Action: The Virtues and Vices of an Incomplete Jurisdiction* (2011) 9 *International Journal of Constitutional Law* 737

Tridimas, T., *Fundamental Rights, General Principles of EU Law, and the Charter* (2014) 16 *Cambridge Yearbook of European Legal Studies* 361–392

Tridimas, T., Gentile, G., *The Essence of Rights: An Unreliable Boundary?* (2019) 20 *German Law Journal* 794

Tubner, G., *Transnational Fundamental Rights: Horizontal Effect?* (2011) 40 *Rechtsfilosofie & Rechtstheorie* 191

Turmo, A., *National Res Judicata in the European Union: Revisiting the Tension between the Temptation of Effectiveness and the Acknowledgement of Domestic Procedural Law* (2021) 58 *Common Market Law Review* 361

Turmo, A., *National Security as an Exception to EU Data Protection Standards: The Judgment of the Conseil d'État in French Data Network and Others* (2022) 59 *Common Market Law Review* 203

Tushnet, M., *State Action, Social Welfare Rights, and the Judicial Role: Some Comparative Observations* (2002) 3 *Chicago Journal of International Law* 435

Urlesberger, F., *Zur Rechtskraft im Gemeinschaftsrecht* (2004) 22 *Zeitschrift für Rechtsvergleichung, internationales Privatrecht und Europarecht* 99

Usher, J., *Direct Effect of Directives: The European Court Holds Firm* (1982) 7 *European Law Review* 193

Van den Brink, M., *When can Religious Employers Discriminate? The Scope of the Religious Ethos Exemption in EU Law* (2022) 1 *European Law Open* 89

Van der Sluis, M., *Similar, Therefore Different: Judicial Review of Another Unconventional Monetary Policy in Weiss* (2019) 46 *Legal Issue of Economic Iintegration* 263

Van Gerven, W., *The Recent Case-Law of the Court of Justice Concerning Articles 30 and 36 of the EEC Treaty* (1977) 14 *Common Market Law Review* 5

Van Gerven, W., *Contribution de l'arret Defrenne au développement du droit Communautaire* (1977) 13 *Cahiers de droit européen* 131

Van Gerven, W., *Bridging the Gap between Community and National Laws: Towards a Principle of Homogeneity in the Field of Legal Remedies?* (1995) 32 *Common Market Law Review* 679

Van Gerven, W., *The Role and Structure of the European Judiciary Now and in the Future* (1996) 21 *European Law Review* 211

Van Gerven, W., *Of Rights, Remedies and Procedures* (2000) 37 *Common Market Law Review* 501

Van Gestel, R., Micklitz, H.-W., *European Integration through Standardization: How Judicial Review is Breaking Down the Club house of Private Standardization Bodies* (2013) 50 *Common Market Law Review* 145

Van Harten, H., Nauta, T., *Towards Horizontal Direct Effect of the Free Movement of Goods? Comment on Fra.bo* (2013) 38 *European Law Review* 677

Van Waeyenberge, A., Pecho, P., *Free Trade Agreements after the Treaty of Lisbon in the Light of the Case Law of the Court of Justice of the European Union* (2014) 20 *European Law Journal* 749

Vandersanden, G., *De l'autorité de chose jugeé des arrêts préjudiciels d'interprétation rendus par la Cour de Justice des Communautés européennes* (1972) 25 *Revue critique de jurisprudence belge* 508

Varner, C. A., *The Effectiveness of European Community Law with Specific Regard to Directives: The Critical Step Not Taken by the European Court of Justice* (2001) 22 *Michigan Journal of International Law* 457–476

Vauchez, A., *The Transnational Politics of Judicialization. Van Gend en Loos and the Making of EU Polity* (2010) 16 *European Law Journal* 1

Vauchez, S. H., *Equality and the Market: The Unhappy Fate of Religious Discrimination in Europe. Bougnaoui, Achbita* (2017) 13 *European Constitutional Law Review* 749

Vergara, M. E., Puig, G. V., *The Quiet Architect Finds its Voice: The Primacy of the Law of the European Union after Press Release No. 58/20 of the Court of Justice of the European Union* (2021) 27 *European Public Law* 673

Verhoeven, J., *La notion d''applicabilité directe' du droit international* (1980) 13 *Revue belge de droit international* 243

Verstraelen, S., *The Temporal Limitation of Judicial Decisions: The Need for Flexibility Versus the Quest for Uniformity* (2013) 14 *German Law Journal* 1687

Vezzani, S., *Pacta sunt servanda? La sentenza della Corte di giustizia nell'affare Intertanko* (caso C-308/06) e l'adattamento dell'ordinamento comunitario al diritto internazionale pattizio (2009) 1 *Studi sull'integrazione europea* 233

Viganò, F., *Il caso Taricco davanti alla Corte costituzionale: qualche riflessione sul merito delle questioni e sulla reale posta in gioco* (2016) *Diritto penale contemporaneo* 9 May 2016

Viganò, F., *Supremacy of EU Law vs. (Constitutional) National Identity: A New Challenge for the Court of Justice from the Italian Constitutional Court* (2017) 7 *European Criminal Law Review* 103

Viganò, F., *La proporzionalità della pena tra diritto costituzionale italiano e diritto dell'Unione europea: sull'effetto diretto dell'art. 49, par. 3, della Carta alla luce di una recentissima sentenza della Corte di giustizia* (2022) *Sistema Penale.it* 1

Villani, U., *Il diritto dell'Unione Europea è ancora materia per internazionalisti?* (2011) 66 *La Comunità Internazionale* 533

Villani, U., *Una rilettura della sentenza Van Gend en Loos dopo cinquant'anni* (2013) 2 *Studi sull'integrazione europea* 225

Vincze, A., Varju, M., *Hungary: The New Fundamental Law* (2012) 18 *European Public Law* 437

Vitale, G., *Il recupero degli aiuti di Stato illegittimamente erogati tra autorità del giudicato ed incompatibilità con il mercato comune in una recente sentenza della Corte di Giustizia* (2008) 3 *Il Diritto dell'Unione europea* 595

Vitale, G., *Il principio dell'autonomia procedurale in due recenti sentenze della Corte di giustizia: i casi Olimpiclub e Asturcom* (2010) 4 *Il Diritto dell'Unione europea* 727

Volker, E. L. M., *The Direct Effect of International Agreements in the Community's Legal Order* (1983) 10 *Legal Issues of Economic Integration* 131

Volpi, M., *La nuova Costituzione ungherese: una democrazia dimezzata* (2012) 3 *Diritto pubblico comparato ed europeo* 1013

Von Bogdandy, A., *Pluralism, Direct Effect, and the Ultimate Say: On the Relationship between International and Domestic Constitutional law* (2008) 6 *International Journal of Constitutional Law* 397

Von Bogdandy, A., Schill, S., *Overcoming Absolute Primacy: Respect for National Identity under the Lisbon Treaty* (2011) 48 *Common Market Law Review* 1417

Von Bogdandy, A., Smrkolj, M., *European Union Law and International Law*, in *Max Planck Encyclopedia of Public International Law*, 2011, available at https://opil.ouplaw.com/display/10.1093/law:epil/9780199231690/law-9780199231690-e620?rskey=jIgrVs&result=3&prd=OPIL

Von Danwitz, T., *Effets juridiques des directives selon la jurisprudence récente de la Cour de justice - Effet anticipé, antérieur à l'expiration du délai de transposition, interprétation conforme aux directives, primauté et application 'combinée' avec les principes généraux du droit* (2007) 4 *Revue trimestrielle de droit européen* 575

Von Oettingen, A., Rabenschlag, D., *Europäische Richtlinien und allgemeiner Gleichheitssatz im innerstaatlichen Recht—Anmerkungen anlässlich des Mangold-Urteils des EuGH* (2006) 9 *Zeitschrift für Europarechtliche Studien* 363

Waelbroeck, M., *May the Court of Justice Limit the Retrospective Operation of Its Judgments?* (1981) 1 *Yearbook of European Law* 115–123

Waldron, J., *The Core Case against Judicial Review* (2006) 115 *Yale Law Journal* 1346

Walker, N., *The Idea of Constitutional Pluralism* (2002) 65 *Modern Law Review* 317

Walker, N., *Constitutional Pluralism Revisited* (2016) 22 *European Law Journal* 333

Ward, A., *Article 47 - Right to an Effective Remedy*, in Peers, S., Hervey, T., Kenner, J., Ward, A. (eds.), *The EU Charter of Fundamental Rights: A Commentary*, 2nd ed., Oxford, Hart, 2021, 1285–1344

Wasserer, S. C., *Rechtskraft contra Gemeinschaftstreue: Überprüfbarkeit einer rechtskräftigen, gemeinschaftsrechtswidrigen Entscheidung eines innerstaatlichen Gerichts* (2006) 6 *European Law Reporter* 198

Wathelet, M., *Arrêt Van Gend en Loos: 50 ans déjà* (2013) 200 *Journal de droit européen* 213

Wattel, P., Köbler, *CILFIT and Welthgrove: We Can't go on Meeting Like This* (2004) 41 *Common Market Law Review* 177

Wattel, P., *National Procedural Autonomy and Effectiveness of EC Law* (2008) 35 *Legal Issues of Economic Integration* 109

Weatherill, S., *Breach of Directives and Breach of Contract* (2001) 26 *European Law Review* 177

Weatherill, S., *Competence Creep and Competence Control* (2004) 23 *Yearbook of European Law* 1–55

Weatherill, S., *Use and Abuse of the EU's Charter of Fundamental Rights: On the Improper Veneration of 'Freedom of Contract'* (2014) 10 *European Review of Contract Law* 167

Weiler, J. H. H., *The Community System: The Dual Character of Supra-Nationalism* (1981) 1 *Yearbook of European Law* 267–306

Weiler, J. H. H., *The Court of Justice on Trial* (1987) 24 *Common Market Law Review* 555

Weiler, J. H. H., *The Transformation of Europe* (1990-1991) 100 *Yale Law Journal* 2403

Weiler, J. H. H., *Journey to an Unknown Destination: A Retrospective and Prospective of the European Court of Justice in the Arena of Political Integration* (1993) 31 *Journal of Common Market Studies* 417

Weiler, J. H. H., Haltern, U., *The Autonomy of the Community Legal Order: through the Looking Glass* (1996) 37 *Harvard International Law Journal* 411

Weiler, J. H. H., *Does Europe Need a Constitution? Demos, Telos and the German Maastricht Decision* (1995) 1 *European Law Journal* 219

Weiler, J. H. H., *Editorial. The 'Lisbon Urteil' and the Fast Food Culture* (2009) 20 *European Journal of International Law* 505

Weiler, J. H. H., *Van Gend en Loos: The Individual as Subject and Object and the Dilemma of European Legitimacy* (2014) 12 *International Journal of Constitutional Law* 94

Weiler, J. H. H., *Je Suis Achbita* (2017) 28 *European Journal of International Law* 989

Weiß, H., *Rechtskraftdurchbrechung bei (mutmaßlichem) Verstoß eines Vertrags gegen EU-Beihilferecht* (2016) 2 *Europäische Zeitschrift für Wirtschaftsrecht* 60

Wendel, M., *Exceeding Judicial Competence in the Name of Democracy: The German Federal Constitutional Court's OMT Reference* (2014) 10 *European Constitutional Law Review* 263

Wendel, M., *The Fog of Identity and Judicial Contestation: Preventive and Defensive Constitutional Identity Review in Germany* (2021) 27 *European Public Law* 465

Wengler, W., *Van Gend & Loos* (1963) 16 *Neue Juristische Wochenschrift* 1751

Wieland, J., *Germany in the European Union. The Maastricht Decision of the Bundesverfassungsgericht* (1994) 5 *European Journal of International Law* 259

Wiesbrock, A., *Case Note—C-555/07, Kücükdeveci v. Swedex, Judgment of the Court (Grand Chamber) of 19 January* (2010) *11 German Law Journal* 539

Wilman, F. G., *The End of the Absence? The Growing Body of EU legislation on Private Enforcement and the Main Remedies it Provides for* (2016) 53 *Common Market Law Review* 887

Winter, J. A., *Direct Applicability and Direct Effect. Two Distinct and Different Concepts in Community Law* (1972) 9 *Common Market Law Review* 425

Wyatt, D., *Prospective Effect of a Holding of Direct Applicability* (1975–1976) 1 *European Law Review* 399

Wyatt, D., *New Legal Order, or Old?* (1982) 7 *European Law Review* 147

Wyatt, D., *The Direct Effect of Community Social Law—Not Forgetting Directives* (1983) 8 *European Law Review* 241

Xenidis, R., *The Polysemy Of Anti-Discrimination Law: The Interpretation Architecture Of The Framework Employment Directive At The Court Of Justice* (2021) 58 *Common Market Law Review* 1649

Zaccaroni, G., *Is the Horizontal Application of General Principles Ultra Vires? Dialogue and Conflict between Supreme European Courts in Dansk Industri* (2018) 9 *Federalismi.it* 1

Zang, M. Q., *Shall We Talk? Judicial Communication between the CJEU and WTO Dispute Settlement* (2017) 28 *European Journal of International Law* 273

Zbiral, R., *A Legal Revolution or Negligible Episode? Court of Justice Decision Proclaimed Ultra Vires* (2012) 49 *Common Market Law Review* 1475

Ziller, J., *The German Constitutional Court's Friendliness Towards European Law: On the Judgment of Bundesverfassungsgericht over the Ratification of the Treaty of Lisbon* (2010) 16 *European Public Law* 53

Ziller, J., *Relire van Gend en Loos (Reading Van Gend en Loos Once Again)* (2012) 3 *Il Diritto dell'Unione europea* 513

Zonnekeyn, G. A., *The Legal Status of WTO Panel Reports in the EC Legal Order. Some Reflections on the Opinion of Advocate General Mischo in the Atlanta Case* (1999) 2 *Journal of International Economic Law* 713

Zonnekeyn, G. A., *The Status of Adopted Panel and Appellate Body Reports in the European Court of Justice and the European Court of First Instance* (2000) 34 *Journal of World Trade* 93

Zonnekeyn, G. A., *The Latest on Indirect Effect of WTO Law in the EC Legal Order: The Nakajima Case Law Misjudged?* (2001) 4 *Journal of International Economic Law* 597

Zonnekeyn, G. A., *The ECJ's Petrotub Judgment: Towards a Revival of the 'Nakajima Doctrine'?* (2003) 30 *Legal Issues of Economic Integration* 249

3. Contributions in edited volumes

Adam, R., *Il rinvio pregiudiziale tra tutela dei diritti soggettivi e controllo delle inadempienze statali*, in Alberti, J., De Cristofaro, G. (eds.), *Il rinvio pregiudiziale come strumento di sviluppo degli ordinamenti*, Pisa, Pacini, 2023, 3–26

Adinolfi, A., *Trattati dell'Unione e 'comuni trattati internazionali': il carattere atipico dei Trattati istitutivi nella giurisprudenza della Corte di giustizia*, in Annoni, A., Forlati, S., Franzina, P. (eds.), *Il diritto internazionale come sistema di valori*, Naples, Jovene, 2021, 213–234

Alì, A., *Some Reflections on the Principle of Consistent Interpretation through the Case Law of the European Court of Justice*, in Boschiero, N., Scovazzi, T., Pitea, C., Ragni, C. (eds.), *International Courts and the Development of International Law*, The Hague, Martinus Nijhoff, 2013, 881–895

Ankersmit, L., *An Incoherent Approach Towards Aarhus and CETA: The Commission and External Oversight Mechanisms*, in Govaere, I., Garben, S. (eds.), *The Interface between EU and International Law: Contemporary Reflections*, Chicago, Hart, 2019, 321–340

Anrò, I., Croci, F., *I simboli religiosi di fronte alla Corte di giustizia: sviluppi recenti e prospettive*, in Negri, A., Ragone, G., Toscano, M., Vanoni, L. P. (eds.), *I simboli religiosi nella società contemporanea*, Turin, Giappichelli, 2022, 5–28

Anrò, I., Alberti, J., *Riflessioni sull'effetto diretto, sul primato e sulla disapplicazione del diritto nazionale*, in Graziadei, M., Iannone, C., Nascimbene, B., Salvato, L., Vincenti, E. (eds.), *Il diritto europeo e il giudice nazionale*, Rome, SSM, 2023, 51–85

Arena, A., *Art. 36. Accesso ai servizi d'interesse economico generale*, in Mastroianni, R., Pollicino, O., Allegrezza, S., Pappalardo, F., Razzolini, O. (eds.), *Carta dei diritti fondamentali dell'Unione europea*, Milan, Giuffrè, 2017, 680–691

Arena, A., *The Twin Doctrines of Primacy and Pre-emption*, in Schütze, R., Tridimas, T., *Oxford Principles of European Union Law: The European Union Legal Order: Volume I*, Oxford, Oxford University Press, 2018, 300–349

Arena, A., *'Notre Nestor, Monsieur le Juge Rossi' (1889-1974): An Internationalist's Contribution to the Making of a Supranational Legal Order*, in Gallo, D., Mastroianni, R., Nicola, F., Cecchetti, L. (eds.), *The Italian Influence on European Law: Judges and Advocates General* (1952-2000), Oxford, Hart, forthcoming

Avbelj, M., Komárek, J., *Introduction*, in Id. (eds.), *Constitutional Pluralism in the European Union and Beyond*, Oxford, Hart, 2012, 1–17

Azoulai, L., *Introduction*, in Azoulai, L. (ed.), *The Question of Competence in the European Union*, Oxford, Oxford University Press, 2014, 1–16

Bamforth, N., *The Public Law-Private Law Distinction: A Comparative and Philosophical Approach*, in Leyland, P., Woods, T. (eds.), *Administrative Law Facing the Future: Old Constraints and New Horizons*, London, Blackstone, 1997, 136–159

Baratta, R., *L'effetto diretto delle disposizioni internazionali* self-executing, inPalmisano, G. (ed.), *Il diritto internazionale ed europeo nei giudizi interni.* Atti del XXIV Convegno SIDI di Roma, 5-6 June 2019, 2020, 75–111

Barav, A., *Applicabilité directe*, in Barav, A., Philip, C., Boutayeb, C. (eds.), in *Dictionnaire juridique des Communautés européennes*, Paris, Pedone, 1993, 104–180

Barav, A., *Rapport Général*, in XVIII Congrès FIDE, Stockholm, 3–6 June 1998, *Les directives communautaires: effets, efficacité, justiciabilité*, 1999, 418

Barceló, J., *Precedent in European Community Law*, in MacCormick, N., Summers, R. S. (eds.), *Interpreting Precedents—A Comparative Study*, London, Routledge, 1997, 407–436

Barents, R., *Some Remarks on the 'Horizontal' Effect of Directives*, in O'Keeffe, D., Schermers, H. G. (eds.), *Essays in European Law and Integration*, Deventer, Kluwer, 1982, 97–104

Barents, R., *Van Gend &. Loos en Costa/Enel*, in Beukers, T. W. B., VanHarten, H. J., Prechal, S. (eds.), *Het recht van de Europese Unie in 50 klassieke arresten*, The Hague, Boom Juridische Uitgevers, 2010, 22–28

Barile, P., *Ancora su diritto comunitario e diritto interno*, in *Studi per il XX anniversario dell'Assemblea costituente*, Florence, Vallecchi, 1969, 35–54

Barnard, C., Van Gend en Loos *to(t) the Future*, in Tizzano, A., Kokott, J.,Prechal, S. (Organising Committee), *50ème anniversaire de l'arrêt Van Gend en Loos: 1963-2013: actes du colloque*, Luxembourg, 13 mai 2013, https://curia.europa.eu/jcms/jcms/P_95693/en/, 117–122

Bebr, G., *Court of Justice: Judicial Protection and the Rule of Law*, in Curtin, D., Heukels, T. (eds.), *Institutional Dynamics of European Integration – Essays in Honour of Henry G. Schermers*, Dordrecht-Boston, Martinus Nijhoff, II, 1994, 303–333

Beljin, S., *Rights in European Union Law*, in Prechal, S., Van Roermund, B., (eds.), *The Coherence of EU Law. The Search for Unity in Divergent Concepts*, Oxford, Oxford University Press, 2008, 91–121

Bengoetxea, J., *Direct Applicability or Effect*, in Hoskins, M., Robinson, W. (eds.), *A True European. Essays for Judge David Edward*, Oxford, Oxford University Press, 2004, 353–366

Bengoetxea, J., *Is Direct Effect a General Principle of European Law?*, in Bernitz, U., Nergelius, J., Cardner, C. (eds.), *General Principles of EC Law in a Process of Development*, The Hague, Wolters Kluwer, 2008, 3–24

Bernardi, A., *Il rinvio pregiudiziale in ambito penale e i problemi posti dalle sentenze interpretative della Corte di giustizia*, in Alberti, J., De Cristofaro, G. (eds.), *Il rinvio pregiudiziale come strumento di sviluppo degli ordinamenti*, Pisa, Pacini, 2023, 309–365

Besson, S., *Comment humaniser le droit privé sans commodifier les droits de l'homme?*, in Werro, F. (ed.), *Droit civil et Convention européenne des droits de l'homme*, Zurich, Schulthess, 2006, 1–51

Biagioni, G., *The EU Charter of Fundamental Rights: In Bad Need of Instructions for Use?*, in Mancaleoni, A. M., Poillot, E. (eds.), *National Judges and the Case Law of the Court of Justice of the European Union* , Rome, Roma Tre Press, 2021, 165–182.

Bleckmann, A., *L'applicabilité directe du droit communautaire*, in Waelbroeck, M., Velu, J. (eds.), *Les recours des individus devant les instances nationales en cas de violation du droit européen*, Brussels, Larcier, 1978, 85–130

Bobek, M., *The Impact of the European Mandate of Ordinary Courts on the Position of Constitutional Courts*, in Claes, M., De Visser, M., Popelier, P., Van de Heyning, C. (eds.), *Constitutional Conversations in Europe: Actors, Topics, and Procedures*, Cambridge-Oxford, Intersentia-Hart, 2012, 287–308

Bobek, M., *Why There is no Principle of 'Procedural Autonomy' of the Member States*, in Micklitz, H.-W., De Witte, B. (eds.), *The European Court of Justice and the Autonomy of the Member States*, Oxford, Intersentia, 2012, 305–323

Bobek, M., *Institutional Report. National Courts and the Enforcement of EU Law*, in Botman, M., Rijpma, J. (eds.), *National Courts and the Enforcement of EU Law: The Pivotal Role of National Courts in the EU Legal Order. The XXIX FIDE Congress Publications*, Vol. 1, The Hague, Eleven International Publishing, 2020, 61–89

Bobek, M., *Van Gend en Loos +50: The Changing Social Context of Direct Effect*, in Tizzano, A., Kokott, J., Prechal, S. (Organising Committee), *50ème anniversaire de l'arrêt Van Gend en Loos: 1963-2013: actes du colloque*, Luxembourg, 13 mai 2013, https://curia.europa.eu/jcms/jcms/P_95693/en/, 181–187

Bobek, M., *The Effects of EU Law in the National Legal Systems*, in Barnard, C., Peers, S. (eds.), *European Union Law*, 3rd ed., Oxford, Oxford University Press, 2020, 154–189

Boulouis, J., *Sur une catégorie nouvelle d'actes juridiques: 'les directives"*, in *Mélanges Eisenmann*, Paris, Pedone, 1975, 191–203

Brand, M., *Discretion, Divergence, and Unity*, in Prechal, S., Van Roermund, B. (eds.), *The Coherence of EU Law. The Search for Unity in Divergent Concepts*, Oxford, Oxford University Press, 2008, 217–232

Brkan, M., Imamovic, S., *Article 52: Twenty-Eight Shades of Interpretation?* in Bobek, M., Adams-Prassl, J. (eds.), *The EU Charter of Fundamental Rights in the Member States*, Oxford, Hart, 2020, 401–420

Broberg, M., *Preliminary References as a Means for Enforcing EU Law*, in Jakab, A., Kochenov, D., *The Enforcement of EU Law and Values: Ensuring Member States' Compliance*, Oxford, Oxford University Press, 2017, 99–111

Bronckers, M., *The Domestic Law Effect of the WTO in the EU—A Dialogue with Jacques Bourgeois*, in Govaere, I., Quick, R., Bronckers, M. (eds.), *Trade and Competition Law in the EU and Beyond*, Cheltenham, Edward Elgar, 2011, 240–256

Cannizzaro, E., *Interpretazione conforme fra tecniche ed effetti normativi*, in Bernardi, A. (ed.), *L'interpretazione conforme al diritto dell'Unione europea*, Naples, Editoriale Scientifica, 2015, 3–16

Capik, A. B., *Five Decades Since Van Gend and Costa Came to Town: Primacy and Indirect Effect Revisited*, in Lazowski, A., Blockmans, S. (eds.), *Research Handbook in EU Institutional Law*, Cheltenham, Edward Elgar, 2016, 379–420

Capotorti, F., *Legal Problems of Directives, Regulations and Their Implementation*, in Siedentopf, H., Ziller, J. (eds.), *Making European Policies Work: The Implementation of Community Legislation in the Member States*, London, Sage, 1988, I, 151–168

Cappelletti, M., Golay, D., *Judicial Branch in the Federal and Transnational Union*, in Cappelletti, M., Seccombe, M., Weiler, J. H. H. (eds.), *Integration through Law: Europe and the American Federal Experience*, Berlin-New York, New York: Walter de Gruyter and Co., 1986, II, 261–351

Cartabia, M., *Fundamental Rights and the Relationship among the Court of Justice*, the National Supreme Courts and the Strasbourg Court, in Tizzano, A., Kokott, J.,Prechal, S. (Organising

Committee), *50ème anniversaire de l'arrêt Van Gend en Loos: 1963-2013: actes du colloque*, Luxembourg, 13 mai 2013, https://curia.europa.eu/jcms/jcms/P_95693/en/, 155–169

Casolari, F., *Giving Indirect Effect to International Law within the EU Legal Order: the Doctrine of Consistent Interpretation*, in Cannizzaro, E., Palchetti, P., Wessel, R. A (eds.), *International Law as Law of the European Union*, The Hague, Martinus Nijhoff, 2012, 395–415

Casolari, F., *The Acknowledgment of the Direct Effect of EU International Agreements: Does Legal Equality Still Matter?*, in Rossi, L. S., Casolari, F. (eds.), *The Principle of Equality in EU Law*, Heidelberg, Springer, 2017, 83–129

Cecchetti, L., Gallo, D., *The Reception of the Narrative of a Europe of Judicial Cooperation in the Italian Jurisprudence and Legal Doctrine: Cooperative Federalism in the Making*, in Bailleux, A., Bernard, E., Jacquot, S., Landenne, Q. (eds.), *Les récits judiciaires de l'Europe: Diffusion, réception et coproduction*, Brussels, Bruylant, 2023, 83–109

Chamon, M., *Constitutional Limits to the Political Choice for Mixity*, in Neframi, E., Gatti, M. (eds.), *Constitutional issues of EU external relations law*, Baden-Baden, Nomos, 2018, 137–166

Chiti, E., *EU Administrative Law in an International Perspective*, in Harlow, C., Leino, P., della Cananea, G. (eds.), *Research Handbook of EU Administrative Law*, Cheltenham, Edward Elgar, 2017, 545–571

Chronowski, N., Szentgáli-Tóth, B., Vincze, A., *Decision 22/2016. (XII. 5.) AB—Constitutional Self-identity of Hungary*, in Gárdos-Orosz, F., Zakariás, K. (eds.), *The Main Lines of the Jurisprudence of the Hungarian Constitutional Court*, Baden-Baden, Nomos, 2022, 441–58

Circolo, A., *Un 'approdo' per le concessioni balneari: l'Adunanza plenaria nega la proroga automatica delle concessioni*, in *Quaderni AISDUE 2021*, Naples, Editoriale Scientifica, 2022, 155–164

Claes, M., *The impact of* Van Gend en Loos *beyond the scope of EU law*, in Tizzano, A., Kokott, J., .Prechal, S. (Organising Committee), *50ème anniversaire de l'arrêt Van Gend en Loos: 1963-2013: actes du colloque*, Luxembourg, 13 mai 2013, https://curia.europa.eu/jcms/jcms/P_95693/en/, 103–110

Clément-Wilz, L., *La Cour de justice de Lagrange, M.*, in Mangenot, M. (ed.), *Un légiste de Vichy à la Communauté européenne. Maurice Lagrange: une biographie professionnelle*, dossier, Civitas Europa n. 50, 2023, 101–120

Clément-Wilz, L., *An Institutional View on the Influence of Italians Judges and Advocates General*, in Gallo, D., Mastroianni, R., Nicola, F., Cecchetti, L. (eds.), *The Italian Influence on European Law: Judges and Advocates General* (1952–2000), Oxford, Hart, forthcoming

Cohen, A., *'Ten Majestic Figures in Long Amaranth Robes': The Formation of the Court of Justice of the European Communities*, in Vauchez, A., De Witte, B. (eds.), *Lawyering Europe: European Law as a Transnational Social Field*, Oxford, Oxford University Press, 2013, 21–42

Colcelli, V., *Individual Rights as Construction of the EU Legal System*, in Arnold, R., Colcelli, V. (eds.), *Europeanization through Private Law Instruments*, Regensburg, Schnell & Steiner, 2015, 35–38

Combrexelle, J., *L'impact de l'arrêt de la Cour: étendue et limites des pouvoirs du juge national*, in Christianos, V. (ed.), *Evolution récente du droit judiciaire communautaire*, European Institute of Public Administration, Maastricht, Vol. I, 1994, 113–115

Condinanzi, M., *Diritti, principi e principi generali nell'ordinamento giuridico dell'Unione europea*, in D'Andrea, L., Moschella, G., Ruggeri, A., Saitta, A. (eds.), *La Carta dei diritti dell'Unione europea e le altre Carte (ascendenze culturali e mutue implicazioni)*, Turin, Giappichelli, 2016, 71–85

Condinanzi, M., *L'invocabilità della Carta dei diritti fondamentali dell'Unione europea nei rapporti orizzontali*, in Amalfitano, C., D'Amico, M., Leone S. (eds.), *La Carta dei diritti fondamentali dell'Unione Europa nel sistema integrato di tutela*, Turin, Giappichelli, 2022, 125–146

Cortese, B., *L'incidenza del diritto comunitario sulle sentenze nazionali definitive: esclusività del sistema giurisdizionale comunitario e nuovi limiti al principio di autonomia procedurale degli Stati membri—Il caso Lucchini*, in Spitaleri, F. (ed.), *L'incidenza del diritto comunitario e della CEDU sugli atti nazionali definitivi*, Milan, Giuffrè, 2009, 36–60

Cottier, T., *A Theory of Direct Effect in Global Law*, in Von Bogdandy, A., Mavroidis, P. C., Mény, Y. (eds.), *European Integration and International Co-ordination*, Alphen aan den Rijn, Kluwer Law International, 2002, 99–123

Craig, P., *Public Law and Control over Private Power*, in Taggart, M. (ed.), *The Province of Administrative Law*, Oxford, Oxford University Press, 1997, 196–216

Craufurd Smith, R., *Remedies for Breaches of EU Law in National Courts: Legal Variation and Selection*, in Craig, P., De Búrca, G. (eds.), *The Evolution of EU Law*, 3rd ed., Oxford, Oxford University Press, 2021, 287–320

Cremona, M., *Defending the Community Interest: the Duties of Cooperation and Compliance*, in Cremona, M., De Witte, B. (eds.), *EU Foreign Relations Law: Constitutional Fundamentals*, Hart, Luiss, 2008, 125–169

Cremona, M., *Member States as Trustees of the Union Interest: Participating in International Agreements on Behalf of the EU*, in Arnull, A., Dashwood, A., Dougan, M., Ross, M., Spaventa, E., Wyatt, D., *Wyatt and Dashwood's European Union Law*, 6th ed., London, Sweet & Maxwell, 2011, 435–457

Cremona, M., *The Judgment—Framing the Argument*, in Tizzano, A., Kokott, J., Prechal, S. (Organising Committee), *50ème anniversaire de l'arrêt Van Gend en Loos: 1963-2013: actes du colloque*, Luxembourg, 13 mai 2013, https://curia.europa.eu/jcms/jcms/P_95693/en/, 23–27

Cremona, M., *External Relations and External Competence of the European Union: The Emergence of an Integrated Policy*', in Craig, P., De Búrca, G. (eds.), *The Evolution of EU Law*, 3rd ed., Oxford, Oxford University Press, 2021, 215–268

Curtin, D., Mortelmans, K. J. M., *Application and Enforcement of Community Law by the Member States*, in Curtin, D., Heukels, T. (eds.), *Institutional Dynamics of European Integration. Essays in Honour of Henry G. Schermers*, The Hague, Martinus Nijhoff, 1994, 423–466

Davies, B., Nicola, F., *Introduction to EU Law Stories. Contextual and Critical Histories in European Jurisprudence*, in Nicola, F., Davies, B. (eds.), *EU Law Stories. Contextual and Critical Histories of European Jurisprudence*, Cambridge, Cambridge University Press, 2017, 1–18

Davis, D. M., *Socio-Economic Rights*, in Rosenfeld, M., Sajó, A. (eds.), *The Oxford Handbook of Comparative Constitutional Law*, Oxford, Oxford University Press, 2012, 1020–1035

De Búrca, G., Kilpatrick, C., Scott, J., *Questioning the EU's 'Principled Openness' to International Law: an Examination of the Court's Reception of the Aarhus Convention and the Convention on the Rights of Persons with Disabilities*, in Claes, M., Vos, E. (eds.), *Making sense of European Union law*, Oxford, Hart, 2022, 3–18

De la Mare, T., Donnelly, C., *Preliminary Rulings and EU Legal Integration: Evolution and Stasis*, in Craig, P., De Búrca, G. (eds.), *The Evolution of EU Law*, 3rd ed., Oxford, Oxford University Press, 2021, 228–274

De Visser, M., Claes, M., *Courts United? On European Judicial Networks*, in Vauchez, A., De Witte, B. (eds.), *Lawyering Europe: European Law as a Transnational Social Field*, Oxford, Oxford University Press, 2013, 75–100

De Vries, S., Van Mastrigt, R., *The Horizontal Direct Effect of the Four Freedoms: From a Hodgepodge of Cases to a Seamless Web of Judicial Protection in the EU Single Market?*, in Bernitz, U., Groussot, X., Schulyok, F. (eds.), *General principles of EU law and European private law*, Alphen aan den Rijn, Kluwer Law International, 2013, 249–280

De Witte, B., *The Continuous Significance of* Van Gend en Loos, in Poiares Maduro, M., Azoulai, L. (eds.), *The Past and Future of EU Law: The Classics of EU Law Revisited on the 50th Anniversary of the Rome Treaty*, Oxford, Hart, 2010, 9–15

De Witte, B., *The Impact of* Van Gend en Loos *on Judicial Protection at European and National Level: Three Types of Preliminary Questions*, in Tizzano, A., Kokott, J., Prechal, S. (Organising Committee), *50ème anniversaire de l'arrêt Van Gend en Loos: 1963-2013: actes du colloque*, Luxembourg, 13 mai 2013, https://curia.europa.eu/jcms/jcms/P_95693/en/, 93–110

De Witte, B., *EU law: Is It International Law?*, in Barnard, C., Peers, S. (eds.), *European Union Law*, Oxford, Oxford University Press, 2020, 177–197

De Witte, B., *Direct Effect, Primacy and the Nature of the Legal Order*, in Craig, P., De Búrca, G. (eds.), *The Evolution of EU Law*, Oxford, Oxford University Press, 2021, 187–227

Di Federico, G., *Il recepimento delle direttive nella giurisprudenza della Corte di Giustizia*, in Di Federico, G., Odone, C. (ed.), *Il recepimento delle direttive dell'Unione europea nella prospettiva delle regioni italiane. Modelli e soluzioni*, Naples, Editoriale Scientifica, 2010, 1–68

Di Federico, G., *Il giudice italiano come giudice europeo*, in Di Federico, G. (ed.), *Ordinamento giudiziario. Uffici giudiziari, CSM e governo della magistratura,* Bologna, Bononia University Press, 2019, 237–265

Domenicucci, D., Filpo, F., *Diritto a un ricorso effettivo e a un giudice imparziale*, in Mastroianni, R., Pollicino, O., Allegrezza, S., Pappalardo, F., Razzolini, O. (eds.), *Carta dei diritti fondamentali dell'Unione europea*, Milan, Giuffrè, 2017, 864–883

Dordi, C., *The Direct Effect of the Agreements Concluded by the EU: Some Inconsistencies in ECJ Case Law?*, in Id. (ed.), *The absence of direct effect of WTO in the EC and in other countries*, Turin, Giappichelli, 2010, 1–11

Dougan, M., *In Defence of* Mangold?, in Arnull, A., Dashwood, A., Dougan, M., Ross, M., Spaventa, E., Wyatt, D., *Wyatt and Dashwood's European Union Law*, 6th ed., London, Sweet & Maxwell, 2011, 219–244

Dougan, M., *The Vicissitudes of Life at the Coalface: Remedies and Procedures for Enforcing Union Law before the National Courts*, in Craig, P., De Búrca, G. (eds.), *The Evolution of EU Law*, 3rd ed., Oxford, Oxford University Press, 2021, 407–438

Douglas-Scott, S., *Fundamental Rights and the Union*, in Schütze, R., Tridimas, T., *Oxford Principles of European Union Law: The European Union Legal Order: Volume I*, Oxford, Oxford University Press, 2018, 383–422

Dubos, O., *Que reste-t-il de l'autonomie procédurale du juge national? Histoire de l'attribution d'une compétence au nom de l'effectivité et de l'efficacité du droit de l'Union*, in Neframi, E. (ed.), *Renvoi préjudiciel et marge d'appréciation du juge national*, Brussels, Bruylant, 2015, 159–182

Edward, D., *Judicial Activism—Myth or Reality?* Van Gend en Loos, Costa v. ENEL *and the* Van Duyn *Family Revisited*, in Campbell, A. I. K., Voyatzi, M. (eds.), *Essays in the Honour of Lord Mackenzie-Stuart*, Trenton, New Jersey, 1996, 29–67

Edward, D., *Direct Effect, the Separation of Powers and the Judicial Enforcement of Obligations*, in *Scritti in onore di Giuseppe Federico Mancini*, Milan, Giuffrè, 1998, 423–445

Edward, D., *Direct Effect: Myth, Mess or Mystery?*, in Prinssen, J. M., Schrauwen, A.,(eds.), *Direct Effect: Rethinking a Classic of EC Legal Doctrine*, Groningen, European Law Publishing, 2002, 1–13

Eeckhout, P., *The Integration of Public International Law in EU Law. Analytical and Normative Questions*, in Eeckhout, P., López Escudero, M. (eds.), *The European Union's External Action in Times of Crisis*, Oxford, Hart, 2019, 189–204

Eijsbouts, T., *Direct Effect, the Test and the Terms*, in Prinssen, J. M., Schrauwen, A. (eds.), *Direct Effect: Rethinking a Classic of EC Legal Doctrine*, Groningen, European Law Publishing, 2002, 237–249

Enchelmaier, S., *Horizontality: The Application of the Four Freedoms to Restrictions Imposed by Private Parties*, in Koutrakos, P., Snell, J. (eds.), *Research Handbook on the Law of the EU's Internal Market*, Cheltenham, Edward Elgar, 2017, 54–81

Epiney, A., *L'arrêt* Van Gend en Loos *et la citoyenneté de l'Union*, in Tizzano, A., Kokott, J., Prechal, S. (Organising Committee), *50ème anniversaire de l'arrêt Van Gend en Loos: 1963-2013: actes du colloque*, Luxembourg, 13 mai 2013, https://curia.europa.eu/jcms/jcms/P_95693/en/, 135–153

Episcopo, F., *The Vicissitudes of Life at the Coalface: Remedies and Procedures for Enforcing Union Law before the National Courts*, 2021, in Craig, P., De Búrca, G. (eds.), *The Evolution of EU Law*, 3rd ed., Oxford, Oxford University Press, 2021, 275–305

Fennelly, N., *The National Judge as Judge of the European Union*, in *The Court of Justice and the Construction of Europe: Analyses and Perspectives on Sixty Years of Case-law*, Berlin, Springer, 2013, 61–80

Ferrari Bravo, L., *Art. 177, in* Quadri, R., Monaco, R., Trabucchi, A. (eds.), *Trattato istitutivo della Comunità economica europea. Commentario, Milan, Giuffrè,* 1965, 1310–1335

Ferraro, F., Lazzerini, N., *Art. 52. Portata e interpretazione dei diritti e dei principi*, in Mastroianni, R., Pollicino, O., Allegrezza, S., Pappalardo, F., Razzolini, O. (eds.), *Carta dei diritti fondamentali dell'Unione europea*, Milan, Giuffrè, 2017, 1062–1083

Forteau, M., *The Role of the International Rules of Interpretation for the Determination of Direct Effect of International Agreements*, in P., Nolte, Aust, H. G. (eds.), *The Interpretation of International Law by Domestic Courts: Uniformity, Diversity, Convergence*, Oxford, Oxford University Press, 2016, 96–112

Gaja, G., Hay, P., Rotunda, D., *Instruments for Legal Integration in the European Community—A Review*, in Cappelletti, M., Seccombe, M., Weiler, J. H. H. (eds.), *Integration through Law: Europe and the American Federal Experience*, Berlin-New York, New York: Walter de Gruyter and Co., 1986, II, 113–160

Gaja, G., *L'esigenza di interpretare le norme nazionali in conformità con il diritto comunitario*, in Panunzio, S. P., Sciso, E. (eds.), *Le riforme istituzionali e la partecipazione dell'Italia all'Unione europea*, Milan, Giuffrè, 2002, 133–143

Gallo, D., *La vexata quaestio dell'efficacia interna delle direttive: l'insostenibile leggerezza del divieto di effetti diretti orizzontali*, in Moavero Milanesi, E., Piccirilli, G. (eds.), *Attuare il diritto dell'Unione europea in Italia. Un bilancio a 5 anni dall'entrata in vigore della legge n. 234 del 2012*, Bari, Cacucci, 2018, 17–36

Gallo, D., *L'evoluzione dell'effetto diretto e dei suoi rapporti con il primato e l'immediata applicazione del diritto UE negli ordinamenti nazionali*, in Palmisano, G. (ed.), *Il diritto internazionale ed europeo nei giudizi interni*, Naples, Editoriale Scientifica, 2020, 131–168

Gallo, D., *La disapplicazione è sempre figlia dell'effetto diretto, non del (solo) primato: Poplawski*, in Caruso, F., Medico, F., Morrone, A. (eds.), *Granital revisited?*, Bologna, Bononia University Press, 2020, 81–89

Gallo, D., Cecchetti L. (eds.), *The Preliminary Ruling Procedure,* Today: *Revisiting Article 267 TFEU's Constitutional Backbone*, Special Issue (2023) 15 *European Journal of Legal Studies* 1

Gallo, D., *The* Taricco *Saga: When Direct Effect and the Duty to Disapply Meet the Principle of Legality in Criminal Matters*, in Craig, P., Schütze, R. (eds.), *Landmark Cases in EU Law*, Oxford, Hart, 2025, forthcoming

Gallo, D., *Un droit opposable à Internet en vertu des obligations de service publique européennes?*, in Millet F.-X. (ed.), *Le constitutionnalisme numérique*, Brussels, Bruylant, forthcoming, 2025

Gaudet, M., *Incidences des Communautés européennes sur le droit interne des Etats membres*, in *Annales de la Faculté de droit de Liège*, 1963, 5

Gori, P., *Quindici anni insieme ad Alberto Trabucchi alla Corte di giustizia CE*, in *La formazione del diritto europeo—Quaderni della Rivista di diritto civile*, Padua, Cedam, 2008, 7183

Gori, P., *Souvenirs d'un survivant*, in Tizzano, A., Kokott, J.,Prechal, S. (Organising Committee), *50ème anniversaire de l'arrêt Van Gend en Loos: 1963-2013: actes du colloque*, Luxembourg, 13 mai 2013, https://curia.europa.eu/jcms/jcms/P_95693/en/, 29–35

Graziadei, M., *Rights in the European Landscape. A Historical and Comparative Profile*, in Prechal, S., Van Roermund, B. (eds.), *The Coherence of EU Law. The Search for Unity in Divergent Concepts*, Oxford, Oxford University Press, 2008, 63–91

Gutman, K., *Article 47: The Right to an Effective Remedy and to a Fair Trial*, in M. Bobek, M. Adams-Prassl, J. (eds.), *The EU Charter of Fundamental Rights in the Member States*, Oxford, Hart, 2020, 371–384

Halberstam, D., *Pluralism in* Marbury *and* Van Gend, in Poiares Maduro, M., Azoulai, L. (eds.), *The Past and Future of EU Law: The Classics of EU Law Revisited on the 50th Anniversary of the Rome Treaty*, Oxford, Hart, 2010, 26–36

Halberstam, D., *Internal Legitimacy and Europe's Piecemeal Constitution: Reflections on* Van Gend *at 50*, in Tizzano, A., Kokott, J., Prechal, S. (Organising Committee), *50ème anniversaire de l'arrêt Van Gend en Loos: 1963-2013: actes du colloque*, Luxembourg, 13 mai 2013, https://curia.europa.eu/jcms/jcms/P_95693/en/, 111–117

Harlow, C., *A Common European Law of Remedies?*, in Kilpatrick, C., Novitz, T., Skidmore, P. (eds.), *The Future of Remedies in Europe*, Oxford, Oxford University Press, 2000, 69–86

Hartkamp, A., *The Concept of (Direct and Indirect) Horizontal Effect of EU Law: The Terminology of European Law Scholars and of Private Law Scholars Compared*, in Bernitz, U., Groussot, X., Schulyok, F. (eds.), *General Principles of EU Law and European Private Law*, Alphen aan den Rijn, Kluwer Law International, 2013, 189–197

Heliskoski, J., *Mixed Agreements: The EU Law Fundamentals*, in Schütze, R., Tridimas, T., *Oxford Principles of European Union Law: The European Union Legal Order: Volume I*, Oxford, Oxford University Press, 2018, 1174–1207

Heukels, T., Tib, J., *Towards Homogeneity in the Field of Legal Remedies: Convergence and Divergence*, in Beaumont, P., Lyons, C., Walker, N. (eds.), *Convergence and Divergence in European Public Law*, Oxford, Hart, 1997, 111–129

Hillion, C., *Tous pour un, un pour tous! Coherence in the External Relations of the Union*, in Cremona, M. (ed.), *Developments in EU External Relations Law*, Oxford, Oxford University Press, 2008, 10–36

Hillion, C., *Conferral, Cooperation and Balance in the Institutional Framework of EU External Action*, in Cremona, M. (ed.), *Structural Principles in EU External Relations Law*, Oxford, Hart, 2018, 117–174

Hunt, J. C., *Fair and Just Working Conditions*, in Hervey, T., Kenner, J. (eds.), *Economic and Social Rights under the EU Charter of Fundamental Rights. A Legal Perspective*, Oxford, Hart, 2003, 45–65

Iancu, B., *Separation of Powers and the Rule of Law in Romania: The Crisis in Concepts and Contexts*, in Von Bogdandy, A., Sonnevend, P. (eds.), *Constitutional Crisis in the European Constitutional Area: Theory, Law and Politics in Hungary and Romania*, Oxford-Portland, Hart, 2015, 153–169

Iglesias Sánchez, S., *Article 51: The Scope of Application of the Charter*, in Bobek, M., Adams-Prassl, J. (eds.), *The EU Charter of Fundamental Rights in the Member States*, Oxford, Hart, 2020, 401–420

Ipsen, H.P., *Richtlinien-Ergebnisse*, in Hallstein, W., Schlochauer, H. J. (eds.), *Zur Integration Europas. Festschrift für Carl Friedrich Ophüls aus Anlass seines siebzigsten Geburtstages*, Karlsruhe, Verlag CF Müller, 1965, 67–84

Ipsen, H.P., *Über Supranationalität*, in Ehmke, H., Kaiser, J. H., Kewenig, W. A., Meessen, K. M., Rüfner, W. (eds.), *Festschrift für Ulrich Scheuner zum 70. Geburtstag*, Berlin, Duncker & Humblot, 1973, 211–225

Jääskinen, N., *Fundamental Social Rights in the Charter – Are They Rights? Are They Fundamental?*, in Peers, S., Hervey, T., Kenner, J., Ward, A. (eds.), *The EU Charter of Fundamental Rights: A Commentary*, 2nd ed., Oxford, Hart, 2021, 1885–1870

Jacobs, F. G., Karst, K., *The 'Federal" Legal Order: The USA and Europe Compared – A Juridical Perspective*, in Cappelletti, M., Seccombe, M., Weiler, J. H. H. (eds.), *Integration through Law: Europe and the American Federal Experience*, Berlin-New York, New York: Walter de Gruyter and Co., 1986, I, 169–243

Jacobs, F. G., *The Effect of Preliminary Rulings in the National Legal Order*, in Andenas, M. (ed.), *Article 177 References to the European Court – Policy and Practice*, London, Butterworths, 1994, 29–45

Jacobs, F. G., *The Role of the ECJ in the Development of Uniform Law*, in Jareborg, N. (ed.), *Towards Universal Law—Trends in National, European and International Lawmaking*, Iustus Forlag, 1995, 193–210

Jacobs, F. G., *Direct effect and interpretation of international agreements in the recent case law of the European Court of Justice*, in Dashwood, A., M. Maresceau (eds.), *Law and Practice of EU External Relations*, Cambridge, Cambridge University Press, 2008, 13–33

Jacqué, J. P., *The Role of Legal Services in the Elaboration of European Legislation*, in Vauchez, A., De Witte, B. (eds.), *Lawyering Europe: European Law as a Transnational Social Field*, Oxford, Oxford University Press, 2013, 43–54

Jans, J. H.. Prinssen, J. M., *Direct Effect: Convergence or Divergence?*, in Prinssen, J. M., Schrauwen, A. (eds.), *Direct Effect: Rethinking a Classic of EC Legal Doctrine*, Groningen, European Law Publishing, 2002, 106–126

Jans, J. H.,Verhoeven, M., *Europeanisation via Consistent Interpretation and Direct Effect*, in Jans, J. H., Prechal, S., Widdershoven, R. J. G. M. (eds.), *Europeanisation of Public Law*, 2nd ed., Groningen, Europa Law Publishing, 2015, 71–132

Jiménez de Aréchaga, E., *Self-Executing Provisions of International Law*, in Hailbronner, K., Resse, G., Stein, T. (eds.), *Staat und Völkerrechtsordnung. Festschrift für Karl Doehring*, Berlin, Springer, 1989, 409–419

Kelemen, K. D., *Eurolegalism and the European Legal Field*, in Vauchez, A., De Witte, B. (eds.), *Lawyering Europe: European Law as a Transnational Social Field*, Oxford, Oxford University Press, 2013, 221–242

Kilpatrick, C., *The Future of Remedies in Europe*, in Kilpatrick, C., Novitz, T., Skidmore, P. (eds.), *The Future of Remedies in Europe*, Oxford, Oxford University Press, 2000, 1–31

Klamert, M., *Article 3 TEU*, in Kellerbauer, M., Klamert, M., Tomkin, J. (eds.), *The EU Treaties and the Charter of Fundamental Rights. A Commentary*, Oxford, Oxford University Press, 2019, 31–34

Koopman, T., Stare Decisis *in European Law*, in O'Keeffe, D., Schermers, H. G. (eds.), *Essays in European Law and Integration*, Deventer, 1982, 11

Kovar, R., *L'intégrité de l'effet direct du droit communautaire selon la jurisprudence de la Cour de Justice de la Communauté*, in Bieber, R., Nickel, D. (eds.), *Das Europa der Zweiten Generation: Gedächtnisschrift für Christoph Sasse*, Baden-Baden, Nomos, 1981, I, 151–163

Kovar, R., *L'incidence du droit communautaire sur l'intangibilité des décisions nationales définitives*, in De Walsche, A., Lévy, A., *Promenades au sein du droit européen. Mélanges en hommage à Georges Vandersanden*, Brussels, Bruylant, 2008, 203–243

Kovar, R., *L'interprétation des droits nationaux en conformité avec le droit communautaire*, in Boev, I (ed.), *La France, l'Europe et le Monde. Mélanges en l'honneur de Jean Charpentier*, Paris, Pedone, 2009, 381–394

Kovar, R., *Observations sur l'intensité normative des directives*, in Kovar, R., *Itinéraire d'un juriste européen*, Brussels, Bruylant, 2010, 141–154

Kuijper, P. J., *Epilogue; Symbiosis?*, in Prinssen, J. M., Schrauwen, A. (eds.), *Direct Effect: Rethinking a Classic of EC Legal Doctrine*, Groningen, European Law Publishing, 2002, 252–267

Labus, C. H. L., *L'esclusione dell'effetto diretto negli accordi internazionali dell'Unione: riflessioni alla luce della prassi recente*, in Poli, S., Marinai, S. (eds.), *L'Unione europea sulla scena internazionale: sfide e trasformazioni sul piano interno ed esterno. Atti del V Convegno AISDUE di Pisa*, Naples, Editoriale Scientifica, forthcoming, 2025

Lane, R., *The Internal Market and the Individual*, in Shuibhne, N. N. (ed.), *Regulating the Internal Market*, Cheltenham, Edward Elgar, 2006, 245–276

Langer, J., *Article 267 TFEU: Celebrating the Jewel in the Crown of the Community Legal Architecture and Some Hot Potatoes*, in Ambtenbrink, F., Davies, G., Kochenov, D., Lindeboom, J. (eds.), *The Internal Market and the Future of European Integration. Essays in Honour of Laurence W. Gormley*, Cambridge, Cambridge University Press, 2019, 455–469

Lecourt, R., *Quel eut été le droit des Communautés sans les arrêts de 1963 et 1964?*, in *Mélanges Jean Boulouis: l'Europe et le droit*, Paris, Dalloz, 1991, 349–350

Leczykiewicz, D., *Horizontal Effect of Fundamental Rights: In Search of Social Justice or Private Autonomy in EU Law?*, in Bernitz, U., Groussot, X., Schulyok, F. (eds.), *General Principles of EU Law and European Private Law*, Alphen aan den Rijn, Kluwer Law International, 2013, 171–186

Leczykiewicz, D., *Effectiveness of EU Law before National Courts*, in *Oxford Handbook of European Union Law*, Oxford, Oxford University Press, 2015, 212–248

Leczykiewicz, D., *Compensatory Remedies in EU Law: The Relationship between EU Law and National Law*, in Giliker, P. (ed.), *Research Handbook on EU Tort Law*, Cheltenham, Edward Elgar, 2017, 63–92

Lenaerts, K., Corthaut, T., *Towards an Internally Consistent Doctrine on Invoking Norms of EU Law*, in Prechal, S., Van Roermund, B. (eds.), *The Coherence of EU Law. The Search for Unity in Divergent Concepts*, Oxford, Oxford University Press, 2008, 495–515

Lenaerts, K., *Direct Applicability and Direct Effect of International Law in the EU Legal Order*, in Govaere, I., Lannon, E., Van Elsuwege, P., Adam, S. (eds.), *The European Union in the World. Essays in Honour of Marc Maresceau*, The Hague, Martinus Nijhoff, 2013, 45–64

Lenaerts, K., *The Decentralised Enforcement of EU Law: The Principles of Equivalence and Effectiveness*, in Leanza, U., Tizzano, A., Vassalli di Dachenhausen, T., Mastroianni, R., De Pasquale, P., Ciccone, R. (Organising Committee), *Scritti in onore di Giuseppe Tesauro* , Naples, Editoriale Scientifica, 2014, 1057–1085

Lenaerts, K., Gutiérrez-Fons, J. A., *The Place of the Charter in the European Legal Space*, in Peers, S., Hervey, T., Kenner, J., Ward, A. (eds.), *The EU Charter of Fundamental Rights: A Commentary*, 2nd ed., Oxford, Hart, 2021, 1711–1734

Lenaerts, K., Gutiérrez-Fons, J. A., *Van Gend en Loos*: A star is born, in Craig, P., Schütze, R. (eds.), *Landmark Cases in EU Law*, Oxford, Hart, 2025, forthcoming

Louis, J.-V., *La primauté du droit de l'Union, un concept dépassé*, in Cohen Jonathan, G., Constantinesco, V., Michel, V. (eds.), *Chemins d'Europe—Mélanges en l'honneur de Jean Paul Jacqué*, Paris, Pedone, 2010, 443–461

Louis, J.-V., *Conclusions générales*, in Tizzano, A., Kokott, J., Prechal, S. (Organising Committee), *50ème anniversaire de l'arrêt Van Gend en Loos: 1963-2013: actes du colloque*, Luxembourg, 13 mai 2013, https://curia.europa.eu/jcms/jcms/P_95693/en/, 205–228

Ludlow, N. P., *Making the New Europe: European Integration Since 1950*, in Gordon, M., (ed.), *A Companion to International History 1900–2001. Blackwell Companions to History*, Oxford, Blackwell, 2007, 327–339

Magen, A., Pech, L., *The Rule of law and the European Union*, in May, C., Winchester, A. (eds.), *Handbook on the Rule of Law*, Cheltenham, Edward Elgar, 2018, 235–256

Martinico, G., *The Autonomy of EU Law: A Joint* Kadi II—Van Gend en Loos *Celebration*, in Avbelj, M., Fontanelli, F., Martinico, G. (eds.), Kadi *on Trial: A Multifaceted Analysis of the* Kadi *Judgment*, Abindgon, Routledge, 2014, 157–171

Mastroianni, R., *Pregiudiziale comunitaria*, in *Digesto delle discipline pubblicistiche*, aggiornamento, vol. IV, Turin, UTET, 2010, 399

Mastroianni, R., Condinanzi, M., *Giuseppe Tesauro—Advocate General at the ECJ—1988-1998. A Paladin of Effective Judicial Protection*, in Gallo, D., Mastroianni, R., Nicola, F., Cecchetti, L. (eds.), *The Italian Influence on European Law: Judges and Advocates General* (1952-2000), Oxford, Hart, forthcoming

Mayer, F. C., *European Law as a Door Opener for Public International Law?*, in Thouvenin, J. M., Tomuschat, C. (eds.), *Droit International et Diversité des Cultures Juridiques – International Law and Diversity of Legal Cultures*, Paris, Pédone, 2008, 241–255

Mayer, F. C., Van Gend en Loos*: The Foundation of a Community of Law*, in Poiares Maduro, M., Azoulai, L. (eds.), *The Past and Future of EU Law: The Classics of EU Law Revisited on the 50th Anniversary of the Rome Treaty*, Oxford, Hart, 2010, 16–25

Mendez, M., *The Application of International Law by the Court of Justice of the European Union*, in Bradley, C. A. (ed.), *The Oxford Handbook of Comparative Foreign Relations Law*, Oxford, Oxford University Press, 2019, 601–621

Mengozzi, P., *Il Rapporto tra Stato e individui nella giurisprudenza comunitaria* in *La formazione del diritto europeo – Quaderni della Rivista di diritto civile*, Padua, Cedam, 2008, 111

Michelman, F. I., *Constitutions and the Public/Private Divide*, in Rosenfeld, M., Sajó, A. (eds.), *The Oxford Handbook of Comparative Constitutional Law*, Oxford, Oxford University Press, 2012, 298–317

Müller, A. T., *The Direct Effect of Customary International Law*, in Lusa Bordin, F., Müller, A. T., Pascual-Vives, F. (eds.), *The European Union and Customary International Law*, Cambridge, Cambridge University Press, 2022, 210–239

Neframi, E., *Le rôle du juge national dans le cadre du renvoi préjudiciel: une marge d'appréciation?*, in Neframi, E. (ed.), *Renvoi préjudiciel et marge d'appréciation du juge national*, Bruxelles, Bruylant, 2015, 21–38

Neframi, E., *Status and Enforceability of EU International Agreements within the Domestic Legal Systems of the Member States: Kupferberg*, in Butler, G., Wessel, R. A. (eds.), *EU External Relations Law: The Cases in Context*, Oxford, Hart, 2022, 155–165

Nicola, F., Tichadou, E., Océano Grupo*: A Transatlantic Victory for the Consumer and a Missed Opportunity for European Law*, in Nicola, F., Davies, B. (eds.), *EU Law Stories. Contextual and Critical Histories of European Jurisprudence*, Cambridge, Cambridge University Press, 2017, 369–390

Nicola, F., *Waiting for the Barbarians: Inside the Archive of the European Court of Justice*, in Kilpatrick, C., Scott, J. (eds.), *New Legal Approaches to Studying the Court of Justice*, Oxford, Oxford University Press, 2020, 62–91

Nicola, F., Mastroianni, R., Gallo, D., Cecchetti, L., *Conclusions*, in Gallo, D., Mastroianni, R., Nicola, F., Cecchetti, L. (eds.), *The Italian Influence on European Law: Judges and Advocates General* (1952-2000), Oxford, Hart, forthcoming

Nipperdey, H. C., *Grundrechte und Privatrecht*, in Id., *Festschrift für Erich Molitor*, Munich, Beck, 1962

Nollkaemper, A., *The Direct Effect of Public International Law*, in Prinssen, J. M., Schrauwen, A. (eds.), *Direct Effect: Rethinking a Classic of EC Legal Doctrine*, Groningen, European Law Publishing, 2002, 156–180

O'Leary, S., *Solidarity and Citizenship Rights in the Charter of Fundamental Rights of the European Union*, in De Búrca, G. (ed.), *EU Law and the Welfare State: In Search of Solidarity*, Oxford, Oxford University Press, 2005, 39–88

O'Leary, S., *Defrenne II revisited*, in Poiares Maduro, M., Azoulai, L. (eds.), *The Past and Future of EU Law: The Classics of EU Law Revisited on the 50th Anniversary of the Rome Treaty*, Oxford, Hart, 2010, 274–285

Oesch, M., *Direct Effect of International Agreements*, in Cottier, T., Nadakavukaren Schefer, K. (eds.), *Elgar Encyclopedia of International Economic Law*, Cheltenham, Edward Elgar, 2017, 277–279

Paciotti, E., *Libertà—Solidarietà*, in Rossi, L. S. (eds.), *Carta dei diritti fondamentali e Costituzione dell'Unione europea*, Milan, Giuffré, 2002, 95–108

Pavone, T., *Making the European Court Work: Nicola Catalano and the Origins of European Legal Integration*, in Gallo, D., Mastroianni, R., Nicola, F., Cecchetti, L. (eds.), *The Italian Influence on European Law: Judges and Advocates General* (1952-2000), Oxford, Hart, forthcoming

Peers, S., *Fundamental Right or Political Whim? WTO Law and the European Court of Justice*, in De Búrca, G., Scott, J. (eds.), *The EU and the WTO: Legal and Constitutional Aspects*, Oxford, Hart, 2001, 111–130

Peers, S., Prechal, S., *Article 52—Scope of Guaranteed Rights*, in Peers, S., Hervey, T., Kenner, J., Ward, A. (eds.), *The EU Charter of Fundamental Rights: A Commentary*, 2nd ed., Oxford, Hart, 2021, 1611–1674

Perillo, E., *Alberto Trabucchi: The Defender of the European Citizens' Rights and the Van Gend & Loos Ruling of the Court of Justice*, in Gallo, D., Mastroianni, R., Nicola, F., Cecchetti, L. (eds.), *The Italian Influence on European Law: Judges and Advocates General* (1952-2000), Oxford, Hart, forthcoming

Perišin, T., Antonakin, E., *Judicial Review of EU Measures in the Light of WTO Rules:* Fediol *and* Nakajima, in Butler, G., Wessel, R. A. (eds.), *EU External Relations Law: The Cases in Context*, Oxford, Hart, 2022, 183–193

Pernice, I., *The Autonomy of the EU Legal Order—Fifty Years after* Van Gend, in Tizzano, A., Kokott, J., Prechal, S. (Organising Committee), *50ème anniversaire de l'arrêt Van Gend en Loos: 1963-2013: actes du colloque*, Luxembourg, 13 mai 2013, https://curia.europa.eu/jcms/jcms/P_95693/en/, 55–80

Pernice, I., *The Right to Effective Judicial Protection and Remedies in the EU*, in Rosas, A., Levits, E., Bot, Y. (eds.), *The Court of Justice and the Construction of Europe: Analyses and Perspectives on Sixty Years of Case-law*, Berlin, Springer, 2013, 381–396

Pescatore, P., *Discussion*, in Waelbroeck, M., Velu, J. (eds.), *Les recours des individus devant les instances nationales en cas de violation du droit européen*, Brussels, Larcier, 1978

Pescatore, P., *Monisme, dualisme et 'effet utile" dans la jurisprudence de la Cour de Justice de la Communauté Européenne*, in Colneric, N., Edward, D., Puissochet, J.-P., Colomer, D. R. (eds.), *Une communauté de droit—Festschrift für G.C. Rodríguez Iglesias*, Berlin, Berliner Wissenschafts-Verlag, 2003, 329–359

Pescatore, P., *Van Gend en Loos, 3 February 1963—A View from within*, in Poiares Maduro, M., Azoulai, L. (eds.), *The Past and Future of EU Law: The Classics of EU Law Revisited on the 50th Anniversary of the Rome Treaty*, Oxford, Hart, 2010, 3–8

Picod, F., *Le statut des particuliers, désormais titulaires de droits individuels*, in Tizzano, A., Kokott, J., Prechal, S. (Organising Committee), *50ème anniversaire de l'arrêt Van Gend en Loos: 1963-2013: actes du colloque*, Luxembourg, 13 mai 2013 https://curia.europa.eu/jcms/jcms/P_95693/en/, 81–92

Podstawa, K., Gwizdak, J., *Judicial Independence: The EU's Prescription in the Making to the Polish (and Other) Maladies*, in Casarosa, F., Moraru, M. (eds.), *The Practice of Judicial Interaction in the Field of Fundamental Rights: The Added Value of the Charter of Fundamental Rights of the EU*, 2022, 112–145

Poiares Maduro, M., *Contrapunctual Law: Europe's Constitutional Pluralism in Action*, in Walker, N. (ed.), *Sovereignty in Transition*, Oxford, Hart, 2003, 501–537

Poiares Maduro, M., *L'État-caméléon. Formes publique et privée de l'Homo Economicus*, in Bot, Y. (ed.), *Mélanges en l'honneur de Philippe Léger. Le droit à la mesure de l'homme*, Paris, Pedone, 2006, 79–91

Poli, S., *La diretta invocabilità degli accordi internazionali*, in Bartoloni, M. E., Poli, S. (eds.), *L'azione esterna dell'Unione europea*, Naples, Editoriale Scientifica, 2021, 93–97

Pollak, M., *Learning from EU Law Stories*, in Nicola, F., Davies, B. (eds.), *EU Law Stories. Contextual and Critical Histories of European Jurisprudence*, Cambridge, Cambridge University Press, 2017, 577–602

Porter, T., *Private Production of Public Goods: Private and Public Norms in Global Governance*, in Grande, E., Pauly, L. W. (eds.), *Complex Sovereignty: Reconstituting Political Authority in the Twenty-first*, Toronto, University of Toronto Press, 2005, 217–237

Potvin-Solis, L., *Qualification des situations purement internes*, in Neframi, E. (ed.), *Renvoi préjudiciel et marge d'appréciation du juge national*, Brussels, Bruylant, 2015, 39–100

Prechal, S., *EC Requirement for an Effective Remedy*, in Lonbay, J. H., Biondi, A. (eds.), *Remedies for Breach of EC Law*, London, Wiley, 1997, 3–13

Prechal, S., *Direct Effect Reconsidered, Redefined and Rejected*, in Prinssen, J. M., Schrauwen, A. (eds.), *Direct Effect: Rethinking a Classic of EC Legal Doctrine*, Groningen, European Law Publishing, 2002, 15–41

Prechal, S., *Rights v. Principles, or How to Remove Fundamental Rights From the Jurisdiction of the Courts*, in De Zwaan, J., Nelissen, F. A., Jans, J., Blockmans, S. (eds.), *The European Union: An Ongoing Process of Integration*, The Hague, TMC Asser Press, 2004, 177–184

Prechal, S., *Direct Effect, Indirect Effect, Supremacy and the Evolving Constitution of the European Union*, in Barnard, C. (ed.), *The Fundamentals of EU Law Revisited. Assessing the Impact of the Constitutional Debate*, Oxford, Oxford University Press, 2007, 35–69

Prechal, S., *Protection of Rights: How Far?*, in Prechal, S., Van Roermund, B. (eds.), *The Coherence of EU Law. The Search for Unity in Divergent Concepts*, Oxford, Oxford University Press, 2008, 155–182

Prechal, S., *The Court of Justice and Effective Judicial Protection: What Has the Charter Changed?*, in Paulussen, C., Takacs, T., Lazic, V., Van Rompuy, B. (eds.), *Fundamental Rights in International and European Law*, The Hauge, M. C. Asser Press, 2015, 143–157

Prechal, S., *Van Duyn and the Nature of Directives*, in Craig, P., Schütze, R. (eds.), *Landmark Cases in EU Law*, Oxford, Hart, 2025, forthcoming

Prek, M., Lefèvre, S., *La dimension 'subjective' de l'invocabilité des accords internationaux*, in Neframi, E., Gatti, M. (eds.), *Constitutional issues of EU external relations law*, Baden-Baden, Nomos, 2018, 231–255

Rasmussen, M., *Constructing and Deconstructing European 'Constitutional' European Law. Some Reflections on How to Study the History of European Law*, in Hagel-Sørensen, K., Koch, H., Haltern, U., Weiler, J. H. H. (eds.), *Europe. The New Legal Realism*, Copenhagen, Djøf Forlag, 2010, 639–660

Rasmussen, M., *Law Meets History*, in Nicola, F., Davies, B. (eds.), *EU Law Stories. Contextual and Critical Histories of European Jurisprudence*, Cambridge, Cambridge University Press, 2017, 103–120

Rodin, S., *Les effets horizontaux du droit de l'Union européenne*, in Tizzano, A., Rosas, A., De Lapuerta, R. S., Lenaerts, K., Kokott, J. (eds.), *La Cour de justice de L'Union européenne sous la présidence de Vassilios Skouris (2003-2015)*. Liber amicorum *Vassilios Skouris*, Brussels, Bruylant, 2015, 491–50

Rosas, A., *Mixed Union: Mixed Agreements*, in Koskenniemi, M. (ed.), *International Law Aspects of the European Union*, The Hague, Kluwer, 1998, 125–148

Rosas, A., *The National Judge as EU Judge*, in Cardonnel, P., Rosas, A., Wahl, N. (eds.), *Constitutionalising the EU Judicial System-Essays in Honour of Pernilla Lindh*, Oxford, Oxford University Press, 2012, 105–121

Rosas, A., *International Law—Union Law—National Law: Autonomy or Common Legal System?*, in Petrlik, D., Bobek, M., Passer, J. M., Masson, A. (eds.), *Évolution des rapports entre les orders juridiques de l'Union européenne, international et nationaux: Liber amicorum Jiří Malenovský*, Brussels, Bruylant, 2020, 261–282

Šadl, U., *National Courts and the Effectiveness of EU Law*, in De Witte, B., Mayoral, J. A., Jaremba, U., Wind, M., Podstawa, K. (eds.), *National Courts and EU Law: New Issues, Theories and Methods*, Cheltenham, Edward Elgar, 2016, 68–103

Sarmiento, D., *Half a Case at a Time: Dealing with Judicial Minimalism at the European Court of Justice*, in Claes, M., De Visser, M., Popelier, P., Van de Heyning, C. (eds.), *Constitutional*

Conversations in Europe: Actors, Topics, and Procedures, Cambridge-Oxford, Intersentia-Hart, 2012, 13–40

Schepisi, C., *Atti amministrativi in contrasto con il Diritto dell'Unione europea e poteri del giudice nazionale*, in Schepisi, C. (ed.), *L'impatto del diritto dell'Unione europea sul processo amministrativo*, Naples, Editoriale Scientifica, 2013, 17–58

Schmidt-Aßman, E., *Öffentliches Recht und Privatrecht: Ihre Funktionen als wechselseitige Auffangordnungen*, in Hoffmann-Riem, W., Schmidt-Aßman, E. (eds.), *Öffentliches Recht und Privatrecht als wechselseitige Auffangordnungen*, Baden-Baden, Nomos, 1996, 7–40

Schockweiler, F., *Effets des directives non transposées en droit national à l'égard des particuliers*, in Pérez González, M. (ed.), *Hacia un nuevo orden internacional y europeo—Estudios en homenaje al Profesor Don Manuel Diez de Velasco*, Madrid, Tecnos, 1993, 1201–1220

Schoukens, H., *Access to Justice before EU Courts in Environmental Cases against the Backdrop of the Aarhus Convention: Balancing Pathological Stubbornness and Cognitive Dissonance?*, in Voigt, C. (ed.), *International Judicial Practice on the Environment: Questions of Legitimacy*, Cambridge, Cambridge University Press, 2019, 74–118

Schütze, R., *Federalism and Foreign Affairs: Mixity as an (Inter)national Phenomenon*, in Hillion, C., Koutrakos, P. (eds.), *Mixed Agreements Revisited*, Oxford, Hart, 2010, 57–86

Schütze, R., *On 'Middle Ground'. The European Union and Public International Law*, in Id., *Foreign Affairs and the EU Constitution.* Selected essays, Cambridge, Cambridge University Press, 2014, 47–90

Schütze, R., *Direct Effects and Indirect Effects of Union Law*, in Schütze, R., Tridimas, T., *Oxford Principles of European Union Law: The European Union Legal Order: Volume I*, Oxford, Oxford University Press, 2018, 265–299

Schütze, R., *Constitutionalism and the European Union*, in Barnard, C., Peers, S. (eds.), *European Union Law*, 3rd ed., Oxford, Oxford University Press, 2020, 71–96

Sharpston, E., *Interim Relief in the National Courts*, in Lonbay, J., Biondi, A. (eds.), *Remedies for Breach of EC Law*, London, Wiley, 1997, 47–54

Sieburgh, C., *General Principles and the Charter in Private Law Relationships: Constructive and Critical Input from Private Law*, in Bernitz, U., Groussot, X., Schulyok, F. (eds.), *General Principles of EU law and European Private Law*, Alphen aan den Rijn, Kluwer Law International, 2013, 233–247

Simon, D., *Les fondements de l'autonomie du droit communautaire. Rapport général*, in *Droit international et Droit communautaire. Perspectives actuelles Actes du colloque de la SFDI 1999*, Paris, Pedone, 2000, 207–249

Simon, D., *SABENA is Dead, Gabrielle Defrenne's Case is Still Alive: The Old Lady's Testament*, in Poiares Maduro, M., Azoulai, L. (eds.), *The Past and Future of EU Law: The Classics of EU Law Revisited on the 50th Anniversary of the Rome Treaty*, Oxford, Hart, 2010, 265–273

Simon, D., *La panacée de l'interprétation conforme: injection homéopathique ou thérapie palliative?*, in D'Alessio, M. T., Placco, V., Kronenberger, V. (eds.), *De Rome à Lisbonne: les juridictions de l'Union européenne à la croisée des chemins. Mélanges en l'honneur de Paolo Mengozzi*, Brussels, Bruylant, 2013, 279–300

Simon, D., Rigaux, A., *Le 'précédent' dans la jurisprudence du juge de l'Union*, in Mestre, C. (ed.), *Europe(s), droit(s) européen(s), Une passion d'universitaire*, Brussels, Bruylant, 2015, 547–578

Skouris, V., *Allocution*, in Tizzano, A., Kokott, J., Prechal, S. (Organising Committee), *50ème anniversaire de l'arrêt Van Gend en Loos: 1963-2013: actes du colloque*, Luxembourg, 13 mai 2013, https://curia.europa.eu/jcms/jcms/P_95693/en/, 7–9

Sonnevend, P., Jakab, A., Csink, L., *The Constitution as an Instrument of Everyday Party Politics: The Basic Law of Hungary*, in Von Bogdandy, A., Sonnevend, P. (eds.), *Constitutional Crisis in the European Constitutional Area: Theory, Law and Politics in Hungary and Romania*, Oxford-Portland, Hart, 2015, 33–109

Spaventa, E., *The Horizontal Application of Fundamental Rights as General Principles of Union Law*, in Arnull, A., Dashwood, A., Dougan, M., Ross, M., Spaventa, E., Wyatt, D., *Wyatt and Dashwood's European Union Law*, 6th ed., London, Sweet & Maxwell, 2011, 199–218

Spitaleri, F., *L'incidenza del diritto comunitario sugli atti definitivi della Pubblica Amministrazione*, in Spitaleri, F., *L'incidenza del diritto comunitario e della CEDU sugli atti amministrativi nazionali*, Milan, Giuffrè, 2009, 7–34

Tancredi, A., *Il ruolo dell'interpretazione conforme al diritto dell'Unione europea fra disapplicazione ed efficacia diretta*, in *Quaderni del Consiglio superiore della magistratura*, Rome, 2010, 1

Tancredi, A., *On the Absence of Direct Effect of the WTO Dispute Settlement Body's Decisions in the EU Legal Order*, in Cannizzaro, E., Palchetti, P., Wessel, R. A. (eds.), *International law as law of the European Union*, The Hague, Martinus Nijhoff, 2012, 249–268

Temple Lang, J., *Article 10 EC—The Most Important 'General Principle' of Community Law*, in Bernitz, U., Nergelius, J., Cardner, C. (eds.), *General Principles of EC Law in a Process of Development*, Alphen aan de Rijn, Kluwer Law International, 2008, 75–113

Tesauro, G., *Art. 19 TUE*, in Tizzano, A., *Trattati dell'Unione europea. Commentario*, 2nd ed., Milan, *Giuffrè*, 2014, 195–215

Tesauro, G., De Pasquale, P., *La doppia pregiudizialità*, in Ferraro, F., Iannone, C. (eds.), *Il rinvio pregiudiziale*, Turin, Giappichelli, 2020, 289–305

Timmermans, C. W. A., *Un nouveau chapitre sur l'invocabilité des directives*, in *Mélanges en l'honneur de Jean-Pierre Puissochet – L'Etat souverain dans le monde d'aujourd'hui*, Paris, Pedone, 2008, 291–302

Tizzano, A., Gencarelli, B., *Union Law and Final Decisions of National Courts in the Recent Case Law of the Court of Justice*, in Arnull, A., Dashwood, A., Dougan, M., Ross, M., Spaventa, E., Wyatt, D., *Wyatt and Dashwood's European Union Law*, 6th ed., London, Sweet & Maxwell, 2011, 267–280

Trabucchi, A., *Incidenza del diritto comunitario sul diritto interno in Italia*, in Rizzo, V. (ed.), *Diritto privato comunitario*, Naples, Editoriale Scientifica, 1997, 37–54

Tridimas, T., *Precedent and the Court of Justice: A Jurisprudence of Doubt?*, in Dickson, J., Eleftheriadis, P. (eds.), *Philosophical Foundations of European Union Law*, Oxford, Oxford University Press, 2012, 307–330

Tridimas, T., *Horizontal Effect of General Principles: Bold Rulings and Fine Distinctions*, in Bernitz, U., Groussot, X., Schulyok, F. (eds.), *General Principles of EU Law and European Private Law*, Alphen aan den Rijn, Kluwer Law International, 2013, 213–232

Tridimas, T., *The Principle of Proportionality*, in Schütze, R., Tridimas, T., *Oxford Principles of European Union Law: The European Union Legal Order: Volume I*, Oxford, Oxford University Press, 2018, 243–264

Triggiani, E., *Sopranazionalità ed internazionalità nell'evoluzione dell'Unione*, in Tufano, M. L. (ed.), *Cantiere Europa—Le riforme istituzionali dell'Europa*, Naples, Editoriale Scientifica, 2004, 37–54

Triggiani, E., *La complessa vicenda dei diritti sociali fondamentali nell'Unione europea*, in Leanza, U., Tizzano, A., Vassalli di Dachenhausen, T., Mastroianni, R., De Pasquale, P., Ciccone, R. (Organising Committee), *Scritti in onore di Giuseppe Tesauro*, Naples, Editoriale Scientifica, 2014, 693–725

Valladares, R., Francovich*: Light at the End of the Marshall Tunnel*, in *The University of Miami Yearbook of International Law*, vol. 3, 1995, 1–52

Van den Bogaert, S., *Horizontality: The Court Attacks?*, in Barnard, C., Scott, J. (eds.), *The Law of the Single Market—Unpacking the Premises*, Oxford, Oxford University Press, 2002, 123–152

Van Gerven, W., *The Horizontal Effect of Directive Provisions Revisited: The Reality of Catchwords*, in Curtin, D., Heukels, T. (eds.), *Institutional Dynamics of European Integration. Essays in Honour of Henry G. Schermers*, The Hague, Martinus Nijhoff, 1994, 335–353

Van Leuken, R., *Direct Horizontal Effect of the Fundamental Freedoms*, in Hartkamp, A., Sieburgh, C. H., Keus, L. A. D., Kortmann, J. S., Wissink, M. H (eds.), *The Influence of EU Law on National Private Law*, Deventer, Kluwer, 2013, 73–94

VanRossem, J. W., *The Autonomy of EU Law: More is less?*, in Wessel, R. A., Blockmans, S. (eds.), *Between Autonomy and Dependence: The EU Legal Order Under the Influence of International Organizations*, The Hague, Martinus Nijhoff, 2013, 13–46

Vandamme, T., *Democracy and Direct Effect: EU and National Perceptions*, in Prechal, S., Van Roermund, B. (eds.), *The Coherence of EU Law. The Search for Unity in Divergent Concepts*, Oxford, Oxford University Press, 2008, 271–290

Vauchez, A., *Judge-Made Law: aux origines du modèle politique communautaire (retour sur* Van Gend en Loos *et* Costa c. ENEL), in Costa, O., Magnette, P. (eds.), *Une Europe des élites? Réflexions sur la fracture démocratique de l'Union européenne*, Brussels, Bruylant, 2007, 139–166

Vauchez, A., *Introduction. Euro-lawyering, Transnational Social Fields and European Polity-Building*, in Vauchez, A., De Witte, B. (eds.), *Lawyering Europe: European Law as a Transnational Social Field*, Oxford, Oxford University Press, 2013, 1–20

Waelbroeck, M., *L'immédiateté communautaire, caractéristique de la supranationalité: quelques consequences pour la pratique*, in Rousseau, C. (ed.), *Le droit international demain*, Neuchâtel, Edition Ides et Calendes, 1974, 81–89

Waelbroeck, M., *Les rapports entre les règles sur la libre circulation des marchandises et les règles de concurrence applicables aux entreprises dans la CEE*, in Capotorti, F., Ehlermann, C., Frowein, J.-A. (eds.), *Du droit international au droit de l'intégration.* Liber amicorum *Pierre Pescatore*, Baden-Baden, Nomos, 1987, 781–803

Waelbroeck, M., Waelbroeck, D., *Article 177*, in Mégret, J., Louis, J. V., Vignes, D., Waelbroeck, W. (eds.), *Commentaire Mégret. Le droit de la Communauté économique européenne*, 2nd ed., vol. X, Brussels, Bruylant, 1993, 197–210

Ward, A., *More than an 'Infant Disease': Individual Rights, EC Directives, and the Case for Uniform Remedies*, in Prinssen, J. M., Schrauwen, A. (eds.), *Direct Effect: Rethinking a Classic of EC Legal Doctrine*, Groningen, European Law Publishing, 2002, 43–75

Warlouzet, L., *Competitiveness and Solidarity in the History of the EU* (1957-2017), in Chiocchetti, P., Allemand, F. (eds.), *Competitiveness and Solidarity in the European Union. Interdisciplinary Perspectives*, Abingdon, Routledge, 2019, 54–72

Wathelet, M., *Du concept de l'effet direct à celui de l'invocabilité au regard de la jurisprudence récente de la Cour de justice*, in Hoskins, M., Robinson, W. (eds.), *A True European. Essays for Judge David Edward*, Oxford, Oxford University Press, 2004, 367–390

Weatherill, S., *Beyond EC Law Rights, National Remedies*, in Caiger, A., Floudas, D. A. (eds.), *1996 Onwards: Lowering the Barriers Further*, Chichester, Chancery Law, 1996, 233–254

Weatherill, S., Viking *and* Laval: *The EU Internal Market Perspective*, in Freedland, M., Prassl, J. (eds.), *Viking, Laval and Beyond* (eds.), Oxford, Oxford University Press, 2014, 23–39

Weiler, J. H. H., *Federalism without Constitutionalism: Europe's Sonderweg*, in Nikoilaidis, K., Howse, R. (eds.), *The Federal Vision: Legitimacy and Levels of Governance in the United States and the European Union*, Oxford, Oxford University Press, 2002, 54–72

Weiler, J. H. H., *Rewriting* Van Gend en Loos: *Towards a Normative Theory of ECJ Hermeneutics*, in Wiklund, O. (ed.), *Judicial Discretion in European Perspective*, Stockholm, Kluwer Law International, 2003, 150–164

Weiler, J. H. H., *Revisiting* Van Gend en Loos: *Subjectifying and Objectifying the Individual*, in Tizzano, A., Kokott, J., Prechal, S. (Organising Committee), *50ème anniversaire de l'arrêt Van Gend en Loos: 1963-2013: actes du colloque*, Luxembourg, 13 mai 2013, https://curia.europa.eu/jcms/jcms/P_95693/en/, 11–22

Weitzel, L., *La Charte des droits fondamentaux de l'Union européenne, avancée ou régression?*, in Weitzel, L., *L'Europe des droits fondamentaux. Mélanges en hommage à Albert Weitzel*, Paris, Pedone, 2013, 225–250

Wessel, R. A., *Reconsidering the Relationship between International and EU Law: Towards a Content-Based Approach?*, in Cannizzaro, E., Palchetti, P., Wessel, R. A. (eds.), *International law as law of the European Union*, The Hague, Martinus Nijhoff, 2012, 7–33

Winter, G., *The Directive: Problems of Construction and Directions for Reform*, in Id., *Sources and Categories of European Union Law*, Baden-Baden, Nomos, 1996, 487–506

Wouters, J., Van Eeckhoutte, D., *Giving Effect to Customary International Law through European Community Law*, in Prinssen, J. M., Schrauwen, A. (eds.), *Direct Effect: Rethinking a Classic of EC Legal Doctrine*, Groningen, European Law Publishing, 2002, 181–234

Ziller, J., *Le fabuleux destin des Explications relative à la Charte des droits fondamentaux*, in Chemins d'Europe—*Mélanges en l'honneur de Jean Paul Jacqué*, Paris, Pedone, 2010, 765–781

Ziller, J., *Les réactions des milieux institutionnels, nationaux et scientifiques de l'époque*, in Tizzano, A., Kokott, J., Prechal, S. (Organising Committee), *50ème anniversaire de l'arrêt Van Gend en Loos: 1963-2013: actes du colloque*, Luxembourg, 13 mai 2013, https://curia.europa.eu/jcms/jcms/P_95693/en/, 7–48.

4. Working papers, blog posts, and contributions in online platforms

Arcuri, A., Poli, S., *What Price for the Community Enforcement of WTO Law?*, EUI Working Papers, Law 2010/01, available at https://cadmus.eui.eu/handle/1814/13534

Arena, A., *How European Law Became Supreme: The Making of Costa v. ENEL*, Jean Monnet Working Paper Series, 2018, 1, 19, available at https://jeanmonnetprogram.org/wp-content/uploads/JMWP-05-Amedeo-Arena.pdf

Bertrand, B., *L'arrêt French Data Network du Conseil d'Etat: un dialogue des juges en trompe l'œil*, in *Le Club des juristes*, 7 May 2021, available at https://www.leclubdesjuristes.com/archives-cdj/larret-french-data-network-du-conseil-detat-un-dialogue-des-juges-en-trompe-loeil-3538/

Cartabia, M., *Taking Dialogue Seriously*, Jean Monnet Working Paper, 2007, available at https://jeanmonnetprogram.org/paper/taking-dialogue-seriously-the-renewed-need-for-a-judicial-dialogue-at-the-time-of-constitutional-activism-in-the-european-union/

Cecchetti, L., Something new under the Sun: The direct effect of directives plus Article 47 Charter in horizontal situations in the K.L. judgment, BlogDUE, 24 April 2024, available at https://www.aisdue.eu/lorenzo-cecchetti-something-new-under-the-sun-the-direct-effect-of-directives-plus-article-47-charter-in-horizontal-situations-in-the-k-l-judgment/

Circolo, A., *La disapplicazione del primato: le eccezioni della Corte di giustizia all'efficacia prevalente del diritto dell'Unione sul diritto interno. Note a margine della pronuncia* Inter Environnement Wallonie II, in *dirittounioneeuropea.eu*, 11 November 2019, available at https://www.dirittounioneeuropea.eu/Tool/Evidenza/Single/view_html?id_evidenza=900

Dani, M., *The 'Partisan Constitution' and the Corrosion of European Constitutional Culture*, LEQS Paper, n., available at https://eprints.lse.ac.uk/55340/1/__libfile_REPOSITORY_Content_European%20Institute_LEQS%20Discussion%20Papers_LEQSPaper68.pdf

De Witte, B., *The Thelen Technopark Berlin judgment: the Court of Justice sticks to its guns on the horizontal effect of directives*, REALaw.blog, 6 May 2022, available at https://realaw.blog/?p=1195

Diverio, D., *Nulla di nuovo... sotto il sole? Qualche considerazione a prima lettura sulla sentenza della Corte di giustizia nella causa* AGCM c. Comune di Ginosa, Blog DUE, 28 April 2023, available at https://www.aisdue.eu/davide-diverio-nulla-di-nuovo-sotto-il-sole-qualche-considerazione-a-prima-lettura-sulla-sentenza-della-corte-di-giustizia-nella-causa-agcm-c-comune-di-ginosa/

Fontanelli, F., *You Can Teach a New Court* Mangold *Tricks—the Horizontal Effect of the Charter Right to Paid Annual Leave*, in *EU Law Analysis*, 11 November, 2018, available at https://eulawanalysis.blogspot.com/2018/11/you-can-teach-new-court-mangold-tricks.html

Figueroa Regueiro, P. V., *Invocability of Substitution and Invocability of Exclusion: Bringing Legal Realism to the Current Developments of the Case-Law of 'Horizontal' Direct Effect of Directives*, Jean Monnet Working Paper 7/02, 2002, available at http://www.jeanmonnetprogram.org/archive/papers/02/020701.pdf

Gallo, D., *Migrants' Social Rights in the Dialogue between the CJEU and the Italian Constitutional Court: Long Live Article 267 TFEU!*, EU Law Live, 8 September 2021, available at https://eulawlive.com/op-ed-migrants-social-rights-in-the-dialogue-between-the-cjeu-and-the-italian-constitutional-court-long-live-article-267-tfeu-by-daniele-gallo/

Gallo, D., Cecchetti, L., *The Principle of Proportionality of Penalties and the Inextricable Knot between Primacy, Direct Effect and Disapplication*, EU Law Live, 30 September 2021, available at https://eulawlive.com/op-ed-the-principle-of-proportionality-of-penalties-and-the-inextricable-knot-between-primacy-direct-effect-and-disapplication-by-daniele-gallo-and-lorenzo-cecchetti/

Groussot, X., Loxa, A., *Of The Practicability of Direct Effect and the 'Doctrine of Change*, EU Law Live, 29 March 2022, available at https://eulawlive.com/op-ed-of-the-practicability-of-direct-effect-and-the-doctrine-of-change-by-xavier-groussot-and-alezini-loxa/

Howard E., *The Court of Justice and headscarves at work: discretion in EU anti-discrimination law: a dangerous precedent (Case C-148/22 OP v Commune d'Ans)*, EU Law Live, 5 December 2023, available at https://eulawlive.com/op-ed-the-court-of-justice-and-headscarves-at-work-discretion-in-eu-anti-discrimination-law-a-dangerous-precedent-case-c-148-22-op-v-commune-dans-by-erica-howard/#

Howard, E., Op-Ed: *Encouraging tolerance and respect and accepting a greater degree of diversity . . . but not for Muslim women (Case C-344/20 LF v SCRL)*, EU Law Live, 2024, available at https://

eulawlive.com/op-ed-encouraging-tolerance-and-respect-and-accepting-a-greater-degree-of-diversity-but-not-for-muslim-women-case-c-344-20-lf-v-scrl-by-erica-howard/

Jacobs, F. G., *Speech for the Walther-Schücking-Institut/Institut für Internationales Recht*, University of Kiel, April 1983, available at https://www.uni-kiel.de/en/law/research/wsi

Lindeboom, J., Op-Ed: *Another Episode on Horizontal Direct Effect of Directives, Or: Who Should Clean Up the Mess? Case C-316/22 Gabel Industria Tessile*, EU Law Live, 30 April 2024, available at https://eulawlive.com/op-ed-another-episode-on-horizontal-direct-effect-of-directives-or-who-should-clean-up-the-mess-case-c-316-22-gabel-industria-tessile-by-justin-lindeboom/

Lonardo, L., Op-Ed: *The will of the legislator and the direct effect of EU international agreements (Case 382/21 P KaiKai Company)*, EU Law Live, 2 May 2024, available at https://eulawlive.com/op-ed-the-will-of-the-legislator-and-the-direct-effect-of-eu-international-agreements-case-c%e2%80%91382-21-p-kaikai-company-by-luigi-lonardo/#

Mańko, R., *Preliminary reference procedure, Briefing of the European Parliamentary Research Service*, EPRS, European Parliament, 608.628, July 2017, available at https://www.europarl.europa.eu/RegData/etudes/BRIE/2017/608628/EPRS_BRI(2017)608628_EN.pdf

Montalivet, P., *Les objectifs de valeur constitutionnelle*, in *Cahiers du Conseil Constitutionnel*, 20 June 2006, available at https://www.conseil-constitutionnel.fr/nouveaux-cahiers-du-conseil-constitutionnel/les-objectifs-de-valeur-constitutionnelle

Ovádek, M., *Legislative Output of the European Union. An Automatically Updated Overview of the EU's Legislative Activity*, available at https://michalovadek.github.io/eulaw/.

Rosas, A., *EU Law and National Law: A Common Legal System*, AEL working paper, 2024, available at https://cadmus.eui.eu/handle/1814/76744

Sanchez-Graells, A., *Interesting Clarification (and Broadening) of the Foster Test on 'Emanation of the State' for Purposes of Direct Effect of EU Directives (C-413/15), How to Cruck a Nut. A Blog on European Law*, 10 October 2017, http://www.howtocrackanut.com/blog/2017/10/10/interesting-clarification-of-the-foster-test-on-emanation-of-the-state-for-purposes-of-direct-effect-of-eu-directives-c-41315

Sanchez-Graells, A., Op-Ed: *Transposing Directives no longer so discretionary! The Court of Justice forces transposition of discretionary exclusion grounds and hints at 'intra-State' vertical direct effect* (C-66/22), Madrid, EU Law Live, 27 February 2024, available at https://eulawlive.com/op-ed-transposing-directives-no-longer-so-discretionary-the-court-of-justice-forces-transposition-of-discretionary-exclusion-grounds-and-hints-at-intra-state-vertical/

Sarmiento, D., *Primacy of EU law and res iudicata in national criminal proceedings, revisited and reversed. A comment on Vueling (C-370/17 and C-37/18)*, 8 April 2020, available at https://eulawlive.com/op-ed-primacy-of-eu-law-and-res-iudicata-in-national-criminal-proceedings-revisited-and-reversed-a-comment-on-vueling-c-370-17-and-c-37-18-by-daniel-sarmiento/

Sarmiento, D., Weiler, J. H. H., *The EU Judiciary after Weiss: Proposing A New Mixed Chamber of the Court of Justice* (2 June 2020) *Verfassungblog*, available at https://verfassungsblog.de/the-eu-judiciary-after-weiss/

Sarmiento, D., *Setting the limits of implementation of national law by EU Institutions: the Corneli v ECB case (T-502/19)*, 22 October 2022, available at https://eulawlive.com/op-ed-setting-the-limits-of-implementation-of-national-law-by-eu-institutions-the-corneli-v-ecb-case-t-502-19-by-daniel-sarmiento/

Sarmiento, D., Iglesias Sánchez, S., *Insight: Is Direct Effect Morphing into Something Different?*, EU Law Live, 4 March 2024, available at https://eulawlive.com/insight-is-direct-effect-morphing-into-something-different-by-daniel-sarmiento-and-sara-iglesias-sanchez/

Stone Sweet, A., *Constitutional Dialogues in the European Communities*, EUI Working Paper RSC, 95/38, 1995

Thym, D., *The Missing Link: Direct Effect, CETA/TTIP and Investor-State-Dispute Settlement*, in *Verfassungsblog*, 4 January 2015, available at https://verfassungsblog.de/en-verhinderte-rechtsanwendung-deutsche-gerichte-cetatiip-und-investor-staat-streitigkeiten-2/, 2015

Vajda, C., *Achmea and the Autonomy of the EU Legal Order*, in *LAwTTIP Working Papers No 1/2019*, 2019, 10

Van der Loo, G., Van Elsuwege, P., Petrov, R., *The EU-Ukraine Association Agreement: Assessment of an Innovative Legal Instrument*, EUI LAW working paper, 2014, available at https://cadmus.eui.eu/handle/1814/32031

Van Reempts, F., Op-Ed: *The Effectiveness of Directives in Horizontal Situations: the Charter Unchained? (K.L. v. X)*, EU Law Live, 2024, available at https://eulawlive.com/op-ed-the-effectiveness-of-directives-in-horizontal-situations-the-charter-unchained-k-l-v-x-by-fien-van-reempts/

Wells, M. L., *European Union Law In The Member State Courts: A Comparative View*, University of Georgia School of Law Research Paper Series, Paper No. 2021-11, 2021, available at https://papers.ssrn.com/sol3/papers.cfm?abstract_id=3911155

Index

For the benefit of digital users, indexed terms that span two pages (e.g., 52–53) may, on occasion, appear on only one of those pages.